KB087677

CEDU(쎄듀)는 A **C**omprehensive **E**nglish e**DU**cation(종합적 영어교육)의 약자입니다.

저자

김기훈 現 ㈜쎄듀 대표이사

現 메가스터디 영어영역 대표강사

前 서울특별시 교육청 외국어 교육정책자문위원회 위원

저서 천일문 / 천일문 Training Book / 천일문 GRAMMAR

어법끝 / 어휘끝 / 첫단추 / 쎈쓰업 / 파워업 / 빈칸백서 / 오답백서

쎄듀 본영어 / 문법의 골든룰 101 / ALL씀 서술형 / 수능실감

거침없이 Writing / Grammar Q / Reading Q / Listening Q 등

쎄듀 영어교육연구센터

쎄듀 영어교육센터는 영어 콘텐츠에 대한 전문지식과 경험을 바탕으로

최고의 교육 콘텐츠를 만들고자 최선의 노력을 다하는 전문가 집단입니다.

장혜승 선임연구원

감수

유원호 (서강대 영미어문과 교수)

마케팅	콘텐츠 마케팅 사업본부
영업	문병구
제작	정승호
인디자인 편집	올댓에디팅
디자인	윤혜영
내지 일러스트	그림숲
영문교열	Janna Christie

LISTENING Q

중학영어듣기
모의고사 24회
②

PREVIEW

STEP 1 최신 기출을 완벽 분석한 유형별 공략

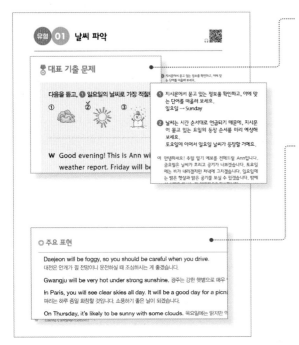

🎖 대표 기출 문제

- 최근 〈시·도교육청 주관 영어듣기능력평가〉에 출제되는 모든 문제 유형을 철저히 분석하여, 유형별 문제 풀이 방법을 제시합니다.
- 오답 함정과 정답 근거를 확인해보며, 각 유형에 대한 이해도를 높일 수 있습니다.

✪ 주요 표현

- 유형별로 가장 많이 출제된 중요 표현을 정리하였습니다.
- 시험 바로 전에 빠르게 훑어볼 수 있습니다.

STEP 2 실전 모의고사로 문제 풀이 감각 익히기

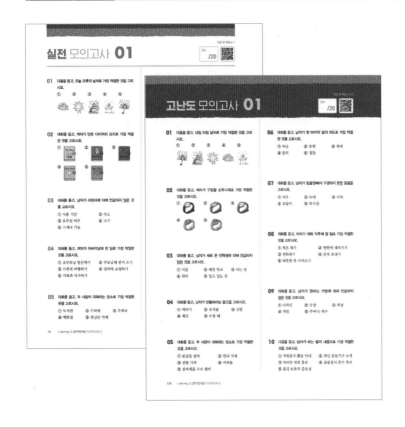

실전 모의고사 20회

- 전국 16개 〈시·도 교육청 주관 영어듣기능력평가〉 최신 5개년 출제 경향이 완벽 반영된 실전 모의고사를 수록했습니다.
- 실전과 동일한 유형 배치 및 엄선된 문항을 통해 영어듣기 평가를 대비하는 동시에 듣기의 기본기를 쌓을 수 있습니다.

고난도 모의고사 4회

점진적으로 문제 풀이 능력을 키워나갈 수 있도록 실전보다 높은 난이도의 문제로 실력을 점검합니다.

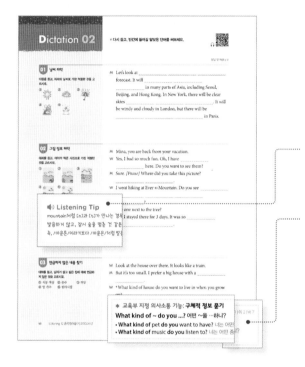

매회 Dictation 수록

- 문제 풀이에 중요한 단서가 되는 핵심 어휘 및 표현들을 연습할 수 있습니다.

- 들은 내용을 다시 한번 확인하며, 중요 표현들과 놓치기 쉬운 연음 등의 집중적인 학습이 가능합니다.

Listening Tip

듣기의 기본기를 쌓을 수 있도록, 더 잘 들리는 발음 팁을 수록하였습니다.

* 교육부 지정 의사소통 기능

개정교과서에 수록된 의사소통 기능 표현을 정리하였습니다.
중요 표현들이 실제 대화에서 어떻게 쓰이는지 확인할 수 있으며,
다른 예시 문장을 제시하여 응용해 볼 수 있도록 구성했습니다.

학습자 혼자서도 충분한 학습이 가능하도록 자세한
해설과 대본 및 해석을 제공합니다.

CEDU MP3 PLAYER

QR코드 하나로 배속 및 문항 선택 재생

- 〈Listening Q 중학영어듣기 모의고사〉 시리즈는 효율적인 듣기 학습을 위해 MP3 PLAYER 기능이 적용되어 있습니다.

- 교재 안에 있는 QR코드를 휴대전화로 인식하면, 기본 배속과 1.2배속, 1.4배속 세 가지 속도 중에 원하는 속도를 선택하여 음원 재생이 가능합니다.

- 각 문항별 파일도 선택하여 재생 가능하기 때문에 더욱 편리하게 받아쓰기를 연습할 수 있습니다.

무료 부가서비스

www.cedubook.com에서 무료 부가서비스 자료를 다운로드하세요.
• MP3 파일 • 어휘리스트 • 어휘테스트

CONTENTS

PART. 03

고난도 모의고사

[책속책] 정답 및 해설

기출 문제 유형 분석표

2018년 ~ 2023년

2023 ← → 2018

2학년	2023년 2회	2023년 1회	2022년 2회	2022년 1회	2021년 2회	2021년 1회	2020년 2회	2020년 1회	2019년 2회	2019년 1회	2018년 2회
날씨 파악	1	1	1	1	1	1	1	1	1	1	1
그림 정보 파악	1	1	1	1	1	1	1	1	1	1	1
의도 파악	1	1	1	1	1	1	1	1	1	1	1
심정 추론	1	1	1	1	1	1					1
한 일 파악	1	1	1	1	2	1	1	1	1		1
대화 장소 추론	1	1	1	1	1	1	1	1	1	1	1
일치하지 않는 내용 찾기	1	1	1	1		1	2	2	1	1	1
일치하는 내용 찾기					1						
특정 정보 파악	1		1	1		2		1	1	2	1
할 일 파악	1	2	1	1	1	1	2	1	1	1	1
장래 희망											
언급하지 않은 내용 찾기	2	2	2	2	2	2	2	2	3	3	2
주제 추론	1	1	1	1	1	1	1	1	1	1	1
목적 파악	1	1	1	1	1	1	1	1	1	1	1
숫자 정보 파악 (시각)									1	1	
숫자 정보 파악 (금액)	1	1	1	1	1		1		1		1
숫자 정보 파악 (날짜)											
관계 추론	1	1	1	1	1	1	1	1	1	1	1
부탁 파악	1	1	1			1	1	1	1	1	1
이유 파악	1		1		1	1	1	1	1	1	1
제안 파악				1	1						
그림 상황에 적절한 대화 고르기	1	1	1	1	1	1	1	1	1	1	1
어색한 대화 고르기											
이어질 응답 찾기	2	2	2	2	2	2	2	2	2	2	2

Study Planner

●● 영어듣기평가 **D-25일**

1일차 유형공략	2일차 실전 모의고사 1회	3일차 실전 모의고사 2회	4일차 실전 모의고사 3회	5일차 실전 모의고사 4회
◯ 월 ◯ 일	◯ 월 ◯ 일 _____ 점	◯ 월 ◯ 일 _____ 점	◯ 월 ◯ 일 _____ 점	◯ 월 ◯ 일 _____ 점
6일차 실전 모의고사 5회	7일차 실전 모의고사 6회	8일차 실전 모의고사 7회	9일차 실전 모의고사 8회	10일차 실전 모의고사 9회
◯ 월 ◯ 일 _____ 점	◯ 월 ◯ 일 _____ 점	◯ 월 ◯ 일 _____ 점	◯ 월 ◯ 일 _____ 점	◯ 월 ◯ 일 _____ 점
11일차 실전 모의고사 10회	12일차 실전 모의고사 11회	13일차 실전 모의고사 12회	14일차 실전 모의고사 13회	15일차 실전 모의고사 14회
◯ 월 ◯ 일 _____ 점	◯ 월 ◯ 일 _____ 점	◯ 월 ◯ 일 _____ 점	◯ 월 ◯ 일 _____ 점	◯ 월 ◯ 일 _____ 점
16일차 실전 모의고사 15회	17일차 실전 모의고사 16회	18일차 실전 모의고사 17회	19일차 실전 모의고사 18회	20일차 실전 모의고사 19회
◯ 월 ◯ 일 _____ 점	◯ 월 ◯ 일 _____ 점	◯ 월 ◯ 일 _____ 점	◯ 월 ◯ 일 _____ 점	◯ 월 ◯ 일 _____ 점
21일차 실전 모의고사 20회	22일차 고난도 모의고사 1회	23일차 고난도 모의고사 2회	24일차 고난도 모의고사 3회	25일차 고난도 모의고사 4회
◯ 월 ◯ 일 _____ 점	◯ 월 ◯ 일 _____ 점	◯ 월 ◯ 일 _____ 점	◯ 월 ◯ 일 _____ 점	◯ 월 ◯ 일 _____ 점

●● 영어듣기평가 **D-15일**

1일차 유형공략	2일차 실전 모의고사 1, 2회	3일차 실전 모의고사 3, 4회	4일차 실전 모의고사 5, 6회	5일차 실전 모의고사 7, 8회
◯ 월 ◯ 일	◯ 월 ◯ 일 _____ 점	◯ 월 ◯ 일 _____ 점	◯ 월 ◯ 일 _____ 점	◯ 월 ◯ 일 _____ 점
6일차 실전 모의고사 9, 10회	7일차 실전 모의고사 11, 12회	8일차 실전 모의고사 13, 14회	9일차 실전 모의고사 15, 16회	10일차 실전 모의고사 17, 18회
◯ 월 ◯ 일 _____ 점	◯ 월 ◯ 일 _____ 점	◯ 월 ◯ 일 _____ 점	◯ 월 ◯ 일 _____ 점	◯ 월 ◯ 일 _____ 점
11일차 실전 모의고사 19, 20회	12일차 고난도 모의고사 1회	13일차 고난도 모의고사 2회	14일차 고난도 모의고사 3회	15일차 고난도 모의고사 4회
◯ 월 ◯ 일 _____ 점	◯ 월 ◯ 일 _____ 점	◯ 월 ◯ 일 _____ 점	◯ 월 ◯ 일 _____ 점	◯ 월 ◯ 일 _____ 점

PART. 01

Listening Q

∧∧∧

중학영어듣기 모의고사

유형공략

영어듣기능력 평가에 자주 출제되는
13가지 대표 유형을 기출문제와 함께 살펴보자!

유형 01 날씨 파악

🎖 대표 기출 문제

다음을 듣고, ❶ 일요일의 날씨로 가장 적절한 것을 고르시오.

① ② ✓ ③ ④ ⑤

✗오답 함정 ○정답 근거

W Good evening! This is Ann with your end-of-the-week weather report. Friday will be cloudy, and the air will be bad. On Saturday, it will rain, but it will stop in the evening. ❷ On Sunday, you can see bright sunshine and
→ 일요일 다음에 이어지는 날씨 정보를 확인하세요.
clear air. Why don't you go out for a walk? Thank you.

❶ 지시문에서 묻고 있는 정보를 확인하고, 이에 맞는 단어를 떠올려 보세요.
일요일 → Sunday

❷ 날씨는 시간 순서대로 언급되기 때문에, 지시문이 묻고 있는 요일의 등장 순서를 미리 예상해 보세요.
토요일에 이어서 일요일 날씨가 등장할 거예요.

여 안녕하세요! 주말 일기 예보를 전해드릴 Ann입니다. 금요일은 날씨가 흐리고 공기가 나쁘겠습니다. 토요일에는 비가 내리겠지만 저녁에 그치겠습니다. 일요일에는 밝은 햇살과 맑은 공기를 보실 수 있겠습니다. 밖에서 산책을 하시는 게 어떨까요? 감사합니다.

⭐ 주요 표현

Daejeon will be foggy, so you should be careful when you drive.
대전은 안개가 낄 전망이니 운전하실 때 조심하시는 게 좋겠습니다.

Gwangju will be very hot under strong sunshine. 광주는 강한 햇볕으로 매우 덥겠습니다.

In Paris, you will see clear skies all day. It will be a good day for a picnic.
파리는 하루 종일 화창할 것입니다. 소풍하기 좋은 날이 되겠습니다.

On Thursday, it's likely to be sunny with some clouds. 목요일에는 맑지만 약간의 구름이 예상됩니다.

In New York, there will be showers and thunderstorms all day long.
뉴욕은 하루 종일 소나기와 폭풍우가 있을 것입니다.

There are strong winds in Seoul because of the rainstorm from the south.
남쪽의 폭풍우로 인하여 서울은 바람이 강하게 붑니다.

Strong winds and heavy rain are expected[forecasted] in Busan. 부산은 강풍과 폭우가 예상됩니다.

🏅 대표 기출 문제

1. 대화를 듣고, 여자가 구입할 휴대폰 케이스로 가장 적절한 것을 고르시오.

①   ②   ③   ④   ⑤

✕ 오답 함정   O 정답 근거

W Excuse me, I'm looking for a cell phone case.

M Oh, look over here. These are our best sellers.

W Oh, it's hard to choose from them.

M How about **this one with a butterfly**?

W Well, I ❷ **prefer a case with a penguin.**
→ 펭귄이 있는 것 중에 정답이 있어요.

M Okay. There are 2 cases with a penguin. Which one do you like more?

W I like **the one with stripes.** ❸ **I'll take that one.**
→ 줄무늬가 있는 케이스로 사겠다는 내용이에요.

❶ 선택지 그림을 보며 각 특징을 의미하는 단어를 떠올려 보세요.
butterfly, penguin, stripe

❷ 단서를 두 번에 걸쳐 언급하기 때문에 등장하는 오답 선택지를 하나씩 제거해 보세요.
→ 펭귄이 있는 것을 선호한다고 했으니, 펭귄이 없는 ①, ②, ⑤는 오답이에요.

❸ 구입을 결정하는 대사까지 확인한 후 정답을 고르세요.
기출 I'll take ~. ~을 살게요.

여 실례합니다, 저 휴대폰 케이스를 찾고 있어요.
남 아, 이쪽을 보세요. 이것들이 저희 가게 베스트셀러입니다.
여 아, 그중에 하나를 고르기가 쉽지 않네요.
남 나비가 있는 이건 어떠세요?
여 음, 저는 펭귄이 있는 케이스가 더 좋아요.
남 알겠습니다. 펭귄이 있는 건 2개가 있는데요. 어느 것이 더 마음에 드시나요?
여 줄무늬가 있는 게 마음에 드네요. 그걸로 살게요.

2. 대화를 듣고, 남자가 만든 강아지 집으로 가장 적절한 것을 고르시오.

①   ②   ③   ④   ⑤

①   ②   ⑤

✕ 오답 함정   O 정답 근거

W Minsu, what's this? Is this house for your puppy?

M Yes, I made it for my puppy, Max.

W Wow, it looks great! Oh, ❷ **there's even a window!**
→ 창문이 있는 것 중 정답이 있어요.

M Yeah, Max can see outside while he's in his house.

W I see. Did you also make ❷ **this sign with his name on it?**
→ Max가 적힌 이름판이 있는 것이 남자가 만든 강아지 집이에요.

M Yes, I did. I think Max will like it.

❶ 선택지 그림을 보며 각 특징을 확인하세요.
Max, window, FIDO

❷ 단서를 두 번에 걸쳐 언급하기 때문에 등장하는 오답 선택지를 하나씩 제거해 보세요.
창문이 있고, 강아지 이름 Max가 쓰인 이름판이 있어요.

여 민수야, 이게 뭐니? 네 강아지 집이니?
남 응, 내가 우리 개 Max를 위해 만들었어.
여 와, 멋져 보인다! 아, 창문도 있네!
남 응, Max가 집에 있을 때 밖을 내다볼 수 있어.
여 그렇구나. 걔 이름이 써진 이름판도 만들었니?
남 응, 내가 만들었어. Max가 좋아할 거야.

유형 03 의도 파악

🎖 대표 기출 문제

대화를 듣고, ❶ 남자의 마지막 말의 의도로 가장 적절한 것을 고르시오.

✓① 허락　② 사과　③ 불평　④ 축하　⑤ 거절

✕ 오답 함정　○ 정답 근거

W Excuse me. Can you tell me what's going on here?

M Oh, I'm preparing for a street performance.

W What kind of performance is it?

M It's a music performance.

W What kind of music are you going to play?

M My band and I are going to play rock music.

W That sounds interesting! ❷ Is it okay to take pictures of
➜ 사진을 찍어도 되는 지 허락을 구하고 있네요.
you?

M ❸ Sure! You can take a lot of pictures.
➜ 사진을 찍어도 된다고 허락하고 있어요.

❶ 마지막 말을 하게 되는 사람이 남자이므로, 남자의 마지막 말에 결정적인 정답 근거가 등장해요.

❷ 의도를 파악하기 위해선 상대방의 마지막 말도 중요해요.
여자가 남자에게 허락을 구하고 있는 상황이에요.

❸ 대화가 언제 끝날지 모르기 때문에 끝까지 집중하면서 대화의 흐름을 놓치지 마세요.

여 실례합니다. 여기서 무슨 일이 있는지 알려주실 수 있나요?
남 아, 길거리 공연을 준비하고 있습니다.
여 어떤 종류의 공연인가요?
남 음악 공연입니다.
여 어떤 종류의 음악을 연주하려고 하시나요?
남 제 밴드하고 저는 락 음악을 연주할겁니다.
여 흥미롭네요! 여러분의 사진을 찍어도 될까요?
남 물론이죠! 많이 찍으셔도 됩니다.

⭐ 주요 표현

조언	You should make eye contact during the speech. 너는 발표하는 동안 눈을 마주쳐야 해. You'd better call the library before it closes. 문 닫기 전에 도서관에 전화해보는 게 좋겠어.
허락	You may watch TV until 7 p.m. 오후 7시까지 TV를 봐도 돼.
동의	That could be a good idea. 그건 좋은 생각인 것 같아.
거절	I'm really sorry. I have a swimming lesson at 4. 정말 미안해. 나 4시에 수영 레슨이 있어.
격려	Good luck with your performance. 네 공연이 잘 되길 바라. I'm sure you'll get on the team next time. Cheer up! 다음번에 팀에 합류할 수 있을 거야. 힘내!
요청	Can you take these cookies to the teacher? 이 쿠키들을 선생님에게 가져다줄래?
충고	You should not give our snacks to animals. 동물들에게 간식을 건네주면 안 됩니다.
칭찬	You did a great job! 잘했어!

🏅 대표 기출 문제

1. 대화를 듣고, ❶ 남자가 겨울방학에 한 일로 가장 적절한 것을 고르시오.

❷ ① 과학관 가기　✓② 드럼 수업 받기　③ 돌고래 먹이 주기
④ 스케이트 타기　⑤ 감귤 농장 체험하기

✗오답 함정　o정답 근거

W　Minsu, it's been a long time!

M　Hi, Jisu. It's good to see you again. How was your winter vacation?

W　It was great! I went to Jeju-do this winter.

M　Wow! What did you do there?

W　❸ I **went to** an aquarium and enjoyed a **dolphin** show there. **How about you?**

M　I was busy ❹ **taking drum lessons.**
　　➜ 드럼 수업을 받았다고 하네요.

W　Cool! I'd like to see you play the drums someday.

❶ 누가, 언제 한 일을 묻고 있는지 확인하세요.

❷ 선택지 내용을 영어로 떠올려 보세요.
science museum, drum lessons, feed dolphins, skate, orange farm

❸ 여자가 한 일로 정답을 고르지 않도록 주의하세요.

❹ 여자의 질문에 이어지는 남자가 한 일을 잘 듣고 정답을 고르세요.
How about you? 너는 어때?

여 민수야, 오랜만이다!
남 안녕, 지수야. 다시 만나니 반갑네. 겨울 방학은 잘 보냈니?
여 아주 좋았어! 이번 겨울에 제주도에 갔었어.
남 와! 거기서 무엇을 했니?
여 수족관에 가서 돌고래 쇼를 즐겼어. 넌 잘 보냈니?
남 나는 드럼 수업을 듣느라 바빴어.
여 멋지다! 언제 한번 네가 드럼을 연주하는 것을 보고 싶네.

2. 대화를 듣고, ❶ 남자가 대화 직후에 할 일로 가장 적절한 것을 고르시오.

❷ ① 메일 확인하기　② 생일 축하하기　③ 친척 방문하기
④ 동생 선물 사기　✓⑤ 문자 메시지 보내기

✗오답 함정　o정답 근거

W　Mike, ❸ **happy birthday!**

M　Thank you, Jin.

W　Did you get many **birthday** messages today?

M　I'm checking my text messages now. *[Pause]* Oh!

W　What? Did you get a special one?

M　Yes, I got a **birthday** card with a **gift** coupon from my **uncle**.

W　Wow, how nice he is!

M　I know, right? I should thank him by ❹ **sending a text message now.**
　　➜ 문자메시지를 지금 보내야 한다고 했어요.

W　Yes, that's a good idea.

❶ 누가 언제 할 일을 묻는지 확인하세요.

❷ 선택지 내용을 영어로 떠올려 보세요.
check e-mails, congratulate, visit cousins, buy presents, send a text message

❸ 선택지 일부의 내용이 대화에 등장해요. 오답 함정에 빠지지 않도록 유의하세요.

❹ 미래를 나타내는 조동사 will 대신, 해야 할 일을 나타내는 표현을 활용해서 앞으로 할 일을 표현하기도 해요.
기출 I should ~ now. 나 지금 ~해야 겠어.

여 Mike, 생일 축하해!
남 고마워, 진아.
여 오늘 생일 축하 메시지 많이 받았니?
남 지금 문자 메시지를 확인하고 있어. *[잠시 후]* 아!
여 무슨 일이야? 특별한 메시지를 받았니?
남 응, 삼촌한테 상품권이 들어있는 생일 축하 카드를 받았어.
여 와, 삼촌이 정말 멋지시구나!
남 맞아, 그렇지? 지금 문자 메시지를 보내서 감사하다고 해야겠어.
여 응, 좋은 생각이야.

유형 05 장소 · 관계 추론

🎖 대표 기출 문제

1. 대화를 듣고, 두 사람이 대화하는 장소로 가장 적절한 곳을 고르시오.

❶ ① 은행   ② 여행사   ③ 사진관   ④ 미술관   ⑤ 야구장

❶ 선택지에 제시된 장소를 확인해 보세요. 특정 장소에 자주 사용되는 어휘나 표현들이 등장하기 때문에 미리 예상해 보면서 대화를 들어보세요.

✕오답 함정 ㅇ정답 근거

M Rosie, let's look around the first floor.

W Okay, Sam. But why don't we **check this guidebook** first?

M Good idea. The first floor has ❷ **Korean paintings.**

W Yes, and **paintings by Picasso** are on the third floor.
  ➥ 피카소 그림을 볼 수 있는 장소라는 단서네요.

M Then, let's go to the third floor first. I like **Picasso.**

W Great! I'm so happy to be able to see his famous **artworks.**

❷ 들리는 힌트를 종합하여 정답을 고르세요.
Korean paintings, paintings by Picasso, artworks

남 Rosie, 1층을 둘러보자.
여 알겠어, Sam. 그런데 이 안내서 먼저 보는 게 어떨까?
남 좋은 생각이야. 1층은 한국 회화들이네.
여 응, 그리고 피카소의 그림은 3층에 있어.
남 그럼 3층부터 가자. 나는 피카소가 좋거든.
여 좋아! 그의 유명한 예술작품들을 볼 수 있어서 정말 기뻐.

---

2. 대화를 듣고, 두 사람의 관계로 가장 적절한 것을 고르시오.

❶ ① 가수 – 팬   ② 제빵사 – 손님
③ 학부모 – 교사   ④ 컴퓨터 수리기사 – 고객
⑤ 관광 가이드 – 여행객

❶ 선택지에 제시된 관계들을 확인해보세요. 특정 직업을 가진 사람이 자주 사용하는 어휘나 표현들이 있으니 선택지들을 보면서 미리 등장할 어휘나 표현을 예상해 보세요.

✕오답 함정 ㅇ정답 근거

M Hello, how can I help you?

W Hi. I'd like to ❷ **order a special cake** for my mom's birthday.

M Oh, I can ❸ **make it for you. What kind of cake would you like?**
  ➥ 남자가 케이크를 만든다고 하네요.

W **Cheesecake.** Could you write something on it?

M Of course! What do you want me to write?

W Please write, "I love you, Mom!" **on the cake.**

M Okay. Do you want me to write it with **chocolate syrup?**

W Yes, thank you.

❷ 첫 대화 초반부터 정답에 대한 힌트가 드러나기도 하지만 그렇지도 않은 경우도 있으니 유의하세요.

❸ 곳곳에 등장하는 장소나 직업에 대한 정보를 통해 관계를 알아낼 수 있어요.

남 안녕하세요, 도와드릴까요?
여 안녕하세요. 저희 엄마의 생일 때 드릴 특별한 케이크를 주문하고 싶어요.
남 아, 만들어 드릴 수 있지요. 어떤 종류의 케이크를 원하시나요?
여 치즈 케이크요. 그 위에 뭔가를 써주실 수 있나요?
남 물론이죠! 무엇을 써드릴까요?
여 케이크 위에 '사랑해요, 엄마!'를 써주세요.
남 알겠습니다. 초콜릿 시럽으로 써드릴까요?
여 네, 감사합니다.

 유형 **06** 특정 정보 파악

🏅 대표 기출 문제

대화를 듣고, ❶ 남자가 빌릴 물건으로 가장 적절한 것을 고르시오.

❷✓① 튜브　② 모자　③ 수건　④ 수영복　⑤ 구명조끼

✗오답 함정　O정답 근거

W　Did you pack everything to go to the swimming pool?

M　Yes, Mom. I put my swimsuit and cap in my bag.
　　→수영복과 모자는 챙겼네요.

W　What about a tube?

M　Oh, I forgot to pack it. *[Pause]* Mom, I can't find it.

W　Ah, I think we lost it last vacation.

M　❸ Can we get a new one?
　　→새로 하나 사도되는지 묻고 있어요.

W　How about **borrowing a tube** at the swimming pool?
　　→여자는 튜브를 빌리자고 제안해요.

M　Okay, I will.
　　→여자의 제안에 동의하네요.

❶ 지시문에서 묻고 있는 특정 정보가 무엇인지 확인해보고 영어로 떠올려 보세요.
borrow 빌리다

❷ 선택지 내용을 확인 후, 관련 단어들을 미리 떠올려 보세요.

❸ 특정 정보에 관해 직접적으로 묻는 경우가 있어요. 이에 이어지는 응답에서 정답 근거를 찾을 수 있어요.

여　수영장에 가져갈 짐을 모두 다 챙겼니?
남　네, 엄마. 가방에 수영복하고 수영 모자를 넣었어요.
여　튜브는 챙겼니?
남　아, 챙기는 걸 깜박했어요. *[잠시 후]* 엄마, 그걸 찾을 수가 없어요.
여　아, 지난 휴가 때 잃어버린 것 같구나.
남　새로 하나 사도 돼요?
여　수영장에서 튜브를 빌리는 게 어떠니?
남　알겠어요, 그럴게요.

⭐ 주요 표현

남자가 선택한 보고서 주제	A: I'm going to write about water for my report. What about you? 내 보고서에 물에 대해 작성할거야. 너는? B: I chose clouds as my report topic. 난 보고서 주제로 구름을 선택했어.
여자가 만든 것	A: Did you make anything there? 그곳에서 뭐라도 만들었어? B: Yes, I made a name tag. Look! 응, 이름표를 만들었어. 봐!
여자가 교환하려는 물건	A: Can you exchange my keyboard? 제 키보드를 교환해주실래요? B: Sure. We'll send you a white one. 물론이죠. 하얀 것으로 보내드릴게요.
여자가 가입하고자 하는 동아리	A: Well, why don't you join the yoga club? 음, 요가 동아리에 가입하는 게 어때? B: Sounds better for me. I'll do that. 나한테 그게 더 좋은 것 같아. 그렇게 할게.

🎖 대표 기출 문제

1. 대화를 듣고, 두 사람이 Power Fitness Club 이용에 대해 언급하지 <u>않은</u> 것을 고르시오.

❶ ① 운동화 착용 여부　　② 개인 수건 필요 여부
③ 사물함 이용 가격　　④ 운동복 대여 장소 ✓
⑤ 샤워실 유무

✗오답 함정　○정답 근거

[Telephone rings.]

W　Hello, Power Fitness Club. How can I help you?

M　I want to exercise in your gym starting today. Should I
　❷ **wear running shoes**?

W　Yes, you should.
　→① 운동화는 착용해야 해요.
M　Do I need to bring my own towel?

W　No, we have towels for you here.
　→② 개인 수건은 필요 없어요.
M　Okay. Are there any lockers?

W　Yes. They cost 5 dollars per month.
　→③ 사물함은 한 달에 $5이에요.
M　I see. Do you have a shower room?

W　Of course! You can use it anytime.
　→⑤ 샤워실은 있고, 언제든지 사용 가능해요.
M　Good. Thank you.

❶ 주어진 선택지를 보면서 어떤 내용들이 등장하는지 미리 예상해 보세요.
running shoes, towel, locker, gym clothes, shower room

❷ 선택지가 등장한 순서대로 대화가 이루어져요. 대화를 들으면서 언급되는 항목은 선택지에서 하나씩 제거해 보세요.

[전화벨이 울린다.]
여　안녕하세요. Power 헬스클럽입니다. 무엇을 도와드릴까요?
남　오늘부터 헬스클럽에서 운동을 하고 싶은데요. 운동화를 신어야 할까요?
여　네, 신으셔야 합니다.
남　제 수건을 가져와야 하나요?
여　아뇨, 여기에 회원님을 위한 수건이 구비되어 있습니다.
남　알겠습니다. 사물함도 있나요?
여　네. 한 달에 5달러입니다.
남　그렇군요. 샤워실도 있나요?
여　물론이죠! 언제든지 사용하실 수 있습니다.
남　잘됐네요. 감사합니다.

---

2. 다음을 듣고, 여자가 Saving Earth 행사에 대해 언급하지 <u>않은</u> 것을 고르시오.

❶ ① 실시 목적　　② 실시 날짜　　③ 시작 시간
④ 참여 국가 ✓　　⑤ 참여 인원

✗오답 함정　○정답 근거

W　Have you heard about the Saving Earth event? This event
is held to encourage people to save electricity. It takes
　→실시 목적: 전기를 아끼도록 장려하기 위함
place every year on June 26th. On this day, people turn
　→실시 날짜: 매년 6월 26일
off their lights for 30 minutes. It begins at 9:00 p.m. and
　→시작 시간: 오후 9시
ends at 9:30 p.m. More than 500 people join this event
　→참여 인원: 500명 이상
every year. Why don't you join us next time? Thank you.

❶ 주어진 선택지를 보면서 어떤 내용들이 등장하는지 미리 예상해 보세요.

❷ 선택지가 등장한 순서대로 대화가 이루어져요. 대화를 들으면서 언급되는 항목은 선택지에서 하나씩 제거해 보세요.

여　Saving Earth 행사에 대해 들어보신 적 있나요? 이 행사는 사람들이 전기를 아끼도록 장려하는 행사입니다. 행사는 매년 6월 26일에 개최됩니다. 이 날에 사람들은 30분 동안 전등을 끕니다. 오후 9시에 시작이 되며 9시 30분에 종료됩니다. 해마다 500명 이상의 사람들이 이 행사에 참여합니다. 다음번에 동참하시는 게 어떠신가요? 감사합니다.

3. 대화를 듣고, 동영상에 관한 정보로 일치하지 <u>않는</u> 것을 고르시오.

❶ ① 미국 문화에 대한 내용이다.　　② 영상 길이는 10분이다.
③ 미국인이 제작했다.　　④ 제작자는 한국에 산다.
✓
⑤ 제작자는 중학교에서 영어를 가르친다.

✗오답 함정　O 정답 근거

M Lisa, what are you looking at on your computer?

W I'm watching ❷ **a video clip about American culture**.
　→ 미국 문화에 대한 내용이다(① 일치)
Let's watch it together.

M Oh, **it's only 10 minutes long**. Who made this video clip?
　→ 영상 길이는 10분이다(② 일치)

W **An American man made it**.
　→ 미국인이 제작했다(③ 일치)

M He speaks Korean very well.

W Yes, **he lives here in Korea**.
　→ 제작자는 한국에 산다(④ 일치)

M Really? What does he do here?

W **He teaches English at a university** here.
　→ 중학교에서 영어를 가르친다(⑤ 불일치)

---

❶ 선택지를 살펴본 후, 관련 어휘들을 하나씩 떠올려 보세요.
about American culture, 10 minutes long, made, lives in Korea, teaches English in middle school

❷ 일치하는 내용은 선택지에서 하나씩 제거해 보세요.
＊불일치 유형에서는 일치하는 내용이 오답이에요.

❸ 일치하지 않는 것은 부분적으로 다른 내용이거나 반대의 내용인 경우가 많아요.
중학교에서(X) → 대학교에서(O) 영어를 가르친다.

남 Lisa, 컴퓨터로 뭘 보고 있니?
여 나는 미국 문화에 대한 동영상을 보고 있어. 같이 보자.
남 아, 겨우 10분짜리네. 이 동영상을 누가 만들었니?
여 한 미국인이 만들었어.
남 그는 한국말을 아주 잘하네.
여 응, 그는 여기 한국에서 살아.
남 정말로? 여기서 무엇을 하는 데?
여 그는 대학교에서 영어를 가르쳐.

---

4. 대화를 듣고, Green Cleanup 행사에 대한 내용과 일치하지 <u>않는</u> 것을 고르시오.

❶ ① 공원을 청소한다.　　② 걸으며 쓰레기를 줍는다.
③ 다음 주 일요일에 열린다.　　④ 활동 시간은 3시간이다.
✓
⑤ 집게를 가져가야 한다.

✗오답 함정　O 정답 근거

M Joy, look at this website. There's a Green Cleanup event in our town.

W Oh, is it for **cleaning up the park**?
　→ 공원을 청소한다(① 일치)

M Yes. Let's sign up for it. We can **pick up trash while we walk**.
　→ 걸으며 쓰레기를 줍는다(② 일치)

W Okay. **It'll be next Sunday**.
　→ 다음 주 일요일에 열린다(③ 일치)

M The event starts at 10 a.m. and finishes at 1 p.m.

W Right. **It's just 3 hours**.
　→ 활동 시간은 3시간이다(④ 일치)

M That's good. What do we need to bring?

W We only **need to bring some gloves**.
　→ 집게를 가져가야 한다(⑤ 불일치)

---

❶ 선택지를 살펴본 후, 관련 어휘들을 하나씩 떠올려 보세요.
clean the park, walk, pick up trash, next Sunday, 3 hours, bring tongs

❷ 일치하는 내용은 선택지에서 하나씩 제거해 보세요.
＊불일치 유형에서는 일치하는 내용이 오답이에요.

❸ 일치하지 않는 것은 부분적으로 다른 내용이거나 반대의 내용인 경우가 많아요.
집게를(X) → 장갑을(O) 가져가야 한다.

남 Joy, 이 웹사이트를 좀 봐. 우리 마을에 Green Cleanup 행사가 있어.
여 아, 공원을 청소하는 행사니?
남 응. 같이 등록하자. 걸으면서 쓰레기를 주울 거래.
여 좋아. 다음 주 일요일이야.
남 이 행사는 오전 10시에 시작해서 오후 1시에 끝나.
여 그렇구나. 3시간뿐이네.
남 그거 좋다. 가져갈 게 있나?
여 장갑만 가져가면 돼.

유형 08 주제 추론

🎖 대표 기출 문제

다음을 듣고, 남자가 하는 말의 내용으로 가장 적절한 것을 고르시오.

① ① 세탁기 사용법　　　　② 감기 예방 방법
③ 바이러스의 종류　　　　④ 숙면에 좋은 운동
⑤ 친환경 비누 제작 과정

╳오답 함정　ㅇ정답 근거

M Hello, students. Today, I'm going to tell you about
② **how to prevent a cold.** First, put on a mask when you
→ 감기를 예방하는 방법을 알려준다고 했어요.
go outside. It will help to block the **virus**. Second, wash
your hands with **soap** often. Lastly, get enough ③ **sleep**
and **exercise** regularly. Please be careful not to **catch a**
cold.

① 선택지를 보고 어떤 내용들이 등장할지 미리 영어로 떠올려 보세요.
washing machine, prevent a cold, virus, exercise, eco-friendly soap

② 주제에 대한 소개가 담화 초반에 등장하고 이에 관련 세부 내용들이 이어서 등장하네요. 반대로 세부 내용들이 등장하고 마지막에 주제가 언급되기도 하니, 늘 처음부터 끝까지 듣고 담화의 중심 내용을 파악하는 습관을 기르세요.

③ 주제가 아닌 세부 내용을 바탕으로 한 오답 선택지가 등장하기 때문에, 일부 내용만 듣고 섣불리 전체 담화의 주제로 선택하지 않도록 하세요.

남 학생 여러분, 안녕하세요. 오늘 감기를 예방하는 방법에 대해 말씀드리겠습니다. 우선, 밖으로 외출하실 때 마스크를 끼세요. 바이러스를 막는 데 도움이 될 겁니다. 두 번째로, 비누로 손을 자주 씻으세요. 마지막으로, 충분한 수면과 규칙적인 운동을 하세요. 부디 감기에 걸리지 않도록 조심하세요.

✪ 주요 표현

화재 대피 훈련	We'll now practice what to do in a fire. You'll learn how to be safe in a real fire. 이제 화재에서 어떻게 대처해야 하는지 연습할 거예요. 여러분은 화재가 일어났을 때 어떻게 안전해지는지 배울 것입니다.
환경 보호 방법	Let's remember these things to protect our environment. 우리 환경을 보호하기 위해, 이것들을 꼭 기억합시다.
올바른 휴대전화 사용방법	Let me tell you how to use your cell phone wisely. 휴대전화를 올바르게 사용하는 방법을 알려 드릴게요.
분실물 습득	We have found a coat and a scarf in the women's restroom on the fifth floor. 5층 여자 화장실에서 코트와 스카프를 찾았습니다.
수영장 안전 수칙	I'd like to tell you about some important rules for using the swimming pool. 수영장을 이용하는 데 몇 가지 중요한 규칙을 말씀 드릴게요.

대표 기출 문제

1. 대화를 듣고, ① 여자가 전화를 건 목적으로 가장 적절한 것을 고르시오.

② ① 분실물을 찾기 위해서   ② 주문을 변경하기 위해서

③ 수리 기사를 요청하기 위해서   ④ 식당 예약을 확인하기 위해서

⑤ 전시회 일정을 알아보기 위해서

✕ 오답 함정   o 정답 근거

[Telephone rings.]

M Hello, Miracle Service. How may I help you?
→ 여자가 어디로 전화했는지를 알 수 있어요.

W Hi, can you ③ **send a repairman** to fix my TV?
→ 수리 기사를 보내달라고 하네요.

M What's wrong with it?

W I can't **change** the channels on my TV.

M Oh, I see. Have you tried putting new batteries in your remote control?

W Yes, I have. But I still can't **change** the channels.

M Okay, I'll **send you a repairman** tomorrow.
→ 수리 기사를 보내주겠다고 다시 한 번 말하네요.

W Good. Thanks.

① 지시문에서 누가 전화했는지 확인하세요. 여자가 전화를 걸었으니, 여자의 말에 집중하세요.

② 선택지 내용을 확인 후, 관련 단어들을 미리 떠올려 보세요.
look for, lost, change order, repairman, check, restaurant reservation

③ 대화 초반에 정답 근거가 등장하더라도 섣불리 정답을 선택하지 않도록 유의하세요. 오답 선택지의 일부 내용이 언급되기도 하므로, 대화를 들으면서 전체 상황을 파악하는 것이 중요해요.

[전화벨이 울린다.]
남 안녕하세요, Miracle Service입니다. 무엇을 도와드릴까요?
여 안녕하세요, 제 TV를 고칠 수리 기사를 보내주실 수 있나요?
남 그것에 어떤 문제가 있나요?
여 제 TV에서 채널을 바꿀 수 없어요.
남 아, 그렇군요. 리모컨에 새 건전지를 넣어보셨나요?
여 네, 넣어봤죠. 그런데 여전히 채널을 바꿀 수가 없어요.
남 알겠습니다, 제가 내일 수리 기사를 보내드리겠습니다.
여 좋아요. 감사합니다.

---

2. 대화를 듣고, ① 남자가 매장을 방문한 목적으로 가장 적절한 것을 고르시오.

② ① 옷을 사기 위해서

② 옷을 환불받기 위해서

③ 옷의 길이를 수선하기 위해서

④ 다른 색상의 옷으로 교환하기 위해서

⑤ 다른 사이즈의 옷으로 교환하기 위해서

✕ 오답 함정   o 정답 근거

W How can I help you?

M I want to ③ **exchange this T-shirt.**

W Do you want to **change the color**? We have blue, black, and red.

M I don't want to change the color. I just **want a bigger size.**
→ 남자는 더 큰 사이즈를 원하네요.

W Let me see. This is a medium. Did you wear this?

M No, I didn't.

W Then, you can **exchange it for a larger size.** Please wait a second.
→ 더 큰 사이즈로 교환해준다고 하네요.

M Thank you.

① 지시문에서 누군가의 행동 목적을 묻고 있는지 확인하세요.

② 선택지 내용을 확인 후, 관련 단어들을 미리 떠올려 보세요.
buy, clothes, refund, exchange, different, size

③ 대화 초반에 정답 근거의 일부만 듣고 섣불리 정답을 선택하지 않도록 유의하세요.

여 어떻게 도와드릴까요?
남 저는 이 티셔츠를 교환하고 싶어요.
여 색상을 바꾸고 싶으신가요? 저희는 파란색, 검은색, 빨간색이 있습니다.
남 색상을 바꾸고 싶진 않아요. 단지 좀 더 큰 사이즈를 원해요.
여 어디 봅시다. 이건 중간 사이즈네요. 이것을 입으셨나요?
남 아뇨, 입지 않았습니다.
여 그러면 더 큰 사이즈로 교환하실 수 있습니다. 잠시만 기다려주세요.
남 감사합니다.

대표 기출 문제

1. 대화를 듣고, ❶ 두 사람이 만날 시각을 고르시오.

① 12:30 p.m.　　② 1:00 p.m.　　③ 1:30 p.m.
④ 2:00 p.m.　　⑤ 2:30 p.m.

✗오답 함정　○정답 근거

M Yuni, do you want to go see a movie this weekend?

W Sounds good, Min. Let's check the movie schedule.

M Okay. What movie do you want to see?

W How about the animation movie? It starts at **2 p.m.** on Saturday.

M That's good. Do you want to meet earlier and have lunch together?

W Sorry. My tennis lesson finishes at **1 o'clock**.

M Then, ❸ **can you meet me at 1:30?**
➜ 남자가 1시 30분에 만나자고 제안해요.

W Sure. See you at the theater.
➜ 남자의 제안에 동의했으니 두 사람이 만날 시각은 정해졌어요.

❶ 어떤 숫자 정보를 파악해야 하는지 지시문을 확인하세요.
meet 만나다

❷ 여러 번 다른 시각을 언급하기 때문에 대화를 들으면서 시각과 내용을 메모하세요.

❸ 두 사람이 만날 시각을 조율하는 상황이니, 제안한 시각에 상대방이 동의를 하는지를 꼭 확인하면서 정답을 고르세요.

남 유니야, 이번 주말에 영화 보러 갈래?
여 그거 좋은 생각이다, 민아. 상영 시간표를 확인해보자.
남 그래. 어떤 영화를 보고 싶니?
여 애니메이션 영화는 어때? 토요일 2시에 시작해.
남 좋아. 좀 더 일찍 만나서 같이 점심 먹을래?
여 미안해. 테니스 수업이 1시에 끝나.
남 그러면 1시 30분에 만날래?
여 알겠어. 영화관에서 보자.

---

2. 대화를 듣고, 여자가 지불해야 할 금액으로 가장 적절한 것을 고르시오.

① $6　　② $8　　③ $12
④ $16　　⑤ $20

✗오답 함정　○정답 근거

M Hello, may I help you?

W I'm looking for a present for my little brother.

M Do you have anything in mind?

W Well... I like these toy cars. How much are they?

M The big one is ❶ **8 dollars**, and the small one is **6 dollars**.

W Then, I'd like to buy **two small cars**.
➜ 6달러짜리 작은 자동차를 2개 구입해요.

M Okay, your total will be **12 dollars**.
➜ 총금액이 12달러라는 직접적인 근거가 나오네요.

W Here you are.

❶ 대화를 들으면서 언급되는 가격을 메모하세요.
자동차 장난감 가격
큰 것: $8　　작은 것: $6

❷ 가격을 확인한 뒤, 구매할 수량에 대한 정보가 등장해요. 수량에 대한 정보도 꼭 확인하고 메모하세요.

❸ 대화 후반에 여자가 지불해야 할 금액이 등장해요.
기출 총금액은 ~입니다.
It will be ~. / Your total will be ~.
It's ~ in total.

남 안녕하세요, 도와드릴까요?
여 제 남동생에게 줄 선물을 찾고 있어요.
남 생각하고 있으신 게 있으신가요?
여 음... 이 자동차 장난감이 마음에 드네요. 얼마인가요?
남 큰 것은 8달러이고, 작은 것은 6달러입니다.
여 그러면 작은 자동차로 2개 살게요.
남 알겠습니다. 총금액은 12달러입니다.
여 여기 있습니다.

대표 기출 문제

1. 대화를 듣고, ❶ 여자가 남자에게 부탁한 일로 가장 적절한 것을 고르시오.

❷ ① 책 꺼내주기 ② 음식 주문하기 ③ 숙제 같이 하기
④ 노트 빌려주기 ⑤ 컴퓨터 수리하기

✕오답 함정 ○정답 근거

M Hi, Jenny. What are you looking for?

W Hi, David. I'm looking for the book, Future ❸ Food.

M Oh, let me help you. Did you look for it on the computer?

W Yes. It says it's here in section B.

M Let me see. *[Pause]* Oh, I found it. It's on the top shelf.

W It's so high up. ❹ Could you get the book for me?
→ 책을 꺼내달라고 부탁하고 있어요.

M Sure.

❶ 지시문에서 누가 누구에게 부탁하는 것인지 확인하세요.

❷ 선택지 내용을 확인 후, 관련 단어들을 미리 떠올려 보세요.

❸ 오답 선택지 내용이 등장하는 경우가 있어요. 오답을 유도하는 함정일 뿐 정답으로 선택하지 않도록 주의하세요.

❹ 부탁할 때 자주 쓰이는 표현을 미리 익혀두세요.
기출 Can[Could] you ~? ~ 해줄래?

남 안녕, Jenny. 무엇을 찾고 있니?
여 안녕, David. 나 'Future Food'라는 책을 찾고 있어.
남 아, 내가 도와줄게. 컴퓨터로 검색해 봤니?
여 응. 여기 B 코너에 있다고 하던데.
남 어디 보자. [잠시 후] 아, 찾았다. 선반 위쪽에 있어.
여 엄청 높이 있네. 내 대신 책 좀 꺼내줄래?
남 물론이지.

---

2. 대화를 듣고, ❶ 여자가 약속에 늦는 이유로 가장 적절한 것을 고르시오.

❷ ① 늦게 일어나서 ② 길을 잃어서 ③ 버스가 늦게 와서
④ 마라톤에 참가해서 ⑤ 지하철이 고장 나서

✕오답 함정 ○정답 근거

[Cell phone rings.]

M Hello, Yoonji.

W Hi, Juwon. Where are you now?

M I'm in front of the shopping mall. We're meeting at 9, right?

W Yes, but I think I'll be about 20 minutes late. I'm still on the bus.

M Really? ❸ Why are you so late?
→ 왜 늦었는지 직접적으로 묻고 있어요.

W The bus came late because of the Daehan Marathon.
→ 마라톤 대회 때문에 버스가 늦게 와서 약속에 늦었어요.
I'm really sorry.

M Oh, I see. How about taking the subway next time?

❶ 지시문에서 어떠한 이유를 묻고 있는 지 확인하세요.

❷ 선택지 내용을 영어로 떠올려 보세요.
got up late, lost, bus came late, in a marathon, subway, broken

❸ 의문사 why를 사용하여 직접적으로 이유를 묻기도 하지만, 그렇지 않은 경우가 더 많이 있어요. 전체 대화 흐름을 이해하고 말하는 사람이 처한 상황에 대해 정확하게 파악하는 것이 중요해요.

[휴대전화가 울린다.]
남 여보세요, 윤지야.
여 안녕, 주원아. 지금 어디니?
남 쇼핑몰 앞에 있어. 9시에 만나기로 한 거, 맞지?
여 응, 근데 나 20분 정도 늦을 것 같아. 아직 버스에 있거든.
남 정말? 왜 이렇게 늦었어?
여 Daehan 마라톤 대회 때문에 버스가 늦게 왔어. 정말 미안해.
남 아, 알겠어. 다음에는 지하철을 타는 게 어떠니?

대표 기출 문제

다음 그림의 상황에 가장 적절한 대화를 고르시오.

① ② ③ ④ ⑤

×오답 함정 ○정답 근거

① **W** Which sport do you like best?

   M I like basketball best.

② **W** Can you help me with my homework?

   M No problem.

③ **W** ❷ Could you check your ticket? I think that's my seat.

   M Oh, I'm sorry. I'll move.

④ **W** I love this shirt. Can I try it on?

   M Sure. Go ahead.

⑤ **W** Excuse me. Where is the bookstore?

   M It's next to the hospital.

❶ 주어진 그림을 보면서 어떤 상황인지 확인하세요. 어떤 상황인지 미리 예측하면 정답을 쉽게 찾을 수 있어요.

그림에서 강조되는 부분은 중요한 근거가 될 수 있으니, 영어로 미리 떠올려 보세요.
ticket, seat, number, E 05

❷ 강조된 부분이 언급되는 대화가 정답인 경우가 많아요.

① 여 어떤 스포츠를 가장 좋아하시나요?
   남 저는 농구를 가장 좋아합니다.
② 여 제 숙제를 도와주실 수 있나요?
   남 물론이죠.
③ 여 가지고 있는 티켓을 확인하시겠어요?
      제 자리에 앉으신 것 같네요.
   남 아, 죄송합니다. 자리를 옮길게요.
④ 여 이 셔츠가 아주 마음에 드네요. 입어 봐도 되나요?
   남 물론이죠. 입어 보세요.
⑤ 여 실례합니다. 서점이 어디에 있나요?
   남 병원 옆에 있습니다.

주어진 그림에 등장하는 일부를 활용한 대화가 등장하기도 해요. 이는 오답을 유도하는 내용이니, 부분적인 내용보다는 전체 상황을 정확히 파악해야 해요.

×오답 함정 ○정답 근거

① **A** There are a lot of pop stars on the stage.

   B So that's why it is crowded now.

② **A** Can you take off your baseball cap inside?

   B Sorry. I forgot to take it off.

✓③ **A** I want to go to a baseball game this Saturday.

   B Great, let's go together.

🎖 대표 기출 문제

1. 대화를 듣고, 남자의 마지막 말에 이어질 여자의 말로 가장 적절한 것을 고르시오.

Woman: _____

❶ ① Don't be late.   ✓② Yes, I love it.
③ Sorry, but you can't.   ④ Please help yourself.
⑤ How have you been?

✕ 오답 함정   ○ 정답 근거

M   Happy birthday, Amy!
W   Oh, thank you for remembering my birthday.
M   What are you planning to do today?
W   My family and I are going to take a family photo.
M   How nice! Oh, I prepared a present for you.
W   You did? What a surprise! What is it?
M   I made this cup for you. ❷ Do you like it?
                  → 여자를 위해 컵을 만들었다고 하면서 마음에 드는지 물어보네요.
W   _____

❶ 선택지가 영문으로 제시되기 때문에, 미리 훑어보는 것이 중요해요.

❷ 남자의 마지막 말이 의문문이므로 주어진 상황을 바탕으로 이어질 응답을 미리 예측해 보세요.

생일 선물을 건네주는 상황이에요.
누군가가 생일 선물을 주면서 마음에 드는지 물었을 때, 가장 일반적인 응답이 무엇일지 생각해 보세요.

남 생일 축하해, Amy!
여 아, 내 생일을 기억해줘서 고마워.
남 오늘 무엇을 할 계획이니?
여 우리 가족하고 나는 가족사진을 찍을 거야.
남 너무 멋지다! 아, 널 위해 선물을 준비했어.
여 정말? 놀랍다! 어떤 거니?
남 너를 위해 이 컵을 만들었어. 마음에 드니?
여 _____

① 늦지 마.   ②응, 정말 마음에 들어.
③ 미안한데, 할 수 없어.   ④ 마음껏 먹어.
⑤ 어떻게 지냈어?

---

2. 대화를 듣고, 남자의 마지막 말에 이어질 여자의 말로 가장 적절한 것을 고르시오.

Woman: _____

❶ ✓① Is 3 p.m. okay?   ② You can say that again!
③ Take an umbrella with you.   ④ What a beautiful house it is!
⑤ I have a terrible stomachache.

✕ 오답 함정   ○ 정답 근거

[Telephone rings.]
M   Hello, this is Dr. Lee's hospital. How may I help you?
W   I'd like to ❷ change my appointment with the doctor.
M   No problem. Can I have your name?
W   Joo-Ah Kim.
M   Your appointment is today at 5 o'clock, right?
W   Yes. Can I change it to 7 o'clock?
M   Sorry, but we close at 6:30.
W   How about tomorrow?
M   Tomorrow? ❸ What time do you want?
            → What time에 대한 응답으로 시각에 대한 내용이 이어져야 해요.
W   _____

❶ 선택지를 훑어보고 어떤 내용의 대화가 이어질지 예상해 보세요.

❷ 질문-대답의 흐름을 놓치지 마세요.
병원 예약을 변경하는 상황이에요.

❸ 마지막 말이 의문사 의문문일 경우, 의문사가 결정적인 정답 근거예요.

[전화벨이 울린다.]
남 안녕하세요, Lee 박사님의 병원입니다. 어떻게 도와드릴까요?
여 진찰 예약을 변경하고 싶습니다.
남 가능합니다. 성함을 알 수 있을까요?
여 김주아입니다.
남 예약이 오늘 5시인데요, 맞으신가요?
여 네, 시간을 7시로 변경해도 될까요?
남 죄송합니다만 저희가 6시 30분에 문을 닫습니다.
여 내일은 어떤가요?
남 내일이요? 몇 시로 원하시나요?
여 _____

① 오후 3시에 가능한가요?   ② 당신 말에 동의해요!
③ 우산을 챙기도록 하세요.   ④ 정말 아름다운 집이구나!
⑤ 배가 너무 아파요.

PART. 02

Listening Q
^^^
중학영어듣기 모의고사

실전 모의고사

실제 시험과 동일한 실전 모의고사 20회로 문제 풀이 감각을 익히고,
받아쓰기 훈련으로 듣기 실력 UP!

실전 모의고사 01

01 다음을 듣고, 오늘 오후의 날씨로 가장 적절한 것을 고르시오.

① ② ③ ④ ⑤

02 대화를 듣고, 여자가 만든 다이어리 표지로 가장 적절한 것을 고르시오.

① ② ③

④ ⑤

03 대화를 듣고, 남자가 프린터에 대해 언급하지 <u>않은</u> 것을 고르시오.

① 사용 기간   ② 속도
③ 유무선 여부   ④ 크기
⑤ 스캐너 기능

04 대화를 듣고, 여자가 어버이날에 한 일로 가장 적절한 것을 고르시오.

① 조부모님 방문하기   ② 부모님께 편지 쓰기
③ 가족과 여행하기   ④ 엄마와 쇼핑하기
⑤ 가족과 식사하기

05 대화를 듣고, 두 사람이 대화하는 장소로 가장 적절한 곳을 고르시오.

① 도서관   ② 기차역   ③ 우체국
④ 백화점   ⑤ 장난감 가게

06 대화를 듣고, 여자의 마지막 말의 의도로 가장 적절한 것을 고르시오.

① 불만   ② 감사   ③ 허락
④ 격려   ⑤ 후회

07 대화를 듣고, 남자가 추천한 모바일 앱의 기능을 고르시오.

① 길 찾기   ② 영어사전
③ 번역기   ④ 지하철 노선도
⑤ 맛집 소개

08 대화를 듣고, 두 사람이 대화 직후에 할 일로 가장 적절한 것을 고르시오.

① 기차역에 가기   ② 해운대 해변에 가기
③ 수영하기   ④ 음식점 가기
⑤ 국수 요리하기

09 대화를 듣고, 여자가 다녀온 여행에 대해 언급하지 <u>않은</u> 것을 고르시오.

① 여행지   ② 교통수단   ③ 날씨
④ 활동   ⑤ 음식

10 다음을 듣고, 여자가 하는 말의 내용으로 가장 적절한 것을 고르시오.

① 건강에 좋은 음식
② 맛있는 식당의 조건
③ 채식을 권하는 이유
④ 패스트푸드를 먹는 건강한 방법
⑤ 패스트푸드를 줄여야 하는 이유

11 다음을 듣고, Stonehenge에 대한 내용으로 일치하지 <u>않는</u> 것을 고르시오.

① 세계의 불가사의한 곳 중 하나이다.
② 거대한 돌로 만들어졌다.
③ 약 5천 년 전에 건설되었을 것이다.
④ 누가 지었는지 알 수 없다.
⑤ 역사학자들이 용도를 알아냈다.

12 대화를 듣고, 여자가 종이꽃을 만든 목적으로 가장 적절한 것을 고르시오.

① 교실을 꾸미기 위해서
② 전시회에 출품하기 위해서
③ 엄마에게 선물을 드리기 위해서
④ 미술 숙제를 제출하기 위해서
⑤ 동아리 회원을 모집하기 위해서

13 대화를 듣고, 남자가 지불해야 할 금액으로 가장 적절한 것을 고르시오.

① $6   ② $8   ③ $12
④ $14   ⑤ $20

14 대화를 듣고, 두 사람의 관계로 가장 적절한 것을 고르시오.

① 영화감독 – 배우
② 신문기자 – 운동선수
③ 자동차 정비사 – 손님
④ 호텔 접수원 – 손님
⑤ 방송 진행자 – 우주 비행사

15 대화를 듣고, 여자가 남자에게 부탁한 일로 가장 적절한 것을 고르시오.

① 학교 잡지 홍보하기
② 전학생과 같이 앉기
③ 학교 잡지에 기사 쓰기
④ 만화 그릴 사람 소개하기
⑤ 재미있는 만화 추천하기

16 대화를 듣고, 남자가 전화한 이유로 가장 적절한 것을 고르시오.

① 쇼핑하러 가기 위해서
② 야구 보러 가기 위해서
③ 선물에 감사하기 위해서
④ 병문안하기 위해서
⑤ 스케이트 타러 가기 위해서

17 다음 그림의 상황에 가장 적절한 대화를 고르시오.

① ② ③ ④ ⑤

18 다음을 듣고, 남자가 김치전에 대해 언급하지 <u>않은</u> 것을 고르시오.

① 좋아하는 이유   ② 주로 먹는 날
③ 재료   ④ 만드는 방법
⑤ 유래

[19-20] 대화를 듣고, 남자의 마지막 말에 이어질 여자의 응답으로 가장 적절한 것을 고르시오.

19 Woman: _____

① Sorry, I'm busy now.
② Yes. That'll be fine.
③ Thanks for your call.
④ Thanks. She's better now.
⑤ I'll ask you again next time.

20 Woman: _____

① See you next time!
② Where are you from?
③ Do you remember me?
④ Sure. That sounds great!
⑤ I don't remember you, either.

Dictation 01

◆ 다시 듣고, 빈칸에 들어갈 알맞은 단어를 써보세요.

정답 및 해설 p.2

01 날씨 파악

다음을 듣고, 오늘 오후의 날씨로 가장 적절한 것을 고르시오.

① ② ③ ④ ⑤

M Good morning, and welcome to the weather forecast. It's cloudy right now, but the sun will come out _____ _____ _____. In the evening, it's going to be _____ _____ _____. And this will continue _____ _____. That's the weather forecast for today. Have a nice day!

02 그림 정보 파악

대화를 듣고, 여자가 만든 다이어리 표지로 가장 적절한 것을 고르시오.

① My Diary ② Dear Diary ③ Dear Diary
④ Dear Diary ⑤ Dear Diary

M Jimin, what are you making?

W I'm making a cover for my diary. Can you help me?

M Sure. Where do you want to _____ _____ _____?

W I want to put "Dear Diary" _____ _____ _____.

M Okay.

W Now, I want to _____ _____ _____ the title. Do you have any ideas?

M How about a big heart?

W Okay. But one heart _____ _____ enough. Let's draw many hearts.

M Great. [Pause] Now it looks better with hearts.

03 언급하지 않은 내용 찾기

대화를 듣고, 남자가 프린터에 대해 언급하지 않은 것을 고르시오.

① 사용 기간   ② 속도
③ 유무선 여부   ④ 크기
⑤ 스캐너 기능

M Mom, this printer is not working again.

W What's wrong with it?

M We bought this 8 years ago. It's _____ _____.

W Okay. Anything else?

M It takes _____ _____ to print papers.

W Well, that's a problem. Let me see if I can fix it.

M You don't need to. ＿＿＿＿＿＿＿＿＿ ＿＿＿＿＿＿＿＿＿
＿＿＿＿＿＿＿＿＿ wireless and has no scanner.

W Okay. Maybe ＿＿＿＿＿＿＿＿＿ ＿＿＿＿＿＿＿＿＿ ＿＿＿＿＿＿＿＿＿
change your printer.

04 한 일 파악

대화를 듣고, 여자가 어버이날에 한 일로 가장 적절한 것을 고르시오.

① 조부모님 방문하기
② 부모님께 편지 쓰기
③ 가족과 여행하기
④ 엄마와 쇼핑하기
⑤ 가족과 식사하기

W Eric, how was your Parents' Day?

M It was nice. I visited my grandparents with my family. We celebrate every Parents' Day together.

W Oh, did you ＿＿＿＿＿＿＿＿＿ ＿＿＿＿＿＿＿＿＿ ＿＿＿＿＿＿＿＿＿
＿＿＿＿＿＿＿＿＿?

M Yes. I also wrote them a card and ＿＿＿＿＿＿＿＿＿
＿＿＿＿＿＿＿＿＿ ＿＿＿＿＿＿＿＿＿ ＿＿＿＿＿＿＿＿＿.

W You're such a good grandson.

M How about you, Julie?

W I ＿＿＿＿＿＿＿＿＿ ＿＿＿＿＿＿＿＿＿ ＿＿＿＿＿＿＿＿＿ my mom.
I bought a scarf for her.

M That's great.

05 장소 추론

대화를 듣고, 두 사람이 대화하는 장소로 가장 적절한 곳을 고르시오.

① 도서관   ② 기차역   ③ 우체국
④ 백화점   ⑤ 장난감 가게

W Hello. How may I help you?

M I'd like to ＿＿＿＿＿＿＿＿＿ ＿＿＿＿＿＿＿＿＿ ＿＿＿＿＿＿＿＿＿ to China.

W How would you like to ＿＿＿＿＿＿＿＿＿ ＿＿＿＿＿＿＿＿＿?

M By airmail, please.

W Okay. What's in the package?

M It's a toy train set for my cousin. *How long will it take?

W ＿＿＿＿＿＿＿＿＿ ＿＿＿＿＿＿＿＿＿ ＿＿＿＿＿＿＿＿＿ 5 days.

M Good. ＿＿＿＿＿＿＿＿＿ ＿＿＿＿＿＿＿＿＿ does it cost?

W It costs $50.

＊ **교육부 지정 의사소통 기능: 소요 시간 묻고 답하기**   동(이) 5 l 능(김) 6

How long does it take ~? (~하는 데) 얼마나 걸리니? – (It takes) 시간.

A: **How long does it take** to finish your homework?
숙제를 끝내는 데 시간이 얼마나 걸리니?
B: About 30 minutes. 약 30분 걸려.

A: **How long does it take** from here to the theater?
여기에서 극장까지 시간이 얼마나 걸리니?
B: It takes an hour. 한 시간 걸려.

대화를 듣고, 여자의 마지막 말의 의도로 가장 적절한 것을 고르시오.

① 불만　　② 감사　　③ 허락
④ 격려　　⑤ 후회

M　Hey, Sumi. What's wrong? You don't look well.

W　I tried everything, but I ＿＿＿＿＿＿ ＿＿＿＿＿＿ hiccuping. What should I do?

M　Try ＿＿＿＿＿＿ ＿＿＿＿＿＿ ＿＿＿＿＿＿. It might help.

W　I already did. But that ＿＿＿＿＿＿ ＿＿＿＿＿＿ ＿＿＿＿＿＿ me.

M　Then hold your breath for ＿＿＿＿＿＿ ＿＿＿＿＿＿ ＿＿＿＿＿＿ you can. That should work.

W　Okay. *[Pause]* Oh, it stopped! Thank you, James.

대화를 듣고, 남자가 추천한 모바일 앱의 기능을 고르시오.

① 길 찾기　　　② 영어사전
③ 번역기　　　④ 지하철 노선도
⑤ 맛집 소개

◀) Listening Tip

[s]가 sorry에서처럼 모음 앞에 있을 때는 'ㅆ'에 가깝게 발음하고 자음 앞이나 단어 끝에 올 때는 'ㅅ'로 발음해요. 그래서 sorry는 /쏘리/로 발음하지만, smile은 /스마일/로, tennis는 /테니스/로 발음해요.

W　I'm ◀)sorry I'm late. I had to help out a tourist on the way.

M　That's all right. What did you help with?

W　I ＿＿＿＿＿＿ ＿＿＿＿＿＿ ＿＿＿＿＿＿ her to City Hall.

M　Why didn't you just ＿＿＿＿＿＿ ＿＿＿＿＿＿ ＿＿＿＿＿＿?

W　She spoke French, and she didn't understand English at all.

M　Why don't you use the mobile app TalkTalk next time?

W　TalkTalk? What is that?

M　It changes ＿＿＿＿＿＿ ＿＿＿＿＿＿ ＿＿＿＿＿＿ ＿＿＿＿＿＿.

W　Really? It sounds very helpful.

대화를 듣고, 두 사람이 대화 직후에 할 일로 가장 적절한 것을 고르시오.

① 기차역에 가기
② 해운대 해변에 가기
③ 수영하기
④ 음식점 가기
⑤ 국수 요리하기

M　Susan, welcome to Busan!

W　Hi, Hajun. I'm so ＿＿＿＿＿＿ ＿＿＿＿＿＿ ＿＿＿＿＿＿.

M　Have you ever been here before?

W　No, it's ＿＿＿＿＿＿ ＿＿＿＿＿＿ ＿＿＿＿＿＿. I went to Haeundae Beach ＿＿＿＿＿＿ ＿＿＿＿＿＿. It was fantastic.

M　Great. Are you hungry?

W　Yes, a little. Why?

M I know a good restaurant around here. It has delicious noodle dishes. What do you think?

W Sure. _____ _____ _____ right now.

---

09 언급하지 않은 내용 찾기

대화를 듣고, 여자가 다녀온 여행에 대해 언급하지 않은 것을 고르시오.

① 여행지   ② 교통수단   ③ 날씨
④ 활동   ⑤ 음식

M Kate! Did you have a good time on your trip?

W I just loved it. I _____ _____ _____ _____ with my family.

M Wow! How did you get to the island?

W I _____ _____ _____. It was fun.

M Great. How was the weather?

W The weather _____ _____. I went snorkeling at the beach. I had _____ _____ _____ _____.

M That sounds like fun!

---

10 주제 추론

다음을 듣고, 여자가 하는 말의 내용으로 가장 적절한 것을 고르시오.

① 건강에 좋은 음식
② 맛있는 식당의 조건
③ 채식을 권하는 이유
④ 패스트푸드를 먹는 건강한 방법
⑤ 패스트푸드를 줄여야 하는 이유

W We know that fast food _____ _____ _____ for us. But I'm sure many of you still enjoy fast food. So, today I'd like to tell you _____ _____ _____ eat fast food. First, choose chicken rather than beef. Second, _____ _____ the sauces. They are high in calories. Finally, if you need something to drink, consider milk _____ _____ _____.

---

11 일치하지 않는 내용 찾기

다음을 듣고, Stonehenge에 대한 내용으로 일치하지 않는 것을 고르시오.

① 세계의 불가사의한 곳 중 하나이다.
② 거대한 돌로 만들어졌다.
③ 약 5천 년 전에 건설되었을 것이다.
④ 누가 지었는지 알 수 없다.
⑤ 역사학자들이 용도를 알아냈다.

W May I have your attention, please? We're finally here at Stonehenge. This is _____ _____ _____ mysterious places on Earth. Stonehenge is _____ _____ _____ huge stones. Historians think it _____ _____ around 5,000 years ago. But _____ _____ _____ who built it or why. Now, let's look around this incredible place!

대화를 듣고, 여자가 종이꽃을 만든 목적으로 가장 적절한 것을 고르시오.

① 교실을 꾸미기 위해서
② 전시회에 출품하기 위해서
③ 엄마에게 선물을 드리기 위해서
④ 미술 숙제를 제출하기 위해서
⑤ 동아리 회원을 모집하기 위해서

M Where did you get these paper flowers?

W Actually, I made them.

M Wow, you're very _____ _____ _____ _____. They look like _____ _____.

W Thanks. I made them as a _____ _____ _____ _____ _____.

M *I'm sure your mom will love them.

W I hope so.

> ✱ **교육부 지정 의사소통 기능: 확신 표현하기**   동(이) 2 | 미 1
>
> **I'm sure ~. 분명히 ~할 거야**
> • **I'm sure** it's going to snow soon. 분명히 곧 눈이 올 거야.
> • **I'm sure** he will get first place in the contest. 그는 분명히 대회에서 1등을 할 거야.

대화를 듣고, 남자가 지불해야 할 금액으로 가장 적절한 것을 고르시오.

① $6   ② $8   ③ $12
④ $14   ⑤ $20

M Excuse me. I'm looking for socks for sports.

W Okay. How about these ones?

M They're nice. How much are they?

W _____ _____ _____ is $6, and _____ _____ _____ is $8.

M I'll take 2 pairs of black socks, please.

W Okay. It's $12 in total.

M Oh, wait! I'd like _____ _____ a pair of blue socks.

W All right. _____ _____ _____ $20 in all.

M Here's my credit card.

대화를 듣고, 두 사람의 관계로 가장 적절한 것을 고르시오.

① 영화감독 – 배우
② 신문기자 – 운동선수
③ 자동차 정비사 – 손님
④ 호텔 접수원 – 손님
⑤ 방송 진행자 – 우주 비행사

M Today, we have a special _____ _____ _____, Jesse Thompson. Jesse, can you hear me?

W Yes. Hi, Ben. Thank you _____ _____ _____.

M Where are you?

W I'm at the International Space Station.

M What are you doing there?

W _____ _____ a satellite and doing some research.

M When are you going to _____ _____ _____ _____ ?

W I've nearly finished my work, and I'll be on Earth in 6 days.

M Thank you for _____ _____ _____ _____ . I hope you get back safely.

15 부탁 파악

대화를 듣고, 여자가 남자에게 부탁한 일로 가장 적절한 것을 고르시오.

① 학교 잡지 홍보하기
② 전학생과 같이 앉기
③ 학교 잡지에 기사 쓰기
④ 만화 그릴 사람 소개하기
⑤ 재미있는 만화 추천하기

W Mark, we're in trouble.

M What's wrong?

W Timmy can't draw cartoons for _____ _____ _____ any longer. So, we have to _____ _____ _____ .

M Hmm... How about Julie?

W Julie? Who's that?

M She is a new student in my class.

W Does she _____ _____ well?

M Yes. I'm sure you will like her cartoons.

W Great. _____ _____ _____ _____ to me?

M Of course.

16 이유 파악

대화를 듣고, 남자가 전화한 이유로 가장 적절한 것을 고르시오.

① 쇼핑하러 가기 위해서
② 야구 보러 가기 위해서
③ 선물에 감사하기 위해서
④ 병문안하기 위해서
⑤ 스케이트 타러 가기 위해서

[Cell phone rings.]

W Hello.

M Hi, Semi. Are you busy right now?

W Not at all. What's up?

M I _____ _____ _____ _____ something. Can you help me?

W Of course. What is it?

M Can you _____ _____ _____ _____ ? I need your help to choose a baseball cap for my sister.

W Okay. Are you planning to go to _____ _____ _____ together?

M No. She broke her arm while she was skating. I just want to

_____ _____ _____.

W Oh, I see. Let's meet at 4 o'clock.

---

17 그림 상황에 적절한 대화 찾기

다음 그림의 상황에 가장 적절한 대화를 고르시오.

① ② ③ ④ ⑤

① W What would you like for _____ _____?

M I'd like a glass of mango juice.

② W _____ _____ _____
_____ the spaghetti?

M It was excellent! I liked it.

③ W Can you tell me _____ _____
_____ this pizza?

M Sure. It's really easy.

④ W Why do you like salad?

M Because it is good for your health.

⑤ W Do you have _____ _____ habits?

M Yes, I eat many vegetables and fruits every day.

---

18 언급하지 않은 내용 찾기

다음을 듣고, 남자가 김치전에 대해 언급하지 않은 것을 고르시오.

① 좋아하는 이유　② 주로 먹는 날
③ 재료　④ 만드는 방법
⑤ 유래

M My favorite food is kimchijeon. I love this food

_____ _____ _____. I usually eat

this food _____ _____ _____.

I made this once with my grandmother. Kimchijeon doesn't

need many things. It _____ _____

_____ flour, kimchi, onions, and seafood. Making

kimchijeon is easy. You just _____ _____

_____ with water. Then _____

_____ on a heated pan with oil.

---

19 이어질 응답 찾기

대화를 듣고, 남자의 마지막 말에 이어질 여자의 응답으로 가장 적절한 것을 고르시오.

Woman: _____

① Sorry, I'm busy now.
② Yes. That'll be fine.
③ Thanks for your call.
④ Thanks. She's better now.
⑤ I'll ask you again next time.

[Telephone rings.]

M Smile Pet Animal Hospital.

W Hello. This is Amy Pitt.

M Hello, Amy. What can I do for you?

W My dog _____ _____ _____ her
food for almost 3 days now. What should I do?

M Okay. Did you try _____ _____

_____ _____?

W Yes, I did. But she didn't eat them.

M I see. Would you like to _____ _____
_____?

W Yes, please.

M Is 2:30 _____ _____ _____?

20 이어질 응답 찾기

대화를 듣고, 남자의 마지막 말에 이어질 여자의
응답으로 가장 적절한 것을 고르시오.

Woman: _____

① See you next time!
② Where are you from?
③ Do you remember me?
④ Sure. That sounds great!
⑤ I don't remember you, either.

M Excuse me. Did you attend Wood Hill Middle School?

W Yes, I did. How _____ _____
_____ that?

M I'm Mingi. We were in _____ _____
_____ 10 years ago.

W Oh, I remember you now. It's been a long time since we last
met.

M Yes, it has. If you are _____ _____
_____, do you want to get some coffee?

실전 모의고사 **02**

점수
/20

01 다음을 듣고, 파리의 날씨로 가장 적절한 것을 고르시오.

①   ②   ③   ④   ⑤

02 대화를 듣고, 여자가 찍은 사진으로 가장 적절한 것을 고르시오.

①   ②   ③

④   ⑤

03 대화를 듣고, 남자가 살고 싶은 집에 대해 언급하지 <u>않은</u> 것을 고르시오.
① 지붕 색상   ② 층수   ③ 전망
④ 방 개수   ⑤ 편의시설

04 대화를 듣고, 여자가 주말에 한 일로 가장 적절한 것을 고르시오.
① 친구 집 가기   ② 스파게티 만들기
③ 번지점프하기   ④ 액션 영화 보기
⑤ 공포 체험하기

05 대화를 듣고, 두 사람이 대화하는 장소로 가장 적절한 곳을 고르시오.
① 병원   ② 수영장   ③ 방송국
④ 세차장   ⑤ 중고차 매장

06 대화를 듣고, 남자의 마지막 말의 의도로 가장 적절한 것을 고르시오.
① 축하   ② 칭찬   ③ 격려
④ 용서   ⑤ 불만

07 대화를 듣고, 남자가 여자에게 가져가라고 한 물건을 고르시오.
① 방수 재킷   ② 모자   ③ 우산
④ 선글라스   ⑤ 지도

08 대화를 듣고, 여자가 대화 직후에 할 일로 가장 적절한 것을 고르시오.
① 머리 말리기
② 미용실 가기
③ 헤어드라이어 환불하기
④ 수리점에 전화하기
⑤ 헤어드라이어 새로 사기

09 대화를 듣고, 전시회에 대해 언급하지 <u>않은</u> 것을 고르시오.
① 전시 기간   ② 작가   ③ 티켓 요금
④ 사진 촬영   ⑤ 전시회 위치

10 다음을 듣고, 여자가 하는 말의 내용으로 가장 적절한 것을 고르시오.
① 건강한 생활 습관
② 환경 보호의 중요성
③ 미세먼지에 대처하는 방법
④ 올바른 양치질 방법
⑤ 물을 자주 마시면 좋은 점

11 다음을 듣고, Jenny Evans에 대한 내용으로 일치하지 <u>않는</u> 것을 고르시오.

① 친절하고 생각이 깊다. ② 남을 도우려고 한다.
③ 훌륭한 리더이다.   ④ 공부를 열심히 한다.
⑤ 이번에 반장이 되었다.

12 대화를 듣고, 여자가 전화를 건 목적으로 가장 적절한 것을 고르시오.

① 약속을 취소하기 위해서
② 계획을 변경하기 위해서
③ 준비물을 확인하기 위해서
④ 스키장 위치를 알려주기 위해서
⑤ 만날 시간을 정하기 위해서

13 대화를 듣고, 여자가 지불해야 할 금액으로 가장 적절한 것을 고르시오.

① $15   ② $18   ③ $20
④ $21   ⑤ $25

14 대화를 듣고, 두 사람의 관계로 가장 적절한 것을 고르시오.

① 택시 기사 – 탑승객
② 택배기사 – 고객
③ 구직자 – 가게 점장
④ 자동차 판매원 – 손님
⑤ 운전자 – 경찰관

15 대화를 듣고, 여자가 남자에게 부탁한 일로 가장 적절한 것을 고르시오.

① 식물에 물주기   ② 병문안 가주기
③ 반려견 목욕시키기   ④ 반려견 돌봐주기
⑤ 집에 잠깐 들르기

16 대화를 듣고, 여자가 반품하려는 이유로 가장 적절한 것을 고르시오.

① 마음에 들지 않아서
② 구멍이 발견되어서
③ 같은 것을 선물 받아서
④ 사이즈가 맞지 않아서
⑤ 수선 서비스에 불만이 있어서

17 다음 그림의 상황에 가장 적절한 대화를 고르시오.

①   ②   ③   ④   ⑤

18 다음을 듣고, 남자가 mooncake에 대해 언급하지 <u>않은</u> 것을 고르시오.

① 먹는 시기   ② 모양   ③ 재료
④ 유래   ⑤ 의미

[19-20] 대화를 듣고, 여자의 마지막 말에 이어질 남자의 응답으로 가장 적절한 것을 고르시오.

19 Man: _____

① Yes, I want to be a rapper.
② Me, too. I like watching movies.
③ I'm sorry, but I don't like them.
④ Sure, I'd love to. I can't wait!
⑤ Right. He's good at dancing and singing.

20 Man: _____

① You should go and see a doctor.
② But I need to check you again.
③ When did you first have the problem?
④ You should turn off your smartphone.
⑤ Bend your wrists back and forth. It's easy.

Dictation 02

◇ 다시 듣고, 빈칸에 들어갈 알맞은 단어를 써보세요.

정답 및 해설 p.8

01 날씨 파악

다음을 듣고, 파리의 날씨로 가장 적절한 것을 고르시오.

① ② ③
④ ⑤

M Let's look at _____ _____ _____ forecast. It will _____ _____ _____ in many parts of Asia, including Seoul, Beijing, and Hong Kong. In New York, there will be clear skies _____ _____ _____. It will be windy and cloudy in London, but there will be _____ _____ _____ in Paris.

02 그림 정보 파악

대화를 듣고, 여자가 찍은 사진으로 가장 적절한 것을 고르시오.

① ② ③
④ ⑤

🔊 Listening Tip

mountain처럼 [n]과 [t]가 만나는 경우에, [t]는 '트'로 발음하지 않고, 잠시 숨을 멈춘 것 같은 소리가 납니다. 즉, /마운튼/이라기보다 /마운은/처럼 발음되는 것이죠.

M Mina, you are back from your vacation.

W Yes, I had so much fun. Oh, I have _____ _____ here. Do you want to see them?

M Sure. *[Pause]* Where did you take this picture? _____ _____.

W I went hiking at Ever 🔊 Mountain. Do you see _____ _____ _____ _____ _____?

M The one next to the tree?

W Yes. I stayed there for 3 days. It was so _____ _____.

03 언급하지 않은 내용 찾기

대화를 듣고, 남자가 살고 싶은 집에 대해 언급하지 않은 것을 고르시오.

① 지붕 색상   ② 층수   ③ 전망
④ 방 개수   ⑤ 편의시설

W Look at the house over there. It looks like a train.

M But it's too small. I prefer a big house with a _____ _____.

W *What kind of house do you want to live in when you grow up?

M I want to live in _____ _____ _____ 2 floors. And in the house, there have to be

_____ _____ _____ my family.
At least 5 rooms.

W That sounds nice. Is there _____ _____
_____ _____ ?

M _____ _____ _____ should be
enough.

✱ 교육부 지정 의사소통 기능: **구체적 정보 묻기** 동(윤) 1|미 2|비 7

What kind of ~ do you ...? 어떤 ~을 …하니?
• **What kind of** pet **do you** want to have? 너는 어떤 종류의 반려동물을 기르고 싶니?
• **What kind of** music **do you** listen to? 너는 어떤 종류의 음악을 듣니?

---

04 한 일 파악

대화를 듣고, 여자가 주말에 한 일로 가장 적절한
것을 고르시오.

① 친구 집 가기　　② 스파게티 만들기
③ 번지점프하기　　④ 액션 영화 보기
⑤ 공포 체험하기

🔊 **Listening Tip**
동사의 과거형을 만드는 '-ed'는 무성음 뒤에서는 [t]로, 유
성음 뒤에서는 [d]로, [d], [t] 소리 뒤에서는 [id]로 발음
해요. jump의 [p]는 무성음이므로 그 뒤에 오는 '-ed'는 [t]
로 발음하지요.

W Did you have a good weekend?

M It was all right. I watched an action movie and made
spaghetti. What about you?

W I went to Gapyeong _____ _____
_____ .

M I see. What did you do there?

W I went bungee jumping _____ _____
_____ _____ .

M How was it?

W It was _____ _____ _____ at
first, but I got over my fear and 🔊jumped.

---

05 장소 추론

대화를 듣고, 두 사람이 대화하는 장소로 가장 적
절한 곳을 고르시오.

① 병원　　　　② 수영장
③ 방송국　　　④ 세차장
⑤ 중고차 매장

M How may I help you?

W This is my first visit here. Can you help me _____
_____ _____ ?

M Sure. Did you change your bills into coins?

W Yes. I have them here.

M All right. First put some coins in this machine. Then water
_____ _____ _____ for 3 minutes.

W Then where do I _____ _____

    _____ for the car?

M You have to put some coins in here again, and then push this soap button.

W Oh, okay. I brought my own brush _____

    _____ _____ _____. Can I use it here?

M Of course.

---

06 의도 파악

대화를 듣고, 남자의 마지막 말의 의도로 가장 적절한 것을 고르시오.

① 축하　　② 칭찬　　③ 격려
④ 용서　　⑤ 불만

M Great work, Jenna!

W But coach, I didn't win today.

M No, you didn't. But you _____ _____ _____ today at the game.

W Do you think so?

M Yes, I know _____ _____ _____ _____ at the game. You also got better at kicking.

W Thanks, but I'm still _____ _____ _____. I was so close to winning.

M Don't get too upset about the result. Losing is _____ _____ _____ _____. You'll win next time.

---

07 특정 정보 파악

대화를 듣고, 남자가 여자에게 가져가라고 한 물건을 고르시오.

① 방수 재킷　　　② 모자
③ 우산　　　　　④ 선글라스
⑤ 지도

W Ethan, are you from New Zealand?

M Yes, I lived in Auckland.

W How is the weather _____ _____ _____? I'm going to visit New Zealand next month.

M March is _____ _____ _____ _____ _____ New Zealand. It's really warm.

W Great! *I'm looking forward to going to the beach and relaxing there.

M There are many _____ _____, but it sometimes rains in March. You should _____ _____ _____.

W Okay. _____ _____ _____.

* 교육부 지정 의사소통 기능: **기대 표현하기**

능(양) 3|비 2|금 2

I'm looking forward to ~. 나는 (~하는 것)을 기대해.
- **I'm looking forward to** seeing you again. 당신을 다시 만나기를 기대하고 있어요.
- **I'm looking forward to** summer break. 난 여름방학을 손꼽아 기다리고 있어.

08 할 일 파악

대화를 듣고, 여자가 대화 직후에 할 일로 가장 적절한 것을 고르시오.

① 머리 말리기
② 미용실 가기
③ 헤어드라이어 환불하기
④ 수리점에 전화하기
⑤ 헤어드라이어 새로 사기

M Amy, are you done with the hair dryer? Can I borrow it?

W I'm _____ _____ _____.
[Pause] Oh no!

M What happened?

W It just _____ _____ _____.

M Again? When did you buy the hair dryer?

W I bought it last month. This is the third time it stopped.

M You should call _____ _____
_____. Since you bought it last month, you can get it fixed for free.

W Really? Maybe I should _____ _____
_____ _____.

09 언급하지 않은 내용 찾기

대화를 듣고, 전시회에 대해 언급하지 <u>않은</u> 것을 고르시오.

① 전시 기간　　② 작가
③ 티켓 요금　　④ 사진 촬영
⑤ 전시회 위치

[Telephone Rings.]

W Hello, Bright Stars Gallery. How may I help you?

M Hello, did the Harrington Photo Exhibition start?

W Yes, it _____ _____ and will continue until May 17.

M The one by Joseph Harrington, right?

W That's right. You'll see his 250 _____ _____
_____ around the world.

M Great. Can I take pictures there?

W No, you can't. We ask all visitors to _____
_____ their cell phones.

M Okay. _____ _____ _____
_____ is the exhibition?

W It's in Room C.

10 주제 추론

다음을 듣고, 여자가 하는 말의 내용으로 가장 적절한 것을 고르시오.

① 건강한 생활 습관
② 환경 보호의 중요성
③ 미세먼지에 대처하는 방법
④ 올바른 양치질 방법
⑤ 물을 자주 마시면 좋은 점

W Hello, everyone. It's hard to see clear skies because of fine dust these days. _____ causes serious diseases. So, it's important to _____ _____ _____ the fine dust. When you go out, _____ _____ _____ to cover your nose and mouth. When you come back, be sure to _____ _____ _____. Lastly, drink as much _____ _____ _____.

11 일치하지 않는 내용 찾기

다음을 듣고, Jenny Evans에 대한 내용으로 일치하지 <u>않는</u> 것을 고르시오.

① 친절하고 생각이 깊다.
② 남을 도우려고 한다.
③ 훌륭한 리더이다.
④ 공부를 열심히 한다.
⑤ 이번에 반장이 되었다.

M Hello, everyone. I'd like to recommend Jenny Evans as our class president. She is a _____ _____ _____ thoughtful person ◀)because she always tries _____ _____ _____. She is a great leader, and she listens to the teacher and _____ _____ _____. I think she will be a _____ _____ _____.

◀) **Listening Tip**

because처럼 끝소리가 [s], [z]인 말 다음에 [ʃ] 소리가 나는 'sh'로 시작하는 단어가 오면 앞 단어의 [s], [z]는 발음하지 않아요. 그래서 because she는 /비코즈 쉬/가 아니라 /비커쉬/로 발음합니다.

12 목적 파악

대화를 듣고, 여자가 전화를 건 목적으로 가장 적절한 것을 고르시오.

① 약속을 취소하기 위해서
② 계획을 변경하기 위해서
③ 준비물을 확인하기 위해서
④ 스키장 위치를 알려주기 위해서
⑤ 만날 시간을 정하기 위해서

[Cell phone rings.]

M Hello.

W Hi, Adam. It's Sumin. I'm calling about _____ _____ _____.

M We're going to go skiing. Is something wrong?

W I heard it's going to _____ _____ _____ this Saturday.

M In that case, I think going skiing _____ _____ a very good idea.

W You're right. So, should we _____ _____ _____ ?

M Why don't we go to the movies instead?

W That sounds good.

13 숫자 정보 파악 (금액)

대화를 듣고, 여자가 지불해야 할 금액으로 가장 적절한 것을 고르시오.

① $15 ② $18 ③ $20
④ $21 ⑤ $25

M Can I help the next person in line, please?

W How much are _____ _____?

M $16 for a vegetable pizza and $18 for _____ _____ _____.

W And are all the sodas $3?

M Yes, they are.

W Okay. Can I get a large cheese pizza and one coke?

M Sure. Your pizza _____ _____ _____ in about 15 minutes.

14 관계 추론

대화를 듣고, 두 사람의 관계로 가장 적절한 것을 고르시오.

① 택시 기사 – 탑승객
② 택배기사 – 고객
③ 구직자 – 가게 점장
④ 자동차 판매원 – 손님
⑤ 운전자 – 경찰관

M I saw your sign on the window. Are you _____ _____ a delivery person?

W Yes, are you interested in applying?

M I am. I'm _____ _____ _____ _____.

W _____ _____ _____ a van before?

M Yes, I have. I drove a delivery van _____ _____ _____.

W Great. When can you _____ _____?

M I can start next Monday.

W Okay. Please fill out this form.

15 부탁 파악

대화를 듣고, 여자가 남자에게 부탁한 일로 가장 적절한 것을 고르시오.

① 식물에 물주기
② 병문안 가주기
③ 반려견 목욕시키기
④ 반려견 돌봐주기
⑤ 집에 잠깐 들르기

W Inho, do you have any plans for this Saturday?

M Nothing special. I think I'll stay home and _____ _____ _____ _____, Max.

W Then could you _____ _____ _____ _____?

M Sure, what is it?

W My family is going to visit my grandmother in the hospital. But we can't take our dog Lily with us. _____ _____ _____ _____ until we come back?

M Of course. Max _____ _____

_____ _____ . He'd love to play with Lily again.

W Thank you so much.

---

16 이유 파악

대화를 듣고, 여자가 반품하려는 이유로 가장 적절한 것을 고르시오.

① 마음에 들지 않아서
② 구멍이 발견되어서
③ 같은 것을 선물 받아서
④ 사이즈가 맞지 않아서
⑤ 수선 서비스에 불만이 있어서

M What can I do for you?

W I'd like to return _____ _____, please.

M Of course. May I see your receipt?

W Sure, here you are.

M Is there _____ _____ with the jeans?

W They are _____ _____ _____ my son.

M I see. The receipt shows you paid in cash. You can

_____ _____ _____

_____ in cash or as a gift card. Which one would you like?

W Cash, please.

---

17 그림 상황에 적절한 대화 찾기

다음 그림의 상황에 가장 적절한 대화를 고르시오.

① ② ③ ④ ⑤

① **M** I want to report a car accident!

W All right. Go ahead.

② **M** Someone _____ _____ _____ my house.

W Okay. What's your address?

③ **M** Did you see _____ _____ about the fire?

W Do you mean _____ _____ at the shopping mall?

④ **M** There's a fire! Call the fire station!

W I have a cell phone. _____ _____ right away!

⑤ **M** The TV is not working again.

W I'll call the _____ _____ right now.

다음을 듣고, 남자가 mooncake에 대해 언급하지 않은 것을 고르시오.

① 먹는 시기 ② 모양 ③ 재료
④ 유래 ⑤ 의미

M The Chinese enjoy eating mooncakes during the Mid-Autumn Festival, one of _____ _____ _____ Chinese festivals. Mooncakes are a traditional Chinese food. They are _____, _____ cakes. The cakes have different fillings, such as _____, _____, _____ _____. The design on the top of the cakes _____ _____ "fortune," so people give them to friends and family during the festival.

대화를 듣고, 여자의 마지막 말에 이어질 남자의 응답으로 가장 적절한 것을 고르시오.

Man: _____

① Yes, I want to be a rapper.
② Me, too. I like watching movies.
③ I'm sorry, but I don't like them.
④ Sure, I'd love to. I can't wait!
⑤ Right. He's good at dancing and singing.

M Minji, what are you going to do this weekend?
W I'm going to go to Super Boys' _____ _____ _____ Bomi.
M That sounds great. I'm a big Super Boys fan, too.
W Really? _____ _____ do you like best?
M I like Juno best. I think he's one of _____ _____ _____ in Korea.
W _____ _____ _____ _____ join us?

대화를 듣고, 여자의 마지막 말에 이어질 남자의 응답으로 가장 적절한 것을 고르시오.

Man: _____

① You should go and see a doctor.
② But I need to check you again.
③ When did you first have the problem?
④ You should turn off your smartphone.
⑤ Bend your wrists back and forth. It's easy.

M _____ _____, Amy?
W Hello, Dr. Jo. My right wrist hurts.
M All right. Let me take a look at it. Do _____ _____ _____ smartphone a lot?
W Yes. I chat a lot with my friends.
M I think you use your _____ _____ _____ too much when you text.
W Then what should I do?
M You should do some _____ _____.
W Okay. How do I _____ _____ _____?

실전 모의고사 03

01 다음을 듣고, 오늘 저녁 날씨로 가장 적절한 것을 고르시오.

① ② ③ ④ ⑤

02 대화를 듣고, 여자가 구입할 목도리로 가장 적절한 것을 고르시오.

① ② ③

④ ⑤

03 대화를 듣고, 남자가 영화에 대해 언급하지 <u>않은</u> 것을 고르시오.

① 장르 ② 스토리 ③ 주연 배우
④ 상영관 ⑤ 상영 시간

04 대화를 듣고, 남자가 어제 한 일로 가장 적절한 것을 고르시오.

① 집에서 쉬기 ② 모자 쇼핑하기
③ 여행사에 가기 ④ 친구와 축구하기
⑤ 할아버지 생신 축하하기

05 대화를 듣고, 두 사람이 대화하는 장소로 가장 적절한 곳을 고르시오.

① 학교 ② 박물관 ③ 놀이공원
④ 백화점 ⑤ 전시회

06 대화를 듣고, 여자의 마지막 말의 의도로 가장 적절한 것을 고르시오.

① 불만 ② 감사 ③ 제안
④ 부탁 ⑤ 칭찬

07 대화를 듣고, 여자가 선택한 과제의 주제를 고르시오.

① 강강술래 ② 음식의 기원
③ 전쟁 영웅들 ④ 승전 비결
⑤ 거북선

08 대화를 듣고, 남자가 대화 직후에 할 일로 가장 적절한 것을 고르시오.

① 책 빌리기 ② 학생증 제시하기
③ 분실 신고하기 ④ 서류 작성하기
⑤ 도서관 카드 발급받기

09 대화를 듣고, 여자가 박물관에 대해 언급하지 <u>않은</u> 것을 고르시오.

① 개관 시간 ② 휴관일 ③ 입장료
④ 주차장 ⑤ 사진 촬영 규칙

10 다음을 듣고, 남자가 하는 말의 내용으로 가장 적절한 것을 고르시오.

① 올림픽의 역사 ② 올림픽 일정 공지
③ 올림픽 방송 홍보 ④ 올림픽 개최지 발표
⑤ 입장권 구입 안내

11 다음을 듣고, December Rain에 대한 내용으로 일치하지 <u>않는</u> 것을 고르시오.

① Tim Spacey가 작곡한 노래이다.
② 1988년에 작곡되었다.
③ 곧바로 전 세계에서 히트했다.
④ 딸을 위한 노래이다.
⑤ 영국에서 아직도 큰 인기를 얻고 있다.

12 대화를 듣고, 여자가 전화를 건 목적으로 가장 적절한 것을 고르시오.

① 케이크를 주문하기 위해서
② 생일을 축하해주기 위해서
③ 생일 선물을 의논하기 위해서
④ 일찍 집에 오라고 하기 위해서
⑤ 식당 예약을 부탁하기 위해서

13 대화를 듣고, 남자가 지불해야 할 금액으로 가장 적절한 것을 고르시오.

① $70   ② $75   ③ $80
④ $85   ⑤ $90

14 대화를 듣고, 두 사람의 관계로 가장 적절한 것을 고르시오.

① 의사 – 환자
② 신문 기자 – 운동선수
③ 마라톤 코치 – 선수
④ 신발가게 점원 – 손님
⑤ 방송 진행자 – 요리사

15 대화를 듣고, 남자가 여자에게 부탁한 일로 가장 적절한 것을 고르시오.

① 차 태워주기
② 치과 예약하기
③ 한 시간 일찍 만나기
④ 과제 기한 연기해 주기
⑤ 남자의 엄마에게 연락하기

16 대화를 듣고, 남자가 애플파이를 태운 이유로 가장 적절한 것을 고르시오.

① 조리법을 몰라서
② 오븐이 고장 나서
③ 음악을 듣느라고
④ 통화를 하느라고
⑤ 오븐에 둔 채로 외출해서

17 다음 그림의 상황에 가장 적절한 대화를 고르시오.

①   ②   ③   ④   ⑤

18 다음을 듣고, 여자가 Colorado Food Festival에 대해 언급하지 <u>않은</u> 것을 고르시오.

① 입장료   ② 개최 시기   ③ 참가 자격
④ 역사   ⑤ 방문객 수

[19-20] 대화를 듣고, 여자의 마지막 말에 이어질 남자의 응답으로 가장 적절한 것을 고르시오.

19 Man: _____

① I love classical music.
② That song makes me happy.
③ They have many popular songs.
④ I just heard that song for the first time.
⑤ I've liked that band since I was a teenager.

20 Man: _____

① I found it at the park.
② I hope you find it soon.
③ It's too heavy for you to carry.
④ Can I borrow your smartphone?
⑤ Did you return the book to the library?

Dictation 03

◆ 다시 듣고, 빈칸에 들어갈 알맞은 단어를 써보세요.

정답 및 해설 p.15

---

01 날씨 파악

다음을 듣고, 오늘 저녁 날씨로 가장 적절한 것을 고르시오.

① ② ③
④ ⑤

W Good morning. I'm Jane Reed, your weather forecaster. It looks like we'll _____ _____ _____ _____ this morning. The snow will stop in the afternoon, but put on your _____ _____ . Strong winds are expected _____ _____ _____ . The temperatures will remain low all day. That's the weather forecast for today. Have a good day!

---

02 그림 정보 파악

대화를 듣고, 여자가 구입할 목도리로 가장 적절한 것을 고르시오.

① ② ③
④ ⑤

M Can I help you?
W Hi. I'm looking for a scarf for my little brother.
M Sure. How about _____ _____ _____ _____ ?
W It looks cute, but he _____ _____ _____ than cats.
M Then, how about this one with stars? This is popular in our shop.
W It's all right. *[Pause]* Oh, I _____ _____ _____ _____ . Can I see it?
M Of course. Here you are.
W It's nice. _____ _____ _____ .

---

03 언급하지 않은 내용 찾기

대화를 듣고, 남자가 영화에 대해 언급하지 <u>않은</u> 것을 고르시오.

① 장르   ② 스토리   ③ 주연 배우
④ 상영관   ⑤ 상영 시간

M *Did you hear about _____ _____ _____ , *Game of Death*?
W No, I didn't. Is it a _____ _____ ?
M Yes. In the movie, 5 people start playing a board game. Then mysterious things _____ _____ _____ .

W That sounds interesting. I like that kind of movie a lot.

M The movie _____ _____ _____ the Cine Box. Why don't we go and see it tomorrow?

W I'd love to! _____ _____ is the movie?

M _____ _____ _____ 4 o'clock and 7 o'clock.

W Then let's see the 4 o'clock show.

✱ 교육부 지정 의사소통 기능: **알고 있는지 묻기 1**   동(윤) 7

Did you hear about ~? ~에 대해 들었니?
• **Did you hear about** the new musical? 너 새 뮤지컬에 대해 들었니?
• **Did you hear about** tomorrow's weather? 너 내일 날씨에 대해 들었니?

04 한 일 파악

대화를 듣고, 남자가 어제 한 일로 가장 적절한 것을 고르시오.

① 집에서 쉬기
② 모자 쇼핑하기
③ 여행사에 가기
④ 친구와 축구하기
⑤ 할아버지 생신 축하하기

W Seho, what did you do yesterday?

M I went to _____ _____ _____ with my parents.

W That's nice. What did you do there?

M It was my grandfather's birthday, so we celebrated _____ _____ _____ _____.

W Did you give him anything?

M Of course. I gave him _____ _____ _____ and a card.

W It sounds like you _____ _____ _____ _____.

05 장소 추론

대화를 듣고, 두 사람이 대화하는 장소로 가장 적절한 곳을 고르시오.

① 학교   ② 박물관   ③ 놀이공원
④ 백화점   ⑤ 전시회

W Dad, thanks for _____ _____ _____ today. It's great to be out of the house.

M Of course, honey. I knew you were a little stressed because of schoolwork. Today, forget about your worries and _____ _____ _____.

W Thanks. I have a map here, but I don't know _____ _____ _____ first.

M Well, how about _____ _____

_____ _____ first? It's right over there.

W It looks like there is a long line for it. How about bumper cars?

M _____ _____ _____

_____ .

06 의도 파악

대화를 듣고, 여자의 마지막 말의 의도로 가장 적절한 것을 고르시오.
① 불만   ② 감사   ③ 제안
④ 부탁   ⑤ 칭찬

M Good afternoon, ma'am.

W Good afternoon. To the international airport, please.

M Are you going _____ _____ international?

W Yes, I'm going to go to Spain.

M What time is your flight?

W I have a 3:30 flight to catch, but there is _____

_____ _____ _____ .

M We need _____ _____ _____ .

W Yes. I have to get there as soon as possible so _____

_____ the highway.

07 특정 정보 파악

대화를 듣고, 여자가 선택한 과제의 주제를 고르시오.
① 강강술래   ② 음식의 기원
③ 전쟁 영웅들   ④ 승전 비결
⑤ 거북선

W Jason, is there any homework from _____

_____ _____ ?

M Yes. You have to write a report about the Imjin War. We learned about it last week.

W Anything about the Imjin War?

M Yes. _____ _____ , Yi Sunshin, the Turtle Ship, and Ganggangsullae.

W Hmm... There are so _____ _____

_____ . I can't choose one.

M How about writing about the Imjin War heroes? It won't

_____ _____ _____ .

W _____ _____ _____ .

대화를 듣고, 남자가 대화 직후에 할 일로 가장 적절한 것을 고르시오.

① 책 빌리기
② 학생증 제시하기
③ 분실 신고하기
④ 서류 작성하기
⑤ 도서관 카드 발급받기

🔊 **Listening Tip**

fill out에서 out처럼 모음으로 시작하는 단어 앞에 자음으로 끝나는 단어가 올 때는 앞의 자음과 뒤 모음 사이에 연음이 일어나서 연결해서 말하게 돼요. 즉, /필아웃/이 아니라 /피라웃/으로 발음해요.

M Excuse me. I'd like to get a library card. I lost mine last week.
W Can I see _____ _____ _____?
M Sure. Here you are. How long does it take to get a new card?
W It takes _____ _____ _____.
M Can I come back _____ _____? I have a class in 15 minutes.
W Yes, you can. And would you 🔊 fill out _____ _____?
M Okay.

대화를 듣고, 여자가 박물관에 대해 언급하지 않은 것을 고르시오.

① 개관 시간   ② 휴관일
③ 입장료   ④ 주차장
⑤ 사진 촬영 규칙

[Telephone rings.]

W The Gyeongju National Museum. How can I help you?
M I'd like to know the opening hours of the museum.
W _____ _____ _____ _____ 10:00 to 6:00.
M Are you open on holidays?
W We _____ _____ _____ New Year's Day and Chuseok.
M I see. And how much is the entrance fee?
W _____ _____.
M Great! One more question. May I _____ _____ inside the museum?
W Yes, you may.

다음을 듣고, 남자가 하는 말의 내용으로 가장 적절한 것을 고르시오.

① 올림픽의 역사
② 올림픽 일정 공지
③ 올림픽 방송 홍보
④ 올림픽 개최지 발표
⑤ 입장권 구입 안내

M At last, the Summer Olympics will start next week! If you are interested in watching the Olympics, be _____ _____ SBN Sports. You can _____ _____ _____ broadcasts all day long. At 11:30 p.m. every night, you can also _____ _____ _____ of the games of the day. If you _____ _____ _____, visit our website at www.SBN.com.

언급하지 않은 내용 찾기

다음을 듣고, December Rain에 대한 내용으로 일치하지 않는 것을 고르시오.

① Tim Spacey가 작곡한 노래이다.
② 1988년에 작곡되었다.
③ 곧바로 전 세계에서 히트했다.
④ 딸을 위한 노래이다.
⑤ 영국에서 아직도 큰 인기를 얻고 있다.

M We started the show with "December Rain." Did you enjoy the song? It was _____ _____ Tim Spacey. He wrote this _____ _____ _____ 1988, and it became an instant hit all over the world. It's a love song _____ _____ _____, and it is still one of the _____ _____ songs in England.

---

12 목적 파악

대화를 듣고, 여자가 전화를 건 목적으로 가장 적절한 것을 고르시오.

① 케이크를 주문하기 위해서
② 생일을 축하해주기 위해서
③ 생일 선물을 의논하기 위해서
④ 일찍 집에 오라고 하기 위해서
⑤ 식당 예약을 부탁하기 위해서

[Cell phone rings.]
M Hello.
W Hi, Mike. Did you remember it's your dad's birthday?
M Of course, Mom. I remembered.
W Can you _____ _____ _____ today? We're going to _____ _____ _____ _____.
M Oh, my study group finishes at 6. Is that okay?
W All right. Just come home _____ _____ _____ you can after studying.
M Don't worry. I will.

---

13 숫자 정보 파악 (금액)

대화를 듣고, 남자가 지불해야 할 금액으로 가장 적절한 것을 고르시오.

① $70   ② $75   ③ $80
④ $85   ⑤ $90

W How may I help you?
M I like these backpacks. _____ _____ _____ _____ ?
W The one with 2 pockets is $85. _____ _____ _____ is $75.
M I'll take _____ _____ _____ 2 pockets.
W Okay. Do you have any coupons?
M Yes, I do. I have a coupon for a $5 discount. Here you are.
W Okay. _____ _____ _____ $80.
M All right. Here's my card.

① 의사 – 환자
② 신문 기자 – 운동선수
③ 마라톤 코치 – 선수
④ 신발가게 점원 – 손님
⑤ 방송 진행자 – 요리사

W Hi, Daniel. I'm Joy Carter from *The Herald*. Congratulations!

M Thank you.

W You won the London Marathon. _____ _____?

M I'm very happy.

W How did you _____ _____ the marathon?

M Besides _____ _____, I followed a healthy diet.

W Anything else?

M It was very important to find the right running shoes.

W Oh, I see. Thank you _____ _____ _____ and congratulations again.

M Thank you.

15 부탁 파악

대화를 듣고, 남자가 여자에게 부탁한 일로 가장 적절한 것을 고르시오.

① 차 태워주기
② 치과 예약하기
③ 한 시간 일찍 만나기
④ 과제 기한 연기해 주기
⑤ 남자의 엄마에게 연락하기

M Excuse me, Ms. Williams.

W Yes, Mike. Can I help you?

M I think I should go to the dentist today.

W Why? _____ _____ _____?

M I _____ _____ _____, and it's getting worse.

W I'm sorry to hear that.

M Could you _____ _____ _____? I'd like to leave an hour early today.

W Of course.

M Thank you so much.

16 이유 파악

대화를 듣고, 남자가 애플파이를 태운 이유로 가장 적절한 것을 고르시오.

① 조리법을 몰라서
② 오븐이 고장 나서
③ 음악을 듣느라고
④ 통화를 하느라고
⑤ 오븐에 둔 채로 외출해서

W Tony, do you smell _____ _____?

M Oh no! I forgot to turn off the oven!

W Turn it off right now!

M *[Pause]* It _____ _____. I'm sorry, Mom.

W _____ _____ _____ forget about the oven?

Listening Tip

next time처럼 두 단어가 같은 자음(ㄷ,ㅌ)으로 끝나고 시작할 때는 같은 자음을 두 번 발음하지 않고 약간 길게 한번만 발음합니다. 그래서 /넥스트 따임/이 아니라 /넥스~따임/으로 발음해요.

M Well, I was talking with Junha _____
_____ _____. Then I completely forgot about my apple pie.

W Don't forget to turn it off ◀)) next time.

M I won't, Mom.

---

17 그림 상황에 적절한 대화 찾기

다음 그림의 상황에 가장 적절한 대화를 고르시오.

① ② ③ ④ ⑤

① M Do you mind if I _____ _____
_____?

W Go ahead.

② M Don't forget to listen to _____ _____
_____.

W Okay, I won't.

③ M What kind of food do you want to eat?

W I want to eat Italian food.

④ M Mom, I'm not feeling well today.

W I think you should _____ _____
_____.

⑤ M _____ _____ _____?

W I'm worried about my dog.

---

18 언급하지 않은 내용 찾기

다음을 듣고, 여자가 Colorado Food Festival에 대해 언급하지 않은 것을 고르시오.

① 입장료　　② 개최 시기
③ 참가 자격　　④ 역사
⑤ 방문객 수

W Hi, I'm Amy Lee. I'm at the Colorado Food Festival now. There is no entrance fee, so you can enjoy this festival _____ _____. This 3-day festival starts on _____ _____ _____ of September every year. The festival _____ _____ _____ 1895 and has been going on since then. Over 500,000 _____ _____ _____ _____ the festival every year.

19 이어질 응답 찾기

대화를 듣고, 여자의 마지막 말에 이어질 남자의 응답으로 가장 적절한 것을 고르시오.

Man: _____

① I love classical music.
② That song makes me happy.
③ They have many popular songs.
④ I just heard that song for the first time.
⑤ I've liked that band since I was a teenager.

W Uncle Jim, what's your favorite band?
M I like the British _____ _____ Queen a lot.
W Oh, I know them. _____ _____ _____ _____ about the band.
M I saw the movie 3 times.
W _____ _____ _____ _____ do you like best?
M I love "Radio Ga Ga" the best.
W _____ _____ _____ _____ _____ so much?

20 이어질 응답 찾기

대화를 듣고, 여자의 마지막 말에 이어질 남자의 응답으로 가장 적절한 것을 고르시오.

Man: _____

① I found it at the park.
② I hope you find it soon.
③ It's too heavy for you to carry.
④ Can I borrow your smartphone?
⑤ Did you return the book to the library?

M You look so down, Mina. Is something wrong?
W I lost my smartphone at the library.
M That's too bad.
W My father gave it to me _____ _____ _____.
M So you got it _____ _____?
W Yes. It's a brand-new smartphone.
M _____ _____ _____ the lost and found?
W Yeah, but _____ _____ _____.

실전 모의고사 **04**

01 다음을 듣고, 금요일 아침 날씨로 가장 적절한 것을 고르시오.

①   ②   ③   ④   ⑤

02 대화를 듣고, 여자가 만든 바구니로 가장 적절한 것을 고르시오.

①   ②   ③

④   ⑤

03 대화를 듣고, 남자의 심정으로 가장 적절한 것을 고르시오.

① thankful   ② happy   ③ proud
④ nervous   ⑤ confident

04 대화를 듣고, 여자가 주말에 한 일로 가장 적절한 것을 고르시오.

① 조카 돌보기
② 이모 도와주기
③ 아빠와 낚시하기
④ 친구 생일 파티에 가기
⑤ 음식 나눔 봉사활동하기

05 대화를 듣고, 두 사람이 대화하는 장소로 가장 적절한 곳을 고르시오.

① 동물 병원   ② 은행
③ 유기견 보호소   ④ 어린이집
⑤ 애견 용품점

06 대화를 듣고, 남자의 마지막 말의 의도로 가장 적절한 것을 고르시오.

① 격려   ② 허락   ③ 제안
④ 불만   ⑤ 칭찬

07 대화를 듣고, 여자가 듣고자 하는 방과 후 수업으로 가장 적절한 것을 고르시오.

① 댄스   ② 요리   ③ 스포츠
④ 유적 답사   ⑤ 독서

08 대화를 듣고, 두 사람이 대화 직후에 할 일로 가장 적절한 것을 고르시오.

① 상자 정리하기
② 초대장 제작하기
③ 동네에 포스터 붙이기
④ 포스터 새로 제작하기
⑤ 축제 준비물 확인하기

09 대화를 듣고, 여자가 송편에 대해 언급하지 <u>않은</u> 것을 고르시오.

① 먹는 시기   ② 모양   ③ 맛
④ 유래   ⑤ 재료

10 다음을 듣고, 남자가 하는 말의 내용으로 가장 적절한 것을 고르시오.

① 나무를 심는 방법
② 종이를 절약하는 방법
③ 환경 파괴의 원인
④ 개인위생의 중요성
⑤ 종이 발명의 과정

11 다음을 듣고, Warka Tower에 대한 내용으로 일치하지 <u>않는</u> 것을 고르시오.

① 공기로부터 물을 모은다.
② 식수를 얻을 수 있다.
③ 만들기 쉽다.
④ 재료는 대나무와 그물이다.
⑤ 만드는 데 8주 걸린다.

12 대화를 듣고, 남자가 박물관에 전화를 건 목적으로 가장 적절한 것을 고르시오.

① 위치를 묻기 위해서
② 입장료를 알기 위해서
③ 투어를 예약하기 위해서
④ 개관 시간을 확인하기 위해서
⑤ 관람 규정을 확인하기 위해서

13 대화를 듣고, 두 사람이 만날 시각을 고르시오.

① 4:00 p.m.　　② 4:10 p.m.　　③ 4:20 p.m.
④ 4:30 p.m.　　⑤ 4:40 p.m.

14 대화를 듣고, 두 사람의 관계로 가장 적절한 것을 고르시오.

① 시험 감독관 – 수험생　　② 수리 기사 – 고객
③ 문구점 점원 – 학생　　④ 주방장 – 웨이터
⑤ 편의점 직원 – 손님

15 대화를 듣고, 여자가 남자에게 부탁한 일로 가장 적절한 것을 고르시오.

① 테이블 세팅하기　　② 숙제 도와주기
③ 식사 재료 사 오기　　④ 동영상 찾아보기
⑤ 스파게티 만들기

16 대화를 듣고, 여자가 스케이트를 타러 갈 수 <u>없는</u> 이유로 가장 적절한 것을 고르시오.

① 다리를 다쳐서
② 결혼식에 가야 해서
③ 스케이트를 타지 못해서
④ 동생 숙제를 도와줘야 해서
⑤ 엄마와 쇼핑을 가기로 해서

17 다음 그림의 상황에 가장 적절한 대화를 고르시오.

①　　②　　③　　④　　⑤

18 다음을 듣고, 여자가 영화에 대해 언급하지 <u>않은</u> 것을 고르시오.

① 제목　　② 개봉 연도　　③ 감독
④ 주인공　　⑤ 상영 시간

[19-20] 대화를 듣고, 여자의 마지막 말에 이어질 남자의 응답으로 가장 적절한 것을 고르시오.

19 Man: _____

① Good. I'll take it.
② I'm just looking around.
③ Okay. Your change is $2.
④ Sorry, but it doesn't look good on me.
⑤ I see. Then I'll just try on this T-shirt.

20 Man: _____

① I'm happy to hear that.
② I'm proud to be your student.
③ I'm always worried about her.
④ She'll try to do better next time.
⑤ I'm sorry to disappoint you again.

Dictation 04

◇ 다시 듣고, 빈칸에 들어갈 알맞은 단어를 써보세요.

정답 및 해설 p.21

---

01 날씨 파악

다음을 듣고, 금요일 아침 날씨로 가장 적절한 것을 고르시오.

① ② ③ ④ ⑤

M Good afternoon. Welcome to the weather forecast. It is _____ _____ _____, and there is a chance of some rain tonight. Tomorrow will be perfect for outdoor activities because it'll be _____ _____ _____. However, it's going to _____ _____ _____ _____, and the rain is expected to turn into snow that night.

---

02 그림 정보 파악

대화를 듣고, 여자가 만든 바구니로 가장 적절한 것을 고르시오.

① ② ③ ④ ⑤

M Seri, what is in the box?
W Take a look. *[Pause]* I made this basket for my mom.
M It looks amazing. _____ _____ _____ old jeans?
W Yes, I used a pair of old jeans. What do you think?
M I really like _____ _____ _____ _____ _____.
W Thanks. My mom _____ _____. So, I added it.
M There are _____ _____ the flower. What does "B.M.W." mean?
W It means, "Best Mom in the World."
M That's so sweet. _____ _____ your mom will love it.

---

03 심정 추론

대화를 듣고, 남자의 심정으로 가장 적절한 것을 고르시오.

① thankful ② happy ③ proud
④ nervous ⑤ confident

W James! You look amazing in that suit.
M Lily, thank you for coming.
W It's your first time in _____ _____ _____. I would not miss it. So, when is it your turn to play?
M I'm next.

W Really? I can't wait to _____ _____ _____.

M I'm so scared right now. I just hope I don't _____ _____ _____ when I play on the stage.

W Don't worry. You are the greatest pianist I know.

동(윤) 4

04 한 일 파악

대화를 듣고, 여자가 주말에 한 일로 가장 적절한
것을 고르시오.

① 조카 돌보기
② 이모 도와주기
③ 아빠와 낚시하기
④ 친구 생일 파티에 가기
⑤ 음식 나눔 봉사활동하기

W Jake, how was your weekend?

M Great. I _____ _____ with my dad. How about you?

W I went to my aunt's house for a birthday party.

M Whose birthday party was it?

W It was my nephew's _____ _____.

M First birthday party? Did you do _____ _____ there?

W Well, I mostly _____ _____ _____ prepare food in the kitchen. But we had so much fun together.

---

05 장소 추론

대화를 듣고, 두 사람이 대화하는 장소로 가장 적
절한 곳을 고르시오.

① 동물 병원   ② 은행
③ 유기견 보호소   ④ 어린이집
⑤ 애견 용품점

M May I help you?

W Yes, please. I heard from the animal clinic that I could find my dog here.

M I see. What does your dog _____ _____?

W She is a brown poodle. Her hair is _____ _____ _____.

M When and where did you lose her?

W I lost her in the park 2 days ago.

M *Can you _____ _____ _____ about her?

W When I lost her, she was wearing pink clothing.

M All right. Let me check _____ _____ _____.

> ★ **교육부 지정 의사소통 기능: 설명 요청하기**   동(윤) 4
>
> **Can you tell me more about ~?** ~에 대해서 더 말해 줄래?
> • **Can you tell me more about** your plans? 네 계획에 대해서 좀 더 말해 줄래?
> • **Can you tell me more about** the singer? 그 가수에 대해서 좀 더 말해 줄래?

대화를 듣고, 남자의 마지막 말의 의도로 가장 적절한 것을 고르시오.

① 격려　　② 허락　　③ 제안
④ 불만　　⑤ 칭찬

W　Mike, have you decided which club to join?

M　Yes, I am going to join _____ _____ _____. What about you?

W　Well, I'm already in a club, but...

M　Is there something wrong?

W　My guitar club only has 3 members. We need more members _____ _____ _____ _____ for a year.

M　I'm sorry to hear that.

W　What should we do to _____ _____ _____?

M　_____ _____ _____ perform in the cafeteria during lunch break?

대화를 듣고, 여자가 듣고자 하는 방과 후 수업으로 가장 적절한 것을 고르시오.

① 댄스　　② 요리　　③ 스포츠
④ 유적 답사　⑤ 독서

◀》 Listening Tip

역할어인 전치사 of의 [v] 소리는 자음 앞에서는 발음하지 않아요. kind의 [d]도 [n] 다음에 쓰여서 발음되지 않는 경우가 많아서 /카인드/가 아니라 /카인/처럼 발음하므로, kind of classes는 /카이 너 클래시즈/로 들려요.

W　Ben, are you going to take any after-school classes?

M　I'm not sure. What about you?

W　I'm going to. There are some interesting classes, and I want to _____ _____ _____.

M　What ◀》kind of classes are there?

W　There are dance, cooking, and sports classes. I'm thinking of _____ _____ _____ _____.

M　I see. Maybe I should try _____ _____ _____ _____.

W　Are you interested in cooking, too?

M　Not really. I think I'll try _____ _____ _____.

대화를 듣고, 두 사람이 대화 직후에 할 일로 가장 적절한 것을 고르시오.

① 상자 정리하기
② 초대장 제작하기
③ 동네에 포스터 붙이기
④ 포스터 새로 제작하기
⑤ 축제 준비물 확인하기

W　There is only one week left until the school festival.

M　Yes. It was a lot of work, but it was fun to _____ _____ _____.

W　Me, too. I hope many people come and enjoy it.

M　Sure. [Pause] What is in that box?

W　I think _____ _____ _____ in the box.

M Didn't we put up posters in the school?

W Yes, but there are _____ _____
_____.

M Then how about posting them in our neighborhood? That
way, _____ _____ will know about the
festival.

W That's a great idea.

09 언급하지 않은 내용 찾기

대화를 듣고, 여자가 송편에 대해 언급하지 <u>않은</u>
것을 고르시오.

① 먹는 시기 ② 모양   ③ 맛
④ 유래   ⑤ 재료

W Ted, I'm going to make some songpyeon. Would you like to
join me?

M What are songpyeon?

W They are _____ _____ _____.
Korean people usually make these and _____
_____ on Chuseok.

M Wow, they look like a half-moon.

W Yes, in Korean history, the people of Silla _____
_____ rice cakes in that shape.

M I see. What do you put inside?

W _____ _____ _____ sesame seeds
and beans. You can also make them in different colors
_____ _____ _____
_____.

M Okay. I'll try making some.

10 주제 추론

다음을 듣고, 남자가 하는 말의 내용으로 가장 적
절한 것을 고르시오.

① 나무를 심는 방법
② 종이를 절약하는 방법
③ 환경 파괴의 원인
④ 개인위생의 중요성
⑤ 종이 발명의 과정

M Did you know that we can save trees _____
_____ _____? That's right. Trees are the
main part of paper. So, I'm going to talk about how to
_____ _____ _____. First,
_____ _____ paper cups. Instead, use your
own cup. Second, you can _____ _____
instead of buying new ones. Last, carry and use a
handkerchief _____ _____ _____
_____ or tissues.

다음을 듣고, Warka Tower에 대한 내용과 일
치하지 <u>않는</u> 것을 고르시오.
① 공기로부터 물을 모은다.
② 식수를 얻을 수 있다.
③ 만들기 쉽다.
④ 재료는 대나무와 그물이다.
⑤ 만드는 데 8주 걸린다.

W Hello, class. I'd like to talk about the Warka Tower. It's a structure to collect water from _____ _____. People use this to _____ _____ _____. The tower is _____ _____ _____. Build a tower out of bamboo and then cover it _____ _____ _____. The net captures water from the air. The Warka Tower can be built with simple tools. But it _____ _____ 4 weeks when 8 people build one.

대화를 듣고, 남자가 박물관에 전화를 건 목적으
로 가장 적절한 것을 고르시오.
① 위치를 묻기 위해서
② 입장료를 알기 위해서
③ 투어를 예약하기 위해서
④ 개관 시간을 확인하기 위해서
⑤ 관람 규정을 확인하기 위해서

[Telephone rings.]

W Korea Art Museum. How can I help you?

M Hello. _____ _____ does the museum _____?

W _____ _____ _____ 5:30 p.m.

M Really? I thought you closed at 7 p.m.

W We close at 7 p.m. only from June to September.

M Then, do you _____ _____ _____ 10 o'clock _____ _____ _____?

W That's right.

M I see. Thank you for letting me know.

대화를 듣고, 두 사람이 만날 시각을 고르시오.
① 4:00 p.m. ② 4:10 p.m.
③ 4:20 p.m. ④ 4:30 p.m.
⑤ 4:40 p.m.

M Mina, there is a new dessert cafe down the street.

W Yes, I know that place. Chocolate cake is _____ _____ _____ dessert at that cafe.

M Really? I want to go there and have a piece.

W Why don't we _____ _____ _____? I don't have plans after school.

M Sure. _____ _____ _____ _____ 10 after 4?

W Oh, I have to stay and clean the classroom. How about 4:30?

M _____ _____. I'll wait for you by the school gate.

14 관계 추론

대화를 듣고, 두 사람의 관계로 가장 적절한 것을
고르시오.

① 시험 감독관 – 수험생
② 수리 기사 – 고객
③ 문구점 점원 – 학생
④ 주방장 – 웨이터
⑤ 편의점 직원 – 손님

M Excuse me, can you help me with something?

W Sure. Is there _____ _____?

M I want to warm this up, but I don't _____
_____ _____ _____ the
microwave.

W I see. Let me do that for you.

M Thanks. *[Pause]* Where are the chopsticks?

W They are on _____ _____ _____
of the counter.

M Oh, I see them.

W When you finish, please _____ _____
_____ garbage.

M I will. Thanks for your help.

15 부탁 파악

대화를 듣고, 여자가 남자에게 부탁한 일로 가장
적절한 것을 고르시오.

① 테이블 세팅하기   ② 숙제 도와주기
③ 식사 재료 사 오기   ④ 동영상 찾아보기
⑤ 스파게티 만들기

M Mom, can you help me with my homework?

W Sorry, honey. I'm pretty _____ _____
_____ _____.

M I see. What are you making?

W I'm making spaghetti, but I _____ _____
_____ _____. I tried everything, but it
won't open.

M I think I saw a video online of how to _____
_____ _____ _____.

W Then can you _____ _____ _____
for me? I need to watch it.

M Sure. I'll do that right now.

16 이유 파악

대화를 듣고, 여자가 스케이트를 타러 갈 수 <u>없는</u>
이유로 가장 적절한 것을 고르시오.

① 다리를 다쳐서
② 결혼식에 가야 해서
③ 스케이트를 타지 못해서
④ 동생 숙제를 도와줘야 해서
⑤ 엄마와 쇼핑을 가기로 해서

W Paul, do you have any special plans for this weekend?

M Yes. I'm going to go ice-skating with my friends.

W _____ _____ _____
_____. I love winter sports, too.

M Then why don't you join us?

W I'd like to, but I _____ _____ _____ to attend.

M Really? _____ _____ _____ _____ get married?

W My aunt. I can't wait to see her _____ _____ _____ _____. She'll look so beautiful.

17 그림 상황에 적절한 대화 찾기

다음 그림의 상황에 가장 적절한 대화를 고르시오.

① ② ③ ④ ⑤

🔊 Listening Tip

center에서처럼 'n' 뒤에 't'가 올 때는 /t/ 소리를 발음하지 않는 경우가 많아요. /쎈터/라고 발음하지 않고 /쎄널/이라고 발음하는 사람이 많다는 거지요. 그래서 winter와 winner가 똑같이 들리기도 해요.

① M May I _____ _____ of the animal?
   W Yes, you may.

② M How can I get to the visitor 🔊 center?
   W Go straight for two blocks.

③ M Excuse me. Is it okay to sit over there?
   W I'm sorry, but you must _____ _____ _____ _____.

④ M Can I help you?
   W Yes. Do you _____ _____ _____ in black?

⑤ M Can I play soccer in the park?
   W Yes. Just be careful _____ _____ _____.

18 언급하지 않은 내용 찾기

다음을 듣고, 여자가 영화에 대해 언급하지 <u>않은</u> 것을 고르시오.

① 제목   ② 개봉 연도
③ 감독   ④ 주인공
⑤ 상영 시간

W Let me tell you about my favorite movie. It's *Titanic*. The movie _____ _____ _____ 1997 and became really popular. It won _____ _____. The movie is about 2 people from different social classes. Rose and Jack _____ _____ _____ _____ and fall in love with each other. The movie is 194 _____ _____, but you won't feel bored at all when you watch it.

대화를 듣고, 여자의 마지막 말에 이어질 남자의 응답으로 가장 적절한 것을 고르시오.

Man: _____

① Good. I'll take it.
② I'm just looking around.
③ Okay. Your change is $2.
④ Sorry, but it doesn't look good on me.
⑤ I see. Then I'll just try on this T-shirt.

M Excuse me. Can I _____ _____ _____ T-shirt?

W Sure. The fitting room is _____ _____.

M Thanks. *[Pause]* Wait a minute! *Is it okay to try on _____ _____ _____, too?

W I'm sorry, but it's _____ _____ _____.

M I really like it. Can't you _____ _____ to me?

W I'm afraid it's only for display.

✳ 교육부 지정 의사소통 기능: **허락 구하기**   동(윤) 8|천(이) 4

Is it OK[okay] to ~? ~해도 괜찮나요?

• **Is it okay to** put up a poster? 포스터를 붙여도 괜찮나요?
• **Is it okay to** take pictures here? 여기에서 사진 찍어도 괜찮나요?

대화를 듣고, 여자의 마지막 말에 이어질 남자의 응답으로 가장 적절한 것을 고르시오.

Man: _____

① I'm happy to hear that.
② I'm proud to be your student.
③ I'm always worried about her.
④ She'll try to do better next time.
⑤ I'm sorry to disappoint you again.

M Hello, Ms. Park. I'm Tom Miller, Cathy's father.

W Oh, Cathy's father! I'm _____ _____ _____ _____.

M I'm happy to meet you, too. How's she doing this year?

W She's doing very well. She _____ _____ and her grades are _____ _____.

M Great. Is she _____ _____ _____ her friends, too?

W Of course. She has _____ _____ _____ _____.

실전 모의고사 05

01 다음을 듣고, 내일 날씨로 가장 적절한 것을 고르시오.

① ② ③ ④ ⑤

02 대화를 듣고, 여자가 구입할 배낭으로 가장 적절한 것을 고르시오.

① ② ③

④ ⑤

03 대화를 듣고, 남자의 심정으로 가장 적절한 것을 고르시오.

① worried　　② excited　　③ bored
④ surprised　　⑤ thankful

04 대화를 듣고, 여자가 서울 도서전에서 한 일로 가장 적절한 것을 고르시오.

① 책 싸게 사기　　② 오디오 북 듣기
③ 작가의 강연 듣기　　④ 책 표지 만들기
⑤ 특별전 관람하기

05 대화를 듣고, 두 사람이 대화하는 장소로 가장 적절한 곳을 고르시오.

① 매표소　　② 옷가게
③ 박물관 안내소　　④ 야구 경기장
⑤ 백화점 분실물 센터

06 대화를 듣고, 남자의 마지막 말의 의도로 가장 적절한 것을 고르시오.

① 격려　　② 동의　　③ 허락
④ 사과　　⑤ 제안

07 대화를 듣고, 두 사람이 보고 있는 박물관 앱을 통해 알 수 없는 것을 고르시오.

① 관람 시간　　② 입장료　　③ 위치
④ 행사 일정　　⑤ 가이드 투어 종류

08 대화를 듣고, 남자가 대화 직후에 할 일로 가장 적절한 것을 고르시오.

① 연극 관람하기
② 연극 동아리 가입하기
③ 상 받은 친구 축하하기
④ 영어 웅변대회 준비하기
⑤ 동아리 홍보 포스터 만들기

09 대화를 듣고, 여자가 음식점에 대해 언급하지 않은 것을 고르시오.

① 위치　　② 개점 시기　　③ 음식 맛
④ 추천 음식　　⑤ 음식 가격

10 다음을 듣고, 여자가 하는 말의 내용으로 가장 적절한 것을 고르시오.

① 체험 활동 공지　　② 미술관 관람 규칙
③ 현대미술 이해 방법　　④ 미술 강습 신청 방법
⑤ 미술관 프로그램 홍보

11 다음을 듣고, Grandma Moses에 대한 내용과 일치하지 <u>않는</u> 것을 고르시오.

① 미국 화가이다.
② 78세에 그림을 시작했다.
③ 농장 생활을 주로 그렸다.
④ 1,500여 점의 그림을 그렸다.
⑤ 100세의 나이로 죽었다.

12 대화를 듣고, 남자가 전화를 건 목적으로 가장 적절한 것을 고르시오.

① 가족의 안부를 묻기 위해서
② 극장의 위치를 확인하기 위해서
③ 함께 영화 보러 가기 위해서
④ 음식점을 추천받기 위해서
⑤ 저녁 식사에 초대하기 위해서

13 대화를 듣고, 두 사람이 만날 시각을 고르시오.

① 8:00 a.m. ② 8:30 a.m. ③ 9:00 a.m.
④ 9:30 a.m. ⑤ 10:00 a.m.

14 대화를 듣고, 두 사람의 관계로 가장 적절한 것을 고르시오.

① 형사 – 범인   ② 의사 – 간호사
③ 가게 점원 – 손님   ④ 구급대원 – 소방관
⑤ 신고 접수원 – 신고자

15 대화를 듣고, 여자가 남자에게 부탁한 일로 가장 적절한 것을 고르시오.

① 영화표 구매하기   ② 집에 일찍 오기
③ 식사 후 설거지하기 ④ 동생 숙제 도와주기
⑤ 아이스크림 사 오기

16 대화를 듣고, 남자가 여자를 멈춰 세운 이유로 가장 적절한 것을 고르시오.

① 속도를 위반해서
② 정지 신호를 무시해서
③ 불법으로 주차해서
④ 불법 유턴을 해서
⑤ 운전 중 휴대전화를 사용해서

17 다음 그림의 상황에 가장 적절한 대화를 고르시오.

①   ②   ③   ④   ⑤

18 다음을 듣고, 남자가 건강한 생활 방식에 대해 언급하지 <u>않은</u> 것을 고르시오.

① 운동 습관   ② 하루 식사량
③ 평소 식단   ④ 피하는 음식
⑤ 수면 시간

[19-20] 대화를 듣고, 남자의 마지막 말에 이어질 여자의 응답으로 가장 적절한 것을 고르시오.

19 Woman: _____

① I'm sure it was beautiful.
② You should put on your raincoat.
③ We stayed at a hotel for 3 days.
④ Then, I should pack my hiking shoes.
⑤ That was fun. We should do it more often.

20 Woman: _____

① I didn't pass the exam.
② Why don't you join the band?
③ You're right. I feel better now.
④ I'm sorry, but I don't need any luck.
⑤ I'm not sure if I can pass the audition.

◆ 다시 듣고, 빈칸에 들어갈 알맞은 단어를 써보세요.

정답 및 해설 p.28

---

01 날씨 파악

다음을 듣고, 내일 날씨로 가장 적절한 것을 고르시오.

① ② ③ ④ ⑤

🔊 Listening Tip

't'나 'd'가 모음 사이에 오면서 강세가 없는 음절의 첫 음일 때는 보통 /ㄹ/로 발음해요. 그래서 later는 /레이터/보다는 /레이럴/에 가깝게, cloudy는 /클라우디/보다는 /클라우리/에 가깝게 발음해요.

W Good morning. It's time for the weather report for this week. It's going to be cloudy and _____ _____.
🔊 Later tonight, it'll _____ _____ _____, and the snow won't stop _____ _____ _____. The good news is that it's going to be _____ _____ _____ on the weekend. So, much of the snow is expected to melt. Thank you.

---

02 그림 정보 파악

대화를 듣고, 여자가 구입할 배낭으로 가장 적절한 것을 고르시오.

① ② ③ ④ ⑤

M May I help you?
W Yes. I need _____ _____ for work. Can you recommend one?
M How about this one _____ _____ _____ _____ _____? This style is very popular these days.
W I like it, but I _____ _____ _____.
M Then how about that one? It has a front pocket and 2 side pockets.
W Oh, that looks convenient. _____ _____ _____.

---

03 심정 추론

대화를 듣고, 남자의 심정으로 가장 적절한 것을 고르시오.

① worried
② excited
③ bored
④ surprised
⑤ thankful

W Ethan, do you have any plans for your vacation?
M Yes, I do. I'm going to _____ _____ _____ _____ _____ next weekend.
W That's nice. Where?

M We're going to visit Sokcho.

W What are you going to do there?

M I'll _____ _____ and ride a boat.

W That sounds like fun. I hope you'll have a great time with your family.

M Yes. _____ _____ _____!

---

04 한 일 파악

대화를 듣고, 여자가 서울 도서전에서 한 일로 가장 적절한 것을 고르시오.

① 책 싸게 사기   ② 오디오 북 듣기
③ 작가의 강연 듣기   ④ 책 표지 만들기
⑤ 특별전 관람하기

W Henry, have you _____ _____ _____ the Seoul Book Fair?

M No, I haven't. Have you?

W Actually, I went _____ _____ _____.

M How was it?

W I liked it a lot. Many people came and enjoyed _____ _____ _____.

M What activities did you do?

W I listened to a lecture by my _____ _____.

M That sounds interesting. I want to _____ _____ next time.

---

05 장소 추론

대화를 듣고, 두 사람이 대화하는 장소로 가장 적절한 곳을 고르시오.

① 매표소   ② 옷가게
③ 박물관 안내소   ④ 야구 경기장
⑤ 백화점 분실물 센터

W Excuse me. Did anyone bring _____ _____ _____?

M Let me see. *[Pause]* We actually have 2 baseball caps.

W I hope one of _____ _____ _____. I lost a blue cap yesterday.

M I'm sorry, but _____ _____ _____ are black. Where did you lose it?

W I don't know. This is _____ _____ _____ _____.

M Can you give me your phone number? I'll call you if _____ _____ a blue baseball cap.

W Okay. It's 048-3742.

대화를 듣고, 남자의 마지막 말의 의도로 가장 적절한 것을 고르시오.

① 격려　　② 동의　　③ 허락
④ 사과　　⑤ 제안

W What is that in your hand, Mike?

M It's _____ _____ _____ _____ at the community center.

W Oh, are there any interesting classes?

M Sure, there are so many. I want to _____ _____ _____ _____, but I don't want to take it alone.

W I want to take a dance class, too. Maybe we both _____ _____ _____ for the same class.

M _____ _____ _____ _____.

대화를 듣고, 두 사람이 보고 있는 박물관 앱을 통해 알 수 없는 것을 고르시오.

① 관람 시간　　② 입장료
③ 위치　　④ 행사 일정
⑤ 가이드 투어 종류

W Eric, look at this app. I'm looking for information about the Seoul History Museum.

M Okay. _____ _____ _____ 9 to 8.

W And _____ _____ _____ _____ entrance fee for students.

M Great. It says _____ _____ Jong-ro.

W Oh, there are many _____ _____ for tourists this Saturday.

M I'd like to visit there. What kind of guided tours are there?

W I don't know. I can't find _____ _____ _____ that.

대화를 듣고, 남자가 대화 직후에 할 일로 가장 적절한 것을 고르시오.

① 연극 관람하기
② 연극 동아리 가입하기
③ 상 받은 친구 축하하기
④ 영어 웅변대회 준비하기
⑤ 동아리 홍보 포스터 만들기

W Did you hear Junsu won the speech contest?

M Yes, I was surprised. I thought he was very _____ _____ _____.

W Yes, he used to be.

M I want to be like him. Do you know _____ _____ _____?

W He has changed a lot since he joined the drama club.

M Really?

W _____ _____ _____ join the

drama club? The club is looking for _____

_____.

M All right. I'll join it right now.

09 언급하지 않은 내용 찾기

대화를 듣고, 여자가 음식점에 대해 언급하지 않은 것을 고르시오.

① 위치   ② 개점 시기
③ 음식 맛   ④ 추천 음식
⑤ 음식 가격

🔊 **Listening Tip**

try에서처럼 'r' 바로 앞에 있는 't'는 /트/보다는 /추/로
발음하는 경우가 많아요. try는 /추라이/로, tree는 /추뤼/
에 가깝게 발음해요.

M Have you been to the new Vietnamese restaurant, Juha?

W Are you talking about _____ _____

_____ _____ the city museum?

M Yes, that's the one.

W _____ _____ _____ 2 weeks ago,

and I went there last Saturday with my aunt.

M How was the food?

W It _____ _____. I really liked the rice

noodles with beef.

M Can you recommend _____ _____

_____ _____? I'm going there for lunch

with my friends.

W Then you should 🔊 try the crispy pancake with seafood.

M It sounds delicious. Thank you.

10 주제 추론

다음을 듣고, 여자가 하는 말의 내용으로 가장 적절한 것을 고르시오.

① 체험 활동 공지
② 미술관 관람 규칙
③ 현대미술 이해 방법
④ 미술 강습 신청 방법
⑤ 미술관 프로그램 홍보

W We are now at Alive Art Gallery. We're going to look around

here for 3 hours. I'll explain _____ _____

_____ before we go in. First, _____

_____ the art. Enjoy it with your eyes only. Second,

you must _____ _____ _____.

Finally, you are not allowed _____ _____

_____ _____ inside the gallery. We'll meet

again at the entrance at 4.

다음을 듣고, Grandma Moses에 대한 내용과 일치하지 <u>않는</u> 것을 고르시오.
① 미국 화가이다.
② 78세에 그림을 시작했다.
③ 농장 생활을 주로 그렸다.
④ 1,500여 점의 그림을 그렸다.
⑤ 100세의 나이로 죽었다.

M Hi, class. I'd like to talk about Grandma Moses. She was an _____ _____. At the age of 78, she _____ _____ _____ pictures. Most of her pictures were _____ _____ _____. During her career, she _____ _____ 1,500 works of art. She died _____ _____ _____ _____ 101.
I learned that you're never too old to learn.

대화를 듣고, 남자가 전화를 건 목적으로 가장 적절한 것을 고르시오.
① 가족의 안부를 묻기 위해서
② 극장의 위치를 확인하기 위해서
③ 함께 영화 보러 가기 위해서
④ 음식점을 추천받기 위해서
⑤ 저녁 식사에 초대하기 위해서

[Cell phone rings.]

W Hello.

M Hi, Susan. It's Noah. You _____ _____ _____ the Miko Cinema House, right?

W Yes, I am. Why?

M I'm going to go to the movies at the Miko Cinema House _____ _____ _____ this Saturday.

W That's nice.

M Yeah. We're going to have dinner before the movie. Do you know _____ _____ _____ _____?

W There's a good Chinese restaurant right _____ _____ _____ _____.

M I see. I should take my family there. Thanks a lot.

대화를 듣고, 두 사람이 만날 시각을 고르시오.
① 8:00 a.m.   ② 8:30 a.m.
③ 9:00 a.m.   ④ 9:30 a.m.
⑤ 10:00 a.m.

W James, why don't we ride bicycles to Chuncheon this Saturday?

M Sure. How long will it take?

W It'll take about 4 hours.

M Well, _____ _____ _____ _____ 10 in the morning?

W I was _____ _____ _____ lunch
in Chuncheon. There are many popular restaurants.

M Then, we should leave earlier. _____ _____
at 8:30.

W All right. I'll _____ _____ _____.

14 관계 추론

대화를 듣고, 두 사람의 관계로 가장 적절한 것을
고르시오.

① 형사 – 범인
② 의사 – 간호사
③ 가게 점원 – 손님
④ 구급대원 – 소방관
⑤ 신고 접수원 – 신고자

[Telephone rings.]

M Nine-one-one. What's the emergency?

W I want to _____ _____ _____.
I see a lot of _____ coming out of a building right
now.

M Where exactly is _____ _____
_____?

W The building is located _____ _____
_____ Rolling Hills Shopping Mall.

M I see. What's your name, ma'am?

W Sandy Evans.

M Okay. We'll _____ _____ _____
and an ambulance _____ _____
_____.

15 부탁 파악

대화를 듣고, 여자가 남자에게 부탁한 일로 가장
적절한 것을 고르시오.

① 영화표 구매하기
② 집에 일찍 오기
③ 식사 후 설거지하기
④ 동생 숙제 도와주기
⑤ 아이스크림 사 오기

W Jake, are you busy right now?

M Not really. Why?

W I'm going out with your dad now. Can you take good care
_____ _____ _____?

M Sure. When are you _____ _____?

W We'll _____ _____ _____
9 o'clock.

M Okay.

W One more thing. Can you help your sister _____
_____ _____? She needs help with science.

M No problem. I'll help her right away.

이유 파악

대화를 듣고, 남자가 여자를 멈춰 세운 이유로 가장 적절한 것을 고르시오.

① 속도를 위반해서
② 정지 신호를 무시해서
③ 불법으로 주차해서
④ 불법 유턴을 해서
⑤ 운전 중 휴대전화를 사용해서

M Excuse me, ma'am. _____ _____ _____ _____ driver's license?

W Here you are, officer. Did I do anything wrong?

M Yes. Do you see the stop sign over there? You didn't _____ _____ _____ _____.

W Oh, I'm sorry. I _____ _____ _____.

M I'm afraid I'm going to have to give you a ticket.

W I understand. It's my fault.

M Here's your license back. _____ _____.

---

17 그림 상황에 적절한 대화 찾기

다음 그림의 상황에 가장 적절한 대화를 고르시오.

① ② ③ ④ ⑤

① M How may I help you?
   W I'm looking for _____ _____.
② M I'd like to have _____ _____ _____.
   W I like it, too.
③ M This ball is on sale. It's only $5.
   W Great! _____ _____ _____.
④ M I'm sorry, but I'm _____ _____ _____.
   W That's all right.
⑤ M Look at this. Isn't it cute?
   W I like _____ _____ _____.
      It's much prettier.

---

18 언급하지 않은 내용 찾기

다음을 듣고, 남자가 건강한 생활 방식에 대해 언급하지 않은 것을 고르시오.

① 운동 습관   ② 하루 식사량
③ 평소 식단   ④ 피하는 음식
⑤ 수면 시간

M Hello, everyone. I'd like to tell you about my healthy lifestyle. I go running every morning and go swimming _____ _____. I have 5 _____ _____ _____ _____. I keep a balanced diet. I try to eat _____ _____ _____ _____ and less red meat. I usually avoid junk food and soda. Do you think I have a healthy lifestyle?

대화를 듣고, 남자의 마지막 말에 이어질 여자의
응답으로 가장 적절한 것을 고르시오.

Woman: _____

① I'm sure it was beautiful.
② You should put on your raincoat.
③ We stayed at a hotel for 3 days.
④ Then, I should pack my hiking shoes.
⑤ That was fun. We should do it more often.

M Jenny, I just finished planning our _____ _____ _____ Gongju this weekend.

W I want to hear about it, Dad. Where are we going _____ _____ _____ _____?

M We are going to visit the national museum first. Then we'll go to Gongsanseong.

W Oh, is that _____ _____ _____?

M Yes, we are _____ _____ _____ _____. It'll take about an hour and a half.

대화를 듣고, 남자의 마지막 말에 이어질 여자의
응답으로 가장 적절한 것을 고르시오.

Woman: _____

① I didn't pass the exam.
② Why don't you join the band?
③ You're right. I feel better now.
④ I'm sorry, but I don't need any luck.
⑤ I'm not sure if I can pass the audition.

M Yuna, you look very tired. What's wrong?

W I _____ _____ _____ _____ last night.

M Why?

W I have an audition for _____ _____ _____ tomorrow. I'm going to play the guitar in front of the band members.

M You must be nervous. Have you _____ _____?

W Not really. I had to prepare _____ _____ _____ today.

M Don't worry. You still _____ _____ _____ to practice until tomorrow.

실전 모의고사 **06**

01 다음을 듣고, 일요일 오후 날씨로 가장 적절한 것을 고르시오.

①   ②   ③   ④   ⑤

02 대화를 듣고, 여자가 구입할 쿠션으로 가장 적절한 것을 고르시오.

①   ②   ③

④   ⑤

03 대화를 듣고, 여자의 심정으로 가장 적절한 것을 고르시오.

① satisfied   ② pleased   ③ scared
④ bored   ⑤ disappointed

04 대화를 듣고, 남자가 잡월드에서 한 일로 가장 적절한 것을 고르시오.

① 게임하기   ② 요리하기
③ 뉴스 보도하기   ④ 옷 디자인하기
⑤ 집 설계하기

05 대화를 듣고, 두 사람이 대화하는 장소로 가장 적절한 것을 고르시오.

① 서점   ② 세탁소   ③ 옷 가게
④ 문구점   ⑤ 신발 가게

06 대화를 듣고, 남자의 마지막 말의 의도로 가장 적절한 것을 고르시오.

① 감사   ② 칭찬   ③ 허락
④ 거절   ⑤ 격려

07 대화를 듣고, 남자가 만들고 있는 것으로 가장 적절한 것을 고르시오.

① 꽃병   ② 목걸이   ③ 케이크
④ 커피 잔   ⑤ 바구니

08 대화를 듣고, 남자가 대화 직후에 할 일로 가장 적절한 것을 고르시오.

① 설거지하기   ② 저녁 준비하기
③ 전화번호 찾아주기   ④ 식료품 사 오기
⑤ 아빠에게 전화하기

09 대화를 듣고, 여자가 듣고 있는 수업에 대해 언급하지 않은 것을 고르시오.

① 장소   ② 수업 일수   ③ 선생님
④ 비용   ⑤ 과제

10 다음을 듣고, 여자가 하는 말의 내용으로 가장 적절한 것을 고르시오.

① 바른 식습관   ② 적절한 수면 시간
③ 초콜릿의 효능   ④ 치아 관리 방법
⑤ 정기 검진 안내

11 다음을 듣고, 영화 수업에 대한 내용으로 일치하지 않는 것을 고르시오.

① 내일부터 이틀간 이루어진다.
② 오전 9시에 시작해서 오후 4시에 끝난다.
③ 첫째 날에는 대본을 쓸 것이다.
④ 둘째 날에는 직접 영화를 찍을 것이다.
⑤ 동아리 회원만 수강할 수 있다.

12 대화를 듣고, 남자가 전화를 건 목적으로 가장 적절한 것을 고르시오.

① 진료를 예약하기 위해서
② 예약 시간을 변경하기 위해서
③ 지각 사유를 말하기 위해서
④ 모임 불참을 알리기 위해서
⑤ 회의 시간 변경을 알리기 위해서

13 대화를 듣고, 두 사람이 만날 시각을 고르시오.

① 3:00 p.m. ② 3:10 p.m. ③ 3:20 p.m.
④ 3:30 p.m. ⑤ 3:40 p.m.

14 대화를 듣고, 두 사람의 관계로 가장 적절한 것을 고르시오.

① 의사 – 환자 ② 아빠 – 딸
③ 코치 – 운동선수 ④ 교사 – 학부모
⑤ 약사 – 손님

15 대화를 듣고, 남자가 여자에게 부탁한 일로 가장 적절한 것을 고르시오.

① 동생 돌봐주기
② 이사 도와주기
③ 여행지 추천해주기
④ 중국어 연습 도와주기
⑤ 중국어 수강 신청해주기

16 대화를 듣고, 여자가 놀이공원에 갈 수 없는 이유로 가장 적절한 것을 고르시오.

① 시험공부를 해야 해서
② 엄마를 도와야 해서
③ 조부모님을 방문해야 해서
④ 부모님이 허락하지 않아서
⑤ 놀이기구 타는 것을 싫어해서

17 다음 그림의 상황에 가장 적절한 대화를 고르시오.

① ② ③ ④ ⑤

18 다음을 듣고, 남자가 Roll's Automotive에 대해 언급하지 않은 것을 고르시오.

① 할인 기간 ② 할인 품목
③ 영업시간 ④ 무료 제공 음식
⑤ 위치

[19-20] 대화를 듣고, 여자의 마지막 말에 이어질 남자의 말로 가장 적절한 것을 고르시오.

19 Man: _____

① You're welcome.
② No, I haven't decided yet.
③ I've already booked a hotel.
④ Sure. Let me check the map.
⑤ Okay. I'll try to do my best at everything.

20 Man: _____

① I can't wait to see it.
② It starts at 7:30 p.m.
③ It will take about 2 hours.
④ She will play Mozart and Shubert.
⑤ Let's meet at 7 o'clock at the concert hall.

Dictation 06

◆ 다시 듣고, 빈칸에 들어갈 알맞은 단어를 써보세요.

정답 및 해설 p.34

01 날씨 파악

다음을 듣고, 일요일 오후 날씨로 가장 적절한 것을 고르시오.

① ② ③ ④ ⑤

W Good evening, everyone. Here is this weekend's weather forecast. This Saturday _____ _____ _____ to have very cold weather. It'll _____ _____ _____ in the morning, and then there will be strong winds in the afternoon. However, the temperature will start to go up on Sunday morning. You'll be able to _____ _____ _____ later in the afternoon.

02 그림 정보 파악

대화를 듣고, 여자가 구입할 쿠션으로 가장 적절한 것을 고르시오.

① ② ③ ④ ⑤

🔊 **Listening Tip**

have a few에서 관사인 a는 강세가 없어요. 따라서 앞 단어인 have와 연음되어 /해버퓨/로 발음해요.

W Excuse me, I'm looking for a cushion.

M They come in many shapes. Do you have _____ _____ _____ _____?

W I don't want _____ _____ _____ because I already 🔊 have a few at home.

M Then how about this square one with hearts?

W It's not bad. But I _____ _____ _____.

M Then you'll like this one with stripes. It's very popular in our store.

W I like it. _____ _____ _____.

03 심정 추론

대화를 듣고, 여자의 심정으로 가장 적절한 것을 고르시오.

① satisfied ② pleased ③ scared
④ bored ⑤ disappointed

W How is your steak, Minsu?

M It's great. This is the perfect medium steak for me. How is your pasta?

W Well, mine is _____ _____ _____ _____ I expected.

M What's wrong with it?

W The pasta is good but _____ _____ _____ for me. Besides, the food was cold when the waiter brought it.

M Really? Let me _____ _____ _____. *[Pause]* Whoa, it is really salty.

W I don't think I can eat _____ _____ _____.

04 한 일 파악

대화를 듣고, 남자가 잡월드에서 한 일로 가장 적절한 것을 고르시오.

① 게임하기　　② 요리하기
③ 뉴스 보도하기　④ 옷 디자인하기
⑤ 집 설계하기

W Jiho, I heard you went to Job World yesterday.

M Yes, I did. There are more than 50 _____ _____ to experience. You can be a chef, game designer, and even news reporter.

W Oh, really? Which job did you try?

M I wanted to experience being a game designer, but I couldn't. The _____ _____ _____ _____.

W Then what did you do?

M I tried being a news reporter instead. I looked into a camera and _____ _____ _____. That was fun.

05 장소 추론

대화를 듣고, 두 사람이 대화하는 장소로 가장 적절한 것을 고르시오.

① 서점　　② 세탁소　　③ 옷 가게
④ 문구점　⑤ 신발 가게

M Hello. Can I help you?

W Yes. I'd like to _____ _____ _____ _____.

M The red ones with the high heels?

W No, I'd like the brown ones _____ _____ _____ heels. I wear a size 6.

M Here you are. Try them on. *[Pause]* How do they feel?

W I think they're too tight for me. Do you have them in _____ _____ _____ ?

M Sure. Could you hold on _____ _____ _____ _____ ?

W Okay. Thanks.

06 의도 파악

대화를 듣고, 남자의 마지막 말의 의도로 가장 적절한 것을 고르시오.

① 감사   ② 칭찬   ③ 허락
④ 거절   ⑤ 격려

M   This spaghetti with meat sauce is so delicious, Olivia.

W   Thanks. It's one of _____ _____

_____ .

M   And this apple pie is good, too. Did you bake this?

W   No. My mom made it this morning.

M   I should ask your mom for the recipe.

W   There is another pie in the oven. So _____

_____ _____ .

M   I wish I could. But _____ _____

_____ .

07 특정 정보 파악

대화를 듣고, 남자가 만들고 있는 것으로 가장 적절한 것을 고르시오.

① 꽃병   ② 목걸이   ③ 케이크
④ 커피 잔   ⑤ 바구니

[Cell phone rings.]

M   Hello.

W   Hi, Liam. Do you want to _____ _____

_____ _____ badminton?

M   Sorry. I can't go out right now. I'm in the middle of something.

W   What are you doing?

M   I'm _____ _____ _____

_____ for my mom.

W   Oh, are you making her a birthday cake?

M   I don't know how to bake. Since she likes flowers, I wanted to give her something to _____ _____

_____ .

W   Oh, you are _____ _____ _____ .

M   Yes. I hope she likes it.

08 할 일 파악

대화를 듣고, 남자가 대화 직후에 할 일로 가장 적절한 것을 고르시오.

① 설거지하기   ② 저녁 준비하기
③ 전화번호 찾아주기   ④ 식료품 사 오기
⑤ 아빠에게 전화하기

W   Mark, your father is going to come home with _____

_____ _____ from work.

M   Now? How many people?

W   4 people. But there is _____ _____

_____ to cook.

M I can go out and _____ _____

_____ you need.

W No, I don't have enough time, either. We should just order some Chinese food. _____ _____

_____ _____ the delivery number?

M Okay. I'll be right back with it.

---

09 언급하지 않은 내용 찾기

대화를 듣고, 여자가 듣고 있는 수업에 대해 언급
하지 않은 것을 고르시오.

① 장소   ② 수업 일수   ③ 선생님
④ 비용   ⑤ 과제

M Narae, what are you studying for?

W I _____ _____ _____ tomorrow in my Japanese class.

M Really? Where do you learn Japanese?

W The public library. You can also learn Chinese, French, and Spanish there.

M I see. _____ _____ do you go to class?

W _____ _____ _____

_____. The teacher is Japanese, but she can speak English and Korean really well.

M Do you get a lot of homework?

W Not much. But I _____ _____

_____ instead.

---

10 주제 추론

다음을 듣고, 여자가 하는 말의 내용으로 가장 적
절한 것을 고르시오.

① 바른 식습관   ② 적절한 수면 시간
③ 초콜릿의 효능   ④ 치아 관리 방법
⑤ 정기 검진 안내

W There are easy and simple ways to _____

_____ _____ _____. First, remember the 3-3-3 rule. _____ _____

_____ for 3 minutes, 3 times a day, and in 3 minutes after each meal. Second, _____ _____

_____ _____ too many sweet things, like chocolate, candy, and cookies. Lastly, _____

_____ _____ _____ go to a dentist.

일치하지 않는 내용 찾기

다음을 듣고, 영화 수업에 대한 내용으로 일치하지 않는 것을 고르시오.

① 내일부터 이틀간 이루어진다.
② 오전 9시에 시작해서 오후 4시에 끝난다.
③ 첫째 날에는 대본을 쓸 것이다.
④ 둘째 날에는 직접 영화를 찍을 것이다.
⑤ 동아리 회원만 수강할 수 있다.

🔊 **Listening Tip**
d나 t가 연속되는 두 단어의 자음 사이에 올 때는 [d]/[t] 소리가 탈락돼요. 따라서 first day는 [퍼스트 데이]가 아니라 [퍼스 데이]로 발음됩니다.

M Hello, students. Our Movie Makers Club will hold a film class _____ _____ 2 days. It'll start at 9 a.m. _____ _____ _____ 4 p.m. On the 🔊first day, you'll learn how to _____ _____ _____. Then you'll write a script for a short movie. On the second day, you'll get into groups of 4 and make a short film. _____ _____ _____ _____ can join the class.

---

12 목적 파악

대화를 듣고, 남자가 전화를 건 목적으로 가장 적절한 것을 고르시오.

① 진료를 예약하기 위해서
② 예약 시간을 변경하기 위해서
③ 지각 사유를 말하기 위해서
④ 모임 불참을 알리기 위해서
⑤ 회의 시간 변경을 알리기 위해서

[Telephone rings.]

W Hello. Dr. Crane's office.

M Hello. This is Alan Tate. I _____ _____ _____ with the doctor this afternoon.

W Yes, Mr. Tate. You have an appointment at 3 p.m.

M That's right. But I forgot I have an important meeting _____ _____ _____ _____.

W So do you want to _____ _____ _____?

M Yes. Can I come in tomorrow?

W Then could you come at 9 tomorrow morning?

M Yes, _____ _____ _____.

---

13 숫자 정보 파악 (시각)

대화를 듣고, 두 사람이 만날 시각을 고르시오.

① 3:00 p.m.　　② 3:10 p.m.
③ 3:20 p.m.　　④ 3:30 p.m.
⑤ 3:40 p.m.

M Sejung, we have a study group meeting at Peter's house. Do you want to join us?

W Sure. What time are you going to go there?

M _____ _____ _____ 3.

W Oh, I have to watch my sister until then. Can I _____ _____ _____ _____?

M Okay. Do you know how to get to his house?

W Actually, _____ _____ _____.

M How about _____ _____ _____
3:30 at the bookstore? We can go together.

W That sounds great. I'll see you then.

14 관계 추론

대화를 듣고, 두 사람의 관계로 가장 적절한 것을
고르시오.

① 의사 – 환자   ② 아빠 – 딸
③ 코치 – 운동선수   ④ 교사 – 학부모
⑤ 약사 – 손님

M Sujin, why are you _____ _____
_____?

W I'm sorry, sir. I had to take my little brother to the doctor
earlier.

M The doctor? Is everything okay?

W Well, he had a terrible stomachache.

M Then, why didn't you call me?

W I was scared. I didn't know _____ _____
_____ at first.

M How is your brother now?

W He's okay. My mom is with him now.

M That's good. _____ _____ _____.
We _____ _____ _____
_____ left before the junior tennis competition.

15 부탁 파악

대화를 듣고, 남자가 여자에게 부탁한 일로 가장
적절한 것을 고르시오.

① 동생 돌봐주기
② 이사 도와주기
③ 여행지 추천해주기
④ 중국어 연습 도와주기
⑤ 중국어 수강 신청해주기

M Do you _____ _____ _____ after
school?

W _____ _____. Why?

M I heard you could speak Chinese well. Is that true?

W Yes, I lived in Shanghai for 3 years.

M I have a Chinese speech contest. Can you _____
_____ _____ for it?

W Sure, but I have to go home before 5. Is that all right?

M It _____ _____ _____
_____. Thanks!

16 이유 파악

대화를 듣고, 여자가 놀이공원에 갈 수 없는 이유로 가장 적절한 것을 고르시오.

① 시험공부를 해야 해서
② 엄마를 도와야 해서
③ 조부모님을 방문해야 해서
④ 부모님이 허락하지 않아서
⑤ 놀이기구 타는 것을 싫어해서

M Hi, Emily.

W Hi, Mason. _____ _____?

M Do you want to go to the amusement park tomorrow?

W I'd love to, but I can't. I have _____ _____ _____.

M You aren't going to study for the exams, are you? It's _____ _____ _____.

W No, I'm not. I have to stay home.

M Why do you _____ _____ _____ _____?

W My grandparents will be visiting. So, I have to clean and _____ _____ _____ in the kitchen.

M Oh, I see.

17 그림 상황에 적절한 대화 찾기

다음 그림의 상황에 가장 적절한 대화를 고르시오.

① ② ③ ④ ⑤

① M *Which do you prefer, roses or tulips?
   W I like tulips _____ _____ roses.

② M Hello, may I help you?
   W Yes. I'm _____ _____ _____ _____ about gardening.

③ M Excuse me, is there a flower shop near here?
   W Yes, there is one _____ _____ _____ _____.

④ M How much is that flower pot?
   W It costs $17.

⑤ M How often do you water your plant?
   W I water my plant _____ _____ _____.

* 교육부 지정 의사소통 기능: **선호 묻기**   동(이) 3│능(양) 1│(박) 5│Y(송) 5│다 3

Which (~) do you prefer, A or B? A와 B 중 어떤 것을[~을] 더 좋아하니?
• **Which do you prefer,** soccer **or** baseball? 축구와 야구 중 어떤 것을 더 좋아하니?
• **Which** season **do you prefer,** summer **or** winter? 여름과 겨울 중 어떤 계절을 더 좋아하니?

다음을 듣고, 남자가 Roll's Automotive에 대해 언급하지 않은 것을 고르시오.

① 할인 기간　　② 할인 품목
③ 영업시간　　④ 무료 제공 음식
⑤ 위치

M Roll's Automotive is going to have a big sale _____ _____ _____. There is a 10% discount _____ _____ _____ _____. It means you can save at least $1,000 on a car. However, the offer does not apply for trucks. During the sale, from 9 a.m. to noon, any visitors to the store will _____ _____ _____ and cookies. So, come down to Roll's Automotive on Main Street. We are _____ _____ the ABC Mall.

대화를 듣고, 여자의 마지막 말에 이어질 남자의 말로 가장 적절한 것을 고르시오.

Man: _____

① You're welcome.
② No, I haven't decided yet.
③ I've already booked a hotel.
④ Sure. Let me check the map.
⑤ Okay. I'll try to do my best at everything.

W There are so many interesting places to visit. I can't decide _____ _____ _____.
M Me neither. We don't _____ _____ _____. We will stay here only for 3 days.
W Well, how about taking a city tour bus first? After that, we can decide which places to go.
M That sounds like a great idea. But we don't have any information _____ _____ _____ _____ or schedule.
W Let's go and find _____ _____ _____ _____.

대화를 듣고, 여자의 마지막 말에 이어질 남자의 말로 가장 적절한 것을 고르시오.

Man: _____

① I can't wait to see it.
② It starts at 7:30 p.m.
③ It will take about 2 hours.
④ She will play Mozart and Shubert.
⑤ Let's meet at 7 o'clock at the concert hall.

M Emma, what are you going to do this Friday night?
W Nothing special. I think I'll _____ _____ _____ and watch TV.
M I see. I got 2 free piano concert tickets. Would you like to come?
W Sure, I'd love to. _____ _____ _____ _____ a piano concert before.
M I read some reviews on this piano concert, and most people said it was good.
W Great. What time does _____ _____ _____?

정답 및 해설 p.40

실전 모의고사 **07**

01 다음을 듣고, 금요일의 날씨로 가장 적절한 것을 고르시오.

①   ②   ③   ④   ⑤

02 대화를 듣고, 남자가 구입할 화병으로 가장 적절한 것을 고르시오.

①   ②   ③

④   ⑤

03 대화를 듣고, 남자의 심정으로 가장 적절한 것을 고르시오.
① relaxed   ② proud   ③ scared
④ bored   ⑤ nervous

04 대화를 듣고, 여자가 벼룩시장에서 한 일로 가장 적절한 것을 고르시오.
① 시계 교환   ② 공연 관람   ③ 가방 구입
④ 쇼핑백 들기   ⑤ 수제 쿠키 판매

05 대화를 듣고, 두 사람이 대화하는 장소로 가장 적절한 것을 고르시오.
① 극장   ② 공항   ③ 매표소
④ 경찰서   ⑤ 분실물 보관소

06 대화를 듣고, 남자의 마지막 말의 의도로 가장 적절한 것을 고르시오.
① 초대   ② 충고   ③ 요청
④ 비난   ⑤ 격려

07 대화를 듣고, 여자가 주문하지 않은 음식을 고르시오.
① 새우 버거   ② 치킨   ③ 감자튀김
④ 콜라   ⑤ 애플파이

08 대화를 듣고, 여자가 대화 직후에 할 일로 가장 적절한 것을 고르시오.
① 사진 찍기   ② 문자 확인하기
③ 수리점 방문하기   ④ 소풍 준비하기
⑤ 이메일로 사진 보내기

09 대화를 듣고, 여자가 건강을 유지하는 방법으로 언급하지 않은 것을 고르시오.
① 균형 잡힌 식사   ② 숙면
③ 규칙적인 운동   ④ 물 마시기
⑤ 많이 걷기

10 다음을 듣고, 남자가 하는 말의 내용으로 가장 적절한 것을 고르시오.
① 봉사활동 계획   ② 신문 구독 안내
③ 신문 동아리 소개   ④ 영어 공부 방법 소개
⑤ 현장 체험 학습 안내

11 다음을 듣고, 학교 축제에 대한 내용으로 일치하지 <u>않는</u> 것을 고르시오.

① 이번 주 금요일에 개최된다.
② 30개 이상의 동아리가 참여한다.
③ 다양한 활동에 참여할 수 있다.
④ 중앙 무대에서 댄스 공연이 있을 것이다.
⑤ 푸드 트럭을 운영할 것이다.

12 대화를 듣고, 남자가 전화를 건 목적으로 가장 적절한 것을 고르시오.

① 연습 장소를 알리기 위해서
② 약속 시간을 변경하기 위해서
③ 공연 시간을 확인하기 위해서
④ 동아리 가입을 권유하기 위해서
⑤ 연극을 보러 가자고 말하기 위해서

13 대화를 듣고, 여자의 식당 예약 시각을 고르시오.

① 6:00 p.m. ② 6:30 p.m. ③ 7:00 p.m.
④ 7:30 p.m. ⑤ 8:00 p.m.

14 대화를 듣고, 두 사람의 관계로 가장 적절한 것을 고르시오.

① 운전자 – 경찰관   ② 배우 – 리포터
③ 감독 – 스턴트맨   ④ 극장 직원 – 관람객
⑤ 운전 강사 – 교육생

15 대화를 듣고, 여자가 남자에게 부탁한 일로 가장 적절한 것을 고르시오.

① 책 빌려주기   ② 집에 데려다주기
③ 숙제 도와주기   ④ 간식 챙겨오기
⑤ 도서관 위치 알려주기

16 대화를 듣고, 남자가 기분이 좋지 <u>않은</u> 이유로 가장 적절한 것을 고르시오.

① 버스를 놓쳐서
② 성적이 좋지 못해서
③ 역사 수업을 듣지 못해서
④ 보고서를 완성하지 못해서
⑤ 보고서를 다시 작성해야 해서

17 다음 그림의 상황에 가장 적절한 대화를 고르시오.

①   ②   ③   ④   ⑤

18 다음을 듣고, 여자가 말하기 대회에 대해 언급하지 <u>않은</u> 것을 고르시오.

① 대회 일시   ② 주제   ③ 참가 자격
④ 제한 시간   ⑤ 수상자 상품

[19-20] 대화를 듣고, 남자의 마지막 말에 이어질 여자의 말로 가장 적절한 것을 고르시오.

19 Woman: _____

① I hope to visit England.
② It has been raining all day.
③ Yes, I went to England last year.
④ I don't speak English very well.
⑤ Yes, I have lived here since I was young.

20 Woman: _____

① Every 20 minutes.
② You can't miss it.
③ Just 10 minutes or so.
④ It's next to the theater.
⑤ You can find it on the second floor.

Dictation 07

◇ 다시 듣고, 빈칸에 들어갈 알맞은 단어를 써보세요.

정답 및 해설 p.40

---

01 날씨 파악

다음을 듣고, 금요일의 날씨로 가장 적절한 것을 고르시오.

① ② ③
④ ⑤

M This is the Joy 365 Forecast. Spring is here, and we'll have many changes this week. It'll be windy and partly cloudy from Monday through Wednesday. On Thursday, there is ＿＿＿＿＿＿ ＿＿＿＿＿＿ ＿＿＿＿＿＿ ＿＿＿＿＿＿ ＿＿＿＿＿＿. You'll be able to enjoy a ＿＿＿＿＿＿ ＿＿＿＿＿＿ ＿＿＿＿＿＿ on Friday. However, ＿＿＿＿＿＿ ＿＿＿＿＿＿ ＿＿＿＿＿＿ ＿＿＿＿＿＿ on the weekend because heavy rain is expected.

---

02 그림 정보 파악

대화를 듣고, 남자가 구입할 화병으로 가장 적절한 것을 고르시오.

① ② ③
④ ⑤

W Hello, may I help you?

M Yes. I'm looking for a vase for my living room.

W ＿＿＿＿＿＿ ＿＿＿＿＿＿ ＿＿＿＿＿＿ rectangular-shaped one? It's very popular these days.

M Hmm... It looks so simple.

W Then, how about this round one ＿＿＿＿＿＿ ＿＿＿＿＿＿ ＿＿＿＿＿＿?

M It's nice, but do you have the ＿＿＿＿＿＿ ＿＿＿＿＿＿ ＿＿＿＿＿＿ ＿＿＿＿＿＿?

W Sure, here you are.

M Perfect. ＿＿＿＿＿＿ ＿＿＿＿＿＿ ＿＿＿＿＿＿.

---

03 심정 추론

대화를 듣고, 남자의 심정으로 가장 적절한 것을 고르시오.

① relaxed ② proud ③ scared
④ bored ⑤ nervous

M Wow, I just found out that I won the writing contest.

W Really? Congratulations!

M Thanks. I ＿＿＿＿＿＿ ＿＿＿＿＿＿ ＿＿＿＿＿＿ ＿＿＿＿＿＿ at all.

W You deserve it. I know you worked ＿＿＿＿＿＿ ＿＿＿＿＿＿ ＿＿＿＿＿＿ ＿＿＿＿＿＿.

M Yes. I _____ _____ _____ every night for 2 weeks to prepare for the contest.

W What did you write about?

M I wrote about my favorite book. Do you want to _____ _____?

W Sure.

04 한 일 파악

대화를 듣고, 여자가 벼룩시장에서 한 일로 가장 적절한 것을 고르시오.

① 시계 교환　　② 공연 관람
③ 가방 구입　　④ 쇼핑백 들기
⑤ 수제 쿠키 판매

M Judy, what did you do last Saturday?

W I went to a flea market with my sister.

M That sounds interesting. Did you _____ _____ _____?

W I wanted to buy a clock for my room, but I couldn't _____ _____ _____.

M Then, did you _____ _____ _____?

W I did. But my sister bought so many things. I had to _____ _____ _____ the shopping bags.

M Well, it sounds like your sister had a good weekend.

05 장소 추론

대화를 듣고, 두 사람이 대화하는 장소로 가장 적절한 것을 고르시오.

① 극장　　② 공항　　③ 매표소
④ 경찰서　　⑤ 분실물 보관소

W May I help you, sir?

M Yes. I left my backpack on the plane. Can I get back _____ _____ _____ and get it?

W Sorry, but _____ _____ _____ _____ enter the plane again.

M What should I do then?

W Wait here for a moment. We'll look for it.

M Thanks a lot.

W Can you tell me your flight number and _____ _____ _____?

M It's TA 724, and my seat was 15C.

대화를 듣고, 남자의 마지막 말의 의도로 가장 적절한 것을 고르시오.

① 초대   ② 충고   ③ 요청
④ 비난   ⑤ 격려

🔊 **Listening Tip**

자음과 반모음 y, w가 만나면 연음현상이 일어나서 자연스럽게 연결되어 발음됩니다. shouldn't you의 경우 n 뒤의 t는 발음이 안 되며 뒤의 반모음인 you와 연음현상이 일어나서 [슈든뉴]와 같이 발음됩니다.

W Dave, what are you doing here?

M I'm _____ _____ _____. I'm going to meet Peter.

W What number is your bus?

M It's the number 2. But it hasn't come for _____ _____ _____. I'm going to be late.

W 🔊 Shouldn't you call him?

M Yes, I should. *[Pause]* Oh no!

W What's wrong?

M I left my cell phone at home. _____ _____ _____ _____ I use yours?

대화를 듣고, 여자가 주문하지 <u>않은</u> 음식을 고르시오.

① 새우 버거   ② 치킨   ③ 감자튀김
④ 콜라   ⑤ 애플파이

M Welcome to Happy Snack. May I take your order?

W Yes, please. _____ _____ _____ have a shrimp burger and french fries.

M Anything _____ _____?

W Oh, I want a small coke, please.

M Okay. If you order a burger, you can buy _____ _____ _____ for $1.

W $1? That's cheap.

M Yes, would you like one?

W Yes, _____ _____ _____.

M _____ _____ _____ _____ _____?

W For here, please.

대화를 듣고, 여자가 대화 직후에 할 일로 가장 적절한 것을 고르시오.

① 사진 찍기   ② 문자 확인하기
③ 수리점 방문하기   ④ 소풍 준비하기
⑤ 이메일로 사진 보내기

M Amy, did you take lots of pictures when we went on the picnic?

W Yes. Do you want me _____ _____ _____ to you?

M My smartphone is broken, so I can't receive them on it.

W Are you going to fix it or get a new one?

M I _____ _____ _____ at the repair shop. Can you _____ _____ by e-mail instead?

W Sure. I'll _____ _____ _____ _____.

09 언급하지 않은 내용 찾기

대화를 듣고, 여자가 건강을 유지하는 방법으로 언급하지 않은 것을 고르시오.
① 균형 잡힌 식사　② 숙면
③ 규칙적인 운동　④ 물 마시기
⑤ 많이 걷기

M Hey, Angela.

W Hi, Steve. Long time no see.

M You look great! How do you _____ _____ _____?

W Thanks. I keep a balanced diet and get 8 hours of sleep a day.

M Do you _____ _____ _____?

W Yes. It's important to _____ _____ _____.

M And what else?

W I try _____ _____ _____ _____ instead of taking public transportation.

M I see. Maybe I should try those things, too.

10 주제 추론

다음을 듣고, 남자가 하는 말의 내용으로 가장 적절한 것을 고르시오.
① 봉사활동 계획
② 신문 구독 안내
③ 신문 동아리 소개
④ 영어 공부 방법 소개
⑤ 현장 체험 학습 안내

M Hello, everyone. Our newspaper club makes a school newspaper _____ _____. The members get together every Wednesday. First, they collect ideas and stories. Then they write and _____ _____ _____ their stories. Lastly, they put all the stories together and _____ _____ _____ a newspaper.

11 일치하지 않는 내용 찾기

다음을 듣고, 학교 축제에 대한 내용으로 일치하지 않는 것을 고르시오.

① 이번 주 금요일에 개최된다.
② 30개 이상의 동아리가 참여한다.
③ 다양한 활동에 참여할 수 있다.
④ 중앙 무대에서 댄스 공연이 있을 것이다.
⑤ 푸드 트럭을 운영할 것이다.

W Hi, students. As you know, the 10th Cherry Middle School Festival is going to be _____ _____ _____. More than 30 school clubs will participate. You can _____ _____ _____, like water balloon fights and face painting. There will be a _____ _____ on the main stage. We won't _____ _____ _____ _____ this year for many reasons.

12 목적 파악

대화를 듣고, 남자가 전화를 건 목적으로 가장 적절한 것을 고르시오.

① 연습 장소를 알리기 위해서
② 약속 시간을 변경하기 위해서
③ 공연 시간을 확인하기 위해서
④ 동아리 가입을 권유하기 위해서
⑤ 연극을 보러 가자고 말하기 위해서

[Cell phone rings.]
W Hello.
M Hi, Lisa. Where are you?
W I'm in the club room. We're supposed to get together and _____ _____ _____ _____.
M Oh, don't you remember? We'll practice in the school hall, _____ _____ _____ _____ today.
W [Pause] Oh, you're right. I completely forgot.
M _____ _____ _____. The practice is going to start soon.
W Okay. I'm leaving right now.

13 숫자 정보 파악 (시각)

대화를 듣고, 여자의 식당 예약 시각을 고르시오.

① 6:00 p.m.   ② 6:30 p.m.
③ 7:00 p.m.   ④ 7:30 p.m.
⑤ 8:00 p.m.

[Telephone rings.]
M King Steak House. How may I help you?
W I'd like to _____ _____ _____ for this evening.
M What time would you like?
W At 7:30.
M I'm sorry, but all the tables _____ _____ _____ that time. But you can still book for 6 and 8 o'clock.

W Then _____ _____ _____
6 o'clock for 8 people.

M Okay. Can I _____ _____ _____,
please?

W My name is Monica Potter.

14 관계 추론

대화를 듣고, 두 사람의 관계로 가장 적절한 것을
고르시오.

① 운전자 – 경찰관
② 배우 – 리포터
③ 감독 – 스턴트맨
④ 극장 직원 – 관람객
⑤ 운전 강사 – 교육생

W Hi, Michael. What is your favorite _____
_____ _____ _____?

M It's the car chase scene. I performed it myself.

W Wasn't it dangerous to film the scene?

M It was, but I try to _____ _____
_____ _____ without a body double.

W You are amazing. Would you like to say anything
_____ _____ _____?

M I really thank you all _____ _____
_____ and support. I hope you enjoy this movie.

W Michael, thank you for your time.

15 부탁 파악

대화를 듣고, 여자가 남자에게 부탁한 일로 가장
적절한 것을 고르시오.

① 책 빌려주기   ② 집에 데려다주기
③ 숙제 도와주기   ④ 간식 챙겨오기
⑤ 도서관 위치 알려주기

W Peter, do you have a second?

M Yes. Why?

W *Do you know _____ _____
_____ _____ the Central Library?

M Sure. It's very close from here.

W I need to borrow some books. Could you _____
_____ _____?

M Actually, I have to go to the library for _____
_____ _____. Let's go together.

W Oh, great. How about eating something _____
_____ _____?

M Good idea.

✱ **교육부 지정 의사소통 기능: 알고 있는지 묻기 2**   동(이) 6 | 천(이) 8 | Y(송) 8

Do you know ~? ~을 아니?

• **Do you know** how to use the copy machine? 복사기 사용하는 법을 아니?
• **Do you know** the name of this flower? 이 꽃의 이름을 아니?

16 이유 파악

대화를 듣고, 남자가 기분이 좋지 <u>않은</u> 이유로 가장 적절한 것을 고르시오.

① 버스를 놓쳐서
② 성적이 좋지 못해서
③ 역사 수업을 듣지 못해서
④ 보고서를 완성하지 못해서
⑤ 보고서를 다시 작성해야 해서

W What's wrong?

M I'm very upset. I ＿＿＿＿＿＿ ＿＿＿＿＿＿ ＿＿＿＿＿＿ on the bus.

W Oh no! Is there ＿＿＿＿＿＿ ＿＿＿＿＿＿ in it?

M Yes. My history homework was in my bag.

W That's too bad. You ＿＿＿＿＿＿ ＿＿＿＿＿＿ ＿＿＿＿＿＿ the homework, didn't you?

M Yes, but now I have to do it again.

W Did you call the bus company's lost and found center? Your bag ＿＿＿＿＿＿ ＿＿＿＿＿＿ ＿＿＿＿＿＿.

M I did, but it isn't there.

17 그림 상황에 적절한 대화 찾기

다음 그림의 상황에 가장 적절한 대화를 고르시오.

① ② ③ ④ ⑤

① M Excuse me, can I ＿＿＿＿＿＿ ＿＿＿＿＿＿ ＿＿＿＿＿＿ ＿＿＿＿＿＿?

W Sure. The fitting room is over there.

② M May I take your order?

W Yes, I'd like a cheeseburger set.

③ M Which T-shirt should I get?

W I think you ＿＿＿＿＿＿ ＿＿＿＿＿＿ in the shirt with the round neck.

④ M What are you doing now?

W I'm ＿＿＿＿＿＿ ＿＿＿＿＿＿ ＿＿＿＿＿＿ ＿＿＿＿＿＿ through the telescope.

⑤ M Hello, may I help you?

W Yes, I'm looking for ＿＿＿＿＿＿ ＿＿＿＿＿＿ ＿＿＿＿＿＿.

18 언급하지 않은 내용 찾기

다음을 듣고, 여자가 말하기 대회에 대해 언급하지 <u>않은</u> 것을 고르시오.

① 대회 일시 ② 주제   ③ 참가 자격
④ 제한 시간 ⑤ 수상자 상품

W Hello, students. I'd like to tell you about the Student Speech Contest. This contest ＿＿＿＿＿＿ ＿＿＿＿＿＿ ＿＿＿＿＿＿ on September 15th. The topic of this year's speech ＿＿＿＿＿＿ "＿＿＿＿＿＿." This contest is ＿＿＿＿＿＿ ＿＿＿＿＿＿ all grades. The speech should be ＿＿＿＿＿＿ ＿＿＿＿＿＿ 5 minutes long. Winners will be announced on October 5. We hope many students will take part in this.

대화를 듣고, 남자의 마지막 말에 이어질 여자의 말로 가장 적절한 것을 고르시오.

Woman: _____

① I hope to visit England.
② It has been raining all day.
③ Yes, I went to England last year.
④ I don't speak English very well.
⑤ Yes, I have lived here since I was young.

🔊 **Listening Tip**

umbrella와 같이 2음절에 강세가 있어서 약모음이나 약음절로 시작하는 단어의 경우 첫 음절은 앞 단어에 연결되어 아주 약하게 발음됩니다. 따라서 an umbrella는 [어넘 브렐러]와 같이 발음됩니다.

W Chanho, what are you doing now?

M I'm making a list _____ _____

_____ .

W Oh, I almost forgot. You are leaving for England next week.

M Right. I'll stay there _____ _____

_____ .

W That's great. Where in England are you _____

_____ _____ ?

M I'm going to visit London first and then Oxford.

W You should take 🔊 an umbrella. It _____

_____ _____ in England.

M Oh, really? Have you been there before?

대화를 듣고, 남자의 마지막 말에 이어질 여자의 말로 가장 적절한 것을 고르시오.

Woman: _____

① Every 20 minutes.
② You can't miss it.
③ Just 10 minutes or so.
④ It's next to the theater.
⑤ You can find it on the second floor.

M Excuse me, but do you know where Smile Department Store is?

W Yes, I do. It's _____ _____ _____

_____ .

M Could you tell me how to get there?

W Just take the number 110 bus from the bus stop

_____ _____ _____ .

M Okay, and then?

W That's it. The bus goes right to the department store.

M Great. _____ _____ _____

_____ _____ ?

실전 모의고사 **08**

01 다음을 듣고, 서울의 날씨로 가장 적절한 것을 고르시오.

①   ②   ③   ④   ⑤

02 대화를 듣고, 남자가 만든 그림엽서로 가장 적절한 것을 고르시오.

①   ②   ③

④   ⑤

03 대화를 듣고, 두 사람이 Oasis Pool에 대해 언급하지 않은 것을 고르시오.
① 위치　　② 놀이 시설　　③ 입장료
④ 교통편　　⑤ 폐장 시각

04 대화를 듣고, 남자가 지난 주말에 한 일로 가장 적절한 것을 고르시오.
① 낚시하기　　② 갯벌 체험하기
③ 요양원 봉사하기　　④ 병원 진료받기
⑤ 할머니 병간호하기

05 대화를 듣고, 두 사람이 대화하는 장소로 가장 적절한 것을 고르시오.
① 서점　　② 도서관　　③ 의상실
④ 가구 판매점　　⑤ 분실물 보관소

06 대화를 듣고, 여자의 마지막 말의 의도로 가장 적절한 것을 고르시오.
① 감사　　② 거절　　③ 충고
④ 비난　　⑤ 격려

07 대화를 듣고, 남자가 보려는 TV 프로그램으로 가장 적절한 것을 고르시오.
① 뉴스　　② TV 드라마　　③ 영화
④ 퀴즈쇼　　⑤ 축구 경기

08 대화를 듣고, 두 사람이 대화 직후에 할 일로 가장 적절한 것을 고르시오.
① 집에 가기　　② 테니스 연습하기
③ 과학 숙제하기　　④ 도서관 가기
⑤ 간식 먹으러 가기

09 대화를 듣고, 여자가 요리 수업에 대해 언급하지 않은 것을 고르시오.
① 만드는 요리　　② 장소　　③ 일정
④ 강습료　　⑤ 재료

10 다음을 듣고, 여자가 하는 말의 내용으로 가장 적절한 것을 고르시오.
① 긴급 대피 안내　　② 분실물 신고 안내
③ 진료 예약 안내　　④ 병원 면회 종료 안내
⑤ 비행기 탑승 안내

11 다음을 듣고, 남자의 동아리에 대한 내용으로 일치하지 <u>않는</u> 것을 고르시오.

① 기타 동아리이다.
② 현재 회원 수는 20명이다.
③ 매주 목요일과 금요일에 만난다.
④ 매년 12월에 연주회를 한다.
⑤ 동아리방은 음악실 옆에 있다.

12 대화를 듣고, 여자가 전화를 건 목적으로 가장 적절한 것을 고르시오.

① 식당을 예약하기 위해서
② 수업 불참을 알리기 위해서
③ 연주회 일정을 알리기 위해서
④ 생일 파티에 초대하기 위해서
⑤ 가족 모임 장소를 정하기 위해서

13 대화를 듣고, 여자가 지불해야 할 금액으로 가장 적절한 것을 고르시오.

① $6   ② $10   ③ $12
④ $18   ⑤ $20

14 대화를 듣고, 두 사람의 관계로 가장 적절한 것을 고르시오.

① 교통경찰 – 보행자
② 매표소 직원 – 손님
③ 버스 운전기사 – 승객
④ 주차 단속원 – 운전자
⑤ 호텔 안내원 – 객실 이용객

15 대화를 듣고, 여자가 남자에게 부탁한 일로 가장 적절한 것을 고르시오.

① 숙제 알려주기   ② 책 추천하기
③ 계단 청소하기   ④ 만화책 가져오기
⑤ 병문안 가기

16 대화를 듣고, 남자가 대회 참가를 망설인 이유로 가장 적절한 것을 고르시오.

① 연습할 시간이 부족해서
② 함께 출전할 파트너가 없어서
③ 참가비용을 마련하기 힘들어서
④ 사람들 앞에 서는 것이 두려워서
⑤ 대회 당일에 중요한 일이 있어서

17 다음 그림의 상황에 가장 적절한 대화를 고르시오.

①   ②   ③   ④   ⑤

18 다음을 듣고, 남자가 하마에 대해 언급하지 <u>않은</u> 것을 고르시오.

① 서식지   ② 수명   ③ 몸길이
④ 몸무게   ⑤ 먹이

[19-20] 대화를 듣고, 여자의 마지막 말에 이어질 남자의 말로 가장 적절한 것을 고르시오.

19 Man: _____

① No. I just eat as usual.
② Okay, I'll have breakfast.
③ No, thank you. I'm full.
④ Yes. I do yoga every morning.
⑤ Eating vegetables is good for you.

20 Man: _____

① I think it's too dangerous.
② I'm planning to visit Hawaii.
③ I enjoy snowboarding in winter.
④ I want to learn figure skating, too.
⑤ I read interesting books about space.

Dictation 08

◆ 다시 듣고, 빈칸에 들어갈 알맞은 단어를 써보세요.

정답 및 해설 p.47

01 날씨 파악

다음을 듣고, 서울의 날씨로 가장 적절한 것을 고르시오.

① ② ③
④ ⑤

W Hello, I'm Sarah Jo for the world weather update. Let's take a look at the weather in Asia. Beijing will be cold _____ _____ _____ _____, and New Delhi will have _____ _____ _____. Stormy weather throughout the day is forecasted in Tokyo. However, it will be _____ _____ _____ _____ in Seoul. Thank you.

02 그림 정보 파악

대화를 듣고, 남자가 만든 그림엽서로 가장 적절한 것을 고르시오.

① ② ③
④ ⑤

W Minho, what are you doing?
M I'm _____ _____ _____ for my French friend, Leo. He'll visit me next week.
W Oh, it's a welcome gift for him.
M That's right. I _____ _____ _____ _____ _____ and the sun on it.
W Do those symbols have any special meaning?
M Yes, this picture means to live _____ _____ _____.
W I think it's a perfect gift for him.

03 언급하지 않은 내용 찾기

대화를 듣고, 두 사람이 Oasis Pool에 대해 언급하지 않은 것을 고르시오.
① 위치   ② 놀이 시설   ③ 입장료
④ 교통편   ⑤ 폐장 시각

W Peter, how about going to a swimming pool this Saturday?
M Good idea. Where?
W How about Oasis Pool?
M Oasis Pool? Do you _____ _____ _____ in Central Park?
W Yes. There is an exciting waterslide _____ _____ _____ _____.

M Great. How much are tickets?

W It's $10 for adults and $7 for students under 16. But we _____ _____ _____ our student card.

M Okay. Let's stay there all day _____ _____ _____ at 6.

---

04 한 일 파악

대화를 듣고, 남자가 지난 주말에 한 일로 가장 적절한 것을 고르시오.
① 낚시하기　　② 갯벌 체험하기
③ 요양원 봉사하기　　④ 병원 진료받기
⑤ 할머니 병간호하기

🔊) **Listening Tip**
모음 사이에 오는 강세가 없는 t는 'ㄹ'로 발음되기 때문에 got a call은 [가러콜]로 발음됩니다.

W Did you have a good time fishing last weekend?

M No, I couldn't go fishing at all.

W Why? _____ _____ _____ ?

M Yes. When my dad and I were leaving, he 🔊got a call from my grandmother. She got really sick, so we had to _____ _____ _____ _____ .

W Oh, I'm sorry to hear that. I hope she _____ _____ _____ .

M Thank you.

---

05 장소 추론

대화를 듣고, 두 사람이 대화하는 장소로 가장 적절한 것을 고르시오.
① 서점　　② 도서관
③ 의상실　　④ 가구 판매점
⑤ 분실물 보관소

M Excuse me. Can I _____ _____ _____ ?

W Of course. What is it?

M Where can I find magazines for interior design?

W They're in Section E on the second floor.

M Thanks. Can I also check out magazines?

W Yes, but you _____ _____ _____ _____ .

M I see. How long can I borrow them for?

W You _____ _____ _____ in a week.

M I understand. Thanks a lot.

대화를 듣고, 여자의 마지막 말의 의도로 가장 적절한 것을 고르시오.

① 감사   ② 거절   ③ 충고
④ 비난   ⑤ 격려

M Hello, how may I help you?

W I _____ _____ _____ in the subway last night.

M What does it _____ _____? Can you describe it?

W It's a gray backpack with a front pocket. And it has 2 black leather straps.

M Does the bag have _____ _____ _____ _____ _____, too?

W Yes, it does.

M Is this your bag?

W Yes, that's mine! _____ _____ _____ _____ for your help.

대화를 듣고, 남자가 보려는 TV 프로그램으로 가장 적절한 것을 고르시오.

① 뉴스   ② TV 드라마
③ 영화   ④ 퀴즈쇼
⑤ 축구 경기

W Steve, how about going to a movie tonight?

M Well, *I'm planning to _____ _____ at home this evening.

W But you don't like watching TV.

M No, but I have to watch it tonight.

W Why? Are there any _____ _____ _____?

M Actually, my uncle is going to be on *I Love Quizzes* _____ _____ _____ _____.

W Wow, I love _____ _____! Let's watch it together.

M Okay.

---

* **교육부 지정 의사소통 기능: 계획 말하기**   동(윤) 6 | 천(이) 1 | 천(정) 2 | 능(김) 6 | Y(송) 1

I'm planning to ~. 나는 ~할 계획이야.

• **I'm planning to** see a movie this Saturday. 나는 이번 주 토요일에 영화를 볼 계획이야.
• **I'm planning to** go hiking. 나는 등산하러 갈 계획이야.

대화를 듣고, 두 사람이 대화 직후에 할 일로 가장 적절한 것을 고르시오.

① 집에 가기　　② 테니스 연습하기
③ 과학 숙제하기　④ 도서관 가기
⑤ 간식 먹으러 가기

M I'm so tired. It's been a long day.

W I just want to go home and ＿＿＿＿＿＿ ＿＿＿＿＿＿ ＿＿＿＿＿＿.

M Me, too. But I have a science test tomorrow.

W Don't you also ＿＿＿＿＿＿ ＿＿＿＿＿＿ ＿＿＿＿＿＿ today?

M Yes, but I'm going to skip it today. I have to go to the library to study.

W Well, would you like to go and ＿＿＿＿＿＿ ＿＿＿＿＿＿ ＿＿＿＿＿＿ with me first?

M Yeah. That sounds good. Let's go.

09 언급하지 않은 내용 찾기

대화를 듣고, 여자가 요리 수업에 대해 언급하지 않은 것을 고르시오.

① 만드는 요리　② 장소
③ 일정　　　　④ 강습료
⑤ 재료

[Telephone rings.]

W Hello, Chloe's Cooking Class. How may I help you?

M Hello. I'm interested in your cooking class.

W Great! You can learn to cook many ＿＿＿＿＿＿ ＿＿＿＿＿＿ ＿＿＿＿＿＿ with me.

M Where is the class?

W The classes are ＿＿＿＿＿＿ ＿＿＿＿＿＿ ＿＿＿＿＿＿ near Hamilton subway station.

M Oh, I see. What time is the class on weekdays?

W The ＿＿＿＿＿＿ ＿＿＿＿＿＿ ＿＿＿＿＿＿ at 7 p.m.

M How much ＿＿＿＿＿＿ ＿＿＿＿＿＿ ＿＿＿＿＿＿?

W $30 per lesson. That includes everything.

10 주제 추론

다음을 듣고, 여자가 하는 말의 내용으로 가장 적절한 것을 고르시오.

① 긴급 대피 안내
② 분실물 신고 안내
③ 진료 예약 안내
④ 병원 면회 종료 안내
⑤ 비행기 탑승 안내

W Attention, all visitors to the hospital. It is now 8 p.m., and ＿＿＿＿＿＿ ＿＿＿＿＿＿ ＿＿＿＿＿＿. We ask that all visitors now leave the building. Normal visiting hours ＿＿＿＿＿＿ ＿＿＿＿＿＿ ＿＿＿＿＿＿ tomorrow at 10 a.m. If you ＿＿＿＿＿＿ ＿＿＿＿＿＿ ＿＿＿＿＿＿, please come to the information desk. Thank you.

다음을 듣고, 남자의 동아리에 대한 내용으로 일치하지 <u>않는</u> 것을 고르시오.

① 기타 동아리이다.
② 현재 회원 수는 20명이다.
③ 매주 목요일과 금요일에 만난다.
④ 매년 12월에 연주회를 한다.
⑤ 동아리방은 음악실 옆에 있다.

M Hello, new students! I'm happy to introduce _____ _____ _____ to you. There are 20 members in the club. We meet twice a week, _____ _____ _____. We have a concert _____ _____. Our club room is _____ _____ _____ _____ _____. Do you want to learn how to play the guitar? Then come and join us!

12 목적 파악

대화를 듣고, 여자가 전화를 건 목적으로 가장 적절한 것을 고르시오.

① 식당을 예약하기 위해서
② 수업 불참을 알리기 위해서
③ 연주회 일정을 알리기 위해서
④ 생일 파티에 초대하기 위해서
⑤ 가족 모임 장소를 정하기 위해서

[Cell phone rings.]

M Hello.

W Hello, Mr. Harris. It's Alice.

M Alice? Don't you have a lesson today?

W I have to go out for dinner with my family tonight. So I don't think I can come over for _____ _____ _____.

M Oh, I see. I hope you have a great time with your family.

W Thank you, sir. I forgot to tell you last week. _____ _____ _____.

M That's okay. Then can you come over for the lesson _____ _____?

W Sure.

13 숫자 정보 파악 (금액)

대화를 듣고, 여자가 지불해야 할 금액으로 가장 적절한 것을 고르시오.

① $6   ② $10   ③ $12
④ $18   ⑤ $20

M Welcome to Hana Aquarium. May I help you?

W Yes, please. I'd like to _____ _____ _____ for the dolphin show.

M Sure. We have S and A _____ _____.

W How much are they?

M The S seats are $10 and A seats are $6.

W I'd like 2 A seats, please.

M Okay. _____ _____ _____ _____ $12.

W All right. _____ _____ _____.

대화를 듣고, 두 사람의 관계로 가장 적절한 것을
고르시오.

① 교통경찰 – 보행자
② 매표소 직원 – 손님
③ 버스 운전기사 – 승객
④ 주차 단속원 – 운전자
⑤ 호텔 안내원 – 객실 이용객

W Excuse me, sir. This bus goes downtown, right?

M Yes, it does. Where exactly are you going?

W I _____ _____ _____ to Star World.

M Okay. I'll let you know when we _____ _____ _____.

W Thank you. Will it take long to get there?

M It usually takes about 30 minutes, but at this time of the day _____ _____ _____.

W That's good. Thank you so much.

M _____ _____.

대화를 듣고, 여자가 남자에게 부탁한 일로 가장
적절한 것을 고르시오.

① 숙제 알려주기   ② 책 추천하기
③ 계단 청소하기   ④ 만화책 가져오기
⑤ 병문안 가기

W Did you hear that Brad is _____ _____ _____?

M I didn't know that. What happened?

W He fell down the stairs and broke his leg.

M Really? That's too bad.

W So I'm going to see him after school.

M I'll _____ _____ _____ then. Should we bring him something?

W How about taking _____ _____ _____ for him? If you have any interesting books, _____ _____ _____ them?

M Okay. I will.

대화를 듣고, 남자가 대회 참가를 망설인 이유로
가장 적절한 것을 고르시오.

① 연습할 시간이 부족해서
② 함께 출전할 파트너가 없어서
③ 참가비용을 마련하기 힘들어서
④ 사람들 앞에 서는 것이 두려워서
⑤ 대회 당일에 중요한 일이 있어서

W What are you looking at?

M I'm looking at the poster for the singing contest.

W Are you going to _____ _____?

M I want to, _____ _____ _____ to sing in front of many people.

W Hmm... You said you wanted to be a singer, didn't you?

M   Yes, that's right.

W   Then, you should _____ _____ in front of an audience.

M   You're right. I should _____ _____ _____ _____ .

다음 그림의 상황에 가장 적절한 대화를 고르시오.

①   ②   ③   ④   ⑤

① M   What do you _____ _____ _____ ?

W   I'd like a hamburger and a coke.

② M   Which bus do I take to go downtown?

W   The number 35 bus will get you there.

③ M   Emily, where are you going?

W   I'm going to the grocery store to _____ _____ _____ .

④ M   Excuse me, but you _____ _____ on the subway.

W   Oh, I'm sorry. I didn't know that.

⑤ M   Mom, I feel _____ _____ _____ .

W   Would you like some apple pie?

다음을 듣고, 남자가 하마에 대해 언급하지 <u>않은</u> 것을 고르시오.

① 서식지   ② 수명   ③ 몸길이
④ 몸무게   ⑤ 먹이

M   Hello, everyone. I'm here to tell you about hippos. Hippos are large animals that _____ _____ _____ . They can live for 40 to 50 years. Hippos can _____ _____ _____ up to 5 meters long. Their weight can be up to 4,500 kilograms. They love to stay in the water to _____ _____ _____ .

대화를 듣고, 여자의 마지막 말에 이어질 남자의 말로 가장 적절한 것을 고르시오.

Man: _____

① No. I just eat as usual.
② Okay, I'll have breakfast.
③ No, thank you. I'm full.
④ Yes. I do yoga every morning.
⑤ Eating vegetables is good for you.

W Hey, Steve. Long time no see.
M Yes. It's been _____ _____ _____ since we last met.
W You've _____ _____ _____ _____ _____!
M Yes, that's right. I'm exercising a lot these days.
W Oh, really? _____ _____ _____ exercise are you doing?
M Just running. I usually run 10 kilometers every day.
W Good for you. Are you _____ _____ _____, too?

대화를 듣고, 여자의 마지막 말에 이어질 남자의 말로 가장 적절한 것을 고르시오.

Man: _____

① I think it's too dangerous.
② I'm planning to visit Hawaii.
③ I enjoy snowboarding in winter.
④ I want to learn figure skating, too.
⑤ I read interesting books about space.

M Did you have a good time during winter vacation?
W Yes. I spent most of my vacation learning figure skating.
M Oh, really? Can you _____ _____ _____ _____?
W Sure. I can even spin in the air.
M That's great! You _____ _____ _____ _____ in such a short time.
W Thanks. How did you _____ _____ _____?

실전 모의고사 **09**

점수 /20

01 다음을 듣고, 부산의 날씨로 가장 적절한 것을 고르시오.

① ② ③ ④ ⑤

02 대화를 듣고, 여자가 만든 가방으로 가장 적절한 것을 고르시오.

① ② ③

④ ⑤

03 대화를 듣고, 두 사람이 Fantasy Film Festival에 대해 언급하지 않은 것을 고르시오.

① 날짜　　　② 장소　　　③ 참가 대상
④ 입장료　　⑤ 강연자

04 대화를 듣고, 여자가 지구의 날에 한 일로 가장 적절한 것을 고르시오.

① 전등 끄기　　　　② 나무 심기
③ 마라톤 참가하기　④ 대중교통 이용하기
⑤ 자전거 타고 등교하기

05 대화를 듣고, 두 사람이 대화하는 장소로 가장 적절한 것을 고르시오.

① 유치원　　② 극장　　③ 음식점
④ 놀이 공원　⑤ 미아보호소

06 대화를 듣고, 여자의 마지막 말의 의도로 가장 적절한 것을 고르시오.

① 감사　　　② 사과　　　③ 부탁
④ 거절　　　⑤ 격려

07 대화를 듣고, 두 사람이 캠프에 가져가기로 한 것이 아닌 것을 고르시오.

① 담요　　② 손전등　　③ 망원경
④ 침낭　　⑤ 수건

08 대화를 듣고, 남자가 대화 직후에 할 일로 가장 적절한 것을 고르시오.

① 비디오 시청하기　　② 집에서 자전거 찾기
③ 지하철 환승하기　　④ 신분증 가져오기
⑤ 자전거 수리점 찾아보기

09 대화를 듣고, 남자가 Happy Guesthouse에 대해 언급하지 않은 것을 고르시오.

① 위치　　② 객실 수　　③ 조식 시간
④ 숙박 요금　⑤ 인터넷 요금

10 다음을 듣고, 남자가 하는 말의 내용으로 가장 적절한 것을 고르시오.

① 화재 대피 훈련　　② 교실 환경 미화
③ 승강기 작동 원리　④ 학급회의 개최 안내
⑤ 지진 발생 시 행동 요령

11 다음을 듣고, 과학 캠프에 대한 내용으로 일치하지 <u>않는</u> 것을 고르시오.

① 쉽고 재밌게 과학을 공부할 수 있다.
② 한국 대학교에서 5일간 진행된다.
③ 모든 학년이 참여할 수 있다.
④ 참가비는 무료다.
⑤ 인원 제한은 20명이다.

12 대화를 듣고, 여자가 전화를 건 목적으로 가장 적절한 것을 고르시오.

① 피자를 주문하기 위해서
② 식당 위치를 묻기 위해서
③ 주소를 확인하기 위해서
④ 음식 주문을 취소하기 위해서
⑤ 온라인 주문 방법을 묻기 위해서

13 대화를 듣고, 남자가 지불할 금액으로 가장 적절한 것을 고르시오.

① $8   ② $12   ③ $16
④ $20   ⑤ $24

14 대화를 듣고, 두 사람의 관계로 가장 적절한 것을 고르시오.

① 사회 교사 – 학생   ② 승무원 – 승객
③ 식당 종업원 – 손님   ④ 교통경찰 – 운전자
⑤ 관광 가이드 – 여행객

15 대화를 듣고, 남자가 여자에게 부탁한 일로 가장 적절한 것을 고르시오.

① 옷 골라 주기   ② 백화점 함께 가기
③ 테니스 가르쳐주기   ④ 점심 식사 준비하기
⑤ 자외선 차단제 사다 주기

16 대화를 듣고, 여자가 병원을 방문한 이유로 가장 적절한 것을 고르시오.

① 약을 찾기 위해서
② 정기검진을 받기 위해서
③ 자원봉사를 하기 위해서
④ 엄마를 간호하기 위해서
⑤ 할아버지 병문안을 하기 위해서

17 다음 그림의 상황에 가장 적절한 대화를 고르시오.

①   ②   ③   ④   ⑤

18 다음을 듣고, 여자가 코알라에 대해 언급하지 <u>않은</u> 것을 고르시오.

① 서식지   ② 크기   ③ 먹이
④ 수명   ⑤ 수면 시간

[19-20] 대화를 듣고, 남자의 마지막 말에 이어질 여자의 말로 가장 적절한 것을 고르시오.

19 Woman: _____

① Sorry, I can't help you.
② Sure. Let's meet at 5 o'clock.
③ No, I'm not good at math.
④ I usually play badminton after school.
⑤ Okay. How about meeting at the library?

20 Woman: _____

① I don't think so.
② Let's buy the gray one.
③ You'd better wear a scarf.
④ Pink is my favorite color.
⑤ I don't have enough money for a present.

Dictation 09

◇ 다시 듣고, 빈칸에 들어갈 알맞은 단어를 써보세요.

01 날씨 파악

다음을 듣고, 부산의 날씨로 가장 적절한 것을 고르시오.

① ② ③
④ ⑤

M This is a special weather report. Because of the influence of the typhoon, it is _____ _____ with strong winds in Jeju-do. In Busan and Gwangju, it is not raining, but the wind _____ _____ _____.
In Seoul and Gyeonggi, it's partly cloudy with _____ _____ _____ _____ in the afternoon, so don't leave home without your umbrella.

02 그림 정보 파악

대화를 듣고, 여자가 만든 가방으로 가장 적절한 것을 고르시오.

① ② ③
④ ⑤

M Angela, did you make this canvas bag yourself?
W Yes, I did it in art class. What do you think?
M I really like the _____ _____ _____ _____ on it. Angie is short for Angela, right?
W That's right. The pocket was not big enough for "Angela."
M I see. You also added _____ _____ _____ the pocket. Do you like sunflowers?
W Yes, they are _____ _____ _____.

03 언급하지 않은 내용 찾기

대화를 듣고, 두 사람이 Fantasy Film Festival에 대해 언급하지 않은 것을 고르시오.

① 날짜 ② 장소 ③ 참가 대상
④ 입장료 ⑤ 강연자

M Did you hear the news about a movie festival in our town?
W You mean the Fantasy Film Festival, right?
M Yes, _____ _____ _____ June 5th. Do you want to go together?
W Sure. Do you know where it is?
M _____ _____ _____ the Daehan Art Center.
W Okay. How much is a ticket?
M It's $15.

🔊 Listening Tip

like처럼 'l'이 단어의 첫 소리로 발음될 때는 우리말의 'ㄹ'에 가깝게 발음되지만 단어 중간이나 끝에 나오면 발음되는 위치에 따라 /어/, /오/, /우/와 가깝게 들리는 애매한 소리로 발음됩니다. film은 [필름]이 아니라 [피엄]과 같이 발음됩니다.

W That's great. Are there any famous people coming to the festival?

M The movie director Kim Menders is coming to _____ _____ _____ .

04 한 일 파악

대화를 듣고, 여자가 지구의 날에 한 일로 가장 적절한 것을 고르시오.

① 전등 끄기
② 나무 심기
③ 마라톤 참가하기
④ 대중교통 이용하기
⑤ 자전거 타고 등교하기

W Did you celebrate Earth Day?

M Yes, I _____ _____ _____ _____ at 8 p.m. Did you do it?

W Actually, I forgot about the time, so I didn't do that.

M Then what did you do?

W I _____ _____ _____ to school instead of taking the bus. And I'm planning to _____ _____ _____ this weekend.

M Good job!

05 장소 추론

대화를 듣고, 두 사람이 대화하는 장소로 가장 적절한 것을 고르시오.

① 유치원   ② 극장   ③ 음식점
④ 놀이 공원 ⑤ 미아보호소

M Let's sit here. What did you _____ _____ _____ _____ ?

W Well, it was better than I expected. The story was very touching.

M I feel the same way. I almost cried when those children cried for their mom.

W Me, too. Anyway, have you decided _____ _____ _____ ?

M Yes. I'll have a cheeseburger set. What about you?

W I'll _____ _____ _____ . Wait here. I'll order and _____ _____ _____ .

06 의도 파악

대화를 듣고, 여자의 마지막 말의 의도로 가장 적절한 것을 고르시오.

① 감사   ② 사과   ③ 부탁
④ 거절   ⑤ 격려

M Judy, can you come here for a minute?

W Yeah, I'm coming. What is it, Dad?

M Do you know what happened to this speaker? It _____ _____ .

W I'm sorry, Dad. I _____ _____.

M What? How did that happen?

W I spilled some hot water on it while I was cooking ramyeon.

M You didn't _____ _____, did you?

W I'm okay, but it's _____ _____.

---

07 특정 정보 파악

대화를 듣고, 두 사람이 캠프에 가져가기로 한 것
이 아닌 것을 고르시오.
① 담요   ② 손전등   ③ 망원경
④ 침낭   ⑤ 수건

W I'm _____ _____ to go to the camp tomorrow.

M Me, too. The weather forecast says we'll have _____ _____ tomorrow.

W But it may _____ _____ _____ _____, so I packed a blanket.

M That's great. What about a flashlight?

W I got that, too. Oh, I don't have a telescope at home. Can you bring one?

M Sure. Do we also need _____ _____ _____?

W No, we are going to stay at a cabin nearby. But we still _____ _____ _____ our own towels.

---

08 할 일 파악

대화를 듣고, 남자가 대화 직후에 할 일로 가장 적
절한 것을 고르시오.
① 비디오 시청하기
② 집에서 자전거 찾기
③ 지하철 환승하기
④ 신분증 가져오기
⑤ 자전거 수리점 찾아보기

M Jamie, are you busy?

W No, Dad. What's up?

M Do you want to do something together then?

W Sure. *[Pause]* We could go out for _____ _____ _____.

M But we have only one bike at home.

W There is a bike rental shop near the subway station. We _____ _____ _____ _____ from there.

M Great! Do I need to _____ _____?

W You might need your ID to borrow a bike.

M Okay. _____ _____ _____ right now.

대화를 듣고, 남자가 Happy Guesthouse에 대해 언급하지 <u>않은</u> 것을 고르시오.

① 위치   ② 객실 수
③ 조식 시간   ④ 숙박 요금
⑤ 인터넷 요금

W   Where did you stay in Jeju-do last summer?

M   At Happy Guesthouse. _____ _____ _____ to go there?

W   Yes, I am. What was the room like?

M   It was nice and quiet. It's a small guesthouse _____ _____ 4 rooms.

W   _____ _____ _____ it per night?

M   It's only $50.

W   That's not expensive.

M   Yes. You can also use the Internet _____ _____.

W   Oh, that sounds great.

---

10 주제 추론

다음을 듣고, 남자가 하는 말의 내용으로 가장 적절한 것을 고르시오.

① 화재 대피 훈련
② 교실 환경 미화
③ 승강기 작동 원리
④ 학급회의 개최 안내
⑤ 지진 발생 시 행동 요령

M   Hello, students. This is Chris, a firefighter from Daelim Fire Station. Today, I came here to talk about _____ _____ _____ in case of an earthquake. If you're in the classroom, _____ _____ _____ the windows and get under a desk. And you _____ _____ _____ the elevators. You _____ _____ _____ and do what your teacher says.

---

11 일치하지 않는 내용 찾기

다음을 듣고, 과학 캠프에 대한 내용으로 일치하지 않는 것을 고르시오.

① 쉽고 재밌게 과학을 공부할 수 있다.
② 한국 대학교에서 5일간 진행된다.
③ 모든 학년이 참여할 수 있다.
④ 참가비는 무료다.
⑤ 인원 제한은 20명이다.

W   Hi, everyone! How about joining a science camp this vacation? With this program, you can enjoy and study science in an _____ _____ _____ _____. This camp will be held at Hanguk University for 5 days. However, it is _____ _____ _____ students over 15. There is _____ _____ _____. Only 20 students can _____ _____ _____, so sign up soon!

12 목적 파악

대화를 듣고, 여자가 전화를 건 목적으로 가장 적절한 것을 고르시오.

① 피자를 주문하기 위해서
② 식당 위치를 묻기 위해서
③ 주소를 확인하기 위해서
④ 음식 주문을 취소하기 위해서
⑤ 온라인 주문 방법을 묻기 위해서

[Telephone rings.]

M   Hello, Joe's Pizza. How may I help you?

W   I ordered a pizza an hour ago, but it _____ _____ _____.

M   Oh, really? What's your address?

W   210 Fine Street.

M   We're really sorry. We'll _____ _____ _____ right away.

W   Actually, I'd like to _____ _____ _____. I don't have enough time to wait.

M   Oh, okay. I'll do that right now. Once again, _____ _____ _____.

13 숫자 정보 파악 (금액)

대화를 듣고, 남자가 지불할 금액으로 가장 적절한 것을 고르시오.

① $8   ② $12   ③ $16
④ $20   ⑤ $24

W   Hello, may I help you?

M   Yes. How much is _____ _____ _____ to the museum?

W   It is $8.

M   Okay. My children are 11 and 12. Do they _____ _____ _____?

W   Yes, they do. For children under 13, the entrance fee is $4.

M   Great. What is _____ _____ _____ an adult and 2 children?

W   _____ _____ $16.

M   Here you are.

W   Thank you. Enjoy the museum.

14 관계 추론

대화를 듣고, 두 사람의 관계로 가장 적절한 것을 고르시오.

① 사회 교사 – 학생
② 승무원 – 승객
③ 식당 종업원 – 손님
④ 교통경찰 – 운전자
⑤ 관광 가이드 – 여행객

W   Please put your seatbelt back on. The seatbelt sign is on again.

M   Oh, I'm sorry. I wanted to _____ _____ _____ for a bit.

W   It's all right, sir. Is this your first time visiting New York?

M   Yes, it is. I'm very excited about my trip.

W There are _____ _____ _____ in the seat pocket. They are _____ _____.

M Great. Thanks. Could I _____ _____ _____, please?

W Sure. Please _____ _____ _____.

M Thank you.

15 부탁 파악

대화를 듣고, 남자가 여자에게 부탁한 일로 가장 적절한 것을 고르시오.

① 옷 골라 주기
② 백화점 함께 가기
③ 테니스 가르쳐주기
④ 점심 식사 준비하기
⑤ 자외선 차단제 사다 주기

🔊 Listening Tip

[t]가 강세를 받는 강모음과 강세를 받지 않는 약모음 사이에 오면, 부드러운 [r] 소리로 발음됩니다. 따라서 matter는 /매터/가 아니라 /매러/로 발음됩니다.

M Mom, when are you going to go to the department store?

W I'll go there after lunch. Why?

M I need to buy something from there. Can you _____ _____ _____ _____?

W What is it?

M I _____ _____ _____ sunblock when I practice tennis. Can you _____ _____ _____?

W No problem. Is there any special brand you want?

M No. It doesn't 🔊 matter to me.

W All right. I'll get one for you.

16 이유 파악

대화를 듣고, 여자가 병원을 방문한 이유로 가장 적절한 것을 고르시오.

① 약을 찾기 위해서
② 정기검진을 받기 위해서
③ 자원봉사를 하기 위해서
④ 엄마를 간호하기 위해서
⑤ 할아버지 병문안을 하기 위해서

M Emily, long time no see!

W Hi, Brian. I didn't _____ _____ _____ _____ here.

M I'm here to see my grandfather. Are you still volunteering at this hospital?

W No, _____ _____ _____ pick up some medicine.

M Oh, I see. Do you have time _____ _____ _____?

W Sorry, I don't. My mom is waiting outside for me.

M Then let's meet _____ _____ _____.

W Sure. See you.

17 그림 상황에 적절한 대화 찾기

다음 그림의 상황에 가장 적절한 대화를 고르시오.

① ② ③ ④ ⑤

① W What did you do last weekend?
  M I visited my grandma in Busan.
② W What do you usually do _____ _____
    _____ _____?
  M I enjoy reading comic books.
③ W *Have you ever heard this song?
  M Sure. It's one of _____ _____
    _____.
④ W When does the baseball season start?
  M It _____ _____ May 12.
⑤ W Can you go to MK's _____ _____
    _____ with me?
  M Sure. I'll go with you.

★ **교육부 지정 의사소통 기능: 경험 묻기**   동(이) 4 | 천(이) 7 | 미 3 | 능(김) 3 | Y(송) 6
Have you ever p.p. ~? ~한 적이 있니?
• **Have you ever eaten** Korean food? 한국 음식 먹어본 적 있니?
• **Have you ever been** to China? 중국에 가 본 적이 있니?

---

18 언급하지 않은 내용 찾기

다음을 듣고, 여자가 코알라에 대해 언급하지 <u>않</u>은 것을 고르시오.

① 서식지   ② 크기   ③ 먹이
④ 수명   ⑤ 수면 시간

W Hello, animal lovers. I'm happy to tell you about a cute
  animal, the koala. _____ _____
  _____ the southeastern part of Australia. The koala
  is about 60 to 85 centimeters long and _____
  _____ 14 kilograms. They only _____
  _____ _____ _____ a special tree
  called eucalyptus. They _____ _____
  _____ 20 hours a day.

---

19 이어질 응답 찾기

대화를 듣고, 남자의 마지막 말에 이어질 여자의 말로 가장 적절한 것을 고르시오.

Woman: _____

① Sorry, I can't help you.
② Sure. Let's meet at 5 o'clock.
③ No, I'm not good at math.
④ I usually play badminton after school.
⑤ Okay. How about meeting at the library?

W Peter, you look worried. What's wrong?
M I don't know how to start my art project. _____
  _____ _____.
W Oh, I see.
M You are very _____ _____ _____,
  aren't you?
W Well, art is my favorite subject.

M I was wondering if you could _____ _____ _____ my art project.

W I'd be happy to help you.

M Thanks a lot. Then _____ _____ _____ _____ the bus stop after school?

20 이어질 응답 찾기

대화를 듣고, 남자의 마지막 말에 이어질 여자의 말로 가장 적절한 것을 고르시오.

Woman: _____

① I don't think so.
② Let's buy the gray one.
③ You'd better wear a scarf.
④ Pink is my favorite color.
⑤ I don't have enough money for a present.

W Mason, what should we buy for Dad's birthday?

M I'm thinking about _____ _____ _____. *[Pause]* How about this one?

W Well, I'm not sure if he needs one.

M It's going to be a cold winter this year. A scarf will be _____ _____ _____ for him.

W Okay. Hmm... I like the design. _____ _____ _____ ?

M I like it, too.

W But there are two colors.

M I like them both, but I think Dad _____ _____ _____.

실전 모의고사 **10**

01 다음을 듣고, 일요일 오전의 날씨로 가장 적절한 것을 고르시오.

① ② ③ ④ ⑤

02 대화를 듣고, 남자가 주문한 음식으로 가장 적절한 것을 고르시오.

① ② ③

④ ⑤

03 대화를 듣고, 남자가 만나려는 사람에 대해 언급되지 않은 것을 고르시오.

① 이름   ② 사무실 위치
③ 직업   ④ 좋아하는 음료
⑤ 생김새

04 대화를 듣고, 남자가 주말에 한 일로 가장 적절한 것을 고르시오.

① 벽지 바르기   ② 집안 청소하기
③ 페인트칠하기   ④ 그림 그리기
⑤ 미술관 가기

05 대화를 듣고, 두 사람이 대화하는 장소로 가장 적절한 곳을 고르시오.

① 시청 민원실   ② 커피숍
③ 버스 정류장   ④ 기차 안
⑤ 레스토랑

06 대화를 듣고, 여자의 마지막 말의 의도로 가장 적절한 것을 고르시오.

① 칭찬   ② 격려   ③ 거절
④ 승낙   ⑤ 부탁

07 대화를 듣고, 두 사람이 선물할 물건으로 가장 적절한 것을 고르시오.

① 시계   ② 자전거   ③ 책
④ 가방   ⑤ 컴퓨터

08 대화를 듣고, 여자가 대화 직후에 할 일로 가장 적절한 것을 고르시오.

① 산책하기   ② 음식 주문하기
③ 과일 사러 가기   ④ 과일 씻기
⑤ 저녁 준비하기

09 대화를 듣고, 남자가 면접에서 자신에 대해 언급하지 않은 것을 고르시오.

① 업무 경험   ② 장단점
③ 어학 실력   ④ 업무 가능 시기
⑤ 취미

10 다음을 듣고, 여자가 하는 말의 내용으로 가장 적절한 것을 고르시오.

① 날씨 예보   ② 기내 안전 교육
③ 여행 일정 소개   ④ 항공편 지연 안내
⑤ 탑승 위치 변경 통보

11 대화를 듣고, 여자가 찾는 곳에 대한 내용으로 일치하지 <u>않는</u> 것을 고르시오.

① 서점이다.　　　　② 새로 개업했다.
③ 9층에 있다.　　　④ 전 층을 사용한다.
⑤ 커피숍도 안에 있다.

12 대화를 듣고, 남자가 해외여행을 자주 하는 목적으로 가장 적절한 것을 고르시오.

① 사진 찍는 것을 좋아해서
② 세계 역사를 배우기 위해서
③ 다양한 문화를 경험하기 위해서
④ 다양한 세계 음식을 맛보고 싶어서
⑤ 세계 곳곳의 건물들을 연구하기 위해서

13 대화를 듣고, 두 사람이 만날 시각을 고르시오.

① 5:00 p.m.　　② 5:10 p.m.　　③ 5:20 p.m.
④ 5:30 p.m.　　⑤ 5:40 p.m.

14 대화를 듣고, 두 사람의 관계로 가장 적절한 것을 고르시오.

① 연예인 – 매니저
② 택시 운전사 – 승객
③ 우체국 직원 – 고객
④ 세관 직원 – 항공 승무원
⑤ 버스 운전사 – 교통경찰

15 대화를 듣고, 여자가 남자에게 부탁한 일로 가장 적절한 것을 고르시오.

① 노트 보여주기　　② 역사책 빌려주기
③ 신문 가져오기　　④ 시험 일정 확인하기
⑤ 약속 시간 변경하기

16 대화를 듣고, 남자가 호텔 예약을 하지 <u>못하는</u> 이유로 가장 적절한 것을 고르시오.

① 위치가 너무 멀어서
② 숙박비가 너무 비싸서
③ 예약 가능한 방이 없어서
④ 반려 동물 출입이 금지라서
⑤ 예약에 필요한 정보를 몰라서

17 다음 그림의 상황에 가장 적절한 대화를 고르시오.

①　　②　　③　　④　　⑤

18 다음을 듣고, 남자가 Premier League에 대해 언급하지 <u>않은</u> 것을 고르시오.

① 소속 팀 수　　　② 창설 연도
③ 팀 당 경기 수　　④ 시즌 시작과 종료 시기
⑤ 승점 부여 방식

[19-20] 대화를 듣고, 남자의 마지막 말에 이어질 여자의 응답으로 가장 적절한 것을 고르시오.

19 Woman: _____

① I often skip breakfast.
② I have lunch at 12:30.
③ I didn't have lunch yesterday.
④ I usually have Korean food for lunch.
⑤ I sometimes have lunch with my friends.

20 Woman: _____

① Okay, here it is.
② What day is it today?
③ You had a great time, didn't you?
④ We should get some flowers for her.
⑤ I think you should throw me a party.

Dictation 10

◇ 다시 듣고, 빈칸에 들어갈 알맞은 단어를 써보세요.

정답 및 해설 p.59

---

01 날씨 파악

다음을 듣고, 일요일 오전의 날씨로 가장 적절한 것을 고르시오.

① ② ③
④ ⑤

M Here is the weather report for the weekend. It will be very hot and sunny _____ _____ _____ on Saturday. The temperatures will _____ _____ across the country.
On Sunday, it will be cloudy in the morning. However, in the afternoon we'll have _____ _____.
And the temperature will be _____ _____ _____ Saturday's. Thank you.

---

02 그림 정보 파악

대화를 듣고, 남자가 주문한 음식으로 가장 적절한 것을 고르시오.

① ② ③
④ ⑤

🎧 Listening Tip

자음으로 끝나는 단어와 모음으로 시작하는 단어가 합쳐져 하나의 단어처럼 발음되기도 해요. and a sandwich의 앞 두 단어인 and와 a가 연음이 되어 /앤드 어/가 아닌 /앤 더/로 발음됩니다.

W Hi. What can I get you?
M I'd like _____ _____ _____ _____, please.
W All right. Would you like something to eat with your coffee?
M I will have _____ _____ _____ _____ 🔊and a sandwich, please.
W Is that everything?
M Yes.
W Okay. Your total comes to $11.
M _____ _____ _____.
W Thanks.

---

03 언급하지 않은 내용 찾기

대화를 듣고, 남자가 만나려는 사람에 대해 언급되지 않은 것을 고르시오.

① 이름 ② 사무실 위치
③ 직업 ④ 좋아하는 음료
⑤ 생김새

M Hello, I came here to see Mike Fox.
W You must be David. Mr. Fox will be with you shortly. Please have a seat.
M All right. By the way, which room is _____ _____?
W It's 201, right _____ _____ _____ _____.

M All right. I brought a drink for him. Do you know

_____ _____ _____

_____ ?

W Sure. He loves black coffee. *[Pause]* Here he comes.

M Which one is Mr. Fox?

W The one _____ _____ _____ .

---

04 한 일 파악

대화를 듣고, 남자가 주말에 한 일로 가장 적절한
것을 고르시오.

① 벽지 바르기　　② 집안 청소하기
③ 페인트칠하기　　④ 그림 그리기
⑤ 미술관 가기

🔊 **Listening Tip**

t나 d로 끝나는 단어에 -ed가 붙으면 [id]로 발음됩니다.
painted가 이 경우에 해당하는데 center처럼 n뒤에서 t
소리가 사라져서 painted는 /페이닌/에 가깝게 발음됩니
다.

W Steve, what did you do on the weekend?

M I worked _____ _____ _____ .

I am so tired.

W What kind of work did you do?

M I made my room _____ _____

_____ .

W You made your room brighter? What did you do?

M Well, my room _____ _____

_____ . So, I 🔊 painted them sky blue. You should

come and see it.

W Sure. Maybe I should _____ _____

_____ , too.

---

05 특정 정보 파악

대화를 듣고, 두 사람이 대화하는 장소로 가장 적
절한 곳을 고르시오.

① 시청 민원실　　② 커피숍
③ 버스 정류장　　④ 기차 안
⑤ 레스토랑

W Excuse me, do you know how to get to City Hall?

M Yes, _____ _____ _____

_____ number 15.

W Okay. Is there a subway station nearby?

M You have to go straight for two blocks. It'll take about 20

minutes to get there on foot.

W 20 minutes? That's too long.

M Then, you'd better _____ _____

_____ to go to City Hall. It's much faster.

Oh, _____ _____ _____

_____ .

W Okay. Thanks for your help.

대화를 듣고, 여자의 마지막 말의 의도로 가장 적절한 것을 고르시오.
① 칭찬　② 격려　③ 거절
④ 승낙　⑤ 부탁

W The weather forecast says we'll have warm weather this weekend.

M I heard that, too. _____, _____ _____ _____.

W I wanted to go hiking during the winter, but it was too dangerous.

M Yes, you could fall _____ _____ _____ _____.

W *I can't wait to go mountain climbing again.

M Well, we could go this weekend. The weather will _____ _____ _____.

W Okay. _____ _____ _____.

> ✱ 교육부 지정 의사소통 기능: **희망·기대 표현하기**　　지7
>
> **I can't wait to ~.** 나는 빨리 ~하고 싶어.
> • **I can't wait to** meet her. 나는 그녀를 빨리 만나고 싶어.
> • **I can't wait to** go fishing. 나는 빨리 낚시하러 가고 싶어.

07 특정 정보 파악

대화를 듣고, 두 사람이 선물할 물건으로 가장 적절한 것을 고르시오.
① 시계　② 자전거　③ 책
④ 가방　⑤ 컴퓨터

W Honey, Jake's birthday is coming up. We need to get something for him.

M You're right. It's next Tuesday, right?

W Yes. Last year, we went to an amusement park instead of _____ _____ _____.

M How about some books? He loves reading.

W Well, he got _____ _____ _____ _____.

M Then _____ _____ _____ _____? His bike is so old.

W You're right. He's too tall for his old bike, too.

M Great! Let's go to _____ _____ _____ with Jake next week.

08 할 일 파악

대화를 듣고, 여자가 대화 직후에 할 일로 가장 적절한 것을 고르시오.
① 산책하기　② 음식 주문하기
③ 과일 사러 가기　④ 과일 씻기
⑤ 저녁 준비하기

W Tom, _____ _____ _____ fruit on your way home?

M Yes, Mom. Here they are: 3 apples, 5 oranges, and a bunch of bananas just like you asked.

W Did you get a pineapple?

M Oh no. I forgot to get one.

W Well, I _____ _____ _____ dinner tonight.

M I'll _____ _____ _____ the store and get one.

W Okay. _____ _____ _____ _____ in the kitchen.

09 언급하지 않은 내용 찾기

대화를 듣고, 남자가 면접에서 자신에 대해 언급
하지 <u>않은</u> 것을 고르시오.

① 업무 경험   ② 장단점
③ 어학 실력   ④ 업무 가능 시기
⑤ 취미

W Do you _____ _____ _____ in this kind of work?

M No, I don't. But I am sure I can do it well.

W Can you tell me about _____ _____?

M Well, I think I am creative and very honest.

W How about your weak points?

M I get nervous when I speak in front of many people.

W _____ _____ do you speak?

M I speak English, French, and a little German.

W Good. And when can _____ _____ _____?

M From the first day of next month.

10 주제 추론

다음을 듣고, 여자가 하는 말의 내용으로 가장 적
절한 것을 고르시오.

① 날씨 예보
② 기내 안전 교육
③ 여행 일정 소개
④ 항공편 지연 안내
⑤ 탑승 위치 변경 통보

W Good afternoon! All passengers, may I _____ _____ _____, please? Because of the bad weather here, all planes at this airport _____ _____ _____ _____ until 3:40 p.m. The first plane to leave will be to Frankfurt at 3:45 p.m. If you _____ _____ _____ _____ the flight schedule, please go to your gate and talk to a staff member.

대화를 듣고, 여자가 찾는 곳에 대한 내용으로 일치하지 않는 것을 고르시오.

① 서점이다.　　　② 새로 개업했다.
③ 9층에 있다.　　④ 전 층을 사용한다.
⑤ 커피숍도 안에 있다.

W Excuse me. Can you tell me the way to the bookstore in this building?

M You are talking about _____ _____ _____, right? I think it's on the 9th floor.

W Do you know how big the bookstore is?

M Yes. It's really big. The bookstore is _____ _____ _____ _____ _____ _____.

W Oh, I see. Is there a coffee shop in the bookstore?

M No. _____ _____ _____ go to the 8th floor for coffee.

W Thanks for your help.

12 목적 파악

대화를 듣고, 남자가 해외여행을 자주 하는 목적으로 가장 적절한 것을 고르시오.

① 사진 찍는 것을 좋아해서
② 세계 역사를 배우기 위해서
③ 다양한 문화를 경험하기 위해서
④ 다양한 세계 음식을 맛보고 싶어서
⑤ 세계 곳곳의 건물들을 연구하기 위해서

W Chris, you travel often, right?

M Yes, I travel a lot. I _____ _____ every year.

W How many countries have you been to?

M More than 50 countries.

W _____ _____ _____ _____ when you travel?

M Since I'm an architect, I always _____ _____. So, I usually take many pictures of interesting _____ _____ _____ _____. Sometimes I draw when I have enough time.

13 숫자 정보 파악 (시각)

대화를 듣고, 두 사람이 만날 시각을 고르시오.

① 5:00 p.m.　　② 5:10 p.m.
③ 5:20 p.m.　　④ 5:30 p.m.
⑤ 5:40 p.m.

[Cell phone rings.]

W Hello.

M Hi, Minji. Are you still home?

W No, I'll be at the shopping center in 5 minutes.

M I'm sorry, but I think I'll be _____ _____ _____.

W Did something happen?

M　_____ _____ _____
_____. So I have to watch my little sister until 5:10.

W　That's okay. I can go to a cafe and _____
_____ _____ _____.

M　Thank you. I'll call you when I'm there. _____
_____ _____ 5:30.

W　All right. See you then.

---

14 관계 추론

대화를 듣고, 두 사람의 관계로 가장 적절한 것을 고르시오.

① 연예인 – 매니저
② 택시 운전사 – 승객
③ 우체국 직원 – 고객
④ 세관 직원 – 항공 승무원
⑤ 버스 운전사 – 교통경찰

W　Hello. How can I help you?

M　I'd like to _____ _____ _____
to Austria.

W　How would you like to send it?

M　_____ _____. How long will it take?

W　About 8 to 10 days.

M　That's fine with me.

W　Is there anything else _____ _____
_____ _____?

M　No, but I'd like to _____ _____
_____, please.

---

15 부탁 파악

대화를 듣고, 여자가 남자에게 부탁한 일로 가장 적절한 것을 고르시오.

① 노트 보여주기
② 역사책 빌려주기
③ 신문 가져오기
④ 시험 일정 확인하기
⑤ 약속 시간 변경하기

W　Let's work on our history project later today.

M　I'm sorry. Can we do it tomorrow?

W　There is not enough time. We _____ _____
_____ it this week.

M　But I'm too tired to focus now.

W　All right. Then let's _____ _____
_____ instead.

M　Thanks. Do I need to bring anything tomorrow?

W　We _____ _____ _____. Can you
bring some?

M　_____ _____. I'll bring them tomorrow.

16 이유 파악

대화를 듣고, 남자가 호텔 예약을 하지 <u>못하는</u> 이유로 가장 적절한 것을 고르시오.

① 위치가 너무 멀어서
② 숙박비가 너무 비싸서
③ 예약 가능한 방이 없어서
④ 반려 동물 출입이 금지라서
⑤ 예약에 필요한 정보를 몰라서

[Telephone rings.]

W King Royal Hotel, how can I help you?

M Yes. I would like a single room for 3 days. From May 7 to 9.

W Let me check if we have a room available.

M I'm planning to visit there _____ _____ _____.

W I'm sorry, sir. Pets _____ _____ _____ in our hotel.

M Really? But I am going to _____ _____ _____.

W I'm sorry. Some guests may have allergies.

M All right. I guess I'll have to _____ _____ _____.

17 그림 상황에 적절한 대화 찾기

다음 그림의 상황에 가장 적절한 대화를 고르시오.

① ② ③ ④ ⑤

① M _____ _____ _____ _____ I use this bike?

W No, I don't. Go ahead.

② M I'd like to _____ _____ now.

W Do you have a reservation?

③ M Excuse me, can you tell me how to get to the city library?

W _____ _____ for two blocks and turn left.

④ M May I _____ _____ _____?

W I'd like to have a steak.

⑤ M What seems to be the problem?

W I have a fever and a sore throat.

18 언급하지 않은 내용 찾기

다음을 듣고, 남자가 Premier League에 대해 언급하지 <u>않은</u> 것을 고르시오.

① 소속 팀 수
② 창설 연도
③ 팀 당 경기 수
④ 시즌 시작과 종료 시기
⑤ 승점 부여 방식

M The Premier League or the EPL, is the English soccer league system. There are 20 _____ _____ this league. The season runs _____ _____ _____ _____ of next year. Most games are played on the weekend. Each team plays 38 matches with 19 other teams. Each team gets 3 points _____

_____ _____. Both teams get 1 point for

a draw. And the loser _____ _____

_____.

---

19 이어질 응답 찾기

대화를 듣고, 남자의 마지막 말에 이어질 여자의 응답으로 가장 적절한 것을 고르시오.

Woman: _____

① I often skip breakfast.
② I have lunch at 12:30.
③ I didn't have lunch yesterday.
④ I usually have Korean food for lunch.
⑤ I sometimes have lunch with my friends.

M　What do you have for breakfast?

W　I have cereal with milk and fruit.

M　Hmm, that sounds _____ _____

_____ _____. Do you eat that every

morning?

W　Well, _____ _____ _____.

I sometimes eat eggs and some bread, but I have fruit at

every breakfast.

M　Wow! You must really enjoy healthy breakfasts.

_____ _____ _____

_____ for lunch?

---

20 이어질 응답 찾기

대화를 듣고, 남자의 마지막 말에 이어질 여자의 응답으로 가장 적절한 것을 고르시오.

Woman: _____

① Okay, here it is.
② What day is it today?
③ You had a great time, didn't you?
④ We should get some flowers for her.
⑤ I think you should throw me a party.

W　Dan, it's July 9, right?

M　That's right.

W　July 9 _____ _____ _____. Is it

your birthday?

M　No, it's not. *[Pause]* Oh, it's Anna's birthday.

W　Really? I saw her this morning, but she didn't say anything.

M　She might be upset because we didn't say anything.

W　How about _____ _____ _____

_____ and giving her a small present?

M　Sure. _____ _____ _____

_____?

실전 모의고사 11

01 다음을 듣고, 광주의 날씨로 가장 적절한 것을 고르시오.

①   ②   ③   ④   ⑤

02 대화를 듣고, 여자가 구입할 접시로 가장 적절한 것을 고르시오.

①   ②   ③

④   ⑤

03 대화를 듣고, 여자가 Sports World에 대해 언급하지 않은 것을 고르시오.

① 상점 위치 ② 영업시간 ③ 할인 기간
④ 할인 품목 ⑤ 할인 가격

04 대화를 듣고, 여자가 학교에서 만들 물건으로 가장 적절한 것을 고르시오.

① 셔츠 ② 베개 ③ 가방
④ 인형 ⑤ 손수건

05 대화를 듣고, 두 사람이 대화하는 장소로 가장 적절한 곳을 고르시오.

① 백화점 ② 은행 ③ 호텔
④ 경찰서 ⑤ 매표소

06 대화를 듣고, 여자가 한 마지막 말의 의도로 가장 적절한 것을 고르시오.

① 기대 ② 후회 ③ 실망
④ 사과 ⑤ 격려

07 대화를 듣고, 여자가 선물로 구입할 것으로 가장 적절한 것을 고르시오.

① 운동화 ② 티셔츠 ③ 야구 모자
④ 농구 반바지 ⑤ 농구공

08 대화를 듣고, 남자가 대화 직후에 할 일로 가장 적절한 것을 고르시오.

① 잠자리에 들기 ② 여행 가방 싸기
③ 침낭 찾기 ④ 자동차에 짐 싣기
⑤ 휴대전화 충전하기

09 대화를 듣고, 두 사람이 International Night에 대해 언급하지 않은 것을 고르시오.

① 개최 시간 ② 장소 ③ 참가 자격
④ 입장료 ⑤ 참가 인원

10 다음을 듣고, 남자가 하는 말의 내용으로 가장 적절한 것을 고르시오.

① 지하철 개통 안내 ② 7분 운동법 소개
③ 열차 운행 지연 안내 ④ 기차 이용 예절
⑤ 도로 공사 공지

11 대화를 듣고, 두 사람의 주말 계획과 일치하지 <u>않는</u> 것을 고르시오.

① 토요일 오전에 조깅을 한다.
② 토요일 점심은 집에서 먹는다.
③ 일요일에 쇼핑을 간다.
④ 일요일 오전에 수영을 한다.
⑤ 토요일 밤 10시 전에 잔다.

12 대화를 듣고, 남자가 전화를 건 목적으로 가장 적절한 것을 고르시오.

① 소화제를 구하기 위해서
② 모닝콜을 부탁하기 위해서
③ 전망 좋은 방으로 바꾸기 위해서
④ 객실 청소를 요구하기 위해서
⑤ 객실의 불편함을 호소하기 위해서

13 대화를 듣고, 두 사람이 만날 시각을 고르시오.
① 5:00 p.m.   ② 5:15 p.m.   ③ 5:30 p.m.
④ 5:45 p.m.   ⑤ 6:00 p.m.

14 대화를 듣고, 두 사람의 관계로 가장 적절한 것을 고르시오.

① 기장 – 승무원
② 공항 직원 – 승객
③ 백화점 안내원 – 손님
④ 부동산 중개인 – 집주인
⑤ 투어 가이드 – 관광객

15 대화를 듣고, 여자가 남자에게 부탁한 일로 가장 적절한 것을 고르시오.

① 교실 꾸미기   ② 사진 찾아주기
③ 친구 찾아주기   ④ 이삿짐 옮겨주기
⑤ 송별회 선물 준비하기

16 대화를 듣고, 남자가 속상한 이유로 가장 적절한 것을 고르시오.

① 동생과 싸워서
② 시험을 잘 못 봐서
③ 부모님께 꾸중을 들어서
④ 아끼던 물건을 잃어버려서
⑤ 친구들과 헤어지기 싫어서

17 다음 그림의 상황에 가장 적절한 대화를 고르시오.

①   ②   ③   ④   ⑤

18 다음을 듣고, 여자가 버스에 대해 언급하지 <u>않은</u> 것을 고르시오.

① 번호   ② 색깔
③ 탑승 가능 인원   ④ 출발 시각
⑤ 요금

[19-20] 대화를 듣고, 남자의 마지막 말에 이어질 여자의 말로 가장 적절한 것을 고르시오.

19 Woman: _____

① No, I'm the only one at school.
② Really? I'm in the book club.
③ I haven't studied hard enough.
④ Yes. I think teachers are friendly.
⑤ You're right. I feel much better now.

20 Woman: _____

① I'm sorry to hear that.
② I can't wait to see you.
③ Yes, I'm going to buy a CD.
④ No, thanks. I'm busy that day.
⑤ Of course. I'm looking forward to it.

Dictation 11

◆ 다시 듣고, 빈칸에 들어갈 알맞은 단어를 써보세요.

정답 및 해설 p.66

---

01 날씨 파악

다음을 듣고, 광주의 날씨로 가장 적절한 것을 고르시오.

① ② ③ ④ ⑤

M Good morning, everyone, and here's your national weather forecast for today. It'll be cool and sunny in Seoul as well as in Incheon. However, it will be very _____ _____ _____ in Daegu. Gwangju won't be hot because it _____ _____ _____. Finally, heavy rain _____ _____ _____ Busan.

---

02 그림 정보 파악

대화를 듣고, 여자가 구입할 접시로 가장 적절한 것을 고르시오.

① ② ③ ④ ⑤

W Hello, how may I help you?

M I'm going to throw a party tomorrow, and I need a big plate.

W This round plate is perfect for a party.

M Well, I _____ _____ _____. Do you have any square plates?

W Yes, we do. Then how about this one with a picture of a tree _____ _____ _____?

M It's not bad, but it is too big. Can you show me a different one?

W Sure. This one has _____ _____ _____ _____ _____ on it. What do you think?

M Great! I'll take it.

---

03 언급하지 않은 내용 찾기

대화를 듣고, 여자가 Sports World에 대해 언급하지 않은 것을 고르시오.

① 상점 위치   ② 영업시간   ③ 할인 기간
④ 할인 품목   ⑤ 할인 가격

[Telephone rings.]

W Thanks for calling Sports World on 5th Avenue and Broadway.

M Hi. What time do you _____ _____ _____ _____?

W We're open from 9 a.m. to 9 p.m. every day.

M Do you have any _____ _____ _____ right now?

W Not yet. But our spring sale event _____
_____ _____ next Monday to Friday.

M Will badminton rackets be on sale, too?

W Yes, _____ _____ _____ will be
on sale.

M Thank you for the information.

대화를 듣고, 여자가 학교에서 만들 물건으로 가
장 적절한 것을 고르시오.
① 셔츠   ② 베개   ③ 가방
④ 인형   ⑤ 손수건

M Somi, where are you going? It's almost time for dinner.

W Dad, I forgot to get _____ _____
_____ _____ school. I have to go and buy
them.

M What do you need?

W I need to get _____ _____ _____
_____ for my art class tomorrow.

M Glue and buttons? What are you going to make?

W I am going to learn to _____ _____
_____.

M _____ _____? That sounds like fun. Do
you need a ride?

W Yes, please.

M Let me get my car key.

대화를 듣고, 두 사람이 대화하는 장소로 가장 적
절한 곳을 고르시오.
① 백화점   ② 은행   ③ 호텔
④ 경찰서   ⑤ 매표소

🔊 **Listening Tip**

pick up에서 pick의 /k/ 발음처럼 강세가 있는 단어의 첫
음절에 오는 k가 아닐 경우 /크/가 아닌 /끄/로 발음하게
되어 pick up는 /피컵/ 보다는 /피껍/에 가까운 소리가 납
니다.

M Can I help the next person _____ _____?

W Hi, I'd like to 🔊 pick up _____ _____,
please.

M May I have your name?

W It's Lisa Moore.

M Let me check. [Pause] I'm sorry, I can't find your name here.
Do you have the _____ _____?

W No, I don't. My dad _____ _____
_____ for me. Then can you try Tom Moore?

M Yes, I have 2 tickets for the show at 5 o'clock.

W That's correct.

대화를 듣고, 여자가 한 마지막 말의 의도로 가장 적절한 것을 고르시오.

① 기대   ② 후회   ③ 실망
④ 사과   ⑤ 격려

M Where are you going, Stephanie?

W I'm going out to _____ _____ _____.

M Do you mean the volleyball game at school?

W Yes. My best friend is going to play and I want to _____ _____ _____.

M Didn't you get the text message? The game _____ _____ _____.

W Why?

M Because of the storm. Everyone should stay home tonight.

W Oh no. I was really _____ _____ _____ it.

대화를 듣고, 여자가 선물로 구입할 것으로 가장 적절한 것을 고르시오.

① 운동화   ② 티셔츠
③ 야구 모자   ④ 농구 반바지
⑤ 농구공

M Hello, can I help you find anything?

W I'm looking for _____ _____ _____ for my younger brother.

M We have a very good selection of sneakers.

W Well, I don't know _____ _____ _____.

M Then how about a T-shirt?

W My brother has too many T-shirts already.

M Baseball caps and basketball shorts are also _____ _____ _____.

W Oh, then I'll get _____ _____ _____ for him.

대화를 듣고, 남자가 대화 직후에 할 일로 가장 적절한 것을 고르시오.

① 잠자리에 들기   ② 여행 가방 싸기
③ 침낭 찾기   ④ 자동차에 짐 싣기
⑤ 휴대전화 충전하기

W It's midnight, honey. We should go to bed.

M Did you finish _____ _____ _____ for the trip?

W Yes, I did. Did you pack your sleeping bag?

M Yes, it's right here. Where's our tent?

W   I _____ _____ _____ in the trunk of the car.

M   Oh, good. Then I think we're ready to go to bed.

W   Make sure to _____ _____ _____ before you go to sleep.

M   Yes. I'll _____ _____ right now.

09 언급하지 않은 내용 찾기

대화를 듣고, 두 사람이 International Night 에 대해 언급하지 <u>않은</u> 것을 고르시오.

① 개최 시간   ② 장소   ③ 참가 자격
④ 입장료   ⑤ 참가 인원

W   Is International Night this Friday?

M   No. _____ _____ _____ from 6 p.m. to 8 p.m.

W   It's held _____ _____ _____ _____, right?

M   Right. Do you know if my cousins can get in, too? They're in elementary school.

W   Of course. Anyone can get in, _____ _____ _____ entrance fee.

M   What do you want to do the most there?

W   I can't wait _____ _____ _____ from many different countries.

10 주제 추론

다음을 듣고, 남자가 하는 말의 내용으로 가장 적절한 것을 고르시오.

① 지하철 개통 안내
② 7분 운동법 소개
③ 열차 운행 지연 안내
④ 기차 이용 예절
⑤ 도로 공사 공지

M   Thank you for using subway line number 11. _____ _____ _____ announce that the train to Songpa _____ _____ _____. The next subway will come in 7 minutes. Because of this, the next train is expected to _____ _____ _____. Once again, we are sorry for this and thank you _____ _____ _____.

11 일치하지 않는 내용 찾기

대화를 듣고, 두 사람의 주말 계획과 일치하지 <u>않</u> 는 것을 고르시오.

① 토요일 오전에 조깅을 한다.
② 토요일 점심은 집에서 먹는다.
③ 일요일에 쇼핑을 간다.
④ 일요일 오전에 수영을 한다.
⑤ 토요일 밤 10시 전에 잔다.

W   Dad, are we going to go jogging on Saturday morning?

M   _____, _____, and then we are going to _____ _____ Joe's Restaurant.

W   Can we go shopping on Sunday?

M   Sure, but first we need to _____ _____ in the morning.

W Dad, don't you think that's too much exercise?

M No. You don't get any exercise on weekdays.

W That's true.

M And *don't forget to _____ _____ _____ _____ 10 on Saturday. We should _____ _____ _____ the next morning.

W All right, Dad.

✱ 교육부 지정 의사소통 기능: **상기시키기**　　천(이) 6 | 미 7 | 비 2 | Y(박) 2 | Y(송) 9

Don't forget to ~. ~하는 것 잊지 마.

• **Don't forget to** bring your umbrella. 우산 가져가는 것 잊지 마.
• **Don't forget to** walk the dog. 개를 산책시키는 걸 잊지 말아라.

---

12 목적 파악

대화를 듣고, 남자가 전화를 건 목적으로 가장 적절한 것을 고르시오.

① 소화제를 구하기 위해서
② 모닝콜을 부탁하기 위해서
③ 전망 좋은 방으로 바꾸기 위해서
④ 객실 청소를 요구하기 위해서
⑤ 객실의 불편함을 호소하기 위해서

🔊 **Listening Tip**

자음 3개가 연달아 나올 때는 대개 가운데 소리는 발음하지 않게 돼요. send someone에서 자음 'n, d , s'가 연달아 오기 때문에 이어서 말할 때 가운데의 [d] 소리는 들리지 않게 됩니다.

[Telephone rings.]

W This is the front desk. How may I help you?

M Hi, I'm calling from room 1509.

W Yes, Mr. Robertson. Is there _____ _____ _____ the room?

M _____ _____ _____ the room has been cleaned.

W I'm really sorry about that, sir.

M Can you 🔊 send someone _____ _____ this room right now?

W Of course, sir. I'll do that _____ _____.

---

13 숫자 정보 파악 (시각)

대화를 듣고, 두 사람이 만날 시각을 고르시오.

① 5:00 p.m.　　② 5:15 p.m.
③ 5:30 p.m.　　④ 5:45 p.m.
⑤ 6:00 p.m.

M Do you want to go to the gym tomorrow?

W Yes. I really need to get some exercise.

M Do you want me to _____ _____ _____ _____ 5 p.m.?

W I need to stay at the office until 5:30 tomorrow.

M Then, *what time and where should we meet?

W _____ _____ _____ at 6 at the gym?

M _____ _____ _____.

✱ 교육부 지정 의사소통 기능: **약속 정하기**   동(윤) 6

What time and where should we meet? 우리 몇 시에 어디에서 만날까?

A: **What time and where should we meet?** 우리 몇 시에 어디에서 만날까?

B: How about meeting at 2:30 in front of Star Movie Theater?
　　Star 영화관 앞에서 2시 반에 만나는 게 어때?

14 관계 추론

대화를 듣고, 두 사람의 관계로 가장 적절한 것을 고르시오.

① 기장 – 승무원
② 공항 직원 – 승객
③ 백화점 안내원 – 손님
④ 부동산 중개인 – 집주인
⑤ 투어 가이드 – 관광객

M Please _____ _____ _____ over here. *[Pause]* You can take it with you. It's under 3 kilograms.

W No. I want to check it in because I have another bag here.

M All right. Are there any _____ _____ _____ in there?

W No. I made sure not to pack anything like those.

M Good. Here _____ _____ _____ and boarding pass. _____ _____ _____.

W Thank you.

15 부탁 파악

대화를 듣고, 여자가 남자에게 부탁한 일로 가장 적절한 것을 고르시오.

① 교실 꾸미기
② 사진 찾아주기
③ 친구 찾아주기
④ 이삿짐 옮겨주기
⑤ 송별회 선물 준비하기

W Steve! I was looking for you everywhere in school.

M Really? Is something wrong?

W Jake is going to move next month, so we will have a farewell party for him.

M Oh, that's right. _____ _____ _____ _____?

W It's next Friday. But we need more people to help with the party. Can you help us with that?

M Of course. _____ _____ _____ _____ _____?

W We need pictures of us with Jake. Can you _____ _____ _____?

M Of course.

16 이유 파악

대화를 듣고, 남자가 속상한 이유로 가장 적절한 것을 고르시오.

① 동생과 싸워서
② 시험을 잘 못 봐서
③ 부모님께 꾸중을 들어서
④ 아끼던 물건을 잃어버려서
⑤ 친구들과 헤어지기 싫어서

W Jayden, you look upset. Is there something wrong?
M My family and I are going _____ _____ _____ Singapore.
W Oh, really? Why?
M My dad's going to work in Singapore for the next 5 years.
W I didn't know that.
M I'm so sad. I don't want to _____ _____ _____.
W Don't be sad. We can still _____ _____ _____ by e-mail.
M Right. Before I leave, we should do _____ _____ together.
W That's a great idea!

17 그림 상황에 적절한 대화 찾기

다음 그림의 상황에 가장 적절한 대화를 고르시오.

① ② ③ ④ ⑤

① M May I see your passport?
  W Sure, here it is.
② M What seems to be the problem, doctor?
  W It's just _____ _____ _____.
③ M Do you _____ _____ _____, ma'am?
  W No, I'm full. Can I have the check?
④ M Excuse me. _____ _____ _____ _____?
  W No, it's not. You can sit here _____ _____ _____.
⑤ M How can I help you, ma'am?
  W I have a flat tire.

18 언급하지 않은 내용 찾기

다음을 듣고, 여자가 버스에 대해 언급하지 않은 것을 고르시오.

① 번호   ② 색깔
③ 탑승 가능 인원   ④ 출발 시각
⑤ 요금

W Good morning, class. We are going to _____ _____ _____ 1547. It's _____ _____ _____ _____, so you won't miss it. Make sure you sit next to someone because the bus _____ _____ _____ 20 people. The bus _____ _____ _____ _____ 9:30. If you need to use the restroom, you still have time.

19 이어질 응답 찾기

대화를 듣고, 남자의 마지막 말에 이어질 여자의 말로 가장 적절한 것을 고르시오.

Woman: _____

① No, I'm the only one at school.
② Really? I'm in the book club.
③ I haven't studied hard enough.
④ Yes. I think teachers are friendly.
⑤ You're right. I feel much better now.

M It's your first day of school tomorrow. How are you feeling, Lisa?

W I'm really nervous right now, Dad.

M What are you _____ _____ _____?

W I'm nervous about meeting new people. It's _____ _____ _____ _____.

M Just relax. It's going to be fine.

W _____ _____ _____ _____?

M Yes. you're not the only one to be worried. Even teachers _____ _____, too.

20 이어질 응답 찾기

대화를 듣고, 남자의 마지막 말에 이어질 여자의 말로 가장 적절한 것을 고르시오.

Woman: _____

① I'm sorry to hear that.
② I can't wait to see you.
③ Yes, I'm going to buy a CD.
④ No, thanks. I'm busy that day.
⑤ Of course. I'm looking forward to it.

W What are you listening to?

M I'm listening to K-pop songs.

W I love listening to K-pop, too. Do you _____ _____ _____ K-pop singers?

M No. I like them all. What about you?

W I like the boy band NTU. In fact, I am _____ _____ _____ of theirs.

M I see. _____ _____ _____ _____ an NTU concert?

W No, because NTU's first concert will take place this September.

M There are still 3 months left. But you are _____ _____ _____, aren't you?

실전 모의고사 12

점수
/20

01 다음을 듣고, 일요일 저녁 날씨로 가장 적절한 것을 고르시오.

①   ②   ③   ④   ⑤

02 대화를 듣고, 두 사람이 보고 있는 사진으로 가장 적절한 것을 고르시오.

①   ②   ③

④   ⑤

03 대화를 듣고, 두 사람이 본 뮤지컬에 대해 언급하지 않은 것을 고르시오.

① 제목   ② 등장인물   ③ 공연 날짜
④ 입장료   ⑤ 관람한 도시

04 대화를 듣고, 남자가 마실 것으로 가장 적절한 것을 고르시오.

① 커피   ② 녹차   ③ 탄산음료
④ 주스   ⑤ 물

05 대화를 듣고, 두 사람이 대화하는 장소로 가장 적절한 곳을 고르시오.

① 영화관   ② 오락실   ③ 수영장
④ 체육관   ⑤ 스케이트장

06 대화를 듣고, 남자가 한 마지막 말의 의도로 가장 적절한 것을 고르시오.

① 승낙   ② 칭찬   ③ 비난
④ 용서   ⑤ 사과

07 대화를 듣고, 두 사람이 저녁에 할 일을 고르시오.

① 영화 보기   ② 산책하기
③ 보드게임하기   ④ TV 보기
⑤ 안경 찾기

08 대화를 듣고, 남자가 대화 직후에 할 일로 가장 적절한 것을 고르시오.

① 음식 만들기   ② 아들 데리러 가기
③ 감사 전화하기   ④ 부엌 청소하기
⑤ 설거지하기

09 대화를 듣고, 두 사람이 햄버거에 대해 언급하지 않은 것을 고르시오.

① 맛   ② 재료   ③ 크기
④ 가격   ⑤ 판매 장소

10 다음을 듣고, 남자가 하는 말의 내용으로 가장 적절한 것을 고르시오.

① 숙면의 중요성
② 좋은 침구의 조건
③ 성공한 사람의 습관
④ 졸음이 올 때 취할 행동
⑤ 불면증을 극복하는 방법

11 대화를 듣고, 두 사람이 본 영화에 대한 내용으로 일치하지 <u>않는</u> 것을 고르시오.

① 상영 시간이 길다.
② 공포 영화이다.
③ 실화를 바탕으로 하고 있다.
④ 연기가 훌륭했다.
⑤ 중국 영화이다.

12 대화를 듣고, 남자가 전화를 건 목적으로 가장 적절한 것을 고르시오.

① 숙제를 확인하기 위해서
② 몸이 아프다고 알리기 위해서
③ 핼러윈 파티에 초대하기 위해서
④ 차를 태워 달라고 부탁하기 위해서
⑤ 핼러윈 파티 의상을 빌리기 위해서

13 대화를 듣고, 두 사람이 다시 통화할 시각을 고르시오.

① 6:30 p.m.   ② 7:00 p.m.   ③ 7:30 p.m.
④ 8:00 p.m.   ⑤ 8:30 p.m.

14 대화를 듣고, 두 사람의 관계로 가장 적절한 것을 고르시오.

① 버스 기사 – 승객
② 육상 선수 – 코치
③ 경찰관 – 운전자
④ 자동차 판매원 – 고객
⑤ 회사원 – 직장 상사

15 대화를 듣고, 남자가 여자에게 부탁한 일로 가장 적절한 것을 고르시오.

① 다친 발 치료하기
② 병원에 함께 가기
③ 축구 경기장에 오기
④ 깨끗한 옷 가져다주기
⑤ 축구 코치에게 전화하기

16 대화를 듣고, 여자가 생일파티에 갈 수 <u>없는</u> 이유로 가장 적절한 것을 고르시오.

① 숙제가 많아서
② 콘서트를 예약해서
③ 가족 여행을 가야 해서
④ 선물을 준비하지 못해서
⑤ 봉사 활동 계획이 있어서

17 다음 그림의 상황에 가장 적절한 대화를 고르시오.

① ② ③ ④ ⑤

18 다음을 듣고, 여자가 Star Fitness에 대해 언급하지 <u>않은</u> 것을 고르시오.

① 창립 시기   ② 위치   ③ 회원 수
④ 회비   ⑤ 회원 혜택

[19-20] 대화를 듣고, 여자의 마지막 말에 이어질 남자의 말로 가장 적절한 것을 고르시오.

19 Man: _____

① Yes, I'm also in a meeting.
② Yes, I can call you back later.
③ No, I don't want to talk to her.
④ Sure, my number is 770-568-3316.
⑤ I'm sorry, but my lawyer is not here.

20 Man: _____

① You don't have to cook next time.
② The food is delicious. Take a bite.
③ I thought pasta was your favorite food.
④ Use soap and wash for 30 seconds.
⑤ You should eat at least 5 times a day.

Dictation 12

◇ 다시 듣고, 빈칸에 들어갈 알맞은 단어를 써보세요.

정답 및 해설 p.73

---

01 날씨 파악

다음을 듣고, 일요일 저녁 날씨로 가장 적절한 것을 고르시오.

① ② ③ ④ ⑤

M Welcome to the weather channel. Here is your weather forecast _____ _____ _____.
After a series of beautiful sunny days this week, it will be mostly cloudy on Saturday. _____ _____ _____ _____ on Saturday or Sunday.
However, there will be _____ _____ _____ Sunday evening, and it will continue to be windy _____ _____ _____.

---

02 그림 정보 파악

대화를 듣고, 두 사람이 보고 있는 사진으로 가장 적절한 것을 고르시오.

① ② ③ ④ ⑤

🔊 Listening Tip
앞 단어의 끝부분 자음과 다음 단어의 첫 부분 자음이 같을 경우 앞의 자음이 탈락하는 현상을 흔히 볼 수 있습니다. next to는 /넥스트 투/가 아니고 /넥스투/로 발음됩니다.

W This is a beautiful picture, James.
M Thank you. It was taken last summer.
W _____ _____ _____ in the picture?
M No, that's my cousin. I took the picture.
W Oh, your cousin _____ _____ _____ _____, right?
M Yes, he does, and that's his dog 🔊 next to him.
W The dog seems really happy _____ _____ _____.
M Yes, he likes _____ _____ _____ _____ much better than walking in the park.

---

03 언급하지 않은 내용 찾기

대화를 듣고, 두 사람이 본 뮤지컬에 대해 언급하지 않은 것을 고르시오.
① 제목 ② 등장인물 ③ 공연 날짜
④ 입장료 ⑤ 관람한 도시

W How did you like the musical, Tom?
M It was as boring as _____ _____, *My Loving Father*.
W I know. I can't believe there were only 2 actors, _____ _____ _____ _____ _____.
M Yes. There were so many empty seats. Now I know why.
W I'm just glad that _____ _____ $50 for the musical.
M We can at least say that we saw _____

_____ _____ New York City.

W Well, that's true.

04 특정 정보 파악

대화를 듣고, 남자가 마실 것으로 가장 적절한 것을 고르시오.

① 커피　② 녹차　③ 탄산음료
④ 주스　⑤ 물

W Are you ready to order?

M We'd like to order our drinks first.

W Okay, _____ _____ _____ coffee?

M It comes in a big mug, right?

W Yes, it comes in a mug.

M Then, my wife will have coffee, and _____
_____ _____ _____.

W Great! I'll be right back _____ _____
_____ _____.

05 장소 추론

대화를 듣고, 두 사람이 대화하는 장소로 가장 적절한 곳을 고르시오.

① 영화관　　② 오락실
③ 수영장　　④ 체육관
⑤ 스케이트장

M Have you done this before, Maggie?

W No, this is my first time.

M Don't worry. I'll teach you.

W I'm nervous. I'm scared to fall down.

M You _____ _____ _____
_____. Everybody falls down.

W Did you bring _____ _____
_____?

M Yes, I did. Now, let's rent a pair of skates for you.

W Okay. Is it expensive _____ _____
_____?

M No, not at all.

06 의도 파악

대화를 듣고, 남자가 한 마지막 말의 의도로 가장 적절한 것을 고르시오.

① 승낙　② 칭찬　③ 비난
④ 용서　⑤ 사과

W Dad, I'm home. Where are you?

M I'm in the garage.

W [Pause] Are you still working on this car?

M Yes, I think I'll be able to fix it this time.

W That's good. Oh, by the way, do you remember the robot competition last month?

M Yes, of course. _____ _____
_____ _____ your robot for a while.

W I _____ _____ _____.

M Great! I knew _____ _____ _____
_____!

대화를 듣고, 두 사람이 저녁에 할 일을 고르시오.

① 영화 보기　　② 산책하기
③ 보드게임하기　④ TV 보기
⑤ 안경 찾기

W　What do you want to do after dinner?
M　Do you want to _____ _____ _____?
W　I can't. I left my glasses at school.
M　We can _____ _____ _____ _____ _____.
W　Don't you think it's a little cold to go for a walk?
M　You're right. Then *how about a board game?
W　_____ _____! It's been a long time since we _____ _____ _____ _____ together.

---

* 교육부 지정 의사소통 기능: **제안하기**　　동(이) 1

How about ~? ~하는 게 어때?
• **How about** going bowling this afternoon? 오늘 오후에 볼링 치러 가는 게 어때?
• **How about** getting some sleep? 잠을 좀 자는 게 어때?

---

08 할 일 파악

대화를 듣고, 남자가 대화 직후에 할 일로 가장 적절한 것을 고르시오.

① 음식 만들기　　② 아들 데리러 가기
③ 감사 전화하기　④ 부엌 청소하기
⑤ 설거지하기

W　Did you enjoy the dinner, Matthew?
M　Yes, it was amazing. How did you prepare all the food so quickly?
W　My friend Jennifer came over and _____ _____ _____.
M　Really? I didn't know that. Why didn't she stay for dinner?
W　She had to pick up her son.
M　_____ _____ _____ and thank her for helping you out.
W　You can do that after we finish cleaning the kitchen.
M　Yes, you're right. I'll _____ _____ _____ _____ right now.

---

09 언급하지 않은 내용 찾기

대화를 듣고, 두 사람이 햄버거에 대해 언급하지 않은 것을 고르시오.

① 맛　　② 재료　　③ 크기
④ 가격　⑤ 판매 장소

W　This is an amazing hamburger. It is _____ _____.
M　I thought you didn't like hamburgers.
W　I don't like hamburgers because they are unhealthy, but this one's different.

M I know. It is completely _____ _____ vegetables.

W But it's _____ _____. $10 for a hamburger?

M It is a little expensive. Are there other restaurants that sell this burger?

W No, you can only _____ _____ _____ at Mike's Diner.

---

10 주제 추론

다음을 듣고, 남자가 하는 말의 내용으로 가장 적절한 것을 고르시오.

① 숙면의 중요성
② 좋은 침구의 조건
③ 성공한 사람의 습관
④ 졸음이 올 때 취할 행동
⑤ 불면증을 극복하는 방법

M Getting a _____ _____ _____ is very important, but many students do not understand the importance. Some students think _____ _____ is the same as being lazy. If you're lazy, you _____ _____ _____. But if you're sleepy most of the day because you didn't get a good night's sleep, _____ _____ _____ a success, either.

---

11 일치하지 않는 내용 찾기

대화를 듣고, 두 사람이 본 영화에 대한 내용으로 일치하지 않는 것을 고르시오.

① 상영 시간이 길다.
② 공포 영화이다.
③ 실화를 바탕으로 하고 있다.
④ 연기가 훌륭했다.
⑤ 중국 영화이다.

M How did you like the movie, Alice?

W *In my opinion, it was pretty good, but it _____ _____ _____.

M I agree. Wasn't it _____ _____ _____, too?

W Yes, it was. The movie is not a horror movie, is it?

M No, it's not. The movie is based on _____ _____ _____.

W I thought the acting was really good.

M It was amazing. It is _____ _____ _____ movie I've ever seen.

---

* **교육부 지정 의사소통 기능: 의견 표현하기**   지6급 3

In my opinion 내 생각에는

• **In my opinion**, he really enjoys dancing. 내 생각에는 그는 정말 춤추는 걸 좋아해.
• **In my opinion**, this is too expensive. 내 생각에는 이건 너무 비싸.

대화를 듣고, 남자가 전화를 건 목적으로 가장 적절한 것을 고르시오.

① 숙제를 확인하기 위해서
② 몸이 아프다고 알리기 위해서
③ 핼러윈 파티에 초대하기 위해서
④ 차를 태워 달라고 부탁하기 위해서
⑤ 핼러윈 파티 의상을 빌리기 위해서

[Telephone rings.]

W Hello.

M Hello. This is Jason, Mike's friend. May I speak to Mike, please?

W He's _____ _____ _____ _____ for the Halloween party.

M Could you tell him to call me back when he's done, ma'am?

W Sure. Are you going to go to the party, too?

M No, I am not. I'm not _____ _____.

W I'm sorry to hear that. Did you _____ _____ _____?

M Yes, I did, so I wanted to ask Mike about _____ _____.

대화를 듣고, 두 사람이 다시 통화할 시각을 고르시오.

① 6:30 p.m. ② 7:00 p.m.
③ 7:30 p.m. ④ 8:00 p.m.
⑤ 8:30 p.m.

[Cell phone rings.]

W Hello.

M Hi, Surin. Is this a good time to talk?

W Sorry, but I'm a little busy now. _____ _____ _____ you back?

M Sure. When?

W I'll call you back _____ _____ _____.

M Okay. That's 7:30, right?

W Oh, I almost forgot. I have a piano lesson at 7:30 this evening.

M Then I'll _____ _____ _____ 8:30. Is that okay?

W _____ _____. I'll talk to you later.

대화를 듣고, 두 사람의 관계로 가장 적절한 것을 고르시오.

① 버스 기사 – 승객
② 육상 선수 – 코치
③ 경찰관 – 운전자
④ 자동차 판매원 – 고객
⑤ 회사원 – 직장 상사

M You were _____ _____ _____.

W I wasn't going over the speed limit, was I?

M The speed limit _____ _____ _____ is 50 kilometers per hour.

W Oh, I didn't know that. I thought it was 60 kilometers per hour.

M Well, _____ _____ _____ at 70 kilometers per hour.

W I'm sorry, officer. I was running late for work.

M Can I see your _____ _____?

W Here it is, sir.

15 부탁 파악

대화를 듣고, 남자가 여자에게 부탁한 일로 가장 적절한 것을 고르시오.

① 다친 발 치료하기
② 병원에 함께 가기
③ 축구 경기장에 오기
④ 깨끗한 옷 가져다주기
⑤ 축구 코치에게 전화하기

W What's the matter, Paul?

M My legs are too tired. I can't feel them, Mom.

W What happened?

M We had a very _____ _____ _____ today.

W Oh, your soccer team is going to play against last year's champion this Saturday, right?

M That's right. Maybe I should relax with my feet up.

W Before you do that, please go and _____ _____ _____.

M Right. Can you _____ _____ _____ _____? I can't walk very well.

W Of course.

16 이유 파악

대화를 듣고, 여자가 생일파티에 갈 수 없는 이유로 가장 적절한 것을 고르시오.

① 숙제가 많아서
② 콘서트를 예약해서
③ 가족 여행을 가야 해서
④ 선물을 준비하지 못해서
⑤ 봉사 활동 계획이 있어서

M Next Wednesday is my birthday! I'm so excited.

W Are you going to _____ _____ _____ _____?

M Yes, it will be this Saturday from 6 to 9 at my house. You should come.

W This Saturday? I'm sorry. I don't think I can _____ _____ _____ _____.

M Do you have other plans?

W I'm going to _____ _____ _____ _____ with my family. I hope you have fun.

다음 그림의 상황에 가장 적절한 대화를 고르시오.

① ② ③ ④ ⑤

① W Nine-one-one. What's your emergency?
   M Somebody _____ _____ _____

   _____ .

② W I'm sorry. I _____ _____ _____

   _____ by accident.

   M It's okay. It didn't hurt at all.

③ W Excuse me. I think you _____ _____ .

   M Oh, that's my cell phone. Thank you!

④ W It's too hot in here. Let's open the window.

   M I don't think that's a good idea.

⑤ W Is there a _____ _____ near here?

   M Yes, there's one right around the corner.

---

18 언급하지 않은 내용 찾기

다음을 듣고, 여자가 Star Fitness에 대해 언급하지 않은 것을 고르시오.

① 창립 시기 ② 위치 ③ 회원 수
④ 회비 ⑤ 회원 혜택

◀» Listening Tip

명사의 복수형을 만드는 -s는 무성음 뒤에서는 같은 무성음
인 [s]로 유성음 뒤에서는 유성음인 [z]로 발음해요. room
의 'm'은 유성음이므로 's'를 [z]로 발음해야 하고, court의
't'는 무성음이므로 's'를 [s]로 발음해야 해요.

W Welcome to Star Fitness! We _____ _____

_____ in 1973, and we have _____

_____ _____ _____ . Becoming

a member is easy. It's $30 _____ _____ ,

and you get to enjoy everything we offer. _____

_____ _____ the training ◀» rooms, pools,

and tennis courts. Become a member today, and take control

of your health!

---

19 이어질 응답 찾기

대화를 듣고, 여자의 마지막 말에 이어질 남자의 말로 가장 적절한 것을 고르시오.

Man: _____

① Yes, I'm also in a meeting.
② Yes, I can call you back later.
③ No, I don't want to talk to her.
④ Sure, my number is 770-568-3316.
⑤ I'm sorry, but my lawyer is not here.

[Telephone rings.]

W Thank you for calling the Taylor Law Group. This is Terry.
   How may I help you?

M _____ _____ _____

   _____ Michelle, please?

W May I ask _____ _____ ?

M This is Joshua Brown. _____ _____

   _____ my car accident.

W Can you _____ _____ _____
_____?

M Sure.

W *[Pause]* Michelle's in a meeting right now. Can I have her
_____ _____ _____ in
10 minutes?

---

20 이어질 응답 찾기

대화를 듣고, 여자의 마지막 말에 이어질 남자의
말로 가장 적절한 것을 고르시오.

Man: _____

① You don't have to cook next time.
② The food is delicious. Take a bite.
③ I thought pasta was your favorite food.
④ Use soap and wash for 30 seconds.
⑤ You should eat at least 5 times a day.

W This pasta looks really delicious, Dad. Did you cook this?

M Of course, I did. Pasta is very easy to make.

W Let's see if this _____ _____, too.

M Wait. Did you _____ _____
_____?

W I did when I got home from school.

M You should always wash your hands _____
_____ _____.

W Okay, Dad. I'll _____ _____
_____.

실전 모의고사 **13**

점수 /20

01 다음을 듣고, 오늘 저녁 날씨로 가장 적절한 것을 고르시오.

① ② ③ ④ ⑤

02 대화를 듣고, 남자가 구입할 바지로 가장 적절한 것을 고르시오.

① ② ③

④ ⑤

03 대화를 듣고, 두 사람이 예술 축제에 대해 언급하지 않은 것을 고르시오.

① 개최일　　② 행사 기간　　③ 장소
④ 행사 내용　　⑤ 입장료

04 대화를 듣고, 여자가 할 수 있는 운동을 고르시오.

① 야구　　　　　② 농구
③ 테니스　　　　④ 피겨 스케이팅
⑤ 스키

05 대화를 듣고, 두 사람이 대화하는 장소로 가장 적절한 곳을 고르시오.

① 콘서트홀　　② 병원　　③ 박물관
④ 영화관　　　⑤ 도서관

06 대화를 듣고, 남자가 한 마지막 말의 의도로 가장 적절한 것을 고르시오.

① 당부　　　② 금지　　　③ 꾸중
④ 칭찬　　　⑤ 사과

07 대화를 듣고, 여자가 한국에 관해 발표할 주제로 가장 적절한 것을 고르시오.

① K-pop　　② 한복　　③ 전통 무용
④ 한옥　　　⑤ 전통 음식

08 대화를 듣고, 남자가 대화 직후에 할 일로 가장 적절한 것을 고르시오.

① 시험 공부하기　　② 책 반납하기
③ 책 읽기　　　　　④ 독후감 쓰기
⑤ 책장 정리하기

09 대화를 듣고, 두 사람이 수영 대회에 대해 언급하지 않은 것을 고르시오.

① 장소　　　② 일정　　　③ 참가 인원
④ 참가 자격　⑤ 티켓 가격

10 다음을 듣고, 남자가 하는 말의 내용으로 가장 적절한 것을 고르시오.

① 학교 사이트 가입 안내
② 학교 연중행사 소개
③ 자원봉사 활동 참여 방법
④ 학급회의 진행 절차
⑤ 선생님과 면담 신청 방법

11 대화를 듣고, 새 음악 선생님에 대한 내용과 일치하지 <u>않는</u> 것을 고르시오.

① 키가 크다.　　　② 취미는 테니스이다.
③ 친절한 성격이다.　　④ 가르친 경험이 많다.
⑤ 예전에 작곡가였다.

12 대화를 듣고, 남자가 할아버지를 방문한 목적으로 가장 적절한 것을 고르시오.

① 스키를 타기 위해서
② 병문안을 하기 위해서
③ 생신을 축하하기 위해서
④ 가족 행사에 참가하기 위해서
⑤ 스마트폰 사용법을 알려 주기 위해서

13 대화를 듣고, 두 사람이 만날 시각을 고르시오.

① 5:00 p.m.　② 5:30 p.m.　③ 6:00 p.m.
④ 6:30 p.m.　⑤ 7:00 p.m.

14 대화를 듣고, 두 사람의 관계로 가장 적절한 것을 고르시오.

① 경찰관 – 운전자
② 자동차 판매원 – 고객
③ 여행 가이드 – 여행자
④ 택시 기사 – 승객
⑤ 식당 종업원 – 손님

15 대화를 듣고, 여자가 남자에게 부탁한 일로 가장 적절한 것을 고르시오.

① 함께 산책하기
② 케이크 사다 주기
③ 생일 축하 카드 쓰기
④ 빵집 가는 길 안내해 주기
⑤ 케이크 만드는 법 알려 주기

16 대화를 듣고, 남자가 티셔츠를 지금 구입할 수 <u>없는</u> 이유로 가장 적절한 것을 고르시오.

① 세일을 하지 않아서
② 신제품을 사고 싶어서
③ 지갑을 차에 놓고 와서
④ 원하는 모델이 품절이라서
⑤ 디자인이 마음에 안 들어서

17 다음 그림의 상황에 가장 적절한 대화를 고르시오.

① 　② 　③ 　④ 　⑤

18 다음을 듣고, 여자가 Reading Club에 대해 언급하지 <u>않은</u> 것을 고르시오.

① 요일　　② 책 제목　　③ 시간
④ 장소　　⑤ 장소 이용 수칙

[19-20] 대화를 듣고, 남자의 마지막 말에 이어질 여자의 말로 가장 적절한 것을 고르시오.

19 Woman: _____

① You'll have to clean the streets.
② Great. I'm going to go there tomorrow.
③ Sure. You should call the city hall about it.
④ The festival will be held this September.
⑤ You have to pay $10 to watch the game.

20 Woman: _____

① You'd better study modern history.
② You need to try to exercise more often.
③ I'll cook while you do your homework.
④ I'm sorry, but I'm really busy right now.
⑤ You should look them up in the dictionary.

Dictation 13

◇ 다시 듣고, 빈칸에 들어갈 알맞은 단어를 써보세요.

정답 및 해설 p.80

---

01 날씨 파악

다음을 듣고, 오늘 저녁 날씨로 가장 적절한 것을 고르시오.

① ② ③ ④ ⑤

W Good morning, and welcome to the weather forecast. It's _____ _____ _____, and it's not raining yet. However, _____ _____ _____ _____ this evening. If you plan to go out in the evening, _____ _____ _____ with you. It will be boiling hot during the day, but _____ _____ _____, it will cool down tonight. That's the weather forecast for today. Have a nice day!

---

02 그림 정보 파악

대화를 듣고, 남자가 구입할 바지로 가장 적절한 것을 고르시오.

① ② ③ ④ ⑤

W Have you decided what to buy, Jack?
M Not yet. Can you help me choose a pair?
W Sure. You're looking for shorts for the summer, right?
M No, I _____ _____ _____. I'm going to get _____ _____.
W All right. How many pockets do you need?
M Two pockets _____ _____ _____.
W How about these ones with a belt? You said you needed _____ _____, too, right?
M You're right. _____ _____ _____.

---

03 언급하지 않은 내용 찾기

대화를 듣고, 두 사람이 예술 축제에 대해 언급하지 않은 것을 고르시오.

① 개최일   ② 행사 기간
③ 장소   ④ 행사 내용
⑤ 입장료

W Are you going to the 20th Annual Art Festival this Saturday?
M Yes. _____ _____ _____ April 13, right? How long is the festival for?
W _____ _____ _____ 5 days until the 17th.
M Okay. I'll be there. It'll _____ _____ _____ the City Museum, right?

W Right. We need to pay $10 _____ _____ _____.

M Should we _____ _____ _____ to the City Museum?

W That's a good idea.

---

04 특정 정보 파악

대화를 듣고, 여자가 할 수 있는 운동을 고르시오.

① 야구　　　　② 농구
③ 테니스　　　④ 피겨 스케이팅
⑤ 스키

W *What are you planning to do this holiday, Ryan?

M I'm planning to see a baseball game with my family. It's my favorite sport.

W That's nice. I _____ _____ _____ baseball, too.

M Really? Do you like to play baseball, too?

W No, I can _____ _____ _____.

M I didn't know you played tennis. When did you start playing?

W When I was 10. My aunt _____ _____ _____ me to play. She was a professional _____ _____.

> ✱ **교육부 지정 의사소통 기능: 계획 묻고 답하기**　　　　천(이) 1 | 능(김) 6 | Y(송) 1
>
> **What are you planning to do ~? ~에 무엇을 할 계획이니?**
> A: **What are you planning to do** this weekend? 이번 주말에 뭘 할 계획이니?
> B: I'm planning to visit my grandparents. 조부모님을 방문할 계획이야.

---

05 장소 추론

대화를 듣고, 두 사람이 대화하는 장소로 가장 적절한 곳을 고르시오.

① 콘서트홀　② 병원　　③ 박물관
④ 영화관　　⑤ 도서관

W Excuse me, sir. _____ _____ _____ your bottle of juice inside here.

M Sorry, I'll throw it away right away.

W Please use the garbage can over there.

M Of course. Can I take pictures here?

W Yes, you can. But you're _____ _____ _____ _____ anything.

M Oh, okay. _____ _____ _____.

W Also, please don't use a flash when you take pictures. The flash _____ _____ _____ _____.

M All right. Thanks.

의도 파악

대화를 듣고, 남자가 한 마지막 말의 의도로 가장 적절한 것을 고르시오.

① 당부   ② 금지   ③ 꾸중
④ 칭찬   ⑤ 사과

M Jina, did you clean your room?

W Not yet, but I'll do it later tonight.

M Tonight?

W I have to go to Tony's house. We _____ _____ _____ our group project by tomorrow.

M What time are you going to come back home?

W I'm not sure. It _____ _____ _____ _____.

M All right, _____ _____ _____ when you are done.

---

07 특정 정보 파악

대화를 듣고, 여자가 한국에 관해 발표할 주제로 가장 적절한 것을 고르시오.

① K-pop   ② 한복   ③ 전통 무용
④ 한옥   ⑤ 전통 음식

M Did you choose the topic for your presentation?

W Yes, I'm going to talk about Korean culture.

M Oh, perfect! K-pop music is getting popular _____ _____ _____ these days.

W Actually, I decided to introduce something more traditional.

M I see. There are _____ _____ _____ _____ about, like traditional food and clothes.

W Yes, but I'm going _____ _____ _____ Korean traditional dance. I saw a video about it, and it was amazing.

---

08 할 일 파악

대화를 듣고, 남자가 대화 직후에 할 일로 가장 적절한 것을 고르시오.

① 시험 공부하기   ② 책 반납하기
③ 책 읽기   ④ 독후감 쓰기
⑤ 책장 정리하기

M Today was such a long day. I had 5 different exams.

W How did you do on the exams?

M I think I did well on all of them. I _____ _____ _____.

W You certainly did. [Pause] You have so many books in your hand. Are they from the library?

M Yes. I _____ _____ _____ them today.

W Really? * You'd better hurry. The library _____ _____ _____ 30 minutes.

M Already? _____ _____ _____.

✽ **교육부 지정 의사소통 기능: 충고하기**   능(김) 2 능(양) 5

You'd better ~. 너는 ~하는 게 좋겠어.

• **You'd better** eat breakfast every day. 너는 매일 아침식사를 하는 게 좋겠어.
• **You'd better** go to bed earlier. 너는 더 일찍 자는 게 좋겠어.

---

09 언급하지 않은 내용 찾기

대화를 듣고, 두 사람이 수영 대회에 대해 언급하지 않은 것을 고르시오.

① 장소   ② 일정
③ 참가 인원   ④ 참가 자격
⑤ 티켓 가격

W Junsu, where were you this morning?

M I was practicing for a swimming competition. So I had to miss my classes.

W Is it _____ _____ _____ Nambu Center?

M Yes, _____ _____ _____ 15th to the 17th.

W That's the biggest competition in the city, right?

M Yes, _____ _____ _____ 150 swimmers this year.

W Are they all in middle school?

M Yes, they _____ _____ _____ _____ 16 to participate. I have tickets. Would you like to come?

W Sure!

---

10 주제 추론

다음을 듣고, 남자가 하는 말의 내용으로 가장 적절한 것을 고르시오.

① 학교 사이트 가입 안내
② 학교 연중행사 소개
③ 자원봉사 활동 참여 방법
④ 학급회의 진행 절차
⑤ 선생님과 면담 신청 방법

M Hello, students! Let me tell you how to _____ _____ _____ volunteer work. First, you should _____ _____ on the school volunteer site. Then you can choose the activity that you _____ _____ _____ for. Lastly, you must _____ _____ _____ _____ to your teacher.

일치하지 않는 내용 찾기

대화를 듣고, 새 음악 선생님에 대한 내용과 일치하지 <u>않는</u> 것을 고르시오.

① 키가 크다.
② 취미는 테니스이다.
③ 친절한 성격이다.
④ 가르친 경험이 많다.
⑤ 예전에 작곡가였다.

W Mike, do you see the man in the blue shirt over there?

M Yes, that's Mr. Han. He is our new music teacher.

W Really? He's very tall.

M Yes. He said his hobby is _____ _____.
He is _____ _____, too.

W I see. He looks young. Is this his _____
_____ _____?

M I think so. He _____ _____ _____
a songwriter before he became a teacher.

W Wow, really? I can't wait until his music class.

---

12 목적 파악

대화를 듣고, 남자가 할아버지를 방문한 목적으로 가장 적절한 것을 고르시오.

① 스키를 타기 위해서
② 병문안을 하기 위해서
③ 생신을 축하하기 위해서
④ 가족 행사에 참가하기 위해서
⑤ 스마트폰 사용법을 알려 주기 위해서

W How was your winter break?

M I had a very relaxing winter break. How was yours?

W I _____ _____ _____ my family
every weekend.

M Where did you go skiing?

W We went to a few ski resorts, but they were mostly in
Gangwon-do.

M Oh, my grandfather lives in Gangwon-do. _____
_____ _____ 2 weeks ago.

W _____ _____ _____
_____?

M No, he didn't know how to use his new smartphone. So I had
to _____ _____ _____.

---

13 숫자 정보 파악 (시각)

대화를 듣고, 두 사람이 만날 시각을 고르시오.

① 5:00 p.m.   ② 5:30 p.m.
③ 6:00 p.m.   ④ 6:30 p.m.
⑤ 7:00 p.m.

M Jane, we have guitar class tonight, right?

W That's right. It begins at 7.

M Do you have anything to do until then?

W Nothing special. What's up?

M I want to practice my guitar _____ _____
_____.

W I see. We could meet earlier and practice together.

M Sure, how about 2 hours earlier?

W   _____ _____ _____. I have to go home and get my guitar.

M   I see. Is 6 o'clock _____ _____ _____ then?

W   That _____ _____ _____ _____.

14 관계 추론

대화를 듣고, 두 사람의 관계로 가장 적절한 것을 고르시오.

① 경찰관 – 운전자
② 자동차 판매원 – 고객
③ 여행 가이드 – 여행자
④ 택시 기사 – 승객
⑤ 식당 종업원 – 손님

M   _____ _____ _____ like to go, ma'am?

W   I'm going to the Claremont Hotel on 5th and Broadway.

M   Okay. I'll put your luggage _____ _____ _____.

W   Thanks. *[Pause]* How long will it take to get there?

M   It won't take long _____ _____ _____ _____ _____ _____. About 15 or 20 minutes.

W   Good. _____ _____ _____ _____ I open a window?

M   Sure. Go ahead.

15 부탁 파악

대화를 듣고, 여자가 남자에게 부탁한 일로 가장 적절한 것을 고르시오.

① 함께 산책하기
② 케이크 사다 주기
③ 생일 축하 카드 쓰기
④ 빵집 가는 길 안내해 주기
⑤ 케이크 만드는 법 알려 주기

🔊 **Listening Tip**

walk의 'l'은 묵음입니다. 묵음은 소리가 나지 않기 때문에 발음할 때는 'l' 소리가 나지 않게 됩니다. walk처럼 'l'이 묵음인 단어로 talk, folk 등이 있습니다.

W   This cake is so delicious. Where did you buy it?

M   I bought it at Jaden's Bakery.

W   How much _____ _____ _____?

M   I only paid $15 for it.

W   Wow, that's cheaper than I expected. _____ _____ _____?

M   _____ _____ _____. It's only a 5-minute 🔊 walk from here.

W   Really? Can you show me _____ _____ _____ _____?

M   Of course.

대화를 듣고, 남자가 티셔츠를 지금 구입할 수 없는 이유로 가장 적절한 것을 고르시오.

① 세일을 하지 않아서
② 신제품을 사고 싶어서
③ 지갑을 차에 놓고 와서
④ 원하는 모델이 품절이라서
⑤ 디자인이 마음에 안 들어서

M Hi, how much are these T-shirts?

W They're $30 each.

M I'll get 2 then.

W Okay. _____ _____ _____ _____ to pay?

M I'll pay _____ _____. *[Pause]* Wait. I have only $50 in my pocket.

W I see. We also _____ _____ _____.

M I'm sorry, but it looks like I _____ _____ _____ in my car. Can I _____ _____ _____?

W No problem.

---

17 그림 상황에 적절한 대화 찾기

다음 그림의 상황에 가장 적절한 대화를 고르시오.

① ② ③ ④ ⑤

◀》 Listening Tip
t가 r과 모음 사이에 오고 t가 포함된 음절에 강세가 없는 경우 [t] 발음이 [r]처럼 바뀌어 party가 /파뤼/로 발음됩니다. forty도 마찬가지 경우입니다.

① W Can I try these on?
   M I'm sorry, but you can't try them on.
② W How much is a haircut?
   M It's $15 _____ _____ and $20 _____ _____.
③ W Did you give your essay to your teacher?
   M Yes, I did that yesterday.
④ W _____ _____ _____ _____ your steak, sir?
   M Well-done, please.
⑤ W _____ _____ are in your ◀》party?
   M Two. My wife's parking the car.

---

18 언급하지 않은 내용 찾기

다음을 듣고, 여자가 Reading Club에 대해 언급하지 않은 것을 고르시오.

① 요일   ② 책 제목   ③ 시간
④ 장소   ⑤ 장소 이용 수칙

W Hello, everyone! My name is Irene Smith, the leader of the Reading Club. Every Thursday, _____ _____ _____ and talk about one novel. It'll take 2 hours from 10 a.m. to noon. The owner of _____ _____ is letting us use this meeting room for free, so we have to keep it clean. _____ _____ _____ _____ any food or drinks to meetings.

19 이어질 응답 찾기

대화를 듣고, 남자의 마지막 말에 이어질 여자의 말로 가장 적절한 것을 고르시오.

Woman: _____

① You'll have to clean the streets.
② Great. I'm going to go there tomorrow.
③ Sure. You should call the city hall about it.
④ The festival will be held this September.
⑤ You have to pay $10 to watch the game.

M Did you hear about the National Sports Festival?

W No, I didn't. What about it?

M I just heard our town _____ _____ _____ _____ this year.

W Really? That's great news!

M Yes. So I'm going to volunteer to help during the festival.

W That sounds like fun. _____ _____ _____ _____ are you going to do?

M I'm not sure. I'm going to go to the city hall and _____ _____ _____ about it.

W I want to take part in it, too. I _____ _____ _____ _____ _____ .

20 이어질 응답 찾기

대화를 듣고, 남자의 마지막 말에 이어질 여자의 말로 가장 적절한 것을 고르시오.

Woman: _____

① You'd better study modern history.
② You need to try to exercise more often.
③ I'll cook while you do your homework.
④ I'm sorry, but I'm really busy right now.
⑤ You should look them up in the dictionary.

M Are you busy, Mom?

W No, I'm not. What is it, Harry?

M _____ _____ _____ do my homework, but I don't know or understand _____ _____ _____ .

W Let me see. [Pause] You're reading an article about ancient history.

M Yes, what should I do?

W You should first try to _____ _____ _____ of the words.

M Okay. Then, _____ _____ _____ _____ _____ ?

실전 모의고사 14

01 다음을 듣고, 뉴욕의 날씨로 가장 적절한 것을 고르시오.

① ② ③ ④ ⑤

02 대화를 듣고, 여자가 구입할 운동화로 가장 적절한 것을 고르시오.

① ② ③

④ ⑤

03 대화를 듣고, 두 사람이 스테이크에 대해 언급하지 않은 것을 고르시오.
① 이름　　　② 가격　　　③ 크기
④ 부위　　　⑤ 굽기 정도

04 대화를 듣고, 여자가 여행 마지막 날에 한 일로 가장 적절한 것을 고르시오.
① 등산하기
② 온천에 가기
③ 친구들에게 엽서쓰기
④ 친구들에게 줄 선물 사기
⑤ 숙소에서 편히 쉬기

05 대화를 듣고, 두 사람이 대화하는 장소로 가장 적절한 곳을 고르시오.
① 책방　　　② 시청　　　③ 박물관
④ 관광안내소　⑤ 지하철역

06 대화를 듣고, 남자가 한 마지막 말의 의도로 가장 적절한 것을 고르시오.
① 불평　　　② 제안　　　③ 칭찬
④ 사과　　　⑤ 허락

07 대화를 듣고, 여자가 여름에 여행갈 도시를 고르시오.
① 경주　　　② 속초　　　③ 부산
④ 여수　　　⑤ 통영

08 대화를 듣고, 남자가 대화 직후에 할 일로 가장 적절한 것을 고르시오.
① 학교에 가기
② 도서관에 가기
③ 가방 속 확인하기
④ 방 안에서 물건 찾기
⑤ 분실물 보관소에 전화하기

09 대화를 듣고, 두 사람이 쇼핑몰에 대해 언급하지 않은 것을 고르시오.
① 위치　　　② 이름　　　③ 영업시간
④ 할인 품목　⑤ 근처 상점

10 다음을 듣고, 남자가 하는 말의 내용으로 가장 적절한 것을 고르시오.
① 감기 예방법
② 숙면의 중요성
③ 올바른 학습 태도
④ 규칙적인 생활의 필요성
⑤ 방학을 알차게 보내는 방법

11 다음을 듣고, Sleep Kingdom에 대한 내용으로 일치하지 않는 것을 고르시오.

① 매트리스를 판매한다.
② 30년 이상 영업하였다.
③ 이번 주말에 세일을 한다.
④ 공공 도서관 근처에 있다.
⑤ 주차장이 없다.

12 대화를 듣고, 남자가 한국을 방문한 목적으로 가장 적절한 것을 고르시오.

① 쇼핑을 하기 위해서
② 아내를 만나기 위해서
③ 영어를 가르치기 위해서
④ 제자들을 만나기 위해서
⑤ 김치 담그는 법을 배우기 위해서

13 대화를 듣고, 여자가 지불해야 할 금액으로 가장 적절한 것을 고르시오.

① $7   ② $10   ③ $14
④ $20   ⑤ $30

14 대화를 듣고, 두 사람의 관계로 가장 적절한 것을 고르시오.

① 의사 – 환자   ② 교사 – 학부모
③ 은행 직원 – 고객   ④ 여행사 직원 – 고객
⑤ 신문 기자 – 교사

15 대화를 듣고, 여자가 남자에게 부탁한 일로 가장 적절한 것을 고르시오.

① 체육관 함께 가기
② 숙제 알려주기
③ 체육복 빌려주기
④ 체육시험 준비 도와주기
⑤ 잃어버린 체육복 찾아주기

16 대화를 듣고, 여자가 집에만 머무른 이유로 가장 적절한 것을 고르시오.

① 동생을 보느라고
② 가족들이 집을 비워서
③ 밀린 공부를 하느라고
④ 심한 감기에 걸려서
⑤ 집에서 쉬는 것을 좋아해서

17 다음 그림의 상황에 가장 적절한 대화를 고르시오.

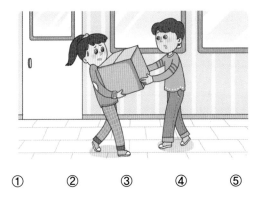

①   ②   ③   ④   ⑤

18 다음을 듣고, 여자가 휴대전화에 대해 언급하지 않은 것을 고르시오.

① 모델명   ② 제조업체   ③ 색깔
④ 크기   ⑤ 요금제

[19-20] 대화를 듣고, 남자의 마지막 말에 이어질 여자의 말로 가장 적절한 것을 고르시오.

19 Woman: _____

① Yes, I am as excited as you are.
② Yes, I'll take you back to the airport.
③ Sure, I'll call you back in 5 minutes.
④ Don't worry about it. Just have fun.
⑤ No, but I'll talk to Matthew's mother about it.

20 Woman: _____

① I never eat out.
② I love Chinese restaurants.
③ My favorite day is Saturday.
④ I like anything but salty food.
⑤ You should also try that restaurant.

정답 및 해설 p.87

01 날씨 파악

다음을 듣고, 뉴욕의 날씨로 가장 적절한 것을 고르시오.

① ② ③
④ ⑤

M Good morning, America! As usual, it'll be sunny in Los Angeles, but it'll be _____ _____ in San Francisco. There is a high chance of rain in Atlanta, and there will be _____ _____ _____ in Dallas. It will be _____ _____ in New York, but no rain is expected.

02 그림 정보 파악

대화를 듣고, 여자가 구입할 운동화로 가장 적절한 것을 고르시오.

① ② ③
④ ⑤

M Can I help you find anything?

W Yes, I'm looking for basketball shoes for myself.

M Okay, how about these? These are really good for _____ _____ _____.

W I actually prefer low basketball shoes, the ones that look like tennis shoes.

M Sure, we have 2 kinds of low basketball shoes. How do you like these?

W Oh, _____ _____ _____ _____ 23 on them. Can you also show me the other kind?

M Sure, instead of the number 23, these have _____ _____ _____ _____.

W Okay, _____ _____ _____. I don't like the number 23.

03 언급하지 않은 내용 찾기

대화를 듣고, 두 사람이 스테이크에 대해 언급하지 않은 것을 고르시오.

① 이름   ② 가격   ③ 크기
④ 부위   ⑤ 굽기 정도

W What are you going to have?

M There are so many things to choose from.

W Well, why don't you _____ _____ _____ here? [Pause] How about Manhattan Night?

M Manhattan Night? Is that _____ _____ _____ the steak?

W Yes, it is, and it's $30.

M I see. _____ _____ is the steak?

W The menu says it's about 200 grams.

M Okay. I'll take it.

W All right. Let's order now. *[Pause]* Oh, _____
_____ _____ _____ your steak?

M Medium, please.

04 한 일 파악

대화를 듣고, 여자가 여행 마지막 날에 한 일로 가
장 적절한 것을 고르시오.

① 등산하기
② 온천에 가기
③ 친구들에게 엽서쓰기
④ 친구들에게 줄 선물 사기
⑤ 숙소에서 편히 쉬기

◀» **Listening Tip**

last day에서 'st+d'처럼 자음 3개가 함께 있을 때는 가운
데 자음은 발음하지 않아요. 그래서 last day는 /래스트
데이/가 아니라 /래스 데이/로 발음해요.

M How was your trip, Janet?

W It was fantastic. The mountain _____
_____ _____.

M Did you do a lot of hiking?

W I went hiking _____ _____ _____
the ◀» last day.

M Did you go to the hot spring and relax _____
_____ _____ _____ ?

W No, I don't like hot springs.

M What did you do then?

W I _____ _____ _____ my friends.
Here's yours.

05 장소 추론

대화를 듣고, 두 사람이 대화하는 장소로 가장 적
절한 곳을 고르시오.

① 책방   ② 시청   ③ 박물관
④ 관광안내소 ⑤ 지하철역

M Hello, how can I help you?

W Hi. Can I _____ _____ _____ of
the city?

M Do you want a map _____ _____ ?

W Yes, please. Can I also get a map of _____
_____ _____ ?

M Of course. Here you are.

W Thank you. This will be very helpful to get around the city.

M We also _____ _____ _____ for
restaurants and tourist attractions. Would you like some?

W Yes, please.

대화를 듣고, 남자가 한 마지막 말의 의도로 가장 적절한 것을 고르시오.

① 불평　② 제안　③ 칭찬
④ 사과　⑤ 허락

W　Can you do me a favor, James?

M　Of course, what is it?

W　Can you show me ＿＿＿＿＿ ＿＿＿＿＿ ＿＿＿＿＿ this question? I know what the answer is, but I don't understand why.

M　I'll give it a try. *[Pause]* This question is not easy at all.

W　No, it's not. So, what did you get?

M　I think the answer is 1,250. ＿＿＿＿＿ ＿＿＿＿＿ ＿＿＿＿＿ ＿＿＿＿＿?

W　No, it's not. The answer is 1,150. I don't understand why.

M　Well, ＿＿＿＿＿ ＿＿＿＿＿ ＿＿＿＿＿ ＿＿＿＿＿ Mike? He's really good at math.

대화를 듣고, 여자가 여름에 여행갈 도시를 고르시오.

① 경주　② 속초　③ 부산
④ 여수　⑤ 통영

M　Do you have any plans for your summer vacation, Sujeong?

W　Not yet. But I really want to ＿＿＿＿＿ ＿＿＿＿＿ this summer.

M　Have you been to Gyeongju? It's a beautiful place.

W　I actually went to Gyeongju and Busan ＿＿＿＿＿ ＿＿＿＿＿.

M　I see. Yeosu is a good place to visit in summer. I went there last summer, and it was amazing.

W　Oh, ＿＿＿＿＿ ＿＿＿＿＿ ＿＿＿＿＿ to go to Yeosu. I should ＿＿＿＿＿ ＿＿＿＿＿ ＿＿＿＿＿ ＿＿＿＿＿ there.

대화를 듣고, 남자가 대화 직후에 할 일로 가장 적절한 것을 고르시오.

① 학교에 가기
② 도서관에 가기
③ 가방 속 확인하기
④ 방 안에서 물건 찾기
⑤ 분실물 보관소에 전화하기

W　What are you looking for, Bill?

M　I'm looking for my phone, Mom.

W　Did you ＿＿＿＿＿ ＿＿＿＿＿ ＿＿＿＿＿?

M　Yes, but it's not in my backpack. I'll check my room.

W　*[Pause]* Did you find it?

M　No, it's not here, either. I think I lost ＿＿＿＿＿

W　*You should go back to school and _____ _____ _____ in the lost and found.

M　Yes. I'll _____ _____ _____ right now.

✳ 교육부 지정 의사소통 기능: 충고하기　　　　　　　　　　Y(송) 2 | 지 2

You should ~. 너는 ~해야 해.
• **You should** exercise regularly. 너는 규칙적으로 운동해야 해.
• **You should** clean your room. 너는 네 방을 청소해야 해.

09 언급하지 않은 내용 찾기

대화를 듣고, 두 사람이 쇼핑몰에 대해 언급하지 않은 것을 고르시오.

① 위치　　② 이름　　③ 영업시간
④ 할인 품목　　⑤ 근처 상점

W　Have you been to the new mall _____ _____ _____ _____?

M　You mean the Mall of California? I went there last week.

W　I'm going with my mom later today. Do you know _____ _____ _____?

M　I think _____ _____ _____ 10 a.m. to 8 p.m. But there are no sports shops.

W　Really? I wanted to get new soccer shoes.

M　There is a big sports shop _____ _____ _____ _____. You should go there instead.

10 주제 추론

다음을 듣고, 남자가 하는 말의 내용으로 가장 적절한 것을 고르시오.

① 감기 예방법
② 숙면의 중요성
③ 올바른 학습 태도
④ 규칙적인 생활의 필요성
⑤ 방학을 알차게 보내는 방법

M　Winter break starts tomorrow. I want you _____ _____ _____ until I see you again. So I'll tell you how to _____ _____ _____. First, drink a lot of water. Second, eat well and sleep well. Exercise is a great way to _____ _____ _____ _____, too. Most importantly, you need to _____ _____ _____ as often as possible.

11 일치하지 않는 내용 찾기

다음을 듣고, Sleep Kingdom에 대한 내용으로 일치하지 않는 것을 고르시오.

① 매트리스를 판매한다.
② 30년 이상 영업하였다.
③ 이번 주말에 세일을 한다.
④ 공공 도서관 근처에 있다.
⑤ 주차장이 없다.

M Are you having sleep problems? _____ _____ _____ a new mattress from Sleep Kingdom. We've _____ _____ _____ for over 30 years, and we're having our spring _____ _____ _____. We are near the public library, and we have _____ _____ _____ _____.

---

12 목적 파악

대화를 듣고, 남자가 한국을 방문한 목적으로 가장 적절한 것을 고르시오.

① 쇼핑을 하기 위해서
② 아내를 만나기 위해서
③ 영어를 가르치기 위해서
④ 제자들을 만나기 위해서
⑤ 김치 담그는 법을 배우기 위해서

W Is this your first visit to Korea, Mr. Jensen?
M This is my first time, but my wife used to _____ _____ _____ a few years.
W Really? Where is she now?
M She went to _____ _____ _____ she used to work at.
W Was she a teacher?
M Yes, she taught English at a high school about 6 years ago.
W Are you going to _____ _____, too?
M No, I came to learn _____ _____ _____ kimchi. I'm a professional chef.

---

13 숫자 정보 파악 (금액)

대화를 듣고, 여자가 지불해야 할 금액으로 가장 적절한 것을 고르시오.

① $7   ② $10   ③ $14
④ $20   ⑤ $30

M _____ _____ _____ _____, ma'am?
W Yes, it is. This mug is $7, right?
M Let me check for you. *[Pause]* It's actually $10.
W Really? The sign said _____ _____ _____ 30 percent off.
M Oh, that sign is for the large mug with a lid. Large mugs are $20 each.
W _____ _____ _____, the large mug is $14, right?
M Yes, you're right.
W Then I'll get _____ _____ _____ instead.

14 관계 추론

대화를 듣고, 두 사람의 관계로 가장 적절한 것을 고르시오.

① 의사 – 환자
② 교사 – 학부모
③ 은행 직원 – 고객
④ 여행사 직원 – 고객
⑤ 신문 기자 – 교사

W Thank you _____ _____ _____, Mr. Carpenter.

M Thank you for taking the time to meet with me, Mrs. Brown.

W I just wanted to talk to you about Paul's grades this year.

M I understand. _____ _____ _____ _____ at school.

W I'm a little worried about him because he rarely _____ _____ _____.

M I'm sorry, Mrs. Brown. I'll make sure that he finishes his homework every night.

W If he just completes his homework, _____ _____ _____.

15 부탁 파악

대화를 듣고, 여자가 남자에게 부탁한 일로 가장 적절한 것을 고르시오.

① 체육관 함께 가기
② 숙제 알려주기
③ 체육복 빌려주기
④ 체육시험 준비 도와주기
⑤ 잃어버린 체육복 찾아주기

🔊 Listening Tip

strict에서 [t]처럼 [t], [p], [k]가 강세가 있는 음절의 첫 음이 아닐 때는 /뜨/, /쁘/, /끄/와 같이 된소리로 발음해요. 그래서 strict는 /스트릭트/가 아니라 /스뜨릭트/로 발음해요.

W Oh no! What am I going to do?

M What's the matter, Lindsey?

W I have gym class right after lunch, but I _____ _____ my gym clothes.

M That's not good. Mr. Brock is 🔊 strict _____ _____ gym clothes.

W I know. Do you have gym class today?

M I had it in the morning. Oh, I think I _____ _____ _____ in my locker.

W Can I _____ _____?

M Sure. I'll be right back.

16 이유 파악

대화를 듣고, 여자가 집에만 머무른 이유로 가장 적절한 것을 고르시오.

① 동생을 보느라고
② 가족들이 집을 비워서
③ 밀린 공부를 하느라고
④ 심한 감기에 걸려서
⑤ 집에서 쉬는 것을 좋아해서

W Did you have a good spring break, David?

M Yes, I had a fantastic break. I went to Jeju-do with my family. How about you? What did you do for the week?

W I couldn't go anywhere. I just _____ _____ _____ during the entire spring break.

M Why couldn't you go anywhere?

W I caught _____ _____ _____, so I stayed in my room.

M Are you better now?

W Yes, _____ _____ _____

_____.

17 그림 상황에 적절한 대화 찾기

다음 그림의 상황에 가장 적절한 대화를 고르시오.

① ② ③ ④ ⑤

① M How much do you weigh?

　 W I weigh about 50 kilograms.

② M Do you _____ _____ _____,

ma'am?

　 W Thank you. This is _____ _____ for me.

③ M I want to _____ _____ _____

to Korea.

　 W Please write _____ _____ on the box.

④ M When did you move to New York?

　 W I moved here 2 months ago.

⑤ M I didn't order any pizza.

　 W I'm sorry. I have _____ _____

_____.

18 언급하지 않은 내용 찾기

다음을 듣고, 여자가 휴대전화에 대해 언급하지 않은 것을 고르시오.

① 모델명　②제조업체　③색깔
④ 크기　　⑤ 요금제

W Do you watch movies a lot on your cell phone? Then Milky Way IV is the perfect one for you. It is _____ _____ _____ _____ Samjeong company. It is lighter and has _____ _____ _____ than the last version. But it is _____ _____ _____! _____ _____ _____ starts at $30.

19 이어질 응답 찾기

대화를 듣고, 남자의 마지막 말에 이어질 여자의 말로 가장 적절한 것을 고르시오.

Woman: _____

① Yes, I am as excited as you are.
② Yes, I'll take you back to the airport.
③ Sure, I'll call you back in 5 minutes.
④ Don't worry about it. Just have fun.
⑤ No, but I'll talk to Matthew's mother about it.

[Telephone rings.]

W Hello.

M Hello, Mom. I'm calling from the airport.

W Are you on _____ _____?

M No, I'll _____ _____ _____

_____ in 5 minutes.

W Is your friend Matthew there with you?

M Yes, he's here. He said he couldn't sleep last night because he was so excited.

W Europe is _____ _____ _____, but don't do anything dangerous. All right?

M Yes, Mom. We'll be careful. Do you _____ _____ _____ _____ anything back for you?

Woman: _____

① I never eat out.
② I love Chinese restaurants.
③ My favorite day is Saturday.
④ I like anything but salty food.
⑤ You should also try that restaurant

M Have you been to the new Chinese restaurant on 6th Street?

W Yes, I have. My dad and I had dinner there last Saturday.

M How was the food? _____ _____ _____ _____.

W My dad loved it, but I thought it _____ _____ _____.

M Chinese food is a bit salty, isn't it?

W That's why I'm not _____ _____ _____ _____ Chinese food.

M What is _____ _____ _____?

실전 모의고사 **15**

점수
/20

01 다음을 듣고, 수요일의 날씨로 가장 적절한 것을 고르시오.

①   ②   ③   ④   ⑤

02 대화를 듣고, 여자가 만든 부채로 가장 적절한 것을 고르시오.

①   ②   ③

④   ⑤

03 대화를 듣고, 두 사람이 여자가 새로 산 청소기에 대해 언급하지 <u>않은</u> 것을 고르시오.
① 제조사   ② 구입 장소   ③ 가격
④ 색상   ⑤ 무게

04 대화를 듣고, 여자가 어제 한 일로 가장 적절한 것을 고르시오.
① 이삿짐 풀기   ② 가구 옮기기
③ 유리 닦기   ④ 이사할 집 가보기
⑤ 발표 자료 준비하기

05 대화를 듣고, 두 사람이 대화하는 장소로 가장 적절한 곳을 고르시오.
① 호텔   ② 백화점   ③ 박물관
④ 극장 매표소   ⑤ 공항

06 대화를 듣고, 여자가 한 마지막 말의 의도로 가장 적절한 것을 고르시오.
① 칭찬   ② 위로   ③ 제안
④ 사과   ⑤ 용서

07 대화를 듣고, 남자가 추천한 음식을 고르시오.
① 와플   ② 피자   ③ 햄버거
④ 스테이크   ⑤ 아이스크림

08 대화를 듣고, 남자가 대화 직후에 할 일로 가장 적절한 것을 고르시오.
① 숙제하기   ② 등산하기
③ 침대 정리하기   ④ 족욕하기
⑤ 따뜻한 물 마시기

09 대화를 듣고, 남자가 본 연극에 대해 언급하지 <u>않은</u> 것을 고르시오.
① 제목   ② 주제   ③ 관람 장소
④ 티켓 가격   ⑤ 함께 본 사람

10 다음을 듣고, 남자가 하는 말의 내용으로 가장 적절한 것을 고르시오.
① 채식의 장단점   ② 점심 메뉴 소개
③ 토론회 일정 안내   ④ 건강한 식사법 소개
⑤ 구내식당 사용 규칙 안내

11 다음을 듣고, 훈련 캠프(training camp)에 대한 내용과 일치하지 <u>않는</u> 것을 고르시오.

① Florida에서 지낸다.
② 기간은 3주이다.
③ 방을 혼자 사용한다.
④ 일요일 외에 매일 아침 7시에 시작한다.
⑤ 매일 밤 10시 반에 불을 끈다.

12 대화를 듣고, 여자가 학교에 가려는 목적으로 가장 적절한 것을 고르시오.

① 선생님과 상담하기 위해서
② 동아리 활동을 하기 위해서
③ 도서관에서 공부하기 위해서
④ 선생님에게 책을 빌리기 위해서
⑤ 두고 온 가방을 가져오기 위해서

13 대화를 듣고, 여자가 지불해야 할 금액으로 가장 적절한 것을 고르시오.

① $5   ② $30   ③ $35
④ $40   ⑤ $45

14 대화를 듣고, 두 사람의 관계로 가장 적절한 것을 고르시오.

① 미용사 – 고객
② 승무원 – 탑승객
③ 음식점 직원 – 손님
④ 도서관 사서 – 이용객
⑤ 호텔 접수원 – 숙박객

15 대화를 듣고, 여자가 남자에게 부탁한 일로 가장 적절한 것을 고르시오.

① 전화 짧게 하기   ② 과제 끝내기
③ 조부모님 모셔오기   ④ 거실 청소하기
⑤ 저녁식사 준비하기

16 대화를 듣고, 남자에게 새 휴대전화가 필요한 이유로 가장 적절한 것을 고르시오.

① 신제품이 나와서
② 전화기가 고장 나서
③ 외국어를 공부하려고
④ 다양한 앱을 사용하려고
⑤ 저장 공간이 부족해서

17 다음 그림의 상황에 가장 적절한 대화를 고르시오.

①   ②   ③   ④   ⑤

18 다음을 듣고, 여자가 현장 학습에 대해 언급하지 <u>않은</u> 것을 고르시오.

① 장소   ② 참가 인원   ③ 활동 내용
④ 준비물   ⑤ 점심시간

[19-20] 대화를 듣고, 여자의 마지막 말에 이어질 남자의 말로 가장 적절한 것을 고르시오.

19 Man: _____

① Sure. I'll wash the dishes now.
② I see. Well, good luck with that.
③ Okay. Thank you for your advice.
④ Wow, you look great with your new shirt.
⑤ No, thanks. I'll borrow some money from my mom.

20 Man: _____

① Mine is too hard for my neck.
② I need a pillow for my brother.
③ I'll go to bed much earlier tonight.
④ I don't know how to make a pillow.
⑤ I'll ask my mom to buy a new pillow.

정답 및 해설 p.94

01 날씨 파악

다음을 듣고, 수요일의 날씨로 가장 적절한 것을 고르시오.

① ② ③
④ ⑤

M Good morning. Here's your weekly weather report. From Monday to Tuesday, we'll have _____ _____ and warm weather. But it's going to be cold with _____ _____ on Wednesday. It's very likely to rain on Thursday. On Friday, it will be very cold and _____ _____ _____ _____.

02 그림 정보 파악

대화를 듣고, 여자가 만든 부채로 가장 적절한 것을 고르시오.

① ② ③
④ ⑤

M It's getting hot out there.
W I made this fan for you. Do you like it?
M I love it. I really like the _____ _____.
W Yes. Long handles are more convenient than short ones.
   *What do you think of the picture?
M It's great. Did you _____ _____ _____ on it?
W I did. And there was _____ _____ _____ add writing, so I wrote "COOL" _____ _____.
M I love it. I'll carry it with me all the time.

> ✱ 교육부 지정 의사소통 기능: 의견 묻기   천(정) 1 | 능(양) 7 | Y(송) 4
> **What do you think of ~?** 너는 ~에 대해 어떻게 생각해?
> • **What do you think of** this diary? 너는 이 일기장에 대해 어떻게 생각해?
> • **What do you think of** my bike? 너는 내 자전거에 대해 어떻게 생각해?

03 언급하지 않은 내용 찾기

대화를 듣고, 두 사람이 여자가 새로 산 청소기에 대해 언급하지 않은 것을 고르시오.
① 제조사   ② 구입 장소   ③ 가격
④ 색상   ⑤ 무게

M Did you get your new vacuum cleaner?
W Yes, I finally did. I bought one at Jackie's Store.
M Is that _____ _____ _____ _____ the subway station?
W Yes. Vacuum cleaners were on sale there last weekend. I _____ _____ _____ $300.

M That's a good price. What color did you get?

W I bought _____ _____ _____.
It works really well, and it's _____ _____
at all.

M I should buy one there, too.

04 한 일 파악

대화를 듣고, 여자가 어제 한 일로 가장 적절한 것을 고르시오.

① 이삿짐 풀기　　② 가구 옮기기
③ 유리 닦기　　　④ 이사할 집 가보기
⑤ 발표 자료 준비하기

🔊 **Listening Tip**

did not의 줄임말인 didn't처럼 'd'와 'n'이 나란히 있을 때는 사이에 모음이 없기 때문에 /디든트/라고 발음하지 않고 [d]는 앞 음절의 받침이 되고 [n]은 가볍게 /은/으로 발음해요. I didn't는 /아이 디든트/가 아니라 /아 딛은/에 가깝게 발음되지요.

M Cindy, why didn't you answer your phone yesterday?

W Yesterday? Oh, I was helping my mom _____
_____.

M Packing? Are you going to move?

W Yes, I'm going to move _____ _____.
Didn't I tell you this?

M No, 🔊 I didn't know that.

W Oh, it's not far. _____ _____
_____ apartment nearby.

M I see. So did you pack a lot?

W Oh, my mom did most of it. _____ _____
_____ _____ _____ the furniture
and cleaned the house.

05 장소 추론

대화를 듣고, 두 사람이 대화하는 장소로 가장 적절한 곳을 고르시오.

① 호텔　　② 백화점　　③ 박물관
④ 극장 매표소　　⑤ 공항

M Can I help the next person in line, please?

W Hi, I'm checking in.

M Do you _____ _____ _____,
ma'am?

W Yes. _____ _____ _____
_____ my last name, Carter.

M Okay. I found a reservation under that name for 3 nights.

W Is it okay to stay _____ _____
_____?

M That should not be a problem, ma'am. _____
_____ _____ your ID, please?

W Sure. Here it is.

06 의도 파악

대화를 듣고, 여자가 한 마지막 말의 의도로 가장 적절한 것을 고르시오.

① 칭찬   ② 위로   ③ 제안
④ 사과   ⑤ 용서

W Tom, what are these in the sink? Are they cupcakes?

M Well, they were. I _____ _____ _____ some but I burned them.

W Why do you need to _____ _____?

M I wanted to make them for my friend, Jenny. She really likes cupcakes.

W Are you going to bake more? I can _____ _____ _____ _____.

M That sounds great. Thanks.

W But first, _____ _____ _____ the kitchen table.

07 특정 정보 파악

대화를 듣고, 남자가 추천한 음식을 고르시오.

① 와플   ② 피자
③ 햄버거   ④ 스테이크
⑤ 아이스크림

M I went to Johnny's Diner last weekend. Have you ever been there?

W I've _____ _____ _____ _____ before. What is it famous for?

M The steak and burgers are good, but _____ _____ _____ _____.

W What dessert do you recommend?

M _____ _____ the waffles. At Johnny's Diner, you get ice cream on it. The waffle is warm, so it makes the ice cream very soft.

W Wow! I should take my family there this weekend.

08 할 일 파악

대화를 듣고, 남자가 대화 직후에 할 일로 가장 적절한 것을 고르시오.

① 숙제하기   ② 등산하기
③ 침대 정리하기 ④ 족욕하기
⑤ 따뜻한 물 마시기

W Jake, why are you still awake? It's past midnight.

M I can't go to sleep, Mom.

W Why not? Is something wrong?

M I went hiking yesterday, and now _____ _____ _____.

W Why don't you _____ _____ _____ _____? It'll relax your feet.

M A foot bath? How do I take a foot bath?

W Fill the bathtub _____ _____ _____ and put your legs into the water.

M Okay, _____ _____ _____ now. I hope it works.

09 언급하지 않은 내용 찾기

대화를 듣고, 남자가 본 연극에 대해 언급하지 않은 것을 고르시오.

① 제목 ② 주제
③ 관람 장소 ④ 티켓 가격
⑤ 함께 본 사람

W What did you do over the weekend, James?

M I saw _____ _____ _____ *Dead or Alive*.

W Where did you see it?

M I _____ _____ _____ the L.A. Cultural Center.

W Aren't _____ _____ _____?

M I thought it was not bad. It was $30 each.

W Who did you go with?

M I went with _____ _____ _____ Susie. You should go and see it, too.

10 주제 추론

다음을 듣고, 남자가 하는 말의 내용으로 가장 적절한 것을 고르시오.

① 채식의 장단점
② 점심 메뉴 소개
③ 토론회 일정 안내
④ 건강한 식사법 소개
⑤ 구내식당 사용 규칙 안내

M It's 12:30, and you'll have _____ _____ _____ until 1:30. There are 2 different meals _____ _____ _____ _____, and one of them is vegetarian. You can choose either a banana or _____ _____ _____ your fruit. However, there are _____ _____ _____, so you'll have to choose between milk and juice.

11 일치하지 않는 내용 찾기

다음을 듣고, 훈련 캠프(training camp)에 대한 내용과 일치하지 않는 것을 고르시오.

① Florida에서 지낸다.
② 기간은 3주이다.
③ 방을 혼자 사용한다.
④ 일요일 외에 매일 아침 7시에 시작한다.
⑤ 매일 밤 10시 반에 불을 끈다.

M Welcome to the training camp, everyone. I hope you're enjoying the beautiful sunshine here in Florida. You will be training here _____ _____ _____ 3 weeks. You'll _____ _____ _____ with 2 other people. We start our training with stretching at 7 every morning, _____ _____ _____. The lights _____ _____ _____ 10:30 every night.

대화를 듣고, 여자가 학교에 가려는 목적으로 가장 적절한 것을 고르시오.

① 선생님과 상담하기 위해서
② 동아리 활동을 하기 위해서
③ 도서관에서 공부하기 위해서
④ 선생님에게 책을 빌리기 위해서
⑤ 두고 온 가방을 가져오기 위해서

M Where are you going out again? You just came back home.
W I'm going back to school, Dad. I'll be _____ _____ _____ _____.

M Did you forget something?
W No. I have to _____ _____ _____ my history teacher.
M Why don't you wait until tomorrow? It's getting dark.
W I can't. She _____ _____ _____ _____ me at school.
M What do you need from her?
W I have to _____ _____ _____ from her. I need them to finish a group project.

13 숫자 정보 파악 (금액)

대화를 듣고, 여자가 지불해야 할 금액으로 가장 적절한 것을 고르시오.

① $5   ② $30   ③ $35
④ $40   ⑤ $45

W Can I _____ _____ _____, please?
M Sure, here it is.
W [Pause] Isn't the T-bone steak set $35?
M It's $35 only on Mondays, ma'am. _____ _____ _____ is $45.
W Oh, I didn't know that. Then can I use this coupon?
M Okay. Can I see the coupon, please?
W Yes, it's a $5 _____ _____ for any steak set.
M You can certainly _____ _____, ma'am.

14 관계 추론

대화를 듣고, 두 사람의 관계로 가장 적절한 것을 고르시오.

① 미용사 – 고객
② 승무원 – 탑승객
③ 음식점 직원 – 손님
④ 도서관 사서 – 이용객
⑤ 호텔 접수원 – 숙박객

M Wow, there are a lot of people waiting.
W Do you have a reservation?
M No, I don't. Do I need a reservation today?
W With a reservation, you don't have to wait for a long time. What would you like to do _____ _____ _____ today?
M I just _____ _____ _____.
W If you come back _____ _____ _____, I can give you a haircut today.
M Great! I'll _____ _____ in an hour.

15 부탁 파악

대화를 듣고, 여자가 남자에게 부탁한 일로 가장 적절한 것을 고르시오.

① 전화 짧게 하기
② 과제 끝내기
③ 조부모님 모셔오기
④ 거실 청소하기
⑤ 저녁식사 준비하기

🔊 **Listening Tip**

dinner에서 'nn'처럼 같은 자음이 두 개 있을 때는 하나만 발음해요. 그래서 /딘너/가 아니라 /디너/로 발음해야 합니다.

[Knock, knock]

W   Can I come in, Jacob?

M   Come on in. I'm not busy now. Do you need something?

W   What were you _____ _____ _____ _____?

M   I was just reading a book. Why?

W   Your grandparents are going to _____ _____ _____ _____.

M   Oh, is it today? I thought it was tomorrow.

W   Well, I'm _____ _____ _____ the kitchen right now. _____ _____ _____ the living room for me?

M   Sure. I'll do that right away.

16 이유 파악

대화를 듣고, 남자에게 새 휴대전화가 필요한 이유로 가장 적절한 것을 고르시오.

① 신제품이 나와서
② 전화기가 고장 나서
③ 외국어를 공부하려고
④ 다양한 앱을 사용하려고
⑤ 저장 공간이 부족해서

M   Mom, can you buy me a _____ _____ _____?

W   A new cell phone? Is there _____ _____ _____ your cell phone?

M   No, there's nothing wrong with it.

W   Then why do you want a new one?

M   My friends downloaded a dictionary app and use it for their homework. But I can't do that because there is _____ _____ _____.

W   Okay. Let me talk to your father about it first.

17 그림 상황에 적절한 대화 찾기

다음 그림의 상황에 가장 적절한 대화를 고르시오.

① ② ③ ④ ⑤

① M   Have you met my cousin?
   W   No, can you introduce me to her?

② M   Do you want me to give you a ride?
   W   No, thanks. My dad's _____ _____ _____.

③ M   Where should we meet tomorrow?
   W   Let's meet at _____ _____ _____.

④ **M** You _____ _____ your drink on the bus.

    W Oh, I'll throw it away then.

⑤ **M** Can I help you find anything?

    W Yes, I'm looking for _____ _____ _____ for my brother.

---

18 언급하지 않은 내용 찾기

다음을 듣고, 여자가 현장 학습에 대해 언급하지 않은 것을 고르시오.

① 장소   ② 참가 인원
③ 활동 내용   ④ 준비물
⑤ 점심시간

W Hello, everyone. Today, we're going to the City Fire Station for our field trip. Mike couldn't come to school today, _____ _____ _____ 15 of us. We'll _____ _____ _____ _____ in case of a fire. Then the firefighters are going to show us how to _____ _____ _____ _____ with the fire truck. We'll _____ _____ _____ 1 p.m. and come back to school by 3 p.m.

---

19 이어질 응답 찾기

대화를 듣고, 여자의 마지막 말에 이어질 남자의 말로 가장 적절한 것을 고르시오.

Man: _____

① Sure. I'll wash the dishes now.
② I see. Well, good luck with that.
③ Okay. Thank you for your advice.
④ Wow, you look great with your new shirt.
⑤ No, thanks. I'll borrow some money from my mom.

M Katie, do you want to go to the cafeteria to _____ _____ _____?

W Sure. *[Pause]* Wait. Oh, I can't. I only have $5.

M I thought you just got your allowance 2 days ago.

W Yes, but I already _____ _____ _____ _____ on clothes.

M Really? Does that mean you have to live off $5 _____ _____ _____?

W Don't worry. I'll _____ _____ _____ by doing chores.

이어질 응답 찾기

대화를 듣고, 여자의 마지막 말에 이어질 남자의
말로 가장 적절한 것을 고르시오.

Man: _____

① Mine is too hard for my neck.
② I need a pillow for my brother.
③ I'll go to bed much earlier tonight.
④ I don't know how to make a pillow.
⑤ I'll ask my mom to buy a new pillow.

🔊 **Listening Tip**
last night처럼 [t]가 단어의 끝에 오는 경우, 약화되어 제
대로 들리지 않아서 /래스나잇/처럼 들려요. first와 just
도 이와 같은 경우예요.

W How are you feeling, Eddie? You don't look very well.

M Oh, I'm okay. I'm just tired.

W Did you _____ _____ _____ to
do your homework 🔊 last night?

M No, I went to sleep early, but I didn't get a _____
_____ _____.

W _____ _____ _____ sleep well?

M I think it was because of my pillow. It's _____
_____. I need a different pillow.

W What's wrong with your pillow?

실전 모의고사 **16**

01 다음을 듣고, 목요일의 날씨로 가장 적절한 것을 고르시오.

①   ②   ③   ④   ⑤

02 대화를 듣고, 남자가 찾는 열쇠로 가장 적절한 것을 고르시오.

①   ②   ③

④   ⑤

03 대화를 듣고, 남자의 심정으로 가장 적절한 것을 고르시오.

① shy ② upset ③ proud
④ excited ⑤ scared

04 대화를 듣고, 여자가 로스앤젤레스에서 한 일로 가장 적절한 것을 고르시오.

① 친척 방문하기 ② 영화 촬영하기
③ 사무실에서 일하기 ④ 친구 만나기
⑤ 관광 명소 방문하기

05 대화를 듣고, 두 사람이 대화하는 장소로 가장 적절한 것을 고르시오.

① 운동장 ② 미술관 ③ 도서관
④ 가구점 ⑤ 놀이공원

06 대화를 듣고, 남자의 마지막 말의 의도로 가장 적절한 것을 고르시오.

① 소망 ② 제안 ③ 불평
④ 칭찬 ⑤ 거절

07 대화를 듣고, 남자가 주문한 음식이 <u>아닌</u> 것을 고르시오.

① 스테이크 ② 구운 감자
③ 치킨 샐러드 ④ 애플파이
⑤ 아이스크림

08 대화를 듣고, 남자가 대화 직후에 할 일로 가장 적절한 것을 고르시오.

① 환불해주기 ② 가격 할인해주기
③ 영수증 발행하기 ④ 운동화 신어보기
⑤ 운동화 가져오기

09 대화를 듣고, 여자가 기내에서 지켜야 할 사항에 대해 언급하지 <u>않은</u> 것을 고르시오.

① 금연하기
② 안전벨트 매기
③ 이륙 시 휴대전화 끄기
④ 가방 앞좌석 밑에 두기
⑤ 이어폰으로 음악 듣기

10 다음을 듣고, 남자가 하는 말의 내용으로 가장 적절한 것을 고르시오.

① 영어 단어 암기법
② 자투리 시간 활용법
③ 우등생의 공부 습관
④ 영어 듣기 잘하는 법
⑤ 다양한 매체를 이용한 학습

11 다음을 듣고, 박쥐에 대한 내용과 일치하지 <u>않는</u> 것을 고르시오.

① 쥐처럼 생겼다.
② 큰 귀와 날개를 가지고 있다.
③ 알을 낳지 않는다.
④ 밤에 주로 사냥을 한다.
⑤ 시력이 뛰어나다.

12 대화를 듣고, 여자가 전화를 건 목적으로 가장 적절한 것을 고르시오.

① 광고를 내기 위해서
② 식당을 예약하기 위해서
③ 일자리를 구하기 위해서
④ 피자를 주문하기 위해서
⑤ 식재료를 구매하기 위해서

13 대화를 듣고, 두 사람이 만날 시각을 고르시오.
① 1:00 p.m. ② 1:30 p.m. ③ 2:00 p.m.
④ 2:30 p.m. ⑤ 3:00 p.m.

14 대화를 듣고, 두 사람의 관계로 가장 적절한 것을 고르시오.

① 경찰관 – 시민
② 택시기사 – 승객
③ 사진작가 – 모델
④ 공원 관리인 – 관광객
⑤ 관광 안내소 직원 – 여행객

15 대화를 듣고, 남자가 여자에게 부탁한 일로 가장 적절한 것을 고르시오.

① 기념우표 사기   ② 소포 부치기
③ 세탁소에 옷 맡기기   ④ 도서 반납하기
⑤ 캐나다 여행 책 사기

16 대화를 듣고, 남자가 어제 피곤했던 이유로 가장 적절한 것을 고르시오.

① 잠을 못 자서
② 시험공부를 해서
③ 늦게까지 통화해서
④ 하프 마라톤에 참가해서
⑤ 체육관에서 운동을 해서

17 다음 그림의 상황에 가장 적절한 대화를 고르시오.

①   ②   ③   ④   ⑤

18 다음을 듣고, 여자가 미아에 대해 언급하지 않은 것을 고르시오.

① 이름   ② 나이   ③ 엄마 이름
④ 생김새   ⑤ 현재 위치

[19-20] 대화를 듣고, 남자의 마지막 말에 이어질 여자의 말로 가장 적절한 것을 고르시오.

19 Woman: _____

① Can I borrow your shirt?
② No, thanks. I'll just take one.
③ Black pants look great on you.
④ Thanks, Dad. I'll get ready soon.
⑤ The white blouse is a medium size.

20 Woman: _____

① How about 3 o'clock?
② It takes about 3 hours.
③ We'll have a good time.
④ I'd like to meet her at 3 p.m.
⑤ I ride my bike 3 times a week.

정답 및 해설 p.100

---

01 날씨 파악

다음을 듣고, 목요일의 날씨로 가장 적절한 것을 고르시오.

① ② ③
④ ⑤

W Good morning! Here is this week's weather report. On Monday, it will _____ _____. But on Tuesday, it will _____ _____ all day long. _____ _____ your umbrella. On Wednesday and Thursday, heavy rain is expected. On Friday, the rain will stop, and it will be _____ _____. And it's likely to be _____ _____ _____ _____ over the weekend.

---

02 그림 정보 파악

대화를 듣고, 남자가 찾는 열쇠로 가장 적절한 것을 고르시오.

① ② ③
④ ⑤

M This drawer _____ _____. Can you get the key for me?

W There are so many keys. Which one is it?

M The _____ _____.

W There are several silver keys. Is it _____ _____ a leather strap?

M No, it's on a _____ _____ _____ _____ _____.

W How many keys are there on the key ring?

M There are 2 _____ _____ _____ _____.

W I got it.

---

03 심정 추론

대화를 듣고, 남자의 심정으로 가장 적절한 것을 고르시오.

① shy ② upset ③ proud
④ excited ⑤ scared

W You seem to be in a _____ _____, Jihun.

M I have a Facebook friend from Russia. Did I tell you about her before?

W Yes, you did. You mean the girl with blond hair, right?

M Right. She is going to come to Seoul next week.

W Really? Is she going to come just _____ _____ _____?

M No. She's going to come with her father. He has a business meeting in Seoul.

W That's great! You _____ _____ _____ _____.

M Yes, I'm _____ _____ _____ meeting her.

04 한 일 파악

대화를 듣고, 여자가 로스앤젤레스에서 한 일로 가장 적절한 것을 고르시오.

① 친척 방문하기
② 영화 촬영하기
③ 사무실에서 일하기
④ 친구 만나기
⑤ 관광 명소 방문하기

W Hi, Joe. _____ _____ _____ _____.

M Hi, Amy. Where have you been?

W I was in Los Angeles _____ _____ for a few months.

M Did you visit any tourist attractions?

W No, not at all. I just _____ _____ _____ _____ _____.

M Oh, I'm sorry to hear that.

W I was so busy. I didn't have time to _____ _____ _____ _____.

05 장소 추론

대화를 듣고, 두 사람이 대화하는 장소로 가장 적절한 것을 고르시오.

① 운동장   ② 미술관   ③ 도서관
④ 가구점   ⑤ 놀이공원

M This place is so crowded.

W Today is the last day of the show. [Pause] Look at the picture of those girls.

M Which one are you talking about? The ones _____ _____ _____ _____?

W No. I mean the girls who are playing the piano.

M Wow, _____ _____ _____ real people, don't they?

W Right. That's why I like _____ _____ of this artist.

M Let's go to the _____ _____. I want to see the paintings of _____ _____.

W Okay.

대화를 듣고, 남자의 마지막 말의 의도로 가장 적절한 것을 고르시오.

① 소망   ② 제안   ③ 불평
④ 칭찬   ⑤ 거절

M You look worried. Is something wrong?

W Well, _____ _____ _____ with Jenny these days.

M Did something happen?

W _____ _____ _____ to me any more. And I don't know why.

M Think carefully.

W *[Pause]* Oh, I think I know why. Last week, she asked me to help her with her homework, _____ _____ _____ _____.

M _____ _____ _____ talk to her first? I'm sure she'll understand.

대화를 듣고, 남자가 주문한 음식이 <u>아닌</u> 것을 고르시오.

① 스테이크   ② 구운 감자
③ 치킨 샐러드   ④ 애플파이
⑤ 아이스크림

W May I take your order?

M Yes. I'll have a steak, please.

W Would you like any side dishes with it?

M I'll have a baked potato. Oh, _____ _____ _____ _____ chicken salad?

W Of course. Anything to drink?

M I'll just _____ _____ _____.

W What would you like for dessert? We have apple pie and ice cream.

M _____ _____ _____ _____.

W All right. I'll be right back with _____ _____ _____ _____ first.

대화를 듣고, 남자가 대화 직후에 할 일로 가장 적절한 것을 고르시오.

① 환불해주기   ② 가격 할인해주기
③ 영수증 발행하기   ④ 운동화 신어보기
⑤ 운동화 가져오기

M May I help you?

W Yes. I'd like _____ _____ _____ sneakers, please.

M What's the matter with them?

W Nothing, actually. I don't think the color looks good on me. _____ _____ _____ _____.

M I see. Do you have your receipt?

W Sure. Here it is.

M Just a moment, please. I'll _____ _____

_____ _____.

W Thank you.

---

09 언급하지 않은 내용 찾기

대화를 듣고, 여자가 기내에서 지켜야 할 사항에
대해 언급하지 <u>않은</u> 것을 고르시오.

① 금연하기
② 안전벨트 매기
③ 이륙 시 휴대전화 끄기
④ 가방 앞좌석 밑에 두기
⑤ 이어폰으로 음악 듣기

M Is the flight leaving on time?

W Yes, it'll be leaving soon. You have to _____

_____ _____ _____

_____.

M I already have. Can I use my cell phone now?

W No, you _____ _____ _____ your
cell phone when the plane is taking off. Please turn off your
cell phone.

M I see. Where can I put this bag?

W You can put it _____ _____
_____ in front of you.

M Okay. Wait, can I listen to music?

W Yes. But please _____ _____
_____.

---

10 주제 추론

다음을 듣고, 남자가 하는 말의 내용으로 가장 적
절한 것을 고르시오.

① 영어 단어 암기법
② 자투리 시간 활용법
③ 우등생의 공부 습관
④ 영어 듣기 잘하는 법
⑤ 다양한 매체를 이용한 학습

M Do you _____ _____ _____ your
English listening skills? Here are some tips. *First, listen to
English _____ _____ _____
_____ every day. Second, make "listening to
English" fun. You can _____ _____
_____ _____ and movies in English.
You'll enjoy the shows and your listening skills
_____ _____ _____, too.

---

* **교육부 지정 의사소통 기능: 열거하기**   천(정) 5|지 5

First, ~. Second[Then/Next], ~. 첫째, ~하세요. 둘째, ~하세요.

• **First,** cut the vegetables into small pieces. **Second,** fry the vegetables with rice.
  첫째, 채소를 작은 조각으로 자르세요. 둘째, 채소를 밥과 볶으세요.
• **First,** draw a circle. **Second,** put a star inside. **Then,** put a triangle on top of the
  circle. 첫째, 원을 그리세요. 둘째, 안에 별을 넣으세요. 그 다음에, 원의 꼭대기에 삼각형을 넣으세요.

다음을 듣고, 박쥐에 대한 내용과 일치하지 않는 것을 고르시오.

① 쥐처럼 생겼다.
② 큰 귀와 날개를 가지고 있다.
③ 알을 낳지 않는다.
④ 밤에 주로 사냥을 한다.
⑤ 시력이 뛰어나다.

W Have you seen a bat? A bat looks like a mouse. It has big ears and wings _____ _____ _____. But it's not a bird because it _____ _____ _____. A bat _____ _____ in the dark. So, it hunts for food at night. Because of _____ _____, a bat can _____ _____ _____ in the dark.

대화를 듣고, 여자가 전화를 건 목적으로 가장 적절한 것을 고르시오.

① 광고를 내기 위해서
② 식당을 예약하기 위해서
③ 일자리를 구하기 위해서
④ 피자를 주문하기 위해서
⑤ 식재료를 구매하기 위해서

🔊 Listening Tip
can이 본동사 앞에 오면 강세를 받지 않아 '컨'으로 발음하지만, Sure, I can.처럼 can이 문장 끝에 쓰이거나 본동사가 뒤따르지 않으면 강세를 받아서 '캔'으로 발음해요.

[Telephone rings.]

M Grandma Mary's Restaurant. How may I help you?
W I'm calling about your advertisement. Are you _____ _____ _____ a part-time waiter?
M Yes, we are.
W How much _____ _____ _____?
M $10 an hour.
W That's pretty good. I'd like to apply for the job.
M Can you come in _____ _____ _____ tomorrow?
W Sure, I 🔊 can. I'll _____ _____ _____ tomorrow.

대화를 듣고, 두 사람이 만날 시각을 고르시오.

① 1:00 p.m.   ② 1:30 p.m.
③ 2:00 p.m.   ④ 2:30 p.m.
⑤ 3:00 p.m.

W Daniel, I have tickets to the musical *Rebecca* on Saturday. Would you like to go with me?
M Of course. What time does _____ _____ _____?
W It starts at 3 o'clock.
M That sounds great. Then, why don't we _____ _____ _____ at 1?
W Sorry, but I have to meet Jessica before the show at 1.
M No problem. _____ _____ in front of the theater at 2:30 then.
W _____ _____ _____ _____.

14 관계 추론

대화를 듣고, 두 사람의 관계로 가장 적절한 것을 고르시오.

① 경찰관 – 시민
② 택시기사 – 승객
③ 사진작가 – 모델
④ 공원 관리인 – 관광객
⑤ 관광 안내소 직원 – 여행객

M May I help you?
W Yes, please. I only have 3 days left in Chicago. _____ _____ _____ I do?
M There are lots of things to see here. You can visit Millennium Park, Chicago Theatre, and the Art Museum. And I suggest you go to the beautiful lake.
W I see. Which one is _____ _____ _____ _____?
M It's Millennium Park. It's a 10-minute walk from here.
W Could I _____ _____ _____ of this area?
M Of course. You can take some _____ _____ _____.
W Thank you.

15 부탁 파악

대화를 듣고, 남자가 여자에게 부탁한 일로 가장 적절한 것을 고르시오.

① 기념우표 사기
② 소포 부치기
③ 세탁소에 옷 맡기기
④ 도서 반납하기
⑤ 캐나다 여행 책 사기

M Where are you going, Mom?
W I'm going to the dry cleaner's. Is there anything you need?
M Can you stop _____ _____ _____ _____?
W The post office? Do you have a package to send?
M Yes, I need to _____ _____ _____ to Anna.
W Isn't Anna in Canada?
M Yes. _____ _____ _____ _____ she wanted.
W All right. _____ _____ _____ for you.
M Thank you.

16 이유 파악

대화를 듣고, 남자가 어제 피곤했던 이유로 가장 적절한 것을 고르시오.

① 잠을 못 자서
② 시험공부를 해서
③ 늦게까지 통화해서
④ 하프 마라톤에 참가해서
⑤ 체육관에서 운동을 해서

M I left a message with your mom yesterday. Did you get it?
W I did. I called you back to ask something else, but you didn't answer.
M Oh, I was really tired. So I _____ _____ _____ than usual.

W Did you _____ _____ _____ the night before?

M No, _____ _____ a half marathon. _____ _____ _____ 2 and a half hours.

W Wow, that's a good time.

---

17 그림 상황에 적절한 대화 찾기

다음 그림의 상황에 가장 적절한 대화를 고르시오.

① ② ③ ④ ⑤

① W Can you _____ _____ _____ _____ to school?

M Sorry, my car is in the repair shop.

② W *Do you mind if I open the window?

M No, I _____ _____ at all.

③ W How can I help you, sir?

M I'm looking for my car.

④ W Thank you for _____ _____ to the theater, Dad.

M You're welcome. _____ _____ with your friends.

⑤ W Where is my car key? Did _____ _____ _____?

M I'm afraid not.

★ 교육부 지정 의사소통 기능: **허락 구하기**   능(양) 6 l 다 6

Do you mind if I ~? 제가 ~해도 될까요?

• **Do you mind if I** go home early? 제가 일찍 집에 가도 될까요?
• **Do you mind if I** take a picture with you? 제가 당신과 사진을 찍어도 될까요?

---

18 언급하지 않은 내용 찾기

다음을 듣고, 여자가 미아에 대해 언급하지 <u>않은</u> 것을 고르시오.

① 이름 ② 나이 ③ 엄마 이름
④ 생김새 ⑤ 현재 위치

W May I have your attention, please? We have found a little girl, _____ _____ _____ _____ Victoria. She is 5 years old, and she says she is looking _____ _____ _____. Victoria _____ _____ _____ _____. She's wearing a pink T-shirt and blue shorts. Right _____ _____ _____ the customer service center on the 5th floor. Thank you.

대화를 듣고, 남자의 마지막 말에 이어질 여자의 말로 가장 적절한 것을 고르시오.

Woman: _____

① Can I borrow your shirt?
② No, thanks. I'll just take one.
③ Black pants look great on you.
④ Thanks, Dad. I'll be ready soon.
⑤ The white blouse is a size medium.

M   Jane, are you looking for something?

W   Yes, I'm looking for _____ _____
    _____. Did you see it, Dad?

M   No. Did you ask your mom?

W   I did, and she said it was _____ _____
    _____. But it's not.

M   Why do you need your white blouse?

W   I need to wear it at my homeroom teacher's wedding.
    Our class is going to sing for her.

M   I see. How about _____ _____ right now?
    _____ _____ _____ a new white
    blouse.

대화를 듣고, 남자의 마지막 말에 이어질 여자의 말로 가장 적절한 것을 고르시오.

Woman: _____

① How about 3 o'clock?
② It takes about 3 hours.
③ We'll have a good time.
④ I'd like to meet her at 3 p.m.
⑤ I ride my bike 3 times a week.

[Cell phone rings.]

M   Hello.

W   Hi, Andrew.

M   Hi, Susie. What's up?

W   Are you busy tomorrow?

M   No, I'm free _____ _____ _____.
    Why?

W   Why don't we _____ _____ _____
    _____ _____?

M   I want to, but I can't. My bike is broken.

W   Don't worry. You can _____ _____
    _____.

M   That'll be great. So, when _____ _____
    _____?

실전 모의고사 **17**

01 다음을 듣고, 주말 날씨로 가장 적절한 것을 고르시오.

① 　② 　③ 　④ 　⑤

02 대화를 듣고, 남자가 구입할 담요로 가장 적절한 것을 고르시오.

① 　② 　③

④ 　⑤

03 대화를 듣고, 남자의 심정으로 가장 적절한 것을 고르시오.

① excited　② angry　③ lonely
④ sad　⑤ surprised

04 대화를 듣고, 여자가 여름 방학에 한 일로 가장 적절한 것을 고르시오.

① 수영하러 가기　② 한 달 여행하기
③ 가족과 등산하기　④ 먼 친척 방문하기
⑤ 한국 음식 요리하기

05 대화를 듣고, 두 사람이 대화하는 장소로 가장 적절한 것을 고르시오.

① 공항　② 호텔　③ 여행사
④ 백화점　⑤ 도서관

06 대화를 듣고, 여자의 마지막 말의 의도로 가장 적절한 것을 고르시오.

① 충고　② 동의　③ 승낙
④ 소망　⑤ 거절

07 대화를 듣고, 여자가 영화에서 가장 마음에 드는 부분을 고르시오.

① 줄거리　② 연기　③ 의상
④ 음악　⑤ 결말

08 대화를 듣고, 여자가 대화 직후에 할 일로 가장 적절한 것을 고르시오.

① 빨래하기　② 단추 달기
③ 셔츠 사기　④ 학교에 가기
⑤ 옷장 정리하기

09 대화를 듣고, 남자가 동물원에서 해야 할 일에 대해 언급하지 <u>않은</u> 것을 고르시오.

① 원숭이 우리 청소하기　② 원숭이 먹이 주기
③ 아기 호랑이 돌보기　④ 울타리 수리하기
⑤ 야외 휴지통 비우기

10 다음을 듣고, 여자가 하는 말의 내용으로 가장 적절한 것을 고르시오.

① 물자 절약 권장　② 벼룩시장 참여 독려
③ 골동품 판매 홍보　④ 기부금 납부 권유
⑤ 봉사활동 참여 독려

11 다음을 듣고, Pizza Kitchen에 대한 내용으로 일치하지 <u>않는</u> 것을 고르시오.

① 매일 신선한 재료를 준비한다.
② 전화와 온라인 주문이 가능하다.
③ 30분 이내로 배달해준다.
④ 배달이 늦어지면 무료이다.
⑤ 첫 배달 주문 시 20% 할인해준다.

12 대화를 듣고, 여자가 전화를 건 목적으로 가장 적절한 것을 고르시오.

① 여행을 취소하기 위해서
② 비행기를 예약하기 위해서
③ 여행 동행을 부탁하기 위해서
④ 비행기 시각을 변경하기 위해서
⑤ 비행기 도착 시각을 알리기 위해서

13 대화를 듣고, 남자가 미용실에 방문할 시각을 고르시오.

① 4:00 p.m.   ② 4:30 p.m.   ③ 5:00 p.m.
④ 5:30 p.m.   ⑤ 7:00 p.m.

14 대화를 듣고, 두 사람의 관계로 가장 적절한 것을 고르시오.

① 연예인 – 매니저   ② 작곡가 – 가수
③ 피아노 강사 – 학생   ④ 피아니스트 – 기자
⑤ 악기 가게 주인 – 손님

15 대화를 듣고, 남자가 여자에게 부탁한 일로 가장 적절한 것을 고르시오.

① 간식 가져오기   ② 등산화 챙겨 오기
③ 친구 소개시켜주기   ④ 주말 날씨 확인하기
⑤ 튤립 축제 같이 가기

16 대화를 듣고, 여자가 딸에 대해 걱정하는 이유로 가장 적절한 것을 고르시오.

① 몸이 아파서   ② 편식이 심해서
③ 게임을 많이 해서   ④ 성적이 좋지 않아서
⑤ 친구를 사귀지 못해서

17 다음 그림의 상황에 가장 적절한 대화를 고르시오.

①   ②   ③   ④   ⑤

18 다음을 듣고, 여자가 백화점 세일에 대해 언급하지 <u>않은</u> 것을 고르시오.

① 할인품목   ② 할인율   ③ 사은품
④ 행사장 위치   ⑤ 판매 시간

[19-20] 대화를 듣고, 남자의 마지막 말에 이어질 여자의 말로 가장 적절한 것을 고르시오.

19 Woman: _____

① Thank you very much.
② Okay, let's go together.
③ I'll get there by subway.
④ It's close. It takes 5 minutes on foot.
⑤ I like walking better than taking a taxi.

20 Woman: _____

① They cost $15.
② Maybe it can help you.
③ You'd better get some rest.
④ You should drink hot water.
⑤ Take these 30 minutes after each meal.

01 날씨 파악

다음을 듣고, 주말 날씨로 가장 적절한 것을 고르시오.

① ② ③ ④ ⑤

W Good morning! This is the weekly weather report. From Monday to Wednesday, it will be very cold and cloudy with _____ _____. Make sure to keep yourself warm. The skies will _____ _____ on Thursday, and you'll have sunny and _____ _____ until Friday. However, we _____ _____ _____ this weekend.

02 그림 정보 파악

대화를 듣고, 남자가 구입할 담요로 가장 적절한 것을 고르시오.

① ② ③ ④ ⑤

W Good afternoon, how may I help you?

M I'm looking for a blanket for my daughter. She needs one for camping this weekend.

W Sure. How about this one _____ _____ _____ in the middle? It's one of the most popular items these days.

M I see. It looks all right, but my daughter likes _____ _____.

W Then how about _____ _____ _____ with a pocket?

M This would be _____ _____ _____. I'll take it.

03 심정 추론

대화를 듣고, 남자의 심정으로 가장 적절한 것을 고르시오.

① excited ② angry ③ lonely
④ sad ⑤ surprised

M I _____ _____ _____ my girlfriend's house for dinner.

W That's great. Are you going to meet her family for the first time?

M Yes. I hope they'll like me. What should I bring to her house?

W You should bring a _____ _____ in that case.

M Can you give me some examples?

W Well, some flowers or a cake would be nice.

M Then, I will ＿＿＿＿＿＿ ＿＿＿＿＿＿ ＿＿＿＿＿＿.
   I ＿＿＿＿＿＿ ＿＿＿＿＿＿ ＿＿＿＿＿＿ meet her family.

04 한 일 파악

대화를 듣고, 여자가 여름 방학에 한 일로 가장 적절한 것을 고르시오.

① 수영하러 가기　② 한 달 여행하기
③ 가족과 등산하기　④ 먼 친척 방문하기
⑤ 한국 음식 요리하기

M Mary, long time no see.

W Lucas, how was your summer vacation?

M It was great. I ＿＿＿＿＿＿ ＿＿＿＿＿＿ ＿＿＿＿＿＿ and went swimming a lot with friends. How about you?

W Oh, ＿＿＿＿＿＿ ＿＿＿＿＿＿ ＿＿＿＿＿＿ a month-long trip to Korea with my family.

M A month? Wow, that's amazing. What did you do?

W We did many things. We visited many places ＿＿＿＿＿＿ ＿＿＿＿＿＿ ＿＿＿＿＿＿ ＿＿＿＿＿＿. Oh, we did a lot of shopping, too.

M That sounds like fun.

W It was. ＿＿＿＿＿＿ ＿＿＿＿＿＿ ＿＿＿＿＿＿ the country one day.

05 장소 추론

대화를 듣고, 두 사람이 대화하는 장소로 가장 적절한 것을 고르시오.

① 공항　② 호텔　③ 여행사
④ 백화점　⑤ 도서관

M Good afternoon. How may I help you?

W Hello. I saw your advertisement from a travel magazine.

M I see. Are you planning to travel alone?

W No. I'll travel with my husband. Do you have ＿＿＿＿＿＿ ＿＿＿＿＿＿ ＿＿＿＿＿＿?

M Of course. We have a 10-day trip to Eastern Europe. The package ＿＿＿＿＿＿ ＿＿＿＿＿＿ ＿＿＿＿＿＿ plane tickets to hotels.

W That sounds great. Will there be ＿＿＿＿＿＿ ＿＿＿＿＿＿ ＿＿＿＿＿＿?

M Yes. When are you ＿＿＿＿＿＿ ＿＿＿＿＿＿ ＿＿＿＿＿＿?

W We would like to travel in April.

06 의도 파악

대화를 듣고, 여자의 마지막 말의 의도로 가장 적절한 것을 고르시오.

① 충고   ② 동의   ③ 승낙
④ 소망   ⑤ 거절

W William, *what's wrong?

M I'm not feeling so good. I think I have a headache and a sore throat.

W That's no good. Did you go and _____ _____ _____ _____?

M I couldn't. I called to make an appointment, but the office _____ _____ _____.

W I see. Then what are you going to do?

M I'll just _____ _____ _____. I should get some sleep.

W Yes. _____ _____ _____ _____.

> ∗ 교육부 지정 의사소통 기능: 증상 묻고 답하기   동(윤) 5|천(이) 3
> **What's wrong (with you)? (너는) 어디가 아프니?**
> A: **What's wrong?** 어디가 아프니?
> B: I have a headache. 두통이 있어[머리가 아파].

07 특정 정보 파악

대화를 듣고, 여자가 영화에서 가장 마음에 드는 부분을 고르시오.

① 줄거리   ② 연기   ③ 의상
④ 음악   ⑤ 결말

M Did you see the movie *Dream Land*?

W Yes. It's one of my favorite movies. I really _____ _____ _____ of the movie.

M Really? Why do you like it so much?

W The movie has a _____ _____ _____. The best part is the music because it _____ _____ _____ the characters' feelings.

M Yeah, I heard a lot about the music. The movie won many awards _____ _____ _____, right?

W Yes. You can watch the movie at my house if you want.

M Sure. Let's go to your house after school.

08 할 일 파악

대화를 듣고, 여자가 대화 직후에 할 일로 가장 적절한 것을 고르시오.

① 빨래하기   ② 단추 달기
③ 셔츠 사기   ④ 학교에 가기
⑤ 옷장 정리하기

W Why aren't you wearing your school uniform?

M You washed my shirt and _____ _____ _____. I couldn't put it on.

W Isn't there another one in your closet?

M That one is _____ _____ _____.

W Why didn't you tell me about it?

M I forgot. Can you put on _____ _____ _____ now?

W All right. I'll do that _____ _____.

M Thanks, Mom.

09 언급하지 않은 내용 찾기

대화를 듣고, 남자가 동물원에서 해야 할 일에 대해 언급하지 <u>않은</u> 것을 고르시오.
① 원숭이 우리 청소하기
② 원숭이 먹이 주기
③ 아기 호랑이 돌보기
④ 울타리 수리하기
⑤ 야외 휴지통 비우기

M I'm so excited about my first day at the zoo. I can't wait to _____ _____ _____.

W Good for you. What do you have to do there?

M Well, in the morning I have to _____ _____ _____.

W I see. What else do you have to do?

M In the afternoon, I'll _____ _____ _____ and take care of baby tigers, too.

W That sounds like fun.

M But sometimes, I'll have to _____ _____ _____.

10 주제 추론

다음을 듣고, 여자가 하는 말의 내용으로 가장 적절한 것을 고르시오.
① 물자 절약 권장
② 벼룩시장 참여 독려
③ 골동품 판매 홍보
④ 기부금 납부 권유
⑤ 봉사활동 참여 독려

W Hello, I'd like to introduce Helping Hands Flea Market. It is open from 10 a.m. to 7 p.m. this Friday. We have various items from furniture to clothes. _____ _____ _____ neighbors by selling and _____ _____ _____. All the money from this flea market will be donated to those in need. _____ _____ _____ your friends and families to help other people.

11 일치하지 않는 내용 찾기

다음을 듣고, Pizza Kitchen에 대한 내용으로 일치하지 <u>않는</u> 것을 고르시오.
① 매일 신선한 재료를 준비한다.
② 전화와 온라인 주문이 가능하다.
③ 30분 이내로 배달해준다.
④ 배달이 늦어지면 무료이다.
⑤ 첫 배달 주문 시 20% 할인해준다.

W We're sure that you'll be happy to have Pizza Kitchen near your home. We _____ _____ _____ dough and toppings every morning. In addition, we don't use the leftovers from the day before. Please _____ _____ _____ _____ _____, and your freshly baked pizza will be delivered to your home in 30 minutes. If the delivery time is longer than 30 minutes, you _____ _____ _____ pay for it. And you can get a 20% discount _____ _____ _____ _____ to buy pizza.

12 목적 파악

대화를 듣고, 여자가 전화를 건 목적으로 가장 적절한 것을 고르시오.

① 여행을 취소하기 위해서
② 비행기를 예약하기 위해서
③ 여행 동행을 부탁하기 위해서
④ 비행기 시각을 변경하기 위해서
⑤ 비행기 도착 시각을 알리기 위해서

[Telephone rings.]

M Joy Travel Agency.

W Hello. Can I speak to Mr. Watson?

M Speaking. Who is calling, please?

W This is Emma Parker calling from New York.

M Oh, hello. I've _____ _____ _____ _____ all afternoon.

W I'm still here in New York.

M Are you going to fly tomorrow?

W Yes. My flight leaves at 10 a.m. and _____ _____ _____ 3:30 p.m.

M Good. I'm going to pick you up _____ _____ _____.

W I appreciate it. I'll see you soon.

13 숫자 정보 파악 (시각)

대화를 듣고, 남자가 미용실에 방문할 시각을 고르시오.

① 4:00 p.m. ② 4:30 p.m.
③ 5:00 p.m. ④ 5:30 p.m.
⑤ 7:00 p.m.

[Telephone rings.]

W Good morning, Hair Design.

M Hi. I'd like to make an appointment on Saturday afternoon, please.

W Sure. Is it _____ _____ _____?

M Yes, it is.

W When would you like to come in?

M Is 4 o'clock all right?

W I'm afraid _____ _____ _____ _____ at 4. Can you come in 30 minutes _____ _____?

M _____ _____ _____.

14 관계 추론

대화를 듣고, 두 사람의 관계로 가장 적절한 것을 고르시오.

① 연예인 – 매니저
② 작곡가 – 가수
③ 피아노 강사 – 학생
④ 피아니스트 – 기자
⑤ 악기 가게 주인 – 손님

M   Good afternoon. How can I help you?

W   I saw your ad "Piano Lessons for Exams" _____ _____ _____.

M   I see. I'm _____ _____ _____ students for entrance exams.

W   I'd like _____ _____ _____.

M   Have you ever taken a piano lesson?

W   Yes, I have.

M   Okay. Have a seat over there. I'll _____ _____ _____ _____ and explain it to you.

W   Thank you.

15 부탁 파악

대화를 듣고, 남자가 여자에게 부탁한 일로 가장 적절한 것을 고르시오.

① 간식 가져오기
② 등산화 챙겨 오기
③ 친구 소개시켜주기
④ 주말 날씨 확인하기
⑤ 튤립 축제 같이 가기

W   It's already the last day of March.

M   I know. The weather is _____ _____.

W   Yes. Oh, I heard about a Tulip Festival nearby this weekend.

M   Oh, really? I wish I could go there.

W   Do you _____ _____ _____ for this weekend?

M   Yes. Since the weather is nice, I'm going to _____ _____ _____ with Chris.

W   That sounds like fun. Can I come, too?

M   Sure. I'll bring some drinks that day. Can you _____ _____ _____?

W   Of course.

16 이유 파악

대화를 듣고, 여자가 딸에 대해 걱정하는 이유로 가장 적절한 것을 고르시오.

① 몸이 아파서
② 편식이 심해서
③ 게임을 많이 해서
④ 성적이 좋지 않아서
⑤ 친구를 사귀지 못해서

M   How's Cindy doing?

W   She's not doing well. * I'm very worried about my daughter.

M   What's wrong? Is it about her grades?

W   No, it's not. Actually, she's doing well in school.

M   Then why are you _____ _____ _____?

W She _____ _____ _____

_____ playing computer games. She even

_____ _____ _____.

M Did you talk to her about it?

W Yes, but she's _____ _____ _____

_____ at all.

★ 교육부 지정 의사소통 기능: **걱정 표현하기**   능(김) 4 l 능(양) 2 l Y(송) 4 l 지 2

I'm worried about ~. 나는 ~ 때문에 걱정이야.

• **I'm worried about** my grades. 나는 성적 때문에 걱정이야.
• **I'm worried about** my future. 나는 나의 미래 때문에 걱정이야.

17 그림 상황에 적절한 대화 찾기

다음 그림의 상황에 가장 적절한 대화를 고르시오.

① ② ③ ④ ⑤

🔊 **Listening Tip**

best student처럼 같은 자음이 연달아 발음되는 경우에는 발음상 편의 때문에 하나가 탈락이 되어서 /베스튜던ㅌ/처럼 발음해요.

① **M** Are you _____ _____ _____?

W Yes. I love collecting stamps.

② **M** Can I take pictures here?

W Sure, go ahead.

③ **M** You're the 🔊best student in our school.

W How _____ _____ _____ to

say so!

④ **M** What do you want to be in the future?

W _____ _____ _____

_____, so I want to be a math teacher.

⑤ **M** Excuse me, can you tell me the way to _____

_____ _____?

W Sure. Go straight for two blocks.

18 언급하지 않은 내용 찾기

다음을 듣고, 여자가 백화점 세일에 대해 언급하지 않은 것을 고르시오.

① 할인 품목   ② 할인율
③ 사은품   ④ 행사장 위치
⑤ 판매 시간

W Good afternoon, ladies and gentlemen. We have a special one-day sale at Grace Department Store. Today, _____ _____ will be 10% off and washing machines will be 15% off. Those are _____ _____ _____ _____ for today only. _____ _____ _____ _____ on the 5th floor. Please hurry because this sale will _____ _____ _____ 5 in the afternoon. Thank you.

Woman: _____

① Thank you very much.
② Okay, let's go together.
③ I'll get there by subway.
④ It's close. It takes 5 minutes on foot.
⑤ I like walking better than taking a taxi.

M Excuse me. How can I get to Seoul N Tower?
W Well, it's not _____ _____ _____ _____ from here.
M What do you mean?
W You have to _____ _____ _____ and then take the Namsan shuttle bus.
M _____ _____ _____ take the shuttle bus?
W I think you can take it in front of Chungmuro Subway Station.
M How far is it _____ _____ _____ _____?

Woman: _____

① They cost $15.
② Maybe it can help you.
③ You'd better get some rest.
④ You should drink hot water.
⑤ Take these 30 minutes after each meal.

W Good afternoon. How can I help you?
M Yes, I have a terrible stomachache.
W I see. _____ _____ _____ _____?
M It began after lunchtime. I think I ate something bad.
W Let me give you _____ _____. *[Pause]* Here you are.
M Thank you.
W _____ _____ _____ 2 pills at a time.
M Okay. _____ _____ _____ take these?

정답 및 해설 p.114

실전 모의고사 **18**

점수 /20

01 다음을 듣고, 토요일의 날씨로 가장 적절한 것을 고르시오.

① ② ③ ④ ⑤

02 대화를 듣고, 여자가 구입할 셔츠로 가장 적절한 것을 고르시오.

① ② ③

④ ⑤

03 대화를 듣고, 여자의 심정으로 가장 적절한 것을 고르시오.

① upset ② bored ③ worried
④ satisfied ⑤ relaxed

04 대화를 듣고, 남자가 스키 리조트에서 한 일로 가장 적절한 것을 고르시오.

① 눈썰매 타기 ② 스키 강습 받기
③ 동계 훈련하기 ④ 가게 청소하기
⑤ 리조트 시설 안내하기

05 대화를 듣고, 두 사람이 대화하는 장소로 가장 적절한 것을 고르시오.

① 배 ② 병원 ③ 기차역
④ 수족관 ⑤ 여객터미널

06 대화를 듣고, 여자의 마지막 말의 의도로 가장 적절한 것을 고르시오.

① 사과 ② 격려 ③ 비난
④ 충고 ⑤ 부탁

07 대화를 듣고, 여자가 여행에서 이용하지 <u>않은</u> 교통수단을 고르시오.

① 버스 ② 배 ③ 택시
④ 자전거 ⑤ 비행기

08 대화를 듣고, 남자가 대화 직후에 할 일로 가장 적절한 것을 고르시오.

① 가방 찾기 ② 잠긴 문 열기
③ 열쇠 가게에 가기 ④ 엄마에게 전화하기
⑤ 카드 분실 신고하기

09 대화를 듣고, 여자가 시간제 일자리에 대해 언급하지 <u>않은</u> 것을 고르시오.

① 나이 ② 시급 ③ 저녁 제공
④ 근무 시간 ⑤ 면접 준비물

10 다음을 듣고, 남자가 하는 말의 내용으로 가장 적절한 것을 고르시오.

① 입학식 ② 학교 체육대회
③ 개교기념일 행사 ④ 우승 축하 파티
⑤ 농구대회 개막식

11 다음을 듣고, Joy's Beauty Shop의 세일에 대한 내용으로 일치하지 <u>않는</u> 것을 고르시오.

① 1월 25일까지이다.
② 대부분의 상품이 세일한다.
③ 헤어 제품은 30% 할인한다.
④ 15달러 이상 구매 시 립스틱이 무료이다.
⑤ 쿠폰도 같이 사용 가능하다.

12 대화를 듣고, 남자가 전화를 건 목적으로 가장 적절한 것을 고르시오.

① 재킷을 빌리기 위해서
② 함께 쇼핑하러 가기 위해서
③ 옷가게 위치를 알기 위해서
④ 테니스 강습을 취소하기 위해서
⑤ 테니스 라켓을 빌리기 위해서

13 대화를 듣고, 두 사람이 만날 시각을 고르시오.

① 5:00 p.m.   ② 5:30 p.m.   ③ 6:00 p.m.
④ 6:30 p.m.   ⑤ 7:00 p.m.

14 대화를 듣고, 두 사람의 관계로 가장 적절한 것을 고르시오.

① 국어 교사 – 학생   ② 소설가 – 독자
③ 출판사 사장 – 직원   ④ 서점 직원 – 손님
⑤ 도서관 사서 – 이용객

15 대화를 듣고, 여자가 남자에게 부탁한 일로 가장 적절한 것을 고르시오.

① 커피 사기   ② 잡지 빌려주기
③ 음료 주문하기   ④ 테이블 맡아주기
⑤ 일자리 소개해주기

16 대화를 듣고, 남자가 화난 이유로 가장 적절한 것을 고르시오.

① 계단에서 넘어져서
② 자전거가 비싸서
③ 자전거가 고장 나서
④ 자전거를 잃어버려서
⑤ 자전거 수리를 할 수 없어서

17 다음 그림의 상황에 가장 적절한 대화를 고르시오.

① ② ③ ④ ⑤

18 다음을 듣고, 여자가 방송에서 703 비행편에 대해 언급하지 <u>않은</u> 것을 고르시오.

① 출발지   ② 연착 이유
③ 연착되는 시간   ④ 도착지
⑤ 새로운 도착 시각

[19-20] 대화를 듣고, 남자의 마지막 말에 이어질 여자의 말로 가장 적절한 것을 고르시오.

19 Woman: _____

① Cheer up!
② That's too bad.
③ Good for you!
④ Thank you for coming.
⑤ I hope he gets well soon.

20 Woman: _____

① It's next Saturday.
② It's at the Sky Stadium.
③ Let's meet at the bus stop.
④ I play baseball at the park.
⑤ We can go there by subway.

Dictation 18

◇ 다시 듣고, 빈칸에 들어갈 알맞은 단어를 써보세요.

정답 및 해설 p.114

01 날씨 파악

다음을 듣고, 토요일의 날씨로 가장 적절한 것을 고르시오.

① ② ③
④ ⑤

W You're listening to Weather Korea. Let's have a look at the weather for this week. On Monday, it will be ＿＿＿＿＿＿ ＿＿＿＿＿＿ ＿＿＿＿＿＿. From Tuesday to Thursday, rain is expected in the morning, so you should be careful when you drive. On Friday, ＿＿＿＿＿＿ ＿＿＿＿＿＿ ＿＿＿＿＿＿ ＿＿＿＿＿＿ cloudy and windy.
On Saturday, it will ＿＿＿＿＿＿ ＿＿＿＿＿＿ ＿＿＿＿＿＿ and will get colder, but ＿＿＿＿＿＿ ＿＿＿＿＿＿ ＿＿＿＿＿＿ on Sunday.

02 그림 정보 파악

대화를 듣고, 여자가 구입할 셔츠로 가장 적절한 것을 고르시오.

① ② ③
④ ⑤

M May I help you, ma'am?
W Yes, I'm looking for a shirt.
M I see. These blue ＿＿＿＿＿＿ ＿＿＿＿＿＿ ＿＿＿＿＿＿ in fashion this spring.
W They are not really my style.
M Then, how about this white shirt with ＿＿＿＿＿＿ ＿＿＿＿＿＿ ＿＿＿＿＿＿ ＿＿＿＿＿＿? It's so pretty.
W Well, that looks good. But the flower print is too big.
M We have shirts with ＿＿＿＿＿＿ ＿＿＿＿＿＿. They're pink.
W ＿＿＿＿＿＿ ＿＿＿＿＿＿ ＿＿＿＿＿＿ ＿＿＿＿＿＿. I'll take one.

03 심정 추론

대화를 듣고, 여자의 심정으로 가장 적절한 것을 고르시오.

① upset   ② bored   ③ worried
④ satisfied   ⑤ relaxed

M Hi, Jane. Where are you going?
W I'm going to the dentist.
M Is there something ＿＿＿＿＿＿ ＿＿＿＿＿＿ ＿＿＿＿＿＿ ＿＿＿＿＿＿?

W My teeth really hurt. I couldn't sleep last night.

M That's too bad.

W _____ _____ _____ it's going to be painful.

M _____ _____. It'll be okay.

04 한 일 파악

대화를 듣고, 남자가 스키 리조트에서 한 일로 가장 적절한 것을 고르시오.

① 눈썰매 타기   ② 스키 강습 받기
③ 동계 훈련하기   ④ 가게 청소하기
⑤ 리조트 시설 안내하기

M Hi, Lucy. Long time no see.

W _____ _____ _____ _____, Brian?

M Pretty good. I stayed at Crystal Mountain Ski Resort during the winter vacation.

W Wow, that sounds like fun. Did you _____ _____ _____?

M No, I worked full-time there.

W Really? What did you do there?

M Well, I mostly _____ _____ _____ and put skis and snowboards in the right places.

05 장소 추론

대화를 듣고, 두 사람이 대화하는 장소로 가장 적절한 것을 고르시오.

① 배   ② 병원
③ 기차역   ④ 수족관
⑤ 여객터미널

W Wow, we were very lucky to see the dolphins _____ _____ _____ _____ today.

M I know. I saw the dolphins so close.

W I heard most people don't get to see them often on a boat tour.

M When are we going to land _____ _____ _____?

W In 20 minutes. *[Pause]* Oh, you _____ _____ _____.

M I'm feeling seasick right now. I want to lie down.

W Take it easy. _____ _____ _____.

의도 파악

대화를 듣고, 여자의 마지막 말의 의도로 가장 적절한 것을 고르시오.

① 사과   ② 격려   ③ 비난
④ 충고   ⑤ 부탁

🔊 **Listening Tip**

embarrassed처럼 [k], [s], [p], [ʃ], [tʃ]로 끝나는 소리 뒤의 ed는 [t]로 발음해요. 이와 같은 말로는 picked, stopped, wished, watched 등이 있어요.

W   Bill, is everything all right?

M   No, I _____ _____ _____ about Kate.

W   Kate? Did something happen between you two?

M   Well, I _____ _____ about Kate's new hat. Then she _____ _____ _____.

W   Oh no. Then what did you do?

M   Nothing. I just left her there. I was so 🔊 embarrassed. I couldn't say anything.

W   It's not _____ _____. _____ _____ apologize to her.

---

07   **특정 정보 파악**

대화를 듣고, 여자가 여행에서 이용하지 <u>않은</u> 교통수단을 고르시오.

① 버스   ② 배   ③ 택시
④ 자전거   ⑤ 비행기

M   How was your summer vacation?

W   I was in Jeju-do for 2 weeks.

M   That sounds great! How did _____ _____ _____?

W   I _____ _____ _____.

M   Did you rent a car there?

W   No. I _____ _____ _____ to get around. And sometimes I took local _____ _____ _____ downtown.

M   What else did you do?

W   I went to U-do by ship. It is a beautiful island.

---

08   **할 일 파악**

대화를 듣고, 남자가 대화 직후에 할 일로 가장 적절한 것을 고르시오.

① 가방 찾기   ② 잠긴 문 열기
③ 열쇠 가게에 가기   ④ 엄마에게 전화하기
⑤ 카드 분실 신고하기

M   Oh no! I can't find my keycard. I have to _____ _____ _____.

W   Did you put it in your bag?

M   Let me see. *[Pause]* It's not here.

W   Did you _____ _____ _____?

M   Yes, but it wasn't there.

W   Wait, you can also open the lock with a password. Do you know the password?

M No, I don't. My mother changed it a few days ago.

W You should _____ _____ _____
and ask.

M Okay. I'll do that right away.

[Telephone rings.]

W Happy Bakery. How may I help you?

M Are you still looking for someone to work part-time?

W Yes, we are. _____ _____ _____
18?

M Yes, I am.

W _____ _____ _____ $10 an hour,
and you have to work from 6 to 10 _____

_____.

M The hours are perfect for me.

W Could you come over to the shop at noon for an interview?

M Sure. Do I _____ _____ _____
_____ to the interview?

W Yes, you need to bring your ID.

10 주제 추론

다음을 듣고, 남자가 하는 말의 내용으로 가장 적
절한 것을 고르시오.

① 입학식　　　　② 학교 체육대회
③ 개교기념일 행사　④ 우승 축하 파티
⑤ 농구대회 개막식

M We're very excited to tell you that our _____
_____ _____ _____ the national
championship. To celebrate this, tomorrow after school, we
are planning _____ _____ _____
_____ for the players at the gym. We hope all the
students will _____ _____ _____.
There will be some _____ _____
_____. We're looking forward to seeing you there.
Thank you.

11 일치하지 않는 내용 찾기

다음을 듣고, Joy's Beauty Shop의 세일에 대한 내용으로 일치하지 않는 것을 고르시오.

① 1월 25일까지이다.
② 대부분의 상품이 세일한다.
③ 헤어 제품은 30% 할인한다.
④ 50달러 이상 구매 시 립스틱이 무료이다.
⑤ 쿠폰도 같이 사용 가능하다.

W Thank you for shopping at Joy's Beauty Shop. We are having a holiday sale _____ _____ _____ January 25. _____ _____ _____ _____ _____ are on sale. Face creams and hair products are 30 percent off. Also, if you spend more than $50 at our shop, _____ _____ _____ _____ lipstick. However, during the sale, we will not _____ _____ _____.

12 목적 파악

대화를 듣고, 남자가 전화를 건 목적으로 가장 적절한 것을 고르시오.

① 재킷을 빌리기 위해서
② 함께 쇼핑하러 가기 위해서
③ 옷가게 위치를 알기 위해서
④ 테니스 강습을 취소하기 위해서
⑤ 테니스 라켓을 빌리기 위해서

[Telephone rings.]
W Hello.
M Hello, this is Tony. Is Wendy there?
W Hi, Tony. This is Wendy. What's up?
M I'm going to _____ _____ _____ _____ a jacket this afternoon. Do you want to _____ _____ _____?
W Sorry, I have a tennis lesson at 3.
M That's too bad. I really _____ _____ _____ with choosing a jacket.
W I can go with you after 5. Will _____ _____ _____ _____ to go shopping then?
M Not at all. Just call me back after your lesson.

13 숫자 정보 파악 (시각)

대화를 듣고, 두 사람이 만날 시각을 고르시오.

① 5:00 p.m.   ② 5:30 p.m.
③ 6:00 p.m.   ④ 6:30 p.m.
⑤ 7:00 p.m.

W Mike, how do you study math at home?
M I check my notes and do my homework.
W I'm trying my best. But I still _____ _____ _____ doing math homework.
M Do you need help? You can come over to my house.
W Really? _____ _____ 5 o'clock after school?
M I have a swimming lesson, _____ _____ _____ _____ 6:30.
W How about 7, then?
M That _____ _____ _____. I'll see you then.

14 관계 추론

대화를 듣고, 두 사람의 관계로 가장 적절한 것을 고르시오.

① 국어 교사 – 학생
② 소설가 – 독자
③ 출판사 사장 – 직원
④ 서점 직원 – 손님
⑤ 도서관 사서 – 이용객

M Excuse me. Where can I find the section on fiction?

W It's on the 3rd floor.

M Are there ＿＿＿＿＿＿ ＿＿＿＿＿＿ ＿＿＿＿＿＿ in the same section?

W No, you can find children's books on the 2nd floor.

M Thank you. What do I need ＿＿＿＿＿＿ ＿＿＿＿＿＿ ＿＿＿＿＿＿ ＿＿＿＿＿＿?

W You need both an ID card and ＿＿＿＿＿＿ ＿＿＿＿＿＿ ＿＿＿＿＿＿.

15 부탁 파악

대화를 듣고, 여자가 남자에게 부탁한 일로 가장 적절한 것을 고르시오.

① 커피 사기   ② 잡지 빌려주기
③ 음료 주문하기   ④ 테이블 맡아주기
⑤ 일자리 소개해주기

W Henry, it's so good to see you. How have you been?

M Great. You look great. What do you do these days?

W I work at a fashion magazine company. I'll tell you ＿＿＿＿＿＿ ＿＿＿＿＿＿ ＿＿＿＿＿＿ ＿＿＿＿＿＿. So what do you want to have?

M I'll have ＿＿＿＿＿＿ ＿＿＿＿＿＿ ＿＿＿＿＿＿ ＿＿＿＿＿＿. What about you?

W ＿＿＿＿＿＿ ＿＿＿＿＿＿ ＿＿＿＿＿＿ ＿＿＿＿＿＿. I'll order the drinks. Can you go ＿＿＿＿＿＿ ＿＿＿＿＿＿ ＿＿＿＿＿＿ ＿＿＿＿＿＿?

M Sure.

16 이유 파악

대화를 듣고, 남자가 화난 이유로 가장 적절한 것을 고르시오.

① 계단에서 넘어져서
② 자전거가 비싸서
③ 자전거가 고장 나서
④ 자전거를 잃어버려서
⑤ 자전거 수리를 할 수 없어서

W You look upset. What's wrong?

M I bought ＿＿＿＿＿＿ ＿＿＿＿＿＿ ＿＿＿＿＿＿ the day before yesterday.

W Right. Your bike was really nice.

M Well, I ＿＿＿＿＿＿ ＿＿＿＿＿＿ ＿＿＿＿＿＿ any more.

W Did somebody steal your bike?

M No, I have it, ＿＿＿＿＿＿ ＿＿＿＿＿＿ ＿＿＿＿＿＿.

W Did you take it to the repair shop?

M I did, but I have to wait 2 weeks ＿＿＿＿＿＿ ＿＿＿＿＿＿ ＿＿＿＿＿＿ ＿＿＿＿＿＿.

17 그림 상황에 적절한 대화 찾기

다음 그림의 상황에 가장 적절한 대화를 고르시오.

① ② ③ ④ ⑤

① M What's _____ _____ _____
   _____ ?
   W There is a Christmas tree in it.
② M Can you _____ _____ _____ ,
   please?
   W Sure. No problem.
③ M I have a present for you.
   W Oh, you're so sweet. Thank you.
④ M Do you know _____ _____
   _____ _____ ?
   W Yes. It's next to the door.
⑤ M _____ _____ _____
   _____ I open the window?
   W Of course not.

18 언급하지 않은 내용 찾기

다음을 듣고, 여자가 방송에서 703 비행편에 대해 언급하지 않은 것을 고르시오.

① 출발지   ② 연착 이유
③ 연착되는 시간   ④ 도착지
⑤ 새로운 도착 시각

🔊 **Listening Tip**

We are sorry to tell you에서는 to가 약화되어 거의 소리 나지 않고, tell you는 반모음 /j/가 앞 자음 /l/의 영향을 받아 '테류'처럼 이어서 소리 나는 것에 유의하세요.

W Ladies and gentlemen, can I have your attention, please? We are sorry to 🔊 tell you that flight 703 from Incheon
_____ _____ _____
_____ because of _____ _____ .
The flight will be an hour and a half late. _____
_____ _____ _____ will be at
7:20 p.m. We'll give you _____ _____
_____ . Thank you.

19 이어질 응답 찾기

대화를 듣고, 남자의 마지막 말에 이어질 여자의 말로 가장 적절한 것을 고르시오.

Woman: _____

① Cheer up!
② That's too bad.
③ Good for you!
④ Thank you for coming.
⑤ I hope he gets well soon.

W You look very tired. What's the problem?
M I have a bad cold.
W Did you see a doctor?
M Not yet. I just _____ _____ _____
   at home.
W I don't think that's enough. Why don't you see a doctor?
M I want to, but I don't _____ _____
   _____ _____ today.
W Why not?
M I _____ _____ _____ my science
   project _____ _____ .

이어질 응답 찾기

대화를 듣고, 남자의 마지막 말에 이어질 여자의 말로 가장 적절한 것을 고르시오.

Woman: _____

① It's next Saturday.
② It's at the Sky Stadium.
③ Let's meet at the bus stop.
④ I play baseball at the park.
⑤ We can go there by subway.

W Eric, what are your plans for this weekend?

M Nothing special. How about you?

W I'm going to go to a baseball game.

M Are you going to _____ _____ _____?

W No, I'm going to go with _____ _____ _____ _____.

M Can I go with you?

W Of course. _____ _____ _____ _____ for you.

M Thank you. Then, I will buy some chicken. By the way, _____ _____ _____ _____?

실전 모의고사 **19**

01 다음을 듣고, 목요일 오후의 날씨로 가장 적절한 것을 고르시오.

① ② ③ ④ ⑤

02 대화를 듣고, 여자가 원하는 티셔츠의 디자인으로 가장 적절한 것을 고르시오.

①   ②   ③

④   ⑤

03 대화를 듣고, 남자가 예약하려는 비행기에 대해 언급하지 <u>않은</u> 것을 고르시오.

① 목적지　　② 출발 요일　　③ 출발지
④ 출발 시각　　⑤ 예매 인원수

04 대화를 듣고, 남자가 가장 좋아하는 책의 종류로 가장 적절한 것을 고르시오.

① 시집　　② 만화책　　③ 수필집
④ 역사책　　⑤ 탐정 소설

05 대화를 듣고, 두 사람이 대화하는 장소로 가장 적절한 것을 고르시오.

① 도서관　　② 공항　　③ 문구점
④ 선물 가게　　⑤ 컴퓨터 수리점

06 대화를 듣고, 여자의 마지막 말의 의도로 가장 적절한 것을 고르시오.

① 부탁　　② 설득　　③ 기원
④ 동의　　⑤ 거절

07 대화를 듣고, 여자가 서울에 돌아올 요일을 고르시오.

① 수요일　　② 목요일　　③ 금요일
④ 토요일　　⑤ 일요일

08 대화를 듣고, 여자가 대화 직후에 할 일로 가장 적절한 것을 고르시오.

① 짐 꾸리기　　② 자러 가기
③ 알람시계 맞추기　　④ 스웨터 찾아주기
⑤ 일기예보 확인하기

09 대화를 듣고, 남자가 소풍에 대해 언급하지 <u>않은</u> 것을 고르시오.

① 장소　　② 날짜　　③ 준비물
④ 활동 내용　　⑤ 복장

10 다음을 듣고, 남자가 하는 말의 내용으로 가장 적절한 것을 고르시오.

① 건강 검진 절차　　② 반입 금지 품목
③ 동물원 안전 수칙　　④ 동물원 시설 안내
⑤ 동물 먹이주기 금지

11 대화를 듣고, 두 사람이 보고 있는 사진에 대한 내용으로 일치하지 <u>않는</u> 것을 고르시오.

① 가족여행 때 찍은 사진이다.
② 사진 속 인물은 10명이다.
③ Jessie는 동그란 안경을 썼다.
④ 엄마는 Jessie 뒤에 서 있다.
⑤ 엄마는 머리가 짧다.

12 대화를 듣고, 남자가 물건을 파는 목적으로 가장 적절한 것을 고르시오.

① 이사 가기 위해서
② 중고 자전거를 사기 위해서
③ 새 컴퓨터를 사기 위해서
④ 자선단체에 기부하기 위해서
⑤ 엄마 생신 선물을 사기 위해서

13 대화를 듣고, 두 사람이 집에서 나갈 시각을 고르시오.
① 10:50 a.m. ② 10:55 a.m. ③ 11:00 a.m.
④ 11:10 a.m. ⑤ 11:15 a.m.

14 대화를 듣고, 두 사람의 관계로 가장 적절한 것을 고르시오.

① 매니저 – 모델   ② 의사 – 환자
③ 체육 교사 – 학생   ④ 가게 점원 – 손님
⑤ 코치 – 축구선수

15 대화를 듣고, 여자가 남자에게 부탁한 일로 가장 적절한 것을 고르시오.

① 보고서 쓰기   ② 치과 예약하기
③ 수영 가르쳐주기   ④ 책 반납하기
⑤ 병원에 같이 가기

16 대화를 듣고, 여자가 친구와 통화할 수 <u>없는</u> 이유로 가장 적절한 것을 고르시오.

① 잠을 자고 있어서
② 샤워를 하고 있어서
③ 슈퍼마켓에 가고 없어서
④ 전화기가 꺼져 있어서
⑤ 전화를 잘못 걸어서

17 다음 그림의 상황에 가장 적절한 대화를 고르시오.

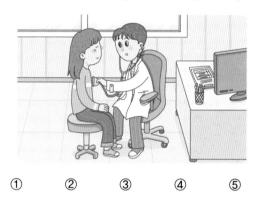

①   ②   ③   ④   ⑤

18 다음을 듣고, 남자가 학교 축제에 대해 언급하지 <u>않은</u> 것을 고르시오.
① 날짜   ② 공연   ③ 공연 시간
④ 음식   ⑤ 체험 행사

[19-20] 대화를 듣고, 남자의 마지막 말에 이어질 여자의 말로 가장 적절한 것을 고르시오.

19 Woman: _____

① I'm glad to see you.
② I'm very proud of myself.
③ She's interested in math.
④ I want her to be a teacher.
⑤ I'm happy to hear that. Thank you.

20 Woman: _____

① There are 5 of us.
② I'll go with my family.
③ I reserved a table for 5.
④ How about meeting at 7?
⑤ I invited 5 people to my birthday party.

정답 및 해설 p.120

---

01 날씨 파악

다음을 듣고, 목요일 오후의 날씨로 가장 적절한 것을 고르시오.

① ② ③ ④ ⑤

W Good morning! Let's check the weekly weather. On Monday and Tuesday, it will snow all day long. On Wednesday, _____ _____ _____ _____, and it will be sunny. On Thursday, it will be cloudy in the morning, but it _____ _____ _____ _____ in the afternoon. Starting Friday, it is going to be sunny, so this weekend will be _____ _____ _____ _____. Thank you for listening.

---

02 그림 정보 파악

대화를 듣고, 여자가 원하는 티셔츠의 디자인으로 가장 적절한 것을 고르시오.

① ② ③ Dragon Fire ④ Dragon Fire ⑤

M Let's make a T-shirt for our band club.
W That's a good idea.
M What type of a T-shirt do you want?
W I think a sleeveless one would be good _____ _____ _____ _____.
M I agree. Then, what about the design on _____ _____ _____ _____?
W I want to _____ _____ _____ on it. Since our band's name is Dragon Fire.
M How about writing "Dragon Fire" _____ _____ _____?
W Great. That will be nice.

---

03 언급하지 않은 내용 찾기

대화를 듣고, 남자가 예약하려는 비행기에 대해 언급하지 않은 것을 고르시오.

① 목적지   ② 출발 요일
③ 출발지   ④ 출발 시각
⑤ 예매 인원수

[Telephone rings.]
M Star Airlines. How may I help you?
W Yes, I'd like to make a reservation.
M Okay. Where are you _____ _____ _____?
W To Vancouver, Canada.

M _____ _____ would you like to leave?

W I'd like to leave _____ _____, the day after tomorrow.

M Okay. We _____ _____ _____ _____ Incheon International Airport at 5 p.m.

W That sounds good.

---

04 특정 정보 파악

대화를 듣고, 남자가 가장 좋아하는 책의 종류로 가장 적절한 것을 고르시오.

① 시집   ② 만화책   ③ 수필집
④ 역사책   ⑤ 탐정 소설

W Wow! You have many books in your room. Do you like reading books?

M Yes, I _____ _____ _____ in my free time.

W What kind of books do you read?

M I read _____ _____ _____ _____, like poetry books, mystery books, and history books.

W Which one do you like the most?

M I like _____ _____ _____ _____.

W _____ _____ _____ one of them to me sometime?

M Sure.

---

05 장소 추론

대화를 듣고, 두 사람이 대화하는 장소로 가장 적절한 것을 고르시오.

① 도서관   ② 공항   ③ 문구점
④ 선물 가게   ⑤ 컴퓨터 수리점

M Hi, _____ _____ _____ some bookmarks.

W Let me show you. *[Pause]* There are metal and plastic ones.

M Metal ones look nice. I'll _____ _____ _____ _____. How much is it?

W It's $3. Do you need anything else?

M Oh, I also need _____ _____ _____ _____ for my son.

W For writing tools, you have to go straight to section A. You can't miss it.

M Thank you so much _____ _____ _____.

06 의도 파악

대화를 듣고, 여자의 마지막 말의 의도로 가장 적절한 것을 고르시오.

① 부탁　② 설득　③ 기원
④ 동의　⑤ 거절

🔊 **Listening Tip**

모음과 자음 사이 또는 단어의 끝에서 /l/ 발음이 거의 들리지 않는 경우가 있어요. 즉, milk는 '밀크'가 아니라 '미역'처럼, film은 '휘염'처럼, oil은 '오여'처럼 들리는 게 여기에 해당해요.

M　Mom, my friend Tom is in the hospital.

W　Did something happen to him?

M　He fell down the subway stairs and _____ _____ _____ yesterday.

W　Oh, I hope it's not serious.

M　I'm going to _____ _____ _____ _____. What should I bring him?

W　How about some drinks? I think juice or soy 🔊milk would be nice.

M　That sounds good. I'll get _____ _____ _____ _____.

W　Good. I hope _____ _____ _____ _____.

07 특정 정보 파악

대화를 듣고, 여자가 서울에 돌아올 요일을 고르시오.

① 수요일　② 목요일　③ 금요일
④ 토요일　⑤ 일요일

M　You must be very excited about your trip to Jeju-do. How long are you planning to stay?

W　Not too long. I _____ _____ _____ _____ to do.

M　That's no good. When are you going to leave?

W　I'm going to leave this Thursday.

M　Then when are you getting back to Seoul?

W　I'll take the last plane _____ _____ _____.

M　You are going to stay there _____ _____ _____ _____? It's too bad you won't have enough time to enjoy the island.

W　I know.

08 할 일 파악

대화를 듣고, 여자가 대화 직후에 할 일로 가장 적절한 것을 고르시오.

① 짐 꾸리기　② 자러 가기
③ 알람시계 맞추기　④ 스웨터 찾아주기
⑤ 일기예보 확인하기

W　You look busy. What are you doing now?

M　I'm packing for a field trip tomorrow.

W　Don't _____ _____ _____. You have to wake up early tomorrow.

M　All right, Mom.

W　Oh, did you check the weather forecast?

M　Yes. The rain will stop late tonight and it'll be fine tomorrow.

W * Make sure you _____ _____
_____. It will get cold after the rain.

M I don't know where it is. Can you _____
_____ _____ _____, please?

W _____, _____ _____.

> ＊ 교육부 지정 의사소통 기능: **당부하기**   동(윤) 5 | Y(송) 2 | 지 4
> **Make sure you ~.** 너는 반드시 ~하도록 해.
> • **Make sure you** wear your seat belt. 너 반드시 안전벨트를 매도록 해.
> • **Make sure you** finish the work by five. 너 5시까지 반드시 그 일을 끝내도록 해.

09 언급하지 않은 내용 찾기

대화를 듣고, 남자가 소풍에 대해 언급하지 <u>않은</u>
것을 고르시오.

① 장소　　② 날짜　　③ 준비물
④ 활동 내용　⑤ 복장

M Did you hear about our school picnic?

W No, I didn't hear anything about it. _____
_____ _____ going to go?

M I heard we are going to go to Wonderland Park.

W The date is still the same, right? April 25th?

M Yes, _____ _____ _____
_____.

W Do I need to bring anything?

M We need to bring some _____ _____
_____ _____.

W Should we wear our school uniform or casual clothes?

M We have to _____ _____ _____.
It's for safety.

W I understand.

10 주제 추론

다음을 듣고, 남자가 하는 말의 내용으로 가장 적
절한 것을 고르시오.

① 건강 검진 절차
② 반입 금지 품목
③ 동물원 안전 수칙
④ 동물원 시설 안내
⑤ 동물 먹이주기 금지

M May I have your attention, please? Thank you for visiting
Singapore Zoo. We'd like to remind _____
_____ _____ _____ the animals
here. A lot of animals at our zoo get sick _____
_____ _____ _____ visitors give
them. We understand you like the animals, but please
_____ _____ _____ _____
_____. We hope you enjoy your time with the
animals. Thank you for listening.

일치하지 않는 내용 찾기

대화를 듣고, 두 사람이 보고 있는 사진에 대한 내용으로 일치하지 않는 것을 고르시오.

① 가족여행 때 찍은 사진이다.
② 사진 속 인물은 10명이다.
③ Jessie는 동그란 안경을 썼다.
④ 엄마는 Jessie 뒤에 서 있다.
⑤ 엄마는 머리가 짧다.

M That's a nice photo. When was this photo taken?

W It was taken _____ _____ _____ last weekend.

M There are 10 people in the photo.

W Yes. We are a big family.

M Who's this woman with the _____ _____ _____?

W She's my sister, Jessie. She is a high school student.

M Oh, I see. Who's the woman _____ _____ _____ _____ _____?

W She is my mother.

M She looks different now because of _____ _____ _____ and sunglasses.

---

12 목적 파악

대화를 듣고, 남자가 물건을 파는 목적으로 가장 적절한 것을 고르시오.

① 이사 가기 위해서
② 중고 자전거를 사기 위해서
③ 새 컴퓨터를 사기 위해서
④ 자선단체에 기부하기 위해서
⑤ 엄마 생신 선물을 사기 위해서

M Are you busy this afternoon?

W Not really. What's up?

M I'm going to the flea market. And I _____ _____ _____.

W Do you need help with something?

M I need to sell some things like my old bike. Can you help me _____ _____ to the market?

W No problem. Why do you _____ _____ _____ _____?

M I'm planning to _____ _____ _____ _____.

---

13 숫자 정보 파악 (시각)

대화를 듣고, 두 사람이 집에서 나갈 시각을 고르시오.

① 10:50 a.m. ② 10:55 a.m.
③ 11:00 a.m. ④ 11:10 a.m.
⑤ 11:15 a.m.

M Honey, what time does the train leave?

W _____ _____ _____ _____ 11:30 in the morning.

M It's 10 to 11 now. I think _____ _____ _____ _____ _____.

W No, we have enough time to get to the station.

M The traffic is terrible at this time. So, we'd better hurry.

W Okay. I'll _____ _____ _____ 5 minutes. _____ _____ _____ _____.

M All right.

W Sam, can I talk to you?

M Sure. Did I do something wrong, ma'am?

W No. _____ _____ _____ _____ the school soccer team?

M The soccer team?

W You run the fastest in the class. You help _____ _____ _____ _____ when you play in a team. I'm sure you'll be a good player.

M _____ _____ _____ _____ of the team?

W No, I'm not. I'm just _____ _____ _____. Mr. Cox is the coach.

M The math teacher?

W Yes, I can talk to him if you are interested.

M I'll think about it.

🔊 **Listening Tip**

서로 다른 자음이 연이어 나올 때, 앞에 오는 자음은 약화되어서 거의 들리지 않아요. 그래서 just found는 [t]가 약화되어 /저스파운드/처럼 들리는 것이에요.

W Jake, are you doing anything later this afternoon?

M Well, I'm _____ _____ _____ _____ to study for some tests.

W I see. Can I ask you a favor?

M Sure. What do you need?

W I 🔊 just found out that I have to _____ _____ _____ by today. But I have a dentist's appointment later.

M Where is your dentist?

W It's next to the fire station.

M _____ _____ _____ _____ the library.

W I know. Since you are going there, could _____ _____ _____ _____ for me?

M Of course.

16 이유 파악

대화를 듣고, 여자가 친구와 통화할 수 <u>없는</u> 이유로 가장 적절한 것을 고르시오.

① 잠을 자고 있어서
② 샤워를 하고 있어서
③ 슈퍼마켓에 가고 없어서
④ 전화기가 꺼져 있어서
⑤ 전화를 잘못 걸어서

[Cell phone rings.]

M　Hello.

W　Hi, Daniel. This is Irene.

M　Sorry, this is Andy, Daniel's brother. He ＿＿＿＿＿＿＿＿＿＿ ＿＿＿＿＿＿＿＿＿＿ ＿＿＿＿＿＿＿＿＿＿ of the house.

W　Hi, Andy. When is he coming back?

M　He ＿＿＿＿＿＿＿＿＿＿ ＿＿＿＿＿＿＿＿＿＿ ＿＿＿＿＿＿＿＿＿＿ ＿＿＿＿＿＿＿＿＿＿ to get something. Would you like to leave a message?

W　Please tell him to call me back when he comes back home.

M　Sure. Should I tell him to ＿＿＿＿＿＿＿＿＿＿ ＿＿＿＿＿＿＿＿＿＿ ＿＿＿＿＿＿＿＿＿＿ ＿＿＿＿＿＿＿＿＿＿ this number?

W　Yes, please.

M　Okay. I'll tell ＿＿＿＿＿＿＿＿＿＿ ＿＿＿＿＿＿＿＿＿＿ ＿＿＿＿＿＿＿＿＿＿.

17 그림 상황에 적절한 대화 찾기

다음 그림의 상황에 가장 적절한 대화를 고르시오.

①　②　③　④　⑤

① W　She had ＿＿＿＿＿＿＿＿＿＿ ＿＿＿＿＿＿＿＿＿＿ ＿＿＿＿＿＿＿＿＿＿ yesterday.

　 M　I'm sorry to hear that.

② W　What does your mother do?

　 M　She is a doctor.

③ W　I have a cough and a sore throat.

　 M　I think you ＿＿＿＿＿＿＿＿＿＿ ＿＿＿＿＿＿＿＿＿＿ ＿＿＿＿＿＿＿＿＿＿ ＿＿＿＿＿＿＿＿＿＿.

④ W　Take ＿＿＿＿＿＿＿＿＿＿ ＿＿＿＿＿＿＿＿＿＿ ＿＿＿＿＿＿＿＿＿＿ ＿＿＿＿＿＿＿＿＿＿.

　 M　I see. How much is it in all?

⑤ W　*I heard that your sister is ＿＿＿＿＿＿＿＿＿＿ ＿＿＿＿＿＿＿＿＿＿ ＿＿＿＿＿＿＿＿＿＿.

　 M　She broke her arm last week.

✳ 교육부 지정 의사소통 기능: 알고 있음 표현하기　　　금7

I heard that ~. 나는 ~라고 들었어.

• **I heard that** "8" is a lucky number in China. 나는 '8'이 중국에서 행운의 숫자라고 들었어.
• **I heard that** Paris is a beautiful city to visit.
　나는 파리가 방문하기에 아름다운 도시라고 들었어.

18 언급하지 않은 내용 찾기

다음을 듣고, 남자가 학교 축제에 대해 언급하지 않은 것을 고르시오.

① 날짜 ② 공연 ③ 공연 시간
④ 음식 ⑤ 체험 행사

M *[Beep]* Hi, Jessica. It's Eric. I'd like to invite you to my school festival. The festival _____ _____ _____ _____ October 14th and 15th. There will be _____ _____ by the famous dance group Dancing Machines. Also, we can buy _____ _____ _____ _____ at the food market. And we can _____ _____ _____ and make bracelets. It will be so much fun.

19 이어질 응답 찾기

대화를 듣고, 남자의 마지막 말에 이어질 여자의 말로 가장 적절한 것을 고르시오.

Woman: _____

① I'm glad to see you.
② I'm very proud of myself.
③ She's interested in math.
④ I want her to be a teacher.
⑤ I'm happy to hear that. Thank you.

W Hello. I'm Alice's mother.
M _____ _____ _____ Mrs. Taylor. I'm glad to meet you.
W Nice to meet you, too. _____ _____ _____ _____ this year?
M She's doing well. She studies hard, and her grades are excellent.
W Is that true? She was poor at math last year.
M Her math grade went up a lot this year. You should be _____ _____ _____ _____.

20 이어질 응답 찾기

대화를 듣고, 남자의 마지막 말에 이어질 여자의 말로 가장 적절한 것을 고르시오.

Woman: _____

① There are 5 of us.
② I'll go with my family.
③ I reserved a table for 5.
④ How about meeting at 7?
⑤ I invited 5 people to my birthday party.

[Telephone rings.]
M Hello. This is Joy Dining. How may I help you?
W I'd like to _____ _____ _____ for dinner.
M Okay. What day and time would you like?
W This Saturday at 7 p.m.
M Sorry, we _____ _____ _____ for 7 o'clock. Is 7:30 okay?
W Yes, that's fine.
M _____ _____ _____ are there _____ _____ _____?

실전 모의고사 **20**

01 다음을 듣고, 수요일 날씨로 가장 적절한 것을 고르시오.

①   ②   ③   ④   ⑤

02 대화를 듣고, 남자가 구입할 찻잔으로 가장 적절한 것을 고르시오.

①   ②   ③

④   ⑤

03 대화를 듣고, 남자가 여름 방학 사진에 대해 언급하지 <u>않은</u> 것을 고르시오.

① 촬영 시기 　　　　② 촬영 장소
③ 촬영한 사람 　　　④ 인화한 장소
⑤ 사진 속 인물

04 대화를 듣고, 여자가 사야 할 것으로 가장 적절한 것을 고르시오.

① 코트 　　② 털모자 　　③ 장갑
④ 목도리 　　⑤ 부츠

05 대화를 듣고, 두 사람이 대화하는 장소로 가장 적절한 것을 고르시오.

① 세탁소 　　② 옷 가게 　　③ 옷 대여점
④ 분실물 센터 　　⑤ 의류 회사

06 대화를 듣고, 여자의 마지막 말의 의도로 가장 적절한 것을 고르시오.

① 제안 　　② 요청 　　③ 사과
④ 경고 　　⑤ 실망

07 대화를 듣고, 남자가 구입할 물건으로 가장 적절한 것을 고르시오.

① 접시 　　② 스케이트보드 　③ 자전거
④ 보드게임 　　⑤ 스웨터

08 대화를 듣고, 여자가 대화 직후에 할 일로 가장 적절한 것을 고르시오.

① 숙제 제출하기 　　② 책 대출하기
③ 서점에 가기 　　④ 인터넷 서핑하기
⑤ 도서관 회원 가입하기

09 대화를 듣고, 남자가 취업 면접 때 언급하지 <u>않은</u> 것을 고르시오.

① 나이 　　② 출신 학교 　③ 직장
④ 연봉 　　⑤ 지원 분야

10 다음을 듣고, 여자가 하는 말의 내용으로 가장 적절한 것을 고르시오.

① 복식 호흡 방법 　　② 달리기의 효과
③ 스트레칭 방법 　　④ 식단 관리
⑤ 부상 위험 요인

11 대화를 듣고, 남자가 탈 기차에 대한 내용으로 일치하지 <u>않는</u> 것을 고르시오.

① 전주 행 기차이다.
② 출발 시각은 6시 30분이다.
③ 5번 플랫폼에서 출발한다.
④ 도착 시각은 3시이다.
⑤ 왕복 요금은 50달러이다.

12 대화를 듣고, 남자가 공원에 가는 목적으로 가장 적절한 것을 고르시오.

① 친구와 약속이 있어서
② 자전거를 타기 위해서
③ 걷기 운동을 하기 위해서
④ 애완견을 산책시키기 위해서
⑤ 길고양이에게 밥을 주기 위해서

13 대화를 듣고, 두 사람이 만날 시각을 고르시오.

① 2:20 p.m. ② 2:30 p.m. ③ 2:40 p.m.
④ 2:50 p.m. ⑤ 3:00 p.m.

14 대화를 듣고, 두 사람의 관계로 가장 적절한 것을 고르시오.

① 경찰관 – 운전자 ② 은행원 – 고객
③ 극장 직원 – 관람객 ④ 버스 기사 – 승객
⑤ 공항 직원 – 탑승객

15 대화를 듣고, 남자가 여자에게 부탁한 일로 가장 적절한 것을 고르시오.

① 드럼 연주하기 ② 면담 시간 정하기
③ 콘서트 표 예매하기 ④ 회의에 참여하기
⑤ 모임 시간 변경하기

16 대화를 듣고, 남자가 테니스 강습에 가지 <u>않은</u> 이유로 가장 적절한 것을 고르시오.

① 늦잠을 자서 ② 다리를 다쳐서
③ 동생을 돌봐야 해서 ④ 병원 예약이 있어서
⑤ 학업에 집중해야 해서

17 다음 그림의 상황에 가장 적절한 대화를 고르시오.

① ② ③ ④ ⑤

18 다음을 듣고, 남자가 자신의 담임 선생님에 대해 언급하지 <u>않은</u> 것을 고르시오.

① 이름 ② 가르치는 과목
③ 사는 곳 ④ 담당 동아리
⑤ 성격

[19-20] 대화를 듣고, 남자의 마지막 말에 이어질 여자의 말로 가장 적절한 것을 고르시오.

19 Woman: _____

① I'm very glad you came.
② Yes, the boxes are for me.
③ Sure. I'll get the door for you.
④ I'm sorry. You cannot be here.
⑤ No, thanks. I don't need any help.

20 Woman: _____

① The book costs $10.
② Return the books on time.
③ It's 100 won a day per book.
④ You don't have to pay for it.
⑤ I left my library card at my house.

Dictation 20

◇ 다시 듣고, 빈칸에 들어갈 알맞은 단어를 써보세요.

정답 및 해설 p.127

---

01 날씨 파악

다음을 듣고, 수요일 날씨로 가장 적절한 것을 고르시오.

① ② ③
④ ⑤

W Hello. Here is the weekly weather report for Seoul. On Monday, it will be _____ _____ _____ because of strong winds. On Tuesday, we will have a lot of rain. On Wednesday, the rain will stop, and the skies _____ _____ _____. From Thursday to Friday, it is _____ _____ _____ _____. Thank you.

---

02 그림 정보 파악

대화를 듣고, 남자가 구입할 찻잔으로 가장 적절한 것을 고르시오.

① ② ③
④ ⑤

W May I help you?

M Yes, please. I'm looking for a gift for my mother.

W How about this blue teacup _____ _____ _____?

M I like it, but my mother has the same one at home.

W Then, _____ _____ _____ pretty cup made of clay?

M You mean the one _____ _____ _____ _____ on it?

W Yes.

M That's nice. _____ _____ _____.

---

03 언급하지 않은 내용 찾기

대화를 듣고, 남자가 여름 방학 사진에 대해 언급하지 않은 것을 고르시오.

① 촬영 시기 ② 촬영 장소
③ 촬영한 사람 ④ 인화한 장소
⑤ 사진 속 인물

M Minji, do you want to see some photos from _____ _____ _____?

W Sure. Where did you go?

M My family visited my cousins in California. I _____ _____ _____ in Long Beach.

W These photos are amazing. [Pause] Who is this girl?

M That's my cousin, Emma.

W Oh, I thought _____ _____ _____ _____.

M No. _____ _____ _____ in this photo.

대화를 듣고, 여자가 사야 할 것으로 가장 적절한 것을 고르시오.

① 코트　　② 털모자　　③ 장갑
④ 목도리　　⑤ 부츠

M What are you going to do this winter vacation?

W I'm planning a ＿＿＿＿＿＿ ＿＿＿＿＿＿
＿＿＿＿＿＿ ＿＿＿＿＿＿.

M When are you ＿＿＿＿＿＿ ＿＿＿＿＿＿
＿＿＿＿＿＿?

W In January.

M What is the weather like in New York in January?

W It's ＿＿＿＿＿＿ ＿＿＿＿＿＿ ＿＿＿＿＿＿
＿＿＿＿＿＿. Actually, I need to buy a scarf and gloves.

M I have a few scarves. I'll give you one.

W Thanks a lot. I just have to ＿＿＿＿＿＿ ＿＿＿＿＿＿,
then.

대화를 듣고, 두 사람이 대화하는 장소로 가장 적절한 것을 고르시오.

① 세탁소　　　　② 옷 가게
③ 옷 대여점　　　④ 분실물 센터
⑤ 의류 회사

M May I help you, ma'am?

W I'd like to complain about this blouse.

M What's wrong with it?

W I wanted to ＿＿＿＿＿＿ ＿＿＿＿＿＿ ＿＿＿＿＿＿
my birthday party, but I couldn't wear it because 2 buttons were missing.

M I'm so sorry. Would you like to ＿＿＿＿＿＿
＿＿＿＿＿＿ or get a refund?

W I'd like to ＿＿＿＿＿＿ ＿＿＿＿＿＿ ＿＿＿＿＿＿,
please.

M Do you ＿＿＿＿＿＿ ＿＿＿＿＿＿ ＿＿＿＿＿＿?

W Yes. Here it is.

대화를 듣고, 여자의 마지막 말의 의도로 가장 적절한 것을 고르시오.

① 제안　　② 요청　　③ 사과
④ 경고　　⑤ 실망

W Matthew, do you know what time it is now?

M Yes, ma'am. It's 9:30.

W By what time ＿＿＿＿＿＿ ＿＿＿＿＿＿ ＿＿＿＿＿＿
to school?

M By 8:30. ＿＿＿＿＿＿ ＿＿＿＿＿＿ ＿＿＿＿＿＿.

W Do you know that this is your third time this week?

M The third time? I promise I _____ _____ _____ _____.

W If you're late again, _____ _____ _____ _____ clean your classroom for a month.

07 특정 정보 파악

대화를 듣고, 남자가 구입할 물건으로 가장 적절한 것을 고르시오.

① 접시
② 스케이트보드
③ 자전거
④ 보드게임
⑤ 스웨터

M There are so many things here at the market.

W People came out to sell those because _____ _____ _____ _____ any more.

M I can't believe everything here is used. Look at that bike. That looks new to me.

W Yes. Are you going to _____ _____ _____?

M I am not sure.

W Look at this sweater. I think it'll _____ _____ _____ _____. It's only $4.

M Really? That's so cheap. _____ _____ _____.

08 할 일 파악

대화를 듣고, 여자가 대화 직후에 할 일로 가장 적절한 것을 고르시오.

① 숙제 제출하기
② 책 대출하기
③ 서점에 가기
④ 인터넷 서핑하기
⑤ 도서관 회원 가입하기

🔊 Listening Tip

t, d는 모음 사이에서 부드럽게 발음되어 'ㄹ'처럼 소리가 나요. 그래서 get enough은 /게리넙/처럼 들리는 것이죠.

M What are you doing here, Vicky?

W I'm doing my art homework. I found _____ _____ _____ here.

M What is your topic?

W It's about artists of the 19th century. I am reading books about the paintings of famous artists at that time.

M It's 5:45. The library will close soon.

W Really? I didn't 🔊 get enough information _____ _____ _____.

M Why don't you search more _____ _____ _____ at home?

W That's a good idea. I'll _____ _____ _____ first.

09 언급하지 않은 내용 찾기

대화를 듣고, 남자가 취업 면접 때 언급하지 않은 것을 고르시오.

① 나이　② 출신 학교　③ 직장
④ 연봉　⑤ 지원 분야

W Can you tell me about yourself?

M Yes, my name is Benjamin Smith. I'm 30 years old. I _____ _____ Yale University 3 years ago. I studied law in school and _____ _____ _____ _____ a law firm in Manhattan.

W How long have you been working there?

M For about 2 years.

W Why do you want to change your job?

M I've been interested in _____ _____ since I was young. I'd really like to work in _____ _____ _____.

10 주제 추론

다음을 듣고, 여자가 하는 말의 내용으로 가장 적절한 것을 고르시오.

① 복식 호흡 방법　② 달리기의 효과
③ 스트레칭 방법　④ 식단 관리
⑤ 부상 위험 요인

W Listen up! Stretching is _____ _____ _____. Follow me. Sit down on the floor. Your legs have to be straight out in front of you. _____ _____ _____ and bend your body forward. When you do that, hold your ankles and take a deep breath. If you _____ _____ _____, you won't get _____ _____ _____.

11 일치하지 않는 내용 찾기

대화를 듣고, 남자가 탈 기차에 대한 내용으로 일치하지 않는 것을 고르시오.

① 전주 행 기차이다.
② 출발 시각은 6시 30분이다.
③ 5번 플랫폼에서 출발한다.
④ 도착 시각은 3시이다.
⑤ 왕복 요금은 50달러이다.

M Excuse me, does _____ _____ _____ Jeonju leave at 7?

W No, _____ _____ _____ 6:30.

M Where do I take it?

W You have to go downstairs.

M How long does it take to Jeonju?

W It takes 3 hours, so _____ _____ _____ _____ 9:30.

M How much is the ticket?

W One way costs $25, and _____ _____ _____ $50.

M 2 round-trip tickets, please.

12 목적 파악

대화를 듣고, 남자가 공원에 가는 목적으로 가장 적절한 것을 고르시오.

① 친구와 약속이 있어서
② 자전거를 타기 위해서
③ 걷기 운동을 하기 위해서
④ 애완견을 산책시키기 위해서
⑤ 길고양이에게 밥을 주기 위해서

M Hi, Susan. What are you doing here?

W I'm _____ _____ _____
_____ my friends. How about you?

M I'm _____ _____ _____
_____. This is my dog, Max.

W He's pretty big. What kind of dog is he?

M He's a Jindo dog. He's 2 years old.

W I see. *How often do you walk him?

M I walk him _____ _____ _____
for an hour every day.

W _____ _____ _____
_____ going to the park.

M That's right.

＊ 교육부 지정 의사소통 기능: 빈도 묻고 답하기　　　　미 8

How often do you ~? 얼마나 자주 ~하니?

A: **How often do you** clean your room? 너는 얼마나 자주 네 방을 청소하니?
B: I clean my room three times a week. 나는 일주일에 세 번 내 방을 청소해.

---

13 숫자 정보 파악 (시각)

대화를 듣고, 두 사람이 만날 시각을 고르시오.

① 2:20 p.m.　　② 2:30 p.m.
③ 2:40 p.m.　　④ 2:50 p.m.
⑤ 3:00 p.m.

M Do you have any plans for tomorrow afternoon?

W No, I don't have anything.

M Do you want to go to a basketball game at the school gym?

W Well, I don't know _____ _____
_____.

M Me neither. But _____ _____
_____ to cheer for our school team.

W You're right. What time does the game start?

M _____ _____ _____ 3:00. How
about meeting 20 minutes _____ _____
_____?

W Sure.

14 관계 추론

대화를 듣고, 두 사람의 관계로 가장 적절한 것을 고르시오.

① 경찰관 – 운전자
② 은행원 – 고객
③ 극장 직원 – 관람객
④ 버스 기사 – 승객
⑤ 공항 직원 – 탑승객

W Good evening. May I _____ _____ _____, please?

M Yes, here it is.

W Thank you. Please do not take any photos or videos _____ _____ _____.

M All right. Can I bring this coffee inside?

W No. You can _____ _____ _____ _____ into the room.

M Okay. Oh, can you tell me where the restroom is?

W It's _____ _____ _____ over there.

M Thanks.

15 부탁 파악

대화를 듣고, 남자가 여자에게 부탁한 일로 가장 적절한 것을 고르시오.

① 드럼 연주하기
② 면담 시간 정하기
③ 콘서트 표 예매하기
④ 회의에 참여하기
⑤ 모임 시간 변경하기

🔊 **Listening Tip**
자음이 중복되는 경우, 자음을 두 번 발음하지 않고 한번만 발음해요. 그래서 drummer는 /드럼머/가 아니라 /드러머/로 발음하죠. summer를 /서머/로 발음하는 것과 같아요.

W Hi, Anthony. Can I talk to you for a minute?

M Sure. What's up?

W We have a band club meeting at 3:30. _____ _____ _____ _____?

M I'm sorry, I can't. I have a meeting with Mr. Evans at 3.

W You _____ _____ _____ _____ you're the 🔊drummer.

M Then, _____ _____ _____ _____ 30 minutes later?

W Okay. See you then.

16 이유 파악

대화를 듣고, 남자가 테니스 강습에 가지 않은 이유로 가장 적절한 것을 고르시오.

① 늦잠을 자서
② 다리를 다쳐서
③ 동생을 돌봐야 해서
④ 병원 예약이 있어서
⑤ 학업에 집중해야 해서

W Mike, I didn't see you at the tennis lesson earlier.

M Right, I had to miss it today. Actually, I don't think I can play tennis for a while.

W What's wrong? _____ _____ _____ _____?

M No. I'm not getting good grades in school. So I have to _____ _____ _____.

W Oh, I'm sorry _____ _____ _____.

M Don't worry. I'll _____ _____ _____ _____ and start taking tennis lessons again.

17 그림 상황에 적절한 대화 찾기

다음 그림의 상황에 가장 적절한 대화를 고르시오.

① ② ③ ④ ⑤

① W I'd like to _____ _____ _____ .

　 M Can you show me _____ _____ _____ ?

② W How long can I borrow these books?

　 M For 10 days.

③ W I'm looking for _____ _____ _____ .

　 M They're in the living section over there.

④ W Could _____ _____ _____ the volume?

　 M Sorry. I didn't know it was so loud.

⑤ W He is being noisy in the library.

　 M I can't stand it any longer.

> ✳ 교육부 지정 의사소통 기능: **화냄 표현하기**　　　　능(양) 8
>
> **I can't stand it.** 나는 정말 참을 수가 없어.
>
> • My brother broke my bike again. **I can't stand it.**
> 　내 남동생이 또 내 자전거를 망가뜨렸어. 나는 정말 참을 수가 없어.
> • The man plays loud music late at night. **I can't stand it.**
> 　그 남자는 밤에 늦게 시끄러운 음악을 틀어. 나는 정말 참을 수가 없어.

18 언급하지 않은 내용 찾기

다음을 듣고, 남자가 자신의 담임 선생님에 대해 언급하지 않은 것을 고르시오.

① 이름　　　　② 가르치는 과목
③ 사는 곳　　　④ 담당 동아리
⑤ 성격

M Let me introduce you to my homeroom teacher. Her name is Emily King and she is 35 years old. _____ _____ _____ . She is married and has a son. She is also _____ _____ _____ _____ badminton. She is the most popular teacher in school because she is very _____ _____ .

19 이어질 응답 찾기

대화를 듣고, 남자의 마지막 말에 이어질 여자의 말로 가장 적절한 것을 고르시오.

Woman: _____

① I'm very glad you came.
② Yes, the boxes are for me.
③ Sure. I'll get the door for you.
④ I'm sorry. You cannot be here.
⑤ No, thanks. I don't need any help.

M Clara, you look so busy. Is there something I can help with?

W Sure. Thanks. *[Pause]* Let's see...

M What are _____ _____ _____ ?

W They're boxes of presents for club members. Oh, can you move those boxes for me?

M Okay. Where do you _____ _____ _____ ?

W To Mr. Lee's office.

M All right. Can you open the door and _____ _____ _____ _____ _____ ?

대화를 듣고, 남자의 마지막 말에 이어질 여자의 말로 가장 적절한 것을 고르시오.

Woman: _____

① The book costs $10.
② Return the books on time.
③ It's 100 won a day per book.
④ You don't have to pay for it.
⑤ I left my library card at my house.

M Excuse me. Can I check out these 5 books?

W No, I'm sorry. You _____ _____ _____ borrow only 3 books at a time.

M Oh, I see. I'll borrow these 3, then. And how long can I _____ _____ _____ ?

W For 3 weeks. If you bring them back late, you have to pay a fee.

M _____ _____ _____ _____ _____ ?

PART. 03

Listening Q

^^^

중학영어듣기 모의고사

고난도 모의고사

✕

실전 모의고사보다 한 단계 높은 고난도 모의고사 4회로
듣기 모의고사 만점을 향해 Listening Q!

고난도 모의고사 01

정답 및 해설 p.133

01 다음을 듣고, 내일 아침 날씨로 가장 적절한 것을 고르시오.

①
②
③
④
⑤

02 대화를 듣고, 여자가 구입할 손목시계로 가장 적절한 것을 고르시오.

①
②
③

④
⑤

03 대화를 듣고, 남자가 새로 온 전학생에 대해 언급하지 않은 것을 고르시오.

① 이름   ② 예전 학교   ③ 사는 곳
④ 취미   ⑤ 입고 있는 옷

04 대화를 듣고, 남자가 반품하려는 물건을 고르시오.

① 넥타이   ② 조각품   ③ 신발
④ 재킷   ⑤ 모형 배

05 대화를 듣고, 두 사람이 대화하는 장소로 가장 적절한 곳을 고르시오.

① 분실물 센터   ② 열쇠 가게
③ 선물 가게   ④ 커피숍
⑤ 전자제품 수리 센터

06 대화를 듣고, 남자가 한 마지막 말의 의도로 가장 적절한 것을 고르시오.

① 비난   ② 후회   ③ 격려
④ 동의   ⑤ 칭찬

07 대화를 듣고, 남자가 동물원에서 구경하지 못한 동물을 고르시오.

① 여우   ② 늑대   ③ 사자
④ 호랑이   ⑤ 북극곰

08 대화를 듣고, 여자가 대화 직후에 할 일로 가장 적절한 것을 고르시오.

① 체온 재기   ② 병원에 데려가기
③ 전화하기   ④ 문자 보내기
⑤ 따뜻한 차 가져오기

09 대화를 듣고, 남자가 원하는 가방에 대해 언급하지 않은 것을 고르시오.

① 디자인   ② 모양   ③ 색상
④ 재질   ⑤ 주머니 개수

10 다음을 듣고, 남자가 하는 말의 내용으로 가장 적절한 것을 고르시오.

① 자원봉사 활동 안내   ② 최신 운동기구 소개
③ 마라톤 대회 홍보   ④ 공공질서 준수 촉구
⑤ 환경 보호의 중요성

228   Listening Q 중학영어듣기 모의고사 2

11 대화를 듣고, 남자의 호주 여행에 대한 내용으로 일치하지 <u>않는</u> 것을 고르시오.

① 2년 전에 갔다.
② 온 가족이 함께 갔다.
③ 가족의 첫 해외여행이었다.
④ 시드니 오페라 하우스에 들렀다.
⑤ 여행 기간이 15일이었다.

12 대화를 듣고, 남자가 전화를 건 목적으로 가장 적절한 것을 고르시오.

① 딸에게 연락하기 위해서
② 교장 선생님을 만나기 위해서
③ 학교 도서관에서 봉사하기 위해서
④ 도서관 이용 시간을 알기 위해서
⑤ 도서관 사서 모집에 지원하기 위해서

13 대화를 듣고, TV 설치 기사가 방문할 시각을 고르시오.
① 3:00 p.m.   ② 3:30 p.m.   ③ 4:00 p.m.
④ 4:30 p.m.   ⑤ 5:00 p.m.

14 대화를 듣고, 두 사람의 관계로 가장 적절한 것을 고르시오.

① 영화배우 – 팬   ② 시장 – 기자
③ 정치인 – 시민   ④ 방송 진행자 – 작가
⑤ 선거 입후보자 – 유권자

15 대화를 듣고, 여자가 남자에게 부탁한 일로 가장 적절한 것을 고르시오.

① 선물 추천하기
② 온라인으로 주문하기
③ 선물 제시간에 전달하기
④ 쇼핑몰에 함께 가기
⑤ 선물 내용 비밀로 하기

16 대화를 듣고, 남자가 숙제를 하지 <u>못한</u> 이유로 가장 적절한 것을 고르시오.

① 게임을 하느라고
② 만화영화를 보느라고
③ 마감 시한을 잘못 알아서
④ 컴퓨터가 고장 나서
⑤ 인터넷 연결에 문제가 생겨서

17 다음 그림의 상황에 가장 적절한 대화를 고르시오.

①   ②   ③   ④   ⑤

18 다음을 듣고, 여자가 New Curry House에 대해 언급하지 <u>않은</u> 것을 고르시오.

① 위치   ② 판매하는 카레 종류
③ 카레 가격   ④ 카레 요리의 장점
⑤ 배달 주문 방법

[19-20] 대화를 듣고, 여자의 마지막 말에 이어질 남자의 말로 가장 적절한 것을 고르시오.

19 Man: _____

① No, I can't call you back.
② Yes, she'll be 15 years old.
③ Yes, I'll make an appointment later.
④ No, please don't leave a message.
⑤ Sorry, but can I come at 9:30 instead?

20 Man: _____

① I gave it to you 2 days ago.
② It was mailed to the wrong house.
③ I had to return it to the teacher.
④ I finished my science report yesterday.
⑤ My teacher sent a Christmas card to me.

Dictation 01

◇ 다시 듣고, 빈칸에 들어갈 알맞은 단어를 써보세요.

정답 및 해설 p.133

---

01 날씨 파악

다음을 듣고, 내일 아침 날씨로 가장 적절한 것을 고르시오.

① ② ③ ④ ⑤

M Good evening, everyone! The weather today was very changeable. It started _____ _____ _____ _____, but it was pouring in the afternoon. Luckily, we won't see anything _____ _____ _____ tomorrow morning, but _____ _____ _____ a little cloudy in the afternoon.

---

02 그림 정보 파악

대화를 듣고, 여자가 구입할 손목시계로 가장 적절한 것을 고르시오.

① ② ③ ④ ⑤

M What can I do for you, ma'am?
W I'm looking for a watch for my younger brother.
M Are you looking for anything in particular?
W I think my brother would prefer one with _____ _____ _____.
M Okay. These digital watches are really popular now.
W They look nice, but he already has one.
M I see. Then how about this round watch? The _____ _____ _____ on it.
W Great. _____ _____ _____ then.

---

03 언급하지 않은 내용 찾기

대화를 듣고, 남자가 새로 온 전학생에 대해 언급하지 않은 것을 고르시오.

① 이름 ② 예전 학교 ③ 사는 곳
④ 취미 ⑤ 입고 있는 옷

M Mina, have you met Adam yet?
W Adam? Adam who?
M It's Adam Brown. Today is his first day. He's _____ _____ _____ _____ Waterloo Middle School.
W I didn't know there was a new student in our school.
M He is also going to join our chess club. _____ _____ is his hobby.
W Great. [Pause] Oh, is that Adam over there?
M Yes, that's him. The one in _____ _____ _____.

대화를 듣고, 남자가 반품하려는 물건을 고르시오.

① 넥타이　② 조각품　③ 신발
④ 재킷　⑤ 모형 배

[Telephone rings.]

W Thank you for calling Fancy Clothing.

M Hello. I ordered a necktie 3 days ago, but I _____ _____ _____ yet.

W Let me check your order. May I have your name, please?

M It's Chris Moon.

W The tie was sent today, so you should get it tomorrow.

M That's great. Oh, also I'd like to return _____ _____ _____ _____. How do I do that?

W First, you have to fill out a request form. Then we'll send the delivery man to _____ _____ _____ _____.

M All right. I'll do that. Thank you very much.

대화를 듣고, 두 사람이 대화하는 장소로 가장 적절한 곳을 고르시오.

① 분실물 센터　② 열쇠 가게
③ 선물 가게　④ 커피숍
⑤ 전자제품 수리 센터

M Can I _____ _____ _____ anything?

W Yes, where can I find candles?

M The candles are _____ _____ _____.

W Okay. Do you also have coffee mugs?

M Yes. They _____ _____ _____ _____ the candles.

W Thanks. I want to get one for my mother.

M _____ _____ _____ _____ I can do for you?

W No, that's all. Thank you.

대화를 듣고, 남자가 한 마지막 말의 의도로 가장 적절한 것을 고르시오.

① 비난　② 후회　③ 격려
④ 동의　⑤ 칭찬

M Are you ready to go, Mary?

W I'll be ready in about 5 minutes.

M Okay. *[Pause]* Oh no! It's pouring out there.

W Really? _____ _____ _____ _____ in the forecast for tonight.

M   I know. I can't believe it.

W   Will it be ＿＿＿＿＿＿ ＿＿＿＿＿＿ ＿＿＿＿＿＿?

M   I don't know if I'll be able to see anything.

W   I think we should just ＿＿＿＿＿＿ ＿＿＿＿＿＿
＿＿＿＿＿＿ ＿＿＿＿＿＿ tonight.

M   ＿＿＿＿＿＿ ＿＿＿＿＿＿ ＿＿＿＿＿＿,
＿＿＿＿＿＿. Driving in this rain is not a good idea.

---

07 특정 정보 파악

대화를 듣고, 남자가 동물원에서 구경하지 <u>못한</u>
동물을 고르시오.

① 여우   ② 늑대   ③ 사자
④ 호랑이   ⑤ 북극곰

W   Did you have fun at the zoo, Jason?

M   Yes, Mom. I saw many animals close up for the first time.

W   What animal did you like most?

M   I liked the wolves and foxes most. The trainer there also
explained ＿＿＿＿＿＿ ＿＿＿＿＿＿ ＿＿＿＿＿＿
＿＿＿＿＿＿.

W   That's nice. Did you get to see lions and tigers too?

M   I ＿＿＿＿＿＿ ＿＿＿＿＿＿ ＿＿＿＿＿＿, but there
weren't any tigers.

W   Oh, I thought ＿＿＿＿＿＿ ＿＿＿＿＿＿ ＿＿＿＿＿＿
＿＿＿＿＿＿ there.

M   The only white animal I saw was a polar bear.

---

08 할 일 파악

대화를 듣고, 여자가 대화 직후에 할 일로 가장 적
절한 것을 고르시오.

① 체온 재기   ② 병원에 데려가기
③ 전화하기   ④ 문자 보내기
⑤ 따뜻한 차 가져오기

M   Mom, I haven't been feeling well since yesterday.

W   Really? Then why didn't you tell me earlier?

M   I thought I was just tired.

W   Let me check. [Pause] Oh, ＿＿＿＿＿＿ ＿＿＿＿＿＿
＿＿＿＿＿＿ ＿＿＿＿＿＿ a fever.

M   I think I have the flu, Mom.

W   I think you'll have to miss school today. I'll call your teacher
now.

M   But it's 6 in the morning. I think it's a little early
＿＿＿＿＿＿ ＿＿＿＿＿＿ ＿＿＿＿＿＿
＿＿＿＿＿＿ now.

W   Yes, you're right. ＿＿＿＿＿＿ ＿＿＿＿＿＿
＿＿＿＿＿＿ a text message instead.

09 언급하지 않은 내용 찾기

대화를 듣고, 남자가 원하는 가방에 대해 언급하지 않은 것을 고르시오.

① 디자인 ② 모양 ③ 색상
④ 재질 ⑤ 주머니 개수

W Isn't your backpack too small, Peter?

M Yes, Mom. I need a new backpack.

W ＿＿＿＿＿＿ ＿＿＿＿＿＿ ＿＿＿＿＿＿
＿＿＿＿＿＿ do you want?

M I want one that I can use in high school, too.

W Then, it ＿＿＿＿＿＿ ＿＿＿＿＿＿ a simple design.

M Right. I'd like a square one ＿＿＿＿＿＿ ＿＿＿＿＿＿.

W Okay. Is there anything else?

M I also ＿＿＿＿＿＿ ＿＿＿＿＿＿ ＿＿＿＿＿＿
2 pockets.

10 주제 추론

다음을 듣고, 남자가 하는 말의 내용으로 가장 적절한 것을 고르시오.

① 자원봉사 활동 안내
② 최신 운동기구 소개
③ 마라톤 대회 홍보
④ 공공질서 준수 촉구
⑤ 환경 보호의 중요성

M Thank you for your time today. Before I let you go, I'd like to tell you about an event called the Green Day Marathon. I know the word "marathon" ＿＿＿＿＿＿ ＿＿＿＿＿＿ ＿＿＿＿＿＿ to some of you, but you can bring your kids and ＿＿＿＿＿＿ ＿＿＿＿＿＿ ＿＿＿＿＿＿ ＿＿＿＿＿＿. We're trying to ＿＿＿＿＿＿ ＿＿＿＿＿＿ ＿＿＿＿＿＿ ＿＿＿＿＿＿ the dangers of global warming. This is a family event that all of you will enjoy!

11 일치하지 않는 내용 찾기

대화를 듣고, 남자의 호주 여행에 대한 내용으로 일치하지 않는 것을 고르시오.

① 2년 전에 갔다.
② 온 가족이 함께 갔다.
③ 가족의 첫 해외 여행이었다.
④ 시드니 오페라 하우스에 들렀다.
⑤ 여행 기간이 15일이었다.

W Have you been to Australia, Paul?

M Yes, I have. I went there 2 years ago.

W Really? Who did you go with?

M I went ＿＿＿＿＿＿ ＿＿＿＿＿＿ ＿＿＿＿＿＿
＿＿＿＿＿＿.

W Was it a family vacation?

M Yes, it was. And it was our ＿＿＿＿＿＿ ＿＿＿＿＿＿
＿＿＿＿＿＿.

W Did you go to Sydney?

M Of course, we did. We took a picture ＿＿＿＿＿＿
＿＿＿＿＿＿ ＿＿＿＿＿＿ the Sydney Opera House.

W Wow, I'm sure you had a wonderful time.

M Yes, we did. It was a 10-day trip, but ＿＿＿＿＿＿
＿＿＿＿＿＿ ＿＿＿＿＿＿ ＿＿＿＿＿＿.

12 목적 파악

대화를 듣고, 남자가 전화를 건 목적으로 가장 적절한 것을 고르시오.

① 딸에게 연락하기 위해서
② 교장 선생님을 만나기 위해서
③ 학교 도서관에서 봉사하기 위해서
④ 도서관 이용 시간을 알기 위해서
⑤ 도서관 사서 모집에 지원하기 위해서

[Telephone rings.]

W Martha Middle School. How may I help you?

M Hi, my name is John Sales, and my daughter goes to your school.

W Do you want to leave a message for her?

M No, I want to know if you still _____ _____ _____.

W Oh, are you calling _____ _____ _____ at the school library?

M Yes, I am.

W Wonderful! Can you _____ _____ _____ _____ sometime between 11 and 1 today?

M Sure. I will come by at 12:30.

---

13 숫자 정보 파악 (시각)

대화를 듣고, TV 설치 기사가 방문할 시각을 고르시오.

① 3:00 p.m. ② 3:30 p.m. ③ 4:00 p.m.
④ 4:30 p.m. ⑤ 5:00 p.m.

[Telephone rings.]

W Hello.

M Hello. Can I speak to Mrs. Larson, please?

W This is she. May I ask who's calling?

M My name is James Carter, and I'm calling to _____ _____ _____ for repairing your TV.

W I think I _____ _____ _____ _____ 3 p.m. today. Is that correct?

M That is correct, ma'am.

W I'm sorry, but _____ _____ _____ _____ 4 instead? I need to pick up my son at 3.

M 4 o'clock _____ _____ _____.

W Thank you so much.

---

14 관계 추론

대화를 듣고, 두 사람의 관계로 가장 적절한 것을 고르시오.

① 영화배우 – 팬
② 시장 – 기자
③ 정치인 – 시민
④ 방송 진행자 – 작가
⑤ 선거 입후보자 – 유권자

M Thank you for your time, Ms. Pederson.

W It's my pleasure, and I'm sorry I only _____ _____ _____ _____.

M It's okay. I understand you are very busy. So, when 🔊 did you start your career?

W When I was _____ _____ _____.

M How did you _____ _____ _____ politics?

W I started working at the mayor's office.

M And now you're _____ _____ _____ _____ of this city.

W Yes. Time really flies.

🔊) Listening Tip

/d/ 소리로 끝나는 단어 뒤에 y로 시작하는 단어가 오면 두 소리가 합쳐져 /쥬/로 발음이 됩니다. 따라서 did you 는 /디드 유/가 아닌 /디쥬/로 소리납니다.

---

15 부탁 파악

대화를 듣고, 여자가 남자에게 부탁한 일로 가장 적절한 것을 고르시오.

① 선물 추천하기
② 온라인으로 주문하기
③ 선물 제시간에 전달하기
④ 쇼핑몰에 함께 가기
⑤ 선물 내용 비밀로 하기

W I need to buy a sweater for my dad. His birthday is this Saturday.

M I know _____ _____ _____ _____ men's clothing.

W I don't think shopping online is a good idea.

M Why do you say that?

W There are only 3 days until Saturday. The delivery could _____ _____ _____ _____.

M You are right. Some deliveries can take 5 days.

W Yes, so I'm planning to go to the shopping mall later today. Can you _____ _____ _____?

M Of course. I was going to _____ _____ _____ _____ today anyway.

---

16 이유 파악

대화를 듣고, 남자가 숙제를 하지 <u>못한</u> 이유로 가장 적절한 것을 고르시오.

① 게임을 하느라고
② 만화영화를 보느라고
③ 마감 시한을 잘못 알아서
④ 컴퓨터가 고장 나서
⑤ 인터넷 연결에 문제가 생겨서

M When do we have history class today?

W I think it is after lunch. Why?

M I need to talk to the teacher before class today.

W Oh, _____ _____ _____ _____ before history class?

M No, I'm not. I didn't do my homework last night.

W You _____ _____ _____. Did something happen?

M Well, there was _____ _____ _____ the 🔊 Internet connection at home. So, I couldn't finish my homework.

W That's too bad.

🔊) Listening Tip

보통 'n' 뒤에 오는 't'는 발음이 되지 않습니다. 따라서 Internet는 /이너넷/ 혹은 /이널넷/으로 소리가 납니다. winter도 마찬가지로 /위널/처럼 발음됩니다.

17 그림 상황에 적절한 대화 찾기

다음 그림의 상황에 가장 적절한 대화를 고르시오.

① ② ③ ④ ⑤

① **M** Excuse me. Where can I find bananas?

   W Fruits are right _____ _____

   _____ _____.

② **M** What do you think of this shirt, Mom?

   W You should get a larger one. _____

   _____ _____ for you.

③ **M** Excuse me. Can I give this to the monkey?

   W No, _____ _____ _____ is not

   allowed in this zoo.

④ **M** Where do you want to _____ _____

   _____ ?

   W I know a really good Italian restaurant.

⑤ **M** Excuse me. How much is the admission?

   W It's $15.

18 언급하지 않은 내용 찾기

다음을 듣고, 여자가 New Curry House에 대해 언급하지 않은 것을 고르시오.

① 위치   ② 판매하는 카레 종류
③ 카레 가격   ④ 카레 요리의 장점
⑤ 배달 주문 방법

W If you've never had real curry, you have to try the New Curry House. It is _____ _____ Vermont Avenue and 3rd Street. At the New Curry House, you can choose from 20 different kinds of _____ _____ all over the world and they are _____ _____ $6! As you may know, curry is not only delicious but also

_____ _____ _____

_____. Pay us a visit, and you won't be disappointed!

19 이어질 응답 찾기

대화를 듣고, 여자의 마지막 말에 이어질 남자의 말로 가장 적절한 것을 고르시오.

Man: _____

① No, I can't call you back.
② Yes, she'll be 15 years old.
③ Yes, I'll make an appointment later.
④ No, please don't leave a message.
⑤ Sorry, but can I come at 9:30 instead?

[Telephone rings.]

M Hello.

W Hello, may I speak to Mr. Woo?

M This is he. May I _____ _____

   _____ ?

W My name is Jennifer Baker from James Middle School.

M Yes, I left you a message about my daughter.

W _____ _____ _____

_____ an appointment with a counselor, right?

M Right, I need to talk about my daughter's _____

_____ .

W Okay. _____ _____ _____

_____ 9 in the morning?

20 이어질 응답 찾기

대화를 듣고, 여자의 마지막 말에 이어질 남자의
말로 가장 적절한 것을 고르시오.

Man: _____

① I gave it to you 2 days ago.
② It was mailed to the wrong house.
③ I had to return it to the teacher.
④ I finished my science report yesterday.
⑤ My teacher sent a Christmas card to
me.

W Have you received your report card, Jamie?

M No, I haven't, Mom.

W That's strange. I received an e-mail from your school saying
that they sent the report cards.

M Oh, I received a report card 3 days ago, but _____

_____ _____ _____ .

W *What do you mean?

M Teacher _____ _____ _____ , so
we're getting a new one tomorrow.

W But the grades were correct, right?

M Yes, they were.

W Then, _____ _____ _____

_____ with the one you received 3 days ago?

★ 교육부 지정 의사소통 기능: **설명 요청하기**   천(정) 6|비 3|Y(박) 7

What do you mean? 무슨 뜻이니[말이야]?
• A Potato clock? **What do you mean?** 감자 시계라고? 그게 무슨 말이야?
• **What do you mean** by that? 그 말이 무슨 뜻이니?

고난도 모의고사 02

01 다음을 듣고, 일요일의 날씨로 가장 적절한 것을 고르시오.

① ② ③ ④ ⑤

02 대화를 듣고, Claire의 집으로 가장 적절한 것을 고르시오.

① ② ③

④ ⑤

03 대화를 듣고, 남자가 여름 캠프에 대해 언급하지 <u>않은</u> 것을 고르시오.

① 장소   ② 기간
③ 참가 인원 수   ④ 참가비
⑤ 활동 내용

04 대화를 듣고, 남자가 파티에 가져갈 음식을 고르시오.

① 스파게티   ② 피자   ③ 애플파이
④ 아이스크림   ⑤ 샌드위치

05 대화를 듣고, 두 사람이 대화하는 장소로 가장 적절한 곳을 고르시오.

① 가구점   ② 스키장
③ 연주회장   ④ 악기 수리점
⑤ 자전거 수리점

06 대화를 듣고, 여자가 한 마지막 말의 의도로 가장 적절한 것을 고르시오.

① 환영   ② 제안   ③ 감사
④ 부탁   ⑤ 비난

07 대화를 듣고, 남자가 가장 좋아하는 행성을 고르시오.

① Mercury   ② Venus   ③ Mars
④ Jupiter   ⑤ Saturn

08 대화를 듣고, 여자가 대화 직후에 할 일로 가장 적절한 것을 고르시오.

① 점심 먹으러 가기
② 체육관에 가기
③ 발표 연습하기
④ 보고서 복사하기
⑤ 발표 슬라이드 만들기

09 대화를 듣고, 남자가 다녀온 여행에 대해 언급하지 <u>않은</u> 것을 고르시오.

① 돌아온 요일   ② 여행 기간
③ 방문한 국가 수   ④ 여행 동반자
⑤ 총 여행 경비

10 다음을 듣고, 남자가 하는 말의 내용으로 가장 적절한 것을 고르시오.

① 화재 방지 대책   ② 체육관 개관 일정
③ 운동복 패션 경향   ④ 체육관 이용 수칙
⑤ 체육관 회원 모집 광고

11 대화를 듣고, Officer Kent에 대한 내용과 일치하지 않는 것을 고르시오.

① TV 프로그램이다.
② 뉴욕 경찰관에 관한 내용이다.
③ Kent의 정체를 아무도 모른다.
④ 금요일 6시에서 7시까지 방송한다.
⑤ 이번 주가 마지막 방송이다.

12 대화를 듣고, 남자가 전화를 건 목적으로 가장 적절한 것을 고르시오.

① 분실물을 찾기 위해서
② 예약을 변경하기 위해서
③ 종업원을 칭찬하기 위해서
④ 체크아웃 시간을 연장하기 위해서
⑤ 아침 식사 시간을 확인하기 위해서

13 대화를 듣고, 남자가 병원에 도착할 시각을 고르시오.
① 12:30 p.m.   ② 1:00 p.m.   ③ 1:30 p.m.
④ 2:00 p.m.   ⑤ 2:30 p.m.

14 대화를 듣고, 두 사람의 관계로 가장 적절한 것을 고르시오.

① 경찰관 – 신고자   ② 은행 직원 – 고객
③ 연예인 – 팬   ④ 음식점 매니저 – 고객
⑤ 여행 가이드 – 여행자

15 대화를 듣고, 여자가 남자에게 부탁한 일로 가장 적절한 것을 고르시오.

① 컴퓨터 수리하기
② 컴퓨터 새 모델 추천하기
③ 컴퓨터 가게 주소 알려주기
④ 아르바이트 자리 소개하기
⑤ 인터넷 중고 거래 사이트 알려주기

16 대화를 듣고, 두 사람이 내일 일찍 일어나야 하는 이유로 가장 적절한 것을 고르시오.

① 일출을 보기 위해서
② 콘택트렌즈를 껴야 해서
③ 수면 습관을 바꾸기 위해서
④ 아침 식사를 준비하기 위해서
⑤ 부모님의 선물을 준비하기 위해서

17 다음 그림의 상황에 가장 적절한 대화를 고르시오.

①   ②   ③   ④   ⑤

18 다음을 듣고, 여자가 황제 펭귄(emperor penguin)에 대해 언급하지 않은 것을 고르시오.
① 키   ② 몸무게   ③ 먹이
④ 수명   ⑤ 서식지

[19-20] 대화를 듣고, 여자의 마지막 말에 이어질 남자의 말로 가장 적절한 것을 고르시오.

19 Man: _____

① Okay, I'll try to drink tea.
② Drinking is bad for you.
③ I guess I can give it a try.
④ I'll call you in the morning.
⑤ You drink too much coffee.

20 Man: _____

① My phone is not working.
② I forgot your email address.
③ I apologized to him yesterday.
④ He left his phone at the library.
⑤ I already did that 30 minutes ago.

Dictation 02

◇ 다시 듣고, 빈칸에 들어갈 알맞은 단어를 써보세요.

정답 및 해설 p.140

---

01 날씨 파악

다음을 듣고, 일요일의 날씨로 가장 적절한 것을 고르시오.

① ② ③ ④ ⑤

M This Friday is a national holiday, and many of you may be planning a trip during this long weekend. _____ _____ _____ _____ as usual, but it will be partly cloudy on Saturday. We won't _____ _____ _____ Monday, but it will _____ _____ _____ on Sunday. I hope you enjoy the long weekend.

---

02 그림 정보 파악

대화를 듣고, Claire의 집으로 가장 적절한 것을 고르시오.

① ② ③ ④ ⑤

M Have you been to Claire's new house?
W Yes, I have. It's a beautiful house.
M It really is. There's a fireplace in the living room.
W I know. There's a real chimney _____ _____ _____ .
M The roof of the house is unique, too.
W You're right. It doesn't have a triangular shape.
M _____ _____ _____ . Claire has a separate garage for her car, too, doesn't she?
W Yes, she does. The garage is _____ _____ _____ _____ .
M I wish I could live in a house like hers.

---

03 언급하지 않은 내용 찾기

대화를 듣고, 남자가 여름 캠프에 대해 언급하지 않은 것을 고르시오.

① 장소 ② 기간
③ 참가 인원 수 ④ 참가비
⑤ 활동 내용

W How was your summer camp, Jaden?
M It wasn't all that interesting.
W Really? Where was the camp?
M It _____ _____ a small campground, Camping Land.
W _____ _____ was the camp?
M It was for 3 days.
W How many people were there?

M A little over 100 _____ _____, and
_____ _____ _____ was $500.

W That was pretty expensive for a 3-day summer camp.

대화를 듣고, 남자가 파티에 가져갈 음식을 고르
시오.
① 스파게티   ② 피자
③ 애플파이   ④ 아이스크림
⑤ 샌드위치

W I'm going to have a potluck party at 6 on Friday. Do you want to come?

M What's a potluck party?

W I throw a party, but all the guests _____
_____ _____ _____.

M I see. Then, the host doesn't have to prepare all the food.

W Right. I heard that _____ _____
_____ good spaghetti.

M I like to cook Italian food. I usually make my own pizza, too.

W Really? Then why don't you bring pizza?

M I may not _____ _____ _____
_____ on Friday. Can I just bring dessert?

W Of course. You can bring anything you want.

M Good. _____ _____ _____
_____.

대화를 듣고, 두 사람이 대화하는 장소로 가장 적
절한 곳을 고르시오.
① 가구점   ② 스키장
③ 연주회장   ④ 악기 수리점
⑤ 자전거 수리점

M What can I do for you?

W Do you think _____ _____ _____
_____?

M Oh, there's a small crack. This is actually a very common problem.

W Do you have to replace _____ _____
_____?

M No, I can just put a small piece of wood in the crack.

W I paid a lot of money _____ _____
_____.

M I see. But this kind of crack happens only to this type of wood.

W I hope it won't cost _____ _____
_____ _____ it.

대화를 듣고, 여자가 한 마지막 말의 의도로 가장
적절한 것을 고르시오.

① 환영　　② 제안　　③ 감사
④ 부탁　　⑤ 비난

M　Are you moving in today?

W　Yes, I'm moving in to the 8th floor.

M　Really? I live ＿＿＿＿＿＿ ＿＿＿＿＿＿ ＿＿＿＿＿＿
＿＿＿＿＿＿. We'll be neighbors.

W　Oh, great! My name is Jennifer.

M　I'm Jason. Do you need help with those boxes?

W　No, thank you. But could you ＿＿＿＿＿＿ ＿＿＿＿＿＿
＿＿＿＿＿＿ ＿＿＿＿＿＿?

M　Of course. [Pause] This is ＿＿＿＿＿＿ ＿＿＿＿＿＿
＿＿＿＿＿＿ ＿＿＿＿＿＿.

W　I really ＿＿＿＿＿＿ ＿＿＿＿＿＿ ＿＿＿＿＿＿ ＿＿＿＿＿＿.

대화를 듣고, 남자가 가장 좋아하는 행성을 고르
시오.

① Mercury　② Venus　③ Mars
④ Jupiter　⑤ Saturn

W　What are you doing, Timothy?

M　I'm just looking at the night sky.

W　Are you looking for anything in particular?

M　I'm looking for Mercury.

W　But can you ＿＿＿＿＿＿ ＿＿＿＿＿＿ ＿＿＿＿＿＿
a telescope?

M　Yes, you can also see Venus, Mars, Jupiter, and Saturn.

W　Oh, I didn't know that. Do you have a favorite planet?

M　Yes, ＿＿＿＿＿＿ ＿＿＿＿＿＿ ＿＿＿＿＿＿ Jupiter.
What's yours?

W　My favorite is Venus. ＿＿＿＿＿＿ ＿＿＿＿＿＿
＿＿＿＿＿＿ ＿＿＿＿＿＿ Jupiter?

M　Because it's ＿＿＿＿＿＿ ＿＿＿＿＿＿ ＿＿＿＿＿＿
in the solar system.

대화를 듣고, 여자가 대화 직후에 할 일로 가장 적
절한 것을 고르시오.

① 점심 먹으러 가기
② 체육관에 가기
③ 발표 연습하기
④ 보고서 복사하기
⑤ 발표 슬라이드 만들기

M　Mary, are you busy right now?

W　Not really. What's up?

M　I have to ＿＿＿＿＿＿ ＿＿＿＿＿＿ my presentation.
It starts at 3 p.m.

W　It's almost 1:30. You ＿＿＿＿＿＿ ＿＿＿＿＿＿
＿＿＿＿＿＿.

M　Not really. I still have to make 30 copies of my report.

W Okay. _____ _____ _____
_____ right now. Just focus on your presentation.

M Thank you so much, Mary.

09 언급하지 않은 내용 찾기

대화를 듣고, 남자가 다녀온 여행에 대해 언급하지 않은 것을 고르시오.

① 돌아온 요일   ② 여행 기간
③ 방문한 국가 수   ④ 여행 동반자
⑤ 총 여행 경비

W When did you come back from your trip?

M I _____ _____ _____ Friday. I'm really tired.

W You must be. How long was your trip?

M It _____ _____ 7 days. It was a very tight schedule.

W _____ _____ _____ _____ did you visit?

M I visited 4 countries.

W That's about 2 days _____ _____
_____. How's that possible?

M That's possible in Europe.

W How much did the whole trip cost?

M _____ _____ _____
3 months' salary, but it was worth it.

10 주제 추론

다음을 듣고, 남자가 하는 말의 내용으로 가장 적절한 것을 고르시오.

① 화재 방지 대책
② 체육관 개관 일정
③ 운동복 패션 경향
④ 체육관 이용 수칙
⑤ 체육관 회원 모집 광고

M May I have your attention, please? The city gym is now open, from 6 a.m. to 10 p.m. Please wear proper _____
_____ _____ _____ only. Also, use your earphones when you listen to music. Music can be noisy to others. _____ _____
_____ _____ put used towels in the basket, which is next to the door. _____ _____
_____ _____ the door when you enter and _____ _____ _____
_____.

11 일치하지 않는 내용 찾기

대화를 듣고, Officer Kent에 대한 내용과 일치하지 않는 것을 고르시오.

① TV 프로그램이다.
② 뉴욕 경찰관에 관한 내용이다.
③ Kent의 정체를 아무도 모른다.
④ 금요일 6시에서 7시까지 방송한다.
⑤ 이번 주가 마지막 방송이다.

W Have you seen the TV show *Officer Kent*?

M No, I haven't. What's it about?

W It's about a New York _____ _____
_____ Kent who's also a superhero.

M That sounds interesting. Does anybody know that he's a superhero?

W His girlfriend is the only person _____

_____ _____ _____.

M When is it on TV?

W _____ _____ _____ 6 to 7 p.m.

every Friday on channel 7.

M I'm busy this Friday. I'll watch it next week.

W _____ _____ _____

_____ the last episode.

M Oh, that's too bad.

12 목적 파악

대화를 듣고, 남자가 전화를 건 목적으로 가장 적절한 것을 고르시오.

① 분실물을 찾기 위해서
② 예약을 변경하기 위해서
③ 종업원을 칭찬하기 위해서
④ 체크아웃 시간을 연장하기 위해서
⑤ 아침 식사 시간을 확인하기 위해서

[Telephone rings.]

W Thank you for calling the Pine Tree Hotel. How may I help you?

M Hello. This is Mark Clayton. I checked out of your hotel earlier today.

W Yes, I remember, Mr. Clayton. What can I do for you?

M Can _____ _____ _____ there is a black hat at the counter?

W Can you please _____ _____ a second? *[Pause]* I'm sorry, _____ _____ _____ _____ here, sir.

M I'm pretty sure I lost it at the hotel.

W I'll give you a call back _____ _____ _____ a black hat.

M Thank you.

13 숫자 정보 파악 (시각)

대화를 듣고, 남자가 병원에 도착할 시각을 고르시오.

① 12:30 p.m.   ② 1:00 p.m.
③ 1:30 p.m.   ④ 2:00 p.m.
⑤ 2:30 p.m.

[Telephone rings.]

W ABC Children's Hospital. How may I help you?

M Can I make an appointment for 2 p.m. today?

W I'm sorry, but we don't _____ _____ _____ Mondays.

M How long do we have to wait until we see a doctor?

W We're very busy on Mondays, so you should expect to

_____ _____ _____

_____.

M If we get to the hospital at 1 p.m., can we see a doctor at 2 p.m.?

W The hospital is _____ _____ _____ _____ 1:30 p.m.

M I see. Then, we'll just have to _____ _____ _____ 1:30.

W I'm sorry I couldn't be more helpful, sir.

---

14 관계 추론

대화를 듣고, 두 사람의 관계로 가장 적절한 것을 고르시오.

① 경찰관 – 신고자
② 은행 직원 – 고객
③ 연예인 – 팬
④ 음식점 매니저 – 고객
⑤ 여행 가이드 – 여행자

M Can I help the next person in line, please?

W Hi, I'd like to _____ _____ _____.

M Could you _____ _____ _____ on the back?

W Yes, of course.

M Would you like 100-dollar bills?

W Yes. I _____ _____ _____ _____, too. Can I have three 100-dollar bills and five 20-dollar bills?

M Yes, of course. *[Pause]* Is there anything else?

W I also want to _____ _____ _____ for my credit card.

M I'm sorry, but you'll have to talk to a credit card specialist for that.

W I see. Thank you for your help.

---

15 부탁 파악

대화를 듣고, 여자가 남자에게 부탁한 일로 가장 적절한 것을 고르시오.

① 컴퓨터 수리하기
② 컴퓨터 새 모델 추천하기
③ 컴퓨터 가게 주소 알려주기
④ 아르바이트 자리 소개하기
⑤ 인터넷 중고 거래 사이트 알려주기

W I need to get a new computer. My old one just stopped working.

M Let me see if I can fix it.

W No. It's _____ _____ _____ twice.

M You used that computer for over 10 years, right?

W Yes. It's time to get a new one.

M Why don't you get a used one? There's a really _____ _____ _____ _____ near my house.

W That's not bad. Can you _____ _____ _____ _____?

M Sure, I'll send it to you right away.

16 이유 파악

대화를 듣고, 두 사람이 내일 일찍 일어나야 하는 이유로 가장 적절한 것을 고르시오.

① 일출을 보기 위해서
② 콘택트렌즈를 껴야 해서
③ 수면 습관을 바꾸기 위해서
④ 아침 식사를 준비하기 위해서
⑤ 부모님의 선물을 준비하기 위해서

M Why are you still up? It's almost midnight.

W I'm putting on my contact lenses. These are the type of lenses I wear while I sleep.

M When did you get them?

W Last week. I want to _____ _____ _____ _____.

M Well, you need to sleep now. We have to _____ _____ _____ to see the sunrise tomorrow.

W Okay. It's my _____ _____ _____ _____ a sunrise on New Year's Day.

---

17 그림 상황에 적절한 대화 찾기

다음 그림의 상황에 가장 적절한 대화를 고르시오.

① ② ③ ④ ⑤

① M *Taking pictures is not allowed here.

　 W I'm sorry. I'll _____ _____ right now.

② M I'm sorry, but you can't borrow magazines.

　 W I didn't know that. Where is _____ _____ _____?

③ M Are you ready to order, ma'am?

　 W Can you _____ _____ _____ _____?

④ M Did you like the movie?

　 W It was so boring. It was _____ _____ _____ _____.

⑤ M I would like to open a bank account.

　 W I can help you with that. What is your name, sir?

> **＊ 교육부 지정 의사소통 기능: 금지하기**　　　　　　동(윤) 8
>
> **~ is not allowed.** ~은 허용되지 않습니다.
> • Sitting **is not allowed** here. 여기에 앉으시면 안 됩니다.
> • Eating **is not allowed** in this room. 이 방 안에서는 음식을 드실 수 없습니다.

---

18 언급하지 않은 내용 찾기

다음을 듣고, 여자가 황제 펭귄(emperor penguin)에 대해 언급하지 <u>않은</u> 것을 고르시오.

① 키　　② 몸무게　　③ 먹이
④ 수명　　⑤ 서식지

W Welcome to Penguin Land, everyone! The penguins in front of you are the world-famous emperor penguins. Adult emperor penguins _____ _____ 1 meter in ◀»height and can _____ _____

_____ 45 kilograms. They usually eat fish, and they

_____ _____ _____ _____ the South

Pole. Now, let's go and meet the smallest penguins.

---

19 이어질 응답 찾기

대화를 듣고, 여자의 마지막 말에 이어질 남자의 말로 가장 적절한 것을 고르시오.

Man: _____

① Okay, I'll try to drink tea.
② Drinking is bad for you.
③ I guess I can give it a try.
④ I'll call you in the morning.
⑤ You drink too much coffee.

W What do you drink in the morning, Paul?

M I drink coffee.

W I used to drink coffee, too, but now I just drink 2 _____ _____ _____.

M _____ _____ _____ _____ drink 2 glasses of water in the morning.

W I drink one glass as soon as I get up. Then I drink another one _____ _____.

M Wow, you have a very healthy lifestyle.

W You should also _____ _____ _____ _____ coffee in the morning.

---

20 이어질 응답 찾기

대화를 듣고, 여자의 마지막 말에 이어질 남자의 말로 가장 적절한 것을 고르시오.

Man: _____

① My phone is not working.
② I forgot your email address.
③ I apologized to him yesterday.
④ He left his phone at the library.
⑤ I already did that 30 minutes ago.

M My friend John is really mad at me, Mom.

W What happened?

M I was supposed to _____ _____ _____ the library, but I forgot.

W That's not good. Why did you forget?

M I was playing basketball with other friends, and I lost track of time.

W Have you apologized to him?

M I wanted to, _____ _____ _____ _____ my phone calls.

W _____ _____ _____ _____ him a text message?

고난도 모의고사 03

01 다음을 듣고, 금요일의 날씨로 가장 적절한 것을 고르시오.

① 　② 　③ 　④ 　⑤

02 대화를 듣고, 여자가 구입할 자전거로 가장 적절한 것을 고르시오.

03 대화를 듣고, 여자가 식탁에 대해 언급하지 <u>않은</u> 것을 고르시오.

① 색깔　② 크기　③ 가격
④ 판매 장소　⑤ 재료

04 대화를 듣고, 남자가 점심 식사 후에 한 일로 가장 적절한 것을 고르시오.

① 피자 먹기　② 농구하기
③ 설거지하기　④ 구내식당 청소하기
⑤ 엄마한테 전화하기

05 대화를 듣고, 두 사람이 대화하는 장소로 가장 적절한 곳을 고르시오.

① 영화관 매표소　② 기차역
③ 휴대전화 판매점　④ 전자 제품 판매점
⑤ 버스 정류장

06 대화를 듣고, 여자가 한 마지막 말의 의도로 가장 적절한 것을 고르시오.

① 거절　② 사과　③ 비난
④ 용서　⑤ 칭찬

07 대화를 듣고, 남자가 좋아하지 <u>않는</u> 과목을 고르시오.

① 사회　② 역사　③ 수학
④ 과학　⑤ 음악

08 대화를 듣고, 여자가 대화 직후에 할 일로 가장 적절한 것을 고르시오.

① 고궁 입장하기
② 안내문 사진 찍기
③ 안내서 구입하기
④ 친구와 기념사진 찍기
⑤ 저장된 사진 보여주기

09 대화를 듣고, 남자가 새로운 이웃에 대해 언급하지 <u>않은</u> 것을 고르시오.

① 이름　② 직업　③ 결혼 여부
④ 나이　⑤ 출생 지역

10 다음을 듣고, 남자가 하는 말의 내용으로 가장 적절한 것을 고르시오.

① 환경 보호의 필요성
② 우유의 다양한 용도
③ 재활용 불가능한 물건들
④ 쓰레기를 줄여야 하는 이유
⑤ 플라스틱 제품의 올바른 재활용 방법

11 대화를 듣고, 두 사람이 언급한 물병에 대한 내용으로 일치하지 않는 것을 고르시오.

① 뜨거운 물을 넣을 수 없다.
② 작은 병이다.
③ 검은색이다.
④ 두 개에 5달러이다.
⑤ 이름을 적을 공간이 있다.

12 대화를 듣고, 남자가 서점에 간 목적으로 가장 적절한 것을 고르시오.

① 작가를 만나기 위해서
② 베스트셀러를 사기 위해서
③ 잃어버린 지갑을 찾기 위해서
④ 건강에 관한 정보를 얻기 위해서
⑤ 독자들에게 사인을 해 주기 위해서

13 대화를 듣고, 두 사람이 보려는 영화의 가격으로 가장 적절한 것을 고르시오.

① $3   ② $5   ③ $7
④ $9   ⑤ $11

14 대화를 듣고, 두 사람의 관계로 가장 적절한 것을 고르시오.

① 아동 작가 – 독자
② 서점 직원 – 고객
③ 동물원 관리인 – 관람객
④ 어린이집 교사 – 학부모
⑤ 장난감 가게 직원 – 고객

15 대화를 듣고, 남자가 여자에게 부탁한 일로 가장 적절한 것을 고르시오.

① 운동 함께 하기   ② 집에 먼저 가기
③ 교실 청소하기   ④ 약속에 늦지 않기
⑤ 잠깐 기다려 주기

16 대화를 듣고, 남자가 꽃을 산 이유로 가장 적절한 것을 고르시오.

① 아버지의 부탁을 받아서
② 어버이날을 기념하기 위해서
③ 집안을 장식하기 위해서
④ 친구와 만남을 기념하기 위해서
⑤ 봉사 단체에 기부하기 위해서

17 다음 그림의 상황에 가장 적절한 대화를 고르시오.

①   ②   ③   ④   ⑤

18 다음을 듣고, 남자가 농구화에 대해 언급하지 않은 것을 고르시오.

① 상품명   ② 기능   ③ 색깔
④ 가격   ⑤ 할인율

[19-20] 대화를 듣고, 여자의 마지막 말에 이어질 남자의 말로 가장 적절한 것을 고르시오.

19 Man: _____

① Sure, I'll return them tomorrow.
② No, I haven't read the cards yet.
③ No, the school was closed today.
④ Yes, I borrowed a few more books.
⑤ Yes, I put them all in the return box.

20 Man: _____

① I don't have a piano at home.
② I often play basketball at the gym.
③ The guitar is my favorite instrument.
④ I play the drums and the bass guitar.
⑤ I learned to play the piano last month.

Dictation 03

◇ 다시 듣고, 빈칸에 들어갈 알맞은 단어를 써보세요.

정답 및 해설 p.147

---

01 날씨 파악

다음을 듣고, 금요일의 날씨로 가장 적절한 것을 고르시오.

① ② ③
④ ⑤

M Here's the weather forecast for the next 5 days. We will
_____ _____ _____
_____ on Monday, Tuesday, and Wednesday. It will
also be _____ _____ _____, but
it will become cloudy and colder again on Thursday. And on
Friday, we should _____ _____
_____ _____ of the winter.

---

02 그림 정보 파악

대화를 듣고, 여자가 구입할 자전거로 가장 적절한 것을 고르시오.

① ② ③
④ ⑤

W Excuse me, I'm looking for a bicycle for myself.
M Okay, these are the bikes for women.
W Do you have bikes _____ _____
_____?
M Yes, we do. They are over here.
W Oh, they _____ _____ _____.
M Yes, but you can replace it with something else.
W Then, can you _____ _____
_____ _____ a basket?
M Of course.
W That's great. _____ _____ _____
_____ then.

---

03 언급하지 않은 내용 찾기

대화를 듣고, 여자가 식탁에 대해 언급하지 <u>않은</u> 것을 고르시오.

① 색깔   ② 크기   ③ 가격
④ 판매 장소   ⑤ 재료

W We need to get a new dining table.
M What's wrong with the one we're using right now?
W I don't like its color. I want to have _____
_____ _____.
M How big a table do you want?
W I want _____ _____ _____
8 people.

Listening Tip

We can get a good table ...에서 문장의 의미를 전달하는 보다 핵심적인 역할을 하는 동사(get), 명사 (good table) 등은 강하게 읽고 상대적으로 중요성이 덜한 역할어인 조동사(can), 관사(a) 등은 짧고 약하게 발음합니다.

M Really? That will be expensive.

W We can go and _____ _____

_____ Tim's Furniture.

M Yes, _____ _____ _____ a lot of

inexpensive furniture.

W We can get a good table for only $500 there.

M Okay, then let's do it.

---

04 한 일 파악

대화를 듣고, 남자가 점심 식사 후에 한 일로 가장 적절한 것을 고르시오.

① 피자 먹기
② 농구하기
③ 설거지하기
④ 구내식당 청소하기
⑤ 엄마한테 전화하기

W How was your day at school, Jake?

M It was good as usual.

W What did you have for lunch?

M We _____ _____ _____

_____ chicken and pizza, so I had pizza.

W What did you do after you had lunch?

M I played basketball with my friends.

W Don't lie to me, Jake. Your teacher called me.

M Oh, I'm sorry, Mom. I _____ _____

_____ the cafeteria after lunch.

W What happened? I heard it _____ _____

_____ _____.

M I was just playing with my friends, and I _____

_____ _____ _____.

---

05 장소 추론

대화를 듣고, 두 사람이 대화하는 장소로 가장 적절한 곳을 고르시오.

① 영화관 매표소   ② 기차역
③ 휴대전화 판매점   ④ 전자 제품 판매점
⑤ 버스 정류장

M Oh no! We're going to be late.

W We'll be fine. We still have 10 minutes.

M Do you have your ticket with you?

W Yes, I have it on my cell phone.

M On your cell phone? Did you print it out?

W Oh, it's an electronic ticket. _____ _____

_____ _____ print it out. You can just

show your cell phone.

M Really? That's _____ _____.

W I know. Let's hurry. _____ _____

_____ _____ _____.

06 의도 파악

대화를 듣고, 여자가 한 마지막 말의 의도로 가장 적절한 것을 고르시오.

① 거절 　 ② 사과 　 ③ 비난
④ 용서 　 ⑤ 칭찬

M Good morning, Sara. How are you?

W I'm well, Mr. Willis. How was your weekend?

M It was great. So, what's my schedule for today?

W First, there is a meeting at 10. After a short break, you have to ＿＿＿＿＿＿ ＿＿＿＿＿＿ ＿＿＿＿＿＿.
Then there is a lunch appointment with Mr. Peterson.

M Mr. Peterson? I thought we ＿＿＿＿＿＿ ＿＿＿＿＿＿ ＿＿＿＿＿＿ with him.

W I didn't hear anything about it.

M ＿＿＿＿＿＿ ＿＿＿＿＿＿ ＿＿＿＿＿＿. I'm sure I told you this before.

W [Pause] Oh, my mistake. ＿＿＿＿＿＿ ＿＿＿＿＿＿ ＿＿＿＿＿＿ I confused you.

07 특정 정보 파악

대화를 듣고, 남자가 좋아하지 <u>않는</u> 과목을 고르시오.

① 사회 　 ② 역사 　 ③ 수학
④ 과학 　 ⑤ 음악

W Did you get your report card today?

M I did. I think my grades are okay. How about you?

W Same here. But I got a C in art.

M Really? ＿＿＿＿＿＿ ＿＿＿＿＿＿. Isn't that your favorite subject?

W No, history is ＿＿＿＿＿＿ ＿＿＿＿＿＿ ＿＿＿＿＿＿.
What's yours?

M I don't have a favorite subject. I ＿＿＿＿＿＿ ＿＿＿＿＿＿ ＿＿＿＿＿＿ the subjects this semester.

W Is there a subject that you really don't like?

M Oh, I ＿＿＿＿＿＿ ＿＿＿＿＿＿ music at all.
I'm ＿＿＿＿＿＿ ＿＿＿＿＿＿ singing.

08 할 일 파악

대화를 듣고, 여자가 대화 직후에 할 일로 가장 적절한 것을 고르시오.

① 고궁 입장하기
② 안내문 사진 찍기
③ 안내서 구입하기
④ 친구와 기념사진 찍기
⑤ 저장된 사진 보여주기

W How many times have you been to this palace, Junha?

M This is actually my first time.

W You live in Seoul, but ＿＿＿＿＿＿ ＿＿＿＿＿＿ ＿＿＿＿＿＿ ＿＿＿＿＿＿ before?

M I've been so busy that I didn't have time to visit.

W Anyway, this is such a beautiful palace.

M I know. That's why I brought you here.

W Look! _____ _____ _____ _____ in English of the whole palace.

M Wow, you can learn so much about Korean history by reading this.

W Let me _____ _____ _____ of this, so I can read it at home.

M Good idea!

09 언급하지 않은 내용 찾기

대화를 듣고, 남자가 새로운 이웃에 대해 언급하지 **않은** 것을 고르시오.

① 이름   ② 직업   ③ 결혼 여부
④ 나이   ⑤ 출생 지역

W Have you met your new neighbor?

M Yes, I have. _____ _____ is Mark Kidd.

W What does he do for a living?

M He's a _____ _____ _____. He teaches geography.

W Is he married?

M I think he's _____ _____. By the way, weren't you born in Boston?

W Yes, I was. Why do you ask?

M He said he _____ _____ _____ Boston, too.

W Really? Can you introduce me to him?

M Of course. I'm sure you two will have a lot in common.

10 주제 추론

다음을 듣고, 남자가 하는 말의 내용으로 가장 적절한 것을 고르시오.

① 환경 보호의 필요성
② 우유의 다양한 용도
③ 재활용 불가능한 물건들
④ 쓰레기를 줄여야 하는 이유
⑤ 플라스틱 제품의 올바른 재활용 방법

M Today, I'd like to talk about the importance of proper recycling. Many of you are _____ _____ _____ from glass bottles, cans, and paper boxes. However, plastic items need to _____ _____ _____ _____. You should _____ _____ before you put plastic items in a recycling bin. And you should also _____ _____ plastic containers for dairy products, such as milk and yogurt.

11 일치하지 않는 내용 찾기

대화를 듣고, 두 사람이 언급한 물병에 대한 내용으로 일치하지 <u>않는</u> 것을 고르시오.

① 뜨거운 물을 넣을 수 없다.
② 작은 병이다.
③ 검은색이다.
④ 두 개에 5달러이다.
⑤ 이름을 적을 공간이 있다.

◀)) Listening Tip

can은 /캔/ 보다는 /큰/에 가깝게 발음되고 can't는 /캔트/가 아니고 /캔/이라고 발음한 뒤에 잠시 숨을 멈추는 느낌으로 발음됩니다.

W Let's get this water bottle, Mike.
M You ◀) can't put hot water in here.
W That's fine. I don't need to carry it for hot water. I just _____ _____ _____ _____.
M But isn't it too small? And it's completely black.
W I know it's small and black. That's why I like it. And it's only $5.
M Okay. _____ _____ _____ are you getting?
W I think I'll get 2, just in case.
M What is this on the bottle?
W Oh, I guess you can _____ _____ _____ on it.

12 목적 파악

대화를 듣고, 남자가 서점에 간 목적으로 가장 적절한 것을 고르시오.

① 작가를 만나기 위해서
② 베스트셀러를 사기 위해서
③ 잃어버린 지갑을 찾기 위해서
④ 건강에 관한 정보를 얻기 위해서
⑤ 독자들에게 사인을 해 주기 위해서

W Can I help the next person in line, please?
M Hi, I was just wondering if there's _____ _____ _____ here today.
W Oh, you just missed it.
M Wasn't the event from 3 p.m. to 5 p.m.?
W Yes, that's right.
M It's only 4:30. Did something happen?
W The author _____ _____ _____, so she left 10 minutes ago.
M I was really looking forward to _____ _____ _____ _____.
W I'm sorry.

13 숫자 정보 파악 (금액)

대화를 듣고, 두 사람이 보려는 영화의 가격으로 가장 적절한 것을 고르시오.

① $3   ② $5   ③ $7
④ $9   ⑤ $11

W Would you like to see a movie tomorrow?
M Sounds good. What do you want to see?
W How about *Little Woman*?
M Oh, sure. What time _____ _____ _____?
W There are shows at 11, 3, and 7:30 tomorrow.
M How much are the tickets?

W Tickets for the 11 o'clock show are $5 and _____ _____ _____ _____ $9 each.

M Then, _____ _____ _____ _____ _____ 11. Is that okay?

W Sure, _____ _____ _____ to me.

대화를 듣고, 두 사람의 관계로 가장 적절한 것을 고르시오.

① 아동 작가 – 독자
② 서점 직원 – 고객
③ 동물원 관리인 – 관람객
④ 어린이집 교사 – 학부모
⑤ 장난감 가게 직원 – 고객

M Hi, I'm looking for a _____ _____ _____ _____.

W Okay. How old is she?

M She just turned 6 last week.

W Is she just starting to read?

M Yes. She _____ _____ _____ _____ a year ago, and she likes to read animal stories.

W Then, I would recommend *The Three Little Pigs*. The book is _____ _____ right now.

M That'll be perfect! How much is it?

W With a 10% discount, _____ _____ _____ to be $9.

대화를 듣고, 남자가 여자에게 부탁한 일로 가장 적절한 것을 고르시오.

① 운동 함께 하기   ② 집에 먼저 가기
③ 교실 청소하기   ④ 약속에 늦지 않기
⑤ 잠깐 기다려 주기

W The study group meeting is in 10 minutes. Let's go.

M I can't leave now. I have to _____ _____ _____ _____.

W Why are you cleaning the classroom?

M I was late for school today for the third time this week, so I'm cleaning.

W Do you want me to _____ _____ _____ the classroom?

M No, I have to do it myself. Can you _____ _____ _____ _____ I finish cleaning the classroom?

W How long will it take?

M I think it's going to take _____ _____ _____ or two.

이유 파악

대화를 듣고, 남자가 꽃을 산 이유로 가장 적절한 것을 고르시오.

① 아버지의 부탁을 받아서
② 어버이날을 기념하기 위해서
③ 집안을 장식하기 위해서
④ 친구와 만남을 기념하기 위해서
⑤ 봉사 단체에 기부하기 위해서

W What beautiful flowers! Where did you get them?
M I _____ _____ _____ yesterday, and they were delivered about an hour ago.
W What are the flowers for?
M I _____ _____ _____ my mother.
W Is it her birthday?
M In Korea, _____ _____ _____ _____ carnations on Parents' Day.
W Oh, I didn't know that. I usually celebrate Mother's Day and Father's Day on 2 different days.
M Not in Korea. There is just one Parents' Day.
W I see.

---

17 **그림 상황에 적절한 대화 찾기**

다음 그림의 상황에 가장 적절한 대화를 고르시오.

① ② ③ ④ ⑤

① M Excuse me. Do you have a lost and found here?
   W Yes, we do. What did _____ _____?
② M Here's the menu. I'll be back to take your orders.
   W Can I _____ _____? I know what I want.
③ M Let's use the restroom before the _____ _____.
   W That's a good idea.
④ M Excuse me. You can't eat in this section of the park.
   W Oh, I'm sorry. Where is _____ _____ _____?
⑤ M I'm sorry, but you can't ride your skateboard here.
   W Where can I ride a skateboard in this park?

---

18 **언급하지 않은 내용 찾기**

다음을 듣고, 남자가 농구화에 대해 언급하지 않은 것을 고르시오.

① 상품명   ② 기능   ③ 색깔
④ 가격   ⑤ 할인율

M Do you want to become a better basketball player? Then, get a pair of these amazing basketball shoes. Why _____ _____ _____ Sky Jump? They will help you _____ _____ _____ _____ higher. $180 a pair may _____ _____, but you won't regret spending that money on a pair of Sky Jump. Order now, and you _____ _____ a 10% discount.

19 이어질 응답 찾기

대화를 듣고, 여자의 마지막 말에 이어질 남자의 말로 가장 적절한 것을 고르시오.

Man: _____

① Sure, I'll return them tomorrow.
② No, I haven't read the cards yet.
③ No, the school was closed today.
④ Yes, I borrowed a few more books.
⑤ Yes, I put them all in the return box.

W How was your last day at school?
M I guess it was the same as usual.
W Did you _____ _____ _____ all of your friends?
M Yes. Some of them gave me a hug, and I also _____ _____ _____ _____ from others.
W That's so sweet of them. Oh, did you _____ _____ _____ that you borrowed from the school library?

20 이어질 응답 찾기

대화를 듣고, 여자의 마지막 말에 이어질 남자의 말로 가장 적절한 것을 고르시오.

Man: _____

① I don't have a piano at home.
② I often play basketball at the gym.
③ The guitar is my favorite instrument.
④ I play the drums and the bass guitar.
⑤ I learned to play the piano last month.

M What do you usually do in your free time?
W I usually play the piano.
M _____ _____ _____ the guitar, too?
W Yes, I do, but I've only been playing for 2 months.
M I saw you playing the guitar last week at Jimmy's place, and you _____ _____ _____.
W I can play a few songs, but I like to play the piano when I'm at home.
M Wow, I want to _____ _____ _____ the piano. You must be great.
W Maybe later. What about you? Do _____ _____ _____ instruments?

고난도 모의고사 04

01 다음을 듣고, 내일 날씨로 가장 적절한 것을 고르시오.

02 대화를 듣고, 여자가 구입할 컵으로 가장 적절한 것을 고르시오.

03 대화를 듣고, 남자의 심정으로 가장 적절한 것을 고르시오.

① happy   ② worried   ③ proud
④ angry   ⑤ bored

04 대화를 듣고, 남자가 Valentine's Day에 한 일로 가장 적절한 것을 고르시오.

① 외식하기   ② 요리하기
③ 쇼핑하기   ④ 축구 시합하기
⑤ 친구에게 선물하기

05 대화를 듣고, 두 사람이 대화하는 장소로 가장 적절한 곳을 고르시오.

① 병원   ② 약국   ③ 경찰서
④ 쇼핑센터   ⑤ 체육관

06 대화를 듣고, 여자가 한 마지막 말의 의도로 가장 적절한 것을 고르시오.

① 거절   ② 부탁   ③ 승낙
④ 비난   ⑤ 후회

07 대화를 듣고, 여자가 여행을 갈 도시를 고르시오.

① 런던   ② 뉴욕   ③ 한국
④ 베이징   ⑤ 도쿄

08 대화를 듣고, 남자가 대화 직후에 할 일로 가장 적절한 것을 고르시오.

① 간식 사러 가기   ② 우산 챙기기
③ 캠핑 장비 챙기기   ④ 친구에게 전화하기
⑤ 일기예보 확인하기

09 대화를 듣고, 여자가 제과점에 대해 언급하지 <u>않은</u> 것을 고르시오.

① 이름   ② 제빵사 이름
③ 개점 날짜   ④ 영업시간
⑤ 위치

10 다음을 듣고, 여자가 하는 말의 내용으로 가장 적절한 것을 고르시오.

① 수영 강습 안내
② 응급 처치 방법
③ 수영장 안전 수칙
④ 규칙적인 운동의 중요성
⑤ 식음료 구입 장소 안내

11 다음을 듣고, 난방기에 대한 내용으로 일치하지 <u>않는</u> 것을 고르시오.

① 에너지를 절약한다.
② 난방비를 줄일 수 있다.
③ 다른 난방기보다 저렴하다.
④ 작고 가볍다.
⑤ 방을 즉시 따뜻하게 해준다.

12 대화를 듣고, 남자가 전화를 건 목적으로 가장 적절한 것을 고르시오.

① 식당을 예약하기 위해서
② 예약을 변경하기 위해서
③ 메뉴를 확인하기 위해서
④ 불만 사항을 말하기 위해서
⑤ 약속에 늦겠다고 알리기 위해서

13 대화를 듣고, 두 사람이 만날 시각을 고르시오.

① 3:00 p.m.　② 3:30 p.m.　③ 4:00 p.m.
④ 4:30 p.m.　⑤ 5:00 p.m.

14 대화를 듣고, 두 사람의 관계로 가장 적절한 것을 고르시오.

① 옷 가게 점원 – 고객　② 간호사 – 환자
③ 자동차 정비사 – 고객　④ 교통경찰 – 운전자
⑤ 주차 관리인 – 운전자

15 대화를 듣고, 남자가 여자에게 부탁한 일로 가장 적절한 것을 고르시오.

① 팝콘 사 오기　　② 영화 추천하기
③ 영화표 예매하기　④ 소설책 빌려주기
⑤ 휴식 방해하지 말기

16 대화를 듣고, 여자가 잠을 자지 <u>못한</u> 이유로 가장 적절한 것을 고르시오.

① 너무 피곤해서　　② 밀린 일을 하느라고
③ 낮잠을 많이 자서　④ 커피를 많이 마셔서
⑤ 프로젝트가 걱정되어

17 다음 그림의 상황에 가장 적절한 대화를 고르시오.

①　　②　　③　　④　　⑤

18 다음을 듣고, 여자가 테니스 라켓에 대해 언급하지 <u>않은</u> 것을 고르시오.

① 상품명　　② 무게　　③ 색깔
④ 길이　　⑤ 가격

[19-20] 대화를 듣고, 여자의 마지막 말에 이어질 남자의 말로 가장 적절한 것을 고르시오.

19 Man: _____

① No, that's not a good idea.
② Our neighbors are so noisy.
③ I'm sorry. I won't forget again.
④ I'll fix the TV right away.
⑤ Yes, you should remember that.

20 Man: _____

① Because life is so precious.
② I don't remember my birthday.
③ Because I don't like getting older.
④ I am going to celebrate this week.
⑤ Because it's important to be happy.

Dictation 04

◇ 다시 듣고, 빈칸에 들어갈 알맞은 단어를 써보세요.

정답 및 해설 p.154

01 날씨 파악

다음을 듣고, 내일 날씨로 가장 적절한 것을 고르시오.

① ② ③ ④ ⑤

M Good afternoon, everyone! I hope you're all having a wonderful weekend. We're finally getting lots of sunshine _____ _____ _____ _____ over the past few weeks. However, we won't have much sunshine tomorrow as _____ _____ _____ _____ throughout the day. The good news is that we won't _____ _____ _____ for the next 10 days.

02 그림 정보 파악

대화를 듣고, 여자가 구입할 컵으로 가장 적절한 것을 고르시오.

① ② ③ ④ ⑤

W Excuse me. Where can I find cups?
M I'll show you where they are. Follow me, please.
W [Pause] Oh, there they are.
M Are you looking for anything in particular?
W I'm looking for something _____ _____ _____.
M There are the ones with handles.
W Do you have any with a picture _____ _____ _____?
M Yes. There's _____ _____ a picture of a rose and _____ _____ a picture of a sunflower.
W Perfect! Then, I'll take the one _____ _____ _____ on it.

03 심정 추론

대화를 듣고, 남자의 심정으로 가장 적절한 것을 고르시오.

① happy   ② worried   ③ proud
④ angry   ⑤ bored

[Cell phone rings.]
W Hello.
M Hi, honey. Have you seen the doctor yet?
W Yes, I have. I just came home.
M What did she say?
W She just told me to _____ _____ _____ _____.

M That doesn't sound good. _____ _____ _____ _____ ?

W The doctor ran some tests. The results _____ _____ _____ next week.

M Do you want me to come home and stay with you?

W No, it's okay. I'll be fine.

M All right. I hope _____ _____ _____ .

04 한 일 파악

대화를 듣고, 남자가 Valentine's Day에 한 일로 가장 적절한 것을 고르시오.

① 외식하기 ② 요리하기
③ 쇼핑하기 ④ 축구 시합하기
⑤ 친구에게 선물하기

W Hey, James. Did you have fun yesterday?

M Yes, I guess. How about you?

W It was the best Valentine's Day ever. My boyfriend and I _____ _____ _____ _____ _____ in the city.

M Do you mean the seafood restaurant by the river?

W Yes, the food was amazing, and the waiter was very friendly.

M I'm _____ _____ _____ that you had a wonderful time.

W What did you do? Did you _____ _____ _____ your girlfriend?

M No, we broke up last week. I _____ _____ _____ my friends.

05 장소 추론

대화를 듣고, 두 사람이 대화하는 장소로 가장 적절한 곳을 고르시오.

① 병원 ② 약국 ③ 경찰서
④ 쇼핑센터 ⑤ 체육관

W What can I do for you?

M Could you take a look at my right hand?

W Oh, it's really swollen. What happened?

M Someone stepped on it by accident.

W _____ _____ _____ a fist?

M I think I can. But it hurts more when I try to _____ _____ _____ .

W I think you _____ _____ _____ _____ .

M I will, but do you have anything I can take for the pain?

W Sure. [Pause] _____ _____ _____ _____ .

대화를 듣고, 여자가 한 마지막 말의 의도로 가장 적절한 것을 고르시오.

① 거절 　② 부탁 　③ 승낙
④ 비난 　⑤ 후회

M What are you doing tonight?
W Nothing in particular. I usually go to bed early on Fridays.
M Do you need to _____ _____
   _____ _____ Saturdays?
W Yes, I have volleyball practice on Saturday mornings. But there's no practice tomorrow.
M Then, you don't have to go to sleep early tonight, right?
   _____ _____ _____
   _____ go to the movies with me?
W _____, _____ _____ a long time since I went to the movies.

---

07 특정 정보 파악

대화를 듣고, 여자가 여행을 갈 도시를 고르시오.

① 런던 　② 뉴욕 　③ 한국
④ 베이징 　⑤ 도쿄

🔊 **Listening Tip**
close는 동사와 형용사가 다 되는 단어입니다. 동사일 때는 끝을 /즈/로 형용사일 때는 /쓰/로 발음하는 것에 유의하세요.

M Have you decided where to go for your vacation?
W Not yet. It's not easy.
M Didn't you want to go to London?
W I went there last year.
M New York is a _____ _____ _____
   _____ in summer.
W But it's too far from Korea. My vacation is only 4 days.
M Then _____ _____ _____
   🔊 close, like Beijing or Tokyo?
W Actually, I've never been to Japan before.
M There is _____ _____ _____
   _____. It'll be perfect for your short vacation.
W _____ _____ _____ Tokyo, then.

---

08 할 일 파악

대화를 듣고, 남자가 대화 직후에 할 일로 가장 적절한 것을 고르시오.

① 간식 사러 가기 　② 우산 챙기기
③ 캠핑 장비 챙기기 　④ 친구에게 전화하기
⑤ 일기예보 확인하기

W Are you excited about this weekend?
M Of course, Mom. It's my first time to go camping with my friends.
W You should start packing today.
M I've _____ _____ _____.

W Really? Do you need more snacks? I can bring you more.
M No, thanks. I think I _____ _____
_____.

W Did you pack an extra jacket and an umbrella?
M I packed extra clothes, but I don't think _____
_____ _____ _____.

W You should _____ _____ _____
_____ to make sure.
M Yes, you're right. I'll do that right now.

09 언급하지 않은 내용 찾기

대화를 듣고, 여자가 제과점에 대해 언급하지 않은 것을 고르시오.

① 이름   ② 제빵사 이름
③ 개점 날짜   ④ 영업시간
⑤ 위치

M Have you been to the new bakery in our building?
W Do you mean Jacob's Bakery?
M Yes. I wonder why it's called Jacob's Bakery.
W Jacob is _____ _____ _____
_____ _____.
M Oh, I didn't know that. When did it open?
W It _____ _____ February 2nd. I heard the
cookies are the most popular.
M Do you know _____ _____ _____?
W Yes. The bakery is open from 9 to 7.
M I'll get some cookies _____ _____
_____ _____ then.

10 주제 추론

다음을 듣고, 여자가 하는 말의 내용으로 가장 적절한 것을 고르시오.

① 수영 강습 안내
② 응급 처치 방법
③ 수영장 안전 수칙
④ 규칙적인 운동의 중요성
⑤ 식음료 구입 장소 안내

W Before you start _____ _____
_____, it's very important that you know and
understand _____ _____ _____.
First, use the pool _____ _____
_____ _____ a lifeguard on duty. Second,
there is _____ _____ in the pool area.
Lastly, eating or drinking is not _____
_____ _____. I hope everyone will stay
safe and have lots of fun!

다음을 듣고, 난방기에 대한 내용으로 일치하지 않는 것을 고르시오.

① 에너지를 절약한다.
② 난방비를 줄일 수 있다.
③ 다른 난방기보다 저렴하다.
④ 작고 가볍다.
⑤ 방을 즉시 따뜻하게 해준다.

M I'd like to tell you about our new heater today. This is an _____ _____ _____, so it will reduce your heating bills. _____ _____ _____ _____, but our new heater will pay for itself in a year or two. It's very _____ _____ _____, but it will warm up your room instantly.

대화를 듣고, 남자가 전화를 건 목적으로 가장 적절한 것을 고르시오.

① 식당을 예약하기 위해서
② 예약을 변경하기 위해서
③ 메뉴를 확인하기 위해서
④ 불만 사항을 말하기 위해서
⑤ 약속에 늦겠다고 알리기 위해서

[Telephone rings.]

W Thank you for calling Martha's Kitchen. How may I help you?

M Can I talk to Elisabeth, please?

W She's not in today.

M She told me to call her if I needed to _____ _____ _____.

W I can _____ _____ _____ _____, sir.

M Oh, great! I have a reservation for tonight under my name.

W May I have your name?

M It is Henry Baker, and could you _____ _____ _____ from 6 p.m. to 7 p.m.?

W Of course. I'll _____ _____ _____ right now.

대화를 듣고, 두 사람이 만날 시각을 고르시오.

① 3:00 p.m.   ② 3:30 p.m.
③ 4:00 p.m.   ④ 4:30 p.m.
⑤ 5:00 p.m.

M Mom, I need a few things for math homework. Can you come and _____ _____ _____ after school today?

W Sure, honey. Where are you going to get them?

M There is a store next to the school. But if I go there, I'll miss the school bus.

W Okay. I finish work at 3:30. How about 4 o'clock?

M Well, _____ _____ _____ 4, but I need time to _____ _____ _____ _____ and buy things.

W I see. How about 4:30? _____ _____

_____ the parking lot.

M Okay. Thanks.

---

14 관계 추론

대화를 듣고, 두 사람의 관계로 가장 적절한 것을 고르시오.

① 옷 가게 점원 – 고객
② 간호사 – 환자
③ 자동차 정비사 – 고객
④ 교통경찰 – 운전자
⑤ 주차 관리인 – 운전자

M How can I help you, ma'am?

W I think there is something wrong _____ _____ _____.

M Can you describe the problem?

W I had a hard time _____ _____ _____ this morning.

M Can you open the hood? I'll take a look.

W Sure, I hope it's nothing serious.

M I don't think _____ _____ _____ _____ the engine.

W What is the problem then?

M I'll have to run some tests. Could you _____ _____ _____ _____ _____?

W Yes, of course.

---

15 부탁 파악

대화를 듣고, 남자가 여자에게 부탁한 일로 가장 적절한 것을 고르시오.

① 팝콘 사 오기
② 영화 추천하기
③ 영화표 예매하기
④ 소설책 빌려주기
⑤ 휴식 방해하지 말기

W Do you have any plans for this holiday?

M I'm just going to relax at home.

W That sounds like a good plan. Why don't you _____ _____ _____?

M No way. I'm not interested in reading at all.

W What are you going to do at home for 3 days then?

M I want to watch movies. I _____ _____ _____ _____ for 2 years.

W Really? A lot of good movies came out last year.

M *Can you recommend _____ _____ _____ for me?

W Sure, I'll text you the names of the movies.

---

* 교육부 지정 의사소통 기능: **추천 요청하기**   동(이) 7 | 미 6

Can[Could] you recommend ~? ~을 추천해 주시겠어요?
• **Can you recommend** a good bike for me? 좋은 자전거 한 대 추천해 줄 수 있을까?
• **Could you recommend** a Spanish dish for me? 스페인 음식 좀 추천해 주시겠어요?

대화를 듣고, 여자가 잠을 자지 <u>못한</u> 이유로 가장 적절한 것을 고르시오.

① 너무 피곤해서
② 밀린 일을 하느라고
③ 낮잠을 많이 자서
④ 커피를 많이 마셔서
⑤ 프로젝트가 걱정되어

M   Megan, you look tired. Do you have a lot of work to do?

W   Well, I've been working on this art project for a while. But it _____ _____ _____ _____ this week.

M   What time did you go to bed last night?

W   I went to bed earlier than usual, but I _____ _____ _____ _____.

M   Were you worried about your project?

W   No, I wasn't. I just _____ _____ _____ _____ in the afternoon.

M   Oh, that happens to me, too.

다음 그림의 상황에 가장 적절한 대화를 고르시오.

① ② ③ ④ ⑤

① M   Do you know _____ _____ _____ _____ now?

   W   Yes, it's 5:30.

② M   Can I get a fork and some napkins?

   W   Yes, I'll bring them right away.

③ M   _____ _____ _____ the salt, please?

   W   Sure, here it is.

④ M   Do you have _____ _____ _____ _____ 12?

   W   I'm sorry. 11 is the biggest size.

⑤ M   Is this washing machine on sale?

   W   No, _____ _____ _____ _____.

다음을 듣고, 여자가 테니스 라켓에 대해 언급하지 <u>않은</u> 것을 고르시오.

① 상품명   ② 무게   ③ 색깔
④ 길이   ⑤ 가격

W   Let me introduce our new tennis racket. _____ _____ Balance Five. You can _____ _____ 3 different weights: 290 grams, 310 grams, and 330 grams. It _____ _____ _____ one color, black. However, it is _____ _____ _____ any other models. Get one today for only $90, and play like a pro!

---

19 이어질 응답 찾기

대화를 듣고, 여자의 마지막 말에 이어질 남자의 말로 가장 적절한 것을 고르시오.

Man: _____

① No, that's not a good idea.
② Our neighbors are so noisy.
③ I'm sorry. I won't forget again.
④ I'll fix the TV right away.
⑤ Yes, you should remember that.

W Where is that sound coming from?
M What sound are you talking about?
W I _____ _____ _____.
M I think it's coming from the bedroom.
W But we just got home. Who could be in our bedroom?
M Let me check. The noise _____ _____ _____ our neighbors downstairs.
W *[Pause]* What was it?
M It was the TV. I forgot _____ _____ _____ _____ when I left home.
W _____ _____ _____ _____ turn off the TV before you leave home.

---

20 이어질 응답 찾기

대화를 듣고, 여자의 마지막 말에 이어질 남자의 말로 가장 적절한 것을 고르시오.

Man: _____

① Because life is so precious.
② I don't remember my birthday.
③ Because I don't like getting older.
④ I am going to celebrate this week.
⑤ Because it's important to be happy.

W When is your birthday, Uncle Bill?
M It's November 9.
W It was just this past weekend.
M Yes, it was. I just turned 31.
W How did _____ _____ _____ _____?
M I _____ _____ my birthday a long time ago.
W Why? It's your happiest day!
M Well, to me it's the saddest day.
W _____ _____ _____ _____ _____?

문법 응용력을 높여주는

GRAMMAR Q

✦ Grammar is Understanding ✦

01
교과서
완벽 해부와 반영

CHAPTER 05 진행형, 미래 표

동아(윤)-2과 | 동아(이)-2과 | 천재(이)-3과 | 미래엔-2과
능률(김)-2과 | 비상-2과

동*(윤)-3과 | 동*(이)-3과 | 천*(이)-4과, 6과 ‥

02
내신 관리
집중 학습

내신 적중 Point

Point 01 어법상 바른 문장 찾기
　　　　　인칭대명사에 따라 be동사가 바르게

Point 02 잘못 바꿔 쓴 문장 찾기
　　　　　주어가 복수일 때 I-I you를 포함하는

Point 03 우리말에 맞게 문장 완성하기
　　　　　주어가 달라질 경우 be동사도 알맞게

03
서술형 만점
모의 시험

Writing Exercises

말과 뜻이 같도록 빈칸에 알맞은 소유격을
완성하세요.

4 다음 사진과 글을 읽고,
　알맞은 말을 쓰세요.

04
예습+복습
무료 부가자료

❶ 어휘리스트, 어휘테스트
❷ 예문영작연습지, 예문해석연습지,
　예문응용연습지
❸ 서술형 추가문제종합평가
❹ Study Planner

쎄듀북닷컴(www.cedubook.com)에서 부가 자료를 무료로 다운로드할 수 있습니다.

쎄듀

1 구문

판매 1위 '천일문' 콘텐츠를 활용하여 정확하고 다양한 구문 학습

(끊어읽기) (해석하기) (문장 구조 분석) (해설·해석 제공) (단어 스크램블링) (영작하기)

2 문법·서술형

쎄듀의 모든 문법 문항을 활용하여 내신까지 해결하는 정교한 문법 유형 제공

 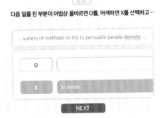  

(객관식과 주관식의 결합) (문법 포인트별 학습) (보기를 활용한 집합 문항) (내신대비 서술형) (어법+서술형 문제)

3 어휘

초·중·고·공무원까지 방대한 어휘량을 제공하며 오프라인 TEST 인쇄도 가능

(영단어 카드 학습) (단어 ↔ 뜻 유형) (예문 활용 유형) (단어 매칭 게임)

4 선생님 보유 문항 이용

(Online Test) (OMR Test)

☕ cafe.naver.com/cedulearnteacher

쎄듀런 학습 정보가 궁금하다면?

쎄듀런 Cafe

· 쎄듀런 사용법 안내 & 학습법 공유
· 공지 및 문의사항 QA
· 할인 쿠폰 증정 등 이벤트 진행

1001개 문장으로 완성하는 중등 필수 영단어

천일문 VOCA

중등 시리즈

하루 20개,
40일 완성
800개

하루 25개,
40일 완성
1,000개

하루 25개,
40일 완성
1,000개

대상: 예비중 ~ 중1

대상: 중2~중3

대상: 중3 ~ 예비고

휴대용
암기장 제공

편리하게 반복 학습 가능해요!

편리한
MP3 player
제공

DAY 01

1001 Sentences
Day 01 - 02

MP3를 직접 들어보세요!

① 중등 교과서 및 교육부 지정 필수 어휘 반영

② 주제별 중등 단어+빈출 표현 수록

③ 쉬운 우리말 풀이와 관련 다양한 tip 제공

④ 문장을 통한 자연스러운 누적 학습

⑤ 쎄듀런을 통한 온라인 단어 암기 서비스

쎄듀북닷컴(www.cedubook.com)에서 부가 자료를 무료로 다운로드할 수 있습니다.

쎄듀

LISTENING Q

[리스닝 큐]

중학영어듣기
모의고사 24회

2

정답 및 해설

김기훈 | 쎄듀 영어교육연구센터

쎄듀

LISTENING Q

중학영어듣기
모의고사 24회

②

정답 및 해설

01 ②	02 ⑤	03 ④	04 ④	05 ③	06 ②	07 ③
08 ④	09 ⑤	10 ④	11 ⑤	12 ③	13 ⑤	14 ⑤
15 ④	16 ①	17 ②	18 ⑤	19 ②	20 ④	

01 ②

[해설] 지금은 흐리지만 오후에는 해가 나겠다고 했다.

[어휘] weather forecast 일기 예보
come out (해·달·별이) 나오다
cool[kuːl] 시원한, 서늘한
continue[kəntínjuː] 계속되다, 지속하다

M Good morning, and welcome to the weather forecast. It's cloudy right now, but the sun will come out in the afternoon. In the evening, it's going to be cool and windy. And this will continue until tonight. That's the weather forecast for today. Have a nice day!

남 안녕하세요, 일기예보를 전해드립니다. 지금은 흐리지만 오후가 되면 해가 나올 것입니다. 저녁에는 선선하고 바람이 불 것입니다. 그리고 이런 상태가 오늘 밤까지 계속되겠습니다. 오늘의 일기예보입니다. 좋은 하루 보내세요!

02 ⑤

[해설] 두 사람은 'Dear Diary' 문구를 맨 위에 두고 그 밑에 하트를 여러 개 그렸다.

[어휘] cover[kʌ́vər] 표지
diary[dáiəri] 다이어리, 일기장
enough[inʌ́f] 충분한

M Jimin, what are you making?
W I'm making a cover for my diary. Can you help me?
M Sure. Where do you want to put the title?
W I want to put "Dear Diary" at the top.
M Okay.
W Now, I want to draw something under the title. Do you have any ideas?
M How about a big heart?
W Okay. But one heart won't be enough. Let's draw many hearts.
M Great. [Pause] Now it looks better with hearts.

남 지민아, 뭐 만들고 있니?
여 다이어리 표지를 만들고 있어. 나 좀 도와줄래?
남 물론이지. 제목을 어디에 두려고 하니?
여 'Dear Diary'를 맨 위에 올려놓고 싶어.
남 알았어.
여 이제 제목 밑에 뭔가를 그리고 싶어. 좋은 생각 있니?
남 큰 하트가 하나 있으면 어떨까?
여 좋아. 하지만 하트 하나로는 충분하지 않아. 하트를 많이 그리자.
남 좋아. [잠시 후] 이제 하트가 있으니 더 나은 것 같아.

03 ④

[해설] 사용 기간(8년), 속도(매우 느림), 유무선 여부(유선), 스캐너 기능(없음)에 대해서 언급하였지만 크기에 대해 언급하지 않았다.

[어휘] printer[príntər] 프린터, 인쇄기
work[wəːrk] (기계, 장치 등이) 작동되다
buy[bai] 사다 (buy-bought-bought)
print 인쇄하다, 프린트하다
fix[fiks] 수리하다
wireless[wáiərlis] 무선 (시스템)
scanner[skǽnər] 스캐너

M Mom, this printer is not working again.
W What's wrong with it?
M We bought this 8 years ago. It's really old.
W Okay. Anything else?
M It takes too long to print papers.
W Well, that's a problem. Let me see if I can fix it.
M You don't need to. It's not even wireless and has no scanner.
W Okay. Maybe it's time to change your printer.

남 엄마, 이 프린터가 또 안 되네요.
여 뭐가 문제인데?
남 8년 전에 이걸 구매했잖아요. 너무 오래됐어요.
여 그래. 그 밖에 또 뭐가 문제니?
남 종이를 인쇄하는 데 너무 오래 걸려요.
여 음, 그건 문제구나. 어디 고칠 수 있는지 보자.
남 그럴 필요 없어요. 심지어 무선도 아니고 스캐너도 없잖아요.
여 알았다. 프린터를 바꿀 때가 됐나 보구나.

04 ④

[해설] 어버이날에 남자는 조부모님을 방문했고, 여자는 엄마와 쇼핑을 했다.

[어휘] Parents' Day 어버이날
celebrate[séləbrèit] 기념하다
grandson[grǽndsʌn] 손자
scarf[ska:rf] 스카프, 목도리

W Eric, how was your Parents' Day?
M It was nice. I visited my grandparents with my family. We celebrate every Parents' Day together.
W Oh, did you give them any flowers?
M Yes. I also wrote them a card and read it to them.
W You're such a good grandson.
M How about you, Julie?
W I went shopping with my mom. I bought a scarf for her.
M That's great.

여 Eric, 어버이날은 어떻게 보냈어?
남 좋았어. 가족과 함께 조부모님을 방문했거든. 우리는 매년 어버이날을 함께 기념해.
여 아, 그분들께 꽃을 드렸니?
남 그래, 카드도 써서 읽어 드렸어.
여 넌 정말 좋은 손자구나.
남 너는 뭐 했어, Julie?
여 나는 엄마랑 쇼핑하러 갔어. 엄마에게 스카프를 사 드렸어.
남 잘했네.

05 ③

[해설] 여자가 남자에게 소포를 중국에 보내는 데 걸리는 소요 시간, 비용을 설명하는 것으로 보아 우체국에서 나누는 대화임을 알 수 있다.

[어휘] mail[meil] (우편으로) 보내다
package[pǽkidʒ] 소포
airmail[éərmeil] 항공 우편

W Hello. How may I help you?
M I'd like to mail this package to China.
W How would you like to send it?
M By airmail, please.
W Okay. What's in the package?
M It's a toy train set for my cousin. How long will it take?
W It'll take about 5 days.
M Good. How much does it cost?
W It costs $50.

여 안녕하세요. 무엇을 도와드릴까요?
남 이 소포를 중국으로 보내려고 해요.
여 어떻게 보내실 건가요?
남 항공우편으로요.
여 알겠습니다. 소포에는 무엇이 들어있나요?
남 제 사촌에게 줄 장난감 기차 세트예요. 얼마나 걸릴까요?
여 5일 정도 걸릴 겁니다.
남 좋습니다. 가격은 얼마죠?
여 50달러입니다.

06 ②

[해설] 여자는 남자가 알려준 대로 숨을 참았고 딸꾹질이 멈추자 남자에게 고맙다고 했다.

[어휘] hiccup[híkʌp] 딸꾹질을 하다
work[wəːrk] 효과가 있다
hold A's breath 숨을 멈추다

M Hey, Sumi. What's wrong? You don't look well.
W I tried everything, but I can't stop hiccuping. What should I do?
M Try drinking some water. It might help.
W I already did. But that didn't work for me.
M Then hold your breath for as long as you can. That should work.
W Okay. [Pause] Oh, it stopped! Thank you, James.

남 Sumi야. 무슨 일 있어? 몸이 안 좋아 보여.
여 모든 걸 다 시도해 봤는데 딸꾹질이 멈추질 않아. 어떡하지?
남 물을 좀 마셔 봐. 도움이 될지도 몰라.
여 이미 마셨어. 하지만 그건 효과가 없더라고.
남 그럼 가능한 한 숨을 참아 봐. 효과가 있을 거야.
여 알았어. [잠시 후] 아, 멈췄다! 고마워, James.

07 ③

[해설] 남자는 모바일 앱의 기능으로 언어의 번역 기능을 소개했다.

[어휘] tourist[túərist] 관광객
on the way 오는 중에
direction[dirékʃən] 방향

W I'm sorry I'm late. I had to help out a tourist on the way.
M That's all right. What did you help with?
W I had to take her to City Hall.
M Why didn't you just give her directions?
W She spoke French, and she didn't understand English at all.

여 늦어서 미안해. 오는 도중에 관광객을 도와야 했어.
남 괜찮아. 뭘 도와줬니?
여 그녀를 시청까지 데려다줘야 했어.
남 왜 그냥 방향을 알려주지 않았어?
여 그녀는 프랑스어를 하는데, 영어를 전혀 이해하지 못했어.

mobile app(= mobile application) 모바일 응용 소프트웨어 language[lǽŋgwidʒ] 언어 helpful[hélpfəl] 도움이 되는	M Why don't you use the mobile app TalkTalk next time? W TalkTalk? What is that? M It changes one language to another. W Really? It sounds very helpful.	남 다음에는 TalkTalk 모바일 앱을 한번 써 보는 거 어때? 여 TalkTalk? 그게 뭔데? 남 한 언어를 다른 언어로 바꿔주는 거야. 여 정말? 매우 도움이 될 것 같네.

08 ④

해설 남자가 근처에 맛있는 국수집이 있다고 하자 여자가 먹으러 가자고 했다. 어휘 fantastic[fæntǽstik] 환상적인 noodle dish 국수 요리	M Susan, welcome to Busan! W Hi, Hajun. I'm so excited to be here. M Have you ever been here before? W No, it's my first time. I went to Haeundae Beach this morning. It was fantastic. M Great. Are you hungry? W Yes, a little. Why? M I know a good restaurant around here. It has delicious noodle dishes. What do you think? W Sure. Let's go there right now.	남 Susan, 부산에 온 것을 환영해! 여 안녕, 하준아. 여기 와서 너무 신나. 남 여기 와 본 적 있어? 여 아니, 처음이야. 오늘 아침에는 해운대 해변에 갔었어. 정말 멋지더라. 남 잘했네. 너 배고프니? 여 응, 조금. 왜? 남 이 근처에 있는 좋은 식당을 알아. 그곳에서 맛있는 국수를 먹을 수 있는데. 어때? 여 그래. 지금 당장 그곳에 가자.

09 ⑤

해설 여행지(섬), 교통수단(배), 날씨(아주 좋았음), 활동(스노클링)에 대해 언급하였으나 음식에 대해서는 언급하지 않았다. 어휘 island[áilənd] 섬 perfect[pə́ːrfikt] 완벽한 go snorkeling 스노클링을 하다	M Kate! Did you have a good time on your trip? W I just loved it. I went to an island with my family. M Wow! How did you get to the island? W I took a boat. It was fun. M Great. How was the weather? W The weather was perfect. I went snorkeling at the beach. I had a lot of fun. M That sounds like fun!	남 Kate! 여행 잘 다녀왔어? 여 그냥 너무 좋았어. 가족과 함께 섬에 갔거든. 남 와! 섬에는 무얼 타고 갔어? 여 배를 탔지. 재미있었어. 남 좋았겠다. 날씨는 어땠어? 여 날씨는 아주 좋았어. 바다에서 스노클링했어. 정말 재미있었어. 남 재미있었겠네!

10 ④

해설 여자는 패스트푸드를 건강하게 먹는 방법을 소개하고 있다. 어휘 rather than ~보다는 beef[biːf] 소고기 cut down on ~을 줄이다 sauce[sɔːs] 소스 calory[kǽləri] 칼로리 consider[kənsídər] 고려하다 instead of ~ 대신에	W We know that fast food can be bad for us. But I'm sure many of you still enjoy fast food. So, today I'd like to tell you healthier ways to eat fast food. First, choose chicken rather than beef. Second, cut down on the sauces. They are high in calories. Finally, if you need something to drink, consider milk instead of soda.	여 우리는 패스트푸드가 우리에게 해로울 수 있다는 것을 압니다. 하지만 분명 여러분 중 많은 사람들이 여전히 패스트푸드를 즐기죠. 그래서 오늘은 패스트푸드를 먹는 건강한 방법을 알려드릴게요. 첫째, 소고기보다는 닭고기를 골라보세요. 둘째, 소스를 줄이세요. 그것은 칼로리가 높아요. 마지막으로, 마실 것이 필요하면, 탄산음료 대신 우유를 고려해보세요.

11 ⑤

해설 스톤헨지를 왜 만들었는지는 아무도 알지 못한다고 하였다.	W May I have your attention, please? We're finally here at Stonehenge. This is one of the	여 주목해 주세요. 우리는 드디어 스톤헨지에 도착했어요. 이곳은 지구상에서

어휘 attention [əténʃən] 주목, 주의
mysterious [mistíəriəs] 불가사의한, 신비한
circle [sə́ːrkl] 원형
huge [hjuːdʒ] 거대한
historian [histɔ́ːriən] 역사학자
incredible [inkrédəbəl] 놀라운, 훌륭한

most mysterious places on Earth. Stonehenge is a circle of huge stones. Historians think it was built around 5,000 years ago. But no one knows who built it or why. Now, let's look around this incredible place!

가장 불가사의한 곳 중 하나이지요. 스톤헨지는 거대한 돌들이 원형으로 둘러서 있는 것이에요. 역사학자들은 이곳이 5,000년쯤 전에 지어졌다고 짐작하고 있어요. 그렇지만 누가 왜 이것을 만들었는지는 아무도 알지 못해요. 자, 이제 이 놀라운 곳을 둘러봅시다!

12 ③

해설 여자는 엄마에게 생신 선물로 드리려고 종이꽃을 만들었다고 했다.

어휘 paper flower 종이꽃

M Where did you get these paper flowers?
W Actually, I made them.
M Wow, you're very good with your hands. They look like real flowers.
W Thanks. I made them as a birthday gift for my mom.
M I'm sure your mom will love them.
W I hope so.

남 이 종이꽃은 어디서 샀니?
여 사실 내가 만들었어.
남 와, 너 손재주가 대단하구나. 그것들은 진짜 꽃처럼 보여.
여 고마워. 우리 엄마께 드릴 생신 선물로 만든 거야.
남 너희 엄마가 분명히 좋아하실 거야.
여 그랬으면 좋겠어.

13 ⑤

해설 6달러짜리 검은 양말 두 켤레에 8달러짜리 파란 양말 한 켤레를 추가해서 모두 20달러를 지불해야 한다.

어휘 sock [sɑːk] 양말
pair [pɛər] (두 개로 된) 한 쌍
credit card 신용 카드

M Excuse me. I'm looking for socks for sports.
W Okay. How about these ones?
M They're nice. How much are they?
W The black pair is $6, and the blue pair is $8.
M I'll take 2 pairs of black socks, please.
W Okay. It's $12 in total.
M Oh, wait! I'd like to add a pair of blue socks.
W All right. That will be $20 in all.
M Here's my credit card.

남 실례합니다. 스포츠 양말을 찾고 있는데요.
여 그렇군요. 이것들은 어때요?
남 그것들은 좋네요. 얼마인가요?
여 검은색 양말은 6달러, 파란색 양말은 8달러입니다.
남 검은 양말 두 켤레 주세요.
여 네. 합쳐서 12달러입니다.
남 아, 잠깐만요! 파란색 양말 한 켤레 추가할게요.
여 알겠습니다. 전부 합해서 20달러입니다.
남 여기 제 신용 카드 드릴게요.

14 ⑤

해설 남자가 우주에서 있는 여자를 특별 손님이라 소개하고, 이어서 여러 질문을 하는 것으로 보아 두 사람의 관계는 방송 진행자와 우주 비행사임을 알 수 있다.

어휘 guest [gest] 특별 출연자, 게스트
space [speis] 우주
International Space Station 국제 우주 정거장
satellite [sǽtəlàit] 인공위성
research [risə́ːrtʃ] 연구, 조사
land [lænd] (비행기나 배를 타고) 도착하다, 착륙하다

M Today, we have a special guest from space, Jesse Thompson. Jesse, can you hear me?
W Yes. Hi, Ben. Thank you for inviting me.
M Where are you?
W I'm at the International Space Station.
M What are you doing there?
W I'm fixing a satellite and doing some research.
M When are you going to land back on Earth?
W I've nearly finished my work, and I'll be on Earth in 6 days.

남 오늘 우리는 우주에서 특별한 손님이신 Jesse Thompson 씨를 모셨는데요. Jesse, 제 말 들리나요?
여 네. 안녕하세요, Ben. 초대해 주셔서 고마워요.
남 어디 계신가요?
여 저는 국제 우주 정거장에 있습니다.
남 그곳에서 무엇을 하시나요?
여 인공위성을 수리하고 연구를 좀 하고 있어요.
남 언제 지구로 돌아오십니까?
여 일을 거의 끝마쳤기 때문에 6일 후에 지구에 도착할 거예요.

nearly[níərli] 거의
Earth[əːrθ] 지구
show[ʃou] (텔레비전 등의) 프로그램

M Thank you for being on my show. I hope you get back safely.

남 프로그램에 나와 주셔서 고맙습니다. 무사히 돌아오길 바랍니다.

15 ④

해설 여자가 학교 잡지에 만화를 그릴 다른 사람을 소개해 달라고 부탁했다.

어휘 trouble[trʌbl] 곤란, 문제
cartoon[ka:rtúːn] 만화
magazine[mæ̀gəzíːn] 잡지
cartoonist[ka:rtúːnist] 만화가
introduce[ìntrədjúːs] 소개하다

W Mark, we're in trouble.
M What's wrong?
W Timmy can't draw cartoons for our school magazine any longer. So, we have to find another cartoonist.
M Hmm... How about Julie?
W Julie? Who's that?
M She is a new student in my class.
W Does she draw cartoons well?
M Yes. I'm sure you will like her cartoons.
W Great. Can you introduce her to me?
M Of course.

여 Mark, 우리가 좀 곤란해졌어.
남 무슨 일이야?
여 Timmy가 우리 학교 잡지에 더 이상 만화를 그릴 수 없게 됐어. 그래서 다른 만화가를 찾아야 해.
남 음… Julie는 어때?
여 Julie? 걔가 누군데?
남 우리 반에 새로 온 애야.
여 그 애는 만화를 잘 그리니?
남 응. 넌 틀림없이 걔가 그린 만화가 마음에 들 거야.
여 좋아. 나한테 소개해 줄 수 있어?
남 물론이지.

16 ①

해설 남자는 여동생에게 줄 모자를 사야 해서 여자에게 쇼핑을 함께 가자고 묻기 위해 전화했다.

어휘 baseball cap 야구 모자
break[breik] 부러뜨리다
cheer up ~을 격려하다

[Cell phone rings.]
W Hello.
M Hi, Semi. Are you busy right now?
W Not at all. What's up?
M I need your help with something. Can you help me?
W Of course. What is it?
M Can you go shopping with me? I need your help to choose a baseball cap for my sister.
W Okay. Are you planning to go to a baseball game together?
M No. She broke her arm while she was skating. I just want to cheer her up.
W Oh, I see. Let's meet at 4 o'clock.

[휴대전화가 울린다.]
여 여보세요.
남 안녕, 세미야. 너 지금 바빠?
여 전혀 바쁘지 않아. 무슨 일이야?
남 나 네 도움이 필요한 게 있는데. 도와 줄 수 있어?
여 물론이지. 그게 뭔데?
남 나랑 같이 쇼핑 가줄래? 여동생에게 줄 야구 모자를 고르는 데 네 도움이 필요하거든.
여 알겠어. 여동생하고 같이 야구 보러 가려고?
남 아니. 걔가 스케이트를 타다가 팔이 부러졌거든. 기운이 나게 해주고 싶어서.
여 아, 그렇구나. 4시에 만나자.

17 ②

해설 식사를 다 마친 후, 음식이 어땠는지 묻는 대화가 적절하다.

어휘 mango[mǽŋgou] 망고
excellent[éksələnt] 훌륭한
healthy[hélθi] 건강한
vegetable[védʒitəbl] 야채
eating habits 식습관

① **W** What would you like for a drink?
　M I'd like a glass of mango juice.
② **W** How did you like the spaghetti?
　M It was excellent! I liked it.
③ **W** Can you tell me how to cook this pizza?
　M Sure. It's really easy.
④ **W** Why do you like salad?
　M Because it is good for your health.
⑤ **W** Do you have healthy eating habits?
　M Yes, I eat many vegetables and fruits every day.

① 여 음료는 어떤 것으로 하시겠습니까?
　남 망고 주스 한 잔 주세요.
② 여 스파게티는 어땠어?
　남 아주 훌륭했어! 난 좋았어.
③ 여 이 피자 어떻게 만들었는지 알려줄 수 있니?
　남 물론이지. 정말 쉬워.
④ 여 왜 샐러드를 좋아하니?
　남 그게 건강에 좋기 때문이야.
⑤ 여 넌 건강한 식습관을 가지고 있니?
　남 응, 나는 매일 야채와 과일을 많이 먹어.

18 ⑤

해설 좋아하는 이유(맛있음), 주로 먹는 날(특별한 날), 재료(밀가루, 김치, 양파, 해산물), 만드는 방법(모든 재료를 섞고, 팬에 조리하기)에 대해 언급하였지만 유래에 대해서는 언급하지 않았다.

어휘 once[wʌns] 한 번
flour[fláuər] 밀가루
onion[ʌnjən] 양파
seafood[síːfud] 해산물
mix[miks] 섞다
heated pan 달궈진 팬

M My favorite food is kimchijeon. I love this food because it's delicious. I usually eat this food on special days. I made this once with my grandmother. Kimchijeon doesn't need many things. It only needs some flour, kimchi, onions, and seafood. Making kimchijeon is easy. You just mix everything together with water. Then cook it on a heated pan with oil.

남 제가 가장 좋아하는 음식은 김치전입니다. 저는 이 음식이 맛있어서 아주 좋아합니다. 저는 특별한 날에 이 음식을 먹는 편입니다. 한번은 할머니와 함께 이것을 만들었습니다. 김치전은 만드는 데 많은 것이 필요하지 않습니다. 밀가루와 김치, 양파, 해산물만 있으면 됩니다. 그냥 물과 함께 모든 것을 섞으면 됩니다. 그러고 나서 달궈진 팬에 기름과 같이 조리해보세요.

19 ②

해설 동물병원에 전화해서 진료 예약을 하는 상황이므로 병원에서 제시한 진료 시간에 대한 가능 여부를 말하는 게 적절하다.

어휘 treat[triːt] 간식
make an appointment 예약을 하다
[선택지]
call[kɔːl] 전화 (통화)

[Telephone rings.]
M Smile Pet Animal Hospital.
W Hello. This is Amy Pitt.
M Hello, Amy. What can I do for you?
W My dog hasn't been eating her food for almost 3 days now. What should I do?
M Okay. Did you try giving her any treats?
W Yes, I did. But she didn't eat them.
M I see. Would you like to make an appointment?
W Yes, please.
M Is 2:30 tomorrow afternoon okay?
W Yes. That'll be fine.

[전화벨이 울린다.]
남 Smile Pet 동물병원입니다.
여 여보세요. 저는 Amy Pitt라고 해요.
남 안녕하세요, Amy 씨. 무엇을 도와드릴까요?
여 우리 개가 거의 3일 동안 음식을 안 먹고 있어요. 어떡하죠?
남 그렇군요. 간식을 줘 보셨나요?
여 네, 줘 봤어요. 하지만 그것들을 먹지 않았어요.
남 알겠습니다. 예약하시겠습니까?
여 네, 그럴게요.
남 내일 오후 2시 30분 괜찮으세요?
여 네. 괜찮아요.

① 미안해요, 지금 바빠요.
③ 전화 줘서 고마워.
④ 고마워요. 그녀는 이제 나아졌어요.
⑤ 다음에 다시 요청할게요.

20 ④

해설 커피를 한잔하자는 남자의 제안에 승낙하거나 거절하는 응답이 적절하다.

어휘 attend[əténd] (~에) 다니다
grade[greid] 학년
remember[rimémbər] 기억하다

M Excuse me. Did you attend Wood Hill Middle School?
W Yes, I did. How do you know that?
M I'm Mingi. We were in the same class 10 years ago.
W Oh, I remember you now. It's been a long time since we last met.
M Yes, it has. If you are not too busy, do you want to get some coffee?
W Sure. That sounds great!

남 실례합니다. Wood Hill 중학교에 다녔죠?
여 네, 그랬어요. 그걸 어떻게 아시죠?
남 나 민기야. 우리 10년 전에 같은 반이었잖아.
여 아, 이제 네가 기억난다. 우리가 마지막으로 보고 꽤 오래 지났네.
남 그래, 오래됐지. 바쁘지 않으면, 커피 한잔할래?
여 그래. 좋아!

① 다음에 봐요!
② 어디 출신이신가요?
③ 나를 기억하세요?
⑤ 나도 당신을 기억하지 못해요.

01 ①	02 ①	03 ③	04 ③	05 ④	06 ③	07 ③
08 ④	09 ③	10 ③	11 ⑤	12 ②	13 ④	14 ③
15 ④	16 ④	17 ④	18 ④	19 ④	20 ⑤	

01 ①

해설 파리는 햇볕이 많이 내리쬘 것이라고 했다.

어휘 continue to-v 계속해서 ~하다
including[inklú:diŋ] ~을 포함하여
all day long 하루 종일
lots of 많은
sunshine[sʌ́nʃàin] 햇빛

M Let's look at today's world weather forecast. It will continue to rain in many parts of Asia, including Seoul, Beijing, and Hong Kong. In New York, there will be clear skies all day long. It will be windy and cloudy in London, but there will be lots of sunshine in Paris.

남 오늘의 세계 일기 예보를 살펴보겠습니다. 서울, 베이징, 그리고 홍콩을 포함한 아시아의 많은 지역에는 비가 계속해서 내리겠습니다. 뉴욕은 하루 종일 맑은 하늘이 이어지겠습니다. 런던은 바람이 불고 흐리겠으나 파리는 햇빛이 많이 내리쬐겠습니다.

02 ①

해설 사진 속에는 산을 배경으로 여자가 머물렀던 집이 나무 옆에 있다.

어휘 back[bæk] 돌아와서
vacation[veikéiʃən] 휴가
go hiking 하이킹을 가다
peaceful[pí:sfəl] 평화로운
quiet[kwáiət] 고요한, 조용한

M Mina, you are back from your vacation.
W Yes, I had so much fun. Oh, I have some pictures here. Do you want to see them?
M Sure. [Pause] Where did you take this picture? It's beautiful.
W I went hiking at Ever Mountain. Do you see the house on the right?
M The one next to the tree?
W Yes. I stayed there for 3 days. It was so peaceful and quiet.

남 미나야, 너 휴가에서 돌아왔구나.
여 그래, 정말 재미있었어. 아, 여기 사진이 몇 장 있어. 보여줄까?
남 물론이지. [잠시 후] 이 사진은 어디서 찍은 거야? 멋지다.
여 Ever Mountain에 등산 갔었어. 오른쪽에 집이 보이니?
남 나무 옆에 있는 거?
여 그래, 거기서 3일 동안 머물렀어. 너무나 평화롭고 고요했어.

03 ③

해설 지붕 색상(빨간색), 층수(2층), 방 개수(5개), 편의시설(수영장)에 대해 언급하였으나 전망에 대해서는 언급하지 않았다.

어휘 prefer[prifə́:r] ~을 (더) 좋아하다, 선호하다
roof[ru(:)f] 지붕
floor[flɔ:r] (건물의) 층

W Look at the house over there. It looks like a train.
M But it's too small. I prefer a big house with a red roof.
W What kind of house do you want to live in when you grow up?
M I want to live in a house with 2 floors. And in the house, there have to be enough rooms for my family. At least 5 rooms.
W That sounds nice. Is there anything else you want?
M A swimming pool should be enough.

여 저기 집 좀 봐. 기차처럼 보여.
남 그런데 너무 작다. 나는 빨간 지붕이 있는 큰 집이 더 좋아.
여 너는 커서 어떤 집에서 살고 싶니?
남 나는 이층집에서 살고 싶어. 그리고 집 안에는 우리 가족에게 맞는 충분한 방이 있어야 해. 적어도 5개의 방.
여 좋은 생각이야. 더 필요한 건 없어?
남 수영장이 있으면 충분할 거야.

04 ③

해설 주말에 남자는 영화를 보고 스파게티를 만들었고 여자는 가평에 가서 번지점프를 했다.

W Did you have a good weekend?
M It was all right. I watched an action movie and made spaghetti. What about you?

여 주말 잘 보냈니?
남 괜찮았어. 나는 액션 영화 한 편 보고 스파게티를 만들었어. 너는?

[어휘] bungee jump 번지점프
for the first time 처음으로
scary[skɛ́(:)əri] 무서운
get over ~을 극복하다
fear[fiər] 두려움, 공포

W I went to Gapyeong <u>with</u> <u>my</u> <u>friends</u>.
M I see. What did you do there?
W I went bungee jumping <u>for</u> <u>the</u> <u>first</u> <u>time</u>.
M How was it?
W It was <u>a</u> <u>little</u> <u>scary</u> at first, but I got over my fear and jumped.

여 나는 친구들과 가평에 갔었어.
남 그렇구나. 거기서 뭐했어?
여 난 처음으로 번지 점프를 했어.
남 어땠어?
여 처음에는 좀 무서웠지만, 두려움을 극복하고 뛰어내렸지.

05 ④

[해설] 동전을 넣으면 물이 나오고 비누를 사용할 수 있으며, 차를 세척할 수 있는 곳은 세차장이다.

[어휘] visit[vízit] 방문
machine[məʃíːn] 기계
bill[bil] (돈의) 지폐
coin[kɔin] 동전
soap[soup] 비누
push a button 버튼을 누르다

M How may I help you?
W This is my first visit here. Can you help me <u>with</u> <u>these</u> <u>machines</u>?
M Sure. Did you change your bills into coins?
W Yes. I have them here.
M All right. First put some coins in this machine. Then water <u>will</u> <u>come</u> <u>out</u> for 3 minutes.
W Then where do I <u>get</u> <u>the</u> <u>soap</u> for the car?
M You have to put some coins in here again, and then push this soap button.
W Oh, okay. I brought my own brush <u>to</u> <u>wash</u> <u>the</u> <u>car</u>. Can I use it here?
M Of course.

남 어떻게 도와드릴까요?
여 이번이 이곳의 첫 방문이에요. 이 기계들 사용하는 걸 좀 도와주시겠어요?
남 물론이죠. 지폐를 동전으로 바꾸셨나요?
여 네. 여기에 있어요.
남 알겠습니다. 먼저 이 기계 안에 동전을 좀 넣으세요. 그러면 물이 3분 동안 나올 거예요.
여 그럼 차 비누는 어디에서 찾을 수 있나요?
남 여기에 다시 동전을 넣은 다음, 이 비누 버튼을 누르셔야 해요.
여 아, 알겠어요. 제 차를 닦을 솔을 가져왔어요. 이곳에서 사용해도 되나요?
남 물론이죠.

06 ③

[해설] 경기에 져서 속상해하는 여자에게 남자는 지는 것도 배우는 하나의 방법이라며 다음에는 이길 거라고 격려했다.

[어휘] win[win] 이기다 (↔ lose[luːz] (시합에서) 지다, 패하다)
do well 잘하다
try A's best 최선을 다하다
kick[kik] (발로) 차다
upset[ʌpsét] 속상한, 마음이 상한
result[rizʌ́lt] 결과
way[wei] 방법

M Great work, Jenna!
W But coach, I didn't win today.
M No, you didn't. But you <u>did</u> <u>really</u> <u>well</u> today at the game.
W Do you think so?
M Yes, I know <u>you</u> <u>tried</u> <u>your</u> <u>best</u> at the game. You also got better at kicking.
W Thanks, but I'm still <u>upset</u> <u>about</u> <u>losing</u>. I was so close to winning.
M Don't get too upset about the result. Losing is <u>a</u> <u>way</u> <u>of</u> <u>learning</u>. You'll win next time.

남 잘했어, Jenna!
여 하지만 감독님, 저는 오늘 이기지 못했어요.
남 그래, 이기지는 못했지. 하지만 너는 오늘 경기에서 정말 잘했어.
여 그렇게 생각하세요?
남 그래, 난 네가 최선을 다했다는 걸 알아. 공을 차는 것도 더 좋아졌어.
여 고맙습니다. 하지만 전 여전히 진 게 속상해요. 거의 이길 뻔했는데.
남 결과에 대해 너무 속상해하지 마. 지는 것도 배우는 하나의 방법이야. 다음에는 네가 이길 거야.

07 ③

[해설] 뉴질랜드는 3월에 맑은 날이 많지만 가끔 비가 오므로 우산을 가져가는 게 좋겠다고 했다.

W Ethan, are you from New Zealand?
M Yes, I lived in Auckland.
W How is the weather <u>there</u> <u>in</u> <u>March</u>? I'm going to visit New Zealand next month.

여 Ethan, 너 뉴질랜드에서 왔지?
남 맞아. 난 오클랜드에 살았어.
여 그곳 3월 날씨는 어때? 다음 달에 뉴질랜드에 갈 거라서.

어휘 warm[wɔːrm] 따뜻한
look forward to ~을 기대하다
beach[biːtʃ] 해변
relax[rilǽks] 휴식을 취하다
pack[pæk] (짐을) 싸다

M March is a good time to visit New Zealand. It's really warm.

W Great! I'm looking forward to going to the beach and relaxing there.

M There are many sunny days, but it sometimes rains in March. You should take an umbrella.

W Okay. I'll pack one.

남 3월은 뉴질랜드를 방문하기에 좋은 시기야. 정말 따뜻해.

여 좋았어! 거기 해변에 가서 휴식을 취하고 싶어.

남 3월에는 맑은 날이 많지만 가끔 비가 와. 우산을 가지고 가는 게 좋겠어.

여 알았어. 하나 챙길게.

08 ④

해설 헤어드라이어가 여러 번 고장이 나자 남자가 수리점에 전화하라고 했고 여자가 당장 그렇게 하겠다고 했다.

어휘 done[dʌn] 다 끝난, 다 된
hair dryer 헤어드라이어
borrow[bárou] 빌리다
work[wəːrk] (기계 등을) 작동시키다
repair shop 수리점
for free 무료로, 무상으로

M Amy, are you done with the hair dryer? Can I borrow it?

W I'm not done yet. [Pause] Oh no!

M What happened?

W It just stopped working again.

M Again? When did you buy the hair dryer?

W I bought it last month. This is the third time it stopped.

M You should call the repair shop. Since you bought it last month, you can get it fixed for free.

W Really? Maybe I should do that right now.

남 Amy, 헤어드라이어 다 썼어? 빌릴 수 있을까?

여 아직 안 다 안 썼어. [잠시 후] 이런!

남 무슨 일이야?

여 이게 방금 또 꺼졌어.

남 또? 그 헤어드라이어 언제 샀니?

여 지난달에 샀어. 이렇게 꺼진 게 이번이 세 번째야.

남 수리점에 전화하는 게 좋겠어. 지난달에 샀으니 무료로 수리가 가능할 거야.

여 정말? 지금 당장 그렇게 해야 할까 봐.

09 ③

해설 전시 기간(어제부터 5월 17일까지), 작가(Joseph Harrington), 사진 촬영(불가능), 전시회 위치(C관)에 대해 언급하였지만 티켓 요금에 대해서는 언급하지 않았다.

어휘 gallery[gǽləri] 미술관; (미술품) 전시실
exhibition[èksəbíʃən] 전시회
continue[kəntínjuː] 계속되다
nature[néitʃər] 자연
around the world 전 세계에
visitor[vízitər] 방문객
turn off ~을 끄다

[Telephone Rings.]

W Hello, Bright Stars Gallery. How may I help you?

M Hello, did the Harrington Photo Exhibition start?

W Yes, it started yesterday and will continue until May 17.

M The one by Joseph Harrington, right?

W That's right. You'll see his 250 pictures of nature around the world.

M Great. Can I take pictures there?

W No, you can't. We ask all visitors to turn off their cell phones.

M Okay. Where in your gallery is the exhibition?

W It's in Room C.

[전화벨이 울린다.]

여 안녕하세요, Bright Stars 미술관입니다. 무엇을 도와드릴까요?

남 안녕하세요, Harrington 사진전이 시작됐나요?

여 네, 어제부터 시작해서 5월 17일까지 계속될 겁니다.

남 Joseph Harrington 전시회가 맞지요?

여 맞습니다. 전 세계의 자연을 찍은 그의 사진 250점을 볼 수 있습니다.

남 좋군요. 거기서 사진 찍어도 되나요?

여 아뇨, 찍을 수 없습니다. 저희는 모든 방문객들에게 휴대전화의 전원을 꺼 달라고 합니다.

남 알겠습니다. 그 전시회는 어느 전시실에서 하나요?

여 C관에서 합니다.

10 ③

해설 여자는 미세먼지에 대처하는 방법 세 가지를 알려주고 있다.

어휘 fine dust 미세먼지
these days 요즘에는
cause[kɔːz] ~의 원인이 되다

W Hello, everyone. It's hard to see clear skies because of fine dust these days. Fine dust causes serious diseases. So, it's important to protect ourselves from the fine dust. When you go out, wear a mask to cover your nose and mouth. When you come back, be sure to

여 안녕하세요, 여러분. 요즘 미세먼지 때문에 맑은 하늘을 보기가 어렵습니다. 미세먼지는 심각한 질병의 원인이 됩니다. 그래서 미세먼지로부터 우리 자신을 보호하는 것이 중요합니다. 외출할 때는 마스크를 착용하여 코와 입

serious[síəriəs] 심각한
disease[dizíːz] 질병
protect A from B B로부터 A를 보호
하다
as ~ as possible 될 수 있는 대로,
가급적

wash your hands. Lastly, drink as much water as possible.

을 가리세요. 돌아와서는 반드시 손을 씻으세요. 마지막으로 가능한 한 물을 많이 마시세요.

11 ⑤

해설 Jenny Evans는 반장 후보로 추천받았다.

어휘 recommend[rèkəménd] 추천하다
class president 반장
thoughtful[θɔ́ːtfəl] 배려심 있는, 친절한
person[pə́ːrsən] 사람
leader[líːdər] 리더, 지도자, 대표

M Hello, everyone. I'd like to recommend Jenny Evans as our class president. She is a very kind and thoughtful person because she always tries to help others. She is a great leader, and she listens to the teacher and studies very hard. I think she will be a great class president.

남 안녕하세요, 여러분. 나는 우리 반 반장으로 Jenny Evans를 추천하고 싶어요. 그녀는 항상 남을 도우려고 하기 때문에 매우 친절하고 배려심 있는 사람입니다. 그녀는 훌륭한 리더이며 선생님의 말씀을 잘 듣고 매우 열심히 공부합니다. 나는 그녀가 훌륭한 반장이 될 거라고 생각합니다.

12 ②

해설 주말에 스키를 타러 가려고 했는데 날씨가 따뜻할 거라고 해서 여자는 계획을 변경하려고 전화했다.

어휘 in that case 그렇다면
instead[instéd] 대신에

[Cell phone rings.]
M Hello.
W Hi, Adam. It's Sumin. I'm calling about our weekend plans.
M We're going to go skiing. Is something wrong?
W I heard it's going to be very warm this Saturday.
M In that case, I think going skiing wouldn't be a very good idea.
W You're right. So, should we change our plans?
M Why don't we go to the movies instead?
W That sounds good.

[휴대전화가 울린다.]
남 여보세요.
여 안녕, Adam. 나 수민이야. 주말 계획 때문에 전화했어.
남 우리 스키 타러 가잖아. 무슨 일이 있니?
여 아니, 그렇진 않아. 하지만 이번 주 토요일에 날씨가 매우 따뜻할 거라고 들었어.
남 그렇다면 스키를 타러 가는 것은 그리 좋은 생각이 아닌 것 같네.
여 맞아. 우리 계획을 바꿔야 할까?
남 대신 영화 보러 가는 건 어때?
여 그거 좋겠다.

13 ④

해설 라지 사이즈 치즈피자는 18달러이고, 콜라 한 잔이 3달러이므로 총 21달러를 지불해야 한다.

어휘 charge[tʃɑːrdʒ] (요금을) 청구하다
soda[sóudə] 탄산음료

M Can I help the next person in line, please?
W How much are large pizzas?
M $16 for a vegetable pizza and $18 for a cheese pizza.
W And are all the sodas $3?
M Yes, they are.
W Okay. Can I get a large cheese pizza and one coke?
M Sure. Your pizza will be ready in about 15 minutes.

남 다음 분 도와드릴까요?
여 라지 사이즈 피자는 얼마인가요?
남 야채 피자는 16달러이고 치즈피자는 18달러입니다.
여 그리고 탄산음료는 모두 3달러인가요?
남 네, 그렇습니다.
여 알겠어요. 라지 사이즈 치즈피자 하나와 콜라 한 잔 주시겠어요?
남 네, 15분 정도면 피자가 준비될 겁니다.

14 ③

해설 배달원에 지원하는 남자와 운전 경험을 묻는 여자의 대화로 보아 두 사람의 관계는 구직자와 가게 점장이다.

어휘 delivery[dilívəri] 배달
person[pə́ːrsən] 사람
apply[əplái] 지원하다
van[væn] 승합차, 밴
form[fɔːrm] 신청서

M I saw your sign on the window. Are you looking for a delivery person?
W Yes, are you interested in applying?
M I am. I'm a very good driver.
W Have you driven a van before?
M Yes, I have. I drove a delivery van for my last job.
W Great. When can you start working?
M I can start next Monday.
W Okay. Please fill out this form.

남 창문에 붙은 공고를 봤어요. 배달원을 구하시나요?
여 네, 지원하고 싶으신가요?
남 그렇습니다. 저는 운전을 아주 잘합니다.
여 승합차를 운전해 본 적이 있나요?
남 네, 있어요. 지난번 직장에서 승합차를 몰았거든요.
여 좋습니다. 언제부터 일을 시작하실 수 있나요?
남 다음 주 월요일부터 일할 수 있습니다.
여 알겠습니다. 이 서류를 작성해 주세요.

15 ④

해설 여자는 가족이 모두 할머니 문병을 가야 해서 남자에게 그동안 개를 돌봐달라고 부탁했다.

어휘 favor[féivər] 부탁
watch[wɑtʃ] (잠깐 동안) 봐 주다

W Inho, do you have any plans for this Saturday?
M Nothing special. I think I'll stay home and play with my dog, Max.
W Then could you do me a favor?
M Sure, what is it?
W My family is going to visit my grandmother in the hospital. But we can't take our dog Lily with us. Could you watch her until we come back?
M Of course. Max played with her before. He'd love to play with Lily again.
W Thank you so much.

여 인호야, 이번 주 토요일에 계획 있니?
남 특별한 건 없어. 집에 있으면서 우리 개 Max랑 놀 것 같아.
여 그럼 부탁 하나만 들어줄래?
남 뭔데?
여 우리 가족이 병원에 계신 할머니한테 갈 거야. 하지만 우리 개 Lily를 데리고 갈 수가 없어. 우리가 돌아올 때까지 걔를 좀 봐 줄래?
남 그래. Max가 전에 걔랑 놀았잖아. Lily랑 다시 놀게 되어 좋아할 거야.
여 정말 고마워.

16 ④

해설 여자는 바지가 아들에게 맞지 않아서 반품하겠다고 했다.

어휘 return[ritə́ːrn] 반품하다
receipt[risíːt] 영수증
tight[tait] (몸에) 꼭 끼는
pay[pei] 지불하다, 내다
(pay-paid-paid)
cash[kæʃ] 현금
gift card 선불카드

M What can I do for you?
W I'd like to return these jeans, please.
M Of course. May I see your receipt?
W Sure, here you are.
M Is there something wrong with the jeans?
W They are too tight for my son.
M I see. The receipt shows you paid in cash. You can get your money back in cash or as a gift card. Which one would you like?
W Cash, please.

남 무엇을 도와드릴까요?
여 이 청바지를 반품하고 싶어요.
남 그러세요. 영수증 좀 보여주시겠습니까?
여 네, 여기 있어요.
남 청바지에 무슨 문제라도 있나요?
여 아들에게 너무 꽉 끼어서요.
남 알겠습니다. 영수증을 보니 현금으로 지불하셨네요. 그 돈은 현금이나 선불카드로 돌려받으실 수 있어요. 어떤 걸로 하시겠습니까?
여 현금으로 주세요.

17 ④

해설 불이 난 것을 발견했으므로 소방서로 전화하겠다는 말이 어울린다.

어휘 report[ripɔ́:rt] 신고하다
accident[ǽksidənt] 사고
Go ahead. 그렇게 하세요.
break into 침입하다
address[ədrés] 주소
mean[mi:n] ~ 뜻으로 말하다
fire station 소방서
repair shop 수리점

① M I want to report a car accident!
　 W All right. Go ahead.
② M Someone has broken into my house.
　 W Okay. What's your address?
③ M Did you see the news about the fire?
　 W Do you mean the fire at the shopping mall?
④ M There's a fire! Call the fire station!
　 W I have a cell phone. I'll call right away!
⑤ M The TV is not working again.
　 W I'll call the repair shop right now.

① 남 자동차 사고를 신고하려고요!
　 여 네. 말씀하세요.
② 남 누군가 우리 집에 침입했어요.
　 여 알겠습니다. 주소가 어딘가요?
③ 남 화재에 관한 뉴스 봤어?
　 여 응. 쇼핑몰에 난 화재 말하는 거지?
④ 남 불이 났어! 소방서에 전화해!
　 여 나한테 휴대전화가 있어. 내가 바로 전화할게!
⑤ 남 TV가 또 고장 났어.
　 여 지금 수리점에 전화할게.

18 ④

해설 먹는 시기(중추절), 모양(둥근), 재료(콩, 씨앗, 꿀 등), 의미(행운)에 대해 언급하였지만 유래에 대해서는 언급하지 않았다.

어휘 mooncake[mú:nkeik] 월병
Mid-Autumn Festival 중추절, 추석
traditional[trədíʃənəl] 전통적인
round[əráund] 둥근
filling[fíliŋ] (음식의) 속, 충전물
bean[bi:n] 콩
seed[si:d] 씨앗
fortune[fɔ́:rtʃən] 행운

M The Chinese enjoy eating mooncakes during the Mid-Autumn Festival, one of the most important Chinese festivals. Mooncakes are a traditional Chinese food. They are round, sweet cakes. The cakes have different fillings, such as beans, seeds, and honey. The design on the top of the cakes usually means "fortune," so people give them to friends and family during the festival.

남 중국인들은 중국의 가장 중요한 축제 중 하나인 중추절 기간 동안 월병을 즐겨 먹습니다. 월병은 중국의 전통 음식입니다. 이것은 둥글고 달콤한 케이크입니다. 이 케이크 속에는 콩, 씨앗, 꿀과 같은 다양한 속 재료가 들어갑니다. 케이크 위의 모양은 대개 '행운'을 의미하기 때문에 사람들은 축제 기간 동안 그것을 친구와 가족에게 선물로 줍니다.

19 ④

해설 대화를 통해 둘 다 Super Boys의 팬인 걸 알게 돼서 여자가 팬 미팅에 같이 가자고 제안했으므로 제안을 수락하는 응답이 이어져야 한다.

어휘 big fan 열혈 팬
rapper[rǽpər] 래퍼

M Minji, what are you going to do this weekend?
W I'm going to go to Super Boys' fan meeting with Bomi.
M That sounds great. I'm a big Super Boys fan, too.
W Really? Which member do you like best?
M I like Juno best. I think he's one of the greatest rappers in Korea.
W Do you want to join us?
M Sure, I'd love to. I can't wait!

남 민지야, 이번 주말에 뭐 할 거야?
여 나 보미랑 Super Boys의 팬 미팅에 갈 거야.
남 좋겠다. 나도 완전 Super Boys 팬인데.
여 정말? 너는 어떤 멤버를 가장 좋아하는데?
남 나는 Juno가 제일 좋아. 나는 그가 한국에서 가장 뛰어난 래퍼 중 한 명인 것 같아.
여 너 우리랑 같이 갈래?
남 좋아, 그렇게 할게. 너무 기대돼!

① 응, 나는 래퍼가 되고 싶어.
② 나도. 나는 영화 보는 것을 좋아해.
③ 미안하지만, 나는 그들을 좋아하지 않아.
⑤ 맞아. 그는 춤도 잘 추고 노래도 잘 불러.

해설 손목이 아픈 여자가 남자에게 스트레칭 하는 방법을 물었으므로, 스트레칭을 하는 방법을 설명하는 응답이 이어져야 한다.

어휘 wrist[rist] 손목
chat[tʃæt] 채팅하다
finger[fíŋgər] 손가락
text[tekst] (휴대전화로) 문자를 보내다
stretching[strétʃiŋ] 스트레칭
[선택지]
bend[bend] 구부리다
back and forth 앞뒤로 움직이는

M What's wrong, Amy?
W Hello, Dr. Jo. My right wrist hurts.
M All right. Let me take a look at it. Do you use your smartphone a lot?
W Yes. I chat a lot with my friends.
M I think you use your fingers and wrists too much when you text.
W Then what should I do?
M You should do some stretching exercises.
W Okay. How do I stretch my wrists?
M Bend your wrists back and forth. It's easy.

남 무슨 문제 있니, Amy?
여 안녕하세요, Jo 선생님. 제 오른쪽 손목이 아파요.
남 그렇구나. 한번 보자. 스마트폰을 많이 쓰니?
여 네. 친구들과 채팅을 많이 해요.
남 네가 문자를 보낼 때 손가락과 손목을 너무 많이 사용하는 것 같구나.
여 그럼 어떻게 해야 하나요?
남 스트레칭 운동을 좀 해야 해.
여 그럴게요. 손목은 어떻게 스트레칭을 하나요?
남 손목을 앞뒤로 구부리면 돼. 쉬워.

① 너는 병원에 가봐야 해.
② 하지만 너를 다시 살펴봐야 해.
③ 언제부터 문제가 생겼니?
④ 스마트폰 전원을 꺼야 해.

실전 모의고사 03

p. 46

01 ③	02 ⑤	03 ③	04 ⑤	05 ③	06 ④	07 ③
08 ④	09 ④	10 ③	11 ④	12 ④	13 ③	14 ②
15 ⑤	16 ④	17 ④	18 ③	19 ②	20 ②	

01 ③

[해설] 아침에 오던 눈이 오후에 그치고 저녁에는 강한 바람이 불 거라고 했다.

[어휘] weather forecaster 일기예보관
heavy[hévi] 두꺼운
temperature[témpərətʃər] 기온
remain[riméin] 계속 ~이다

W Good morning. I'm Jane Reed, your weather forecaster. It looks like we'll <u>have a little snow</u> this morning. The snow will stop in the afternoon, but put on your <u>heavy coats</u>. Strong winds are expected <u>in the evening</u>. The temperatures will remain low all day. That's the weather forecast for today. Have a good day!

여 안녕하세요. 일기예보관 Jane Reed 입니다. 오늘 아침에는 눈이 조금 올 것 같습니다. 오후에는 눈이 그치겠지 만, 두꺼운 코트를 입으세요. 저녁에 는 강한 바람이 예상됩니다. 기온은 종일 낮을 것입니다. 오늘의 일기예보 입니다. 멋진 하루 보내세요!

02 ⑤

[해설] 남자가 별 그림이 있는 목도리를 권했지만 여자는 줄무늬가 있는 것을 사 겠다고 했다.

[어휘] scarf[ska:rf] 목도리, 스카프
popular[pápulər] 인기 있는
striped[straipt] 줄무늬가 있는

M Can I help you?
W Hi. I'm looking for a scarf for my little brother.
M Sure. How about <u>this one with cats</u>?
W It looks cute, but he <u>likes dogs better</u> than cats.
M Then, how about this one with stars? This is popular in our shop.
W It's all right. [Pause] Oh, I like <u>that striped one</u>. Can I see it?
M Of course. Here you are.
W It's nice. <u>I'll take it</u>.

남 도움이 필요하신가요?
여 안녕하세요. 남동생에게 줄 목도리를 찾고 있어요.
남 네. 고양이가 있는 이건 어떠세요?
여 귀여워 보이는데, 동생이 고양이보다 개를 더 좋아해요.
남 그럼 별들이 있는 이건 어떠세요? 저 희 가게에서 인기 있는 거예요.
여 괜찮군요. [잠시 후] 아, 저 줄무늬가 마음에 들어요. 볼 수 있을까요?
남 물론이죠. 여기 있어요.
여 좋네요. 이걸 살게요.

03 ③

[해설] 장르(무서운 영화), 스토리(다섯 사 람이 보드게임을 시작하면서 기이한 일이 일어나는 이야기), 상영관(Cine Box), 상 영 시간(4시와 7시)에 대해 언급하였지만 주연 배우에 대해서는 언급하지 않았다.

[어휘] scary[skɛ́(:)əri] 무서운
mysterious[mistíəriəs] 기이한
happen[hǽpən] (사건 등이) 생기다. 일 어나다
show[ʃou] 상영하다; 상영

M Did you hear about <u>the new movie</u>, *Game of Death*?
W No, I didn't. Is it a <u>scary movie</u>?
M Yes. In the movie, 5 people start playing a board game. Then mysterious things <u>start to happen</u>.
W That sounds interesting. I like that kind of movie a lot.
M The movie <u>is playing</u> at the Cine Box. Why don't we go and see it tomorrow?
W I'd love to! <u>What time</u> is the movie?
M <u>It's showing at</u> 4 o'clock and 7 o'clock.
W Then let's see the 4 o'clock show.

남 너 새 영화 〈죽음의 게임〉에 대해 들 어봤어?
여 아니, 못 들었어. 무서운 영화니?
남 응. 이 영화에서 다섯 명의 사람들이 보드게임을 하기 시작해. 그러자 기이 한 일들이 일어나지.
여 재미있을 것 같네. 나는 그런 영화를 아주 좋아해.
남 그 영화는 Cine Box에서 상영되고 있 어. 내일 그거 보러 가지 않을래?
여 나야 좋지! 영화는 몇 시에 상영하니?
남 4시와 7시에 상영되고 있어.
여 그럼 4시 영화로 보자.

04 ⑤

[해설] 남자는 어제 조부모님 댁을 방문해 서 할아버지의 생신을 축하해 드렸다.

W Seho, what did you do yesterday?
M I went to <u>my grandparent's house</u> with my

여 세호야, 어제 뭐 했어?
남 부모님과 함께 조부모님 댁에 갔어.

어휘 celebrate[séləbrèit] 축하하다

W That's nice. What did you do there?
M It was my grandfather's birthday, so we celebrated his birthday with dinner.
W Did you give him anything?
M Of course. I gave him a nice hat and a card.
W It sounds like you had a great time.

여 좋았겠다. 거기서 뭐 했어?
남 할아버지 생신이라서 우리는 저녁 식사를 하면서 생신을 축하해 드렸어.
여 할아버지께 뭐라도 드렸니?
남 물론이지. 할아버지에게 멋진 모자와 카드를 드렸어.
여 좋은 시간을 보낸 것 같네.

05 ③

해설 롤러코스터와 범퍼카 등을 타자는 것으로 보아 놀이공원에서 나누는 대화임을 알 수 있다.

어휘 take A out A를 데리고 나가다, 외출을 시켜 주다
stressed[strest] 스트레스를 받는
worry[wə́ːri] 걱정, 우려
ride[raid] (탈 것에) 타다
roller coaster 롤러코스터
bumper car 범퍼카

W Dad, thanks for taking me out today. It's great to be out of the house.
M Of course, honey. I knew you were a little stressed because of schoolwork. Today, forget about your worries and just have fun.
W Thanks. I have a map here, but I don't know where to go first.
M Well, how about riding the roller coaster first? It's right over there.
W It looks like there is a long line for it. How about bumper cars?
M That sounds like fun.

여 아빠, 오늘 데리고 나와 주셔서 고마워요. 집 밖에 나오니까 정말 좋아요.
남 물론이지, 얘야. 네가 학업 때문에 스트레스를 좀 받고 있다는 거 알고 있단다. 오늘은 걱정은 잊어버리고 그냥 재미있게 보내렴.
여 감사해요. 여기 지도가 있는데 어딜 먼저 가야 할지 모르겠어요.
남 그렇다면, 롤러코스터를 먼저 타는 건 어떨까? 바로 저쪽에 있네.
여 그건 줄이 긴 것 같아요. 범퍼카를 타는 거 어때요?
남 그거 재미있겠다.

06 ④

해설 여자는 빨리 공항에 가야 한다고 하면서 고속도로로 가 달라고 남자에게 부탁했다.

어휘 international[ìntərnǽʃənəl] 국제의
airport[ɛ́ərpɔ̀ːrt] 공항
flight[flait] 항공편
as soon as possible 되도록 빨리
highway[háiwèi] 고속도로

M Good afternoon, ma'am.
W Good afternoon. To the international airport, please.
M Are you going to fly international?
W Yes, I'm going to go to Spain.
M What time is your flight?
W I have a 3:30 flight to catch, but there is not much time left.
M We need to hurry then.
W Yes. I have to get there as soon as possible so please take the highway.

남 안녕하세요.
여 안녕하세요. 국제공항으로 가 주세요.
남 국제선을 타실 건가 봐요?
여 네, 스페인에 가려고요.
남 몇 시 비행기인가요?
여 3시 30분 비행기를 타야 하는데, 시간이 별로 얼마 남지 않았어요.
남 그럼 서둘러야겠군요.
여 네, 가능한 한 빨리 거기에 도착해야 하니 고속도로로 가주세요.

07 ③

해설 남자가 임진왜란의 영웅에 대해 쓰라고 하자 여자가 좋은 생각이라고 했으므로 전쟁 영웅들에 대해 쓸 것이다.

어휘 war[wɔːr] 전쟁
for example 예를 들면
topic[tápik] 주제
hero[hí(ː)ərou] 영웅

W Jason, is there any homework from today's history class?
M Yes. You have to write a report about the Imjin War. We learned about it last week.
W Anything about the Imjin War?
M Yes. For example, Yi Sunshin, the Turtle Ship, and Ganggangsullae.
W Hmm... There are so many good topics. I can't choose one.

여 Jason, 오늘 역사 시간에 숙제가 있었니?
남 응. 임진왜란에 대한 보고서를 써야 해. 우리 지난주에 그거 배웠잖아.
여 임진왜란에 대해 아무거나?
남 응. 예를 들면 이순신이나 거북선, 강강술래 같은 거.
여 음. 좋은 주제들이 너무 많은데. 하나를 선택할 수가 없네.

M How about writing about the Imjin War heroes? It won't <u>be that difficult</u>.
W <u>That</u> <u>sounds</u> <u>good</u>.

남 임진왜란의 영웅들에 대해 쓰는 건 어때? 그렇게 어렵지는 않을 거야.
여 그거 좋은 것 같아.

08 ④

[해설] 여자가 남자에게 도서관 카드를 발급받기 위한 신청서를 작성하라고 했다.

[어휘] student ID 학생증
fill out (양식, 서식을) 작성하다
form[fɔːrm] 신청서, (문서의) 양식

M Excuse me. I'd like to get a library card. I lost mine last week.
W Can I see <u>your student ID</u>?
M Sure. Here you are. How long does it take to get a new card?
W It takes <u>about an hour</u>.
M Can I come back <u>after school</u>? I have a class in 15 minutes.
W Yes, you can. And would you fill out <u>this form</u>?
M Okay.

남 실례합니다. 도서관 카드를 발급받고 싶은데요. 지난주에 잃어버렸거든요.
여 학생증 좀 보여주실래요?
남 네, 여기 있습니다. 새 카드를 받는 데 얼마나 걸리나요?
여 한 시간 정도 걸려요.
남 방과 후에 다시 와도 되나요? 15분 후에 수업이 있어서요.
여 네, 그러세요. 그리고 이 신청서를 작성해 주실래요?
남 그러죠.

09 ④

[해설] 개관 시간(10시부터 6시), 휴관일(설날과 추석), 입장료(무료), 사진 촬영 규칙(내부 사진 촬영 가능)에 대해 언급하였으나 주차장에 대해서는 언급하지 않았다.

[어휘] National Museum 국립 박물관
opening hours 개관 시간
holiday[hάlədèi] 공휴일, 휴일
entrance fee 입장료

[Telephone rings.]
W The Gyeongju National Museum. How can I help you?
M I'd like to know the opening hours of the museum.
W <u>We are open from</u> 10:00 to 6:00.
M Are you open on holidays?
W We <u>are closed on</u> New Year's Day and Chuseok.
M I see. And how much is the entrance fee?
W <u>It's free</u>.
M Great! One more question. May I <u>take pictures</u> inside the museum?
W Yes, you may.

[전화벨이 울린다.]
여 국립경주박물관입니다. 무엇을 도와드릴까요?
남 네. 박물관 개관 시간을 알고 싶어요.
여 10시부터 6시까지입니다.
남 휴일에도 여나요?
여 저희는 설날과 추석에는 쉽니다.
남 알겠습니다. 그리고 입장료는 얼마지요?
여 무료입니다.
남 좋군요! 질문 하나만 더 할게요. 박물관 안에서 사진을 찍어도 되나요?
여 네, 괜찮습니다.

10 ③

[해설] 방송국에서 자사 하계 올림픽 방송을 홍보하는 내용이다.

[어휘] at last 드디어, 마침내
be sure to-v 꼭[반드시] ~하다
live broadcast 생방송
highlight[hάilàit] 하이라이트, 가장 중요한[흥미로운] 부분

M At last, the Summer Olympics will start next week! If you are interested in watching the Olympics, be <u>sure to watch</u> SBN Sports. You can <u>enjoy our live</u> broadcasts all day long. At 11:30 p.m. every night, you can also <u>enjoy the highlights</u> of the games of the day. If you <u>miss any games</u>, visit our website at www.SBN.com.

남 드디어 다음 주에 하계 올림픽이 시작되네요! 올림픽에 관심이 있으시다면, SBN 스포츠를 꼭 시청하세요. 하루 종일 생방송으로 즐길 수 있습니다. 매일 밤 11시 30분부터 그날 경기의 하이라이트도 볼 수 있습니다. 놓친 경기가 있다면 www.SBN.com 웹사이트를 방문하세요.

11 ④

해설 딸을 위한 노래가 아니라 아내에 대한 사랑 노래이다.

어휘 instant[ínstənt] 즉시의
hit[hit] 히트 (곡), 인기 작품
popular[pápulər] 인기 있는

M We started the show with "December Rain." Did you enjoy the song? It was written by Tim Spacey. He wrote this beautiful song in 1988, and it became an instant hit all over the world. It's a love song for his wife, and it is still one of the most popular songs in England.

남 '12월의 비'로 방송을 시작했습니다. 노래를 즐겁게 들으셨나요? 이 곡은 Tim Spacey가 작곡했습니다. 그는 1988년에 이 아름다운 노래를 썼고, 곧바로 전 세계에서 히트했지요. 아내에 대한 사랑 노래인데, 지금도 영국에서 가장 인기 있는 노래 중 하나입니다.

12 ④

해설 여자는 남자에게 외식할 예정이니 일찍 집에 오라고 전화했다.

어휘 eat out 외식하다
study[stʌ́di] 공부; 공부하다

[Cell phone rings.]
M Hello.
W Hi, Mike. Did you remember it's your dad's birthday?
M Of course, Mom, I remembered.
W Can you come home earlier today? We're going to eat out this evening.
M Oh, my study group finishes at 6. Is that okay?
W All right. Just come home as soon as you can after studying.
M Don't worry. I will.

[휴대전화가 울린다.]
남 여보세요.
여 여보세요, Mike. 오늘이 아빠 생일인 거 기억하지?
남 물론이죠, 엄마. 기억하죠.
여 오늘 집에 좀 더 일찍 올 수 있니? 저녁에 우리 외식하려고 하거든.
남 아, 제가 하는 스터디 그룹이 6시에 끝나는데, 괜찮으세요?
여 알겠어. 공부 끝나고 가능한 한 빨리 집에 와.
남 걱정하지 마세요. 그럴게요.

13 ③

해설 85달러짜리 배낭을 5달러 할인받아서 80달러에 사기로 했다.

어휘 coupon[kú:pan] 쿠폰
discount[dískaunt] 할인

W How may I help you?
M I like these backpacks. How much are they?
W The one with 2 pockets is $85. The other one is $75.
M I'll take the one with 2 pockets.
W Okay. Do you have any coupons?
M Yes, I do. I have a coupon for a $5 discount. Here you are.
W Okay. Then that'll be $80.
M All right. Here's my card.

여 무엇을 도와드릴까요?
남 이 배낭들이 맘에 드네요. 이것들은 얼마인가요?
여 주머니가 두 개 달린 건 85달러이고, 나머지는 75달러입니다.
남 주머니가 두 개 있는 것을 살게요.
여 알겠습니다. 어떤 쿠폰이라도 있으신가요?
남 네, 있어요. 5달러 할인 쿠폰이 있어요. 여기 있습니다.
여 알겠습니다. 그럼 80달러입니다.
남 알겠어요. 제 카드 여기 있어요.

14 ②

해설 여자가 자신이 기자라고 밝히면서 남자에게 우승 소감과 비결에 대해 묻고 있으므로 두 사람의 관계는 신문 기자와 운동선수임을 알 수 있다.

어휘 Congratulations! 축하합니다!
marathon[mǽrəθàn] 마라톤
daily[déili] 하루하루

W Hi, Daniel. I'm Joy Carter from The Herald. Congratulations!
M Thank you.
W You won the London Marathon. How do you feel?
M I'm very happy.
W How did you prepare for the marathon?

여 안녕하세요, Daniel. 저는 The Herald의 Joy Carter입니다. 축하합니다!
남 감사합니다.
여 런던 마라톤에서 우승하셨어요. 기분이 어떤가요?
남 정말 행복합니다.
여 마라톤 준비는 어떻게 하셨나요?

follow [fálou] 따르다, 따라 하다
healthy diet 건강식
right [rait] 적절한, 적당한

M Besides training daily, I followed a healthy diet.
W Anything else?
M It was very important to find the right running shoes.
W Oh, I see. Thank you for your time and congratulations again.
M Thank you.

남 매일 훈련하는 것 외에 건강한 식단을 따랐어요.
여 그 밖에 또 다른 건요?
남 그리고 적절한 신발을 찾는 것도 매우 중요했지요.
여 아, 그렇군요. 시간 내주셔서 감사드리며 다시 한번 축하합니다.
남 고맙습니다.

15 ⑤

해설 남자는 여자에게 치통이 심해져서 조퇴하기 위해 엄마한테 전화해달라고 부탁했다.

어휘 dentist [déntist] 치과의사
toothache [tuːθeik] 치통
get worse 악화되다

M Excuse me, Ms. Williams.
W Yes, Mike. Can I help you?
M I think I should go to the dentist today.
W Why? Is something wrong?
M I have a toothache, and it's getting worse.
W I'm sorry to hear that.
M Could you call my mother? I'd like to leave an hour early today.
W Of course.
M Thank you so much.

남 저, Williams 선생님.
여 그래, Mike. 도와줄까?
남 오늘 치과에 가야 할 것 같아서요.
여 왜 그러니? 어디가 안 좋니?
남 치통이 있는데, 점점 심해지고 있어요.
여 안됐구나.
남 저희 엄마한테 전화 좀 해주시겠어요? 오늘 한 시간 일찍 조퇴하려고요.
여 물론이지.
남 고맙습니다.

16 ④

해설 남자는 친구와 통화를 하다가 오븐을 끄는 것을 잊어버렸다.

어휘 burn [bəːrn] 타다
turn off 끄다
oven [ʌvən] 오븐
terrible [térəbl] 심한
forget [fərɡét] 잊다
(forget-forgot-forgotten)
completely [kəmplíːtli] 완전히

W Tony, do you smell something burning?
M Oh no! I forgot to turn off the oven!
W Turn it off right now!
M [Pause] It smells terrible. I'm sorry, Mom.
W How could you forget about the oven?
M Well, I was talking with Junha on the phone. Then I completely forgot about my apple pie.
W Don't forget to turn it off next time.
M I won't, Mom.

여 Tony, 뭔가 타는 냄새 안 나니?
남 이런! 오븐 끄는 걸 깜빡했어요!
여 지금 당장 꺼!
남 [잠시 후] 냄새가 지독해요. 죄송해요, 엄마.
여 그걸 어떻게 잊을 수가 있니?
남 저, 준하와 통화하고 있었거든요. 그리고 나서 애플파이를 완전히 잊었어요.
여 다음에는 끄는 걸 잊지 마.
남 잊지 않을게요, 엄마.

17 ④

해설 남자가 아파서 침대에 누워있으므로 여자가 병원에 가 보라고 권하는 대화가 적절하다.

어휘 Do you mind if I ~? 제가 ~해도 될까요?
weather forecast 일기예보

① M Do you mind if I open the window?
W Go ahead.
② M Don't forget to listen to the weather forecast.
W Okay, I won't.
③ M What kind of food do you want to eat?
W I want to eat Italian food.
④ M Mom, I'm not feeling well today.
W I think you should see a doctor.
⑤ M What's the matter?
W I'm worried about my dog.

① 남 창문 좀 열어도 될까요?
여 그렇게 하세요.
② 남 일기예보 듣는 거 잊지 마.
여 알았어, 잊지 않을게.
③ 남 어떤 종류의 음식을 먹고 싶니?
여 나는 이탈리아 음식을 먹고 싶어.
④ 남 엄마, 나 오늘 몸이 안 좋아요.
여 병원에 가는 게 좋겠다.
⑤ 남 무슨 일 있니?
여 우리 개가 너무 걱정돼.

18 ③

해설 입장료(무료), 개최 시기(매년 9월 첫 번째 금요일부터 3일간), 역사(1895년에 시작되어 지금까지 이어짐), 방문객 수(매년 50만 명 이상)에 대해 언급하였지만 참가 자격에 대해서는 언급하지 않았다.

어휘 festival[féstivəl] 축제
entrance fee 입장료
begin[bigín] 시작되다
(begin-began-begun)
since then 그때부터

W Hi, I'm Amy Lee. I'm at the Colorado Food Festival now. There is no entrance fee, so you can enjoy this festival for free. This 3-day festival starts on the first Friday of September every year. The festival first began in 1895 and has been going on since then. Over 500,000 visitors come to enjoy the festival every year.

여 안녕하세요, Amy Lee입니다. 저는 Colorado 푸드 페스티벌에 와 있습니다. 입장료가 없으니 무료로 이 축제를 즐길 수 있습니다. 이 3일간의 축제는 매년 9월 첫 번째 금요일에 시작됩니다. 이 축제는 1895년에 처음 시작되었고 그때부터 계속되어 왔습니다. 매년 50만 명 이상의 방문객들이 이 축제를 즐기기 위해 옵니다.

19 ②

해설 'Radio Ga Ga'라는 노래를 가장 좋아하는 이유를 물었으므로 그 이유에 해당하는 응답이 이어져야 한다.

어휘 British[brítiʃ] 영국의
rock band 록 음악 밴드
[선택지]
classical[klǽsikl] 클래식의
teenager[tíːnèidʒər] 십 대

W Uncle Jim, what's your favorite band?
M I like the British rock band Queen a lot.
W Oh, I know them. I've seen a movie about the band.
M I saw the movie 3 times.
W Which of their songs do you like best?
M I love "Radio Ga Ga" the best.
W Why do you love it so much?
M The song makes me feel happy.

여 Jim 삼촌, 어떤 밴드를 제일 좋아해요?
남 나는 영국 록 밴드 퀸을 아주 좋아해.
여 아, 저도 그들을 알아요. 그 밴드에 관한 영화를 본 적이 있어요.
남 나는 그 영화를 세 번 봤어.
여 그들의 노래 중에서 어떤 노래를 가장 좋아하세요?
남 나는 'Radio Ga Ga'를 가장 좋아해.
여 왜 그 노래를 그렇게 좋아하세요?
남 그 노래를 들으면 행복해지거든.

① 나는 고전 음악을 매우 좋아해.
③ 그들은 히트곡이 매우 많아.
④ 나는 방금 그 노래를 처음 들었어.
⑤ 나는 십 대 때부터 그 밴드를 좋아했어.

20 ②

해설 여자가 잃어버린 스마트폰을 분실물 취급소에서도 찾지 못했다고 했으므로 위로하는 말이 이어져야 한다.

어휘 down[daun] 우울한
brand-new 완전 새것인
the lost and found 분실물 취급소
[선택지]
return[ritə́ːrn] 반납하다

M You look so down, Mina. Is something wrong?
W I lost my smartphone at the library.
M That's too bad.
W My father gave it to me for my birthday.
M So you got it last week?
W Yes. It's a brand-new smartphone.
M Did you check the lost and found?
W Yeah, but it wasn't there.
M I hope you find it soon.

남 미나야, 너 기분이 안 좋은 것 같구나. 무슨 일 있니?
여 나 도서관에서 스마트폰을 잃어버렸어.
남 그것참 안 됐네.
여 아버지가 내 생일날 선물하신 거였어.
남 그렇다면 지난주에 받은 거네?
여 그래, 완전 새 스마트폰이야.
남 분실물 센터는 확인해 봤니?
여 응, 하지만 거기에는 없다고 하네.
남 빨리 찾았으면 좋겠다.

① 내가 그걸 공원에서 찾았어.
③ 이건 네가 들고 다니기에는 너무 무거워.
④ 네 스마트폰을 빌려줄 수 있니?
⑤ 도서관에 책을 반납했니?

01 ⑤	02 ②	03 ④	04 ②	05 ③	06 ③	07 ②
08 ③	09 ③	10 ②	11 ⑤	12 ④	13 ④	14 ⑤
15 ④	16 ②	17 ③	18 ③	19 ⑤	20 ①	

01 ⑤

해설 금요일 아침에는 다시 비가 왔다가 밤에 눈으로 바뀔 거라고 했다.

어휘 perfect[pə́ːrfikt] 더할 나위 없는
outdoor[áutdɔ̀ːr] 야외의
activity[æktívəti] 활동
turn into ~으로 변하다

M Good afternoon. Welcome to the weather forecast. It is cloudy right now, and there is a chance of some rain tonight. Tomorrow will be perfect for outdoor activities because it'll be sunny all day. However, it's going to rain again Friday morning, and the rain is expected to turn into snow that night.

남 안녕하세요. 일기예보를 전해드립니다. 지금은 흐리고, 오늘 밤에는 비가 올 가능성이 있습니다. 내일은 하루 종일 맑아서 야외 활동하기에 좋을 겁니다. 하지만 금요일 아침에 다시 비가 올 것이며, 그날 밤에 비가 눈으로 바뀔 것으로 예상됩니다.

02 ②

해설 청바지로 만든 바구니 중앙에는 꽃이 있고 꽃 아래에 B.M.W.라는 글자가 새겨져 있다.

어휘 basket[bǽskit] 바구니
amazing[əméiziŋ] 굉장한
jeans[dʒiːnz] 청바지
letter[létər] 글자
sweet[swiːt] 다정한, 상냥한

M Seri, what is in the box?
W Take a look. [Pause] I made this basket for my mom.
M It looks amazing. Did you use old jeans?
W Yes, I used a pair of old jeans. What do you think?
M I really like the flower in the middle.
W Thanks. My mom loves flowers. So, I added it.
M There are letters under the flower. What does "B.M.W." mean?
W It means, "Best Mom in the World."
M That's so sweet. I'm sure your mom will love it.

남 세리야, 상자 안에 뭐가 있니?
여 한번 봐봐. [잠시 후] 우리 엄마 드리려고 이 바구니를 만들었어.
남 정말 멋져 보인다. 낡은 청바지를 사용했니?
여 그래, 내 오래된 청바지를 사용했어. 어떤 거 같아?
남 가운데 있는 꽃이 정말 맘에 든다.
여 고마워. 우리 엄마가 꽃을 좋아하셔. 그래서 그것을 넣었어.
남 꽃 아래에 글자가 있네. 'B.M.W.'는 무슨 뜻이니?
여 '세계 최고의 엄마'라는 뜻이야.
남 참 다정하다. 너희 엄마가 분명히 좋아하실 거야.

03 ④

해설 경연대회에서 피아노 연주를 앞둔 남자는 너무 무섭다고 하면서 실수할까봐 걱정하는 걸로 보아 긴장하고 있다는 것을 알 수 있다.

어휘 suit[suːt] 정장
turn[təːrn] 순서
mistake[mistéik] 실수, 잘못
stage[steidʒ] 무대

W James! You look amazing in that suit.
M Lily, thank you for coming.
W It's your first time in the piano contest. I would not miss it. So, when is it your turn to play?
M I'm next.
W Really? I can't wait to hear you play.
M I'm so scared right now. I just hope I don't make any mistakes when I play on the stage.
W Don't worry. You are the greatest pianist I know.

여 James! 그 정장을 입으니 정말 멋져 보인다.
남 Lily, 와 줘서 고마워.
여 네가 피아노 경연대회에 나온 것은 처음이잖아. 내가 그것을 놓칠 리 없지. 그래, 네 연주 순서는 언제니?
남 나는 다음이야.
여 그래? 네 연주를 정말 듣고 싶어.
남 너무 흥분하지 마. 나는 무대에서 연주할 때 실수하지 않기만을 바라고 있어.
여 걱정하지 마. 넌 내가 아는 최고의 피아니스트야.

04 ②

해설 주말에 남자는 아빠랑 낚시를 하러 갔고 여자는 조카의 돌잔치에 가서 요리 하는 이모를 도왔다고 했다.

어휘 go fishing 낚시하러 가다
aunt[ænt] 이모, 고모
nephew[néfjuː] 조카
mostly[móustli] 주로

W Jake, how was your weekend?
M Great. I went fishing with my dad. How about you?
W I went to my aunt's house for a birthday party.
M Whose birthday party was it?
W It was my nephew's first birthday.
M First birthday party? Did you do anything special there?
W Well, I mostly helped my aunt prepare food in the kitchen. But we had so much fun together.

여 Jake, 주말은 어떻게 보냈니?
남 좋았어. 아빠랑 낚시하러 갔었어. 너 는 어땠어?
여 나는 생일 파티가 있어서 이모네 집에 갔었어.
남 누구 생일 파티였는데?
여 내 조카의 첫 번째 생일이었어.
남 돌잔치말이야? 거기서 특별한 거라도 했니?
여 음, 나는 주로 부엌에서 숙모가 음식 준비하시는 걸 도왔어. 하지만 우리는 함께 정말 즐거운 시간을 보냈어.

05 ③

해설 여자가 잃어버린 개를 찾으러 와서 개의 특징을 알려주고 남자가 이곳에 있 는지 확인해 보겠다고 하는 대화로 보아 장소는 유기견 보호소임을 알 수 있다.

어휘 animal clinic 동물 병원
clothing[klóuðiŋ] 옷, 의복

M May I help you?
W Yes, please. I heard from the animal clinic that I could find my dog here.
M I see. What does your dog look like?
W She is a brown poodle. Her hair is a little short.
M When and where did you lose her?
W I lost her in the park 2 days ago.
M Can you tell me more about her?
W When I lost her, she was wearing pink clothing.
M All right. Let me check if she's here.

남 도와드릴까요?
여 네. 동물병원에서 우리 개를 여기서 찾을 수 있다고 들어요.
남 알겠습니다. 개가 어떻게 생겼나요?
여 갈색 푸들이에요. 털이 좀 짧아요.
남 언제 어디서 잃어버리셨어요?
여 이틀 전에 공원에서 잃어버렸어요.
남 개에 대해 좀 더 말해 주실래요?
여 개를 잃어버렸을 때, 분홍색 옷을 입 고 있었어요.
남 알겠습니다. 여기에 있는지 확인해 볼 게요.

06 ③

해설 남자는 동아리 회원을 모집하기 위 해 점심시간에 구내식당에서 공연할 것을 제안하고 있다.

어휘 decide[disáid] 결정하다
join[dʒɔin] 가입하다
keep[kiːp] 유지하다
perform[pərfɔ́ːrm] 공연하다
cafeteria[kæfətíəriə] 구내식당
lunch break 점심시간

W Mike, have you decided which club to join?
M Yes, I am going to join the dance club. What about you?
W Well, I'm already in a club, but...
M Is there something wrong?
W My guitar club only has 3 members. We need more members to keep the club for a year.
M I'm sorry to hear that.
W What should we do to get more members?
M Why don't you perform in the cafeteria during lunch break?

여 Mike, 어느 동아리에 가입할지 결정했 니?
남 응, 댄스 동아리에 가입할 거야. 너는?
여 음, 난 이미 동아리에 가입했어, 그런 데…
남 무슨 문제라도 있니?
여 우리 기타 동아리는 회원이 3명밖에 없어. 동아리를 1년 동안 유지하려면 더 많은 회원이 필요해.
남 안 됐네.
여 회원 수를 늘리려면 어떻게 해야 할 까?
남 점심시간에 구내식당에서 공연을 하 는 게 어떨까?

07 ②

해설 남자는 방과 후 수업으로 댄스 수 업을 들으려고 하고 여자는 요리 수업을 수강하고자 한다.

W Ben, are you going to take any after-school classes?
M I'm not sure. What about you?

여 Ben, 방과 후 수업 들을 거니?
남 잘 모르겠어. 너는 어때?

어휘 after-school 방과 후의

W I'm going to. There are some interesting classes, and I want to <u>learn something new</u>.
M What kind of classes are there?
W There are dance, cooking, and sports classes. I'm thinking of <u>taking the cooking class</u>.
M I see. Maybe I should try <u>one of the classes</u>.
W Are you interested in cooking, too?
M Not really. I think I'll try <u>the dance class</u>.

여 그러려고. 재미있는 수업이 몇 가지 있는데, 나는 새로운 걸 배우고 싶어.
남 어떤 수업이 있는데?
여 댄스, 요리, 스포츠 수업이 있어. 요리 수업을 들을까 생각 중이야.
남 그렇구나. 나도 그 수업 중에서 하나를 들어봐야겠네.
여 너도 요리에 관심이 있니?
남 그렇진 않아. 나는 댄스 수업을 들어 볼까 해.

08 ③

해설 두 사람은 축제에 더 많은 사람들이 올 수 있도록 동네에도 포스터를 붙이기로 했다.

어휘 prepare[pripέər] 준비하다
put up 붙이다, 게시하다
post[poust] 게시하다
neighborhood[néibərhùd] 근처, 이웃

W There is only one week left until the school festival.
M Yes. It was a lot of work, but it was fun to <u>prepare for it</u>.
W Me, too. I hope many people come and enjoy it.
M Sure. *[Pause]* What is in that box?
W I think <u>there are posters</u> in the box.
M Didn't we put up posters in the school?
W Yes, but there are <u>some posters left</u>.
M Then how about posting them in our neighborhood? That way, <u>more people</u> will know about the festival.
W That's a great idea.

여 학교 축제날까지 일주일밖에 남지 않았어.
남 그래. 일이 많긴 했지만, 준비하는 게 재미있었어.
여 나도 그래. 많은 사람들이 와서 즐겼으면 좋겠어.
남 그러게. *[잠시 후]* 그 상자 안에는 뭐가 들어 있니?
여 상자 안에 포스터가 있는 것 같아.
남 우리가 학교에 포스터를 붙이지 않았나?
여 그랬지, 그런데 포스터가 좀 남았어.
남 그럼 그것을 우리 동네에 게시하는 건 어떨까? 그래야 더 많은 사람들이 축제에 대해 알게 될 거야.
여 좋은 생각이야.

09 ③

해설 먹는 시기(추석), 모양(반달), 유래(신라 때부터 먹기 시작함), 재료(참깨, 콩, 야채, 과일)에 대해 언급하였지만 맛에 대해서는 언급하지 않았다.

어휘 traditional[trədíʃənəl] 전통의, 전통적인
rice cake 떡
half-moon[hǽf-mùːn] 반달
shape[ʃeip] 모양
sesame seed 참깨
bean[biːn] 콩

W Ted, I'm going to make some songpyeon. Would you like to join me?
M What are songpyeon?
W They are <u>traditional rice cakes</u>. Korean people usually make these and <u>eat them</u> on Chuseok.
M Wow, they look like a half-moon.
W Yes, in Korean history, the people of Silla <u>started</u> making rice cakes in that shape.
M I see. What do you put inside?
W <u>Most people use</u> sesame seeds and beans. You can also make them in different colors <u>with vegetables and fruits</u>.
M Okay. I'll try making some.

여 Ted, 나는 송편을 좀 만들려고 해. 너도 같이 만들래?
남 송편이 뭔데?
여 그건 전통 떡이야. 한국 사람들은 보통 추석에 이것을 만들어 먹어.
남 와, 반달 같이 생겼네.
여 맞아, 한국 역사를 보면, 신라 사람들이 그런 모양으로 떡을 만들기 시작했대.
남 그렇구나. 그 안에 무엇을 넣니?
여 대부분의 사람은 깨와 콩을 이용해. 채소와 과일로 다양한 색깔로도 만들 수 있어.
남 알았어. 나도 한번 만들어 볼게.

10 ②

해설 남자는 나무를 살리기 위해 종이를 절약하는 방법 세 가지를 알려주고 있다.

M Did you know that we can save trees <u>by saving paper</u>? That's right. Trees are the main

남 우리가 종이를 절약하게 되면 나무를 살릴 수 있다는 것을 알고 있었나요?

어휘 save[seiv] 구하다; 절약하다
instead of ~ 대신에
handkerchief[hǽŋkərtʃi(ː)f] 손수건
paper towel 종이 타월
tissue[tíʃuː] 휴지, 화장지

part of paper. So, I'm going to talk about how to use less paper. First, stop using paper cups. Instead, use your own cup. Second, you can borrow books instead of buying new ones. Last, carry and use a handkerchief instead of paper towels or tissues.

그렇습니다. 나무는 종이의 주요한 부분이지요. 그래서 저는 종이를 덜 쓰는 방법에 대해 이야기하려고 합니다. 첫째, 종이컵 사용을 멈추세요. 대신, 자신의 컵을 사용하세요. 둘째, 책을 새로 사는 대신 빌릴 수 있어요. 마지막으로, 종이 타월이나 휴지 대신 손수건을 가지고 다니며 사용하세요.

11 ⑤

해설 Warka Tower는 제작하는 데 4주 걸린다고 했다.

어휘 tower[táuər] 탑
structure[strʌ́ktʃər] 구조물
collect[kəlékt] 모으다
bamboo[bæmbúː] 대나무
net[net] 그물
capture[kǽptʃər] 붙잡다

W Hello, class. I'd like to talk about the Warka Tower. It's a structure to collect water from the air. People use this to drink clean water. The tower is easy to make. Build a tower out of bamboo and then cover it with a net. The net captures water from the air. The Warka Tower can be built with simple tools. But it usually takes 4 weeks when 8 people build one.

여 여러분, 안녕하세요. 저는 Warka Tower에 대해 이야기하려고 해요. 이것은 공기 중에서 물을 모으는 구조물입니다. 사람들은 깨끗한 물을 마시기 위해 이것을 사용해요. 이 탑은 만들기 쉬워요. 대나무로 탑을 쌓은 다음 그물로 그 탑을 덮어요. 그물이 공기 중에서 물을 끌어들여요. 간단한 도구로도 만들 수 있어요. 하지만 8명이 하나를 만들 때 4주가 걸려요.

12 ④

해설 남자는 박물관의 개관 시간을 물어보기 위해 전화하였다.

어휘 art museum 미술관
all year round 일 년 내내

[Telephone rings.]
W Korea Art Museum. How can I help you?
M Hello. What time does the museum close?
W We close at 5:30 p.m.
M Really? I thought you closed at 7 p.m.
W We close at 7 p.m. only from June to September.
M Then, do you always open at 10 o'clock all year round?
W That's right.
M I see. Thank you for letting me know.

[전화벨이 울린다.]
여 한국 미술관입니다. 무엇을 도와드릴까요?
남 안녕하세요. 박물관은 몇 시에 문을 닫나요?
여 저희는 오후 5시 30분에 폐관합니다.
남 정말요? 저는 오후 7시에 문을 닫는 줄 알았는데요.
여 6월부터 9월까지만 오후 7시에 문을 닫습니다.
남 그럼 일 년 내내 항상 10시에 문을 여나요?
여 그렇습니다.
남 알겠습니다. 알려주셔서 감사합니다.

13 ④

해설 디저트 카페에 가기 위해 4시 10분에 만나자고 했으나 여자가 교실 청소를 해야 한다고 해서 4시 30분에 만나기로 했다.

어휘 dessert[dizə́ːrt] 디저트
piece[piːs] 조각
school gate 교문

M Mina, there is a new dessert cafe down the street.
W Yes, I know that place. Chocolate cake is the most popular dessert at that cafe.
M Really? I want to go there and have a piece.
W Why don't we go there today? I don't have plans after school.
M Sure. How about meeting at 10 after 4?

남 미나야, 길 아래쪽에 새로운 디저트 카페가 있어.
여 그래, 나도 거기 알아. 그 카페에서 제일 인기 있는 디저트는 초콜릿 케이크이지.
남 그래? 거기 가서 한 조각 먹고 싶네.
여 우리 오늘 거기 갈까? 나는 방과 후에 아무 계획도 없어.
남 좋아. 4시 10분에 만나면 어떨까?

W Oh, I have to stay and clean the classroom. How about 4:30?

M All right. I'll wait for you by the school gate.

여 아, 난 남아서 교실을 청소해야 해. 4시 30분은 어때?

남 괜찮아. 교문에서 기다릴게.

14 ⑤

해설 남자가 여자에게 전자레인지의 사용법을 묻고 있고 여자가 음식을 먹고 나서 쓰레기를 버려달라고 하는 것으로 보아 두 사람의 관계는 편의점 직원과 손님임을 알 수 있다.

어휘 **warm up** (음식을) 데우다
microwave[máikrəwèiv] 전자레인지
chopsticks[tʃápstiks] 젓가락
counter[káuntər] 계산대
throw away 버리다
garbage[gáːrbidʒ] 쓰레기

M Excuse me, can you help me with something?

W Sure. Is there something wrong?

M I want to warm this up, but I don't know how to use the microwave.

W I see. Let me do that for you.

M Thanks. [Pause] Where are the chopsticks?

W They are on the right side of the counter.

M Oh, I see them.

W When you finish, please throw away your garbage.

M I will. Thanks for your help.

남 실례합니다만, 좀 도와주시겠어요?

여 그러죠. 뭐가 잘못됐나요?

남 이걸 데우고 싶은데, 전자레인지를 사용하는 법을 모르겠어요.

여 그렇군요. 제가 대신 눌러 드릴게요.

남 고맙습니다. [잠시 후] 젓가락은 어디에 있나요?

여 계산대 오른쪽에 있어요.

남 아, 보이네요.

여 다 드시고 나면 쓰레기를 버려 주세요.

남 그럴게요. 도와줘서 고마워요.

15 ④

해설 남자가 병을 쉽게 여는 방법을 알려주는 동영상을 본 것 같다고 하자 엄마는 그 동영상을 찾아달라고 부탁했다.

어휘 **jar**[dʒɑːr] 병, 단지
pretty[príti] 아주, 매우

M Mom, can you help me with my homework?

W Sorry, honey. I'm pretty busy in the kitchen.

M I see. What are you making?

W I'm making spaghetti, but I can't open this jar. I tried everything, but it won't open.

M I think I saw a video online of how to open a jar easily.

W Then can you find the video for me? I need to watch it.

M Sure. I'll do that right now.

남 엄마, 숙제 좀 도와주실래요?

여 미안하다, 얘야. 나는 부엌에서 아주 바쁘거든.

남 알겠어요. 뭘 만드시는데요?

여 스파게티를 만들고 있는데 이 병을 열 수가 없어. 할 수 있는 건 다 해 봤는데 열리지 않네.

남 온라인에서 병을 쉽게 여는 방법에 대한 동영상을 본 것 같아요.

여 그럼 그 동영상 좀 찾아봐 줄래? 그걸 봐야겠어.

남 네, 지금 당장 찾아볼게요.

16 ②

해설 남자가 같이 스케이트를 타러 가자고 제안했지만 여자는 이모의 결혼식이 있어서 갈 수 없다고 했다.

어휘 **wedding**[wédiŋ] 결혼식
attend[əténd] 참석하다
get married 결혼하다

W Paul, do you have any special plans for this weekend?

M Yes. I'm going to go ice-skating with my friends.

W That sounds like fun. I love winter sports, too.

M Then why don't you join us?

W I'd like to, but I have a wedding to attend.

M Really? Who is going to get married?

W My aunt. I can't wait to see her in a wedding dress. She'll look so beautiful.

여 Paul, 이번 주말에 특별한 계획 있니?

남 응, 나는 친구들과 아이스 스케이트를 타러 갈 거야.

여 재미있겠다! 나도 겨울 스포츠를 좋아하는데.

남 그럼 우리랑 같이 가지 않을래?

여 가고 싶지만 결혼식에 참석해야 해.

남 그래? 누가 결혼하는데?

여 우리 이모. 웨딩드레스를 입은 모습을 빨리 보고 싶어. 이모는 정말 예뻐 보일 거야.

17 ③

해설 남자가 잔디를 가리키고 있고 여자의 말풍선에 들어가면 안 된다는 표시가 있으므로 잔디에 들어가도 되는지 묻는 대화가 적절하다.

어휘 grass[græs] 잔디
visitor center 관광 안내소
keep off 멀리하다, 피하다

① M May I take pictures of the animal?
   W Yes, you may.
② M How can I get to the visitor center?
   W Go straight for two blocks.
③ M Excuse me. Is it okay to sit over there?
   W I'm sorry, but you must keep off the grass.
④ M Can I help you?
   W Yes. Do you have this skirt in black?
⑤ M Can I play soccer in the park?
   W Yes. Just be careful with the ball.

① 남 그 동물의 사진을 찍어도 되나요?
   여 네, 그러세요.
② 남 관광 안내소는 어떻게 가나요?
   여 두 블록을 직진하세요.
③ 남 실례합니다만, 저기에 앉아도 되나요?
   여 죄송하지만, 잔디밭에 들어가시면 안 됩니다.
④ 남 도와드릴까요?
   여 네. 이 치마로 검정색이 있나요?
⑤ 남 공원에서 축구를 해도 되나요?
   여 네. 공만 좀 주의해 주세요.

18 ③

해설 제목(타이타닉), 개봉 연도(1997년), 주인공(Rose와 Jack), 상영 시간(194분)에 대해 언급하였지만 감독에 대해서는 언급하지 않았다.

어휘 come out 나오다, 개봉하다
award[əwɔ́ːrd] 상
social class 사회 계층
fall in love with ~와 사랑에 빠지다
bored[bɔːrd] 지루해 하는

W Let me tell you about my favorite movie. It's *Titanic*. The movie came out in 1997 and became really popular. It won many awards. The movie is about 2 people from different social classes. Rose and Jack meet on a ship and fall in love with each other. The movie is 194 minutes long, but you won't feel bored at all when you watch it.

여 내가 가장 좋아하는 영화에 대해 말할게요. 그것은 〈타이타닉〉이에요. 1997년에 개봉해서 큰 인기를 얻었어요. 이 영화는 많은 상을 받았어요. 이 영화는 사회 계층이 다른 두 사람에 관한 이야기예요. Rose와 Jack은 배에서 만나 서로 사랑에 빠져요. 이 영화는 194분짜리이지만, 보다 보면 전혀 지루하지 않을 거예요.

19 ⑤

해설 전시된 빨간 모자가 마음에 들어서써 보려고 했지만 전시용이라 팔지 않는다고 했으므로 티셔츠만 입어보겠다고 응답해야 적절하다.

어휘 try on ~을 입어 보다
fitting room 탈의실
for sale 판매 중인
display[displéi] 전시, 진열
[선택지]
change[tʃeindʒ] 거스름돈

M Excuse me. Can I try on this T-shirt?
W Sure. The fitting room is over there.
M Thanks. [Pause] Wait a minute! Is it okay to try on that red hat, too?
W I'm sorry, but it's not for sale.
M I really like it. Can't you sell it to me?
W I'm afraid it's only for display.
M I see. Then I'll just try on this T-shirt.

남 실례합니다만, 이 티셔츠를 입어 봐도 될까요?
여 물론이죠. 탈의실은 저쪽이에요.
남 고맙습니다. [잠시 후] 잠깐만요! 저 빨간 모자도 써 봐도 되나요?
여 죄송하지만, 그건 파는 물건이 아닙니다.
남 정말 마음에 드는데. 저한테 판매하시면 안 되나요?
여 죄송합니다만 전시용이라서요.
남 알겠습니다. 그럼 이 티셔츠만 입어 볼게요.

① 좋아요. 그걸 살게요.
② 그냥 둘러보는 겁니다.
③ 네. 거스름돈은 2달러입니다.
④ 죄송하지만, 저한테 잘 안 어울리네요.

20 ①

해설 남자의 딸이 학교생활을 잘하고 있고 친구도 많다고 여자가 칭찬했으므로 남자는 그 이야기를 들어서 기쁘다고 응답하는 것이 적절하다.

어휘 grade[greid] 성적
get along with ~와 잘 지내다
[선택지]
disappoint[dìsəpɔ́int] 실망시키다

M Hello, Ms. Park. I'm Tom Miller, Cathy's father.
W Oh, Cathy's father! I'm pleased to meet you.
M I'm happy to meet you, too. How's she doing this year?
W She's doing very well. She studies hard and her grades are getting better.
M Great. Is she getting along with her friends, too?
W Of course. She has a lot of friends.
M I'm happy to hear that.

남 안녕하세요, 박 선생님. 저는 Cathy의 아버지인 Tom Miller입니다.
여 아, Cathy의 아버님! 뵙게 돼서 반갑습니다.
남 저도 만나서 반갑습니다. Cathy는 올해 어떻게 지내고 있나요?
여 아주 잘 지내고 있습니다. 열심히 공부해서 성적도 좋아지고 있어요.
남 잘됐네요. 친구들과도 잘 지내나요?
여 물론이죠. 친구가 아주 많답니다.
남 그 얘기를 들으니 기쁘네요.

② 제가 당신의 학생인 것이 자랑스러워요.
③ 저는 그 애가 항상 걱정됩니다.
④ 걔가 다음에 더 잘하려고 노력할 거예요.
⑤ 또 실망시켜서 죄송합니다.

01 ④	02 ④	03 ②	04 ③	05 ⑤	06 ②	07 ⑤
08 ②	09 ⑤	10 ②	11 ⑤	12 ④	13 ②	14 ⑤
15 ④	16 ②	17 ⑤	18 ⑤	19 ④	20 ③	

01 ④

해설 오늘 밤 늦게 눈이 내리기 시작해서 내일 저녁까지 그치지 않을 거라고 했으므로 내일은 눈이 오는 날씨이다.

어휘 melt[melt] 녹다
expected[ikspéktid] 예상되는

W Good morning. It's time for the weather report for this week. It's going to be cloudy and windy today. Later tonight, it'll start to snow, and the snow won't stop until tomorrow evening. The good news is that it's going to be sunny and warm on the weekend. So, much of the snow is expected to melt. Thank you.

여 좋은 아침입니다. 이번 주 일기예보 시간입니다. 오늘은 흐리고 바람이 불 것입니다. 오늘 밤 늦게 눈이 내리기 시작해서 내일 저녁까지 그치지 않을 것입니다. 주말에는 날씨가 화창하고 따뜻할 것이라는 좋은 소식입니다. 따라서 눈이 많이 녹을 것으로 예상됩니다. 감사합니다.

02 ④

해설 여자는 주머니가 앞에 1개, 옆에 2개인 배낭을 사겠다고 했다.

어휘 recommend[rèkəménd] 추천하다
front[frʌnt] 앞쪽의
popular[pápulər] 인기 있는
side[said] 옆면
convenient[kənvíːnjənt] 편리한

M May I help you?
W Yes. I need a backpack for work. Can you recommend one?
M How about this one with a big front pocket? This style is very popular these days.
W I like it, but I need more pockets.
M Then how about that one? It has a front pocket and 2 side pockets.
W Oh, that looks convenient. I'll take it.

남 도와드릴까요?
여 네. 출근할 때 쓸 배낭이 필요해요. 하나 추천해 주시겠어요?
남 큰 앞주머니가 있는 이건 어때요? 이게 요즘 아주 인기 있어요.
여 그것도 좋은데, 저는 주머니가 더 필요해요.
남 그럼 저건 어때요? 앞주머니가 하나 있고 옆 주머니가 두 개 있어요.
여 아, 편리해 보이네요. 그걸로 할게요.

03 ②

해설 남자는 가족 여행을 기다리며 매우 신이 난 상태이다.

어휘 go hiking 하이킹을 가다

W Ethan, do you have any plans for your vacation?
M Yes, I do. I'm going to go on a family trip next weekend.
W That's nice. Where?
M We're going to visit Sokcho.
W What are you going to do there?
M I'll go hiking and ride a boat.
W That sounds like fun. I hope you'll have a great time with your family.
M Yes. I can't wait!

여 Ethan, 너 방학에 특별한 계획 있니?
남 응, 있어. 다음 주말에 가족 여행을 갈 거거든.
여 좋겠다. 어디로?
남 속초에 갈 거야.
여 거기서 뭐 할 건데?
남 등산도 하고 보트도 탈 거야.
여 재미있겠다. 가족들과 즐거운 시간 보내길 바랄게.
남 그래. 빨리 가고 싶어!

04 ③

해설 여자는 도서 전시회에서 자신이 좋아하는 작가의 강연을 들었다고 했다.

어휘 book fair 도서 전시회

W Henry, have you ever been to the Seoul Book Fair?
M No, I haven't. Have you?
W Actually, I went there last week.

여 Henry, 서울 도서전에 가본 적 있니?
남 아니, 안 가 봤어. 너는?
여 사실 난 지난주에 갔었어.
남 어땠어?

activity [æktívəti] 활동
lecture [léktʃər] 강연

M How was it?
W I liked it a lot. Many people came and enjoyed many fun activities.
M What activities did you do?
W I listened to a lecture by my favorite writer.
M That sounds interesting. I want to join you next time.

여 굉장히 좋았어. 많은 사람들이 와서 많은 재미있는 활동을 즐겼어.
남 너는 어떤 활동을 했니?
여 나는 내가 좋아하는 작가의 강연을 들었어.
남 재미있었겠다. 다음엔 나도 같이 가고 싶어.

05 ⑤

해설 모자를 어디서 잃어버렸는지 묻는 남자의 말에 여자가 '이곳은 너무 큰 백화점이에요.'라고 직접적으로 말했으며, 읽어버린 물건이 들어오면 전화하겠다는 것으로 보아 백화점 분실물 센터에서 나누는 대화임을 알 수 있다.

어휘 baseball cap 야구 모자
both [bouθ] 둘 다
huge [hju:dʒ] 거대한
department store 백화점

W Excuse me. Did anyone bring a baseball cap?
M Let me see. [Pause] We actually have 2 baseball caps.
W I hope one of them is blue. I lost a blue cap yesterday.
M I'm sorry, but both of them are black. Where did you lose it?
W I don't know. This is a huge department store.
M Can you give me your phone number? I'll call you if someone brings a blue baseball cap.
W Okay. It's 048-3742.

여 실례합니다만. 누가 야구 모자 가져왔나요?
남 잠시만요. [잠시 후] 사실 야구 모자가 두 개 있네요.
여 그중 하나가 파란색이었으면 좋겠네요. 제가 어제 파란 모자를 잃어버렸거든요.
남 죄송하지만 둘 다 검은색이네요. 어디서 잃어버리셨어요?
여 모르겠어요. 이 백화점이 너무 커서요.
남 전화번호 알려주실 수 있나요? 누군가 파란 야구 모자를 가져오면 전화드릴게요.
여 그렇게 해주세요. 048-3742예요.

06 ②

해설 댄스 수업을 혼자 듣고 싶지 않다는 남자에게 여자가 자신도 듣겠다고 하며 같은 반에 등록하자고 했고 남자가 좋은 생각이라며 동의하고 있다.

어휘 list [list] 목록
community center 주민 센터
alone [əlóun] 혼자
sign up 등록하다, 가입하다

W What is that in your hand, Mike?
M It's a list of programs at the community center.
W Oh, are there any interesting classes?
M Sure, there are so many. I want to take a dance class, but I don't want to take it alone.
W I want to take a dance class, too. Maybe we both can sign up for the same class.
M That's a great idea.

여 Mike, 네 손에 있는 게 뭐야?
남 주민 센터에서 하는 프로그램 목록이야.
여 아, 재미있는 수업이라도 있어?
남 물론이지, 아주 많이 있어. 나는 댄스 수업을 듣고 싶은데 혼자 듣기는 싫어.
여 나도 댄스 수업을 듣고 싶어. 아마 우리 둘 다 같은 반에 등록할 수 있을 거야.
남 좋은 생각이야.

07 ⑤

해설 가이드 투어에 대한 정보는 없다고 했다.

어휘 app(= application) [æp] 앱, 응용 프로그램
entrance fee 입장료
tourist [túərist] 관광객
information [ìnfərméiʃən] 정보
guided tour 안내인이 있는 투어

W Eric, look at this app. I'm looking for information about the Seoul History Museum.
M Okay. It's open from 9 to 8.
W And there is no entrance fee for students.
M Great. It says it's near Jong-ro.
W Oh, there are many interesting events for tourists this Saturday.
M I'd like to visit there. What kind of guided tours are there?

여 Eric, 이 앱 좀 봐. 나는 서울 역사박물관에 대한 정보를 찾고 있거든.
남 그래. 9시부터 8시까지 여는구나.
여 그리고 학생들은 입장료가 없대.
남 잘됐네. 박물관은 종로 근처래.
여 아, 이번 토요일에 관광객들을 위한 재미있는 행사가 있어.
남 나 거기 가보고 싶어. 가이드 투어는 어떤 게 있어?

W   I don't know. I can't find <u>any information</u> <u>about</u> that.

여   모르겠어. 그것에 대해서는 정보를 찾을 수가 없네.

08 ②

해설 조용하고 수줍음을 타던 준수가 변하게 된 비결이 연극 동아리라는 걸 알게 된 남자는 자신도 당장 가입하겠다고 했다.

어휘 speech[spiːtʃ] 연설
quiet[kwáiət] 조용한
shy[ʃai] 소심한, 부끄럼을 타는
used to-v ~하곤 했다
since[sins] ~한 이후로

W   Did you hear Junsu won the speech contest?
M   Yes, I was surprised. I thought he was very <u>quiet and shy</u>.
W   Yes, he used to be.
M   I want to be like him. Do you know <u>what changed him</u>?
W   He has changed a lot since he joined the drama club.
M   Really?
W   <u>Why don't you</u> join the drama club? The club is looking for <u>new members</u>.
M   All right. I'll join it right now.

여   준수가 연설 대회에서 우승했다는 소식 들었어?
남   응, 놀랐어. 나는 걔가 아주 조용하고 수줍음을 탄다고 생각했는데.
여   그래, 그랬었지.
남   나도 걔처럼 되고 싶어. 무엇이 준수를 변하게 했는지 아니?
여   준수는 연극 동아리에 가입하고 나서 많이 변했어.
남   정말?
여   너 연극 동아리에 가입하는 게 어때? 그 동아리에서 새 멤버를 찾고 있거든.
남   좋아. 당장 가입해야겠다.

09 ⑤

해설 위치(시립박물관 옆), 개점 시기(2주 전), 음식 맛(맛있음), 추천 음식(쇠고기 쌀국수와 해물을 넣은 바삭한 부침개)에 대해 언급하였지만 음식 가격에 대해서는 언급하지 않았다.

어휘 Vietnamese[vìètnəːmíːz] 베트남의
rice noodle 쌀국수
crispy[kríspi] 바삭바삭한

M   Have you been to the new Vietnamese restaurant, Juha?
W   Are you talking about <u>the one next to</u> the city museum?
M   Yes, that's the one.
W   <u>The restaurant opened</u> 2 weeks ago, and I went there last Saturday with my aunt.
M   How was the food?
W   It <u>was great</u>. I really liked the rice noodles with beef.
M   Can you recommend <u>a dish for me</u>? I'm going there for lunch with my friends.
W   Then you should try the crispy pancake with seafood.
M   It sounds delicious. Thank you.

남   주하야, 새로 생긴 베트남 음식점에 가 봤니?
여   시립박물관 옆에 있는 곳 말하는 거니?
남   응, 바로 그곳.
여   그 음식점은 2주 전에 영업을 시작했는데, 나는 지난 토요일에 그곳에 이모와 함께 갔었어.
남   음식은 어땠니?
여   아주 좋았어. 나는 쇠고기 쌀국수가 정말 맛있었어.
남   나한테 요리 좀 추천해 줄래? 친구랑 점심 먹으러 갈 거라서.
여   그러면, 해물을 넣은 바삭한 부침개를 먹어 봐.
남   맛있겠다. 고마워.

10 ②

해설 여자는 미술관에서 지켜야 할 규칙 세 가지를 알려주고 있다.

어휘 look around 둘러보다
art gallery 미술관
rule[ruːl] 규칙
entrance[éntrəns] 입구

W   We are now at Alive Art Gallery. We're going to look around here for 3 hours. I'll explain <u>some rules here</u> before we go in. First, <u>don't touch</u> the art. Enjoy it with your eyes only. Second, you must <u>not talk loudly</u>. Finally, you are not allowed <u>to eat or drink</u> inside the gallery. We'll meet again at the entrance at 4.

여   우리는 지금 Alive 미술관에 있어요. 우리는 세 시간 동안 이곳을 둘러볼 거예요. 들어가기 전에 이곳의 몇 가지 규칙을 설명할게요. 첫째, 예술품을 만지지 마세요. 눈으로만 감상하세요. 둘째, 큰 소리로 이야기해서는 안 됩니다. 마지막으로, 미술관 안에서 먹거나 마시는 것은 허용되지 않아요. 우리는 4시에 입구에서 다시 만나기로 해요.

11 ⑤

해설 Grandma Moses는 101살 때 세상을 떠났다.

어휘 artist[ɑ́:rtist] 화가
career[kəríər] 이력, 생애
works of art 미술 작품

M Hi, class. I'd like to talk about Grandma Moses. She was an American artist. At the age of 78, she started to paint pictures. Most of her pictures were about farm life. During her career, she created about 1,500 works of art. She died at the age of 101. I learned that you're never too old to learn.

남 안녕하세요, 여러분. Grandma Moses에 대해 이야기하려고 해요. 그녀는 미국의 화가였어요. 78세의 나이에 그림을 그리기 시작했지요. 그녀의 그림 대부분은 농장 생활에 대한 거였어요. 화가로 지내면서 그녀는 1,500여 점의 미술 작품을 그렸어요. 그녀는 101세에 세상을 떠났어요. 저는 배우기에 너무 늦은 나이는 없다는 사실을 알게 됐어요.

12 ④

해설 남자는 영화관 근처에 사는 여자에게 그 부근에 있는 좋은 음식점을 추천해 달라고 전화했다.

어휘 cinema[sínəmə] 영화관
nearby[nìərbái] 근처에, 가까이에
Chinese restaurant 중국 식당
theater[θí(:)ətər] 극장

[Cell phone rings.]
W Hello.
M Hi, Susan. It's Noah. You are living near the Miko Cinema, right?
W Yes, I am. Why?
M I'm going to go to the movies at the Miko Cinema House with my family this Saturday.
W That's nice.
M Yeah. We're going to have dinner before the movie. Do you know any good restaurants nearby?
W There's a good Chinese restaurant right next to the theater.
M I see. I should take my family there. Thanks a lot.

[휴대전화가 울린다.]
여 여보세요.
남 안녕, Susan. 나 Noah야. 너 Miko 영화관 근처에 살고 있지?
여 응, 맞아. 왜?
남 이번 주 토요일에 가족과 함께 Miko 영화관으로 영화를 보러 갈 예정이야.
여 좋겠네.
남 응. 우리는 영화 보기 전에 저녁을 먹을 예정이야. 근처에 좋은 음식점 아는 데 있니?
여 극장 바로 옆에 괜찮은 중국 식당이 있어.
남 그렇구나. 그곳으로 가족을 데려가야겠다. 정말 고마워.

13 ②

해설 여자가 목적지인 춘천에서 점심을 먹고 싶다고 했고, 남자는 그러면 더 일찍 출발하자고 해서 8시 반에 만나기로 했다.

어휘 ride[raid] 타다
early[ə́:rli] 일찍, 빨리

W James, why don't we ride bicycles to Chuncheon this Saturday?
M Sure. How long will it take?
W It'll take about 4 hours.
M Well, how about leaving at 10 in the morning?
W I was thinking about having lunch in Chuncheon. There are many popular restaurants.
M Then, we should leave earlier. Let's meet at 8:30.
W All right. I'll see you then.

여 James, 이번 주 토요일에 우리 춘천으로 자전거 타러 가는 게 어때?
남 좋아, 얼마나 걸릴까?
여 4시간 정도 걸릴 거야.
남 음, 아침 10시에 출발하는 게 어때?
여 나는 춘천에서 점심을 먹을까 했었거든. 그곳에 인기 있는 식당들이 많대.
남 그러면, 좀 더 일찍 출발해야겠다. 8시 반에 만나자.
여 알겠어. 그때 보자.

14 ⑤

해설 건물에서 불이 나는 것을 목격한 여자가 소방서에 신고하고 있고 남자가 소방차와 응급차를 보내주겠다는 상황으로 보아 두 사람의 관계는 신고 접수원과

[Telephone rings.]
M Nine-one-one. What's the emergency?
W I want to report a fire. I see a lot of smoke coming out of a building right now.

[전화벨이 울린다.]
남 911입니다. 어떤 응급 상황인가요?
여 화재 신고를 하려고요. 지금 건물에서 연기가 많이 나고 있는 것이 보여요.

신고자임을 알 수 있다.

어휘 nine-one-one 긴급 전화 번호
(911)
emergency[imə́:rdʒənsi] 비상 (사태)
report[ripɔ́:rt] 신고하다
smoke[smouk] 연기
located[lóukeitəd] ~에 위치한
fire truck 소방차
ambulance[ǽmbjuləns] 구급차

M	Where exactly is the fire happening?
W	The building is located in front of Rolling Hills Shopping Mall.
M	I see. What's your name, ma'am?
W	Sandy Evans.
M	Okay. We'll send fire trucks and an ambulance there right away.

남	정확히 어디서 불이 나고 있나요?
여	Rolling Hills 쇼핑몰 앞에 있는 건물이에요.
남	알겠습니다. 선생님의 성함이 어떻게 되십니까?
여	Sandy Evans입니다.
남	알겠습니다. 소방차와 구급차를 즉시 그곳으로 보내겠습니다.

15 ④

해설 여자가 남자에게 동생의 숙제를 도와주라고 부탁했다.

어휘 take good care of ~을 잘 돌보다

W	Jake, are you busy right now?
M	Not really. Why?
W	I'm going out with your dad now. Can you take good care of your sister?
M	Sure. When are you coming home?
W	We'll be back before 9 o'clock.
M	Okay.
W	One more thing. Can you help your sister with her homework? She needs help with science.
M	No problem. I'll help her right away.

여	Jake, 지금 바쁘니?
남	그렇지 않아요. 왜요?
여	난 네 아빠와 이제 외출할 거야. 동생을 잘 돌봐 줄 수 있겠니?
남	물론이죠. 언제 집에 오세요?
여	우리는 9시 전에 돌아올 거야.
남	알겠어요.
여	한 가지 더. 네 동생의 숙제를 도와줄 수 있겠니? 걔가 과학 과목에서 도움이 필요하거든.
남	그럴게요. 바로 도울게요.

16 ②

해설 교통경찰인 남자는 여자가 정지 신호를 무시하고 달렸기 때문에 여자를 멈춰 세웠다.

어휘 driver's license 운전 면허증
officer[ɔ́(:)fisər] 경(찰)관
sign[sain] 표시, 표지
ticket[tíkit] (위반) 딱지
fault[fɔ:lt] 잘못, 과실
carefully[kɛ́ərfəli] 주의하여

M	Excuse me, ma'am. Can I see your driver's license?
W	Here you are, officer. Did I do anything wrong?
M	Yes. Do you see the stop sign over there? You didn't stop for that sign.
W	Oh, I'm sorry. I didn't see it.
M	I'm afraid I'm going to have to give you a ticket.
W	I understand. It's my fault.
M	Here's your license back. Drive carefully.

남	실례합니다. 운전 면허증을 볼 수 있을까요?
여	여기 있어요, 경관님. 제가 뭘 잘못했나요?
남	네. 저기 정지 표시가 보입니까? 저 표시에 정지하지 않으셨어요.
여	아, 죄송해요. 못 봤어요.
남	죄송하지만 딱지를 끊겠습니다.
여	알겠습니다. 제 잘못이니까요.
남	여기 면허증 돌려드립니다. 조심해서 운전하세요.

17 ⑤

해설 남자가 곰 인형을 권하고 있지만 여자는 다른 인형을 더 마음에 들어 하는 상황이 적절하다.

어휘 on sale 할인 중인
cute[kju:t] 귀여운

① M How may I help you?
　 W I'm looking for a toy car.
② M I'd like to have that toy train.
　 W I like it, too.
③ M This ball is on sale. It's only $5.
　 W Great! I'll take it.
④ M I'm sorry, but I'm busy this afternoon.
　 W That's all right.
⑤ M Look at this. Isn't it cute?
　 W I like this doll better. It's much prettier.

① 남 무엇을 도와드릴까요?
　 여 네, 장난감 차를 찾고 있는데요.
② 남 나는 저 장난감 기차를 갖고 싶어.
　 여 저도 그게 마음에 들어요.
③ 남 이 공은 세일 중이네. 겨우 5달러야.
　 여 잘됐네요! 그거 살게요.
④ 남 미안하지만 오늘 오후에는 내가 바쁘구나.
　 여 괜찮아요.
⑤ 남 이것 봐. 귀엽지 않니?
　 여 저는 이 인형이 더 좋아요. 이게 훨씬 더 예뻐요.

18 ⑤

해설 운동 습관(달리기와 수영), 하루 식사량(다섯 끼), 평소 식단(균형 잡힌 식사), 피하는 음식(인스턴트 식품, 탄산음료)에 대해 언급하였지만 수면 시간에 대해서는 언급하지 않았다.

어휘 lifestyle[láifstàil] 생활 방식
meal[miːl] 식사
balanced diet 균형 잡힌 식사
avoid[əvɔ́id] 피하다
junk food 인스턴트식품
soda[sóudə] 탄산음료

M Hello, everyone. I'd like to tell you about my healthy lifestyle. I go running every morning and go swimming twice a week. I have 5 small meals each day. I keep a balanced diet. I try to eat more vegetables and fruits and less red meat. I usually avoid junk food and soda. Do you think I have a healthy lifestyle?

남 여러분, 안녕하세요. 제 건강한 생활 방식에 대해 말씀드릴게요. 저는 매일 아침 달리기를 하고 일주일에 두 번 수영을 해. 매일 다섯 끼의 양이 적은 식사를 해요. 균형 잡힌 식단을 유지하지요. 채소와 과일을 더 많이 먹고 붉은 고기를 덜 먹으려고 노력한답니다. 주로 인스턴트식품과 탄산음료를 먹지 않지요. 제 생활 방식이 건강한 것 같나요?

19 ④

해설 여행에서 등산을 하게 될 거라고 했으므로 등산화를 가져가야겠다는 응답이 가장 어울린다.

어휘 national museum 국립 박물관
pack[pæk] (짐을) 챙기다, 싸다
[선택지]
put on ~을 입다
raincoat[réinkòut] 비옷

M Jenny, I just finished planning our family trip to Gongju this weekend.
W I want to hear about it, Dad. Where are we going on the first day?
M We are going to visit the national museum first. Then we'll go to Gongsanseong.
W Oh, is that on a mountain?
M Yes, we are going to hike there. It'll take about an hour and a half.
W Then, I should pack my hiking shoes.

남 Jenny, 이번 주말에 공주로 가는 가족 여행 계획을 막 끝냈단다.
여 아빠, 계획에 대해 듣고 싶어요. 첫날에 우리 어디로 가요?
남 먼저 국립 박물관을 방문할 거야. 그러고 나서 공산성으로 갈 거야.
여 아, 그곳은 산에 있는 건가요?
남 그래. 거기서 하이킹을 할 거야. 1시간 반 정도 걸릴 거야.
여 그럼, 등산화를 챙겨야겠어요.

① 그건 분명 아름다웠을 거예요.
② 비옷을 입어야 해요.
③ 우리는 호텔에 3일간 머물렀어요.
⑤ 재밌었어요. 우리 더 자주 그걸 해요.

20 ③

해설 내일까지 연습할 시간이 있다고 격려하는 남자의 말을 듣고 여자는 기분이 좀 더 나아졌다고 응답하는 것이 가장 적절하다.

어휘 audition[ɔːdíʃən] 오디션
practice[prǽktis] 연습하다
[선택지]
luck[lʌk] 행운

M Yuna, you look very tired. What's wrong?
W I didn't get much sleep last night.
M Why?
W I have an audition for a rock band tomorrow. I'm going to play the guitar in front of the band members.
M You must be nervous. Have you practiced enough?
W Not really. I had to prepare for my exam today.
M Don't worry. You still have some time to practice until tomorrow.
W You're right. I feel better now.

남 윤아야. 너 무척 피곤해 보여. 왜 그래?
여 어젯밤에 잠을 많이 못 잤어.
남 왜?
여 나는 내일 록 밴드 오디션이 있거든. 밴드 멤버들 앞에서 기타를 쳐야 해.
남 긴장되겠다. 연습은 충분히 했니?
여 그렇진 않아. 오늘 시험을 준비해야 했거든.
남 걱정하지 마. 내일까지 연습할 시간이 좀 남아 있잖아.
여 네 말이 맞아. 이제 기분이 좀 나아졌어.

① 나 시험에 합격하지 못했어.
② 밴드에 가입하는 게 어때?
④ 미안하지만, 난 어떤 행운도 필요 없어.
⑤ 오디션에 합격할 수 있을지 모르겠어.

01 ③	02 ④	03 ⑤	04 ③	05 ⑤	06 ④	07 ①
08 ③	09 ④	10 ④	11 ⑤	12 ②	13 ④	14 ③
15 ④	16 ②	17 ③	18 ③	19 ④	20 ②	

01 ③

[해설] 토요일에는 눈이 오고 춥겠지만 일요일 오전에 기온이 올라가서 오후에는 맑은 하늘을 볼 수 있을 거라고 했다.

[어휘] weather forecast 일기예보
expect[ikspékt] 예상하다
temperature[témpərətʃər] 기온, 온도

W Good evening, everyone. Here is this weekend's weather forecast. This Saturday we are expecting to have very cold weather. It'll start to snow in the morning, and then there will be strong winds in the afternoon. However, the temperature will start to go up on Sunday morning. You'll be able to see clear skies later in the afternoon.

여 여러분, 안녕하세요. 이번 주말 일기예보입니다. 이번 토요일에는 매우 추운 날씨가 예상됩니다. 오전에는 눈이 오기 시작하겠고 오후에는 강한 바람이 불 것입니다. 하지만 일요일 오전에 기온이 올라가기 시작할 것입니다. 오후 늦게는 맑은 하늘을 보실 수 있을 겁니다.

02 ④

[해설] 단순한 모양을 선호한다는 여자에게 남자가 정사각형에 줄무늬가 있는 쿠션을 권하자 그걸 사겠다고 했다.

[어휘] cushion[kúʃən] 쿠션
shape[ʃeip] 모양
have ~ in mind ~을 마음에 두다
a few (수가) 여러, 몇
square[skwɛər] 정사각형 모양의
prefer[prifə́ːr] 더 좋아하다, 선호하다
stripe[straip] 줄무늬
popular[pápulər] 인기 있는

W Excuse me, I'm looking for a cushion.
M They come in many shapes. Do you have a shape in mind?
W I don't want any round ones because I already have a few at home.
M Then how about this square one with hearts?
W It's not bad. But I prefer something simple.
M Then you'll like this one with stripes. It's very popular in our store.
W I like it. I'll take it.

여 실례지만, 쿠션을 찾고 있어요.
남 쿠션이 다양한 모양으로 나와요. 마음에 두신 모양이라도 있나요?
여 둥근 모양은 집에 이미 몇 개 있어서 원하지 않아요.
남 그럼 하트가 그려진 이 정사각형 쿠션은 어떠세요?
여 나쁘지 않네요. 하지만 전 단순한 걸 더 좋아해요.
남 그럼 줄무늬가 있는 이게 마음에 드실 거예요. 저희 가게에서 무척 인기 있어요.
여 좋아요. 그걸로 살게요.

03 ⑤

[해설] 자신의 음식이 짜고 식었다고 하면서 더 이상 못 먹겠다는 여자의 말로 보아 실망했다는 것을 알 수 있다.

[어휘] perfect[pə́ːrfikt] 완벽한
medium[míːdiəm] 중간 정도로 구워진
expect[ikspékt] 기대하다
salty[sɔ́ːlti] 짠
besides[bisáidz] 게다가
have a bite 한 입 먹다

W How is your steak, Minsu?
M It's great. This is the perfect medium steak for me. How is your pasta?
W Well, mine is not as good as I expected.
M What's wrong with it?
W The pasta is good but a little salty for me. Besides, the food was cold when the waiter brought it.
M Really? Let me have a bite. [Pause] Whoa, it is really salty.
W I don't think I can eat this any more.

여 민수야, 네 스테이크 어떠니?
남 아주 맛있어. 이건 나에게 완벽한 미디움 스테이크야. 네 파스타는 어때?
여 글쎄, 내건 기대한 것만큼 좋지 않아.
남 뭐가 문제야?
여 파스타는 괜찮지만 나에겐 조금 짜. 게다가, 웨이터가 그것을 가져왔을 때 음식이 차가웠어.
남 정말? 내가 한 입 먹어볼게. [잠시 후] 워, 정말 짜다.
여 더 이상 못 먹을 것 같아.

① 만족한 ② 기쁜 ③ 무서워하는
④ 지루한 ⑤ 실망한

04 ③

해설 남자는 게임 디자이너를 체험하고 싶었으나 줄이 길어서 못하고 대신 뉴스 리포터를 체험했다고 했다.

어휘 experience[ikspíəriəns] 체험하다, 경험하다
chef[ʃef] 요리사
news reporter 뉴스 보도 기자
instead[instéd] 대신에
report[ripɔ́:rt] 보도하다

W Jiho, I heard you went to Job World yesterday.
M Yes, I did. There are more than 50 different jobs to experience. You can be a chef, game designer, and even news reporter.
W Oh, really? Which job did you try?
M I wanted to experience being a game designer, but I couldn't. The line was too long.
W Then what did you do?
M I tried being a news reporter instead. I looked into a camera and reported the news. That was fun.

여 지호야, 어제 Job World에 갔었다며.
남 응, 갔었어. 50여 가지의 다양한 직업을 체험할 수 있거든. 요리사, 게임 디자이너, 심지어 뉴스 리포터도 될 수 있어.
여 아, 정말? 너는 어떤 직업을 체험했니?
남 게임 디자이너를 체험하고 싶었지만 할 수 없었어. 줄이 너무 길었거든.
여 그럼 뭘 했니?
남 대신 뉴스 리포터를 체험했어. 카메라를 보고 뉴스를 보도했어. 재미있었어.

05 ⑤

해설 여자가 부츠를 신어보고 있고 남자가 사이즈를 확인해주는 상황이므로 신발 가게에서 이루어지는 대화임을 알 수 있다.

어휘 try on ~을 신어[입어] 보다
heel[hi:l] 굽
tight[tait] (옷 등이) 꼭 끼는
hold on 기다리다

M Hello. Can I help you?
W Yes. I'd like to try on those boots.
M The red ones with the high heels?
W No, I'd like the brown ones with the low heels. I wear a size 6.
M Here you are. Try them on. [Pause] How do they feel?
W I think they're too tight for me. Do you have them in a larger size?
M Sure. Could you hold on while I get them?
W Okay. Thanks.

남 안녕하세요. 도와드릴까요?
여 네. 저 부츠를 신어보고 싶은데요.
남 높은 굽이 있는 빨간 부츠 말씀이신가요?
여 아니요, 낮은 굽이 있는 갈색 부츠요. 저는 사이즈 6을 신어요.
남 여기 있습니다. 신어보세요. [잠시 후] 어때세요?
여 너무 꽉 끼는 것 같아요. 더 큰 사이즈가 있나요?
남 그럼요. 그걸 가져올 동안 잠시 기다려주시겠어요?
여 알겠습니다. 감사합니다.

06 ④

해설 파이가 많이 있다며 더 먹으라는 여자의 말에 남자는 배가 부르다며 거절하고 있다.

어휘 delicious[dilíʃəs] 맛있는
dish[diʃ] 음식; 접시
recipe[résəpi] 조리[요리]법
slice[slais] 한 조각
full[ful] 배부른

M This spaghetti with meat sauce is so delicious, Olivia.
W Thanks. It's one of my best dishes.
M And this apple pie is good, too. Did you bake this?
W No. My mom made it this morning.
M I should ask your mom for the recipe.
W There is another pie in the oven. So have another slice.
M I wish I could. But I'm too full.

남 이 미트소스 스파게티는 정말 맛있어, Olivia.
여 고마워. 내가 가장 잘하는 요리 중 하나야.
남 그리고 이 애플파이도 맛있어. 이것도 네가 구웠니?
여 아니. 엄마가 오늘 아침에 만드셨어.
남 너희 엄마께 요리법을 여쭤봐야겠다.
여 오븐에 다른 파이가 더 있어. 한 조각 더 먹어봐.
남 먹을 수 있으면 좋을 텐데. 근데 너무 배가 불러.

07 ①

해설 남자는 꽃을 좋아하는 엄마를 위해 꽃을 꽂을 수 있는 꽃병을 만들고 있다고 했다.

[Cell phone rings.]
M Hello.
W Hi, Liam. Do you want to come out and play

[휴대전화가 울린다.]
남 여보세요.
여 안녕, Liam. 나와서 배드민턴 칠래?

[어휘] come out (밖으로) 나오다
be in the middle of 한창 ~하는 중이다
bake[beik] (음식을) 굽다
vase[veis] 꽃병

M badminton?
M Sorry. I can't go out right now. I'm in the middle of something.
W What are you doing?
M I'm making a birthday present for my mom.
W Oh, are you making her a birthday cake?
M I don't know how to bake. Since she likes flowers, I wanted to give her something to put flowers in.
W Oh, you are making a vase.
M Yes. I hope she likes it.

남 미안. 지금 당장은 나갈 수 없어. 뭔가를 하고 있는 중이거든.
여 뭐 하고 있는데?
남 엄마에게 드릴 생일 선물을 만들고 있어.
여 아, 생일 케이크를 만들고 있니?
남 케이크 굽는 법을 몰라. 엄마가 꽃을 좋아하셔서 꽃을 꽂을 수 있는 뭔가를 만들어드리고 싶었어.
여 아, 너 꽃병 만들고 있구나.
남 그래. 엄마가 그걸 마음에 들어 하시면 좋겠어.

08 ③

[해설] 요리할 재료나 시간이 부족해서 대신 중국 요리를 주문해야겠다면서 여자는 남자에게 배달 전화번호를 찾아 달라고 했다.

[어휘] guest[gest] 손님
enough[inʌf] 충분한
order[ɔ́ːrdər] 주문하다
delivery[dilívəri] 배달

W Mark, your father is going to come home with a few guests from work.
M Now? How many people?
W 4 people. But there is not enough food to cook.
M I can go out and get the things you need.
W No, I don't have enough time, either. We should just order some Chinese food. Can you find me the delivery number?
M Okay. I'll be right back with it.

여 Mark, 아빠가 직장에서 손님 몇 분과 함께 집에 오실 거라는 구나.
남 지금요? 몇 분이나요?
여 네 분. 근데 요리할 재료가 충분하지가 않네.
남 제가 나가서 필요한 것을 사 올게요.
여 아니, 시간도 충분하지 않아. 그냥 중국 요리를 좀 주문해야겠다. 배달 전화번호를 좀 찾아줄래?
남 알겠어요. 금방 가지고 올게요.

09 ④

[해설] 장소(공공도서관), 수업 일수(일주일에 한 번), 선생님(일본인), 과제(많지 않음)에 대해 언급했지만 비용에 대해서는 언급하지 않았다.

[어휘] quiz[kwiz] 퀴즈, 시험[테스트]
public[pʌ́blik] 공공의

M Narae, what are you studying for?
W I have a quiz tomorrow in my Japanese class.
M Really? Where do you learn Japanese?
W The public library. You can also learn Chinese, French, and Spanish there.
M I see. How often do you go to class?
W Only once a week. The teacher is Japanese, but she can speak English and Korean really well.
M Do you get a lot of homework?
W Not much. But I get many quizzes instead.

남 나래야, 뭘 공부하고 있니?
여 내일 일본어 수업에 시험이 있거든.
남 정말? 어디에서 일본어를 배우니?
여 공공도서관에서. 그곳에서 중국어, 프랑스어, 스페인어도 배울 수 있어.
남 그렇구나. 수업에 얼마나 자주 가니?
여 일주일에 한 번만. 선생님이 일본인이신데 영어와 한국어도 정말 잘하셔.
남 숙제가 많니?
여 많지는 않아. 하지만 대신 퀴즈를 많이 봐.

10 ④

[해설] 여자는 치아를 건강하게 관리하는 방법으로 3가지를 언급하고 있다.

[어휘] teeth[tiːθ] tooth(이, 치아)의 복수형
healthy[hélθi] 건강한
brush A's teeth 이를 닦다, 양치질하다
meal[miːl] 식사, 끼니
lastly[lǽstli] 마지막으로
go to a dentist 치과에 가다

W There are easy and simple ways to keep your teeth healthy. First, remember the 3-3-3 rule. Brush your teeth for 3 minutes, 3 times a day, and in 3 minutes after each meal. Second, try not to eat too many sweet things, like chocolate, candy, and cookies. Lastly, don't be afraid to go to a dentist.

여 치아를 건강하게 유지하는 쉽고 간단한 방법이 있습니다. 우선, 3-3-3 규칙을 기억하세요. 3분 동안, 하루에 3번, 매 식사 후 3분 안에 이를 닦으세요. 둘째, 초콜릿, 사탕, 쿠키 같은 단 것을 너무 많이 먹지 않으려고 노력하세요. 마지막으로, 치과에 가는 것을 두려워하지 마세요.

36 정답 및 해설

11 ⑤

해설 재학생은 누구든 영화 수업에 참여할 수 있다고 했다.

어휘 film[film] 영화
script[skript] 대본, 원고
get into ~에 들어가다

M Hello, students. Our Movie Makers Club will hold a film class starting tomorrow for 2 days. It'll start at 9 a.m. and end at 4 p.m. On the first day, you'll learn how to make a story. Then you'll write a script for a short movie. On the second day, you'll get into groups of 4 and make a short film. Anyone in our school can join the class.

남 안녕하세요, 학생 여러분. 저희 Movie Makers Club에서는 내일부터 이틀간 영화 수업을 진행할 것입니다. 수업은 오전 9시에 시작해서 오후 4시에 끝납니다. 첫날에는 이야기를 구성하는 방법을 배울 것입니다. 그런 후에 짧은 영화를 위한 대본을 쓸 것입니다. 둘째 날에는 4명이 한 그룹으로 짧은 영화를 만들 것입니다. 우리 학교에 재학 중인 누구나 수업에 참여할 수 있습니다.

12 ②

해설 남자는 오늘 3시로 예약한 진료 시간에 못 올 것 같아 내일로 예약을 변경하고자 전화했다.

어휘 appointment[əpɔ́intmənt]
예약, 약속
change[tʃeindʒ] 변경하다, 바꾸다

[Telephone rings.]
W Hello. Dr. Crane's office.
M Hello. This is Alan Tate. I have an appointment with the doctor this afternoon.
W Yes, Mr. Tate. You have an appointment at 3 p.m.
M That's right. But I forgot I have an important meeting at the same time.
W So do you want to change your appointment?
M Yes. Can I come in tomorrow?
W Then could you come at 9 tomorrow morning?
M Yes, that sounds fine.

[전화벨이 울린다.]
여 여보세요. Crane 박사 진료소입니다.
남 여보세요. 저는 Alan Tate인데요. 오늘 오후에 진료 예약이 되어 있는데요.
여 네, Tate 씨. 오후 3시에 예약이 되어 있네요.
남 맞아요. 하지만 같은 시간에 중요한 회의가 있었다는 걸 깜박했어요.
여 그래서 예약을 변경하고 싶으신가요?
남 네. 내일 가도 될까요?
여 그럼 내일 아침 9시에 오실 수 있나요?
남 네, 좋아요.

13 ④

해설 스터디 모임에 3시까지 여동생을 돌봐야 하는 여자를 위해 3시 30분에 서점에서 만나서 같이 가기로 했다.

어휘 join[dʒɔin] 합류하다, 함께 하다
actually[ǽktʃuəli] 실제로, 정말로
bookstore[búkstɔ̀:r] 서점

M Sejung, we have a study group meeting at Peter's house. Do you want to join us?
W Sure. What time are you going to go there?
M It starts at 3.
W Oh, I have to watch my sister until then. Can I join you after that?
M Okay. Do you know how to get to his house?
W Actually, I'm not sure.
M How about meeting me at 3:30 at the bookstore? We can go together.
W That sounds great. I'll see you then.

남 세정아, Peter네 집에서 스터디 모임이 있어. 우리와 같이할래?
여 물론이지. 몇 시에 그곳에 가니?
남 3시에 시작해.
여 아, 3시까지 내 여동생을 돌봐야 해. 그 이후에 합류해도 될까?
남 그래. 걔네 집 가는 길은 아니?
여 사실, 잘 모르겠어.
남 서점에서 3시 30분에 나와 만나는 게 어때? 같이 가자.
여 좋아. 그때 보자.

14 ③

해설 남자가 여자에게 일주일 남은 대회를 위해 연습하자고 말하는 것으로 보아 두 사람의 관계는 코치와 운동선수임을 알 수 있다.

M Sujin, why are you late for practice?
W I'm sorry, sir. I had to take my little brother to the doctor earlier.
M The doctor? Is everything okay?
W Well, he had a terrible stomachache.

남 수진아, 왜 연습에 늦었니?
여 죄송해요, 선생님. 아까 전에 남동생을 병원에 데려가야 했어요.
남 병원에? 괜찮은 거야?
여 음, 걔한테 심한 복통이 있었거든요.

어휘 practice[prǽktis] 연습
terrible[térəbl] 심한, 지독한
stomachache[stʌ́məkeik] 복통
scared[skɛərd] 무서운, 두려운
junior[dʒúːnjər] 주니어의, 청소년의
competition[kàmpətíʃən] 대회, 시합

M Then, why didn't you call me?
W I was scared. I didn't know what to do at first.
M How is your brother now?
W He's okay. My mom is with him now.
M That's good. Let's start training. We only have a week left before the junior tennis competition.

남 그럼, 왜 나한테 전화하지 않았니?
여 무서웠어요. 먼저 뭘 해야 할지 몰랐어요.
남 네 동생은 지금은 어떠니?
여 괜찮아요. 지금은 엄마가 그 애와 함께 계세요.
남 다행이네. 훈련을 시작하자. 주니어 테니스 대회가 일주일밖에 안 남았어.

15 ④

해설 남자는 여자가 중국어를 잘 한다는 것을 알고 중국어 말하기 연습을 도와 달라고 부탁하고 있다.

어휘 speak[spiːk] (언어를) 말하다
speech[spiːtʃ] 말하기, 발언
long[lɔ(ː)ŋ] (시간 상으로) 오랜, 긴

M Do you have any plans after school?
W Nothing special. Why?
M I heard you could speak Chinese well. Is that true?
W Yes, I lived in Shanghai for 3 years.
M I have a Chinese speech contest. Can you help me practice for it?
W Sure, but I have to go home before 5. Is that all right?
M It won't be too long. Thanks!

남 방과 후에 어떤 계획이 있니?
여 특별한 일 없어. 왜?
남 네가 중국어를 잘한다고 들었어. 정말이야?
여 응, 3년 동안 상하이에서 살았어.
남 중국어 말하기 대회가 있거든. 나 연습하는 것 좀 도와줄래?
여 물론이지, 그런데 5시 전에 집에 가야 해. 괜찮니?
남 오래 걸리지 않을 거야. 고마워!

16 ②

해설 여자는 내일 집에 조부모님이 오실 예정이라 엄마를 도와야 해서 놀이공원에 못 간다고 했다.

어휘 amusement park 놀이공원
be away 떨어져 있다

M Hi, Emily.
W Hi, Mason. What's up?
M Do you want to go to the amusement park tomorrow?
W I'd love to, but I can't. I have something to do.
M You aren't going to study for the exams, are you? It's many days away.
W No, I'm not. I have to stay home.
M Why do you have to stay home?
W My grandparents will be visiting. So, I have to clean and help my mom in the kitchen.
M Oh, I see.

남 안녕, Emily.
여 안녕, Mason. 무슨 일이야?
남 내일 놀이공원에 갈래?
여 그러고 싶지만 갈 수 없어. 해야 할 일이 있거든.
남 시험공부를 하는 건 아니지, 그렇지? 시험은 한참 남았잖아.
여 아니야. 집에 있어야 하거든.
남 왜 집에 있어야 하는데?
여 조부모님이 방문하실 거라서. 그래서 청소하고 부엌에서 엄마를 도와드려야 해.
남 아, 그렇구나.

17 ③

해설 남자와 여자가 꽃가게의 위치를 묻고 답하는 대화가 적절하다.

어휘 prefer[prifə́ːr] ~을 더 좋아하다
gardening[gáːrdniŋ] 정원 가꾸기, 원예
pot[pat] 항아리
water[wɔ́ːtər] 물을 주다
once a week 일주일에 한 번

① M Which do you prefer, roses or tulips?
  W I like tulips better than roses.
② M Hello, may I help you?
  W Yes. I'm looking for a book about gardening.
③ M Excuse me, is there a flower shop near here?
  W Yes, there is one next to the bookstore.
④ M How much is that flower pot?
  W It costs $17.
⑤ M How often do you water your plant?
  W I water my plant once a week.

① 남 장미와 튤립 중 어떤 게 더 좋니?
  여 장미보다 튤립을 더 좋아해.
② 남 안녕하세요, 도와드릴까요?
  여 네. 정원 가꾸기에 관한 책을 찾고 있어요.
③ 남 실례지만 이 근처에 꽃 가게가 있나요?
  여 네, 서점 옆에 하나 있어요.
④ 남 화분이 얼마인가요?
  여 17달러예요.
⑤ 남 식물에 물을 얼마나 자주 주니?
  여 일주일에 한 번 물을 줘.

18 ③

해설 할인 기간(이번 주말에만), 할인 품목(트럭을 제외한 모든 자동차), 무료 제공 음식(커피와 쿠키), 위치(Main 가)에 대해 언급하였지만 영업시간에 대해서는 언급하지 않았다.

어휘 discount[dískaunt] 할인
at least 적어도
offer[ɔ́(:)fər] 할인; 제안
apply[əplái] 적용하다

M Roll's Automotive is going to have a big sale <u>this weekend only</u>. There is a 10% discount <u>on any car</u>. It means you can save at least $1,000 on a car. However, the offer does not apply for trucks. During the sale, from 9 a.m. to noon, any visitors to the store will <u>get free coffee</u> and cookies. So, come down to Roll's Automotive on Main Street. We are <u>next to</u> the ABC Mall.

남 Roll's Automotive가 이번 주말에만 큰 세일을 합니다. 어떤 차든 10퍼센트 할인이 됩니다. 그건 차 한 대에 적어도 천 달러를 아낄 수 있다는 것을 의미합니다. 하지만 트럭은 할인이 적용되지 않습니다. 세일 기간 동안, 오전 9시부터 정오까지 가게에 방문하는 어떤 분이든 쿠키와 커피를 무료로 제공받으실 수 있습니다. 그러니 Main 가에 있는 Roll's Automotive에 오세요. 저희 매장은 ABC Mall 옆에 있습니다.

19 ④

해설 남자가 시티 투어 버스를 타는 것에 동의했으므로 관광 안내소에 가서 버스 정류장과 일정에 대해 알아보는 여자의 제안을 수락하는 응답이 이어져야 한다.

어휘 interesting[íntərestiŋ] 흥미로운
place[pleis] 장소
information[ìnfərméiʃən] 정보
schedule[skédʒuːl] 일정
[선택지]
book[buk] 예약하다

W There are so many interesting places to visit. I can't decide <u>where to go</u>.
M Me neither. We don't <u>have enough time</u>. We will stay here only for 3 days.
W Well, how about taking a city tour bus first? After that, we can decide which places to go.
M That sounds like a great idea. But we don't have any information <u>about the bus stop</u> or schedule.
W Let's go and find <u>the tourist information center</u>.
M Sure. Let me check the map.

여 가 볼 만한 흥미로운 곳들이 정말 많네. 어디를 가야 할지 결정이 안 돼.
남 나도, 그래. 우리는 시간이 충분하지 않아. 우린 여기서 3일만 머물 거야.
여 음, 우선 시티 투어 버스를 타는 게 어때? 그다음에 갈 곳을 정할 수 있잖아.
남 좋은 생각인 것 같아. 하지만 버스 정류장이나 일정에 대한 정보가 없어.
여 관광 안내소에 가서 알아보자.
남 좋아. 내가 지도를 확인해볼게.

① 천만에.
② 아니, 아직 결정하지 못했어.
③ 이미 호텔을 예약했어.
⑤ 알겠어. 모든 것에 최선을 다할게.

20 ②

해설 여자는 콘서트가 시작하는 시각을 묻고 있으므로 콘서트 시작 시각을 알려주는 응답이 이어져야 한다.

어휘 review[rivjúː] 리뷰, 비평

M Emma, what are you going to do this Friday night?
W Nothing special. I think I'll <u>just stay home</u> and watch TV.
M I see. I got 2 free piano concert tickets. Would you like to come?
W Sure, I'd love to. <u>I've never been to</u> a piano concert before.
M I read some reviews on this piano concert, and most people said it was good.
W Great. What time does <u>this concert start</u>?
M It starts at 7:30 p.m.

남 Emma, 금요일 밤에 뭐 할 거니?
여 특별한 거 없어. 집에서 TV나 볼 것 같아.
남 그렇구나. 무료 피아노 콘서트 표가 두 장 있거든. 같이 갈래?
여 좋아, 그러고 싶어. 전에 피아노 콘서트를 가 본 적이 없거든.
남 나도. 이 피아노 콘서트에 대한 리뷰를 좀 읽었는데 대부분의 사람들이 좋았다고 하더라고.
여 잘됐다. 이 콘서트가 몇 시에 시작하니?
남 오후 7시 30분에 시작해.

① 빨리 보고 싶어 죽겠어.
③ 대략 2시간 정도 걸릴 거야.
④ 그녀는 모차르트와 슈베르트를 연주할 거야.
⑤ 콘서트홀에서 7시에 만나자.

01 ③	02 ④	03 ②	04 ④	05 ②	06 ③	07 ②
08 ⑤	09 ④	10 ③	11 ⑤	12 ①	13 ①	14 ②
15 ⑤	16 ⑤	17 ③	18 ⑤	19 ③	20 ③	

01 ③

[해설] 금요일에는 맑고 화창한 날씨를 즐길 수 있다고 했다.

[어휘] forecast[fɔ́ːrkæst] 예측, 예보
a high chance of ~의 높은 가능성
indoors[ìndɔ́ːrz] 실내에서
expected[ikspéktid] 예상되는

M This is the Joy 365 Forecast. Spring is here, and we'll have many changes this week. It'll be windy and partly cloudy from Monday through Wednesday. On Thursday, there is a high chance of rain. You'll be able to enjoy a beautiful sunny day on Friday. However, you'd better stay indoors on the weekend because heavy rain is expected.

남 Joy 365 일기예보입니다. 봄이 왔고 이번 주에는 많은 기온 변화가 있겠습니다. 월요일부터 수요일까지는 바람이 불고 부분적으로 구름이 끼겠습니다. 목요일에는 비가 올 가능성이 높습니다. 금요일에는 맑고 화창한 날씨를 즐기실 수 있을 겁니다. 하지만 주말에는 많은 비가 예상되므로 실내에 머무르시는 게 좋겠습니다.

02 ④

[해설] 원형에 손잡이가 하나 있고 줄무늬가 없는 화병을 산다고 했다.

[어휘] vase[veis] 화병
rectangular[rektǽŋgulər] 직사각형의
handle[hǽndl] 손잡이
stripe[straip] 줄무늬

W Hello, may I help you?
M Yes. I'm looking for a vase for my living room.
W How about this rectangular-shaped one? It's very popular these days.
M Hmm... It looks so simple.
W Then, how about this round one with a handle?
M It's nice, but do you have the same one without stripes?
W Sure, here you are.
M Perfect. I'll take it.

여 안녕하세요, 도와드릴까요?
남 네. 거실에 둘 화병을 찾고 있어요.
여 이 직사각형 모양의 화병은 어떠세요? 요즘 무척 인기 있어요.
남 음… 너무 단순한 것 같아요.
여 그럼 손잡이가 하나 달린 이 원형 화병은 어떠세요?
남 좋네요, 하지만 줄무늬 없는 것으로 같은 모양의 화병이 있나요?
여 그럼요, 여기 있어요.
남 완벽하네요. 그걸로 살게요.

03 ②

[해설] 매일 밤 2주 동안 준비한 글로 상을 받은 남자가 여자에게 자신이 쓴 글에 대해 설명하는 내용으로 보아 남자가 자랑스러워하는 것을 알 수 있다.

[어휘] writing contest 글짓기 대회
Congratulations. 축하해.
expect[ikspékt] 예상하다, 기대하다
deserve[dizɔ́ːrv] ~을 받을 만하다
stay up late 늦게까지 깨어 있다
favorite[féivərit] 가장 좋아하는

M Wow, I just found out that I won the writing contest.
W Really? Congratulations!
M Thanks. I didn't expect to win at all.
W You deserve it. I know you worked very hard for it.
M Yes. I stayed up late every night for 2 weeks to prepare for the contest.
W What did you write about?
M I wrote about my favorite book. Do you want to read it?
W Sure.

남 와, 내가 글짓기 대회에서 우승했다는 걸 방금 알았어.
여 정말? 축하해!
남 고마워. 우승할 거라고 전혀 예상하지 못했어.
여 너는 받을 만해. 네가 정말 열심히 했다는 거 내가 알지.
남 그래. 그 대회를 준비하기 위해 매일 밤 2주 동안 늦게까지 깨어 있었으니까.
여 뭐에 대해 썼어?
남 내가 가장 좋아하는 책에 대해 썼어. 내 글을 읽어 볼래?
여 물론이지.

① 편안한 ② 자랑스러운 ③ 무서워하는
④ 따분해하는 ⑤ 긴장한

04 ④

해설 여자는 벼룩시장에 가서 언니가 산 물건이 든 쇼핑백을 들어줬다고 했다.

어휘 flea market 벼룩시장
look around 둘러보다

M Judy, what did you do last Saturday?
W I went to a flea market with my sister.
M That sounds interesting. Did you buy anything there?
W I wanted to buy a clock for my room, but I couldn't find anything good.
M Then, did you just look around?
W I did. But my sister bought so many things. I had to help her carry the shopping bags.
M Well, it sounds like your sister had a good weekend.

남 Judy, 지난 토요일에 뭘 했니?
여 우리 언니와 벼룩시장에 갔었어.
남 재미있었겠다. 거기에서 뭐 좀 샀어?
여 내 방에 둘 시계를 사고 싶었는데 괜찮은 걸 찾지 못했어.
남 그럼 그냥 구경만 했니?
여 응. 하지만 우리 언니는 이것저것 엄청 많이 샀어. 내가 쇼핑백 드는 걸 도와줘야 했어.
남 음. 너희 언니는 즐거운 주말을 보낸 것 같구나.

05 ②

해설 남자가 배낭을 두고 내려서 비행기에 다시 돌아가도 되는지 묻고 있고 여자는 항공편 번호와 좌석 번호를 확인하는 것으로 보아 두 사람은 공항에 있다는 것을 알 수 있다.

어휘 backpack[bǽkpæ̀k] 배낭
allow[əláu] 허락하다
enter[éntər] 들어가다
for a moment 잠시 동안
look for 찾다, 구하다
flight[flait] 항공편
seat[si:t] 좌석, 자리

W May I help you, sir?
M Yes. I left my backpack on the plane. Can I get back on the plane and get it?
W Sorry, but you're not allowed to enter the plane again.
M What should I do then?
W Wait here for a moment. We'll look for it.
M Thanks a lot.
W Can you tell me your flight number and the seat number?
M It's TA 724, and my seat was 15C.

여 도와드릴까요, 고객님?
남 네. 제가 비행기에 배낭을 두고 내렸어요. 비행기로 돌아가서 그것을 가져올 수 있나요?
여 죄송하지만, 비행기에 다시 들어가는 건 허용되지 않습니다.
남 그럼 어떻게 해야 하나요?
여 여기서 잠시만 기다려주세요. 저희가 찾아보겠습니다.
남 정말 감사합니다.
여 고객님의 항공편 번호와 좌석 번호를 말씀해주시겠어요?
남 TA 724편이고, 제 좌석은 15C였습니다.

06 ③

해설 집에 휴대전화를 두고 온 남자가 여자에게 여자의 휴대전화를 사용해도 되는지 요청하고 있다.

어휘 half an hour 30분
Do you mind if ~? ~해도 될까요?

W Dave, what are you doing here?
M I'm waiting for the bus. I'm going to meet Peter.
W What number is your bus?
M It's the number 2. But it hasn't come for half an hour. I'm going to be late.
W Shouldn't you call him?
M Yes, I should. [Pause] Oh no!
W What's wrong?
M I left my cell phone at home. Do you mind if I use yours?

여 Dave, 여기서 뭐 하고 있니?
남 버스를 기다리고 있어. Peter를 만나기로 했거든.
여 몇 번 버스를 타니?
남 2번 버스야. 그런데 30분째 오지 않고 있어. 늦을 것 같아.
여 걔한테 전화해야 하지 않을까?
남 응, 해야겠다. [잠시 후] 이런!
여 무슨 일 있니?
남 집에 휴대전화를 두고 왔어. 네 걸 좀 사용해도 될까?

07 ②

해설 새우 버거, 감자튀김, 콜라, 애플파이는 주문했지만 치킨은 주문하지 않았다.

어휘 order[ɔ́:rdər] 주문; 주문하다

M Welcome to Happy Snack. May I take your order?
W Yes, please. I'd like to have a shrimp burger and french fries.

남 Happy Snack에 오신 것을 환영합니다. 주문하시겠어요?
여 네. 새우 버거 하나와 감자튀김 주세요.

shrimp[ʃrimp] 새우
cheap[tʃi:p] 값이 싼

| | M | Anything to drink? | 남 | 음료는 어떤 걸로 하시겠어요? |

M Anything to drink?
W Oh, I want a small coke, please.
M Okay. If you order a burger, you can buy an apple pie for $1.
W $1? That's cheap.
M Yes, would you like one?
W Yes, I'll take one.
M For here or to go?
W For here, please.

남 음료는 어떤 걸로 하시겠어요?
여 아, 콜라 작은 것 하나 주세요.
남 알겠습니다. 버거를 하나 주문하면 1달러에 애플파이를 하나 살 수 있어요.
여 1달러요? 저렴하네요.
남 네, 하나 드시겠어요?
여 네, 하나 살게요.
남 여기서 드실 건가요, 가져가실 건가요?
여 여기서 먹을 거예요.

08 ⑤

해설 남자가 여자에게 이메일로 사진을 보내달라고 했고 여자가 바로 보내겠다고 했다.

어휘 take a picture 사진 찍다
go on a picnic 소풍 가다
broken[bróukən] 고장 난
receive[risí:v] 받다
fix[fiks] 고치다, 수리하다
leave[li:v] 맡기다

M Amy, did you take lots of pictures when we went on the picnic?
W Yes. Do you want me to send them to you?
M My smartphone is broken, so I can't receive them on it.
W Are you going to fix it or get a new one?
M I already left it at the repair shop. Can you send them by e-mail instead?
W Sure. I'll do that right now.

남 Amy, 우리 소풍 갔을 때 사진 많이 찍었니?
여 응. 너한테 사진 보내줄까?
남 내 스마트폰이 고장이 나서 사진을 받을 수가 없어.
여 스마트폰을 고치거나 새로 살 예정이니?
남 이미 수리점에 맡겼어. 대신 이메일로 사진을 보내줄래?
여 그래. 지금 당장 보내줄게.

09 ④

해설 여자는 건강을 유지하는 방법으로 균형 잡힌 식사, 수면 시간, 규칙적인 운동, 많이 걷는 것에 대해 언급했지만 물 마시기에 대해서는 언급하지 않았다.

어휘 Long time no see. 오랜만이야.
stay in shape 건강을 유지하다
balanced[bǽlənst] 균형 잡힌
diet[dáiət] 식단, 식이
regular[régjələr] 규칙적인
instead of ~ 대신에
public transportation 대중교통

M Hey, Angela.
W Hi, Steve. Long time no see.
M You look great! How do you stay in shape?
W Thanks. I keep a balanced diet and get 8 hours of sleep a day.
M Do you exercise as well?
W Yes. It's important to do regular exercise.
M And what else?
W I try to walk a lot instead of taking public transportation.
M I see. Maybe I should try those things, too.

남 안녕, Angela.
여 안녕, Steve. 오랜만이야.
남 너 멋져 보인다! 어떻게 그렇게 건강하게 유지하는 거야?
여 고마워. 나는 균형 잡힌 식단을 유지하고 하루에 8시간 자거든.
남 운동도 하니?
여 응. 규칙적인 운동을 하는 게 중요해.
남 또 다른 건?
여 대중교통을 이용하는 대신 많이 걸으려고 해.
남 그렇구나. 나도 그 방법대로 한번 해 봐야겠다.

10 ③

해설 남자는 학교 신문 동아리에서 하는 활동을 소개하고 있다.

어휘 get together 모이다
collect[kəlékt] 모으다, 수집하다
put A together (이것저것을 모아) 준비하다, 만들다

M Hello, everyone. Our newspaper club makes a school newspaper every month. The members get together every Wednesday. First, they collect ideas and stories. Then they write and make changes to their stories. Lastly, they put all the stories together and make it into a newspaper.

남 안녕하세요, 여러분. 저희 신문 동아리는 매달 학교 신문을 만듭니다. 회원들은 매주 수요일에 모입니다. 우선, 회원들은 아이디어와 이야기를 모읍니다. 그리고 나서 글을 쓰고 수정합니다. 마지막으로, 글을 모두 모아서 신문으로 만듭니다.

11 ⑤

해설 올해에는 푸드 트럭을 운영하지 않을 것이라고 했다.

어휘 festival[féstivəl] 축제
be held 열리다
participate[pɑːrtísəpèit] 참가하다
various[vériəs] 다양한
performance[pərfɔ́ːrməns] 공연
main[mein] 주된, 주요한
stage[steidʒ] 무대
food truck 푸드 트럭

W Hi, students. As you know, the 10th Cherry Middle School Festival is going to be held this Friday. More than 30 school clubs will participate. You can join various activities, like water balloon fights and face painting. There will be a dance performance on the main stage. We won't have any food trucks this year for many reasons.

여 안녕하세요, 학생 여러분. 아시다시피 제10회 Cherry 중학교 축제가 이번 주 금요일에 열릴 예정입니다. 30여 개의 학교 동아리가 참여할 것입니다. 여러분은 풍선 싸움과 얼굴 페인팅과 같은 다양한 활동에 참여할 수 있습니다. 주 무대에서는 댄스 공연이 있을 것입니다. 푸드 트럭은 여러 가지 이유로 올해에는 운영되지 않을 것입니다.

12 ①

해설 남자는 여자에게 연습 장소는 학교 강당이라고 알려주려고 전화했다.

어휘 be supposed to-v ~하기로 되어 있다
practice[præktis] 연습하다; 연습
play[plei] 연극
hall[hɔːl] 강당
completely[kəmplíːtli] 완전히
quickly[kwíkli] 빨리, 빠르게

[Cell phone rings.]
W Hello.
M Hi, Lisa. Where are you?
W I'm in the club room. We're supposed to get together and practice for the play.
M Oh, don't you remember? We'll practice in the school hall, not the club room today.
W *[Pause]* Oh, you're right. I completely forgot.
M Come here quickly. The practice is going to start soon.
W Okay. I'm leaving right now.

[휴대전화가 울린다.]
여 여보세요.
남 여보세요, Lisa. 너 어디에 있니?
여 동아리방에 있어. 모여서 연극 연습하기로 되어 있잖아.
남 아, 기억 안 나? 오늘은 동아리방이 아니라 학교 강당에서 연습할 거야.
여 *[잠시 후]* 아, 네 말이 맞네. 완전히 깜빡했어.
남 여기로 빨리 와. 연습이 곧 시작될 거야.
여 알겠어. 지금 당장 갈게.

13 ①

해설 6시와 8시에 예약이 가능하다는 남자의 말에 여자는 6시에 예약하겠다고 했다.

어휘 reserve[rizə́ːrv] 예약하다
book[buk] 예약하다

[Telephone rings.]
M King Steak House. How may I help you?
W I'd like to reserve a table for this evening.
M What time would you like?
W At 7:30.
M I'm sorry, but all the tables are booked for that time. But you can still book for 6 and 8 o'clock.
W Then I'll make it 6 o'clock for 8 people.
M Okay. Can I have your name, please?
W My name is Monica Potter.

[전화벨이 울린다.]
남 King Steak House입니다. 무엇을 도와드릴까요?
여 오늘 저녁에 자리를 예약하고 싶은데요.
남 몇 시를 원하시나요?
여 7시 30분이요.
남 죄송하지만, 그 시간에는 모든 좌석이 예약이 되어 있어요. 하지만 6시와 8시에는 예약이 가능합니다.
여 그럼 6시에 8명 예약할게요.
남 알겠습니다. 성함을 말씀해주시겠어요?
여 Monica Potter입니다.

14 ②

해설 남자가 대역 없이 모든 장면을 직접 연기한다고 했고 여자가 남자를 인터

W Hi, Michael. What is your favorite scene of the movie?

여 안녕하세요, Michael. 영화에서 당신이 가장 좋아하는 장면은 무엇인가요?

뷰하는 것으로 보아 두 사람의 관계는 배우와 리포터임을 알 수 있다.

어휘 scene[siːn] 장면
chase[tʃeis] 추격
perform[pərfɔ́ːrm] 연기하다
dangerous[déindʒərəs] 위험한
act out 실연해보이다
body double 대역 (배우)
amazing[əméiziŋ] 놀라운
fan[fæn] 팬
support[səpɔ́ːrt] 지지, 지원

M It's the car chase scene. I performed it myself.
W Wasn't it dangerous to film the scene?
M It was, but I try to act out every scene without a body double.
W You are amazing. Would you like to say anything to your fans?
M I really thank you all for your love and support. I hope you enjoy this movie.
W Michael, thank you for your time.

남 자동차 추격 장면이요. 제가 직접 연기했거든요.
여 그 장면을 촬영하는 데 위험하지 않았나요?
남 위험했지만, 저는 대역 없이 모든 장면을 직접 연기하려고 노력해요.
여 놀랍네요. 당신의 팬들에게 하고 싶은 말씀이라도 있나요?
남 여러분 모두의 사랑과 응원에 정말 감사드려요. 이 영화를 즐겁게 보셨으면 좋겠네요.
여 Michael, 시간 내주셔서 감사합니다.

15 ⑤

해설 여자는 남자에게 Central 도서관에 가는 길을 알려달라고 부탁했다.

어휘 second[sékənd] (아주) 잠깐
central[séntrəl] 중앙의
close[klous] 가까운
direction[dirékʃən] 방향
borrow[bárou] 빌리다
report[ripɔ́ːrt] 보고서

W Peter, do you have a second?
M Yes. Why?
W Do you know how to get to the Central Library?
M Sure. It's very close from here.
W I need to borrow some books. Could you give me directions?
M Actually, I have to go to the library for a science report. Let's go together.
W Oh, great. How about eating something before we go?
M Good idea.

여 Peter, 잠깐 시간 있어?
남 응. 왜?
여 Central 도서관에 어떻게 가는지 아니?
남 물론이지. 여기서 무척 가까워.
여 책을 몇 권 빌려야 하거든. 가는 길을 알려줄 수 있니?
남 실은, 나도 과학 보고서를 쓰기 위해서 도서관에 가야 해. 같이 가자.
여 잘됐다. 가기 전에 뭐 좀 먹는 게 어때?
남 좋은 생각이야.

16 ⑤

해설 남자가 기분이 좋지 않은 이유는 역사 보고서를 다시 써야 하기 때문이다.

어휘 upset[ʌpsét] 속상한, 마음이 상한
backpack[bǽkpæk] 배낭, 책가방
history[hístəri] 역사
lost and found center 분실물 보관소

W What's wrong?
M I'm very upset. I left my backpack on the bus.
W Oh no! Is there anything important in it?
M Yes. My history homework was in my bag.
W That's too bad. You worked hard on the homework, didn't you?
M Yes, but now I have to do it again.
W Did you call the bus company's lost and found center? Your bag might be there.
M I did, but it isn't there.

여 무슨 일 있어?
남 너무 속상해. 버스에 가방을 놓고 내렸어.
여 이런! 가방 안에 뭐 중요한 거라도 있니?
남 응. 가방 안에 내 역사 숙제가 있었어.
여 안 됐다. 너는 숙제를 열심히 준비했었잖아, 그렇지 않아?
남 그래, 하지만 이제 그걸 다시 써야 해.
여 그 버스 회사의 분실물 보관소에 전화해봤니? 네 가방이 거기에 있을지도 모르잖아.
남 해봤는데, 그곳에 없대.

17 ③

해설 어느 티셔츠를 사야 할지 묻고 답하는 대화가 적절하다.

어휘 try on ~을 입어 보다
fitting room 탈의실

① M Excuse me, can I try this shirt on?
   W Sure. The fitting room is over there.
② M May I take your order?
   W Yes, I'd like a cheeseburger set.

① 남 죄송하지만, 이 셔츠 입어 봐도 되나요?
   여 그럼요. 탈의실은 저쪽에 있어요.
② 남 주문하시겠어요?
   여 네, 치즈버거 세트 하나 주세요.

through[θru:] ~을 통해
telescope[téləskòup] 망원경
striped[straipt] 줄무늬의

③ M Which T-shirt should I get?
  W I think you look better in the shirt with the round neck.
④ M What are you doing now?
  W I'm looking at the stars through the telescope.
⑤ M Hello, may I help you?
  W Yes, I'm looking for a striped skirt.

③ 남 어떤 티셔츠를 사야 할까?
  여 너한테 라운드 넥 셔츠가 더 잘 어울리는 것 같아.
④ 남 지금 뭐 하고 있니?
  여 망원경으로 별을 보고 있어.
⑤ 남 안녕하세요, 도와드릴까요?
  여 네, 줄무늬 치마를 찾고 있는데요.

18 ⑤

해설 대회 일시(9월 15일), 주제(우정), 참가 자격(모든 학년), 제한 시간(5분 이내)에 대해 언급했으나 수상자 상품에 대해서는 언급하지 않았다.

어휘 speech contest 말하기 대회
topic[tápik] 주제
friendship[fréndʃip] 우정
grade[greid] 학년, 등급
announce[ənáuns] 발표하다, 알리다
take part in ~에 참가하다

W Hello, students. I'd like to tell you about the Student Speech Contest. This contest will be held on September 15th. The topic of this year's speech is "friendship." This contest is open to all grades. The speech should be less than 5 minutes long. Winners will be announced on October 5. We hope many students will take part in this.

여 안녕하세요, 학생 여러분. 학생 말하기 대회에 대해 말씀드리겠습니다. 이 대회는 9월 15일에 열릴 것입니다. 올해 말하기 주제는 '우정'입니다. 이 대회는 모든 학년의 학생들이 참가할 수 있습니다. 말하기는 5분 이내의 길이여야 합니다. 수상자는 10월 5일에 발표될 것입니다. 많은 학생들이 참가하길 기대합니다.

19 ③

해설 전에 영국에 가 본 적이 있는지 물었으므로 이어질 응답으로 영국 방문의 여부를 답하는 것이 적절하다.

어휘 make a list 목록을 만들다
trip[trip] 여행

W Chanho, what are you doing now?
M I'm making a list for my trip.
W Oh, I almost forgot. You are leaving for England next week.
M Right. I'll stay there for a week.
W That's great. Where in England are you planning to visit?
M I'm going to visit London first and then Oxford.
W You should take an umbrella. It rains a lot in England.
M Oh, really? Have you been there before?
W Yes, I went to England last year.

여 찬호야, 지금 뭐 하고 있니?
남 여행에 필요한 목록을 만들고 있어.
여 아, 거의 깜빡했다. 너 다음 주에 영국으로 떠나지.
남 맞아. 일주일 동안 거기에 머물 거야.
여 잘됐네. 영국에서 어디를 방문할 계획이니?
남 우선 런던에 간 뒤에 옥스퍼드에 방문할 거야.
여 너는 우산을 가져가야 해. 영국에는 비가 많이 오거든.
남 아, 정말? 전에 그곳에 가봤니?
여 응, 작년에 영국에 갔었어.

① 영국에 방문하고 싶어.
② 하루 종일 비가 오고 있어.
④ 나는 영어를 아주 잘하진 못해.
⑤ 응, 나는 어릴 때부터 이곳에 살았어.

20 ③

해설 백화점에 가는 데 버스로 걸리는 시간을 물었으므로 이어질 응답으로 소요 시간을 답하는 것이 적절하다.

어휘 department store 백화점

M Excuse me, but do you know where Smile Department Store is?
W Yes, I do. It's not far from here.
M Could you tell me how to get there?

남 실례지만, Smile 백화점이 어디에 있는지 아시나요?
여 네. 여기서 멀지 않아요.
남 거기에 어떻게 가는지 말해주시겠어요?

far[fɑːr] 먼, 멀리 떨어져 있는
across[əkrɔ́ːs] 건너서, 가로질러
[선택지]
every[évri] 매 ~, ~마다

W Just take the number 110 bus from the bus stop <u>across</u> <u>the</u> <u>street</u>.
M Okay, and then?
W That's it. The bus goes right to the department store.
M Great. <u>How</u> <u>long</u> <u>does</u> <u>it</u> <u>take</u>?
W <u>Just 10 minutes or so.</u>

여 길 건너 버스정류장에서 110번 버스를 타시면 돼요.
남 알겠습니다. 그다음은요?
여 그게 다예요. 그 버스가 백화점 바로 앞으로 가거든요.
남 잘됐네요. 얼마나 걸리나요?
여 <u>10분 정도 걸려요.</u>

① 20분마다 있어요.
② 틀림없이 찾을 수 있을 거예요.
④ 영화관 옆에 있어요.
⑤ 2층에서 찾을 수 있어요.

01 ④	02 ④	03 ④	04 ⑤	05 ②	06 ①	07 ④
08 ⑤	09 ⑤	10 ④	11 ③	12 ②	13 ③	14 ③
15 ④	16 ④	17 ④	18 ⑤	19 ①	20 ⑤	

01 ④

해설 서울은 화창하고 맑을 것이라고 했다.

어휘 update[ʌ̀pdéit] 최신 뉴스
take a look at ~을 살펴보다
because of ~ 때문에
stormy[stɔ́ːrmi] 폭풍우가 몰아치는
throughout[θruːáut] ~동안 쭉, 내내
forecast[fɔ́ːrkæ̀st] 예보[예측]하다

W Hello, I'm Sarah Jo for the world weather update. Let's take a look at the weather in Asia. Beijing will be cold because of strong winds, and New Delhi will have lots of rain. Stormy weather throughout the day is forecasted in Tokyo. However, it will be mostly sunny and clear in Seoul. Thank you.

여 안녕하세요. 최신 세계 날씨의 뉴스를 전해드릴 Sarah Jo입니다. 아시아 날씨를 살펴보겠습니다. 베이징은 강풍으로 인해 춥겠고 뉴델리는 많은 비가 오겠습니다. 도쿄는 하루 종일 폭풍우가 휘몰아치는 날씨가 예보됩니다. 하지만 서울은 대체로 화창하고 맑겠습니다. 감사합니다.

02 ④

해설 엽서 위에 흰 새 한 마리와 해를 그렸다고 했다.

어휘 postcard[póustkàrd] 그림엽서
welcome[wélkəm] 환영
symbol[símbəl] 상징
meaning[míːniŋ] 의미
long life 장수, 오래도록 삶

W Minho, what are you doing?
M I'm making a postcard for my French friend, Leo. He'll visit me next week.
W Oh, it's a welcome gift for him.
M That's right. I drew a white bird and the sun on it.
W Do those symbols have any special meaning?
M Yes, this picture means to live a long life.
W I think it's a perfect gift for him.

여 민호야, 뭐 하고 있니?
남 프랑스 친구인 Leo를 위해 그림엽서를 만들고 있어. 다음 주에 그가 방문할 거거든.
여 아, 그건 환영 선물이구나.
남 맞아. 엽서 위에 흰색 새와 해를 그렸어.
여 이 상징들이 특별한 의미라도 있니?
남 응. 이 그림은 장수하는 것을 의미해.
여 그에게 완벽한 선물이 되겠구나.

03 ④

해설 위치(Central 공원 안), 놀이 시설(워터슬라이드), 입장료(성인 10달러, 학생 7달러), 폐장 시각(6시)에 대해 언급했지만 교통편에 대해서는 언급하지 않았다.

어휘 swimming pool 수영장
mean[miːn] 의미하다
exciting[iksáitiŋ] 신나는
waterslide[wɔ́ːtərslàid] 워터 슬라이드, 물 미끄럼틀
main[mein] 가장 큰, 주된
adult[ədʌ́lt] 성인
under[ʌ́ndər] (나이 등이) ~ 미만의

W Peter, how about going to a swimming pool this Saturday?
M Good idea. Where?
W How about Oasis Pool?
M Oasis Pool? Do you mean the one in Central Park?
W Yes. There is an exciting waterslide in the main pool.
M Great. How much are tickets?
W It's $10 for adults and $7 for students under 16. But we have to show our student card.
M Okay. Let's stay there all day until it closes at 6.

여 Peter, 이번 주 토요일에 수영장에 가는 게 어때?
남 좋은 생각이야. 어디로?
여 Oasis 수영장은 어때?
남 Oasis 수영장? Central 공원 안에 있는 거 말하는 거니?
여 맞아. 가장 큰 풀장 안에는 신나는 워터슬라이드가 있어.
남 좋네. 티켓은 얼마니?
여 성인은 10달러이고 16세 미만의 학생은 7달러야. 하지만 우리는 학생증을 보여줘야 해.
남 알겠어. 6시에 끝날 때까지 거기에서 하루 종일 있자.

04 ⑤

해설 남자는 지난 주말에 할머니가 아프셔서 병간호했다고 했다.

어휘 go fishing 낚시하러 가다
get well 병이 나아지다

W Did you have a good time fishing last weekend?
M No, I couldn't go fishing at all.
W Why? Did something happen?
M Yes. When my dad and I were leaving, he got a call from my grandmother. She got really sick, so we had to take care of her.
W Oh, I'm sorry to hear that. I hope she gets well soon.
M Thank you.

여 지난 주말에 낚시하면서 즐거운 시간 보냈니?
남 아니, 낚시하러 가지도 못했어.
여 왜? 무슨 일 있었니?
남 응. 아빠와 내가 출발하려고 했을 때 할머니에게서 전화가 왔거든. 할머니가 많이 아프셔서 병간호해야 했어.
여 아, 그것참 안 됐구나. 할머니가 얼른 회복하셨으면 좋겠네.
남 고마워.

05 ②

해설 찾고 있는 책의 위치, 대출 기간 등을 묻고 답하고 있으므로 도서관에서 이루어지는 대화임을 알 수 있다.

어휘 magazine[mǽgəzíːn] 잡지
interior design 인테리어 디자인, 실내장식
section[sékʃən] 구역, 구획
check out (도서관에서) 대출받다
ID card 신분증
return[ritə́ːrn] 반납하다

M Excuse me. Can I ask you something?
W Of course. What is it?
M Where can I find magazines for interior design?
W They're in Section E on the second floor.
M Thanks. Can I also check out magazines?
W Yes, but you need an ID card.
M I see. How long can I borrow them for?
W You must return them in a week.
M I understand. Thanks a lot.

남 실례합니다. 뭐 좀 여쭤봐도 될까요?
여 그럼요. 뭔가요?
남 인테리어 디자인에 관한 잡지를 어디에서 찾을 수 있을까요?
여 2층 E구역에 있어요.
남 감사합니다. 잡지도 대출할 수 있나요?
여 네, 하지만 신분증이 있어야 해요.
남 알겠습니다. 대출 기간은 얼마나 되나요?
여 일주일 안에 반납하셔야 해요.
남 그렇군요. 정말 감사합니다.

06 ①

해설 여자는 남자가 잃어버렸던 가방을 찾아주자 감사해하고 있다.

어휘 subway[sʌ́bwèi] 지하철
describe[diskráib] 묘사하다
backpack[bǽkpæ̀k] 배낭
front[frʌnt] 앞쪽(의)
leather[léðər] 가죽
strap[stræp] 끈
name tag 이름표

M Hello, how may I help you?
W I left my bag in the subway last night.
M What does it look like? Can you describe it?
W It's a gray backpack with a front pocket. And it has 2 black leather straps.
M Does the bag have a name tag on it, too?
W Yes, it does.
M Is this your bag?
W Yes, that's mine! Thank you very much for your help.

남 안녕하세요, 무엇을 도와드릴까요?
여 어젯밤에 제 가방을 지하철에 두고 내렸어요.
남 어떻게 생겼나요? 모양을 설명해주시겠어요?
여 앞주머니가 달린 회색 배낭이에요. 그리고 두 개의 검정 가죽 끈이 달려 있어요.
남 가방에 이름표도 붙어있나요?
여 네, 맞아요.
남 이게 당신 가방인가요?
여 네, 제 가방이에요! 도와주셔서 정말 감사합니다.

07 ④

해설 남자는 저녁 뉴스 뒤에 방송하는 퀴즈쇼인 'I Love Quizzes'를 본다고 했다.

W Steve, how about going to a movie tonight?
M Well, I'm planning to watch TV at home this evening.

여 Steve, 오늘 밤에 영화 보러 가는 거 어때?
남 글쎄, 난 오늘 저녁에 집에서 TV를 볼 거야.

| 어휘 actually [ǽktʃuəli] 사실은 quiz [kwiz] 퀴즈 | W But you don't like watching TV.
M No, but I have to watch it tonight.
W Why? Are there any soccer games on?
M Actually, my uncle is going to be on *I Love Quizzes* after the evening news.
W Wow, I love quiz shows! Let's watch it together.
M Okay. | 여 근데 너 TV 보는 거 좋아하지 않잖아.
남 그래, 하지만 오늘 밤에는 TV를 봐야 해.
여 왜? 축구 경기라도 있니?
남 실은 삼촌이 저녁 뉴스 뒤에 하는 'I Love Quizzes'에 출연하시거든.
여 와, 나 퀴즈쇼 좋아하는데! 같이 보자.
남 좋아. |

08 ⑤

| 해설 여자가 도서관에 가기 전에 간식을 먹으러 가자고 했다.

어휘 tired [táiərd] 피곤한
get some rest 약간의 휴식을 취하다
skip [skip] (일을) 거르다[빼먹다]
snack [snæk] 간식 | M I'm so tired. It's been a long day.
W I just want to go home and get some rest.
M Me, too. But I have a science test tomorrow.
W Don't you also have tennis practice today?
M Yes, but I'm going to skip it today. I have to go to the library to study.
W Well, would you like to go and eat a snack with me first?
M Yeah. That sounds good. Let's go. | 남 정말 피곤하다. 긴 하루였어.
여 집에 가서 좀 쉬고 싶다.
남 나도. 하지만 난 내일 과학 시험이 있어.
여 오늘 테니스 연습도 있지 않니?
남 맞아, 하지만 오늘은 빠질 거야. 공부하러 도서관에 가야 하거든.
여 음. 먼저 나와 함께 간식이나 좀 먹으러 가는 게 어때?
남 그래. 좋은 것 같다. 가자. |

09 ⑤

| 해설 만드는 요리(프랑스 요리), 장소 (Hamilton 지하철역 근처의 자기 집), 일 정(수요일 저녁 7시), 강습료(1회에 30달 러)에 대해 언급했지만 재료에 대해서는 언급하지 않았다.

어휘 be interested in ~에 흥미[관심] 가 있다
dish [diʃ] 요리
weekday [wíkdei] 평일
cost [kɔːst] (비용이) ~이다[들다]
per [pəːr] ~마다
include [inklúːd] 포함하다 | [Telephone rings.]
W Hello, Chloe's Cooking Class. How may I help you?
M Hello. I'm interested in your cooking class.
W Great! You can learn to cook many different French dishes with me.
M Where is the class?
W The classes are at my house near Hamilton subway station.
M Oh, I see. What time is the class on weekdays?
W The Wednesday class starts at 7 p.m.
M How much does it cost?
W $30 per lesson. That includes everything. | [전화벨이 울린다.]
여 여보세요, Chloe's Cooking Class입니다. 무엇을 도와드릴까요?
남 안녕하세요. 요리 수업에 관심이 있어서요.
여 잘됐네요! 저와 함께 많고 다양한 프랑스 요리를 배우실 수 있어요.
남 수업은 어디에서 하나요?
여 Hamilton 지하철역 근처에 있는 저희 집에서 합니다.
남 아, 그렇군요. 주중에는 수업 시간이 어떻게 되나요?
여 수요일 수업이 저녁 7시에 시작해요.
남 수업료는 얼마인가요?
여 수업 한 번에 30달러예요. 그건 모든 걸 포함해요. |

10 ④

| 해설 여자는 면회 시간이 종료됨을 알리 며 방문객들이 병원에서 떠나기를 요청하 고 있다.

어휘 Attention. [əténʃən] (안내 방송에 서) 알립니다.
normal [nɔ́ːrməl] 보통의, 정상적인
visiting hours 면회 시간
begin [bigín] 시작하다
information desk 안내 데스크 | W Attention, all visitors to the hospital. It is now 8 p.m., and visiting hours are ending. We ask that all visitors now leave the building. Normal visiting hours will begin again tomorrow at 10 a.m. If you have any questions, please come to the information desk. Thank you. | 여 병원에 오신 모든 방문객에게 알립니다. 현재 저녁 8시이며, 면회 시간이 종료되었습니다. 모든 방문객께서는 이제 건물을 떠나주시기 바랍니다. 정상 방문 시간은 내일 오전 10시에 다시 시작됩니다. 문의 사항이 있으시면 안내데스크로 와주세요. 감사합니다. |

11 ③

해설 일주일에 두 번, 화요일과 금요일에 만난다고 했다.

어휘 introduce[intrədjúːs] 소개하다
member[mémbər] 회원
have a concert 연주회를 열다

M Hello, new students! I'm happy to introduce <u>my guitar club</u> to you. There are 20 members in the club. We meet twice a week, <u>Tuesday and Friday</u>. We have a concert <u>every December</u>. Our club room is <u>next to the music room</u>. Do you want to learn how to play the guitar? Then come and join us!

남 안녕하세요, 신입생 여러분! 여러분들에게 저희 기타 동아리를 소개하게 되어 기쁩니다. 저희 동아리에는 스무 명의 회원이 있습니다. 저희는 일주일에 두 번, 화요일과 금요일에 만납니다. 매년 12월에는 연주회를 엽니다. 저희 동아리방은 음악실 옆에 있습니다. 기타 연주하는 법을 배우고 싶으신가요? 그렇다면 저희 동아리에 가입하세요!

12 ②

해설 여자는 남자에게 바이올린 수업에 갈 수 없다고 말하기 위해 전화했다.

어휘 come over 오다, 들르다
lesson[lésən] 레슨, 수업

[Cell phone rings.]
M Hello.
W Hello, Mr. Harris. It's Alice.
M Alice? Don't you have a lesson today?
W I have to go out for dinner with my family tonight. So I don't think I can come over for <u>my violin lesson</u>.
M Oh, I see. I hope you have a great time with your family.
W Thank you, sir. I forgot to tell you last week. <u>I'm really sorry</u>.
M That's okay. Then can you come over for the lesson <u>tomorrow afternoon</u>?
W Sure.

[휴대전화가 울린다.]
남 여보세요.
여 안녕하세요, Harris 선생님. 저 Alice예요.
남 Alice니? 오늘 수업이 있지 않니?
여 저 오늘 밤에 가족들과 저녁 식사하러 가야 해요. 그래서 바이올린 레슨에 갈 수 없을 것 같아요.
남 아, 그렇구나. 가족들과 좋은 시간을 보내렴.
여 감사합니다, 선생님. 지난주에 말씀드리는 걸 깜빡했어요. 정말 죄송해요.
남 괜찮아. 그러면 내일 오후에는 레슨을 받으러 올 수 있니?
여 물론이죠.

13 ③

해설 6달러짜리 A 좌석 표 두 장을 산다고 했으므로 총 12달러를 지불할 것이다.

어휘 aquarium[əkwéəriəm] 수족관
dolphin[dɑ́lfin] 돌고래
available[əvéiləbl] 이용할 수 있는
total[tóutl] 합계, 총액

M Welcome to Hana Aquarium. May I help you?
W Yes, please. I'd like to <u>buy some tickets</u> for the dolphin show.
M Sure. We have S and A <u>seats available</u>.
W How much are they?
M The S seats are $10 and A seats are $6.
W I'd like 2 A seats, please.
M Okay. <u>Your total will be</u> $12.
W All right. <u>Here you are</u>.

남 Hana 수족관에 오신 것을 환영합니다. 도와드릴까요?
여 네. 돌고래쇼 티켓을 구매하려고 합니다.
남 네. S 좌석과 A 좌석이 이용 가능합니다.
여 얼마인가요?
남 S 좌석은 10달러이고, A 좌석은 6달러입니다.
여 A 좌석 두 장으로 주세요.
남 알겠습니다. 총금액은 12달러입니다.
여 알겠습니다. 여기 있습니다.

14 ③

해설 버스가 어느 방향으로 향하는지 묻는 여자의 말과 목적지 근처에 도착하면 알려주겠다는 남자의 말로 보아 두 사람의 관계는 버스 운전기사와 승객임을 알 수 있다.

W Excuse me, sir. This bus goes downtown, right?
M Yes, it does. Where exactly are you going?
W I <u>need to get</u> to Star World.
M Okay. I'll let you know when we <u>get near</u>

여 실례합니다. 이 버스가 시내로 가는 것 맞나요?
남 네, 맞아요. 정확히 어디로 가나요?
여 Star World에 가야 하거든요.
남 알겠습니다. 그곳 근처에 도착하면 알

어휘 downtown[dàuntáun] 시내에[로]
exactly[igzǽktli] 정확히
at this time of (the) day 하루 중 이 시간에
less[les] 보다 적은 수[양, 액]

there.
W Thank you. Will it take long to get there?
M It usually takes about 30 minutes, but at this time of the day it'll take less.
W That's good. Thank you so much.
M No problem.

려드릴게요.
여 감사합니다. 거기까지 가는 데 오래 걸릴까요?
남 보통은 30분쯤 걸리지만 지금 시간에는 덜 걸릴 거예요.
여 잘됐네요. 정말 감사합니다.
남 천만에요.

15 ④

해설 여자는 남자에게 재미있는 만화책이 있으면 가져오라고 부탁했다.

어휘 be in the hospital 입원해 있다
stairs[stɛərz] 계단
break A's leg 다리가 부러지다
comic book 만화책

W Did you hear that Brad is in the hospital?
M I didn't know that. What happened?
W He fell down the stairs and broke his leg.
M Really? That's too bad.
W So I'm going to see him after school.
M I'll go with you then. Should we bring him something?
W How about taking some comic books for him? If you have any interesting books, can you bring them?
M Okay. I will.

여 Brad가 입원했다는 얘기 들었어?
남 몰랐어. 무슨 일이 있었는데?
여 계단에서 넘어져서 다리가 부러졌대.
남 정말? 안 됐다.
여 그래서 방과 후에 그 애를 보러 가려고.
남 그럼 나도 너와 같이 갈게. 뭐 좀 가져다줘야 하지 않을까?
여 만화책을 몇 권 가져가는 게 어때? 재미있는 책이 있으면 좀 가져와 줄래?
남 알겠어. 가져올게.

16 ④

해설 남자가 대회 참가를 망설인 이유는 사람들 앞에서 노래하는 것이 무섭기 때문이라고 했다.

어휘 poster[póustər] 포스터, 벽보
enter[éntər] 참가하다
scary[skɛ́(:)əri] 무서운, 겁나는
audience[ɔ́:diəns] 관객, 청중
give it a try 한번 해보다

W What are you looking at?
M I'm looking at the poster for the singing contest.
W Are you going to enter it?
M I want to, but it's scary to sing in front of many people.
W Hmm... You said you wanted to be a singer, didn't you?
M Yes, that's right.
W Then, you should practice singing in front of an audience.
M You're right. I should give it a try.

여 뭘 보고 있니?
남 노래자랑 대회 포스터를 보고 있어.
여 대회에 참가하려고?
남 그러고 싶지만 많은 사람들 앞에서 노래하는 게 무서워.
여 음… 너 가수가 되고 싶다고 말했었지, 그렇지?
남 응, 맞아.
여 그럼, 관객 앞에서 노래하는 것을 연습해야 해.
남 네 말이 맞아. 한번 해보는 게 좋겠어.

17 ④

해설 지하철 안에서 음식을 먹을 수 없다고 말하는 대화가 적절하다.

어휘 grocery[gróusəri] 식료품점
subway[sʌ́bwèi] 지하철

① M What do you want for lunch?
   W I'd like a hamburger and a coke.
② M Which bus do I take to go downtown?
   W The number 35 bus will get you there.
③ M Emily, where are you going?
   W I'm going to the grocery store to buy some milk.
④ M Excuse me, but you can't eat on the subway.
   W Oh, I'm sorry. I didn't know that.

① 남 점심으로 뭘 먹을 거니?
   여 햄버거와 콜라를 먹을래.
② 남 시내로 가려면 어떤 버스를 타야 하나요?
   여 35번 버스가 시내로 갈 거예요.
③ 남 Emily, 어디에 가고 있니?
   여 우유를 사러 식료품점에 가고 있어.
④ 남 실례지만 지하철에서 음식을 드시면 안 됩니다.
   여 아, 죄송해요. 몰랐어요.

⑤ M Mom, I feel a little hungry.
　　W Would you like some apple pie?

⑤ 남 엄마, 배가 조금 고파요.
　　여 애플파이를 좀 먹을래?

18 ⑤

해설 서식지(아프리카), 수명(40~50년), 몸길이(5미터), 몸무게(4,500kg)에 대해 언급했지만 먹이에 대해서는 언급하지 않았다.

어휘 hippo[hípou] 하마
up to ~까지
weight[weit] 무게
cool A down A를 시원하게 하다

M Hello, everyone. I'm here to tell you about hippos. Hippos are large animals that live in Africa. They can live for 40 to 50 years. Hippos can grow to be up to 5 meters long. Their weight can be up to 4,500 kilograms. They love to stay in the water to cool themselves down.

남 안녕하세요, 여러분. 저는 하마에 대해 말씀드리려고 합니다. 하마는 아프리카 지역에 사는 덩치가 큰 동물입니다. 하마는 40년에서 50년까지 살 수 있습니다. 하마는 5미터까지 자랄 수 있습니다. 몸무게는 4,500킬로그램까지 나갈 수 있습니다. 하마는 열을 식히기 위해서 물속에서 지내는 것을 무척 좋아합니다.

19 ①

해설 달리기를 해서 살을 뺀 남자에게 식이요법도 하는지 물었으므로 이어질 응답으로 식이요법의 여부를 답하는 것이 적절하다.

어휘 almost[ɔ́ːlmoust] 거의
since[sins] ~이후로
lose weight 살을 빼다
on a diet 식이요법을 하다
[선택지]
usual[júːʒuəl] 평소의, 보통의
do yoga 요가를 하다

W Hey, Steve. Long time no see.
M Yes. It's been almost a month since we last met.
W You've lost a lot of weight!
M Yes, that's right. I'm exercising a lot these days.
W Oh, really? What kind of exercise are you doing?
M Just running. I usually run 10 kilometers every day.
W Good for you. Are you on a diet, too?
M No. I just eat as usual.

여 안녕, Steve. 오랜만이야.
남 그래. 마지막으로 만난 지 거의 한 달이 되었어.
여 너 살이 정말 많이 빠졌구나!
남 그래, 맞아. 요즘 운동을 많이 하고 있거든.
여 아, 정말? 어떤 종류의 운동을 하고 있니?
남 그냥 달리기. 보통 매일 10km를 달려.
여 잘됐네. 식이요법도 하니?
남 아니. 그냥 평소처럼 먹어.

② 알겠어. 아침을 먹을게.
③ 아니, 괜찮아. 배불러.
④ 응. 매일 아침 요가를 해.
⑤ 채소를 먹는 것은 너에게 좋아.

20 ⑤

해설 방학을 어떻게 보냈는지 물었으므로 이어질 응답으로 방학에 한 활동을 말하는 것이 적절하다.

어휘 during[djúəriŋ] ~ 동안
spend+시간+v-ing ~하는 데 시간을 보내다
spin[spin] 회전하다
in the air 공중에서

M Did you have a good time during winter vacation?
W Yes. I spent most of my vacation learning figure skating.
M Oh, really? Can you jump on the ice?
W Sure. I can even spin in the air.
M That's great! You have learned a lot in such a short time.
W Thanks. How did you spend your vacation?
M I read interesting books about space.

남 겨울 방학 동안 즐거운 시간 보냈니?
여 응. 방학 대부분을 피겨스케이팅을 배우면서 보냈어.
남 아, 정말? 얼음 위에서 점프를 할 수 있니?
여 물론이지. 심지어 공중에서 회전도 할 수 있는걸.
남 대단하다! 그렇게 짧은 시간 동안 많은 걸 배웠구나.
여 고마워. 너는 방학을 어떻게 보냈니?
남 우주에 관한 흥미로운 책들을 읽었어.

① 그건 너무 위험한 것 같아.
② 하와이를 방문할 계획이야.
③ 겨울에는 스노보드 타기를 즐겨.
④ 나도 피겨스케이팅 배우고 싶다.

01 ⑤	02 ④	03 ③	04 ⑤	05 ③	06 ②	07 ④
08 ④	09 ③	10 ⑤	11 ③	12 ④	13 ③	14 ②
15 ⑤	16 ①	17 ⑤	18 ④	19 ②	20 ②	

---

01 ⑤

해설 부산과 광주는 바람이 심하게 불고 있다고 했다.

어휘 influence[ínfluəns] 영향
typhoon[taifúːn] 태풍
blow[blou] (바람이) 불다
hard[hɑːrd] 심하게

M This is a special weather report. Because of the influence of the typhoon, it is raining heavily with strong winds in Jeju-do. In Busan and Gwangju, it is not raining, but the wind is blowing hard. In Seoul and Gyeonggi, it's partly cloudy with a chance of showers in the afternoon, so don't leave home without your umbrella.

남 기상 특보입니다. 태풍의 영향으로 제주도에는 강한 바람과 함께 많은 비가 내리고 있습니다. 부산과 광주는 비가 오고 있지는 않지만 바람이 강하게 불고 있습니다. 서울과 경기는 부분적으로 흐리고 오후에 소나기가 올 가능성이 있으니 우산 없이 외출하지 마시기 바랍니다.

---

02 ④

해설 주머니에 Angie를 쓰고 주변에 작은 해바라기들을 그렸다고 했다.

어휘 canvas[kǽnvəs] 캔버스
pocket[pάkit] 주머니
be short for ~의 줄임말이다
sunflower[sʌ́nflauər] 해바라기

M Angela, did you make this canvas bag yourself?
W Yes, I did it in art class. What do you think?
M I really like the pocket with your name on it. Angie is short for Angela, right?
W That's right. The pocket was not big enough for "Angela."
M I see. You also added small sunflowers around the pocket. Do you like sunflowers?
W Yes, they are my favorite flower.

남 Angela, 이 캔버스 가방 네가 직접 만들었니?
여 응, 미술 시간에 만들었어. 어떤 것 같아?
남 네 이름이 쓰여 있는 주머니가 정말 마음에 들어. Angie가 Angela를 줄인 말 맞지?
여 맞아. 주머니가 'Angela'를 쓸 만큼 충분히 크지 않았거든.
남 그렇구나. 주머니 주변에 작은 해바라기들도 그려 넣었구나. 너 해바라기 좋아하니?
여 응, 내가 제일 좋아하는 꽃이야.

---

03 ③

해설 날짜(6월 5일), 장소(Daehan 아트 센터), 입장료(15달러), 강연자(Kim Menders)에 대해 언급하였지만 참가 대상에 대해서는 언급하지 않았다.

어휘 famous[féiməs] 유명한
movie director 영화감독
give a lecture 강연하다

M Did you hear the news about a movie festival in our town?
W You mean the Fantasy Film Festival, right?
M Yes, it'll start on June 5th. Do you want to go together?
W Sure. Do you know where it is?
M It'll be at the Daehan Art Center.
W Okay. How much is a ticket?
M It's $15.
W That's great. Are there any famous people coming to the festival?
M The movie director Kim Menders is coming to give a lecture.

남 우리 시에서 하는 영화 축제에 대한 소식 들었니?
여 Fantasy 영화 축제 말하는 거지, 그렇지?
남 응. 6월 5일에 시작할 거래. 같이 갈래?
여 그래. 어디에서 하는지 아니?
남 Daehan 아트센터에서 열릴 거야.
여 알겠어. 티켓은 얼마니?
남 15달러야.
여 잘됐어. 축제에 유명한 사람들이라도 오니?
남 영화감독 Kim Menders가 강연을 하러 올 거야.

04 ⑤

해설 여자는 지구의 날에 버스 대신에 자전거로 등교했다고 했다.

어휘 celebrate[séləbrèit] 기념하다, 축하하다
turn off (불을) 끄다
forget[fərgét] 잊다
(forget-forgot-forgotten)
instead of ~ 대신에
plant[plænt] 심다

W   Did you celebrate Earth Day?
M   Yes, I turned off the lights at 8 p.m. Did you do it?
W   Actually, I forgot about the time, so I didn't do that.
M   Then what did you do?
W   I rode my bike to school instead of taking the bus. And I'm planning to plant a tree this weekend.
M   Good job!

여   너 지구의 날을 기념했니?
남   응, 저녁 8시에 전등을 껐어. 너도 그렇게 했니?
여   사실, 시간을 깜빡해서 그건 하지 못했어.
남   그럼 뭘 했니?
여   버스를 타는 대신에 학교에 자전거를 타고 갔어. 그리고 이번 주말에 나무를 심을 계획이야.
남   잘했네!

05 ③

해설 무엇을 주문할지를 서로 묻고 나서, 주문 후에 음식을 가져오겠다는 여자의 말로 보아 두 사람은 음식점에 있다는 것을 알 수 있다.

어휘 expect[ikspékt] 기대하다
touching[tʌtʃiŋ] 감동적인
anyway[éniwèi] 그건 그렇고

M   Let's sit here. What did you think of the play?
W   Well, it was better than I expected. The story was very touching.
M   I feel the same way. I almost cried when those children cried for their mom.
W   Me, too. Anyway, have you decided what to order?
M   Yes. I'll have a cheeseburger set. What about you?
W   I'll get the same. Wait here. I'll order and bring the food.

남   여기 앉자. 연극은 어땠어?
여   내가 기대했던 것보다 더 좋았어. 이야기가 정말 감동적이었거든.
남   나도 같은 생각이야. 아이들이 엄마를 찾으면서 울었을 때 나도 울 뻔했어.
여   나도. 그건 그렇고, 뭘 주문할지 결정했니?
남   응. 치즈버거 세트를 먹을 거야. 너는?
여   나도 같은 거 먹어야겠다. 여기서 기다려. 내가 주문해서 음식을 가져올게.

06 ②

해설 여자는 자신이 스피커를 고장 냈다고 말하며 자신의 잘못이라고 말하며 사과하고 있다.

어휘 happen[hǽpən] 발생하다, 일어나다
spill[spil] 쏟다
get hurt 다치다
fault[fɔːlt] 잘못, 책임

M   Judy, can you come here for a minute?
W   Yeah, I'm coming. What is it, Dad?
M   Do you know what happened to this speaker? It doesn't work.
W   I'm sorry, Dad. I broke it.
M   What? How did that happen?
W   I spilled some hot water on it while I was cooking ramyeon.
M   You didn't get hurt, did you?
W   I'm okay, but it's my fault.

남   Judy, 잠깐 여기로 와볼래?
여   네, 가요. 무슨 일이에요, 아빠?
남   이 스피커에 무슨 일이 있었는지 아니? 작동을 안 하는구나.
여   죄송해요, 아빠. 제가 고장 냈어요.
남   뭐라고? 어떻게 된 일이니?
여   라면을 끓이다가 뜨거운 물을 거기에 쏟았어요.
남   다치지는 않았지, 그렇지?
여   전 괜찮지만, 제 잘못이에요.

07 ④

해설 담요, 손전등, 망원경, 수건을 가져가기로 했으나 침낭은 가져가지 않아도 된다고 했다.

어휘 excited[iksáitid] 흥분된
pack[pæk] (짐을) 챙기다
blanket[blǽŋkit] 담요

W   I'm so excited to go to the camp tomorrow.
M   Me, too. The weather forecast says we'll have clear skies tomorrow.
W   But it may get cold at night, so I packed a blanket.
M   That's great. What about a flashlight?
W   I got that, too. Oh, I don't have a telescope at

여   내일 캠프에 가게 되어 너무 설레어.
남   나도. 일기예보에 따르면 내일 맑은 하늘일 거래.
여   하지만 밤에는 추워질지도 몰라서 담요를 챙겼어.
남   잘했어. 손전등은 챙겼어?
여   그것도 챙겼지. 아, 나 집에 망원경이

flashlight[flǽʃlàit] 손전등
telescope[téləskòup] 망원경
sleeping bag 침낭
cabin[kǽbin] 오두막집
nearby[nìərbài] 근처에, 가까이에

home. Can you bring one?

M Sure. Do we also need <u>a sleeping bag</u>?

W No, we are going to stay at a cabin nearby. But we still <u>need to bring</u> our own towels.

없어. 하나 가져와줄래?

남 그래. 우리가 침낭도 필요할까?

여 아니. 우리는 근처에 있는 오두막집에서 머물 거야. 하지만 수건은 직접 가져가야 해.

08 ④

해설 자전거를 빌리려면 신분증이 필요할 수 있다는 여자의 말에 남자가 당장 가져오겠다고 했다.

어휘 rental shop 대여쇼
borrow[bárou] 빌리다

M Jamie, are you busy?

W No, Dad. What's up?

M Do you want to do something together then?

W Sure. *[Pause]* We could go out for <u>a bike ride</u>.

M But we have only one bike at home.

W There is a bike rental shop near the subway station. We <u>could borrow one</u> from there.

M Great! Do I need to <u>bring anything</u>?

W You might need your ID to borrow a bike.

M Okay. <u>I'll get it</u> right now.

남 Jamie, 너 바쁘니?

여 아니요, 아빠. 무슨 일이에요?

남 그럼 같이 뭔가 할래?

여 물론이죠. *[잠시 후]* 자전거 타러 나가도 돼요.

남 하지만 집에 자전거가 하나 밖에 없잖니.

여 지하철 역 근처에 자전거 대여소가 있어요. 거기에서 하나 빌릴 수 있을 거예요.

남 잘됐다! 뭐라도 가져가야 할까?

여 자전거를 대여하려면 신분증이 필요할지도 몰라요.

남 알겠다. 지금 당장 가져올게.

09 ③

해설 위치(제주도), 객실 수(4개), 숙박 요금(1박 5만원), 인터넷 요금(무료)에 대해 언급하였으나 조식 시간에 대해서는 언급하지 않았다.

어휘 quiet[kwáiət] 조용한
expensive[ikspénsiv] 비싼
for free 무료로

W Where did you stay in Jeju-do last summer?

M At Happy Guesthouse. <u>Are you planning</u> to go there?

W Yes, I am. What was the room like?

M It was nice and quiet. It's a small guesthouse <u>with only</u> 4 rooms.

W <u>How much is</u> it per night?

M It's only $50.

W That's not expensive.

M Yes. You can also use the Internet <u>for free</u>.

W Oh, that sounds great.

여 너 지난 여름에 제주도에서 어디에서 지냈지?

남 Happy 게스트하우스에서 지냈어. 그곳에 갈 계획이니?

여 응. 방은 어땠어?

남 좋았고 조용했어. 방이 4개뿐인 작은 게스트하우스거든.

여 하룻밤에 얼마니?

남 겨우 50달러야.

여 비싸지 않네.

남 맞아. 무료로 인터넷도 이용할 수 있어.

여 아, 그거 좋다.

10 ⑤

해설 소방관인 남자가 지진 발생 시 무엇을 해야 하는지 설명하고 있다.

어휘 firefighter[fáiəfàitər] 소방관
fire station 소방서
in case of ~의 경우
earthquake[ə́ːrθkwèik] 지진
stay away from ~에서 떨어져 있다
get under 밑에 들어가다[숨다]
stay calm 침착함을 유지하다

M Hello, students. This is Chris, a firefighter from Daelim Fire Station. Today, I came here to talk about <u>what to do</u> in case of an earthquake. If you're in the classroom, <u>stay away from</u> the windows and get under a desk. And you <u>should never use</u> the elevators. You <u>must stay calm</u> and do what your teacher says.

남 안녕하세요, 학생 여러분. 저는 Daelim 소방서의 소방관인 Chris입니다. 오늘은 지진 발생 시 행동 요령에 대해 알려드리려고 왔습니다. 만약 여러분이 교실에 있다면 창문에서 멀리 떨어져서 책상 밑으로 들어가세요. 그리고 절대로 엘리베이터를 이용하면 안 됩니다. 침착함을 유지하고 선생님의 지시대로 해야 합니다.

11 ③

해설 15세 이상인 학생들만 참여할 수 있다고 했다.

어휘 entry fee 참가비
sign up ~을 등록하다

W Hi, everyone! How about joining a science camp this vacation? With this program, you can enjoy and study science in an easy and fun way. This camp will be held at Hanguk University for 5 days. However, it is only open to students over 15. There is no entry fee. Only 20 students can join this camp, so sign up soon!

여 안녕하세요, 여러분! 이번 방학에 과학 캠프에 참여하는 게 어떠세요? 이 프로그램을 통해 여러분은 쉽고 재미있는 방법으로 과학을 즐기고 공부할 수 있어요. 이 캠프는 한국 대학교에서 5일 간 열릴 예정입니다. 하지만 15세 이상인 학생들만 참여할 수 있습니다. 참가비는 무료입니다. 단 20명의 학생만이 이 캠프에 참가할 수 있으니 얼른 등록하세요!

12 ④

해설 여자는 한 시간 전에 주문한 피자가 도착하지 않아서 배달을 취소하기 위해 전화를 하였다.

어휘 address[ədrés] 주소
cancel[kǽnsəl] 취소하다

[Telephone rings.]
M Hello, Joe's Pizza. How may I help you?
W I ordered a pizza an hour ago, but it hasn't come yet.
M Oh, really? What's your address?
W 210 Fine Street.
M We're really sorry. We'll check your order right away.
W Actually, I'd like to cancel my order. I don't have enough time to wait.
M Oh, okay. I'll do that right now. Once again, we're very sorry.

[전화벨이 울린다.]
남 여보세요, Joe's Pizza입니다. 어떻게 도와드릴까요?
여 한 시간 전에 피자를 주문했는데 배달이 아직 안 왔어요.
남 아, 정말요? 주소가 어떻게 되시죠?
여 Fine 가 210번지예요.
남 정말 죄송합니다. 주문을 바로 확인하겠습니다.
여 실은, 제 주문을 취소하고 싶어요. 기다릴 시간이 없거든요.
남 아, 알겠습니다. 지금 당장 그렇게 해드릴게요. 다시 한 번 정말 죄송합니다.

13 ③

해설 성인 한 장과 13세 미만 어린이 두 장을 구입했으므로 총 16달러를 지불할 것이다.

어휘 entrance fee 입장료
museum[mjuːzíːəm] 박물관
get a discount 할인을 받다
total[tóutl] 총액, 총금액
adult[ədʌ́lt] 성인

W Hello, may I help you?
M Yes. How much is the entrance fee to the museum?
W It is $8.
M Okay. My children are 11 and 12. Do they get a discount?
W Yes, they do. For children under 13, the entrance fee is $4.
M Great. What is the total for an adult and 2 children?
W It'll be $16.
M Here you are.
W Thank you. Enjoy the museum.

여 안녕하세요, 도와드릴까요?
남 네. 박물관 입장료가 얼마인가요?
여 8달러입니다.
남 알겠습니다. 제 아이들은 11살 그리고 12살인데요. 할인을 받을 수 있나요?
여 네, 받을 수 있습니다. 13세 미만 어린이는 입장료가 4달러입니다.
남 잘됐네요. 성인 한 명과 어린이 두 명 모두 다 해서 얼마인가요?
여 16달러입니다.
남 여기 있습니다.
여 감사합니다. 즐거운 관람되세요.

14 ②

해설 여자가 안전벨트 표시등이 켜져 있으니 안전벨트를 매라고 말하고, 남자가 물을 가져다 달라고 요청하는 것으로 보아 두 사람의 관계는 승무원과 승객임을

W Please put your seatbelt back on. The seatbelt sign is on again.
M Oh, I'm sorry. I wanted to stretch my legs for a bit.

여 안전벨트를 다시 매 주세요. 안전벨트 표시등이 다시 켜졌습니다.
남 아, 죄송합니다. 다리를 좀 펴고 싶었거든요.

알 수 있다.

어휘 put on ~을 매다
seat belt 안전벨트
stretch[stretʃ] 펴다, 당기다
magazine[mæ̀gəzíːn] 잡지
helpful[hélpfəl] 도움이 되는

W	It's all right, sir. Is this your first time visiting New York?	여 괜찮습니다, 선생님. 이번이 뉴욕 첫 방문이신가요?
M	Yes, it is. I'm very excited about my trip.	남 네, 맞아요. 여행을 가니 무척 신이 나네요.
W	There are some travel magazines in the seat pocket. They are quite helpful.	여 좌석 앞주머니에 몇 가지 여행 잡지가 있습니다. 도움이 많이 될 거예요.
M	Great. Thanks. Could I get some water, please?	남 잘됐네요. 고맙습니다. 물을 좀 가져다주실 수 있나요?
W	Sure. Please wait a moment.	여 물론이죠. 잠시만 기다려주세요.
M	Thank you.	남 감사합니다.

15 ⑤

해설 남자는 여자에게 자외선 차단제를 사다 달라고 부탁했다.

어휘 department store 백화점
sunblock[sʌ́nblak] 자외선 차단제
special[spéʃəl] 특정한, 특유의
brand[brænd] 브랜드, 상표
as long as ~하는 한, ~하기만 하면
sticky[stíki] 끈적이는

M	Mom, when are you going to go to the department store?	남 엄마, 언제 백화점에 가실 건가요?
W	I'll go there after lunch. Why?	여 점심을 먹고 나서 갈 거야. 왜 그러니?
M	I need to buy something from there. Can you get it for me?	남 거기에서 뭐 좀 살 게 있어서요. 그걸 사다 주실래요?
W	What is it?	여 어떤 건데?
M	I need to wear sunblock when I practice tennis. Can you buy me some?	남 테니스 연습할 때 자외선차단제를 발라야 하거든요. 좀 사다주실래요?
W	No problem. Is there any special brand you want?	여 그래. 원하는 특정 브랜드라도 있니?
M	No. It doesn't matter to me.	남 아니요. 브랜드는 저한테 중요하지 않아요.
W	All right. I'll get one for you.	여 알겠다. 하나 사다줄게.

16 ①

해설 여자는 약을 찾기 위해 병원을 방문했다.

어휘 expect[ikspékt] 기대하다, 예상하다
volunteer[vàləntíər] 자원 봉사하다
pick up (어디에서) ~을 찾대[찾아오다]
medicine[médisn] 약

M	Emily, long time no see!	남 Emily, 오랜만이다!
W	Hi, Brian. I didn't expect to see you here.	여 안녕, Brian. 여기서 널 볼 줄 몰랐네.
M	I'm here to see my grandfather. Are you still volunteering at this hospital?	남 나는 할아버지를 뵈러 왔어. 너 이 병원에서 아직도 자원 봉사하니?
W	No, I'm here to pick up some medicine.	여 아니, 나는 약을 좀 찾으러 왔어.
M	Oh, I see. Do you have time for a coffee?	남 아, 그렇구나. 너 혹시 커피 마실 시간 있니?
W	Sorry, I don't. My mom is waiting outside for me.	여 미안하지만, 시간이 없어. 엄마가 밖에서 기다리고 계시거든.
M	Then let's meet some other time.	남 그럼 다음에 만나자.
W	Sure. See you.	여 그래. 또 보자.

17 ⑤

해설 여자가 남자에게 콘서트에 가자고 물어보는 대화가 적절하다.

어휘 usually[júːʒuəli] 보통, 대개
free time 자유 시간
season[síːzn] (운동 경기 등의) 시즌

① W	What did you do last weekend?	① 여 지난 주말에 뭘 했니?
M	I visited my grandma in Busan.	남 부산에 계신 할머니를 방문했어.
② W	What do you usually do in your free time?	② 여 너는 자유 시간에 주로 뭘 하니?
M	I enjoy reading comic books.	남 나는 만화책 읽는 걸 즐겨.
③ W	Have you ever heard this song?	③ 여 이 노래 들어본 적 있니?
M	Sure. It's one of my favorite songs.	남 물론이지. 이건 내가 가장 좋아하는 노래 중 하나야.
④ W	When does the baseball season start?	④ 여 야구 시즌이 언제 시작하지?
M	It starts on May 12.	남 5월 12일에 시작해.
⑤ W	Can you go to MK's concert this Friday with me?	⑤ 여 이번 주 금요일에 하는 MK의 콘서트에 나와 함께 갈래?
M	Sure. I'll go with you.	남 좋아. 같이 가자.

18 ④

해설 서식지(호주 남동부), 크기(60~85cm), 먹이(유칼립투스 잎사귀), 수면 시간(하루에 20시간)에 대해서는 언급하였으나 수명에 대해서는 언급하지 않았다.

어휘 animal lover 동물 애호가
southeastern[sàuθí:stərn]
남동부의
weigh[wei] 무게가 ~나가다[이다]
eucalyptus[jù:kəlíptəs] 유칼립투스
(오스트레일리아산 나무)

W Hello, animal lovers. I'm happy to tell you about a cute animal, the koala. They live in the southeastern part of Australia. The koala is about 60 to 85 centimeters long and weighs about 14 kilograms. They only eat the leaves from a special tree called eucalyptus. They usually sleep for 20 hours a day.

여 안녕하세요, 동물 애호가 여러분. 귀여운 동물인 코알라에 대해 말씀드리게 되어 기쁘네요. 코알라는 호주의 남동부 지역에 삽니다. 코알라는 대략 60에서 85센티미터 정도의 길이이며, 몸무게는 약 14킬로그램 나갑니다. 코알라는 유칼립투스라고 불리는 특별한 나무의 잎사귀만을 먹습니다. 그들은 보통 하루에 20시간 잠을 잡니다.

19 ②

해설 여자가 미술 프로젝트를 도와주겠다고 했으므로 남자의 약속 제안에 수락하는 응답이 이어져야 한다.

어휘 be good at ~을 잘하다
subject[sʌ́bdʒikt] 과목

W Peter, you look worried. What's wrong?
M I don't know how to start my art project. It's too difficult.
W Oh, I see.
M You are very good at drawing, aren't you?
W Well, art is my favorite subject.
M I was wondering if you could help me with my art project.
W I'd be happy to help you.
M Thanks a lot. Then could we meet at the bus stop after school?
W Sure. Let's meet at 5 o'clock.

여 Peter, 걱정돼 보인다. 무슨 일이니?
남 미술 프로젝트를 어떻게 시작해야 할지 모르겠어. 너무 어려워.
여 아, 그렇구나.
남 너 그림 엄청 잘 그리지 않니?
여 음, 미술은 내가 좋아하는 과목이긴 해.
남 내가 하는 미술 프로젝트를 도와 줄 수 있나 해서.
여 기꺼이 도와줄게.
남 정말 고마워. 그럼 방과 후에 버스 정류장에 만날 수 있을까?
여 그래. 5시에 만나자.

① 미안하지만 도와줄 수 없어.
③ 아니, 나는 수학을 잘 못해.
④ 나는 보통 방과 후에 배드민턴을 쳐.
⑤ 알겠어. 도서관에서 만나는 게 어때?

20 ②

해설 아빠가 회색을 더 좋아하실 것 같다는 남자의 말에 회색 목도리를 사자는 응답이 적절하다.

어휘 scarf[skɑːrf] 목도리
present[prézənt] 선물
design[dizáin] 디자인
prefer[prifɔ́ːr] ~을 좋아하다

W Mason, what should we buy for Dad's birthday?
M I'm thinking about buying a scarf. [Pause] How about this one?
W Well, I'm not sure if he needs one.
M It's going to be a cold winter this year. A scarf will be a good present for him.
W Okay. Hmm... I like the design. What do you think?
M I like it, too.
W But there are two colors.
M I like them both, but I think Dad would prefer gray.
W Let's buy the gray one.

여 Mason, 아빠 생신 선물로 뭘 사야 할까?
남 목도리를 살까 생각 중이야. [잠시 후] 이건 어때?
여 음, 아빠가 그게 필요하실지 모르겠어.
남 이번 겨울은 추울 거야. 목도리는 아빠에게 좋은 선물이 될 거야.
여 알겠어. 음… 이 디자인이 마음에 드는데. 네 생각은 어때?
남 나도 마음에 들어.
여 그런데 색상이 두 가지네.
남 난 둘 다 마음에 들긴 하지만, 아빠가 회색을 더 좋아하실 것 같아.
여 회색 목도리를 사자.

① 나는 그렇게 생각하지 않아.
③ 너는 목도리를 하는 게 좋겠다.
④ 분홍색은 내가 가장 좋아하는 색이야.
⑤ 선물 사기엔 돈이 충분하지 않아.

01 ⑤	02 ③	03 ③	04 ③	05 ③	06 ④	07 ②
08 ④	09 ⑤	10 ④	11 ⑤	12 ⑤	13 ④	14 ③
15 ③	16 ④	17 ④	18 ②	19 ④	20 ④	

01 ⑤

해설 일요일 오전에는 흐리고 오후에는 맑을 것으로 예보하고 있다.

어휘 temperature[témpərətʃər] 기온, 온도
remain[riméin] 계속 ~이다
across the country 전국적으로
clear[kliər] (날씨가) 맑은

M Here is the weather report for the weekend. It will be very hot and sunny without any rain on Saturday. The temperatures will remain high across the country. On Sunday, it will be cloudy in the morning. However, in the afternoon we'll have clear skies. And the temperature will be as high as Saturday's. Thank you.

남 주말 일기 예보입니다. 토요일에는 비가 내리지 않고 아주 덥고 화창할 예정입니다. 기온은 전국적으로 계속 높을 예정입니다. 일요일에는 오전에 흐리겠습니다. 하지만, 오후에는 맑은 하늘을 볼 수 있을 것으로 예상됩니다. 그리고 기온은 토요일만큼 높겠습니다. 감사합니다.

02 ③

해설 남자는 커피 한 잔과 케이크 한 조각, 그리고 샌드위치 한 개를 주문했다.

어휘 a piece of ~ 한 조각
come to (총계가) ~이 되다
Here you go. 여기 있어요. 〈물건 등을 건네 줄 때〉

W Hi. What can I get you?
M I'd like a cup of coffee, please.
W All right. Would you like something to eat with your coffee?
M I will have a piece of cake and a sandwich, please.
W Is that everything?
M Yes.
W Okay. Your total comes to $11.
M Here you go.
W Thanks.

여 어서 오세요. 뭘 드릴까요?
남 커피 한 잔 주세요.
여 알겠습니다. 커피와 함께 드실 것도 좀 드릴까요?
남 케이크 한 조각과 샌드위치 한 개 주세요.
여 그게 전부 인가요?
남 네.
여 알겠습니다. 전부 합해서 11달러 되겠습니다.
남 여기 있습니다.
여 감사합니다.

03 ③

해설 이름(Mike Johnson), 사무실 위치(201호, 엘리베이터 옆), 좋아하는 음료(블랙커피), 생김새(회색 머리)에 대해 언급하였지만 직업에 대해서는 언급하지 않았다.

어휘 must be 틀림없이 ~이다
shortly[ʃɔ́ːrtli] 곧
by the way 그런데
gray[gréi] 회색의

M Hello, I came here to see Mike Fox.
W You must be David. Mr. Fox will be with you shortly. Please have a seat.
M All right. By the way, which room is his office?
W It's 201, right next to the elevator.
M All right. I brought a drink for him. Do you know if he likes coffee?
W Sure. He loves black coffee. [Pause] Here he comes.
M Which one is Mr. Fox?
W The one with gray hair.

남 안녕하세요. Mike Fox 씨를 만나러 왔습니다.
여 David 씨군요. Fox 씨는 곧 오실 거예요. 앉아계세요.
남 알겠습니다. 근데, 어느 방이 Fox 씨의 사무실인가요?
여 바로 엘리베이터 옆에 있는 201호입니다.
남 그렇군요. 그 분께 드릴 커피를 가져왔어요. 커피를 좋아하시는지 아시나요?
여 물론이죠. 블랙커피를 좋아하세요. [잠시 후] 저기 오시네요.
남 어떤 분이 Fox 씨인가요?
여 회색 머리이신 분이에요.

04 ③

해설 남자는 주말에 자신의 방을 더 밝게 만들기 위해 페인트를 칠했다고 했다.

어휘 all day (long) 하루 종일
bright[brait] (색깔이) 밝은, 선명한
paint[peint] 페인트를 칠하다
sky blue 하늘색

W Steve, what did you do on the weekend?
M I worked all day long. I am so tired.
W What kind of work did you do?
M I made my room a little brighter.
W You made your room brighter? What did you do?
M Well, my room had gray walls. So, I painted them sky blue. You should come and see it.
W Sure. Maybe I should change my room, too.

여 Steve, 주말에 뭐 했니?
남 하루 종일 일했어. 정말 피곤해.
여 어떤 일을 했는데?
남 내 방을 좀 더 밝게 만들었어.
여 네 방을 더 밝게 만들었다고? 어떻게 했는데?
남 음, 내 방의 벽이 회색이었잖아. 그래서 벽을 하늘색 페인트로 칠했어. 와서 봐봐.
여 좋아. 내 방도 바꿔봐야 겠다.

05 ③

해설 여자가 가려는 시청으로 향하는 버스가 여기로 들어오고 있다는 대화로 보아 장소는 버스 정류장임을 알 수 있다.

어휘 city hall 시청
subway station 지하철 역
nearby[nìərbái] 근처에, 가까이에
much[mʌtʃ] 훨씬 〈비교급 앞에서〉

W Excuse me, do you know how to get to City Hall?
M Yes, you should take bus number 15.
W Okay. Is there a subway station nearby?
M You have to go straight for two blocks. It'll take about 20 minutes to get there on foot.
W 20 minutes? That's too long.
M Then, you'd better take the bus to go to City Hall. It's much faster. Oh, here comes your bus.
W Okay. Thanks for your help.

여 실례합니다만, 시청에 어떻게 가는지 아시나요?
남 네, 15번 버스를 타시면 됩니다.
여 알겠습니다. 그런데 근처에 지하철이 있나요?
남 두 블록을 직진해서 가셔야 해요. 거기로 가는 데 걸어서 약 20분 걸릴 거예요.
여 20분이라고요? 너무 오래 걸리네요.
남 그럼 시청까지 버스를 타시는 것이 좋아요. 그게 훨씬 빠르거든요. 아, 여기에 버스가 오네요.
여 알겠습니다. 도와주셔서 감사합니다.

06 ④

해설 날씨가 좋아졌으니 주말에 같이 산에 갈 수 있을 것 같다는 남자의 제안에 여자가 승낙했다.

어휘 finally[fáinəli] 마침내, 드디어
go hiking 등산[하이킹]을 가다
dangerous[déindʒərəs] 위험한
can't wait to-v 빨리 ~하고 싶다

W The weather forecast says we'll have warm weather this weekend.
M I heard that, too. Finally, spring is here.
W I wanted to go hiking during the winter, but it was too dangerous.
M Yes, you could fall because of the ice.
W I can't wait to go mountain climbing again.
M Well, we could go this weekend. The weather will be warm enough.
W Okay. Let's do that.

여 일기 예보에서 이번 주말에 날씨가 따뜻할 거래.
남 나도 들었어. 드디어 봄이 왔네.
여 겨울 동안에 등산을 가고 싶었는데, 너무 위험했거든.
남 그래, 얼음 때문에 넘어질 수 있어.
여 빨리 다시 등산을 하고 싶다.
남 음, 이번 주말에 갈 수 있을 것 같아. 날씨가 충분히 따뜻해 질 테니까.
여 그래. 그렇게 하자.

07 ②

해설 두 사람은 아들의 자전거가 너무 낡아서 새 자전거를 사 주기로 했다.

어휘 amusement park 놀이 공원
instead of ~ 대신에

W Honey, Jake's birthday is coming up. We need to get something for him.
M You're right. It's next Tuesday, right?
W Yes. Last year, we went to an amusement park instead of giving him presents.

여 여보, Jake의 생일이 다가오네요. 걔를 위한 선물을 사야 해요.
남 당신 말이 맞아요. 다음 주 화요일이죠, 맞죠?
여 맞아요. 작년에 우리는 선물을 주는 대신에 놀이공원에 갔잖아요.

M	How about some books? He loves reading.	남	책은 어때요? Jake는 독서를 아주 좋아하잖아요.
W	Well, he got <u>new</u> <u>books</u> <u>last</u> <u>month</u>.	여	음, 지난달에 새 책들을 샀어요.
M	Then <u>how</u> <u>about</u> <u>a</u> <u>bike</u>? His bike is so old.	남	그럼 자전거는 어떨까요? 이미 있는 건 너무 낡았잖아요.
W	You're right. He's too tall for his old bike, too.	여	당신 말이 맞아요. 그 낡은 자전거를 타기엔 키도 너무 커요.
M	Great! Let's go to <u>the</u> <u>bike</u> <u>shop</u> with Jake next week.	남	좋아요! 다음 주에 Jake랑 자전거 가게에 갑시다.

08 ④

해설 여자는 남자가 파인애플을 사러 가는 사이 부엌에서 과일을 씻겠다고 했다.

어휘 on A's way home A가 집에 오는 길에
a bunch of 한 송이의
get[get] (물건을) 사다 (get-got-gotten)
forget to-v ~할 것을 잊다

W	Tom, <u>did</u> <u>you</u> <u>buy</u> fruit on your way home?	여	Tom, 집에 오는 길에 과일을 샀니?
M	Yes, Mom. Here they are: 3 apples, 5 oranges, and a bunch of bananas just like you asked.	남	네, 엄마. 여기 있어요. 엄마가 부탁한 대로 사과 세 개, 오렌지 다섯 개, 그리고 바나나 한 송이예요.
W	Did you get a pineapple?	여	파인애플은 샀니?
M	Oh no. I forgot to get one.	남	아, 이런. 파인애플 사는 것을 잊었네요.
W	Well, I <u>need</u> <u>it</u> <u>for</u> dinner tonight.	여	글쎄, 오늘 저녁 요리에 그게 필요한데.
M	I'll <u>go</u> <u>back</u> <u>to</u> the store and get one.	남	제가 가게에 다시 가서 하나 사 올게요.
W	Okay. I'll <u>wash</u> <u>the</u> <u>fruit</u> in the kitchen.	여	그래. 나는 부엌에서 과일을 씻을게.

09 ⑤

해설 업무 경험(없음), 장단점(창의적이고 정직하지만 많은 사람들 앞에서 긴장함), 어학 실력(영어, 프랑스어, 독일어), 업무 가능 시기(다음 달 1일)에 대해 언급하였지만 취미에 대해서는 언급하지 않았다.

어휘 experience[ikspíəriəns] 경험
strength[streŋθ] 장점, 강점
creative[kriéitiv] 창의적인
honest[ánist] 정직한
weak point 약점
nervous[nə́ːrvəs] 긴장한
language[læŋgwidʒ] 언어
speak[spiːk] (특정한 언어를) 할 줄 알다 [구사하다]

W	Do you <u>have</u> <u>any</u> <u>experience</u> in this kind of work?	여	이런 일에 경험이 있으신가요?
M	No, I don't. But I am sure I can do it well.	남	아뇨, 없습니다. 하지만 잘 할 수 있을 거라 확신해요.
W	Can you tell me about <u>your</u> <u>strengths</u>?	여	당신의 장점에 대해 말해 보시겠어요?
M	Well, I think I am creative and very honest.	남	음, 저는 창의적이고 아주 정직하다고 생각합니다.
W	How about your weak points?	여	단점은 어떤가요?
M	I get nervous when I speak in front of many people.	남	많은 사람들 앞에서 말할 때 긴장합니다.
W	<u>What</u> <u>languages</u> do you speak?	여	어떤 언어를 할 줄 아시나요?
M	I speak English, French, and a little German.	남	영어와 프랑스어를 할 수 있고 독일어도 조금 합니다.
W	Good. And when can <u>you</u> <u>start</u> <u>working</u>?	여	좋습니다. 그러면 언제부터 일을 시작할 수 있으세요?
M	From the first day of next month.	남	다음 달 1일부터요.

10 ④

해설 공항에서 승객들에게 비행기 출발 시간이 지연되었음을 알리는 안내 방송이다.

W	Good afternoon! All passengers, may I <u>have</u> <u>your</u> <u>attention</u>, please? Because of the bad weather here, all planes at this airport <u>will</u> <u>not</u> <u>fly</u> <u>out</u> until 3:40 p.m. The first plane to leave	여	안녕하세요! 모든 승객 여러분, 주목해 주시겠습니까? 이곳 날씨가 좋지 못해서 이 공항의 모든 항공기는 오후 3시 40분까지는 출발하지 못합니다.

어휘 passenger[pǽsəndʒər] 승객
fly out 비행기로 출발하다
not ~ until … (때가) …가 되어야 ~하다
flight schedule 항공 스케줄
staff member 직원

will be to Frankfurt at 3:45 p.m. If you have any questions about the flight schedule, please go to your gate and talk to a staff member.

가장 먼저 출발하는 비행기는 3시 45분발 프랑크푸르트 행이 되겠습니다. 항공 스케줄에 대해 문의 사항이 있으시면 게이트로 가셔서 직원에게 문의하시기 바랍니다.

11 ⑤

해설 여자가 찾고 있는 서점 안에는 커피숍이 없다고 했다.

어휘 floor[flɔːr] (건물의) 층

W Excuse me. Can you tell me the way to the bookstore in this building?
M You are talking about the new one, right? I think it's on the 9th floor.
W Do you know how big the bookstore is?
M Yes. It's really big. The bookstore is the only shop on that floor.
W Oh, I see. Is there a coffee shop in the bookstore?
M No. You'll have to go to the 8th floor for coffee.
W Thanks for your help.

여 실례합니다. 이 건물에서 서점에 가는 길 좀 알려주실 수 있나요?
남 새로운 서점 말씀하시는 거죠, 그렇죠? 그건 9층에 있는 것 같아요.
여 그 서점이 얼마나 큰지 아시나요?
남 네. 정말 커요. 그 층에 그 서점만 유일하게 있어요.
여 아, 그렇군요. 서점 안에 커피숍도 있나요?
남 아니요. 커피를 드시려면 8층으로 가셔야 해요.
여 도와주셔서 감사합니다.

12 ⑤

해설 남자는 직업이 건축가라서 세계 곳곳의 건물을 연구하기 위해 해외여행을 자주 한다고 했다.

어휘 a lot 많이
go abroad 해외에 나가다
architect[áːrkətèkt] 건축가
around the world 세계 곳곳의

W Chris, you travel often, right?
M Yes, I travel a lot. I go abroad every year.
W How many countries have you been to?
M More than 50 countries.
W What do you do when you travel?
M Since I'm an architect, I always study buildings. So, I usually take many pictures of interesting buildings around the world. Sometimes I draw when I have enough time.

여 Chris, 여행을 자주 하지, 맞니?
남 응, 여행을 많이 하지. 매년마다 해외로 나가.
여 몇 개국에 가봤어?
남 50개국 이상 가봤어.
여 여행을 가면 무슨 일을 하니?
남 내가 건축가라서 항상 건물들을 연구해. 그래서 세계 곳곳의 흥미로운 건물의 사진을 많이 찍어. 시간이 충분하면 가끔씩 그림을 그리기도 해.

13 ④

해설 남자는 도착하면 전화한다고 했으며 5시 30분이 될 것이라 했다.

어휘 still[stil] 아직도
a little 약간
happen[hǽpən] (일이) 일어나다
watch[watʃ] 봐 주다
probably[prábəbli] 아마도

[Cell phone rings.]
W Hello.
M Hi, Minji. Are you still home?
W No, I'll be at the shopping center in 5 minutes.
M I'm sorry, but I think I'll be a little late.
W Did something happen?
M My mom's not home. So I have to watch my little sister until 5:10.
W That's okay. I can go to a cafe and wait for you there.
M Thank you. I'll call you when I'm there. It'll be around 5:30.
W All right. See you then.

[휴대전화가 울린다]
여 여보세요.
남 안녕, 민지야. 아직 집에 있니?
여 아니, 5분 뒤에 쇼핑센터에 도착할 예정이야.
남 미안해, 내가 조금 늦을 것 같아.
여 무슨 일 있었니?
남 엄마가 집에 안 계시거든. 그래서 여동생을 5시 10분까지 돌봐야 해.
여 괜찮아. 카페에 가서 기다리면 돼.
남 고마워. 쇼핑센터에 도착하면 전화할게. 5시 30분쯤 될 것 같아.
여 알겠어. 그때 봐.

14 ③

해설 남자가 소포를 보내고 우표도 사려는 것으로 보아 두 사람의 관계는 우체국 직원과 고객임을 알 수 있다.

어휘 package[pǽkidʒ] 소포
by airmail 항공 우편으로
anything else 다른 어떤 것
stamp[stæmp] 우표

W   Hello. How can I help you?
M   I'd like to send this package to Austria.
W   How would you like to send it?
M   By airmail. How long will it take?
W   About 8 to 10 days.
M   That's fine with me.
W   Is there anything else you'd like to send?
M   No, but I'd like to get some stamps, please.

여   안녕하세요. 무엇을 도와드릴까요?
남   이 소포를 오스트리아로 보내고 싶습니다.
여   어떻게 보내시길 원하세요?
남   항공 우편으로요. 얼마나 걸릴까요?
여   대략 8일에서 10일 걸리겠네요.
남   괜찮습니다.
여   보내고 싶은 것이 또 있으세요?
남   아뇨, 우표를 좀 살게요.

15 ③

해설 여자는 역사 프로젝트를 위해 남자에게 신문을 가져다 달라고 부탁했다.

어휘 history[hístəri] 역사
later today 오늘 더 늦은 때에, 이따가
too ~ to-v 너무 ~해서 …할 수 없는
focus[fóukəs] 집중하다
get together 만나다, 모이다

W   Let's work on our history project later today.
M   I'm sorry. Can we do it tomorrow?
W   There is not enough time. We have to finish it this week.
M   But I'm too tired to focus now.
W   All right. Then let's get together tomorrow instead.
M   Thanks. Do I need to bring anything tomorrow?
W   We need more newspapers. Can you bring some?
M   Of course. I'll bring them tomorrow.

여   오늘 이따가 우리 역사 프로젝트 좀 하자.
남   미안해. 내일 하면 안 될까?
여   시간이 충분하지 않아. 우리 이번 주에 끝내야 해.
남   하지만 너무 피곤해서 지금은 집중을 할 수가 없네.
여   알겠어. 그러면 대신 내일 다시 만나자.
남   고마워. 내일 내가 가져가야 할 것이 있니?
여   우리는 신문이 더 필요해. 좀 가져올 수 있겠니?
남   물론이지. 내일 갖고 올게.

16 ④

해설 호텔에 반려 동물의 출입이 금지되어서 남자는 다른 호텔을 찾을 것이라 했다.

어휘 single room 1인용 침실
available[əvéiləbl] 이용할 수 있는
be allowed 허락되다
even if ~일지라도
cage[keidʒ] (짐승의) 우리
I'm afraid not. 그렇지 않아서 유감입니다.
allergy[ǽlərdʒi] 알레르기

[Telephone rings.]
W   King Royal Hotel, how can I help you?
M   Yes. I would like a single room for 3 days. From May 7 to 9.
W   Let me check if we have a room available.
M   I'm planning to visit there with my bird.
W   I'm sorry, sir. Pets are not allowed in our hotel.
M   Really? But I am going to bring his cage.
W   I'm sorry. Some guests may have allergies.
M   All right. I guess I'll have to find another hotel.

[전화벨이 울린다.]
여   King Royal 호텔입니다. 무엇을 도와드릴까요?
남   네. 5월 7일부터 9일까지 3일 동안 1인용 침실을 예약하고 싶습니다.
여   이용가능한 방이 있는지 확인해 보겠습니다.
남   제 새를 데려 갈 예정이에요.
여   죄송합니다. 반려 동물은 저희 호텔에는 허용되지 않습니다.
남   정말인가요? 하지만 새장을 가져갈 건데요.
여   죄송합니다. 알레르기가 있는 손님이 있을 수 있거든요.
남   알겠습니다. 다른 호텔을 찾아봐야 하겠네요.

17 ④

[해설] 레스토랑에서 주문을 받는 웨이터와 스테이크를 주문하는 여자 고객의 대화 내용을 고른다.

[어휘] mind[maind] 꺼려하다, 싫어하다
Go ahead. 어서 하세요.
reservation[rèzərvéiʃən] 예약
go straight 직진하다
turn left 좌회전하다
order[ɔ́:rdər] 주문
sore throat 인후염

① M Do you mind if I use this bike?
　 W No, I don't. Go ahead.
② M I'd like to check in now.
　 W Do you have a reservation?
③ M Excuse me, can you tell me how to get to the city library?
　 W Go straight for two blocks and turn left.
④ M May I take your order?
　 W I'd like to have a steak.
⑤ M What seems to be the problem?
　 W I have a fever and a sore throat.

① 남 이 자전거 좀 써도 될까요?
　 여 물론 되죠. 어서 쓰세요.
② 남 지금 체크인을 하려고요.
　 여 예약하셨나요?
③ 남 실례합니다. 시립 도서관으로 가는 길 좀 알려 주시겠어요?
　 여 두 블록을 직진한 뒤 좌회전 하세요.
④ 남 주문하시겠습니까?
　 여 스테이크로 할게요.
⑤ 남 어디가 안 좋으신가요?
　 여 열이 나고 목이 아파요.

18 ②

[해설] 소속 팀 수(20개), 팀 당 경기 수(38경기), 시즌 시작과 종료 시기(8월에서 이듬해 5월까지), 승점 부여 방식(이기면 3점, 비기면 1점, 지면 0점)이 대해 언급하였으나 창설 연도에 대해서는 언급하지 않았다.

[어휘] premier[prímiər] 최고의, 제1의
league[li:g] (스포츠 경기의) 리그
or[ər] 즉, 다시 말해서
English[íŋgliʃ] 잉글랜드의; 영국의
system[sístəm] 조직 (체계)
match[mætʃ] 경기, 시합
win[win] 승리
draw[drɔ:] 무승부
loser[lú:zər] 패자

M The Premier League or the EPL, is the English soccer league system. There are 20 teams in this league. The season runs from August to May of next year. Most games are played on the weekend. Each team plays 38 matches with 19 other teams. Each team gets 3 points for a win. Both teams get 1 point for a draw. And the loser gets no points.

남 프리미어 리그 즉, EPL은 잉글랜드의 축구 리그 조직이다. 이 리그에는 20개 팀이 있다. 시즌은 8월에서 이듬해 5월까지 진행된다. 대부분의 경기는 주말에 치러진다. 각 팀은 19개의 상대팀과 38경기를 치른다. 각 팀은 승리할 경우 3점을 얻는다. 비기면 양 팀이 1점을 얻는다. 그리고 패배한 팀은 점수를 얻지 못한다.

19 ④

[해설] 점심 식사로 뭘 먹는지 묻고 있으므로 음식의 종류로 대답하는 것이 자연스럽다.

[어휘] for breakfast 아침식사로
cereal[síəriəl] 시리얼
not every ~ 모든 ~은 아닌
healthy[hélθi] 건강에 좋은
[선택지]
skip[skip] (식사를) 거르다, 건너뛰다

M What do you have for breakfast?
W I have cereal with milk and fruit.
M Hmm, that sounds good for your health. Do you eat that every morning?
W Well, not every morning. I sometimes eat eggs and some bread, but I have fruit at every breakfast.
M Wow! You must really enjoy healthy breakfasts. What do you eat for lunch?
W I usually have Korean food for lunch.

남 아침 식사로 무엇을 드시나요?
여 우유와 과일을 곁들인 시리얼을 먹습니다.
남 음, 건강에 좋겠네요. 그것들을 매일 아침에 드시나요?
여 글쎄, 매일 아침은 아니에요. 가끔 계란과 빵을 먹기도 하는데요, 하지만 아침 식사 때 과일은 꼭 먹어요.
남 와! 건강에 좋은 아침 식사를 즐기시네요. 점심은 뭘 드세요?
여 점심으로 주로 한식을 먹습니다.

① 종종 아침 식사를 거릅니다.
② 12시 30분에 점심을 먹습니다.
③ 어제는 점심을 먹지 않았습니다.
⑤ 가끔 친구들과 점심 식사를 합니다.

해설 생일 선물을 주기로 하고 어떤 것이 좋을지 묻고 있으므로 구체적인 선물로 답하는 것이 자연스럽다.

어휘 familiar[fəmíljər] 익숙한
upset[ʌpsét] 화난
[선택지]
throw A a party A에게 파티를 열어 주다

W Dan, it's July 9, right?
M That's right.
W July 9 sounds so familiar. Is it your birthday?
M No, it's not. [Pause] Oh, it's Anna's birthday.
W Really? I saw her this morning, but she didn't say anything.
M She might be upset because we didn't say anything.
W How about going to her house and giving her a small present?
M Sure. What should we get?
W We should get some flowers for her.

여 Dan, 오늘이 7월 9일이지, 맞지?
남 맞아.
여 7월 9일이 아주 친숙한 것 같은데. 네 생일이니?
남 아니, 그렇지 않아. [잠시 후] 아, Anna의 생일이네.
여 정말? 오늘 아침에 걜 봤는데 아무 말 없던데.
남 우리가 아무 말도 안 해서 속상할지도 몰라.
여 Anna의 집에 가서 작은 선물을 하는 게 어떨까?
남 좋아. 뭘 사야 할까?
여 꽃을 좀 사주는 것이 좋을 것 같아.

① 알았어, 여기 있어.
② 오늘이 무슨 요일이지?
③ 넌 즐거운 시간을 보냈니?
⑤ 네가 나에게 파티를 열어 줘야 할 것 같아.

01 ②	02 ⑤	03 ⑤	04 ④	05 ⑤	06 ③	07 ③
08 ⑤	09 ⑤	10 ③	11 ②	12 ④	13 ⑤	14 ②
15 ②	16 ⑤	17 ④	18 ⑤	19 ⑤	20 ⑤	

01 ②

해설 광주는 흐릴 것이라고 했다.

어휘 national[nǽʃənəl] 전국의
A as well as B B뿐 아니라 A도
humid[hjú:mid] 습한
finally[fáinəli] 마지막으로
heavy rain 폭우

M Good morning, everyone, and here's your national weather forecast for today. It'll be cool and sunny in Seoul as well as in Incheon. However, it will be very hot and humid in Daegu. Gwangju won't be hot because it will be cloudy. Finally, heavy rain is expected in Busan.

남 안녕하세요, 여러분. 오늘의 전국 날씨 예보를 전해드립니다. 인천뿐만 아니라 서울도 선선하고 화창하겠습니다. 하지만 대구는 몹시 덥고 습한 날씨가 되겠습니다. 광주는 흐릴 것이기 때문에 덥지는 않겠습니다. 마지막으로 부산은 폭우가 예상됩니다.

02 ⑤

해설 눈사람이 그려진 네모난 접시를 사기로 했다.

어휘 throw a party 파티를 열다
plate[pleit] 접시
round[raund] 둥근
square[skwɛər] 네모난, 정사각형 모양의
snowman[snoumæn] 눈사람

W Hello, how may I help you?
M I'm going to throw a party tomorrow, and I need a big plate.
W This round plate is perfect for a party.
M Well, I prefer square ones. Do you have any square plates?
W Yes, we do. Then how about this one with a picture of a tree in the middle?
M It's not bad, but it is too big. Can you show me a different one?
W Sure. This one has a picture of a snowman on it. What do you think?
M Great! I'll take it.

여 어서 오세요, 무엇을 도와드릴까요?
남 내일 파티를 열 계획이라서 커다란 접시가 하나 필요해요.
여 이 둥근 접시가 파티에 딱 어울려요.
남 글쎄요, 전 네모난 모양이 더 좋아요. 네모난 접시 있나요?
여 네, 있습니다. 그러시면 가운데에 나무 그림이 있는 이건 어떠세요?
남 나쁘지는 않은데, 너무 크네요. 다른 것 좀 보여 주시겠어요?
여 물론이죠. 이건 눈사람이 그려져 있는데요. 어떠세요?
남 좋아요! 이걸로 주세요.

03 ⑤

해설 상점 위치(5번가와 Broadway가 만나는 모퉁이), 영업시간(오전 9시부터 오후 9시까지), 할인 기간(다음 주 월요일부터 금요일까지), 할인 품목(라켓)에 대해 언급하였으나 제품 가격에 대해서는 언급하지 않았다.

어휘 avenue[ǽvənjù:] (도시의) -가, 거리
open[óupən] 문을 열다
(↔ close[klouz] 문을 닫다)
go on (일이) 일어나다
racket[rǽkit] (배드민턴 등의) 라켓
be on sale 세일 중이다

[Telephone rings.]
W Thanks for calling Sports World on 5th Avenue and Broadway.
M Hi. What time do you open and close today?
W We're open from 9 a.m. to 9 p.m. every day.
M Do you have any sales going on right now?
W Not yet. But our spring sale event will be from next Monday to Friday.
M Will badminton rackets be on sale, too?
W Yes, all the rackets will be on sale.
M Thank you for the information.

[전화벨이 울린다.]
여 5번가와 Broadway가 만나는 모퉁이에 있는 Sports World에 전화 주셔서 감사합니다.
남 안녕하세요. 오늘 몇 시에 문을 열고 닫으시나요?
여 저희는 매일 오전 9시부터 오후 9시까지 문을 엽니다.
남 지금 세일 중인 품목이 있나요?
여 아직은 없는데요. 저희 봄 세일 행사는 다음 주 월요일부터 금요일까지입니다.
남 배드민턴 라켓도 세일하나요?
여 네. 라켓 전부 세일합니다.
남 알려 주셔서 정말 고마워요.

04 ④

해설 여자는 내일 학교에서 인형 만드는
걸 배울 것이라 했다.

어휘 almost[ɔ́:lmoust] 거의
glue[gluː] 접착제, 풀
button[bʌ́tən] 단추
ride[raid] (차에) 태움, 탐

M Somi, where are you going? It's almost time for dinner.
W Dad, I forgot to get a few things for school. I have to go and buy them.
M What do you need?
W I need to get glue and some buttons for my art class tomorrow.
M Glue and buttons? What are you going to make?
W I am going to learn to make a doll.
M A doll? That sounds like fun. Do you need a ride?
W Yes, please.
M Let me get my car key.

남 소미야, 어디 가는 거니? 저녁 먹을 시간이 거의 다 되었단다.
여 아빠, 저 학교에 필요한 것들을 준비 하는 걸 깜빡했어요. 가서 사야 해요.
남 무엇이 필요하니?
여 내일 미술 수업에 사용할 접착제와 단추 몇 개가 필요해요.
남 접착제와 단추? 무엇을 만들거니?
여 인형을 만드는 걸 배울 거예요.
남 인형? 재미있겠구나. 태워다 줄까?
여 네, 태워주세요.
남 자동차 열쇠를 가져올게.

05 ⑤

해설 여자가 예매한 티켓을 찾고 있고
남자가 확인 후 티켓을 건네주는 것으로
보아 장소는 매표소임을 알 수 있다.

어휘 in line 줄에 서 있는
pick up (어디에서) ~을 찾다[찾아오다]
reservation[rèzərvéiʃən] 예약
book[buk] 예약하다
correct[kərékt] 정확한

M Can I help the next person in line?
W Hi, I'd like to pick up my tickets, please.
M May I have your name?
W It's Lisa Moore.
M Let me check. [Pause] I'm sorry, I can't find your name here. Do you have the reservation number?
W No, I don't. My dad booked the tickets for me. Then can you try Tom Moore?
M Yes, I have 2 tickets for the show at 5 o'clock.
W That's correct.

남 줄에 서 계신 다음 분 도와드리겠습니 다.
여 안녕하세요, 제 티켓을 찾으려고요.
남 성함이 어떻게 되시죠?
여 Lisa Moore입니다.
남 확인해 볼게요. [잠시 후] 죄송하지만 여기에 이름이 없으시네요. 예약 번호 가 있으신가요?
여 아뇨, 없어요. 저희 아빠가 예약해 주 셨는데요. Tom Moore로 찾아보시겠 어요?
남 네, 5시 공연으로 티켓 2장이 있네요.
여 맞습니다.

06 ③

해설 배구 경기가 폭풍우로 인해 취소되
었다는 말을 듣고 여자는 기대했었다며
실망하고 있다.

어휘 mean[miːn] 의미하다
volleyball[válibɔ̀ːl] 배구
text message 문자 메시지
cancel[kǽnsəl] 취소하다
storm[stɔːrm] 폭풍우
look forward to ~을 기대하다

M Where are you going, Stephanie?
W I'm going out to watch the game.
M Do you mean the volleyball game at school?
W Yes. My best friend is going to play and I want to cheer her up.
M Didn't you get the text message? The game has been canceled.
W Why?
M Because of the storm. Everyone should stay home tonight.
W Oh no. I was really looking forward to it.

남 어디 가니, Stephanie?
여 경기를 보러 나가려고요.
남 학교에서 하는 배구 시합을 말하는 거 니?
여 맞아요. 제일 친한 친구가 경기를 해 서 걔를 응원하고 싶어서요.
남 문자 메시지 못 받았니? 그 경기는 취 소되었잖아.
여 왜?
남 폭풍우 때문이야. 오늘 밤에는 모두 집에 있어야 해.
여 이런. 정말 기대했었는데.

07 ③

[해설] 여자는 남동생에게 줄 생일 선물로 야구 모자를 사기로 했다.

[어휘] selection[silékʃən] 선택 가능한 것들(의 집합)
sneaker[sníːkər] 운동화
shorts[ʃɔːrts] 반바지
popular[pápulər] 인기 있는

M Hello, can I help you find anything?
W I'm looking for a birthday present for my younger brother.
M We have a very good selection of sneakers.
W Well, I don't know his shoe size.
M Then how about a T-shirt?
W My brother has too many T-shirts already.
M Baseball caps and basketball shorts are also popular birthday presents.
W Oh, then I'll get a baseball cap for him.

남 어서 오세요, 찾으시는 것 도와드릴까요?
여 남동생에게 줄 생일 선물을 찾고 있어요.
남 저희 가게에는 여러 가지 아주 좋은 운동화들을 갖추고 있습니다.
여 음, 제가 동생의 신발 사이즈를 몰라서요.
남 그러면 티셔츠는 어떠세요?
여 제 남동생은 이미 티셔츠가 너무 많아요.
남 야구 모자와 농구 반바지도 생일 선물로 인기 있습니다.
여 아, 그럼 야구 모자를 사줄래요.

08 ⑤

[해설] 자기 전에 전화기 충전을 꼭 하라는 여자의 말에 남자가 지금 바로 하겠다고 했다.

[어휘] midnight[midnáit] 자정
pack[pæk] (짐을) 싸다
sleeping bag 침낭
trunk[trʌŋk] (자동차 뒷부분의) 트렁크
Make sure to-v. 꼭 ～하세요.
charge[tʃɑːrdʒ] 충전하다

W It's midnight, honey. We should go to bed.
M Did you finish packing your bag for the trip?
W Yes, I did. Did you pack your sleeping bag?
M Yes, it's right here. Where's our tent?
W I already put it in the trunk of the car.
M Oh, good. Then I think we're ready to go to bed.
W Make sure to charge your phone before you go to sleep.
M Yes, I'll do that right now.

여 자정이에요, 여보. 자야 해요.
남 여행에 가져 갈 가방 싸는 건 다 끝냈셨어요?
여 네, 끝냈지요. 침낭은 챙겼어요?
남 네, 바로 여기 있어요. 저희 텐트는 어디에 있죠?
여 벌써 차 트렁크에 넣어 뒀어요.
남 아, 잘했어요. 그럼 자러 갈 준비가 끝난 것 같네요.
여 자기 전에 전화기를 꼭 충전하세요.
남 네. 지금 바로 할게요.

09 ⑤

[해설] 개최 시간(저녁 6시에서 8시까지), 장소(학교 체육관), 참가 자격(제한 없음), 입장료(무료)에 대해 언급하였으나 참가 인원에 대해서는 언급하지 않았다.

[어휘] be held 개최되다
gym(= gymnasium)[dʒim] 체육관
cousin[kʌ́zən] 사촌
get in 들어가다
entrance fee 입장료
try[trai] (음식을) 먹어 보다

W Is International Night this Friday?
M No. It's on Thursday from 6 p.m. to 8 p.m.
W It's held in the school gym, right?
M Right. Do you know if my cousins can get in, too? They're in elementary school.
W Of course. Anyone can get in, and there's no entrance fee.
M What do you want to do the most there?
W I can't wait to try food from many different countries.

여 International Night가 이번 주 금요일이니?
남 아니. 목요일 저녁 6시에서 8시까지야.
여 학교 체육관에서 열리지, 맞지?
남 맞아. 우리 사촌들도 들어갈 수 있는지 아니? 걔네들은 초등학생인데.
여 물론이지. 누구나 들어갈 수 있고 입장료도 없어.
남 너는 거기서 뭘 가장 하고 싶니?
여 나는 많은 다양한 나라의 음식을 먹어 보고 싶어.

10 ③

[해설] 송파 방면 열차 운행이 지연되어 승객들의 이해를 구한다는 안내 방송이다.

M Thank you for using subway line number 11. I'm sorry to announce that the train to Songpa will be late. The next subway will

남 지하철 11호선을 이용해 주셔서 감사드립니다. 송파 방면 열차가 지연되게 됨을 알려드리게 되어 죄송합니다. 다

어휘 subway line 지하철 노선
announce[ənáuns] 발표하다, 알려 주다
be expected to-v ~할 것으로 기대[예상]되다
crowded[kráudid] 혼잡한, 붐비는
once again 다시 한번

come in 7 minutes. Because of this, the next train is expected to be very crowded. Once again, we are sorry for this and thank you for your understanding.

음 열차는 7분 뒤에 도착하겠습니다. 이러한 이유로 다음 열차가 대단히 혼잡할 것으로 예상됩니다. 다시 한번 지연에 대해 죄송하다는 말씀드리면서 이해해 주셔서 감사드립니다.

11 ②

해설 토요일 점심은 Joe's 레스토랑에서 먹는다고 하였다.

어휘 go jogging 조깅하러 가다
on weekdays 평일에
get up early 일찍 일어나다

W Dad, are we going to go jogging on Saturday morning?
M Yes, we are, and then we are going to have lunch at Joe's Restaurant.
W Can we go shopping on Sunday?
M Sure, but first we need to go swimming in the morning.
W Dad, don't you think that's too much exercise?
M No. You don't get any exercise on weekdays.
W That's true.
M And don't forget to go to bed before 10 on Saturday. We should get up early the next morning.
W All right, Dad.

여 아빠, 저희 토요일 아침에 조깅하러 가나요?
남 응. 그럴 거야. 그리고 나서 Joe's 레스토랑에서 점심을 먹을 거야.
여 일요일에 우리 쇼핑하러 가도 돼요?
남 물론이지, 하지만 먼저 일요일 오전에 수영하러 가야 해.
여 아빠, 운동이 지나친 것 같지 않으세요?
남 아니. 너는 평일에는 전혀 운동하지 않잖아.
여 그건 그래요.
남 그리고 토요일에 10시 전에 잠자리에 드는 것 잊지 마. 다음 날 아침에 일찍 일어나야 하니까.
여 알았어요, 아빠.

12 ④

해설 남자는 객실이 깨끗하지 않아서 프런트 데스크에 전화하여 청소해 달라고 요구했다.

어휘 front desk 프런트[안내] 데스크

[Telephone rings.]
W This is the front desk. How may I help you?
M Hi, I'm calling from room 1509.
W Yes, Mr. Robertson. Is there something wrong with the room?
M I don't think the room has been cleaned.
W I'm really sorry about that, sir.
M Can you send someone to clean this room right now?
W Of course, sir. I'll do that right away.

[전화벨이 울린다.]
여 프런트 데스크입니다. 무엇을 도와드릴까요?
남 안녕하세요, 1509호에서 전화하는데요.
여 네, Robertson 씨. 방에 무슨 문제가 생겼나요?
남 방이 청소가 안 된 것 같아요.
여 그 점에 대해 정말 죄송합니다. 고객님.
남 이 방을 지금 청소할 사람을 보내 주실래요?
여 물론이죠, 고객님. 바로 그렇게 하겠습니다.

13 ⑤

해설 여자가 5시 30분은 되어야 사무실에서 나올 수 있어서 두 사람은 6시에 체육관에서 만나기로 했다.

어휘 go to the gym 체육관에 가다
get some exercise 운동을 하다

M Do you want to go to the gym tomorrow?
W Yes. I really need to get some exercise.
M Do you want me to pick you up at 5 p.m.?
W I need to stay at the office until 5:30 tomorrow.
M Then, what time and where should we meet?

남 내일 체육관에 갈래?
여 그래, 나는 정말 운동을 좀 해야 해.
남 오후 5시에 너를 태우러 갈까?
여 나는 내일 5시 30분까지 사무실에 있어야 해.
남 그럼, 우리 몇 시에 어디에서 만날까?

pick A up A를 (차에) 태우러 가다
until [əntíl] ~때까지

14 ②

[해설] 남자가 가방의 무게를 재고 나서 여자에게 여권과 티켓을 건네주는 상황으로 보아 두 사람의 관계는 공항 직원과 승객임을 알 수 있다.

[어휘] check A in (비행기 탈 때) A를 부치다
battery [bǽtəri] 건전지, 배터리
lighter [láitər] 라이터
passport [pǽspɔːrt] 여권
boarding pass 탑승권

W How about meeting at 6 at the gym?
M That sounds good.

M Please put your bag over here. [Pause] You can take it with you. It's under 3 kilograms.
W No. I want to check it in because I have another bag here.
M All right. Are there any batteries or lighters in there?
W No. I made sure not to pack anything like those.
M Good. Here are your passport and boarding pass. Enjoy your trip.
W Thank you.

여 6시에 체육관에서 만나는 게 어때?
남 그거 좋겠다.

남 이쪽에 가방을 놓아주세요. [잠시 후] 그 가방은 가지고 계셔도 됩니다. 그건 3킬로그램 이하이네요.
여 아니에요. 여기 다른 가방이 있어서 그 가방을 부치고 싶어요.
남 알겠습니다. 그 가방 안에 배터리나 라이터가 들어있나요?
여 아니요. 그런 것을 넣지 않도록 확실히 확인했어요.
남 좋습니다. 여권과 탑승권 여기 있습니다. 즐거운 여행 보내세요.
여 감사합니다.

15 ②

[해설] 여자는 송별회에 쓰기 위해 친구들이 같이 나오는 사진을 남자에게 찾아 달라고 부탁했다.

[어휘] everywhere [évrihwὲər] 모든 곳에서
move [muːv] 이사하다
farewell party 송별회

W Steve! I was looking for you everywhere in school.
M Really? Is something wrong?
W Jake is going to move next month, so we will have a farewell party for him.
M Oh, that's right. When is the party?
W It's next Friday. But we need more people to help with the party. Can you help us with that?
M Of course. What should I do first?
W We need pictures of us with Jake. Can you find some pictures?
M Of course.

여 Steve! 학교 곳곳에 널 찾아다녔어.
남 정말? 무슨 일 있니?
여 Jake가 다음 달에 이사를 가서 그에게 송별회를 해 주려고 하고 있어.
남 아, 맞다. 송별회는 언제야?
여 다음 주 금요일이야. 하지만 우리는 송별회를 도와줄 사람이 더 필요해. 우리를 도와줄 수 있니?
남 물론이지. 내가 먼저 뭘 하면 될까?
여 우리가 Jake하고 같이 찍은 사진이 필요해. 사진을 좀 찾아 줄 수 있겠니?
남 물론이야.

16 ⑤

[해설] 남자는 가족과 함께 해외로 이주하게 되어 친구들과 헤어져야 하는 사실에 속상해 하고 있다.

[어휘] upset [ʌpsét] 속상한, 화난
move to 이사 가다
keep in touch 연락하고 지내다
by e-mail 이메일로

W Jayden, you look upset. Is there something wrong?
M My family and I are going to move to Singapore.
W Oh, really? Why?
M My dad's going to work in Singapore for the next 5 years.
W I didn't know that.
M I'm so sad. I don't want to leave my friends.
W Don't be sad. We can still keep in touch by e-mail.
M Right. Before I leave, we should do something fun together.
W That's a great idea!

여 Jayden, 너 속상해 보이네. 무슨 일 있니?
남 우리 가족하고 내가 싱가포르로 이사를 가게 되었어.
여 아, 정말? 왜?
남 우리 아빠가 앞으로 5년 동안 싱가포르에서 일하실 예정이시거든.
여 그건 몰랐어.
남 난 너무 슬퍼. 친구들을 떠나고 싶지 않아.
여 슬퍼하지 마. 계속해서 이메일로 연락하고 지낼 수 있잖아.
남 맞아. 내가 떠나기 전에 우리 같이 재미있는 거 하자.
여 좋은 생각이야!

17 ④

해설 옆자리에 앉아도 되는지 묻는 대화가 적절하다.

어휘 Here it is. 여기 있어요. 〈물건을 건네줄 때〉
bad cold 독감
dessert [dizə́ːrt] 디저트, 후식
check [tʃek] 계산서
seat [siːt] 자리, 좌석
have a flat tire 타이어가 펑크 나다

① M May I see your passport?
　 W Sure, here it is.
② M What seems to be the problem, doctor?
　 W It's just a bad cold.
③ M Do you want any dessert, ma'am?
　 W No, I'm full. Can I have the check?
④ M Excuse me. Is this seat taken?
　 W No, it's not. You can sit here if you want.
⑤ M How can I help you, ma'am?
　 W I have a flat tire.

① 남 여권 좀 볼 수 있을까요?
　 여 네, 여기 있습니다.
② 남 어디가 이상이 있나요, 의사 선생님?
　 여 그냥 독감입니다.
③ 남 디저트 드릴까요, 고객님?
　 여 아니요, 배가 부르네요. 계산서 좀 갖다주시겠어요?
④ 남 실례합니다. 여기 자리 있나요?
　 여 아니요, 없습니다. 원하시면 여기에 앉아도 됩니다.
⑤ 남 무엇을 도와드릴까요, 고객님?
　 여 타이어가 펑크 났어요.

18 ⑤

해설 번호(1547번), 색깔(파란색), 탑승 가능 인원(20명), 출발 시각(9시 30분)에 대해 언급하였지만 요금에 대해서는 언급하지 않았다.

어휘 miss [mis] (못 보고) 놓치다, 지나치다
next to ~옆에
seat [siːt] (건물·차량 등에 특정한 수의) 좌석이 있다

W Good morning, class. We are going to take bus number 1547. It's the only blue bus, so you won't miss it. Make sure you sit next to someone because the bus can seat only 20 people. The bus will leave at 9:30. If you need to use the restroom, you still have time.

여 안녕하세요, 학생 여러분. 저희는 1547번 버스를 타게 됩니다. 이 버스는 색깔이 파란 유일한 버스라서 여러분이 놓치지 않을 겁니다. 이 버스는 20명의 좌석뿐이니 여러분은 반드시 누군가의 옆에 앉아야 합니다. 버스는 9시 30분에 출발합니다. 화장실을 사용해야 한다면 아직 시간이 있습니다.

19 ⑤

해설 첫 등교를 앞두고 긴장하고 있는 여자에게 남자가 선생님들도 긴장한다며 안심시켜주고 있으므로 기분이 나아졌다고 응답하는 것이 적절하다.

어휘 nervous [nə́ːrvəs] 긴장한
relax [rilǽks] 편안히 하다, 안심하다
even [íːvən] ~조차도
[선택지]
friendly [fréndli] 친절한

M It's your first day of school tomorrow. How are you feeling, Lisa?
W I'm really nervous right now, Dad.
M What are you so nervous about?
W I'm nervous about meeting new people. It's not easy for me.
M Just relax. It's going to be fine.
W Do you think so?
M Yes. you're not the only one to be worried. Even teachers get nervous, too.
W You're right. I feel much better now.

남 내일이 너의 첫 등교일이구나, 기분이 어때, Lisa?
여 지금 정말로 긴장돼요, 아빠.
남 뭐가 그렇게 긴장되니?
여 새로운 사람들을 만나는 것이 긴장돼요. 저에게는 쉽지 않거든요.
남 마음을 편하게 가져라. 잘 될 거야.
여 그렇게 생각하세요?
남 그럼. 너만 걱정하고 있는 게 아니란다. 심지어 선생님들도 긴장하거든.
여 아빠 말이 맞아요. 기분이 한결 좋아졌어요.

① 아니요, 학교에서 저만 그래요.
② 정말요? 저는 독서 동아리예요.
③ 전 공부를 충분히 하지 않았어요.
④ 네, 선생님들이 친절한 것 같아요.

해설 여자에게 9월에 있을 콘서트에 갈 것인지 물었으므로 이어질 응답으로 갈 것인지 여부를 답하는 것이 적절하다.

어휘 can't wait to-v 빨리 ~하고 싶다
big fan 열혈 팬
plan to-v ~할 계획이다

W What are you listening to?
M I'm listening to K-pop songs.
W I love listening to K-pop, too. Do you <u>have any favorite</u> K-pop singers?
M No. I like them all. What about you?
W I like the boy band NTU. In fact, I am <u>a big fan</u> of theirs.
M I see. <u>Have you been to</u> an NTU concert?
W No, because NTU's first concert will take place this September.
M There are still 3 months left. But you are <u>planning to go</u>, aren't you?
W Of course. I'm looking forward to it.

여 뭘 듣고 있니?
남 K-pop 노래를 듣고 있어.
여 나도 K-pop 듣는 걸 정말 좋아해. 가장 좋아하는 K-pop 가수라도 있니?
남 아니. 나는 전부 다 좋아. 너는 어때?
여 나는 보이 밴드 NTU가 좋아. 사실 그들의 열혈 팬이야.
남 그렇구나. NTU 콘서트에 가 본 적 있니?
여 아니, 왜냐하면 이번 9월에 첫 콘서트를 할 예정이거든.
남 아직 세 달이나 남았네. 하지만 너 갈 거지, 그렇지 않니?
여 물론이지, 기대하고 있는걸.

① 그 말을 들으니 안됐네.
② 너를 어서 빨리 보고 싶어.
③ 응, CD를 한 장 살 거야.
④ 아니, 괜찮아. 그 날은 바쁘거든.

01 ④	02 ②	03 ③	04 ②	05 ⑤	06 ②	07 ③
08 ⑤	09 ③	10 ①	11 ②	12 ①	13 ⑤	14 ③
15 ④	16 ③	17 ②	18 ②	19 ④	20 ④	

01 ④

해설 일요일 저녁에 강한 바람이 분다고 했다.

어휘 weather forecast 일기 예보
a series of 연속적인
mostly[móustli] 주로, 대부분
continue to-v 계속 ~하다
throughout ~동안 쭉, 내내

M Welcome to the weather channel. Here is your weather forecast for this weekend. After a series of beautiful sunny days this week, it will be mostly cloudy on Saturday. No rain is expected on Saturday or Sunday. However, there will be strong winds on Sunday evening, and it will continue to be windy throughout the night.

남 날씨 채널을 함께 하고 계신 여러분 환영합니다. 이번 주말의 일기 예보입니다. 이번 주에 연속적으로 화창한 날이 지나면 토요일에는 구름이 많이 끼겠습니다. 토요일이나 일요일에 비가 오지 않겠습니다. 하지만, 일요일 저녁에 강한 바람이 불겠고 밤새 바람 부는 날씨가 이어지겠습니다.

02 ②

해설 남자의 사촌과 그 옆에 개 한 마리가 해변을 걷고 있는 사진이다.

어휘 cousin[kʌ́zən] 사촌
by[bai] ~옆에
beach[biːtʃ] 해변
seem[siːm] ~처럼 보이다, ~인 듯하다
much[mʌtʃ] 훨씬 〈비교급 앞에서〉

W This is a beautiful picture, James.
M Thank you. It was taken last summer.
W Is this you in the picture?
M No, that's my cousin. I took the picture.
W Oh, your cousin lives by the beach, right?
M Yes, he does, and that's his dog next to him.
W The dog seems really happy on the beach.
M Yes, he likes walking on the beach much better than walking in the park.

여 이건 아름다운 사진이구나, James.
남 고마워. 지난여름에 찍은 거야.
여 사진 속에 이 사람이 너니?
남 아니, 내 사촌이야. 내가 그 사진을 찍었거든.
여 아, 사촌이 해변 근처에 사는구나, 그렇지?
남 응, 맞아. 그리고 옆에 있는 것은 그의 개야.
여 개가 해변에서 아주 행복해 보인다.
남 응, 저 개는 공원에서 걷는 것보다 해변에서 걷는 것을 훨씬 더 좋아해.

03 ③

해설 제목(My Loving Father), 등장인물(딸과 아버지), 입장료(50달러), 관람한 도시(뉴욕시)에 대해 언급하였지만 공연 날짜에 대해서는 언급하지 않았다.

어휘 boring[bɔ́ːriŋ] 지루한, 따분한
loving[lʌ́viŋ] 사랑하는
actor[ǽktər] 배우
pay A for B B에 대해 A를 지불하다
empty[émpti] 비어 있는
seat[siːt] 좌석, 자리
glad[glæd] 만족한
at least 최소한, 적어도

W How did you like the musical, Tom?
M It was as boring as its title, My Loving Father.
W I know. I can't believe there were only 2 actors, a daughter and a father.
M Yes. There were so many empty seats. Now I know why.
W I'm just glad that we only paid $50 for the musical.
M We can at least say that we saw a musical in New York City.
W Well, that's true.

여 뮤지컬이 맘에 들었니, Tom?
남 〈사랑하는 우리 아빠〉 제목만큼이나 지루했어.
여 맞아. 딸과 아버지 두 명의 배우만 나왔다는 것이 믿어지지 않아.
남 그래. 빈 좌석이 아주 많았지. 이제 그 이유를 알겠어.
여 나는 우리가 그 뮤지컬에 50달러만 지불했다는 사실에 만족해.
남 우리는 최소한 뉴욕시에서 뮤지컬 한 편을 보았다고 말할 수는 있겠네.
여 음, 그건 사실이지.

04 ②

[해설] 남자는 아내를 위해 커피를 주문했고 자신은 녹차를 마신다고 했다.

[어휘] order[ɔ́:rdər] 주문하다; 주문품
drink[driŋk] 음료
come in (물건이) ~로 나오다
mug[mʌg] 머그잔
green tea 녹차
I'll be right back. 금방 돌아올게요.

W Are you ready to order?
M We'd like to order our drinks first.
W Okay, would you like coffee?
M It comes in a big mug, right?
W Yes, it comes in a mug.
M Then, my wife will have coffee, and I'll have green tea.
W Great! I'll be right back with your drink orders.

여 주문하시겠습니까?
남 저희 음료 먼저 주문할게요.
여 그러세요, 커피 드시겠어요?
남 그건 큰 머그잔에 담겨서 나오죠, 맞나요?
여 네, 머그잔으로 나옵니다.
남 그러면, 제 아내는 커피를 마시고, 저는 녹차를 마실게요.
여 좋습니다! 주문하신 음료 준비해서 금방 오겠습니다.

05 ⑤

[해설] 스케이트 타는 것을 가르쳐 주겠다고 하고 스케이트를 대여하려는 것으로 보아 스케이트장에서 나누는 대화임을 알 수 있다.

[어휘] fall down 넘어지다
get back up (넘어졌다가) 일어나다
own[oun] 자신의
rent[rent] (사용료를 내고) 빌리다
a pair of 한 켤레

M Have you done this before, Maggie?
W No, this is my first time.
M Don't worry. I'll teach you.
W I'm nervous. I'm scared to fall down.
M You just get back up. Everybody falls down.
W Did you bring your own skates?
M Yes, I did. Now, let's rent a pair of skates for you.
W Okay. Is it expensive to rent skates?
M No, not at all.

남 이거 예전에 해본 적 있니, Maggie?
여 아니, 이번이 처음이야.
남 걱정하지 마. 너한테 가르쳐 줄게.
여 나 긴장돼. 넘어질까 봐 무서워.
남 다시 일어서면 되지. 누구나 넘어져.
여 너는 네 스케이트를 갖고 왔니?
남 응, 갖고 왔어. 이제, 네가 신을 스케이트를 빌리자.
여 알겠어. 스케이트 빌리는 거 비싸니?
남 아니, 전혀 그렇지 않아.

06 ②

[해설] 남자가 경연대회에서 수상한 여자에게 해낼 줄 알았다며 칭찬하고 있다.

[어휘] garage[gərá:dʒ] 차고
work on ~에 노력을 들이다
fix[fiks] 고치다, 수리하다
competition[kàmpətíʃən] (경연) 대회, 시합
for a while 잠시 동안, 당분간
win first prize 1등을 하다

W Dad, I'm home. Where are you?
M I'm in the garage.
W [Pause] Are you still working on this car?
M Yes, I think I'll be able to fix it this time.
W That's good. Oh, by the way, do you remember the robot competition last month?
M Yes, of course. You were working on your robot for a while.
W I won first prize.
M Great! I knew you could do it!

여 아빠, 저 집에 왔어요. 어디 계세요?
남 차고에 있단다.
여 [잠시 후] 아직도 이 차에 몰두하고 계세요?
남 응, 이번에는 고칠 수 있을 것 같아.
여 잘됐네요. 아, 그건 그렇고, 지난달에 있었던 로봇 경연대회 기억하세요?
남 그럼, 기억하지. 너는 한동안 로봇 작업에 매진했었잖아.
여 제가 1등을 했어요.
남 멋지다! 네가 해낼 줄 알았어.

07 ③

[해설] 두 사람은 저녁 식사 후에 보드게임을 하기로 했다.

[어휘] glasses[glǽsiz] 안경
leave[li:v] ~을 두고 오다
go out for a walk 산책 나가다
chilly[tʃíli] (날씨가) 쌀쌀한

W What do you want to do after dinner?
M Do you want to watch a movie?
W I can't. I left my glasses at school.
M We can go out for a walk.
W Don't you think it's a little cold to go for a walk?
M You're right. Then how about a board game?

여 저녁 식사 후에 뭐 할 거야?
남 너 영화 보러 갈래?
여 나는 못 봐. 안경을 학교에 두고 왔거든.
남 우리가 같이 산책하러 나갈 수는 있어.
여 산책하기에는 약간 추운 것 같지 않니?
남 네 말이 맞네. 그럼 보드게임을 하는 건 어때?

W Good idea! It's been a long time since we played a board game together.

여 좋은 생각이야! 우리가 보드게임을 같이 한지 한참 지났네.

08 ⑤

해설 남자는 부엌 청소를 먼저 하자는 여자의 의견에 동의하며 바로 설거지를 하기로 했다.

어휘 amazing[əméiziŋ] 놀라운
prepare[pripέər] 준비하다
come over ~에 들르다
do the dishes 설거지하다

W Did you enjoy the dinner, Matthew?
M Yes, it was amazing. How did you prepare all the food so quickly?
W My friend Jennifer came over and helped me cook.
M Really? I didn't know that. Why didn't she stay for dinner?
W She had to pick up her son.
M I should call and thank her for helping you out.
W You can do that after we finish cleaning the kitchen.
M Yes, you're right. I'll start doing the dishes right now.

여 저녁 식사 맛있게 했어요, Matthew?
남 네, 아주 맛있었어요. 어떻게 모든 음식을 그렇게 빨리 준비했나요?
여 내 친구 Jennifer가 와서 제가 요리하는 것을 도와줬어요.
남 정말요? 몰랐네요. 왜 저녁을 먹지 않고 갔나요?
여 그녀는 아들을 태우러 가야 했어요.
남 전화해서 당신을 도와준 것에 대해 고마움을 전해야겠네요.
여 우리가 부엌 청소를 다 마치고 나서 해도 돼요.
남 네, 당신 말이 맞아요. 지금 바로 설거지를 시작할게요.

09 ③

해설 맛(좋음), 재료(야채), 가격(10달러), 판매 장소(Mike's Diner)에 대해 언급하였으나 크기에 대해서는 언급하지 않았다.

어휘 so[sou:] 아주, 대단히
unhealthy[ʌnhélθi] 건강에 해로운
completely[kəmplí:tli] 완전히
be made of ~으로 만들어지다
vegetable[védʒitəbl] 채소, 야채
quite[kwait] 상당히, 꽤
expensive[ikspénsiv] (가격이) 비싼
diner[dáinər] (작은) 식당

W This is an amazing hamburger. It is so delicious.
M I thought you didn't like hamburgers.
W I don't like hamburgers because they are unhealthy, but this one's different.
M I know. It is completely made of vegetables.
W But it's quite expensive. $10 for a hamburger?
M It is a little expensive. Are there other restaurants that sell this burger?
W No, you can only get it here at Mike's Diner.

여 이거 굉장한 햄버거야. 너무 맛있어.
남 나는 네가 햄버거를 좋아하지 않는다고 생각했어.
여 나는 햄버거가 건강에 나빠서 좋아하지 않아. 그런데 이 햄버거는 다르네.
남 맞아. 완전히 야채로만 만들었어.
여 근데 꽤 비싸긴 해. 햄버거 한 개에 10달러라고?
남 좀 비싸긴 하지. 다른 레스토랑에서도 이 햄버거를 파니?
여 아니, 여기 Mike's Diner에서만 먹을 수 있어.

10 ①

해설 충분히 자는 것은 게으른 것이 아닌 좋은 컨디션으로 성공하는 길이라고 하며 숙면의 중요성을 강조하고 있다.

어휘 get a good night's sleep 충분히 숙면을 취하다
importance[impɔ́:rtəns] 중요성
same as ~와 같은
successful[səksésfəl] 성공적인, 성공한
success[səksés] 성공한 사람; 성공

M Getting a good night's sleep is very important, but many students do not understand the importance. Some students think getting enough sleep is the same as being lazy. If you're lazy, you can't be successful. But if you're sleepy most of the day because you didn't get a good night's sleep, you will never become a success, either.

남 숙면을 충분히 취하는 것은 아주 중요하지만 많은 학생들이 그 중요성을 이해하지 못합니다. 일부 학생들은 충분히 자는 것과 게으른 것이 똑같다고 생각합니다. 만약 여러분이 게으르다면, 성공할 수 없습니다. 하지만 숙면을 충분히 취하지 못해 하루 중 대부분의 시간에 졸리다면 여러분은 역시 성공한 사람이 될 수 없습니다.

11 ②

해설 여자가 공포 영화냐고 묻자 공포 영화가 아닌 실화를 다룬 영화라고 했다.

어휘 pretty[príti] 꽤, 상당히
scary[skέ(:)əri] 무서운
horror movie 공포 영화
be based on ~에 근거를 두고 있다
true story 실화
acting[ǽktiŋ] 연기

M How did you like the movie, Alice?
W In my opinion, it was pretty good, but it was too long.
M I agree. Wasn't it a little scary, too?
W Yes, it was. The movie is not a horror movie, is it?
M No, it's not. The movie is based on a true story.
W I thought the acting was really good.
M It was amazing. It is the best Chinese movie I've ever seen.

남 영화가 마음에 들었니, Alice?
여 내 생각엔 꽤 괜찮았지만 너무 길었어.
남 나도 동의해. 좀 무섭기도 하지 않았니?
여 맞아, 무서웠어. 이 영화가 공포 영화는 아니지, 그렇지?
남 응, 공포 영화는 아니야. 이 영화는 실화를 바탕으로 하고 있어.
여 나는 연기가 정말 좋은 것 같았어.
남 놀라웠어. 내가 여태껏 본 중국 영화 중에서 가장 최고야.

12 ①

해설 남자는 몸이 아파 학교에 못 갔기 때문에 숙제를 확인하기 위해 전화했다.

어휘 put on (옷을) 입다, 착용하다
costume[kástuːm] 복장, 의상
call A back A에게 다시 전화를 하다
miss school 학교를 쉬다

[Telephone rings.]
W Hello.
M Hello. This is Jason, Mike's friend. May I speak to Mike, please?
W He's putting on his costume for the Halloween party.
M Could you tell him to call me back when he's done, ma'am?
W Sure. Are you going to go to the party, too?
M No, I am not. I'm not feeling well.
W I'm sorry to hear that. Did you miss school today?
M Yes, I did, so I wanted to ask Mike about today's homework.

[전화벨이 울린다.]
여 여보세요.
남 여보세요. 저 Mike 친구 Jason인데요. Mike와 통화할 수 있을까요?
여 Mike는 핼러윈 파티 옷을 입는 중이란다.
남 옷을 다 입으면 저에게 다시 전화하라고 전해 주시겠어요?
여 그럴게. 너도 파티에 갈 예정이니?
남 아뇨, 저는 못 가요. 몸이 안 좋거든요.
여 그거 안됐네. 오늘 학교에 결석했니?
남 네, 그래서 Mike에게 오늘 숙제에 대해 물어보려고 했어요.

13 ⑤

해설 8시 30분에 다시 전화하겠다는 남자의 말에 여자는 동의했다.

어휘 in an hour 한 시간 뒤에
almost[ɔ́ːlmoust] 거의
longer than ~보다 긴

[Cell phone rings.]
W Hello.
M Hi, Surin. Is this a good time to talk?
W Sorry, but I'm a little busy now. Can I call you back?
M Sure. When?
W I'll call you back in an hour.
M Okay. That's 7:30, right?
W Oh, I almost forgot. I have a piano lesson at 7:30 this evening.
M Then I'll call you at 8:30. Is that okay?
W That's perfect. I'll talk to you later.

[휴대전화가 울린다.]
여 여보세요.
남 수린아, 안녕. 지금 통화하기 괜찮니?
여 미안하지만, 나 지금 조금 바쁜데. 내가 다시 전화해도 될까?
남 물론이지. 언제?
여 한 시간 뒤에 다시 전화할게.
남 알겠어. 7시 30분이지, 그렇지?
여 아, 하마터면 잊어버릴 뻔했네. 오늘 저녁 7시 30분에 피아노 레슨이 있어.
남 그러면 내가 8시 30분에 전화할게. 그건 괜찮아?
여 그게 좋겠다. 나중에 얘기하자.

14 ③

해설 남자가 여자에게 제한 속도와 실제로 주행한 속도를 일러 준 뒤 운전 면허증 제시를 요구하고 있으므로 두 사람의 관계는 경찰관과 운전자이다.

어휘 go over ~을 초과하다
speed limit 제한 속도
per hour 시간당
run late 늦어지다
driver's license 운전 면허증

M You were going too fast.
W I wasn't going over the speed limit, was I?
M The speed limit on this road is 50 kilometers per hour.
W Oh, I didn't know that. I thought it was 60 kilometers per hour.
M Well, you were driving at 70 kilometers per hour.
W I'm sorry, officer. I was running late for work.
M Can I see your driver's license?
W Here it is, sir.

남 운전자분 너무 빨리 가셨어요..
여 제한 속도를 넘지는 않았죠, 그렇죠?
남 이 도로의 제한 속도는 시속 50킬로미터입니다.
여 아, 몰랐네요. 저는 시속 60킬로미터인 줄 알았어요.
남 음, 운전자분 시속 70킬로미터로 운전하셨어요.
여 죄송합니다, 경찰관님. 제가 회사에 늦었거든요.
남 운전 면허증 좀 볼 수 있을까요?
여 여기 있습니다.

15 ④

해설 다리가 아파 제대로 걸을 수 없는 남자는 여자에게 깨끗한 옷을 가져다 달라고 부탁했다.

어휘 matter[mǽtər] 문제
play against ~를 상대로 경기하다
champion[tʃǽmpiən] (경기의) 챔피언, 우승자
relax[rilǽks] 긴장을 풀다
take a shower 샤워하다

W What's the matter, Paul?
M My legs are too tired. I can't feel them, Mom.
W What happened?
M We had a very long soccer practice today.
W Oh, your soccer team is going to play against last year's champion this Saturday, right?
M That's right. Maybe I should relax with my feet up.
W Before you do that, please go and take a shower.
M Right. Can you bring me clean clothes? I can't walk very well.
W Of course.

여 무슨 문제 있니, Paul?
남 제 다리가 너무 피곤해요. 다리에 감각이 없어요, 엄마.
여 어떻게 된 거니?
남 오늘 축구 연습을 아주 오래 했거든요.
여 아, 이번 토요일에 너희 축구팀이 작년 챔피언을 상대로 시합을 하게 되지?
남 맞아요. 발을 올려놓고 좀 풀어줘야 할 것 같아요.
여 그러기 전에 가서 샤워를 먼저 하렴.
남 알았어요. 깨끗한 옷을 좀 갖다주시겠어요? 제대로 걸을 수가 없어서요.
여 알았어.

16 ③

해설 여자는 가족과 함께 여행을 갈 예정이라서 생일 파티에 갈 수 없다고 했다.

어휘 excited[iksáitid] 신이 난, 흥분한
go on a trip 여행가다

M Next Wednesday is my birthday! I'm so excited.
W Are you going to have a birthday party?
M Yes, it will be this Saturday from 6 to 9 at my house. You should come.
W This Saturday? I'm sorry. I don't think I can come to your party.
M Do you have other plans?
W I'm going to go on a trip with my family. I hope you have fun.

남 다음 주 수요일이 내 생일이야! 나 너무 신나.
여 생일 파티 할 거니?
남 응, 이번 토요일에 우리 집에서 6시부터 9시까지야. 너 와야 해.
여 이번 토요일이라고? 미안해. 네 파티에 못 갈 것 같아.
남 다른 계획이라도 있어?
여 가족과 함께 여행을 가기로 했어. 재밌게 보내길 바랄게.

17 ②

해설 발을 밟아 미안하다고 사과를 하고 괜찮다고 답하는 대화가 적절하다.

어휘 nine-one-one 긴급 전화 번호
(911)

① W Nine-one-one. What's your emergency?
   M Somebody broke into our house.
② W I'm sorry. I stepped on your foot by accident.

① 여 911입니다. 어떤 긴급 상황인가요?
   남 누군가가 우리 집에 침입했어요.
② 여 죄송합니다. 실수로 당신 발을 밟았어요.

emergency [imə́:rdʒənsi] 긴급 (상황)

break into ~에 침입하다

step on ~을 밟다

by accident 실수로, 우연히

hurt [hə:rt] 아프다

not ~ at all 전혀 ~ 아닌

drop [drɑp] 떨어뜨리다

M It's okay. It didn't hurt at all.

③ W Excuse me. I think you <u>dropped this</u>.

M Oh, that's my cell phone. Thank you!

④ W It's too hot in here. Let's open the window.

M I don't think that's a good idea.

⑤ W Is there a <u>subway station</u> near here?

M Yes, there's one right around the corner.

남 괜찮습니다. 전혀 아프지 않았어요.

③ 여 실례합니다. 이것을 떨어뜨리셨어요.

남 아, 제 휴대전화네요. 감사합니다!

④ 여 여기 너무 덥네요. 창문을 좀 열죠.

남 그건 좋은 생각이 아닌 것 같네요.

⑤ 여 근처에 지하철역이 있나요?

남 네, 모퉁이를 돌면 바로 거기에 있어요.

18 ②

해설 창립 시기(1973년), 회원 수(백만 명 이상), 회비(월 30달러), 회원 혜택(훈련실, 수영장, 테니스 코트 이용)에 대해 언급하였지만 위치에 대해서는 언급하지 않았다.

어휘 fitness [fítnis] 신체 단련, 건강

million [míljən] 100만

get to-v ~하게 되다

pool [pu:l] 수영장

take control of ~을 통제하다

W Welcome to Star Fitness! We <u>started our business</u> in 1973, and we have <u>over a million members</u>. Becoming a member is easy. It's $30 <u>a month</u>, and you get to enjoy everything we offer. <u>You can use</u> the training rooms, pools, and tennis courts. Become a member today, and take control of your health!

여 Star Fitness에 오신 것을 환영합니다! 저희는 1973년도에 개업했고 회원 수가 백만 명이 넘습니다. 회원이 되기는 쉽습니다. 한 달에 30달러면 여러분은 저희가 제공하는 모든 것을 누리게 되실 겁니다. 여러분은 트레이닝 룸, 수영장, 테니스 코트를 이용할 수 있습니다. 오늘 회원이 되셔서, 여러분의 건강을 관리하세요.

19 ④

해설 여자가 Michelle이 다시 전화하도록 전달하겠다고 했으므로 이를 수락하거나 거절하는 말이 이어져야 한다.

어휘 lawyer [lɔ́:jər] 변호사

law [lɔ:] 법, 법률

call about ~일로 전화하다

hold [hould] (통화 도중에) 기다리다

for a second 잠시 동안

[Telephone rings.]

W Thank you for calling the Taylor Law Group. This is Terry. How may I help you?

M <u>Can I talk to</u> Michelle, please?

W May I ask <u>who's calling</u>?

M This is Joshua Brown. <u>I'm calling about</u> my car accident.

W Can you <u>hold for a second</u>?

M Sure.

W [Pause] Michelle's in a meeting right now. Can I have her <u>call you back</u> in 10 minutes?

M Sure, my number is 770-568-3316.

[전화벨이 울린다.]

여 Taylor Law Group에 전화 주셔서 감사합니다. 제 이름은 Terry입니다. 무엇을 도와드릴까요?

남 Michelle 좀 바꿔 주시겠어요?

여 전화하시는 분은 누구신가요?

남 저는 Joshua Brown이라고 합니다. 제 자동차 사고 때문에 전화 드립니다.

여 잠깐 기다려 주시겠어요?

남 그럴게요.

여 [잠시 후] Michelle이 지금 다른 직원과 미팅 중인데요. 10분 뒤에 다시 전화 드리라고 해도 될까요?

남 그러세요, 제 전화번호는 770-568-3316입니다.

① 네, 저도 미팅 중입니다.

② 네, 나중에 전화 드릴 수 있어요.

③ 아뇨, 그녀와 통화하고 싶지 않아요.

⑤ 죄송합니다만 제 변호사가 여기에 없네요.

20 ④

해설 남자가 손 씻는 것의 중요성을 강조하고 있으므로 씻으러 가려는 여자에게 구체적으로 손 씻는 방법을 일러주는 말이 이어져야 한다.

어휘 taste[teist] ~한 맛이 나다
get home 집에 도착하다
[선택지]
take a bite 한 입 베어 물다

W This pasta looks really delicious, Dad. Did you cook this?
M Of course, I did. Pasta is very easy to make.
W Let's see if this tastes good, too.
M Wait. Did you wash your hands?
W I did when I got home from school.
M You should always wash your hands before you eat.
W Okay, Dad. I'll be right back.
M Use soap and wash for 30 seconds.

여 이 파스타 정말 맛있어 보여요, 아빠. 아빠가 요리했어요?
남 물론 내가 했지. 파스타는 만들기가 아주 쉽단다.
여 맛도 좋은지 어디 볼게요.
남 기다려. 너 손 씻었니?
여 학교에서 집으로 돌아왔을 때 씻었어요.
남 음식을 먹기 전에는 항상 손을 씻어야 한단다.
여 알겠어요, 아빠. 금방 돌아올게요.
남 비누를 사용해서 30초 동안 씻으렴.

① 다음에는 네가 요리 할 필요 없어.
② 음식이 맛있어. 한 입 먹어 봐.
③ 파스타는 네가 가장 좋아하는 음식이라고 생각했어.
⑤ 너는 적어도 하루에 다섯 번은 먹어야 해.

01 ②	02 ④	03 ④	04 ③	05 ③	06 ①	07 ③
08 ②	09 ⑤	10 ③	11 ④	12 ⑤	13 ③	14 ④
15 ④	16 ③	17 ⑤	18 ②	19 ②	20 ⑤	

01 ②

해설 오늘 저녁에는 비가 온다고 했다.

어휘 expect[ikspékt] 예상하다
plan[plæn] 계획하다
boil[bɔil] 끓다
during[djúəriŋ] ~동안
cool down 시원해지다

W Good morning, and welcome to the weather forecast. It's cloudy outside now, and it's not raining yet. However, we're expecting some rain this evening. If you plan to go out in the evening, take your umbrella with you. It will be boiling hot during the day, but after the rain, it will cool down tonight. That's the weather forecast for today. Have a nice day!

여 안녕하세요. 일기예보를 전해드립니다. 지금 밖은 흐리고 아직 비가 오지 않습니다. 하지만 오늘 저녁에는 비가 올 것으로 예상됩니다. 저녁에 외출할 계획이라면 우산을 가져가세요. 낮에는 찌는 듯이 덥겠지만 비 온 뒤 밤에는 시원해지겠습니다. 오늘의 일기예보였습니다. 좋은 하루 보내세요!

02 ④

해설 긴 바지에 주머니가 2개이고 벨트가 있는 것을 사기로 했다.

어휘 decide on ~으로 정하다
pants[pænts] 바지
pair[pɛər] (바지 등의) 한 벌
shorts[ʃɔːrts] 반바지
change A's mind 생각을 바꾸다
instead[instéd] 대신에

W Have you decided what to buy, Jack?
M Not yet. Can you help me choose a pair?
W Sure. You're looking for shorts for the summer, right?
M No, I changed my mind. I'm going to get pants instead.
W All right. How many pockets do you need?
M Two pockets will be enough.
W How about these ones with a belt? You said you needed a belt, too, right?
M You're right. I'll get those.

여 무엇을 살지 정했니, Jack?
남 아직 못 정했어요. 바지 고르는 것 좀 도와주실래요?
여 좋아. 여름에 입을 반바지를 찾고 있는 거지, 그렇지?
남 아뇨, 생각을 바꿨어요. 대신 긴 바지를 사려고 해요.
여 알겠어. 주머니가 몇 개 있으면 되니?
남 두 개면 충분해요.
여 벨트가 있는 이건 어떠니? 너는 벨트도 필요하다고 했지, 맞니?
남 맞아요. 그걸로 살게요.

03 ④

해설 개최일(4월 13일), 행사 기간(5일), 장소(시립 박물관), 입장료(10달러)에 대해 언급하였으나 행사 내용에 대해서는 언급하지 않았다.

어휘 annual[ǽnjuəl] 연례의, 매년의
almost 거의
be held 열리다, 개최되다
get in 들어가다
share a taxi 택시에 합승하다

W Are you going to the 20th Annual Art Festival this Saturday?
M Yes. It starts on April 13, right? How long is the festival for?
W It'll be for 5 days until the 17th.
M Okay. I'll be there. It'll be held at the City Museum, right?
W Right. We need to pay $10 to get in.
M Should we share a taxi to the City Museum?
W That's a good idea.

여 이번 토요일에 개최되는 20회 연례 예술 축제에 갈 거니?
남 응. 4월 13일에 시작하지, 그렇지? 축제 기간이 얼마 동안이야?
여 17일까지 5일 동안 열릴 거야.
남 알겠어. 거기에 갈 거야. 시립 박물관에서 열리는 것 맞지?
여 맞아. 입장하려면 10달러를 내야 해.
남 시립 박물관까지 같이 택시 탈래?
여 좋은 생각이야.

04 ③

해설 여자는 이모에게 배워서 10살 때부터 테니스를 쳤다.

W What are you planning to do this holiday, Ryan?
M I'm planning to see a baseball game with my

여 이번 공휴일에 뭘 할 계획이니, Ryan?
남 가족과 함께 야구 경기를 보러 갈 계획이야. 내가 가장 좋아하는 스포츠거

어휘 holiday[hálədèi] 공휴일
used to-v (과거에) ~하곤 했다
professional[prəféʃənəl] 직업적인,
전문적인

family. It's my favorite sport.

W That's nice. I like to watch baseball, too.

M Really? Do you like to play baseball, too?

W No, I can only play tennis.

M I didn't know you played tennis. When did you start playing?

W When I was 10. My aunt used to teach me to play. She was a professional tennis player.

든.

여 그거 좋네. 나도 야구 경기 보는 것을 좋아해.

남 정말? 야구를 하는 것도 좋아하니?

여 아니, 나는 테니스만 칠 줄 알아.

남 네가 테니스를 친다는 건 몰랐네. 언제부터 치기 시작했니?

여 열 살 때 시작했어. 이모가 가르쳐 주시곤 했어. 이모는 프로 테니스 선수였거든.

05 ③

해설 안으로 음료를 가져올 수 없으며, 아무것도 만지면 안 되고, 사진을 찍을 때는 플래시 기능을 사용하면 안 된다는 것으로 보아 두 사람이 대화하는 장소는 박물관임을 알 수 있다.

어휘 bottle[bátl] 병
throw away 버리다
garbage can 쓰레기 통
be allowed to-v ~하는 것이 허용되다
flash[flæʃ] (카메라) 플래시
damage[dǽmidʒ] 훼손하다

W Excuse me, sir. You can't bring your bottle of juice inside here.

M Sorry, I'll throw it away right away.

W Please use the garbage can over there.

M Of course. Can I take pictures here?

W Yes, you can. But you're not allowed to touch anything.

M Oh, okay. I'll be careful.

W Also, please don't use a flash when you take pictures. The flash may damage things here.

M All right. Thanks.

여 실례합니다. 주스 병을 이 안으로 가지고 들어오시면 안 됩니다.

남 죄송합니다. 바로 버릴게요.

여 저쪽에 있는 쓰레기통을 이용해주세요.

남 알겠습니다. 여기서 사진을 촬영해도 되나요?

여 네, 됩니다. 하지만 어떤 것도 만지시면 안 됩니다.

남 아, 알겠습니다. 조심할게요.

여 또한, 사진을 찍으실 때 플래시를 사용하시면 안 됩니다. 플래시가 여기에 있는 것들을 훼손시킬 수도 있거든요.

남 알겠습니다. 감사합니다.

06 ①

해설 남자는 프로젝트가 다 끝나면 전화해달라고 당부하고 있다.

어휘 finish[fíniʃ] 끝내다, 완성하다
by[bai] ~까지
come back home 집으로 돌아오다

M Jina, did you clean your room?

W Not yet, but I'll do it later tonight.

M Tonight?

W I have to go to Tony's house. We have to finish our group project by tomorrow.

M What time are you going to come back home?

W I'm not sure. It could be really late.

M All right, but call me when you are done.

남 지나야, 네 방 청소했니?

여 아직 안 했어요, 하지만 이따 밤에 할게요.

남 밤에 한다고?

여 Tony의 집에 가야 해요. 내일까지 그룹 프로젝트를 끝내야 하거든요.

남 집에 몇 시에 올거니?

여 모르겠어요. 많이 늦을 수도 있어요.

남 알았다. 하지만 다 끝나면 전화하렴.

07 ③

해설 여자는 전통적인 한국 문화 중에서도 전통 무용에 대해 발표하기로 했다.

어휘 topic[tápik] 주제, 토픽
presentation[prèzəntéiʃən] 발표
culture[kʌ́ltʃər] 문화
popular[pápulər] 인기 있는
all over the world 전 세계적으로
traditional[trədíʃənəl] 전통적인

M Did you choose the topic for your presentation?

W Yes, I'm going to talk about Korean culture.

M Oh, perfect! K-pop music is getting popular all over the world these days.

W Actually, I decided to introduce something more traditional.

M I see. There are many things to talk about, like traditional food and clothes.

남 발표할 주제를 정했니?

여 응, 한국 문화에 대해 발표할 생각이야.

남 아, 멋지다! 요즘에 K-pop 음악이 전 세계적으로 인기를 얻고 있지.

여 실은, 좀 더 전통적인 것을 소개하려고 해.

남 알겠어. 전통 음식이나 의복처럼 이야기 할 것들이 많지.

clothes[klouðz] 옷

| W | Yes, but I'm going to talk about Korean traditional dance. I saw a video about it, and it was amazing. | 여 | 맞아. 그런데 나는 한국의 전통 무용에 대해 이야기 할 거야. 그것에 대한 동영상을 보았는데 놀라웠거든. |

08 ②

해설 남자는 도서관에 빌린 책들을 반납할 것이라 했다.

어휘 certainly[sə́ːrtnli] 틀림없이, 분명히
almost[ɔ́ːlmoust] 거의
return[ritə́ːrn] 반납하다
had better ~하는 것이 낫다
hurry[hə́ːri] 서두르다

M	Today was such a long day. I had 5 different exams.	남	오늘은 아주 긴 하루였어. 시험이 5개나 있었거든.
W	How did you do on the exams?	여	시험은 다 잘 봤어?
M	I think I did well on all of them. I studied really hard.	남	다 잘 본 것 같아. 정말 열심히 공부했거든.
W	You certainly did. [Pause] You have so many books in your hand. Are they from the library?	여	넌 정말로 열심히 했지. [잠시 후] 손에 책을 많이 들고 있네. 도서관에서 빌린 거야?
M	Yes. I have to return them today.	남	응. 오늘 반납해야 해.
W	Really? You'd better hurry. The library is closing in 30 minutes.	여	정말이니? 서두르는 게 좋아. 도서관이 30분 뒤에 문을 닫거든.
M	Already? I should run.	남	벌써? 뛰어야겠다.

09 ⑤

해설 장소(남부 센터), 일정(6월 15~17일), 참가 인원(150명), 참가 자격(16세 미만)에 대해 언급하였지만 티켓 가격에 대해서는 언급하지 않았다.

어휘 practice[prǽktis] 연습하다
competition[kàmpətíʃən] 대회, 시합
under[ʌ́ndər] ~ 미만의
participate[paːrtísəpèit] 참가하다

W	Junsu, where were you this morning?	여	준수야, 오늘 오전에 어디에 있었니?
M	I was practicing for a swimming competition. So I had to miss my classes.	남	수영 대회를 위해 연습을 했어. 그래서 수업에 빠져야 했어.
W	Is it the one at Nambu Center?	여	남부 센터에서 열리는 대회 말이니?
M	Yes, it's from June 15th to the 17th.	남	응. 6월 15일부터 17일까지 열려.
W	That's the biggest competition in the city, right?	여	시에서 가장 큰 대회지, 그렇지?
M	Yes, there will be 150 swimmers this year.	남	응. 올해 150명의 수영 선수가 참가할 예정이래.
W	Are they all in middle school?	여	모두 중학생들이니?
M	Yes, they have to be under 16 to participate. I have tickets. Would you like to come?	남	맞아. 참가하려면 16세 미만이어야 해. 나에게 티켓이 있는데. 너 오지 않을래?
W	Sure!	여	좋아!

10 ③

해설 자원봉사 활동에 참여하는 방법을 세 단계로 설명하는 안내 방송이다.

어휘 take part in ~에 참여[참가]하다
volunteer[vàləntíər] 자원봉사(자); 자원봉사하다
sign up 가입하다, ~에 등록하다
choose[tʃuːz] 선택하다
activity[æktívəti] 활동
lastly[lǽstli] 마지막으로
hand in 제출하다
form[fɔːrm] 신청 용지

| M | Hello, students! Let me tell you how to take part in volunteer work. First, you should sign up on the school volunteer site. Then you can choose the activity that you want to volunteer for. Lastly, you must hand in a form to your teacher. | 남 | 안녕하세요, 학생 여러분! 자원봉사 활동에 참여하는 법을 알려드리겠습니다. 우선, 학교 봉사 사이트에 가입해야 합니다. 그러면 여러분이 자원봉사하고 싶은 활동을 선택할 수 있습니다. 마지막으로, 여러분은 신청서를 담임 선생님께 제출해야 합니다. |

11 ④

해설 새 음악 선생님은 선생님이 되기
전에 작곡을 했지만 가르치는 일은 이번
이 처음이다.

어휘 over there 저쪽에
hobby[hábi] 취미
friendly[fréndli] 친절한, 상냥한
songwriter[sɔ́(:)ŋràitər] 작곡가, 작사
가

W Mike, do you see the man in the blue shirt over there?

M Yes, that's Mr. Han. He is our new music teacher.

W Really? He's very tall.

M Yes. He said his hobby is playing tennis. He is very friendly, too.

W I see. He looks young. Is this his first teaching job?

M I think so. He used to be a songwriter before he became a teacher.

W Wow, really? I can't wait until his music class.

여 Mike, 저 쪽에 파란 셔츠 입은 남자 보이니?

남 응, 저분은 한 선생님이야. 우리의 새 음악 선생님이지.

여 정말이니? 키가 아주 크시네.

남 맞아. 선생님은 취미가 테니스라고 말씀하셨어. 아주 친절하시기도 해.

여 그렇구나. 젊어 보이시네. 가르치는 일은 처음이시래?

남 그럴 거야. 선생님이 되기 전에 작곡 가셨어.

여 와, 정말? 음악 수업이 너무 기다려진다.

12 ⑤

해설 남자는 스마트폰 사용법을 가르쳐
드리러 할아버지 댁에 갔다.

어휘 winter break 겨울 방학
relaxing[riláeksiŋ] 여유로운, 편안한
go skiing 스키 타러 가다
mostly[móustli] 주로, 대부분
how to-v ~하는 방법
use[juːz] 사용하다

W How was your winter break?

M I had a very relaxing winter break. How was yours?

W I went skiing with my family every weekend.

M Where did you go skiing?

W We went to a few ski resorts, but they were mostly in Gangwon-do.

M Oh, my grandfather lives in Gangwon-do. I visited him 2 weeks ago.

W Was it his birthday?

M No, he didn't know how to use his new smartphone. So I had to show him how.

여 겨울 방학 어떻게 보냈니?

남 아주 여유로운 겨울 방학을 보냈어. 너는 어땠어?

여 나는 주말마다 가족들과 스키를 타러 갔어.

남 어디서 스키를 탔는데?

여 스키 리조트를 몇 군데 갔는데 대부분 강원도에 있었어.

남 아, 우리 할아버지가 강원도에 사시는데. 나는 2주 전에 할아버지를 찾아뵈었어.

여 할아버지의 생신이었니?

남 아니, 할아버지가 스마트폰을 사용할 줄 모르셔. 그래서 사용법을 알려 드려야 했지.

13 ③

해설 여자가 집에 가서 기타를 가져와야
한다고 해서 6시에 만나서 연습하기로
했다.

어휘 until then 그때까지
What's up? 무슨 일인데?
work for (시간 등이) ~에게 편하다. 괜찮
다

M Jane, we have guitar class tonight, right?

W That's right. It begins at 7.

M Do you have anything to do until then?

W Nothing special. What's up?

M I want to practice my guitar before today's class.

W I see. We could meet earlier and practice together.

M Sure, how about 2 hours earlier?

W That's too early. I have to go home and get my guitar.

M I see. Is 6 o'clock okay with you then?

W That works better for me.

남 Jane, 우리 오늘 밤에 기타 수업 있지, 그렇지?

여 맞아. 7시에 시작해.

남 너 그때까지 할 일 있니?

여 특별한 일은 없어. 무슨 일로 그러는데?

남 오늘 수업 전에 기타 연습을 좀 하고 싶거든.

여 그렇구나. 우리가 일찍 만나서 같이 연습할 수는 있어.

남 그래, 두 시간 일찍 가는 게 어떨까?

여 그건 너무 일러. 나는 집에 가서 내 기타를 갖고 와야 하거든.

남 알겠어. 그럼 6시는 괜찮니?

여 그게 나한테 더 낫겠다.

14 ④

[해설] 남자는 여자에게 목적지를 물은 뒤 짐을 트렁크에 넣어 주겠다고 하고 여자는 원하는 목적지와 소요 시간 등을 묻고 있으므로 택시 기사와 승객의 대화임을 알 수 있다.

[어휘] luggage[lʌ́gidʒ] 짐, 수하물
take long 오래 걸리다
at this time of day 이맘때에

M Where would you like to go, ma'am?
W I'm going to the Claremont Hotel on 5th and Broadway.
M Okay. I'll put your luggage in the trunk.
W Thanks. *[Pause]* How long will it take to get there?
M It won't take long at this time of day. About 15 or 20 minutes.
W Good. Is it okay if I open a window?
M Sure. Go ahead.

남 어디로 가십니까, 손님?
여 5번가와 브로드웨이가 만나는 모퉁이에 있는 Claremont 호텔로 가 주세요.
남 알겠습니다. 짐은 트렁크에 넣어 드리겠습니다.
여 고맙습니다. *[잠시 후]* 거기까지 얼마나 걸릴까요?
남 지금 시간에는 그리 오래 걸리지 않을 겁니다. 대략 15분에서 20분 정도입니다.
여 좋아요. 창문 좀 열어도 될까요?
남 물론입니다. 어서 여세요.

15 ④

[해설] 여자는 남자가 케이크를 산 빵집에 가는 방법을 알려달라고 부탁했다.

[어휘] delicious[dilíʃəs] 맛있는
cost[kɔːst] 비용이 들다
walk[wɔːk] 보행 거리
get there (어떤 장소에) 도착하다

W This cake is so delicious. Where did you buy it?
M I bought it at Jaden's Bakery.
W How much did it cost?
M I only paid $15 for it.
W Wow, that's cheaper than I expected. Where's the bakery?
M It's very close. It's only a 5-minute walk from here.
W Really? Can you show me how to get there?
M Of course.

여 이 케이크 정말 맛있다. 이거 어디에서 샀니?
남 Jaden's bakery에서 샀어.
여 가격은 얼마였니?
남 15달러만 내고 샀어.
여 와, 예상했던 것보다 더 저렴하네. 그 빵집은 어디에 있니?
남 아주 가까워. 여기서 걸어서 5분 거리야.
여 정말? 거기에 어떻게 가는지 가르쳐 줄 수 있니?
남 물론이지.

16 ③

[해설] 남자는 지갑을 차에 두고 와서 티셔츠를 구입할 수 없었다.

[어휘] each[iːtʃ] 각각
cash[kæʃ] 현금
credit card 신용 카드
look like ~처럼 보이다
wallet[wálit] 지갑

M Hi, how much are these T-shirts?
W They're $30 each.
M I'll get 2 then.
W Okay. How would you like to pay?
M I'll pay with cash. *[Pause]* Wait. I have only $50 in my pocket.
W I see. We also take credit cards.
M I'm sorry, but it looks like I left my wallet in my car. Can I come back later?
W No problem.

남 안녕하세요, 이 티셔츠 얼마인가요?
여 한 장에 30달러입니다.
남 그럼 두 장 주세요.
여 네. 계산은 어떻게 하시겠어요?
남 현금으로 지불할게요. *[잠시 후]* 주머니에 50달러밖에 없네요.
여 그렇군요. 저희는 신용 카드도 받습니다.
남 죄송하지만, 지갑을 차에 두고 온 것 같네요. 나중에 다시 와도 되나요?
여 물론이죠.

17 ⑤

[해설] 여자가 일행이 몇 명인지 묻고 남자가 아내는 차를 주차하는 중이라고 대답하는 대화가 적절하다.

① W Can I try these on?
   M I'm sorry, but you can't try them on.
② W How much is a haircut?
   M It's $15 for men and $20 for women.

① 여 이것들을 입어 볼 수 있을까요?
   남 죄송하지만, 입어 보실 수 없습니다.
② 여 머리 커트하는 데 얼마죠?
   남 남성은 15달러, 여성은 20달러입

어휘 try on (옷 등을) 입어 보다
haircut[héərkλt] 머리 깎기, 헤어스타일
turn in 제출하다
essay[ései] 과제물, 에세이
party[pá:rti] 일행
park[pɑ:rk] 주차하다

③ W Did you give your essay to your teacher?
   M Yes, I did that yesterday.
④ W How would you like your steak, sir?
   M Well-done, please.
⑤ W How many are in your party?
   M Two. My wife's parking the car.

니다.
③ 여 너 선생님에게 과제물 드렸니?
   남 응, 어제 드렸어.
④ 여 스테이크를 어떻게 해 드릴까요,
      손님?
   남 완전히 익혀 주세요.
⑤ 여 일행이 몇 명인가요?
   남 둘입니다. 제 아내는 주차 중이에요.

18 ②

해설 요일(매주 목요일), 시간(오전 10시
~12시), 장소(서점), 장소 이용 수칙(음식,
음료 반입 금지)에 대해 언급하였으나 책
제목에 대해서는 언급하지 않았다.

어휘 get together 모이다
novel[nάvəl] 소설
owner[óunər] 주인, 소유자
for free 무료로
careful[kέərfəl] 주의하는, 조심하는

W Hello, everyone! My name is Irene Smith, the leader of the Reading Club. Every Thursday, we'll get together and talk about one novel. It'll take 2 hours from 10 a.m. to noon. The owner of this bookstore is letting us use this meeting room for free, so we have to keep it clean. Please do not bring any food or drinks to meetings.

여 안녕하세요, 여러분! 제 이름은 Irene Smith이고, Reading Club의 모임장입니다. 우리는 매주 목요일에 모여서 소설 한 편을 가지고 토론할 거예요. 오전 10시부터 정오까지 두 시간이 걸릴 겁니다. 이 서점의 주인분이 우리가 무료로 이 회의실을 쓰도록 허락해 주셨으니 깨끗하게 사용해야 합니다. 모임에 음식이나 음료를 가지고 오지 마세요.

19 ②

해설 시청에 같이 가겠다는 여자의 말에
이어서 언제 갈 예정인지 응답하는 것이
적절하다.

어휘 town[taun] 도시
host[houst] 주최하다
volunteer[vὰləntíər] 자원하다, 지원
하다
take part in ~에 참여하다

M Did you hear about the National Sports Festival?
W No, I didn't. What about it?
M I just heard our town will host the festival this year.
W Really? That's great news!
M Yes. So I'm going to volunteer to help during the festival.
W That sounds like fun. What kind of work are you going to do?
M I'm not sure. I'm going to go to the city hall and ask some questions about it.
W I want to take part in it, too. I will go there with you.
M Great. I'm going to go there tomorrow.

남 전국체전에 관해 들었니?
여 아니, 못 들었어. 그거에 대해서 어떤 거?
남 우리 도시가 올해 전국체전을 주최한다고 방금 들었어.
여 정말? 그거 좋은 소식이네!
남 그래. 그래서 난 축제 동안 돕기 위해 자원하려고.
여 그거 재미있겠다. 어떤 일을 하게 되는데?
남 잘 모르겠어. 시청에 가서 몇 가지 물어볼거야.
여 나도 참여하고 싶어. 너랑 같이 갈게.
남 좋아. 난 내일 갈 거야.

① 넌 거리를 청소해야 할 거야.
③ 물론이지. 그것에 대해 시청에 전화해야 해.
④ 축제는 이번 9월에 열릴 거야.
⑤ 경기를 보려면 10달러를 내야 해.

20 ⑤

해설 글을 읽을 때 모르는 단어를 추측
해서 해결하는 것이 더 좋지만 그것이 안
될 때는 사전을 찾아보라고 조언하는 말
이 이어지면 적절하다.

M Are you busy, Mom?
W No, I'm not. What is it, Harry?
M I'm trying to do my homework, but I don't know or understand many words here.

남 바쁘세요, 엄마?
여 아니, 바쁘지 않아. 무슨 일인데, Harry?
남 숙제를 하려는 데요, 모르거나 이해가

어휘 try[trai] 시도하다
article[áːrtikl] (신문 등의) 기사
ancient[éinʃənt] 고대의
guess[ges] 추측하다
meaning[míːniŋ] 의미
[선택지]
modern[mádərn] 현대의, 근대의
look A up (사전에서) A를 찾아보다
dictionary[díkʃənèri] 사전
exercise[éksərsàiz] 운동하다
more often 더 자주

W Let me see. *[Pause]* You're reading an article about ancient history.
M Yes, what should I do?
W You should first try to guess the meanings of the words.
M Okay. Then, what do I do next?
W You should look them up in the dictionary.

안 되는 단어가 많아서요.
여 어디 보자. *[잠시 후]* 네가 고대사에 대한 기사를 읽고 있어서 그렇구나.
남 그럼, 어떻게 해야 해요?
여 우선 모르는 단어의 의미를 추측하려 고 해 봐.
남 알겠어요. 의미가 추측이 안 되면 어 떻게 해야 하죠?
여 사전에서 그 단어들을 찾아봐야지.

① 너는 현대사를 공부하는 것이 낫겠어.
② 너는 운동을 더 자주 해야 해.
③ 네가 숙제를 하는 동안 나는 요리를 할 게.
④ 미안한데 지금은 정말 바쁘단다.

01 ④	02 ④	03 ④	04 ③	05 ④	06 ②	07 ④
08 ①	09 ④	10 ①	11 ⑤	12 ⑤	13 ③	14 ②
15 ③	16 ④	17 ②	18 ③	19 ④	20 ④	

01 ④

해설 뉴욕은 흐리지만 비는 오지 않을 것이라고 했다.

어휘 as usual 늘 그렇듯이
chance[tʃæns] 가능성
a few 약간의, 몇
shower[ʃáuər] 소나기

M Good morning, America! As usual, it'll be sunny in Los Angeles, but it'll be very windy in San Francisco. There is a high chance of rain in Atlanta, and there will be a few showers in Dallas. It will be very cloudy in New York, but no rain is expected.

남 좋은 아침입니다, 미국! 늘 그렇듯이 로스앤젤레스는 맑겠지만 샌프란시스코는 바람이 많이 불 것입니다. 애틀랜타에는 비가 올 가능성이 높고, 댈러스에는 몇 차례 소나기가 내릴 것입니다. 뉴욕은 매우 흐리겠지만 비는 오지 않을 것으로 예상됩니다.

02 ④

해설 여자는 농구공이 그려진 발목 낮은 농구화를 사겠다고 했다.

어휘 basketball shoes 농구화
myself[maisélf] 나 자신
protect[prətékt] 보호하다
ankle[æ̃ŋkl] 발목
tennis shoes 테니스화
kind[kaind] 종류
instead of ~ 대신에

M Can I help you find anything?
W Yes, I'm looking for basketball shoes for myself.
M Okay, how about these? These are really good for protecting your ankles.
W I actually prefer low basketball shoes, the ones that look like tennis shoes.
M Sure, we have 2 kinds of low basketball shoes. How do you like these?
W Oh, these have the number 23 on them. Can you also show me the other kind?
M Sure, instead of the number 23, these have a basketball on them.
W Okay, I'll take these. I don't like the number 23.

남 찾으시는 게 있나요?
여 네, 제가 신을 농구화를 사려고요.
남 알겠습니다. 이건 어떠세요? 발목을 보호하는 데 아주 좋아요.
여 사실 저는 테니스화처럼 보이는 발목 낮은 농구화가 좋아요.
남 네, 낮은 농구화도 두 가지 종류가 있습니다. 이것들은 어떠세요?
여 아, 여기에는 숫자 23이 적혀 있네요. 다른 종류도 보여주실래요?
남 그러죠, 이건 숫자 23 대신 농구공이 그려져 있습니다.
여 좋아요, 이걸로 할게요. 23이라는 숫자를 별로 좋아하지 않거든요.

03 ④

해설 이름(Manhattan Night), 가격(30달러), 크기(200g), 굽기 정도(중간 굽기)에 대해 언급하였지만 부위에 대해서는 언급하지 않았다.

어휘 decide[disáid] 결정하다
choose[tʃuːz] 고르다
medium[míːdiəm] (스테이크가) 중간 정도로 구워진

W What are you going to have?
M There are so many things to choose from.
W Well, why don't you try a steak here? [Pause] How about Manhattan Night?
M Manhattan Night? Is that the name of the steak?
W Yes, it is, and it's $30.
M I see. How big is the steak?
W The menu says it's about 200 grams.
M Okay. I'll take it.
W All right. Let's order now. [Pause] Oh, how do you want your steak?
M Medium, please.

여 너 뭐 먹을 거야?
남 선택할 게 너무 많아.
여 음, 여기서 스테이크를 먹어보는 게 어때? [잠시 후] Manhattan Night는 어떨까?
남 Manhattan Night? 그게 스테이크 이름이야?
여 응, 맞아. 그리고 그건 30달러야.
남 그렇구나. 그 스테이크는 얼마나 크니?
여 메뉴판에는 약 200그램이라고 나와 있네.
남 좋았어. 나는 그걸로 할게.
여 알았어. 지금 주문하자. [잠시 후] 아, 스테이크 굽기 정도는 어떻게 하면 될까?
남 중간 정도로 해 줘.

04 ③

해설 여자는 여행 마지막 날에 친구들에게 줄 엽서를 썼다고 했다.

어휘 fantastic[fæntǽstik] 환상적인, 멋진
peaceful[píːsfəl] 평화로운
hiking[háikiŋ] 하이킹, 도보여행
except[iksépt] ~을 제외하고
last[læst] 마지막의
hot spring 온천
relax[rilǽks] 휴식을 취하다, 쉬다
postcard[póustkɑ̀rd] 엽서

M How was your trip, Janet?
W It was fantastic. The mountain was so peaceful.
M Did you do a lot of hiking?
W I went hiking every day except the last day.
M Did you go to the hot spring and relax on the last day?
W No, I don't like hot springs.
M What did you do then?
W I wrote postcards to my friends. Here's yours.

남 Janet, 여행은 어땠어?
여 환상적이었어. 산은 너무나 평화로웠고
남 하이킹 많이 했어?
여 마지막 날은 빼고 매일 했어.
남 마지막 날에는 온천에 가서 쉬었니?
여 아니, 난 온천을 싫어해.
남 그럼 뭘 했는데?
여 나는 친구들에게 줄 엽서를 썼어. 이건 네 거야.

05 ④

해설 여자가 지도나 지하철 노선도 등 관광객을 위한 다양한 정보를 구하는 것으로 보아 관광안내소에서 나누는 대화임을 알 수 있다.

어휘 subway system 지하철
helpful[hélpfəl] 유용한, 도움이 되는
get around 돌아다니다
coupon[kúːpan] 쿠폰
attraction[ətrǽkʃən] 명소

M Hello, how can I help you?
W Hi. Can I get a map of the city?
M Do you want a map in English?
W Yes, please. Can I also get a map of the subway system?
M Of course. Here you are.
W Thank you. This will be very helpful to get around the city.
M We also have some coupons for restaurants and tourist attractions. Would you like some?
W Yes, please.

남 안녕하세요, 어떻게 도와드릴까요?
여 안녕하세요. 도시 지도를 좀 얻을 수 있을까요?
남 영어로 된 지도를 원하세요?
여 네. 지하철 노선도도 구할 수 있을까요?
남 물론이죠. 여기 있어요.
여 고맙습니다. 도시를 둘러볼 때 아주 유용하겠어요.
남 식당과 관광지를 위한 쿠폰도 있어요. 좀 드릴까요?
여 네, 주세요.

06 ②

해설 두 사람 다 수학 문제를 풀지 못하자 남자가 수학을 잘하는 Mike에게 물어보라고 제안하고 있다.

어휘 do A a favor ~의 부탁을 들어주다
solve[salv] (문제를) 풀다
give it a try 시도하다, 한번 해보다
correct[kərékt] 맞는, 정확한

W Can you do me a favor, James?
M Of course, what is it?
W Can you show me how to solve this question? I know what the answer is, but I don't understand why.
M I'll give it a try. [Pause] This question is not easy at all.
W No, it's not. So, what did you get?
M I think the answer is 1,250. Is that correct?
W No, it's not. The answer is 1,150. I don't understand why.
M Well, why don't you ask Mike? He's really good at math.

여 부탁 하나 들어줄래, James?
남 물론이지, 뭔데?
여 이 문제를 푸는 방법을 가르쳐 줄 수 있니? 정답은 아는데, 왜 정답인지 모르겠어.
남 내가 한번 풀어 볼게. [잠시 후] 이 문제는 전혀 쉽지 않네.
여 그래, 쉽지 않아. 그래서 답이 얼마 나왔니?
남 1,250인 것 같은데. 맞니?
여 아니, 그렇지 않아. 정답은 1,150이야. 왜 그런지 모르겠어.
남 음, Mike에게 물어보는 게 어떨까? 걔 수학 정말 잘하거든.

07 ④

해설 여름휴가 계획으로 남자가 여수를 추천했고 여자는 가고 싶었던 곳이라고 하며 여수로 여행 갈 계획을 짜겠다고 했다.

어휘 somewhere[sʌ́mhwɛ̀ər] 어딘가에
amazing[əméiziŋ] 놀라운, 멋진

M	Do you have any plans for your summer vacation, Sujeong?
W	Not yet. But I really want to go somewhere this summer.
M	Have you been to Gyeongju? It's a beautiful place.
W	I actually went to Gyeongju and Busan last summer.
M	I see. Yeosu is a good place to visit in summer. I went there last summer, and it was amazing.
W	Oh, I've always wanted to go to Yeosu. I should start planning a trip there.

남 수정아, 너 여름휴가 계획 있어?
여 아직 없어. 하지만 이번 여름에는 어딘가로 꼭 가고 싶어.
남 경주에 가 봤니? 거긴 아름다운 곳이야.
여 나는 사실 지난여름에 경주와 부산에 갔었어.
남 그렇구나. 여수는 여름에 방문하기 좋은 곳이야. 나는 지난여름에 갔었는데, 정말 놀라웠어.
여 아, 난 항상 여수에 가고 싶었어. 거기로 여행 갈 계획을 짜야겠다.

08 ①

해설 남자는 전화기를 학교에서 잃어버린 것 같다고 하며 학교에 가서 확인해 보겠다고 했다.

어휘 backpack[bǽkpæ̀k] 책가방
either[íːðər] ~도 역시, 또한
lost and found 분실물 보관소

W	What are you looking for, Bill?
M	I'm looking for my phone, Mom.
W	Did you check your backpack?
M	Yes, but it's not in my backpack. I'll check my room.
W	[Pause] Did you find it?
M	No, it's not here, either. I think I lost it at school.
W	You should go back to school and see if it's in the lost and found.
M	Yes. I'll go back there right now.

여 Bill, 뭘 찾고 있니?
남 제 전화기를 찾고 있어요, 엄마.
여 네 책가방은 확인했니?
남 네, 그런데 책가방에는 없어요. 제 방을 확인해 볼게요.
여 [잠시 후] 찾았니?
남 아뇨, 여기에도 없어요. 학교에서 잃어버린 것 같아요.
여 학교로 돌아가서 분실물 보관소에 있는지 알아보는 게 좋겠다.
남 네. 지금 바로 돌아가서 확인해 볼게요.

09 ④

해설 위치(시청 근처), 이름(Mall of California), 영업시간(오전 10시~오후 8시), 근처 상점(스포츠 상점)에 대해 언급하였으나 할인 품목에 대해서는 언급하지 않았다.

어휘 city hall 시청
business hours 영업시간
a sports shop 스포츠 용품점
soccer shoes 축구화
across from ~의 건너편에

W	Have you been to the new mall near the city hall?
M	You mean the Mall of California? I went there last week.
W	I'm going with my mom later today. Do you know the business hours?
M	I think it's open from 10 a.m. to 8 p.m. But there are no sports shops.
W	Really? I wanted to get new soccer shoes.
M	There is a big sports shop across from the mall. You should go there instead.

여 시청 근처에 새로 생긴 쇼핑몰에 가 봤니?
남 California 몰을 말하는 거니? 나는 지난주에 그곳에 갔었어.
여 난 오늘 늦게 엄마랑 가려고 해. 영업시간을 알고 있니?
남 오전 10시부터 오후 8시까지 영업하는 것 같아. 하지만 스포츠 상점은 없어.
여 그래? 나는 새 축구화를 사고 싶었는데.
남 쇼핑몰 건너편에 큰 스포츠 상점이 있어. 너는 대신 그곳에 가는 게 좋겠다.

10 ①

해설 남자는 감기를 예방하는 방법에 대해 소개하고 있다.

어휘 winter break 겨울방학
healthy[hélθi] 건강한
avoid[əvɔ́id] 피하다
exercise[éksərsàiz] 운동
fit[fit] 건강한
importantly[impɔ́ːrtəntli] 중요하게
as often as possible 가능한 한 자주

M Winter break starts tomorrow. I want you to stay healthy until I see you again. So I'll tell you how to avoid a cold. First, drink a lot of water. Second, eat well and sleep well. Exercise is a great way to stay fit and healthy, too. Most importantly, you need to wash your hands as often as possible.

남 내일부터 겨울방학이 시작됩니다. 여러분들을 다시 볼 때까지 건강했으면 좋겠어요. 그러니 감기에 걸리지 않는 방법을 알려줄게요. 먼저, 물을 많이 마십니다. 두 번째로, 잘 먹고 잘 자야 해요. 운동은 좋은 체격과 건강 또한 유지하는 데 좋은 방법이기도 합니다. 가장 중요한 것은, 가능한 한 자주 손을 씻어야 합니다.

11 ⑤

해설 Sleep Kingdom에 거대한 주차장이 있다고 했다.

어휘 mattress[mǽtris] 매트리스
kingdom[kíŋdəm] 왕국
be in business 영업을 하고 있다
public[pʌ́blik] 공공의
huge[hjuːdʒ] 거대한
parking lot 주차장

M Are you having sleep problems? Then you need a new mattress from Sleep Kingdom. We've been in business for over 30 years, and we're having our spring sale this weekend. We are near the public library, and we have a huge parking lot.

남 수면 장애가 있으신가요? 그렇다면 Sleep Kingdom에서 새 매트리스가 필요하시네요. 저희는 30년 넘게 사업을 해 왔으며, 이번 주말에 봄 세일을 할 예정입니다. 저희는 공공 도서관 근처에 있고, 거대한 주차장도 구비하고 있습니다.

12 ⑤

해설 남자는 전문 요리사이며 김치 담그는 법을 배우려고 한국에 왔다고 했다.

어휘 visit[vízit] 방문; 방문하다
used to-v (과거에) ~하곤 했다
professional[prəféʃənəl] 전문적인
chef[ʃef] 요리사

W Is this your first visit to Korea, Mr. Jensen?
M This is my first time, but my wife used to live here for a few years.
W Really? Where is she now?
M She went to visit the school she used to work at.
W Was she a teacher?
M Yes, she taught English at a high school about 6 years ago.
W Are you going to teach English, too?
M No, I came to learn how to make kimchi. I'm a professional chef.

여 Jensen 씨, 한국에 처음 오셨나요?
남 저는 이번이 처음인데, 아내는 몇 년 동안 이곳에 산 적이 있어요.
여 정말요? 지금 아내 분은 어디 계세요?
남 아내가 전에 일했었던 학교에 찾아갔어요.
여 그녀는 선생님이었나요?
남 네, 대략 6년 전에 고등학교에서 영어를 가르쳤어요.
여 당신도 영어를 가르칠 건가요?
남 아니요, 저는 김치 만드는 법을 배우러 왔어요. 저는 전문 요리사예요.

13 ③

해설 여자는 30% 할인이 적용된 큰 머그잔을 14달러에 샀다.

어휘 mug[mʌg] 머그잔
lid[lid] 뚜껑
discount[dískaunt] 할인

M Will this be all, ma'am?
W Yes, it is. This mug is $7, right?
M Let me check for you. [Pause] It's actually $10.
W Really? The sign said the mugs were 30 percent off.

남 이게 전부입니까, 손님?
여 네, 그래요. 이 머그잔은 7달러이죠, 맞나요?
남 확인해 드릴게요. [잠시 후] 그건 실은 10달러입니다.
여 정말요? 표시에는 머그잔이 30퍼센트 할인된다고 쓰여 있는데요.

M	Oh, that sign is for the large mug with a lid. Large mugs are $20 each.	남	아, 그 표시는 뚜껑 달린 큰 머그잔에 해당됩니다. 큰 머그 잔은 각 20달러입니다.
W	With the discount, the large mug is $14, right?	여	할인해서 큰 머그잔이 14달러라는 거네요, 그렇죠?
M	Yes, you're right.	남	네, 맞습니다.
W	Then I'll get a large one instead.	여	그렇다면 대신 큰 것으로 살게요.

14 ②

해설 숙제를 안 하는 남자의 아들을 걱정하고 있는 여자에게 남자가 죄송하다며 숙제를 끝내도록 하겠다는 대화로 보아 두 사람의 관계는 교사와 학부모임을 알 수 있다.

어휘 grade[greid] 성적
do well at school 성적이 좋다
rarely[réərli] 좀처럼 ~하지 않는
complete[kəmplí:t] 끝마치다
make sure 확실히 하다
improve[imprú:v] 향상되다, 나아지다

W	Thank you for coming in, Mr. Carpenter.	여	갑작스러운 요청에도 와주셔서 감사합니다, Carpenter 씨.
M	Thank you for taking the time to meet with me, Mrs. Brown.	남	시간을 내어 저를 만나주셔서 감사합니다, Brown 선생님.
W	I just wanted to talk to you about Paul's grades this year.	여	Paul의 올해 성적에 대해 말씀드리려고 합니다.
M	I understand. He's not doing well at school.	남	알고 있습니다. 학교 성적이 좋지 않지요.
W	I'm a little worried about him because he rarely completes his homework.	여	Paul이 좀처럼 숙제를 하지 않아서 조금 걱정됩니다.
M	I'm sorry, Mrs. Brown. I'll make sure that he finishes his homework every night.	남	죄송합니다, Brown 선생님. 그 애가 매일 밤 숙제를 끝내도록 하겠습니다.
W	If he just completes his homework, his grades will improve.	여	그 애가 숙제만 잘한다면, 성적이 올라갈 거예요.

15 ③

해설 체육복을 가져오지 않아서 곤란해 하던 여자는 남자에게 여분의 체육복이 있다고 하자 빌려달라고 부탁했다.

어휘 matter[mǽtər] 문제, 일
gym class 체육 수업
gym clothes 체육복
strict[strikt] 엄격한
extra[ékstrə] 여분의
locker[lákər] 사물함
be right back 다시 돌아오다

W	Oh no! What am I going to do?	여	이런! 어떡하지?
M	What's the matter, Lindsey?	남	무슨 일이야, Lindsey?
W	I have gym class right after lunch, but I forgot to bring my gym clothes.	여	점심 후에 바로 체육 수업이 있는데 체육복을 가져오는 걸 깜빡했어.
M	That's not good. Mr. Brock is strict about wearing gym clothes.	남	저런. Brock 선생님은 체육복을 입는 것에 대해 엄격하잖아.
W	I know. Do you have gym class today?	여	맞아. 너 오늘 체육 수업 있니?
M	I had it in the morning. Oh, I think I have extra clothes in my locker.	남	오전에 있었어. 아, 내 사물함에 체육복이 하나 더 있을 것 같아.
W	Can I borrow them?	여	그것 좀 빌려줄래?
M	Sure. I'll be right back.	남	그래. 금방 가지고 돌아올게.

16 ④

해설 봄방학 동안 남자는 가족과 함께 제주도에 갔고 여자는 심한 감기에 걸려서 방안에만 있었다.

어휘 spring break 봄방학
anywhere[énihwèər] 어디에도, 아무데도
entire[intáiər] 전체의
catch a cold 감기에 걸리다
terrible[térəbl] 심한
stay in (밖으로) 나가지 않다[집에 있다]

W	Did you have a good spring break, David?	여	봄방학은 잘 보냈니, David?
M	Yes, I had a fantastic break. I went to Jeju-do with my family. How about you? What did you do for the week?	남	응, 정말 멋진 방학을 보냈어. 가족과 함께 제주도에 갔거든. 넌 어때? 일주일 동안 뭐 했어?
W	I couldn't go anywhere. I just stayed at home during the entire spring break.	여	난 아무 데도 갈 수 없었어. 봄방학 내내 집에 있었어.
M	Why couldn't you go anywhere?	남	왜 아무 데도 못 갔니?
W	I caught a terrible cold, so I stayed in my room.	여	감기가 심하게 걸려서 방에만 있었어.
M	Are you better now?	남	지금은 괜찮아졌니?
W	Yes, I'm much better now.	여	응, 지금은 훨씬 나아졌어.

17 ②

해설 무거운 박스를 들고 가는 여자에게 남자가 도와주겠다고 하는 대화가 적절하다.

어휘 weigh[wei] 무게가 ~이다
need a hand 도움이 필요하다
address[ədrés] 주소
move to ~로 이사하다
wrong[rɔ(ː)ŋ] 잘못된

① M How much do you weigh?
  W I weigh about 50 kilograms.
② M Do you need a hand, ma'am?
  W Thank you. This is too heavy for me.
③ M I want to send this box to Korea.
  W Please write the address on the box.
④ M When did you move to New York?
  W I moved here 2 months ago.
⑤ M I didn't order any pizza.
  W I'm sorry. I have the wrong house.

① 남 너는 몸무게가 얼마니?
  여 내 몸무게는 한 50Kg쯤 돼.
② 남 도와드릴까요, 부인?
  여 고마워요. 이건 저에게 너무 무겁네요.
③ 남 이 상자를 한국으로 보내고 싶어요.
  여 상자에 주소를 써 주세요.
④ 남 언제 뉴욕으로 이사 오셨어요?
  여 두 달 전에 여기로 이사 왔어요.
⑤ 남 저는 피자를 주문하지 않았어요.
  여 미안합니다. 집을 잘못 찾았어요.

18 ③

해설 모델명(Milky Way IV), 제조업체(삼정사), 크기(이전 버전과 동일), 요금제(월 30달러)에 대해 언급하였지만 색깔에 대해서는 언급하지 않았다.

어휘 latest[léitist] 최신의, 최근의
company[kʌ́mpəni] 회사
screen[skriːn] 스크린, 화면
last[læst] 지난, 가장 최근의
version[və́ːrʒən] 버전, 판
monthly plan 월 요금제

W Do you watch movies a lot on your cell phone? Then Milky Way IV is the perfect one for you. It is the latest model from Samjeong company. It is lighter and has a bigger screen than the last version. But it is the same size! The monthly plan starts at $30.

여 휴대전화로 영화를 많이 보시나요? 그렇다면 Milky Way IV가 당신에게 아주 딱 맞습니다. 이것은 삼정사에서 나온 최신 모델입니다. 지난 버전보다 가볍고 화면도 더 큽니다. 하지만 크기는 같습니다! 월 요금제는 월 30달러부터 시작됩니다.

19 ④

해설 여행을 떠나는 남자가 무엇을 사 올 지 묻는 말에 대한 응답이므로 사 올지 여부와 함께 당부의 말이 와야 적절하다.

어휘 airport[ɛ́ərpɔ̀ːrt] 공항
get on 탑승하다
excited[iksáitid] 신이 난
exciting[iksáitiŋ] 흥미로운
dangerous[déindʒərəs] 위험한
careful[kɛ́ərfəl] 조심하는
bring[briŋ] 가져오다
[선택지]
take A back A를 데려다주다

[Telephone rings.]
W Hello.
M Hello, Mom. I'm calling from the airport.
W Are you on the airplane?
M No, I'll get on the plane in 5 minutes.
W Is your friend Matthew there with you?
M Yes, he's here. He said he couldn't sleep last night because he was so excited.
W Europe is an exciting place, but don't do anything dangerous. All right?
M Yes, Mom. We'll be careful. Do you want me to bring anything back for you?
W Don't worry about it. Just have fun.

[전화벨이 울린다.]
여 여보세요.
남 저예요, 엄마. 공항에서 전화하는 거예요.
여 너 비행기 탔니?
남 아뇨, 탑승은 5분 후에 시작될 거예요.
여 네 친구 Matthew도 거기 있니?
남 네, 여기 있어요. 걔는 너무 신이 나서 어젯밤에 잠을 잘 수 없었대요.
여 유럽은 확실히 흥미로운 곳이지만, 위험한 일은 하지 마라. 알겠지?
남 네, 엄마. 저희는 조심할게요. 돌아올 때 뭐 사다드릴까요?
여 그건 걱정하지 마. 그냥 재밌게 놀아.

① 그래, 나도 너만큼 신이 나네.
② 응, 공항까지 다시 데려다줄게.
③ 그래, 5분 후에 다시 전화할게.
⑤ 아니, 하지만 Matthew의 어머니와 얘기해 볼게.

20 ④

해설 짠 음식을 별로 좋아하지 않는 여자에게 남자가 가장 좋아하는 음식이 무엇이냐고 물었으므로 이어질 응답으로 짠 음식이 아닌 것을 좋아한다는 말이 와야 적절하다.

어휘 salty[sɔ́:lti] 짠, 짭짤한
huge fan 열혈 팬
[선택지]
eat out 외식하다
try[trai] (음식을) 맛보다

M Have you been to the new Chinese restaurant on 6th Street?
W Yes, I have. My dad and I had dinner there last Saturday.
M How was the food? I've never been there.
W My dad loved it, but I thought it was too salty.
M Chinese food is a bit salty, isn't it?
W That's why I'm not a huge fan of Chinese food.
M What is your favorite food?
W I like anything but salty food.

남 6번가에 새로 생긴 중국 식당에 가 봤니?
여 응, 가 봤어. 아빠랑 지난 토요일에 그곳에서 저녁을 먹었거든.
남 음식은 어땠어? 나는 그곳에 가 본 적이 없어.
여 아빠는 좋아했는데, 나는 너무 짠 것 같았어.
남 중국 음식은 좀 짠 편이지?
여 그래서 내가 중국 음식을 별로 좋아하지 않는 거야.
남 네가 가장 좋아하는 음식은 뭐니?
여 난 짠 음식 말고는 다 좋아해.

① 나는 외식을 절대 하지 않아.
② 나는 중국 식당을 좋아해.
③ 내가 가장 좋아하는 날은 토요일이다.
⑤ 너도 그 식당에 가 봐야 해.

01 ③

해설 수요일에는 바람이 강하게 불면서 추울 거라고 했다.

어휘 weekly[wíːkli] 주간의
partly[páːrtli] 부분적으로
be likely to-v ~할 가능성이 많다

M Good morning. Here's your weekly weather report. From Monday to Tuesday, we'll have partly cloudy and warm weather. But it's going to be cold with strong winds on Wednesday. It's very likely to rain on Thursday. On Friday, it will be very cold and rainy all day long.

남 안녕하세요. 주간 일기예보 전해드립니다. 월요일부터 화요일까지는 부분적으로 흐리고 따뜻한 날씨가 이어지겠습니다. 그러나 수요일에는 강한 바람이 불면서 춥겠습니다. 목요일에는 비가 올 가능성이 매우 높습니다. 금요일은 매우 춥고 하루 종일 비가 올 것입니다.

02 ③

해설 여자가 남자에게 준 부채에는 무지개가 그려져 있고 아래에 Cool이라고 쓰여 있다.

어휘 hot[hɑt] 더운
handle[hǽndl] 손잡이
convenient[kənvíːnjənt] 편리한
rainbow[réinbòu] 무지개
space[speis] 공간
writing[ráitiŋ] 글자, 글씨

M It's getting hot out there.
W I made this fan for you. Do you like it?
M I love it. I really like the long handle.
W Yes. Long handles are more convenient than short ones. What do you think of the picture?
M It's great. Did you draw the rainbow on it?
W I did. And there was enough space to add writing, so I wrote "COOL" under it.
M I love it. I'll carry it with me all the time.

남 밖이 점점 더워지고 있어.
여 내가 널 위해 이 부채를 만들었어. 마음에 드니?
남 너무 맘에 들어. 긴 손잡이가 정말 좋다.
여 그래. 긴 손잡이가 짧은 손잡이보다 더 편리하지. 그 그림은 어때?
남 멋지다. 그 위에 무지개를 그린 거니?
여 맞아. 그리고 글자를 쓸 수 있는 공간이 충분해서 그 밑에 'Cool'이라고 썼어.
남 아주 맘에 들어. 항상 가지고 다닐게.

03 ①

해설 가격(300달러), 색상(검정색), 무게(무겁지 않음), 구입 장소(Jackie's 가게)에 대해 언급하였지만 제조사에 대해서는 언급하지 않았다.

어휘 vacuum cleaner 진공청소기
price[prais] 가격
heavy[hévi] 무거운
whole[houl] 전체의, 모든

M Did you get your new vacuum cleaner?
W Yes, I finally did. I bought one at Jackie's Store.
M Is that the store next to the subway station?
W Yes. Vacuum cleaners were on sale there last weekend. I bought mine for $300.
M That's a good price. What color did you get?
W I bought a black one. It works really well, and it's not heavy at all.
M I should buy one there, too.

남 진공청소기 새로 샀어?
여 응, 드디어 샀어. Jackie's 가게에서 하나 구매했어.
남 지하철역 옆에 있는 가게 말이지?
여 응. 지난 주말에 그곳에서 청소기를 세일했어. 내건 300달러에 샀어.
남 좋은 가격이네. 무슨 색으로 샀니?
여 검정색을 샀어. 작동이 정말 잘 되고, 전혀 무겁지 않아.
남 나도 그곳에서 하나 사야겠어.

04 ②

해설 여자는 어제 이사를 앞두고 가구를 옮기고 집 청소를 했다고 했다.

M Cindy, why didn't you answer your phone yesterday?
W Yesterday? Oh, I was helping my mom with

남 Cindy, 어제 왜 전화를 안 받았니?
여 어제? 아, 엄마 짐 싸는 거 돕고 있었어.

어휘 pack[pæk] 짐을 싸다
move[muːv] 이사하다
apartment[əpáːrtmənt] 아파트
nearby[nìərbái] 가까운
furniture[fɔ́ːrnitʃər] 가구

packing.
M Packing? Are you going to move?
W Yes, I'm going to move <u>next weekend</u>. Didn't I tell you this?
M No, I didn't know that.
W Oh, it's not far. <u>Just to another</u> apartment nearby.
M I see. So did you pack a lot?
W Oh, my mom did most of it. <u>My dad and I moved</u> the furniture and cleaned the house.

남 짐을 싸? 너 이사 가니?
여 그래, 다음 주말에 이사 갈 거야. 너한테 말 안 했니?
남 아니, 나는 그건 몰랐어.
여 멀지 않아. 바로 근처에 있는 다른 아파트야.
남 그렇구나. 그래서 짐은 다 쌌어?
여 아, 엄마가 거의 다 하셨어. 아빠와 나는 가구들을 옮기고 집을 청소했어.

05 ①

해설 여자가 체크인을 하면서 신분증을 제시하고 남자가 예약을 확인해주는 것으로 보아 장소는 호텔임을 알 수 있다.

어휘 check in 체크인하다, 투숙 수속을 밟다
have a reservation 예약이 되어있다
last name 성(姓)
ID(= identification) [àidíː] 신분증

M Can I help the next person in line, please?
W Hi, I'm checking in.
M Do you <u>have a reservation</u>, ma'am?
W Yes. <u>It should be under</u> my last name, Carter.
M Okay. I found a reservation under that name for 3 nights.
W Is it okay to stay <u>one more night</u>?
M That should not be a problem, ma'am. <u>Can I have</u> your ID, please?
W Sure. Here it is.

남 다음 고객님 도와드릴까요?
여 안녕하세요, 체크인하려고요.
남 예약하셨나요?
여 네, 제 성인 Carter로 되어 있을 거예요.
남 네. 그 이름으로 3박 예약되어 있네요.
여 하룻밤 더 묵어도 괜찮을까요?
남 가능합니다. 고객님. 신분증을 좀 주시겠습니까?
여 네. 여기 있어요.

06 ③

해설 여자는 컵케이크 만드는 것을 도와주겠다고 하면서 남자에게 먼저 식탁부터 치우자고 제안하고 있다.

어휘 sink[siŋk] 싱크대
cupcake[kʌpkèik] 컵케이크
burn[bəːrn] 태우다

W Tom, what are these in the sink? Are they cupcakes?
M Well, they were. I <u>tried to bake</u> some but I burned them.
W Why do you need to <u>bake cupcakes</u>?
M I wanted to make them for my friend, Jenny. She really likes cupcakes.
W Are you going to bake more? I can <u>help you with it</u>.
M That sounds great. Thanks.
W But first, <u>we should clean</u> the kitchen table.

여 Tom, 싱크대에 있는 이것들은 뭐야? 컵케이크니?
남 음, 그랬었지. 조금 만들려고 했었는데 다 태워버렸어.
여 컵케이크는 왜 만드니?
남 내 친구 Jenny한테 만들어주고 싶었어. 걔가 컵케이크를 정말 좋아하거든.
여 컵케이크 더 구울 거니? 내가 도와줄 수 있는데.
남 그거 좋지. 고마워.
여 하지만 먼저 부엌 식탁부터 치워야겠다.

07 ①

해설 남자는 디저트로 와플을 추천했다.

어휘 be famous for ~으로 유명하다
recommend[rèkəménd] 추천하다
waffle[wάfl] 와플

M I went to Johnny's Diner last weekend. Have you ever been there?
W I've <u>heard of that place</u> before. What is it famous for?
M The steak and burgers are good, but <u>the desserts are great</u>.
W What dessert do you recommend?
M <u>I recommend</u> the waffles. At Johnny's Diner, you get ice cream on it. The waffle is warm, so it makes the ice cream very soft.

남 나는 지난 주말에 Johnny's Diner 갔었어. 거기에 가본 적 있니?
여 전에 그곳에 대해 들은 적이 있어. 그곳은 뭐가 유명하니?
남 스테이크와 햄버거도 좋지만, 디저트가 정말 맛있어.
여 추천할 만한 디저트가 뭐니?
남 와플을 추천할게. Johnny's Diner에서는 그 위에 아이스크림을 얹거든. 와플이 따뜻하니까 아이스크림을 매우

W Wow! I should take my family there this weekend.

부드럽게 만들지.

여 와! 이번 주말에 가족들이랑 거기에 가봐야겠다.

08 ④

해설 다리가 아파서 잠을 못 자는 남자에게 여자가 족욕을 권하자 남자는 해보겠다고 했다.

어휘 awake[əwéik] 잠들지 않은, 깨어 있는
foot bath 족욕
relax[rilǽks] (근육 등이) 긴장이 풀리다
bathtub[bǽθtəb] 욕조

W Jake, why are you still awake? It's past midnight.
M I can't go to sleep, Mom.
W Why not? Is something wrong?
M I went hiking yesterday, and now my legs really hurt.
W Why don't you take a foot bath? It'll relax your feet.
M A foot bath? How do I take a foot bath?
W Fill the bathtub with warm water and put your legs into the water.
M Okay, I'll try that now. I hope it works.

여 Jake, 왜 아직 안 자고 있어? 12시가 넘었는데.
남 잠이 안 와요, 엄마.
여 왜 안 오니? 어디 안 좋니?
남 어제 등산을 갔더니 지금 다리가 너무 아파요.
여 족욕을 좀 하는 게 어떠니? 그렇게 하면 발의 긴장이 풀릴 거야.
남 족욕이요? 족욕은 어떻게 하는 건데요?
여 욕조에 따뜻한 물을 채우고 다리를 물속에 넣으면 돼.
남 알았어요, 지금 그렇게 해 볼게요. 효과가 있으면 좋겠어요.

09 ②

해설 제목(Dead or Alive), 관람 장소(LA 문화센터), 티켓 가격(30달러), 함께 본 사람(Susie)에 대해 언급하였지만 주제에 대해서는 언급하지 않았다.

어휘 play[plei] 연극
Cultural Center 문화센터
expensive[ikspénsiv] 비싼
reasonable[rí:zənəbl] 적당한, 합리적인

W What did you do over the weekend, James?
M I saw a play called Dead or Alive.
W Where did you see it?
M I saw it at the L.A. Cultural Center.
W Aren't tickets expensive there?
M I thought it was not bad. It was $30 each.
W Who did you go with?
M I went with my older sister Susie. You should go and see it, too.

여 James, 주말에 뭐 했어?
남 나는 〈Dead or Alive〉라는 연극을 봤어.
여 어디서 봤는데?
남 LA 문화센터에서 봤어.
여 거긴 입장료가 비싸지 않니?
남 적당한 것 같았어. 한 사람당 30달러였거든.
여 누구랑 갔었니?
남 Susie 누나랑 갔어. 너도 가서 봐.

10 ②

해설 점심 메뉴로 식사의 종류와 선택할 수 있는 과일, 음료에 대해서 알려주고 있다.

어휘 lunch break 점심시간
meal[mi:l] 식사
vegetarian[vèdʒətɛ́əriən] 채식주의자
soft drink 청량음료

M It's 12:30, and you'll have a lunch break until 1:30. There are 2 different meals you can choose from, and one of them is vegetarian. You can choose either a banana or an apple for your fruit. However, there are no soft drinks, so you'll have to choose between milk and juice.

남 지금은 12시 반이고, 1시 30분까지 점심시간을 갖도록 해요. 점심으로 선택할 수 있는 두 가지 식단이 있는데 그중 하나는 채식주의자용입니다. 과일은 바나나와 사과 중에서 선택할 수 있어요. 하지만 청량음료는 없으니 우유와 주스 중에서 선택해야 합니다.

11 ③

해설 다른 두 사람과 함께 방을 사용한다고 했다.

M Welcome to the training camp, everyone. I hope you're enjoying the beautiful sunshine here in Florida. You will be training here for

남 여러분, 훈련 캠프에 오신 것을 환영합니다. 여기 플로리다의 아름다운 햇살을 즐기셨으면 좋겠습니다. 이번 훈

어휘 training[tréiniŋ] 훈련, 트레이닝
sunshine[sʌ́nʃàin] 햇빛
share[ʃɛər] 함께 쓰다
stretching[strétʃiŋ] 스트레칭
except[iksépt] ~을 제외하고
out[aut] (전등 등이) 꺼진

the next 3 weeks. You'll share a room with 2 other people. We start our training with stretching at 7 every morning, except on Sundays. The lights will be out at 10:30 every night.

련은 3주 동안 계속됩니다. 여러분은 다른 두 사람과 함께 방을 쓰게 될 겁니다. 일요일을 제외하고 매일 아침 7시에 스트레칭으로 훈련을 시작합니다. 매일 밤 10시 30분에 소등하겠습니다.

12 ④

해설 여자는 역사 선생님께 필요한 책을 빌리기 위해 학교에 다시 가야 한다고 했다.

어휘 borrow[bárou] 빌리다
without[wiðáut] ~ 없이

M Where are you going out again? You just came back home.
W I'm going back to school, Dad. I'll be back in an hour.
M Did you forget something?
W No. I have to get something from my history teacher.
M Why don't you wait until tomorrow? It's getting dark.
W I can't. She is already waiting for me at school.
M What do you need from her?
W I have to borrow some books from her. I need them to finish a group project.

남 어디 나가려고 하니? 너 방금 집에 왔잖아.
여 학교로 도로 가려고요, 아빠. 한 시간 안에 돌아올게요.
남 뭐 잊은 거 있니?
여 아뇨. 역사 선생님께 뭘 좀 받아와야 해서요.
남 내일까지 기다리는 게 어떠니? 점점 어두워지고 있어.
여 안 돼요. 선생님께서 이미 저를 학교에서 기다리고 계세요.
남 알겠다. 선생님한테서 뭐가 필요한데?
여 선생님께 책을 몇 권 빌려야 해요. 그룹 과제를 하려면 그 책들이 필요하거든요.

13 ④

해설 여자가 스테이크의 정가인 45달러에서 쿠폰으로 5달러를 할인 받았으므로 40달러를 지불해야 한다.

어휘 bill[bil] 계산서
regular price 정상 가격
coupon[kú:pan] 쿠폰
discount[dískaunt] 할인

W Can I have the bill, please?
M Sure, here it is.
W [Pause] Isn't the T-bone steak set $35?
M It's $35 only on Mondays, ma'am. The regular price is $45.
W Oh, I didn't know that. Then can I use this coupon?
M Okay. Can I see the coupon, please?
W Yes, it's a $5 discount coupon for any steak set.
M You can certainly use this, ma'am.

여 계산서 좀 주시겠습니까?
남 네, 여기 있어요.
여 [잠시 후] 티본 스테이크 세트는 35달러 아닌가요?
남 월요일에만 35달러입니다, 손님. 정가는 45달러이고요.
여 아, 몰랐어요. 그럼 이 쿠폰을 사용할 수 있나요?
남 네. 쿠폰 좀 보여주시겠습니까?
여 네, 모든 스테이크 세트에 쓸 수 있는 5달러 할인 쿠폰이에요.
남 이건 당연히 쓸 수 있으세요.

14 ①

해설 남자가 머리를 커트하러 갔고 여자가 사람이 많으니 한 시간 후에 다시 오라고 하는 것으로 보아 두 사람의 관계는 미용사와 고객임을 알 수 있다.

어휘 reservation[rèzərvéiʃən] 예약
haircut[hɛ́ərkʌ̀t] 이발, 머리 깎기

M Wow, there are a lot of people waiting.
W Do you have a reservation?
M No, I don't. Do I need a reservation today?
W With a reservation, you don't have to wait for a long time. What would you like to do with your hair today?
M I just need a haircut.

남 와, 기다리는 사람이 많네요.
여 예약하셨나요?
남 아뇨, 안 했어요. 오늘 예약이 필요한가요?
여 예약을 하시면 오래 기다릴 필요가 없죠. 오늘은 머리를 어떻게 하시려고요?
남 그냥 머리만 자르려고요.

| W | If you come back in an hour, I can give you a haircut today. | 여 | 한 시간 후에 다시 오시면, 오늘 이발해 드릴게요. |
| M | Great! I'll be back in an hour. | 남 | 잘됐네요! 한 시간 후에 다시 올게요. |

15 ④

해설 여자는 남자의 조부모님이 오실 예정이니 거실 청소를 해달라고 부탁했다.

어휘 get off the phone 전화를 끊다
living room 거실

[Knock, knock]
W Can I come in, Jacob?
M Come on in. I'm not busy now. Do you need something?
W What were you doing in your room?
M I was just reading a book. Why?
W Your grandparents are going to come for dinner tonight.
M Oh, is it today? I thought it was tomorrow.
W Well, I'm quite busy in the kitchen right now. Can you clean the living room for me?
M Sure. I'll do that right away.

[똑똑]
여 들어가도 되니, Jacob?
남 들어오세요. 지금은 바쁘지 않아요. 필요한 것 있으세요?
여 방에서 뭐 하고 있었어?
남 그냥 책을 읽고 있었어요. 왜요?
여 오늘 밤에 저녁 식사를 하러 조부모님이 오신단다.
남 아, 그게 오늘이에요? 내일인 줄 알았어요.
여 음, 지금 내가 부엌에서 꽤 바쁘거든. 나 대신 거실을 청소해 줄 수 있니?
남 그럼요. 지금 바로 할게요.

16 ⑤

해설 남자는 사전 앱을 쓸 저장 공간이 부족해서 새 휴대전화가 필요하다고 했다.

어휘 download[dáunlòud] 다운로드하다, 내려 받다
dictionary[díkʃənèri] 사전

M Mom, can you buy me a new cell phone?
W A new cell phone? Is there something wrong with your cell phone?
M No, there's nothing wrong with it.
W Then why do you want a new one?
M My friends downloaded a dictionary app and use it for their homework. But I can't do that because there is not enough space.
W Okay. Let me talk to your father about it first.

남 엄마, 나 새 휴대전화 사줄 수 있어요?
여 새 휴대전화? 네 휴대전화에 무슨 문제라도 있니?
남 아니요, 문제는 없어요.
여 그럼 왜 새 걸 원하는데?
남 제 친구들은 사전 앱을 다운받아서 숙제할 때 사용해요. 하지만 저는 그걸 다운로드하기에 저장 공간이 충분하지 않아서 숙제할 때 사용할 수 없어요.
여 알겠어. 우선 네 아버지와 이야기해 볼게.

17 ④

해설 커피를 들고 버스에 타려는 여자에게 남자가 마실 것을 들고 타면 안 된다고 말하는 대화가 적절하다.

어휘 cousin[kʌ́zən] 사촌
give A a ride A를 태워 주다
pick up ~을 차에 태우다
throw away 없애다, 버리다

① M Have you met my cousin?
　 W No, can you introduce me to her?
② M Do you want me to give you a ride?
　 W No, thanks. My dad's picking me up.
③ M Where should we meet tomorrow?
　 W Let's meet at the bus stop.
④ M You can't bring your drink on the bus.
　 W Oh, I'll throw it away then.
⑤ M Can I help you find anything?
　 W Yes, I'm looking for a toy bus for my brother.

① 남 내 사촌 만나 봤니?
　 여 아니, 그녀를 소개해 줄 수 있니?
② 남 내가 태워다 줄까?
　 여 아니, 괜찮아. 아빠가 데리러 올 거야.
③ 남 내일 어디서 만날까?
　 여 버스 정거장에서 만나자.
④ 남 버스에서는 음료를 마실 수 없습니다.
　 여 아, 그럼 버릴게요.
⑤ 남 찾으시는 거 도와드릴까요?
　 여 네, 남동생에게 줄 장난감 버스를 찾고 있어요.

18 ④

[해설] 장소(시 소방서), 참가 인원(15명), 활동 내용(화재 예방법을 배우고 소방관의 화재 진압 시범 관람), 점심시간(오후 1시)에 대해 언급하였지만 준비물에 대해서는 언급하지 않았다.

[어휘] fire station 소방서
field trip 현장 학습, 견학
in case of ~의 경우
firefighter[fáiəfáitər] 소방관
put out (불을) 끄다

W Hello, everyone. Today, we're going to the City Fire Station for our field trip. Mike couldn't come to school today, so it'll be 15 of us. We'll learn what to do in case of a fire. Then the firefighters are going to show us how to put a fire out with the fire truck. We'll have lunch at 1 p.m. and come back to school by 3 p.m.

여 여러분, 안녕하세요. 오늘은 시 소방서로 현장 학습을 하러 갈 거예요. Mike가 오늘 학교에 못 왔으니 우리 일행은 15명이 될 거예요. 우리는 불이 났을 때 무엇을 해야 하는지 배울 거예요. 그리고 나서 소방관들이 소방차로 어떻게 불을 끄는지 보여줄 겁니다. 우리는 오후 1시에 점심을 먹고 오후 3시까지 학교로 돌아올 예정입니다.

19 ②

[해설] 다음 달까지 집안일을 하면서 용돈을 벌겠다고 했으므로 남자의 응답으로 잘 되길 바란다는 내용이 적절하다.

[어휘] cafeteria[kæfətíəriə] 구내식당
snack[snæk] 간식
live off ~로 살아나가다
do chores 집안일을 하다
[선택지]
advice[ədváis] 충고, 조언

M Katie, do you want to go to the cafeteria to get some snacks?
W Sure. [Pause] Wait. Oh, I can't. I only have $5.
M I thought you just got your allowance 2 days ago.
W Yes, but I already spent most of it on clothes.
M Really? Does that mean you have to live off $5 until next month?
W Don't worry. I'll make some money by doing chores.
M I see. Well, good luck with that.

남 Katie, 간식 먹으러 구내식당에 갈래?
여 좋아. [잠시 후] 잠깐만. 아, 안 돼. 나는 5달러밖에 없어.
남 네가 이틀 전에 용돈을 받은 줄 알았어.
여 그랬는데, 이미 대부분의 돈을 옷 사는 데 썼어.
남 그래? 그럼 다음 달까지 5달러를 가지고 살아야 한다는 말이니?
여 걱정하지 마. 나는 집안일을 해서 돈을 좀 벌 거야.
남 그렇구나. 그럼 잘 되기를 바랄게.

① 그래. 내가 지금 설거지할게.
③ 그래. 충고 고마워.
④ 와, 새 셔츠가 잘 어울리네.
⑤ 아니, 괜찮아. 엄마한테 돈을 좀 빌릴 거야.

20 ①

[해설] 베개 때문에 잠을 제대로 못 잔 남자에게 문제가 무엇인지 물었으므로 이어질 응답으로 베개의 문제를 말해주는 것이 적절하다.

[어휘] stay up 깨어 있다
pillow[pílou] 베개
uncomfortable[ʌnkʌ́mfərtəbl] 불편한
different[dífərənt] 다른

W How are you feeling, Eddie? You don't look very well.
M Oh, I'm okay. I'm just tired.
W Did you stay up late to do your homework last night?
M No, I went to sleep early, but I didn't get a good night's sleep.
W Why couldn't you sleep well?
M I think it was because of my pillow. It's really uncomfortable. I need a different pillow.
W What's wrong with your pillow?
M Mine is too hard for my neck.

여 몸은 좀 어때, Eddie? 안색이 별로 안 좋아 보여.
남 아, 난 괜찮아. 그냥 피곤해서 그래.
여 어젯밤 숙제하느라 늦게까지 밤 새웠니?
남 아니, 일찍 잤는데, 잠을 제대로 못 잤어.
여 왜 잠을 잘못 잤는데?
남 내 베개 때문인 것 같아. 베개가 정말 불편해. 다른 베개가 필요해.
여 네 베개에 무슨 문제라도 있니?
남 내 건 내 목에 너무 딱딱해.

② 나는 내 동생을 위한 베개가 필요해.
③ 오늘 밤은 훨씬 일찍 잘 거야.
④ 나는 베개를 어떻게 만드는지 몰라.
⑤ 엄마에게 새 베개를 사 달라고 할 거야.

01 ②	02 ⑤	03 ④	04 ③	05 ②	06 ②	07 ⑤
08 ⑤	09 ①	10 ④	11 ⑤	12 ③	13 ④	14 ⑤
15 ②	16 ④	17 ④	18 ③	19 ④	20 ①	

01 ②

[해설] 목요일에는 큰 비가 올 것으로 예상된다고 했다.

[어휘] **all day long** 하루 종일
heavy rain 폭우, 호우
mostly[móustli] 대체로

W Good morning! Here is this week's weather report. On Monday, it will be sunny. But on Tuesday, it will be rainy all day long. Don't forget your umbrella. On Wednesday and Thursday, heavy rain is expected. On Friday, the rain will stop, and it will be mostly cloudy. And it's likely to be sunny with some clouds over the weekend.

여 안녕하세요! 이번 주 일기예보입니다. 월요일에는 날씨가 화창하겠습니다. 그러나 화요일에는 하루 종일 비가 오겠습니다. 우산 잊지 마세요. 수요일과 목요일에는 폭우가 예상됩니다. 금요일에는 비가 그치고 대체로 흐리겠습니다. 그리고 주말 동안에는 약간의 구름이 낀 맑은 날씨가 되겠습니다.

02 ⑤

[해설] 남자가 찾는 열쇠는 은색에 하트가 달린 열쇠고리에 걸려 있으며, 고리에 같은 열쇠 두 개가 걸려 있다고 했다.

[어휘] **be locked** 자물쇠가 잠겨 있다
silver[sílvər] 은색
several[sévərəl] 몇 개의
hang on ~에 걸려 있다
leather strap 가죽끈
ring[riŋ] 고리

M This drawer is locked. Can you get the key for me?
W There are so many keys. Which one is it?
M The silver one.
W There are several silver keys. Is it hanging on a leather strap?
M No, it's on a key ring with a heart.
W How many keys are there on the key ring?
M There are 2 keys on the ring.
W I got it.

남 이 서랍이 자물쇠로 잠겨 있네요. 열쇠 좀 가져다줄래요?
여 열쇠가 너무 많은데요. 어떤 거예요?
남 은색 열쇠예요.
여 은색 열쇠가 여러 개인데요. 가죽끈에 걸려 있나요?
남 아니요, 하트가 달린 열쇠고리에 달려 있어요.
여 열쇠고리에 몇 개의 열쇠가 있나요?
남 고리에 두 개의 열쇠가 있어요.
여 찾았어요.

03 ④

[해설] 남자는 러시아에 있는 친구가 서울에 올 거라고 하면서 신이 나 있다.

[어휘] **be in a good mood** 기분이 좋다
mean[mi:n] 의미하다
blond[bland] 금발의
business meeting 업무 회의
look forward to v-ing ~하기를 기대하다

W You seem to be in a good mood, Jihun.
M I have a Facebook friend from Russia. Did I tell you about her before?
W Yes, you did. You mean the girl with blond hair, right?
M Right. She is going to come to Seoul next week.
W Really? Is she going to come just to see you?
M No. She's going to come with her father. He has a business meeting in Seoul.
W That's great! You must be so happy.
M Yes, I'm looking forward to meeting her.

여 지훈아, 너 기분이 좋아 보이네.
남 나한테 러시아 출신의 페이스북 친구가 있는데. 너에게 그녀에 대해 전에 말했었지?
여 응, 그랬지. 금발 머리의 여자아이 말이지, 맞지?
남 맞아. 다음 주에 그 애가 서울에 올 거래.
여 정말? 단지 너를 만나러 온다는 거야?
남 아니. 그 애는 아버지와 함께 올 거야. 아버지가 서울에서 업무 회의가 있으시대.
여 잘됐다! 너 아주 행복하겠구나.
남 응, 나는 걔를 만나기를 기대하고 있어.

04 ③

해설 여자는 업무상 로스앤젤레스에 다녀왔는데, 일하느라 사무실에만 있었다고 했다.

어휘 Long time no see. 오랜만이야.
on business 업무상
tourist attraction 관광 명소
keep v-ing 계속 ~하다
look around 둘러보다

W Hi, Joe. Long time no see.
M Hi, Amy. Where have you been?
W I was in Los Angeles on business for a few months.
M Did you visit any tourist attractions?
W No, not at all. I just kept working in the office.
M Oh, I'm sorry to hear that.
W I was so busy. I didn't have time to look around the city.

여 안녕, Joe. 오랜만이야.
남 안녕, Amy. 너 어디에 갔었니?
여 업무상 몇 달 동안 로스앤젤레스에 다녀왔어.
남 관광 명소에 가봤니?
여 아니, 전혀. 나는 사무실에서 계속 일만 했어.
남 아, 그 말을 들으니 안됐구나.
여 나는 너무 바빴어. 도시를 둘러볼 시간이 없었어.

05 ②

해설 두 사람이 어떤 화가의 그림을 감상하면서 나누는 대화이므로, 대화 장소는 미술관임을 알 수 있다.

어휘 crowded[kráudid] 붐비는
show[ʃou] 전시회
real[ríːəl] 진짜의
painting[péintiŋ] 그림
artist[áːrtist] 화가, 예술가
painter[péintər] 화가

M This place is so crowded.
W Today is the last day of the show. [Pause] Look at the picture of those girls.
M Which one are you talking about? The ones dancing on the stage?
W No. I mean the girls who are playing the piano.
M Wow, they look like real people, don't they?
W Right. That's why I like the paintings of this artist.
M Let's go to the next room. I want to see the paintings of other painters.
W Okay.

남 이곳이 많이 붐비네.
여 오늘이 전시 마지막 날이거든. [잠시 후] 저 소녀들을 봐.
남 어떤 걸 말하는 거야? 무대 위에서 춤추는 소녀들?
여 아니. 피아노를 치는 소녀들 말이야.
남 와, 그들은 진짜 사람처럼 보여. 그렇지 않니?
여 맞아. 그것이 내가 이 화가의 그림을 좋아하는 이유야.
남 다음 방으로 가자. 다른 화가들의 그림을 보고 싶어.
여 좋아.

06 ②

해설 여자가 친구와의 문제에 대해 고민하자 남자는 먼저 이야기해보라고 제안하고 있다.

어휘 worried[wɔ́ːrid] 걱정스러운
have trouble with ~와 문제가 있다
these days 요즘
say no 거절하다
understand[ʌ̀ndərstǽnd] 이해하다

M You look worried. Is something wrong?
W Well, I'm having trouble with Jenny these days.
M Did something happen?
W She doesn't talk to me any more. And I don't know why.
M Think carefully.
W [Pause] Oh, I think I know why. Last week, she asked me to help her with her homework, and I said no.
M Why don't you talk to her first? I'm sure she'll understand.

남 너 걱정스러워 보여. 무슨 일이 있니?
여 음, 나 요즘 Jenny와 문제가 있어.
남 무슨 일이 있었니?
여 걔가 나랑 더 이상 말하지 않아. 그리고 나는 이유를 모르겠어.
남 잘 생각해봐.
여 [잠시 후] 아, 이유를 알 것 같아. 지난주에, Jenny가 나에게 숙제 좀 도와달라고 부탁했는데, 내가 거절했어.
남 걔한테 먼저 이야기해보는 게 어때? 걔는 분명히 이해할 거야.

07 ⑤

해설 남자는 스테이크, 구운 감자, 치킨샐러드와 후식으로 애플파이를 주문했다.

W May I take your order?
M Yes. I'll have a steak, please.
W Would you like any side dishes with it?

여 주문하시겠어요?
남 네. 전 스테이크로 할게요.
여 그것과 같이 어떤 곁들인 음식을 드릴까요?

어휘 order[ɔ́ːrdər] 주문
side dish 곁들임 요리
baked[beik] 구운
dessert[dizə́ːrt] 디저트, 후식

M I'll have a baked potato. Oh, <u>can I also add</u> chicken salad?
W Of course. Anything to drink?
M I'll just <u>have some water</u>.
W What would you like for dessert? We have apple pie and ice cream.
M <u>I'll take apple pie</u>.
W All right. I'll be right back with <u>your drink and salad</u> first.

남 구운 감자로 할게요. 아, 치킨 샐러드도 추가해도 되나요?
여 물론이죠. 마실 건요?
남 그냥 물 좀 주세요.
여 후식으로 어떤 걸 드릴까요? 애플파이와 아이스크림이 있어요.
남 애플파이로 할게요.
여 알겠습니다. 먼저 마실 것과 샐러드를 가지고 다시 오겠습니다.

08 ⑤

해설 여자가 운동화를 파란색으로 교환하고 싶다고 했고, 남자는 영수증을 확인한 후 가져오겠다고 했다.

어휘 exchange[ikstʃéindʒ] 교환하다
actually[ǽktʃuəli] 사실
look good on ~와 어울리다
receipt[risíːt] 영수증
right away 바로

M May I help you?
W Yes. I'd like <u>to exchange these</u> sneakers, please.
M What's the matter with them?
W Nothing, actually. I don't think the color looks good on me. <u>I'd like blue ones</u>.
M I see. Do you have your receipt?
W Sure. Here it is.
M Just a moment, please. I'll <u>bring them right away</u>.
W Thank you.

남 도와드릴까요?
여 네. 저는 이 운동화를 교환하고 싶어요.
남 그것에 무슨 문제가 있나요?
여 사실 아무 문제 없어요. 색이 저와 어울리지 않는 것 같아서요. 저는 파란색 운동화를 원해요.
남 알겠습니다. 영수증 있으신가요?
여 물론이요. 여기 있어요.
남 잠시 기다려 주세요. 바로 가져다드릴게요.
여 고맙습니다.

09 ①

해설 여자는 금연에 대해서는 언급하지 않았다.

어휘 on time 제시간에
put on ~을 입다
seat belt 안전벨트
take off (항공기 등이) 이륙하다, 날아오르다
earphones 이어폰

M Is the flight leaving on time?
W Yes, it'll be leaving soon. You have to <u>put on your seat belt</u>.
M I already have. Can I use my cell phone now?
W No, you <u>may not use</u> your cell phone when the plane is taking off. Please turn off your cell phone.
M I see. Where can I put this bag?
W You can put it <u>under the seat</u> in front of you.
M Okay. Wait, can I listen to music?
W Yes. But please <u>use your earphones</u>.

남 비행기가 제시간에 출발하나요?
여 네, 곧 출발할 겁니다. 안전벨트를 매셔야 합니다.
남 이미 매고 있어요. 지금 제 휴대전화를 사용해도 되나요?
여 아니요, 비행기 이륙 시에는 휴대전화를 사용할 수 없습니다. 휴대전화의 전원을 꺼주시기 바랍니다.
남 알겠습니다. 이 가방을 어디에 놓으면 되나요?
여 그건 앞좌석 아래에 두십시오.
남 알겠어요. 잠깐만요, 음악을 들어도 되나요?
여 네. 하지만 이어폰을 사용해 주십시오.

10 ④

해설 영어 듣기 실력을 기르기 위한 방법을 알려 주고 있다.

어휘 skill[skil] 기술
tip[tip] 조언
as ~ as possible 가능한 한 ~하게

M Do you <u>want to practice</u> your English listening skills? Here are some tips. First, listen to English <u>as often as possible</u> every day. Second, make "listening to English" fun. You can <u>watch popular TV shows</u> and movies in English. You'll enjoy the shows and

남 영어 듣기 실력을 연습하고 싶은가요? 여기 몇 가지 조언이 있습니다. 첫째, 매일 가능한 한 자주 영어를 들으세요. 둘째, '영어 듣기'를 재미있게 하세요. 인기 있는 TV 프로그램과 영화를 영어로 볼 수 있습니다. 그 프로

popular[pápulər] 인기 있는
TV show TV 프로그램
get better 좋아지다

your listening skills will get better, too.

여 그램을 즐기면서 듣기 실력도 좋아질
겁니다.

11 ⑤

해설 박쥐는 청력이 뛰어나다고 했다.

어휘 bat[bæt] 박쥐
look like ~처럼 생기다
made of ~로 만든
skin[skin] 피부
lay eggs 알을 낳다
active[金ktiv] 활동적인
hunt[hʌnt] 사냥하다
hearing[hí:əriŋ] 청력
easily[í:zili] 쉽게

W Have you seen a bat? A bat looks like a mouse. It has big ears and wings made of skin. But it's not a bird because it doesn't lay eggs. A bat is active in the dark. So, it hunts for food at night. Because of good hearing, a bat can find food easily in the dark.

여 박쥐를 본 적이 있나요? 박쥐는 쥐처럼 생겼어요. 그것은 큰 귀와 피부로 만들어진 날개가 있어요. 하지만 알을 낳지 않기 때문에 새가 아니에요. 박쥐는 어둠 속에서 활동적이랍니다. 그래서 밤에는 먹이를 사냥해요. 좋은 청력 때문에, 박쥐는 어둠 속에서 쉽게 먹이를 찾을 수 있답니다.

12 ③

해설 여자는 광고를 보고 식당에 일자리를 구하기 위해 전화했다.

어휘 advertisement[ædvərtáizmənt] 광고
part-time 시간제의
pay[pei] 지불하다
pretty[príti] 꽤
apply for ~에 지원하다
interview[íntərvjù:] 면접

[Telephone rings.]
M Grandma Mary's Restaurant. How may I help you?
W I'm calling about your advertisement. Are you still looking for a part-time waiter?
M Yes, we are.
W How much do you pay?
M $10 an hour.
W That's pretty good. I'd like to apply for the job.
M Can you come in for an interview tomorrow?
W Sure, I can. I'll visit your restaurant tomorrow.

[전화벨이 울린다.]
남 Grandma Mary's 식당입니다. 무엇을 도와드릴까요?
여 광고를 보고 전화 드립니다. 아직도 시간제 웨이터를 찾고 계신가요?
남 네, 그렇습니다.
여 얼마를 주시나요?
남 시간당 10달러입니다.
여 아주 괜찮네요. 제가 그 일에 지원하고 싶은데요.
남 내일 인터뷰 하러 오실 수 있나요?
여 네, 가능합니다. 내일 식당으로 갈게요.

13 ④

해설 두 사람은 뮤지컬 공연 전인 2시 30분에 만나기로 했다.

어휘 show[ʃou] 공연
in front of ~의 앞에
theater[θí(:)ətər] 극장

W Daniel, I have tickets to the musical *Rebecca* on Saturday. Would you like to go with me?
M Of course. What time does the show start?
W It starts at 3 o'clock.
M That sounds great. Then, why don't we have lunch together at 1?
W Sorry, but I have to meet Jessica before the show at 1.
M No problem. Let's meet in front of the theater at 2:30 then.
W That's fine with me.

여 Daniel, 나는 토요일에 하는 뮤지컬 〈Rebecca〉의 티켓이 있어. 너 나랑 갈래?
남 물론이지. 공연이 몇 시에 시작하니?
여 3시에 시작해.
남 좋은데. 그럼, 1시에 함께 점심을 먹는 게 어떠니?
여 미안하지만, 나는 공연 보기 전에 1시에 Jessica를 만나야 해.
남 괜찮아. 그럼 2시 30분에 극장 앞에서 만나자.
여 그게 좋겠다.

14 ⑤

해설 여자가 시카고에서 가 볼 만한 곳을 추천해 달라고 했고 남자가 몇 군데를 소개해 주면서 여행객을 위한 쿠폰을 가져가라고 했으므로 두 사람의 관계는 관광 안내소 직원과 여행객이다.

어휘 left[left] 남은
suggest[sədʒést] 제안하다
area[έəriə] 지역
coupon[kú:pan] 쿠폰, 할인권
tourist[túərist] 여행객

M May I help you?
W Yes, please. I only have 3 days left in Chicago. What do you suggest I do?
M There are lots of things to see here. You can visit Millennium Park, Chicago Theatre, and the Art Museum. And I suggest you go to the beautiful lake.
W I see. Which one is the closest from here?
M It's Millennium Park. It's a 10-minute walk from here.
W Could I get a map of this area?
M Of course. You can take some coupons for tourists.
W Thank you.

남 도와드릴까요?
여 네. 저는 시카고에서 3일을 머무를 건데요. 무엇을 하면 좋을까요?
남 여기에는 볼거리가 많이 있어요. 밀레니엄 공원, 시카고 극장, 그리고 미술관에 가도 되고요. 그리고 아름다운 호수에 가보는 것을 추천합니다.
여 알겠습니다. 어느 곳이 여기서 가장 가까운가요?
남 밀레니엄 공원이요. 여기서 걸어서 10분 거리입니다.
여 이 지역 지도를 얻을 수 있을까요?
남 물론이지요. 여행객을 위한 쿠폰을 좀 가져가셔도 돼요.
여 감사합니다.

15 ②

해설 남자는 여자에게 우체국에 들러서 Anna에게 보낼 소포를 부쳐 달라고 부탁했다.

어휘 dry cleaner's 세탁소
stop by ~에 들르다
package[pǽkidʒ] 소포

M Where are you going, Mom?
W I'm going to the dry cleaner's. Is there anything you need?
M Can you stop by the post office?
W The post office? Do you have a package to send?
M Yes, I need to send a package to Anna.
W Isn't Anna in Canada?
M Yes. These are the books she wanted.
W All right. I'll do it for you.
M Thank you.

남 어디 가세요, 엄마?
여 세탁소에 갈 거야. 뭐 필요한 거라도 있니?
남 우체국에 들르실 수 있나요?
여 우체국? 보낼 소포가 있니?
남 네, 소포 하나를 Anna에게 보내야 해요.
여 Anna가 캐나다에 있지 않니?
남 맞아요. 이건 그 애가 원하는 책들이에요.
여 알겠다. 그렇게 해줄게.
남 감사합니다.

16 ④

해설 남자는 어제 참가한 하프 마라톤 때문에 피곤하다고 했다.

어휘 leave a message 메시지를 남기다
answer[ǽnsər] (전화에) 응답하다
fall asleep 잠이 들다
than usual 평소보다
half marathon 하프 마라톤
time[taim] (시간) 기록

M I left a message with your mom yesterday. Did you get it?
W I did. I called you back to ask something else, but you didn't answer.
M Oh, I was really tired. So I fell asleep earlier than usual.
W Did you stay up late the night before?
M No, I finished a half marathon. I ran for 2 and a half hours.
W Wow, that's a good time.

남 내가 어제 너의 엄마께 메시지를 남겼는데. 받았니?
여 받았어. 내가 너한테 뭘 좀 묻기 위해서 다시 전화했는데, 안 받더라.
남 아, 내가 정말 피곤했거든. 그래서 평소보다 더 일찍 잠들었지.
여 전날 밤에 늦게까지 깨어 있었니?
남 아니, 내가 하프 마라톤을 했거든. 2시간 반 동안 달렸어.
여 와, 그거 좋은 기록이네.

17 ④

해설 남자가 여자를 차로 극장에 데려 다주고 나서 인사를 나누는 대화가 적절 하다.

어휘 give A a ride 차로 데려다 주다
repair shop 정비소
mind[maind] 꺼리다
theater[θí(ː)ətər] 극장

① W Can you give me a ride to school?
　M Sorry, my car is in the repair shop.
② W Do you mind if I open the window?
　M No, I don't mind at all.
③ W How can I help you, sir?
　M I'm looking for my car.
④ W Thank you for driving me to the theater, Dad.
　M You're welcome. Have fun with your friends.
⑤ W Where is my car key? Did you see it?
　M I'm afraid not.

① 여 학교에 차로 데려다주실 수 있어 요?
　남 미안한데, 내 차가 정비소에 있단 다.
② 여 창문을 열어도 될까요?
　남 네, 괜찮습니다.
③ 여 어떻게 도와드릴까요?
　남 제 차를 찾고 있어요.
④ 여 극장에 저를 데려다 주셔서 고마 워요, 아빠.
　남 천만에. 친구들과 재미있게 놀아 라.
⑤ 여 내 차 열쇠가 어디 있지? 열쇠 봤 어요?
　남 아니요.

18 ③

해설 이름(Victoria), 나이(5살), 생김새 (금발 곱슬머리, 분홍색 티셔츠, 파란색 반바지), 현재 위치(5층 고객 서비스 센터) 에 대해 언급하였으나 엄마 이름에 대해 서는 언급하지 않았다.

어휘 curly[kə́ːrli] 곱슬머리의
blond[blɔnd] 금발의
shorts[ʃɔːrts] 반바지
customer service center 고객 서비 스센터

W May I have your attention, please? We have found a little girl, and her name is Victoria. She is 5 years old, and she says she is looking for her mom. Victoria has curly blond hair. She's wearing a pink T-shirt and blue shorts. Right now she's at the customer service center on the 5th floor. Thank you.

여 주목해 주십시오. 저희가 어린 소녀를 발견했으며, 이름은 Victoria입니다. 5살이고, 엄마를 찾고 있다고 합니다. Victoria는 금발의 곱슬머리를 가지고 있습니다. 그녀는 분홍색 티셔츠와 파 란색 반바지를 입고 있습니다. 지금 그녀는 5층에 있는 고객 서비스센터 에 있습니다. 감사합니다.

19 ④

해설 여자에게 남자가 블라우스를 사주 겠다며 쇼핑을 하러 갈 것을 제안했으므 로 이를 수락하거나 거절하는 말이 이어 져야 한다.

어휘 closet[klɑ́zit] 옷장
wedding[wédiŋ] 결혼식
homeroom teacher 담임 선생님

M Jane, are you looking for something?
W Yes, I'm looking for my white blouse. Did you see it, Dad?
M No. Did you ask your mom?
W I did, and she said it was in my closet. But it's not.
M Why do you need your white blouse?
W I need to wear it at my homeroom teacher's wedding. Our class is going to sing for her.
M I see. How about going shopping right now? I'll buy you a new white blouse.
W Thanks, Dad. I'll get ready soon.

남 얘야, 뭐 찾고 있니?
여 네, 제 흰색 블라우스를 찾고 있어요.
남 엄마에게 물어봤니?
여 물어봤는데, 엄마는 그게 제 옷장에 있다고 하셨어요. 하지만 없네요.
남 왜 흰색 블라우스가 필요한 거니?
여 저희 담임 선생님 결혼식에 입어야 해 요. 저희 반이 노래를 부를 거거든요.
남 그렇구나. 지금 쇼핑하러 가는 게 어 떠니? 새 흰색 블라우스를 사 줄게.
여 감사합니다, 아빠. 곧 준비할게요.

① 셔츠를 빌릴 수 있나요?
② 아니요, 감사합니다. 하나만 가져갈게 요.
③ 검은색 바지가 아빠에게 잘 어울려요.
⑤ 흰색 블라우스는 중간 크기예요.

해설 여자가 나가서 자전거를 타러 가자고 제안했고 남자가 몇 시에 만날지 물었으므로 여자가 괜찮은 시간을 말하는 것이 적절하다.

어휘 busy[bízi] 바쁜
free[fri:] 한가한

[Cell phone rings.]
M Hello.
W Hi, Andrew.
M Hi, Susie. What's up?
W Are you busy tomorrow?
M No, I'm free <u>all day tomorrow</u>. Why?
W Why don't we <u>go out and ride bikes</u>?
M I want to, but I can't. My bike is broken.
W Don't worry. You can <u>use my brother's</u>.
M That'll be great. So, when <u>shall we meet</u>?
W How about 3 o'clock?

[전화벨이 울린다.]
남 여보세요.
여 안녕, Andrew.
남 안녕, Susie. 무슨 일이니?
여 너 내일 바쁘니?
남 아니, 나 내일 하루 종일 한가해. 왜?
여 밖에 나가서 자전거 타지 않을래?
남 그러고 싶은데, 탈 수 없어. 내 자전거가 고장이 났거든.
여 걱정하지 마. 내 남동생 거를 타면 돼.
남 그거 좋겠네. 그래서 언제 만날까?
여 3시 어때?

② 3시간 정도 걸려.
③ 우리는 즐겁게 지낼 거야.
④ 나는 오후 3시에 그녀를 만나고 싶어.
⑤ 나는 일주일에 세 번 자전거를 타.

01 ⑤	02 ②	03 ①	04 ②	05 ③	06 ②	07 ④
08 ②	09 ⑤	10 ②	11 ⑤	12 ⑤	13 ②	14 ③
15 ①	16 ③	17 ⑤	18 ③	19 ④	20 ⑤	

01 ⑤

해설 주말에는 비가 올 것이라 했다.

어휘 weekly[wíːkli] 주간의, 매주의
make sure to-v 반드시 ~하다
clear[kliər] 맑은, 갠
chance[tʃæns] 가능성

W Good morning! This is the weekly weather report. From Monday to Wednesday, it will be very cold and cloudy with strong winds. Make sure to keep yourself warm. The skies will be clear on Thursday, and you'll have sunny and warm weather until Friday. However, we will have rain this weekend.

여 안녕하세요! 주간 일기예보입니다. 월요일부터 수요일까지 강한 바람에 의해 매우 춥고 흐리겠습니다. 반드시 몸을 따뜻하게 유지하십시오. 목요일에 하늘이 맑아지면서 금요일까지 화창하고 따뜻한 날씨가 되겠습니다. 그러나 이번 주말에는 비가 오겠습니다.

02 ②

해설 남자는 딸이 좋아하는 체크무늬에 주머니가 있는 담요를 선택했다.

어휘 blanket[blǽŋkit] 담요
camping[kǽmpiŋ] 캠핑
pocket[pákit] 주머니
in the middle 중앙에
popular[pápulər] 인기 있는
item[áitəm] 물품, 품목
check[tʃek] 체크무늬
pattern[pǽtərn] 패턴, 양식

W Good afternoon, how may I help you?
M I'm looking for a blanket for my daughter. She needs one for camping this weekend.
W Sure. How about this one with a pocket in the middle? It's one of the most popular items these days.
M I see. It looks all right, but my daughter likes check patterns.
W Then how about this check one with a pocket?
M This would be perfect for her. I'll take it.

여 안녕하세요, 어떻게 도와드릴까요?
남 딸에게 줄 담요를 찾고 있어요. 이번 주말에 캠핑용 담요가 하나 필요하거든요.
여 네. 중앙에 주머니가 달린 이 담요는 어떠세요? 요즘 인기 있는 품목 중 하나입니다.
남 그렇군요. 괜찮은 것 같지만, 제 딸은 체크무늬 패턴을 좋아해서요.
여 그럼 주머니가 달린 이 체크무늬 담요는 어떠세요?
남 이건 제 딸에게 딱 맞네요. 그걸 살게요.

03 ①

해설 남자는 여자 친구의 가족을 처음으로 만나게 되어 신이 나있다.

어휘 invite[inváit] 초대하다
for the first time 처음으로
in that case 그렇다면, 그런 경우에는
example[igzǽmpl] 예, 예시
can't wait to-v ~하고 싶다

M I was invited to my girlfriend's house for dinner.
W That's great. Are you going to meet her family for the first time?
M Yes. I hope they'll like me. What should I bring to her house?
W You should bring a small gift in that case.
M Can you give me some examples?
W Well, some flowers or a cake would be nice.
M Then, I will buy some roses. I can't wait to meet her family.

남 나 여자 친구의 집으로 저녁 식사를 초대받았어.
여 좋겠네. 그녀의 가족들을 처음으로 만나는 거니?
남 그래. 나를 좋아해 주셨으면 좋겠어. 그녀의 집에 뭘 가져가야 할까?
여 그렇다면, 작은 선물을 가져가는 게 좋을 것 같아.
남 몇 가지 예를 좀 들어줄래?
여 음, 꽃이나 케이크가 좋을 것 같아.
남 그럼 장미꽃을 좀 사야겠다. 빨리 그녀의 가족들을 만나고 싶어.

04 ②

해설 여자는 여름 방학에 가족과 함께 한국으로 한 달간의 여행을 갔다고 했다.

어휘 month-long 한 달간의
amazing [əméiziŋ] 놀라운
tasty [téisti] 맛있는
one day 언젠가

M Mary, long time no see.
W Lucas, how was your summer vacation?
M It was great. I read many books and went swimming a lot with friends. How about you?
W Oh, I went on a month-long trip to Korea with my family.
M A month? Wow, that's amazing. What did you do?
W We did many things. We visited many places and had tasty food. Oh, we did a lot of shopping, too.
M That sounds like fun.
W It was. You should visit the country one day.

남 Mary, 오랜만이야.
여 Lucas, 여름 방학은 어떻게 보냈어?
남 좋았어. 나는 책을 많이 읽었고 친구들과 자주 수영하러 갔었어. 너는 어땠니?
여 아, 나는 가족과 한국으로 한 달간의 여행을 갔었어.
남 한 달이나? 와, 놀랍다. 무엇을 했니?
여 우리는 많은 일들을 했어. 여러 곳을 방문했고 맛있는 음식을 먹었어. 아, 우리는 쇼핑도 많이 했어.
남 재미있었겠다.
여 그랬지. 너도 언젠가 그 나라에 가봐야 해.

05 ③

해설 여자가 여행 패키지를 추천해달라고 하고, 남자는 여행 패키지에 대해 설명하는 걸로 보아 두 사람이 대화하는 장소는 여행사임을 알 수 있다.

어휘 advertisement [ædvərtáizmən]
광고
magazine [mǽgəzíːn] 잡지
tour package 여행 패키지
Eastern Europe 동부 유럽
include [inklúːd] 포함하다
tour guide 여행 가이드

M Good afternoon. How may I help you?
W Hello. I saw your advertisement from a travel magazine.
M I see. Are you planning to travel alone?
W No. I'll travel with my husband. Do you have any tour packages?
M Of course. We have a 10-day trip to Eastern Europe. The package includes everything from plane tickets to hotels.
W That sounds great. Will there be a tour guide?
M Yes. When are you planning to travel?
W We would like to travel in April.

남 안녕하세요. 어떻게 도와드릴까요?
여 안녕하세요. 제가 여행 잡지에서 광고를 보았는데요.
남 그렇군요. 혼자 여행을 가실 계획이신가요?
여 아뇨. 남편과 같이 갈 거예요. 저희에게 맞는 여행 패키지가 있을까요?
남 물론이죠. 동유럽으로 10일짜리 여행이 있습니다. 그 패키지는 비행기 티켓부터 호텔까지 모든 걸 포함하죠.
여 좋은 것 같네요. 여행 가이드도 있을까요?
남 네. 언제 여행 갈 계획이신가요?
여 저희는 4월에 가고 싶어요.

06 ②

해설 몸이 좋지 않은 남자가 집에 가서 자야겠다고 하자, 여자는 좋은 생각이라고 말하면서 동의했다.

어휘 sore throat 인후통, 목통증
make an appointment 예약을 하다
head [hed] 가다, 향하다

W William, what's wrong?
M I'm not feeling so good. I think I have a headache and a sore throat.
W That's no good. Did you go and see a doctor today?
M I couldn't. I called to make an appointment, but the office was already closed.
W I see. Then what are you going to do?
M I'll just head home now. I should get some sleep.
W Yes. That's a good idea.

여 William, 어디가 아프니?
남 몸이 별로 좋지 않아. 두통이 있고, 목이 아픈 것 같아.
여 좋지 않구나. 오늘 의사에게 진료를 받았니?
남 못 받았어. 예약하려고 전화했는데, 이미 문을 닫았더라고.
여 그렇구나. 그럼 어떻게 할 거야?
남 난 그냥 집에 가려고. 좀 자야겠어.
여 그래. 그게 좋을 것 같아.

07 ④

해설 여자는 음악이 등장인물들의 감정을 이해하는 데 도움을 주기 때문에 가장 좋은 부분이라고 했다.

어휘 scene[siːn] 장면
story line 줄거리
character[kǽriktər] 등장인물
feeling[fíːliŋ] 감정
win awards 상을 받다

M Did you see the movie *Dream Land*?
W Yes. It's one of my favorite movies. I really enjoyed every scene of the movie.
M Really? Why do you like it so much?
W The movie has a great story line. The best part is the music because it helps me understand the characters' feelings.
M Yeah, I heard a lot about the music. The movie won many awards because of it, right?
W Yes. You can watch the movie at my house if you want.
M Sure. Let's go to your house after school.

남 너 영화 〈Dream Land〉 봤니?
여 응. 내가 가장 좋아하는 영화 중 하나야. 나는 영화의 모든 장면을 정말 재밌게 봤어.
남 정말? 너는 그 영화를 왜 그렇게 좋아하니?
여 그 영화는 줄거리가 훌륭해. 가장 좋은 부분은 음악인데, 등장인물들의 감정을 이해하는 데 도움을 줬거든.
남 그래, 나 그 음악에 대해 많이 들었어. 그 영화는 음악 때문에 많은 상을 받았잖아, 맞지?
여 맞아. 원한다면 우리 집에서 그 영화를 봐도 돼.
남 그래. 방과 후에 너네 집에 가자.

08 ②

해설 남자의 셔츠에 단추가 하나 떨어져 있다고 하자 여자는 지금 바로 단추를 달아주겠다고 했다.

어휘 school uniform 교복
wash[waʃ] 옷을 세탁하다
wet[wet] 젖은
put on (옷을) 입다
closet[klázit] 옷장
missing[mísiŋ] 없는, 빠진
button[bʌ́tən] 단추

W Why aren't you wearing your school uniform?
M You washed my shirt and it's still wet. I couldn't put it on.
W Isn't there another one in your closet?
M That one is missing a button.
W Why didn't you tell me about it?
M I forgot. Can you put on a new button now?
W All right. I'll do that right now.
M Thanks, Mom.

여 왜 네 교복을 입지 않았니?
남 엄마가 제 셔츠를 빨아서 아직 젖어 있어요. 그걸 입을 수가 없었어요.
여 옷장에 셔츠가 하나 더 있지 않니?
남 그 셔츠는 단추가 하나 떨어졌어요.
여 왜 나한테 그걸 말하지 않았니?
남 깜빡했어요. 지금 새로 단추를 좀 달아 주실래요?
여 알겠다. 지금 바로 할게.
남 감사해요, 엄마.

09 ⑤

해설 남자가 동물원에서 해야 할 일로 야외 휴지통 비우기는 언급되지 않았다.

어휘 cage [keidʒ] 우리
feed[fiːd] 먹이를 주다
take care of ~을 돌보다
repair[ripɛ́ər] 수리하다
fence[fens] 울타리

M I'm so excited about my first day at the zoo. I can't wait to work with animals.
W Good for you. What do you have to do there?
M Well, in the morning I have to clean monkey cages.
W I see. What else do you have to do?
M In the afternoon, I'll feed the monkeys and take care of baby tigers, too.
W That sounds like fun.
M But sometimes, I'll have to repair the fences.

남 나는 동물원에서 일하는 첫날이 너무 기대돼. 빨리 동물들과 함께 일하고 싶어.
여 잘됐다. 넌 거기서 무엇을 해야 하니?
남 음, 아침에는 원숭이 우리를 청소해야 해.
여 그렇구나. 그밖에 무엇을 해야 하니?
남 오후에는 원숭이에게 먹이를 주고 아기 호랑이도 돌볼 거야.
여 재미있겠다.
남 하지만 가끔 울타리를 수리해야 할 거야.

10 ②

해설 벼룩시장에서 중고품을 판매 및 구매함으로써 어려운 이웃을 도울 수 있으니 많이 참여하라고 했다.

어휘 introduce[ìntrədjúːs] 소개하다
flea market 벼룩시장
various[vérias] 다양한
furniture[fə́ːrnitʃər] 가구
neighbor[néibər] 이웃
donate[dóuneit] 기부하다
in need 어려움에 처한

W Hello, I'd like to introduce Helping Hands Flea Market. It is open from 10 a.m. to 7 p.m. this Friday. We have various items from furniture to clothes. You can also help neighbors by selling and buying used items. All the money from this flea market will be donated to those in need. Please come with your friends and families to help other people.

여 안녕하세요, Helping Hands 벼룩시장을 소개하겠습니다. 벼룩시장은 이번 금요일, 오전 10시부터 오후 7시까지 엽니다. 가구부터 옷까지 다양한 물품이 있습니다. 여러분은 또한 중고품을 판매 및 구매함으로써 이웃을 도울 수 있습니다. 이 벼룩시장에서 나온 수익금 전액은 어려움에 처한 사람들에게 기부될 겁니다. 다른 사람들을 돕기 위해, 친구와 가족들과 함께 방문하세요.

11 ⑤

해설 직접 방문해서 피자를 사면 20% 할인을 받을 수 있다고 했다.

어휘 prepare[pripέər] 준비하다
fresh[freʃ] 신선한
cf. freshly[fréʃli] 신선하게
dough[dou] 피자 반죽
topping[tápiŋ] 토핑
leftover[léftòuvər] 남은 재료
the day before 전날
deliver[dilívər] 배달하다
delivery time 배달 시간
be delayed 지연되다

W We're sure that you'll be happy to have Pizza Kitchen near your home. We prepare fresh pizza dough and toppings every morning. In addition, we don't use the leftovers from the day before. Please call us or order online, and your freshly baked pizza will be delivered to your home in 30 minutes. If the delivery time is longer than 30 minutes, you won't have to pay for it. And you can get a 20% discount if you visit us to buy pizza.

여 여러분의 집 가까이에 Pizza Kitchen이 생겨서 행복하실 겁니다. 저희는 매일 아침 신선한 피자 반죽과 토핑들을 준비합니다. 게다가, 저희는 전날의 남은 재료들은 사용하지 않습니다. 저희에게 전화하거나 온라인으로 주문하세요. 그러면 갓 구운 여러분의 피자가 30분 이내에 집으로 배달될 겁니다. 배달이 30분 이상 길어지면, 피자 값을 내지 않으셔도 됩니다. 그리고 저희를 방문하셔서 피자를 구매하시면, 20퍼센트 할인을 받으실 수 있습니다.

12 ⑤

해설 여자는 내일 오전 10시 비행기로 뉴욕에서 출발해서 3시 30분에 공항에 도착한다고 알리기 위해 전화했다.

어휘 all afternoon 오후 내내
still[stil] 아직도
flight[flait] 항공편
appreciate[əpríːʃièit] 감사하다

[Telephone rings.]
M Joy Travel Agency.
W Hello. Can I speak to Mr. Watson?
M Speaking. Who is calling, please?
W This is Emma Parker calling from New York.
M Oh, hello. I've waited for your call all afternoon.
W I'm still here in New York.
M Are you going to fly tomorrow?
W Yes. My flight leaves at 10 a.m. and arrives there at 3:30 p.m.
M Good. I'm going to pick you up at the airport.
W I appreciate it. I'll see you soon.

[전화벨이 울린다.]
남 Joy 여행사입니다.
여 여보세요. Watson 씨와 통화할 수 있나요?
남 전데요. 누구시죠?
여 저는 뉴욕에서 전화 드리는 Emma Parker예요.
남 아, 안녕하세요. 오후 내내 당신의 전화를 기다렸어요.
여 저는 아직 여기 뉴욕에 있어요.
남 내일 비행기로 오시나요?
여 네. 제 비행기는 오전 10시에 떠나서 오후 3시 30분에 도착해요.
남 좋아요. 제가 공항으로 데리러 가겠습니다.
여 감사합니다. 곧 뵐게요.

13 ②

해설 남자는 이발 예약을 4시에 하려고 했으나, 그 시간에는 이미 예약이 되어 있어서 4시 30분에 가기로 했다.

어휘 haircut[hέərkʌt] 머리 이발하기

[Telephone rings.]
W Good morning, Hair Design.
M Hi. I'd like to make an appointment on Saturday afternoon, please.
W Sure. Is it for a haircut?
M Yes, it is.
W When would you like to come in?
M Is 4 o'clock all right?
W I'm afraid there is somebody else at 4. Can you come in 30 minutes after that?
M That'll be fine.

[전화벨이 울린다.]
여 안녕하세요, Hair Design입니다.
남 안녕하세요. 토요일 오후에 예약하고 싶습니다.
여 네. 머리 커트를 하실 건가요?
남 네, 맞습니다.
여 언제 오실 건가요?
남 4시 괜찮은가요?
여 4시에는 다른 사람이 이미 있네요. 그 시간 30분 후에 오실 수 있나요?
남 좋습니다.

14 ③

해설 여자가 입시 피아노 레슨 광고를 보고 레슨을 받고 싶어 하자, 남자가 신청서를 작성하라고 했으므로 두 사람은 피아노 강사와 학생임을 알 수 있다.

어휘 entrance[éntrəns] 입학
have a seat 앉다
form[fɔːrm] 신청 용지
explain[ikspléin] 설명하다

M Good afternoon. How can I help you?
W I saw your ad "Piano Lessons for Exams" on your window.
M I see. I'm teaching piano to students for entrance exams.
W I'd like to take lessons.
M Have you ever taken a piano lesson?
W Yes, I have.
M Okay. Have a seat over there. I'll bring you a form and explain it to you.
W Thank you.

남 안녕하세요. 어떻게 도와드릴까요?
여 학원 창문에 붙은 광고 '입시 피아노 레슨'을 봤는데요.
남 그렇군요. 저는 학생들에게 입시를 위한 피아노를 가르치고 있습니다.
여 저는 그 수업을 듣고 싶어요.
남 피아노 레슨을 받아 본 적이 있나요?
여 네, 있습니다.
남 알겠습니다. 저쪽에 앉으세요. 신청서를 가져와서 설명할게요.
여 감사합니다.

15 ①

해설 두 사람은 이번 주말에 함께 등산을 하기로 하고 남자가 여자에게 간식을 가져오라고 부탁했다.

어휘 nearby[nìərbái] 인근에, 가까운 곳에
climb[klaim] 오르다
snack[snæk] 간식

W It's already the last day of March.
M I know. The weather is getting warmer.
W Yes. Oh, I heard about a Tulip Festival nearby this weekend.
M Oh, really? I wish I could go there.
W Do you have other plans for this weekend?
M Yes. Since the weather is nice, I'm going to go mountain climbing with Chris.
W That sounds like fun. Can I come, too?
M Sure. I'll bring some drinks that day. Can you bring some snacks?
W Of course.

여 벌써 3월의 마지막 날이야.
남 알아. 날씨가 점점 따뜻해지고 있어.
여 맞아. 아, 나는 이번 주말에 근처에서 하는 튤립 축제에 대해 들었어.
남 아, 정말? 갈 수만 있으면 가고 싶네.
여 너 이번 주말에 다른 계획이 있니?
남 응. 날씨가 좋아서, Chris와 함께 등산할 거야.
여 재미있겠다. 나도 가도 되니?
남 물론이지. 내가 그날 음료를 좀 가져올게. 너는 간식을 좀 가져올래?
여 그래.

16 ③

해설 여자는 딸이 식사를 거르고 게임을 너무 많이 해서 걱정하고 있다.

어휘 be worried about ~에 대해 걱정하다
grade[greid] 성적
even[íːvən] 심지어
skip[skip] (일 등을) 거르다, 빼먹다
meal[miːl] 식사, 끼니

M How's Cindy doing?
W She's not doing well. I'm very worried about my daughter.
M What's wrong? Is it about her grades?
W No, it's not. Actually, she's doing well in school.
M Then why are you worried about her?
W She spends too much time playing computer games. She even skips her meals.
M Did you talk to her about it?
W Yes, but she's not listening to me at all.

남 Cindy는 어떻게 지내요?
여 잘 지내지 못해요. 저는 제 딸이 매우 걱정돼요.
남 무슨 일 있어요? 성적 때문인가요?
여 아니에요. 실은 제 딸은 학교에서는 잘하고 있어요.
남 그럼 Cindy가 왜 걱정이 되나요?
여 걔가 컴퓨터 게임을 너무 많이 해요. 심지어 식사도 거르고요.
남 그 일에 대해 얘기를 해보셨어요?
여 네, 하지만 제 말을 전혀 듣지 않네요.

17 ⑤

해설 남자가 우체국을 찾고 있고, 여자가 위치를 알려주는 대화가 적절하다.

어휘 be interested in ~에 관심이 있다
collect[kəlékt] 모으다, 수집하다
stamp[stæmp] 우표
in the future 미래에
be good at ~을 잘하다

① M Are you interested in stamps?
　W Yes. I love collecting stamps.
② M Can I take pictures here?
　W Sure, go ahead.
③ M You're the best student in our school.
　W How nice of you to say so!
④ M What do you want to be in the future?
　W I'm good at math, so I want to be a math teacher.
⑤ M Excuse me, can you tell me the way to the post office?
　W Sure. Go straight for two blocks.

① 남 당신은 우표에 관심이 있나요?
　여 네. 저는 우표 모으는 걸 아주 좋아해요.
② 남 여기서 사진을 찍어도 되나요?
　여 물론이죠, 어서 찍으세요.
③ 남 당신은 우리 학교에서 가장 뛰어난 학생이에요.
　여 그렇게 말해주니 고마워요!
④ 남 미래에 무엇이 되고 싶나요?
　여 저는 수학을 잘해서, 수학 선생님이 되고 싶어요.
⑤ 남 실례합니다. 우체국에 가는 길을 알려주시겠어요?
　여 네. 두 블록 직진하세요.

18 ③

해설 할인 품목(TV, 에어컨), 할인율(각각 10%, 15%), 행사장 위치(5층), 판매 시간(오후 5시까지)에 대해 언급하였으나, 사은품에 대해서는 언급하지 않았다.

어휘 one-day 하루 동안의
event hall 행사장
hurry[hə́ːri] 서두르다
last[læst] 계속되다

W Good afternoon, ladies and gentlemen. We have a special one-day sale at Grace Department Store. Today, television sets will be 10% off and washing machines will be 15% off. Those are our special sale items for today only. The event hall is on the 5th floor. Please hurry because this sale will last only until 5 in the afternoon. Thank you.

여 신사 숙녀 여러분, 안녕하세요. Grace 백화점에서 특별 일일 할인 행사가 있습니다. 오늘, 텔레비전은 10퍼센트 할인하고 세탁기는 15퍼센트 할인합니다. 오늘만 하는 특별 할인 품목들입니다. 행사장은 5층에 있습니다. 오후 5시까지만 계속되므로 서둘러 주십시오. 감사합니다.

19 ④

해설 남자가 셔틀버스를 타는 장소를 물은 후에 지하철역까지 걸어갈 수 있는지 물었으므로 갈 수 있는 지 여부를 말해주는 것이 적절하다.

M Excuse me. How can I get to Seoul N Tower?
W Well, it's not easy to get there from here.
M What do you mean?

여 실례합니다. 서울 N 타워에 어떻게 가나요?
남 음, 여기서 그곳까지 가는 게 쉽지 않아요.
여 무슨 말씀이세요?

어휘 get to ~에 도착하다
mean[miːn] 의미하다
take the subway 지하철을 타다
shuttle bus 셔틀버스, 근거리 왕복 버스

W You have to take the subway and then take the Namsan shuttle bus.
M Where can I take the shuttle bus?
W I think you can take it in front of Chungmuro Subway Station.
M How far is it to the nearest station?
W It's close. It takes 5 minutes on foot.

남 지하철을 타고 그다음에 남산 셔틀 버스를 타야 해요.
여 셔틀버스는 어디서 타나요?
남 충무로 지하철역 앞에서 탈 수 있어요.
여 가장 가까운 역까지 얼마나 먼가요?
남 가까워요. 걸어서 5분 걸려요.

① 정말 감사합니다.
② 좋아요, 함께 갑시다.
③ 저는 지하철로 그곳에 갈 거예요.
⑤ 저는 택시를 타는 것보다 걷는 것을 좋아해요.

20 ⑤

해설 남자가 약을 언제 먹어야 하는지 묻고 있으므로 약을 먹는 시간을 말해주는 것이 적절하다.

어휘 stomachache[stʌ́məkeik] 복통
lunchtime[lʌ́ntʃtàim] 점심시간
pill[pil] 알약
at a time 한번에

W Good afternoon. How can I help you?
M Yes, I have a terrible stomachache.
W I see. When did it begin?
M It began after lunchtime. I think I ate something bad.
W Let me give you some medicine. [Pause] Here you are.
M Thank you.
W You should take 2 pills at a time.
M Okay. When should I take these?
W Take these 30 minutes after each meal.

여 안녕하세요. 어떻게 도와드릴까요?
남 네, 저 배가 심하게 아파요.
여 그렇군요. 언제부터 아프기 시작했나요?
남 점심시간 이후부터 아프기 시작했어요. 뭔가 잘못 먹은 것 같아요.
여 약을 좀 드릴게요. [잠시 후] 여기 있습니다.
남 감사합니다.
여 한 번에 두 알씩 드세요.
남 알겠습니다. 이것들을 언제 먹어야 하나요?
여 식후 30분에 드세요.

① 그 약은 15달러입니다.
② 아마 그건 당신에게 도움이 될 겁니다.
③ 당신은 쉬는 게 좋겠어요.
④ 당신은 뜨거운 물을 마셔야 해요.

01 ④	02 ③	03 ③	04 ④	05 ①	06 ④	07 ③
08 ④	09 ③	10 ④	11 ⑤	12 ②	13 ⑤	14 ⑤
15 ④	16 ③	17 ②	18 ④	19 ②	20 ②	

01 ④

해설 토요일에 눈이 내리기 시작해서 더 추워진다고 했다.

어휘 have a look 살펴보다
be expected 예상되다
careful[kέərfəl] 조심하는
partly[pάːrtli] 부분적으로

W You're listening to Weather Korea. Let's have a look at the weather for this week. On Monday, it will be cloudy all day. From Tuesday to Thursday, rain is expected in the morning, so you should be careful when you drive. On Friday, it will be partly cloudy and windy. On Saturday, it will start to snow and will get colder, but the snow will stop on Sunday.

여 여러분은 〈Weather Korea〉를 듣고 계십니다. 이번 주 날씨를 살펴보겠습니다. 월요일에는 하루 종일 흐리겠습니다. 화요일부터 목요일까지, 아침에 비가 올 것으로 예상되므로 운전에 유의하십시오. 금요일에는 부분적으로 흐리고 바람이 불겠습니다. 토요일에 눈이 내리기 시작해서 더 추워지겠지만, 일요일에 눈이 그치겠습니다.

02 ③

해설 여자는 작은 꽃 모양이 있는 셔츠를 샀다.

어휘 striped[straipt] 줄무늬
be in fashion 유행이다
style[stail] 스타일, 모양
sunflower[sʌnfláuər] 해바라기
print[print] 무늬
pattern[pǽtərn] 무늬

M May I help you, ma'am?
W Yes, I'm looking for a shirt.
M I see. These blue striped shirts are in fashion this spring.
W They are not really my style.
M Then, how about this white shirt with a sunflower on it? It's so pretty.
W Well, that looks good. But the flower print is too big.
M We have shirts with small flowers. They're pink.
W That would be better. I'll take one.

남 도와드릴까요, 손님?
여 네, 셔츠를 찾고 있어요.
남 그러시군요. 이 파란색 줄무늬 셔츠가 이번 봄에 유행이에요.
여 그건 정말 제 스타일이 아니네요.
남 그럼, 해바라기가 그려진 이 흰색 셔츠는 어때세요? 아주 예뻐요.
여 음, 좋아 보이네요. 하지만 꽃무늬가 너무 커요.
남 작은 꽃이 있는 셔츠들도 있습니다. 그것은 분홍색이에요.
여 그게 더 낫겠어요. 그걸로 주세요.

03 ③

해설 여자는 치과에 치료를 받으러 가면서 아플까 봐 걱정하고 있다.

어휘 dentist[déntist] 치과 의사
toothache[túːθeik] 치통
for a while 한동안, 잠깐 동안
painful[péinfəl] 고통스러운

M Hi, Jane. Where are you going?
W I'm going to the dentist.
M Is there something wrong with your teeth?
W My teeth really hurt. I couldn't sleep last night.
M That's too bad.
W I'm really afraid it's going to be painful.
M Don't worry. It'll be okay.

남 안녕, Jane. 너 어디 가니?
여 치과에 가는 중이야.
남 치아에 무슨 문제가 있니?
여 내 치아가 너무 아파. 어젯밤에 잠을 잘 수 없었거든.
남 그거 안됐구나.
여 아플까 봐 너무 무서워.
남 걱정 마. 괜찮을 거야.

04 ④

해설 남자는 스키 리조트에서 가게를 청소하며 일했다고 했다.

어휘 full-time 전임으로, 전시간제로
mostly[móustli] 주로

M Hi, Lucy. Long time no see.
W How have you been, Brian?
M Pretty good. I stayed at Crystal Mountain Ski Resort during the winter vacation.

남 안녕, Lucy. 오랜만이야.
여 어떻게 지냈니, Brian?
남 잘 지냈어. 나는 겨울 방학 내내 Crystal Mountain 스키 리조트에서 지냈어.

snowboard[snóubɔ̀ːrd] 스노보드

W Wow, that sounds like fun. Did you learn to ski?
M No, I worked full-time there.
W Really? What did you do there?
M Well, I mostly cleaned the shops and put skis and snowboards in the right places.

여 와, 재미있었겠다. 너 스키를 배웠니?
남 아니, 나는 거기에서 전임으로 일했어.
여 정말? 거기서 뭘 했는데?
남 음, 나는 주로 가게를 청소했고, 스키와 스노보드를 제자리에 두었어.

05 ①

해설 남자가 뱃멀미를 한다고 했고 여자가 곧 섬에 도착한다는 것으로 보아 배에서 나누는 대화임을 알 수 있다.

어휘 dolphin[dɑ́lfin] 돌고래
air[ɛər] 공중
land[lænd] (배를 타고) 도착하다
seasick[síːsik] 뱃멀미
lie down 눕다
Take it easy. 진정해.

W Wow, we were very lucky to see the dolphins jump in the air today.
M I know. I saw the dolphins so close.
W I heard most people don't get to see them often on a boat tour.
M When are we going to land on the island?
W In 20 minutes. [Pause] Oh, you don't look well.
M I'm feeling seasick right now. I want to lie down.
W Take it easy. We're almost there.

여 와, 돌고래가 공중으로 점프하는 걸 보다니 우린 정말 운이 좋았어.
남 맞아. 아주 가까이에서 돌고래를 봤어.
여 대부분의 사람들이 보트 투어에서 돌고래를 자주 보지 못한다고 들었어.
남 우리가 언제 섬에 도착해?
여 20분 후에. [잠시 후] 아, 너 몸이 안 좋아 보이네.
남 나 뱃멀미가 나고 있어. 눕고 싶네.
여 진정해. 우리 거의 다 왔어.

06 ④

해설 여자는 친구와 다툰 남자에게 사과하라고 충고하고 있다.

어휘 between[bitwíːn] 사이에
make a joke 농담하다
embarrassed[imbǽrəst] 당황한
apologize[əpɑ́lədʒàiz] 사과하다

W Bill, is everything all right?
M No, I feel really bad about Kate.
W Kate? Did something happen between you two?
M Well, I made a joke about Kate's new hat. Then she started to cry.
W Oh no. Then what did you do?
M Nothing. I just left her there. I was so embarrassed. I couldn't say anything.
W It's not too late. You should apologize to her.

여 Bill, 잘 지내?
남 아니, 나는 Kate에 대해서 정말 기분이 안 좋아.
여 Kate? 너희 둘 사이에 무슨 일이 있었니?
남 음, 내가 Kate가 산 새 모자에 대해 농담을 했거든. 그러고 나서 걔가 울기 시작했어.
여 이런. 그다음에 넌 뭘 했어?
남 아무것도. 나는 그냥 거기에 걔 내버려 뒀어. 너무 당황했거든. 아무 말도 할 수 없었어.
여 너무 늦지 않았어. 너는 걔한테 사과해야 해.

07 ③

해설 여자는 제주도 여행에서 택시를 이용하지 않았다.

어휘 rent[rent] 빌리다
sometimes[sʌ́mtàimz] 가끔
local[lóukəl] 지역의
downtown[dáuntáun] 시내

M How was your summer vacation?
W I was in Jeju-do for 2 weeks.
M That sounds great! How did you get there?
W I took an airplane.
M Did you rent a car there?
W No. I rented a bike to get around. And sometimes I took local buses to visit downtown.
M What else did you do?
W I went to U-do by ship. It is a beautiful island.

남 여름 방학 어떻게 보냈니?
여 난 2주 동안 제주도에 있었어.
남 멋지다! 거기에 어떻게 갔니?
여 비행기를 탔어.
남 거기서 자동차를 빌렸니?
여 아니. 돌아다니려고 자전거를 빌렸어. 그리고 가끔 시내를 방문하러 지역 버스를 탔지.
남 그밖에 또 뭘 했니?
여 배를 타고 우도에 갔어. 아름다운 섬이더라.

08 ④

[해설] 엄마에게 비밀번호를 물어보기 위해 전화하라는 여자의 말에 남자는 알겠다고 했다.

[어휘] keycard[kíkàːrd] 키 카드
get into ~에 들어가다
check[tʃek] 확인하다
lock[lɑk] 잠금장치
password[pǽswərd] 비밀번호
right away 곧바로

M Oh no! I can't find my keycard. I have to get into my house.
W Did you put it in your bag?
M Let me see. [Pause] It's not here.
W Did you check your pockets?
M Yes, but it wasn't there.
W Wait, you can also open the lock with a password. Do you know the password?
M No, I don't. My mother changed it a few days ago.
W You should call your mom and ask.
M Okay. I'll do that right away.

남 이런! 내 키 카드를 못 찾겠어. 집에 들어가야 하는데.
여 그걸 가방 안에 넣어 두었니?
남 어디 보자. [잠시 후] 여기에 없어.
여 네 주머니는 확인해봤어?
남 물론이지, 하지만 거기에 없었어.
여 잠깐, 비밀번호로 잠긴 문을 열 수도 있잖아. 비밀번호를 알고 있니?
남 아니, 몰라. 어머니가 며칠 전에 그것을 바꾸셨거든.
여 엄마에게 전화해서 물어봐.
남 알았어. 지금 바로 그럴게.

09 ③

[해설] 나이(18세 이상), 시급(10달러), 근무 시간(매일 저녁 6시~10시), 면접 준비물(신분증)에 대해 언급하였으나 저녁 제공에 대해서는 언급하지 않았다.

[어휘] part-time 시간제로, 파트 타임으로
pay[pei] 급료, 보수
perfect[pə́ːrfikt] 완벽한
come over ~에 들르다
interview[íntərvjùː] 면접
ID(= identification) 신분증

[Telephone rings.]
W Happy Bakery. How may I help you?
M Are you still looking for someone to work part-time?
W Yes, we are. Are you over 18?
M Yes, I am.
W The pay is $10 an hour, and you have to work from 6 to 10 every evening.
M The hours are perfect for me.
W Could you come over to the shop at noon for an interview?
M Sure. Do I need to bring anything to the interview?
W Yes, you need to bring your ID.

[전화벨이 울린다.]
여 Happy 제과점입니다. 어떻게 도와드릴까요?
남 아직도 시간제로 일할 사람을 찾고 계시나요?
여 네, 그렇습니다. 나이가 18세 이상인가요?
남 네, 맞아요.
여 시간당 급료는 10달러이고, 매일 저녁 6시에서 10시까지 근무해야 해요.
남 그 시간이 저에게 딱 맞네요.
여 12시에 면접 보러 가게에 들를 수 있나요?
남 물론이죠. 면접에 뭘 가져가야 하나요?
여 네, 신분증을 가져오셔야 해요.

10 ④

[해설] 학교 농구팀이 대회에서 우승한 것을 축하하기 위한 파티에 대해 안내하는 내용이다.

[어휘] national championship 전국 선수권대회
celebrate[séləbrèit] 축하하다
gym[dʒim] 체육관
join[dʒɔin] 함께하다
snack[snæk] 간식

M We're very excited to tell you that our school basketball team won the national championship. To celebrate this, tomorrow after school, we are planning to have a party for the players at the gym. We hope all the students will join the party. There will be some snacks and drinks. We're looking forward to seeing you there. Thank you.

남 여러분에게 우리 학교의 농구팀이 전국 선수권대회에서 우승한 것을 말하게 되어 매우 기쁩니다. 이 일을 축하하기 위해서, 내일 방과 후에, 체육관에서 선수들을 위한 파티를 열 계획입니다. 전교생이 파티를 함께하기를 바랍니다. 간식과 음료가 있을 겁니다. 그곳에서 여러분을 만날 것을 기대하겠습니다. 감사합니다.

11 ⑤

[해설] 세일 기간에는 어떤 쿠폰도 받지 않는다고 했다.

W Thank you for shopping at Joy's Beauty Shop. We are having a holiday sale from today until January 25. Most of our beauty

여 Joy's Beauty Shop에서 쇼핑해주셔서 감사합니다. 오늘부터 1월 25일까지 휴일 세일이 있습니다. 저희 미용 제

어휘 holiday[hálədèi] 휴일
most[moust] 대부분
beauty product 미용 제품
off[ɔːf] 할인되어
spend[spend] 쓰다, 소비하다
free [friː] 무료의
accept[əksépt] 받아 주다, 수락하다

products are on sale. Face creams and hair products are 30 percent off. Also, if you spend more than $50 at our shop, you'll get a free lipstick. However, during the sale, we will not accept any coupons.

품의 대부분이 세일 중입니다. 얼굴 크림과 헤어 제품은 30퍼센트 할인됩니다. 또한, 저희 가게에서 50달러 이상을 쓰시면, 무료 립스틱을 받으실 겁니다. 그러나 세일 기간에는 어떤 쿠폰도 받지 않습니다.

12 ②

해설 남자는 함께 쇼핑하러 가서 재킷을 고르는 것을 도와 달라고 여자에게 전화했다.

어휘 choose[tʃuːz] 고르다
late[leit] 늦은

[Telephone rings.]
W Hello.
M Hello, this is Tony. Is Wendy there?
W Hi, Tony. This is Wendy. What's up?
M I'm going to go shopping to buy a jacket this afternoon. Do you want to go with me?
W Sorry, I have a tennis lesson at 3.
M That's too bad. I really needed your help with choosing a jacket.
W I can go with you after 5. Will it be too late to go shopping then?
M Not at all. Just call me back after your lesson.

[전화벨이 울린다.]
여 여보세요.
남 여보세요, 저 Tony인데요. Wendy 있나요?
여 안녕, Tony. 나 Wendy야. 무슨 일이니?
남 나 오늘 오후에 재킷을 사러 쇼핑을 하려고 해. 나랑 같이 갈래?
여 미안해. 나는 3시에 테니스 강습이 있어.
남 아쉽다. 재킷을 고르는 데 네 도움이 정말로 필요했거든.
여 내가 5시 이후에 너와 함께 갈 수 있는데. 그때 쇼핑하러 가면 너무 늦을까?
남 전혀. 수업 끝나고 나한테 다시 전화해 줘.

13 ⑤

해설 남자가 6시 반까지 수영 강습이 있어서 대신 7시에 만나기로 했다.

어휘 note[nout] 필기
try A's best 최선을 다하다
have difficulty in v-ing
~하는 데 어려움이 있다
come over to ~에 오다, 합류하다

W Mike, how do you study math at home?
M I check my notes and do my homework.
W I'm trying my best. But I still have difficulty in doing math homework.
M Do you need help? You can come over to my house.
W Really? How about 5 o'clock after school?
M I have a swimming lesson, and it finishes at 6:30.
W How about 7, then?
M That will be fine. I'll see you then.

여 Mike, 너는 집에서 수학 공부를 어떻게 하니?
남 나는 필기한 것을 확인하고 숙제를 해.
여 나는 최선을 다하고 있거든. 하지만 여전히 수학 숙제를 하는 데 어려움이 있어.
남 도움이 필요하니? 네가 우리 집으로 와도 돼.
여 정말? 방과 후 5시 어때?
남 내가 수영 강습이 있는데 그건 6시 30분에 끝나.
여 그럼, 7시는 어때?
남 그게 좋을 것 같아. 그때 보자.

14 ⑤

해설 책을 빌리기 위해 신분증과 도서 대출 카드가 필요하다는 내용으로 보아 두 사람의 관계는 도서관 사서와 이용객임을 알 수 있다.

M Excuse me. Where can I find the section on fiction?
W It's on the 3rd floor.
M Are there storybooks for children in the same section?

남 실례합니다. 소설 코너가 어디에 있나요?
여 3층에 있어요.
남 어린이용 이야기책도 같은 코너에 있나요?

어휘 section[sékʃən] 코너, 분야
fiction[fíkʃən] 소설
storybook[stɔ́:ribùk] 이야기책
same[seim] 같은
 borrow[bárou] 빌리다
ID card 신분증
library card 도서 대출 카드

W No, you can find children's books on the 2nd floor.

M Thank you. What do I need to borrow the books?

W You need both an ID card and a library card.

여 아뇨, 어린이 책은 2층에서 찾을 수 있어요.

남 감사합니다. 책을 빌리려면 뭐가 필요하나요?

여 신분증과 도서 대출 카드 둘 다 필요해요.

15 ④

해설 여자는 남자에게 음료를 주문하는 동안 테이블을 맡아 달라고 부탁했다.

어휘 company[kʌ́mpəni] 회사
later[léitər] 나중에
order[ɔ́:rdər] 주문하다

W Henry, it's so good to see you. How have you been?

M Great. You look great. What do you do these days?

W I work at a fashion magazine company. I'll tell you more about it later. So what do you want to have?

M I'll have a cup of coffee. What about you?

W I'll get the same. I'll order the drinks. Can you go and find a table?

M Sure.

여 Henry, 만나서 너무 반가워요. 어떻게 지냈어요?

남 잘 지냈어요. 당신은 좋아 보이네요. 요즘 뭐 하세요?

여 저는 패션 잡지 회사에서 일해요. 나중에 자세히 알려 드릴게요. 그래서 무엇을 마시고 싶으세요?

남 저는 커피 한 잔 마실게요. 당신은요?

여 저도 같은 것으로 할게요. 저는 음료를 주문할게요. 가서 테이블을 찾아주실래요?

남 알겠어요.

16 ③

해설 남자는 새로 산 자전거가 고장이 나서 화가 났다.

어휘 upset[ʌpsét] 속상한, 화가 난
the day before yesterday 그저께
ride[raid] 타다
steal[sti:l] 훔치다
be broken 고장 나다
repair shop 수리점

W You look upset. What's wrong?

M I bought a new bike the day before yesterday.

W Right. Your bike was really nice.

M Well, I can't ride it any more.

W Did somebody steal your bike?

M No, I have it, but it's broken.

W Did you take it to the repair shop?

M I did, but I have to wait 2 weeks until it is fixed.

여 너 화가 나 보여. 무슨 일 있니?

남 내가 그저께 새 자전거를 샀잖아.

여 맞아. 네 자전거 엄청 좋은 거였어.

남 글쎄, 난 더 이상 그것을 탈 수가 없어.

여 누군가 네 자전거를 훔쳤니?

남 아니, 자전거를 가지고는 있는데, 그게 고장이 났거든.

여 그걸 수리점에 가져갔니?

남 그랬는데, 수리가 끝나려면 2주나 기다려야 해.

17 ②

해설 상자를 들고 있는 남자가 여자에게 문을 열어 달라고 부탁하는 대화가 적절하다.

어휘 present[prézənt] 선물
next to ~의 옆에
mind[maind] 꺼리다, 싫어하다

① M What's in this big box?
　　W There is a Christmas tree in it.
② M Can you open the door, please?
　　W Sure. No problem.
③ M I have a present for you.
　　W Oh, you're so sweet. Thank you.
④ M Do you know where my box is?
　　W Yes. It's next to the door.
⑤ M Do you mind if I open the window?
　　W Of course not.

① 남 이 큰 상자 안에 무엇이 들어있나요?
　　여 그 안에 크리스마스트리가 있어요.
② 남 문을 열어 주시겠어요?
　　여 네. 그럼요.
③ 남 당신에게 줄 선물이 있어요.
　　여 정말 자상하시네요. 고마워요.
④ 남 제 상자가 어디에 있는지 아세요?
　　여 네. 문 옆에 있어요.
⑤ 남 창문을 열어도 되나요?
　　여 물론이죠.

18 ④

해설 출발지(인천), 연착 이유(폭설), 연착되는 시간(1시간 반), 새로운 도착 시각(오후 7시 20분)에 대해 언급했지만, 도착지에 대해서는 언급하지 않았다.

어휘 have A's attention 주의를 기울이다
flight[flait] 비행편
land[lænd] 도착하다
on time 제시간에
heavy snow 폭설
arrival time 도착 시간

W Ladies and gentlemen, can I have your attention, please? We are sorry to tell you that flight 703 from Incheon won't land on time because of heavy snow. The flight will be an hour and a half late. The new arrival time will be at 7:20 p.m. We'll give you more information later. Thank you.

여 신사 숙녀 여러분. 주목해 주시겠습니까? 인천에서 오는 703 비행편이 폭설로 인하여 제시간에 도착하지 못한다는 말씀을 드리게 되어 죄송합니다. 비행기는 1시간 반 정도 늦겠습니다. 새로운 도착 시각은 오후 7시 20분이 되겠습니다. 추후에 더 자세한 정보를 알려 드리겠습니다. 감사합니다.

19 ②

해설 아프지만 병원에 갈 시간이 없다는 남자의 말에 위로하는 말이 와야 적절하다.

어휘 bad cold 독감
medicine[médisn] 약
enough[ináf] 충분한
finish[fíniʃ] 끝내다
by[bai] ~까지

W You look very tired. What's the problem?
M I have a bad cold.
W Did you see a doctor?
M Not yet. I just took some medicine at home.
W I don't think that's enough. Why don't you see a doctor?
M I want to, but I don't have time for that today.
W Why not?
M I have to finish my science project by tomorrow.
W That's too bad.

여 너 매우 피곤해 보여. 무슨 일 있니?
남 나 독감에 걸렸어.
여 병원에 갔었니?
남 아직. 그냥 집에서 약을 좀 먹었어.
여 그것으로 충분할 것 같지 않은데. 병원에 가 보지 그러니?
남 그러고 싶은데 오늘 갈 시간이 없어.
여 왜?
남 나는 내일까지 과학 과제를 끝내야 하거든.
여 안됐구나.

① 기운 내!
③ 잘했어!
④ 와줘서 고마워.
⑤ 그가 얼른 나았으면 좋겠다.

20 ②

해설 남자가 야구 경기가 어디에서 열리는지 장소를 묻고 있으므로 야구 경기를 하는 장소를 알려주는 응답이 적절하다.

어휘 special[spéʃəl] 특별한
alone[əlóun] 혼자서
[선택지]
stadium[stéidiəm] 경기장, 스타디움

W Eric, what are your plans for this weekend?
M Nothing special. How about you?
W I'm going to go to a baseball game.
M Are you going to go there alone?
W No, I'm going to go with some of my friends.
M Can I go with you?
W Of course. I'll buy a ticket for you.
M Thank you. Then, I will buy some chicken. By the way, where is the game?
W It's at the Sky Stadium.

여 Eric, 이번 주말 계획이 뭐니?
남 특별한 건 없어. 너는 어때?
여 나는 야구 경기를 보러 갈 거야.
남 너 혼자 가는 거니?
여 아니, 내 친구들 몇 명이랑 같이 가.
남 나도 같이 가도 되니?
여 물론이지. 내가 표를 사줄게.
남 좋아. 그럼 내가 치킨을 살게. 그런데 경기는 어디서 하니?
여 Sky 경기장에서 해.

① 다음 주 토요일이야.
③ 버스 정류장에서 만나자.
④ 나는 공원에서 야구를 해.
⑤ 우리는 지하철을 타고 거기 가면 돼.

01 ④	02 ⑤	03 ⑤	04 ⑤	05 ③	06 ③	07 ③
08 ④	09 ④	10 ⑤	11 ④	12 ③	13 ②	14 ③
15 ④	16 ③	17 ③	18 ③	19 ⑤	20 ①	

01 ④

해설 목요일 오전에는 흐리지만, 오후에는 비가 많이 온다고 했다.

어휘 weekly[wíːkli] 주간의, 매주의
all day long 하루 종일
starting[stάːrtiŋ] ~부터
outdoor activity 야외 활동

W Good morning! Let's check the weekly weather. On Monday and Tuesday, it will snow all day long. On Wednesday, the snow will stop, and it will be sunny. On Thursday, it will be cloudy in the morning, but it will rain a lot in the afternoon. Starting Friday, it is going to be sunny, so this weekend will be good for outdoor activities. Thank you for listening.

여 안녕하세요! 주간 날씨를 살펴보겠습니다. 월요일과 화요일에는 하루 종일 눈이 내리겠습니다. 수요일에는 눈이 그치고 화창하겠습니다. 목요일에는 아침에는 흐리지만, 오후에는 비가 많이 오겠습니다. 금요일부터는 화창해서, 이번 주말은 야외 활동하기에 좋은 날이 되겠습니다. 들어주셔서 감사합니다.

02 ⑤

해설 용 그림 아래에 Dragon Fire라고 쓰여진 민소매 티셔츠이다.

어휘 sleeveless[slíːvlis] 소매 없는
front[frʌnt] 앞쪽, 앞면
dragon[drǽgən] 용

M Let's make a T-shirt for our band club.
W That's a good idea.
M What type of a T-shirt do you want?
W I think a sleeveless one would be good because it's getting hot.
M I agree. Then, what about the design on the front of it?
W I want to put a dragon on it. Since our band's name is Dragon Fire.
M How about writing "Dragon Fire" under the dragon?
W Great. That will be nice.

남 우리 밴드 동아리 티셔츠 만들자.
여 그거 좋은 생각이야.
남 어떤 종류의 티셔츠를 원하니?
여 날이 더워지고 있으니까 소매가 없는 게 좋을 것 같아.
남 나도 동의해. 그러면 티셔츠 앞쪽 디자인은 어때?
여 나는 그 위에 용 그림을 넣고 싶어. 우리 밴드 이름이 Dragon Fire잖아.
남 용 그림 아래에 Dragon Fire라고 쓰는 게 어때?
여 좋아. 멋질 거야.

03 ⑤

해설 목적지(캐나다 밴쿠버), 출발 요일(수요일), 출발지(인천), 출발 시각(오후 5시)에 대해 언급했으나, 예매 인원수에 대해서는 언급하지 않았다.

어휘 airline[ɛ́ərlàin] 항공사
the day after tomorrow 모레
Incheon International Airport 인천 국제 공항

[Telephone rings.]
M Star Airlines. How may I help you?
W Yes, I'd like to make a reservation.
M Okay. Where are you going to go?
W To Vancouver, Canada.
M What date would you like to leave?
W I'd like to leave this Wednesday, the day after tomorrow.
M Okay. We have a flight leaving Incheon International Airport at 5 p.m.
W That sounds good.

[전화벨이 울린다.]
여 Star 항공입니다. 어떻게 도와드릴까요?
남 네, 예약을 하고 싶은데요.
여 알겠습니다. 어디로 가실 예정이십니까?
남 캐나다 밴쿠버로요.
여 어떤 날짜에 떠나고 싶으신가요?
남 모레인 이번 주 수요일에 떠나고 싶습니다.
여 알겠습니다. 오후 5시에 인천국제공항에서 출발하는 비행기가 있습니다.
남 좋습니다.

04 ⑤

해설 남자는 탐정 소설을 가장 좋아한다고 했다.

어휘 free time 여가 시간
what kind of 어떤 종류의
poetry book 시집
mystery book 탐정 소설
most[moust] 가장 많이
lend[lend] 빌려주다
sometimes[sʌ́mtàimz] 언젠가

W Wow! You have many books in your room. Do you like reading books?
M Yes, I enjoy reading books in my free time.
W What kind of books do you read?
M I read all kinds of books, like poetry books, mystery books, and history books.
W Which one do you like the most?
M I like mystery books the most.
W Can you lend one of them to me sometime?
M Sure.

여 와! 네 방에 책이 많네. 너는 책 읽는 걸 좋아하니?
남 응, 나는 여가 시간에 책 읽는 걸 좋아해.
여 너는 어떤 종류의 책을 읽니?
남 시집, 탐정 소설, 역사책과 같은 모든 종류의 책을 읽어.
여 어떤 것을 가장 좋아하니?
남 나는 탐정 소설이 가장 좋아.
여 언젠가 그것 중에 하나를 나에게 빌려줄래?
남 물론이지.

05 ③

해설 여자가 남자에게 책갈피를 보여주면서 가격을 알려주고, 필기구가 어디에 있는지 설명하는 상황으로 보아 두 사람이 대화하는 장소는 문구점임을 알 수 있다.

어휘 bookmark[búkmà:rk] 책갈피
metal[métəl] 금속(의)
plastic[plǽstik] 플라스틱(으로 된)
writing tool 필기구
section[sékʃən] 부분, 구분
You can't miss it. 찾기 쉬워요.

M Hi, I'm looking for some bookmarks.
W Let me show you. [Pause] There are metal and plastic ones.
M Metal ones look nice. I'll take one of those. How much is it?
W It's $3. Do you need anything else?
M Oh, I also need some pencils and erasers for my son.
W For writing tools, you have to go straight to section A. You can't miss it.
M Thank you so much for your help.

남 안녕하세요. 책갈피를 좀 찾고 있는데요.
여 제가 보여드릴게요. [잠시 후] 금속이나 플라스틱으로 된 것이 있어요.
남 금속으로 된 게 좋은 것 같네요. 이거 하나 가져갈게요. 얼마인가요?
여 3달러입니다. 또 필요하신 게 있으신가요?
남 아, 제 아들에게 줄 연필이랑 지우개도 필요해요.
여 필기구는 A 구역까지 곧장 가셔야 해요. 찾기 쉬워요.
남 도와주셔서 감사합니다.

06 ③

해설 여자는 남자의 친구가 곧 낫기를 바란다고 하면서 친구의 회복을 기원하고 있다.

어휘 fall down 넘어지다
stairs[stɛə́rz] 계단
serious[síəriəs] 심한
soy milk 두유
get better (병이) 나아지다

M Mom, my friend Tom is in the hospital.
W Did something happen to him?
M He fell down the subway stairs and broke his leg yesterday.
W Oh, I hope it's not serious.
M I'm going to visit him this afternoon. What should I bring him?
W How about some drinks? I think juice or soy milk would be nice.
M That sounds good. I'll get orange juice for him.
W Good. I hope he'll get better soon.

남 엄마, 제 친구 Tom이 병원에 있어요.
여 걔한테 무슨 일이 있었니?
남 걔가 어제 지하철 계단에서 넘어져서 다리가 부러졌거든요.
여 아, 심하지 않았으면 좋겠네.
남 저는 오늘 오후에 Tom을 보러 가려고요. 뭘 가져가야 할까요?
여 음료수 어때? 주스나 두유가 좋을 것 같네.
남 그거 좋네요. 저는 오렌지 주스를 사다 줄래요.
여 좋아. 걔가 얼른 나았으면 좋겠네.

07 ③

해설 여자는 목요일에 제주도에 가서 금요일에 마지막 비행기로 서울에 돌아온다고 했다.

M You must be very excited about your trip to Jeju-do. How long are you planning to stay?
W Not too long. I have too much work to do.

남 너 제주도 여행 때문에 정말 신나겠다. 얼마나 오래 머무를 계획이니?
여 별로 길지는 않아. 나는 할 일이 너무

어휘 be planning to-v ~할 계획이다
get back to ~로 돌아오다
island[áilənd] 섬

M That's no good. When are you going to leave?
W I'm going to leave this Thursday.
M Then when are you getting back to Seoul?
W I'll take the last plane the next day.
M You are going to stay there for only one day? It's too bad you won't have enough time to enjoy the island.
W I know.

많거든.
남 좋지 않네. 언제 떠나니?
여 나는 이번 목요일에 떠날 거야.
남 그럼 언제 서울로 돌아오니?
여 나는 그 다음 날 마지막 비행기를 탈 거야.
남 너 하루만 그곳에 머무르는 거야? 섬을 즐길 시간이 충분하지 않아서 안 됐네.
여 그래.

08 ④

해설 남자가 여자에게 스웨터를 찾아 달라고 하자, 여자는 알겠다고 했다.

어휘 pack[pæk] 짐을 꾸리다
field trip 수학여행
stay up late 늦게까지 깨어 있다
make sure 확인하다

W You look busy. What are you doing now?
M I'm packing for a field trip tomorrow.
W Don't stay up late. You have to wake up early tomorrow.
M All right, Mom.
W Oh, did you check the weather forecast?
M Yes. The rain will stop late tonight and it'll be fine tomorrow.
W Make sure you bring your sweater. It will get cold after the rain.
M I don't know where it is. Can you find it for me, please?
W Okay, I will.

여 너 바빠 보인다. 지금 뭐 하고 있니?
남 내일 수학여행 갈 짐을 챙기고 있어요.
여 너무 늦지 않게 자렴. 내일 일찍 일어나야 하잖니.
남 알겠어요, 엄마.
여 아, 일기 예보는 확인했니?
남 네. 오늘 밤에 늦게 비가 그치고 내일은 맑을 거예요.
여 네 스웨터를 반드시 챙기도록 해. 비가 온 후에는 추워질 거야.
남 그게 어디 있는지 모르겠어요. 그걸 찾아주실래요?
여 알았다. 그럴게.

09 ④

해설 장소(Wonderland Park), 날짜(4월 25일), 준비물(점심값), 복장(교복)에 대해서는 언급했지만 활동 내용에 대해서는 언급하지 않았다.

어휘 date[deit] 날짜
school uniform 교복
casual clothes 평상복
safety[séifti] 안전

M Did you hear about our school picnic?
W No, I didn't hear anything about it. Where are we going to go?
M I heard we are going to go to Wonderland Park.
W The date is still the same, right? April 25th?
M Yes, it's still that day.
W Do I need to bring anything?
M We need to bring some money for our lunch.
W Should we wear our school uniform or casual clothes?
M We have to wear school uniforms. It's for safety.
W I understand.

남 우리 학교 소풍에 대해 들었니?
여 아니. 나는 아무것도 들은 게 없어. 우리 어디로 가?
남 나는 우리가 Wonderland Park에 간다고 들었어.
여 날짜는 여전히 같지, 맞지? 4월 25일?
남 응, 여전히 그날이야.
여 내가 뭘 가져가야 하니?
남 우리는 점심을 사 먹을 돈을 좀 가져가야 해.
여 교복을 입어야 할까 아니면 평상복을 입어야 할까?
남 우리는 교복을 입어야 해. 안전을 위해서야.
여 알겠어.

10 ⑤

해설 방문객들이 준 먹이 때문에 동물들이 병이 나므로 먹이를 주지 말라는 내용의 안내 방송이다.

M May I have your attention, please? Thank you for visiting Singapore Zoo. We'd like to remind you not to feed the animals here. A lot of

남 주목해 주시겠습니까? 싱가포르 동물원을 방문해 주셔서 감사합니다. 여러분께 이곳 동물들에게 먹이를 주지 말

<table>
<tr><td>어휘</td><td colspan="2">remind[rimáind] 상기시키다</td></tr>
</table>

어휘 remind[rimáind] 상기시키다
feed[fi:d] 먹이를 주다
get sick 병에 걸리다
visitor[vízitər] 방문객
care about ~에 대해 신경을 쓰다

animals at our zoo get sick <u>because of the food</u> visitors give them. We understand you like the animals, but please <u>care about their health</u>. We hope you enjoy your time with the animals. Thank you for listening.

라고 상기시켜 드리고자 합니다. 저희 동물원에 있는 많은 동물들이 방문객이 주는 먹이로 인해 병에 걸립니다. 여러분이 동물들을 좋아하는 것은 이해하지만, 동물들의 건강에 신경을 써 주십시오. 동물들과 즐거운 시간 보내시기를 바랍니다. 들어주셔서 감사합니다.

11 ④

해설 사진 속에서 엄마는 여자와 여자의 언니인 Jessie의 사이에 있다고 했다.

어휘 photo[fóutou] 사진
big family 대가족
sunglasses[sʌ́ŋglæsiz] 선글라스

M That's a nice photo. When was this photo taken?
W It was taken <u>during my family trip</u> last weekend.
M There are 10 people in the photo.
W Yes. We are a big family.
M Who's this woman with the <u>round black glasses</u>?
W She's my sister, Jessie. She is a high school student.
M Oh, I see. Who's the woman <u>between you and your sister</u>?
W She is my mother.
M She looks different now because of <u>her short hair</u> and sunglasses.

남 멋진 사진이네. 이 사진 언제 찍은 거야?
여 지난 주말 가족 여행 중에 찍은거야.
남 사진에 사람들이 10명이나 있구나.
여 응. 우리는 대가족이거든.
남 동그란 검은색 안경을 쓰고 있는 이 여자는 누구니?
여 우리 언니, Jessie야. 언니는 고등학생이야.
남 아, 알겠다. 너와 네 언니 사이에 있는 여자는 누구니?
여 우리 어머니잖아.
남 지금은 짧은 머리와 선글라스 때문에 다르게 보이셔.

12 ③

해설 남자는 벼룩시장에서 물건을 판매한 돈으로 새 컴퓨터를 살 계획이라고 했다.

어휘 busy[bízi] 바쁜
flea market 벼룩시장

M Are you busy this afternoon?
W Not really. What's up?
M I'm going to the flea market. And I <u>need your help</u>.
W Do you need help with something?
M I need to sell some things like my old bike. Can you help me <u>take those</u> to the market?
W No problem. Why do you <u>want to sell them</u>?
M I'm planning to <u>buy a new computer</u>.

남 너 오늘 오후에 바쁘니?
여 별로. 무슨 일이야?
남 내가 벼룩시장에 갈 건데. 네 도움이 필요해.
여 뭐 도와줄까?
남 나는 내 오래된 자전거와 같은 물건들을 좀 팔아야 해. 그것들을 시장으로 가져가는 걸 도와줄래?
여 문제없어. 그것들을 왜 팔려고 하니?
남 새 컴퓨터를 살 계획이거든.

13 ②

해설 현재 시각은 11시 10분 전(10:50)이고 여자가 5분 안에 준비할 테니 그때 나가자고 했으므로 10시 55분에 집에서 나갈 것이다.

어휘 enough[inʌ́f] 충분한
traffic[trǽfik] 교통
terrible[térəbl] 끔찍한

M Honey, what time does the train leave?
W It leaves at 11:30 in the morning.
M It's 10 to 11 now. I think <u>we should leave now</u>.
W No, we have enough time to get to the station.
M The traffic is terrible at this time. So, we'd better hurry.

남 여보, 기차가 몇 시에 떠나요?
여 오전 11시 30분에 떠나요.
남 지금 11시 10분 전이에요. 우리가 지금 떠나야 할 것 같아요.
여 아뇨, 역에 도착할 시간은 충분해요.
남 이 시간에는 교통이 막혀요. 그래서 서두르는 게 좋겠어요.

had better ~하는 게 좋다
hurry[hə́:ri] 서두르다
ready[rédi] 준비가 된

W Okay. I'll be ready in 5 minutes. We can leave then.
M All right.

여 알겠어요. 5분 안에 준비할게요. 우리는 그때 떠나면 돼요.
남 좋아요.

14 ③

해설 체육 수업에서 반에서 제일 빠르고 팀으로 경기할 때 다른 사람들을 도와주는 남자에게 축구팀 가입을 제안하는 상황으로 보아 두 사람의 관계는 체육 교사와 학생임을 알 수 있다.

어휘 be interested in ~에 관심이 있다
gym class 체육 시간
coach[koutʃ] 코치

W Sam, can I talk to you?
M Sure. Did I do something wrong, ma'am?
W No. Are you interested in the school soccer team?
M The soccer team?
W You run the fastest in the class. You help others in gym class when you play in a team. I'm sure you'll be a good player.
M Are you the coach of the team?
W No, I'm not. I'm just a gym teacher. Mr. Cox is the coach.
M The math teacher?
W Yes, I can talk to him if you are interested.
M I'll think about it.

여 Sam, 너와 이야기를 좀 할 수 있니?
남 네. 제가 잘못한 게 있었나요, 선생님?
여 아니야. 너 학교 축구팀에 관심이 있니?
남 축구팀이요?
여 너는 수업에서 가장 빨리 달리잖니. 체육 수업에서 팀으로 경기할 땐 다른 사람들을 돕고, 넌 분명히 좋은 선수가 될 거야.
남 선생님이 축구팀 코치세요?
여 아니. 나는 그냥 체육 교사야. Cox 선생님이 코치이셔.
남 수학 선생님이요?
여 그래. 네가 관심이 있다면 선생님에게 말씀드릴게.
남 생각해 볼게요.

15 ④

해설 여자는 치과에 가야 해서 도서관을 가는 남자에게 자신의 책을 대신 반납해 달라고 부탁했다.

어휘 ask A a favor A에게 부탁하다
find out 알게 되다
return[ritə́:rn] 반납하다
have an appointment 예약이 되어 있다
dentist[déntist] 치과의사
far from ~에서 먼

W Jake, are you doing anything later this afternoon?
M Well, I'm going to the library to study for some tests.
W I see. Can I ask you a favor?
M Sure. What do you need?
W I just found out that I have to return this book by today. But I have a dentist's appointment later.
M Where is your dentist?
W It's next to the fire station.
M That's too far from the library.
W I know. Since you are going there, could you return this book for me?
M Of course.

여 Jake, 오늘 오후 늦게 하는 일 있니?
남 글쎄, 시험공부를 하려고 도서관에 갈 거야.
여 그렇구나. 부탁 하나 해도 될까?
남 그래. 뭐가 필요하니?
여 내가 오늘까지 이 책을 돌려줘야 한다는 것을 방금 알았어. 근데 내가 이따가 치과 진료 예약이 있거든.
남 치과가 어디에 있는데?
여 소방서 옆에 있어.
남 도서관에서 꽤 머네.
여 맞아. 네가 그곳에 가니까, 나 대신에 이 책을 돌려줄 수 있겠니?
남 물론이야.

16 ③

해설 여자는 친구가 식료품을 사러 나가서 통화를 하지 못해서 대신 그의 동생에게 메시지를 남겼다.

어휘 step out 나가다
supermarket[sùpərmá:rkit] 슈퍼마켓
leave a message 메시지를 남기다

[Cell phone rings.]
M Hello.
W Hi, Daniel. This is Irene.
M Sorry, this is Andy, Daniel's brother. He just stepped out of the house.
W Hi, Andy. When is he coming back?

[휴대전화 벨이 울린다.]
남 여보세요.
여 안녕, Daniel. 나 Irene이야.
남 미안하지만, 저는 Daniel의 남동생 Andy인데요. 형은 방금 집 밖에 나갔어요.
여 안녕, Andy. 걔는 언제 집에 오니?

call A back A에게 다시 전화하다

M He went to the supermarket to get something. Would you like to leave a message?

W Please tell him to call me back when he comes back home.

M Sure. Should I tell him to call you back at this number?

W Yes, please.

M Okay. I'll tell him you called.

남 형은 뭘 좀 사기 위해 슈퍼마켓에 갔어요. 전할 말이 있나요?

여 Daniel이 집에 오면, 나한테 전화해 달라고 전해줘.

남 네. 이 번호로 다시 전화하라고 형에게 전해 드릴까요?

여 응, 부탁해.

남 알겠어요. 형에게 누나가 전화했었다고 전할게요.

17 ③

해설 독감에 걸린 여자를 남자가 진찰하고 있는 상황의 대화가 적절하다.

어휘 car accident 교통사고
cough[kɔ(ː)f] 기침
sore throat 인후염
bad cold 독감
medicine[médisn] 약
after meals 식후에
in all 모두 합쳐서
be in the hospital 입원해 있다

① W She had a car accident yesterday.
   M I'm sorry to hear that.
② W What does your mother do?
   M She is a doctor.
③ W I have a cough and a sore throat.
   M I think you have a bad cold.
④ W Take this medicine after meals.
   M I see. How much is it in all?
⑤ W I heard that your sister is in the hospital.
   M She broke her arm last week.

① 여 그녀는 어제 교통사고를 당했어요.
   남 유감이네요.
② 여 당신의 어머니는 무슨 일을 하시나요?
   남 어머니는 의사세요.
③ 여 기침이 나고 목이 아파요.
   남 당신은 독감에 걸린 것 같네요.
④ 여 이 약을 식후에 드세요.
   남 알겠습니다. 모두 합쳐서 얼마인가요?
⑤ 여 네 여동생이 입원했다고 들었어.
   남 지난주에 팔이 부러졌거든.

18 ③

해설 날짜(10월 14~15일), 공연(Dancing Machines의 춤 공연), 음식(간식과 음료), 체험 행사(얼굴 페인팅, 팔찌 만들기)에 대해 언급했지만 공연 시간에 대해서는 언급하지 않았다.

어휘 invite[inváit] 초대하다
festival[féstivəl] 축제
take place 열리다
performance[pərfɔ́ːrməns] 공연
famous[féiməs] 유명한
snack[snæk] 간식
bracelet[bréislit] 팔찌

M [Beep] Hi, Jessica. It's Eric. I'd like to invite you to my school festival. The festival will take place on October 14th and 15th. There will be dance performances by the famous dance group Dancing Machines. Also, we can buy some snacks and drinks at the food market. And we can do face painting and make bracelets. It will be so much fun.

남 [삐] 안녕, Jessica. 나 Eric이야. 나는 너를 우리 학교 축제에 초대하고 싶어. 축제는 10월 14일과 15일에 열릴 거야. 유명한 댄스 그룹인 Dancing Machines의 춤 공연이 있을 거고. 우리는 푸드 마켓에서 간식과 음료도 좀 살 수 있어. 그리고 우리는 얼굴 페인팅과 팔찌 만들기도 할 수 있지. 정말 재미있을 거야.

19 ⑤

해설 남자가 여자에게 딸의 수학 성적이 많이 오른 것을 칭찬하면서 자랑스럽겠다고 했으므로 감사하다는 말이 와야 적절하다.

어휘 must be ~임이 틀림없다
this year 올해

W Hello. I'm Alice's mother.

M You must be Mrs. Taylor. I'm glad to meet you.

W Nice to meet you, too. How is she doing this year?

M She's doing well. She studies hard, and her grades are excellent.

여 안녕하세요. 저는 Alice의 엄마입니다.

남 Taylor 씨군요. 만나서 반갑습니다.

여 저도 만나서 반갑습니다. Alice가 올해 어떻게 하고 있나요?

남 그 애는 잘하고 있어요. 열심히 공부해서, 성적이 우수해요.

excellent[éksələnt] 우수한
be poor at ~을 못하다
go up 오르다
be proud of ~을 자랑스러워하다

W Is that true? She was poor at math last year.
M Her math grade went up a lot this year. You should be very proud of her.
W I'm happy to hear that. Thank you.

여 정말요? 그 애가 작년에 수학을 못했거든요.
남 올해는 수학 성적이 많이 올랐어요. 아주 자랑스러우시겠어요.
여 그 말을 들으니 기쁘네요. 감사합니다.

① 만나 뵙게 되어 기뻐요.
② 내가 너무 자랑스러워요.
③ 그 애는 수학에 흥미가 있어요.
④ 나는 그 애가 교사가 되길 원해요.

20 ①

해설 저녁 식사 예약을 하려는 여자에게 일행이 몇 명인지 묻고 있으므로 일행의 수를 말하는 응답이 적절하다.

어휘 room[ru(ː)m] 자리, 공간
party[páːrti] 일행
[선택지]
reserve[rizə́ːrv] 예약하다
invite[inváit] 초대하다

[Telephone rings.]
M Hello. This is Joy Dining. How may I help you?
W I'd like to make a reservation for dinner.
M Okay. What day and time would you like?
W This Saturday at 7 p.m.
M Sorry, we have no room for 7 o'clock. Is 7:30 okay?
W Yes, that's fine.
M How many people are there in your party?
W There are 5 of us.

[전화벨이 울린다.]
남 안녕하세요. Joy Dining입니다. 어떻게 도와드릴까요?
여 저녁 식사 예약을 하고 싶습니다.
남 네. 어느 요일과 시간을 원하시나요?
여 이번 토요일 오후 7시요.
남 죄송합니다만, 저희는 7시에 자리가 없습니다. 7시 30분 괜찮으시겠어요?
여 네, 괜찮아요.
남 일행이 몇 분이세요?
여 다섯 명이에요.

② 저는 가족과 함께 갈 거예요.
③ 제가 5명 자리를 예약했어요.
④ 7시에 만나는 게 어때요?
⑤ 저는 제 생일 파티에 5명을 초대했어요.

01 ②	02 ②	03 ④	04 ③	05 ②	06 ④	07 ⑤
08 ②	09 ④	10 ③	11 ④	12 ④	13 ③	14 ③
15 ⑤	16 ⑤	17 ④	18 ③	19 ③	20 ③	

01 ②

[해설] 수요일에는 비가 그치고 맑겠다고
했다.

[어휘] weekly[wíːkli] 매주의
strong winds 강풍
from A to B A에서 B까지
get warm 따뜻해지다

W Hello. Here is the weekly weather report for Seoul. On Monday, it will be cold all day because of strong winds. On Tuesday, we will have a lot of rain. On Wednesday, the rain will stop, and the skies will become clear. From Thursday to Friday, it is going to get warm. Thank you.

여 안녕하세요. 서울의 주간 일기예보입니다. 월요일에는 강한 바람 때문에 하루 종일 춥겠습니다. 화요일에는 비가 많이 오겠습니다. 수요일에는 비가 그치고 맑게 개겠습니다. 목요일부터 금요일까지는 따뜻해지겠습니다. 그러나 주말 동안에는 흐리겠습니다. 감사합니다.

02 ②

[해설] 남자가 사려는 찻잔은 꽃과 새들이
있는 점토로 된 것이다.

[어휘] teacup[tíːkəp] 찻잔
made of ~으로 만들어진
clay[klei] 점토

W May I help you?
M Yes, please. I'm looking for a gift for my mother.
W How about this blue teacup made of glass?
M I like it, but my mother has the same one at home.
W Then, how about this pretty cup made of clay?
M You mean the one with flowers and birds on it?
W Yes.
M That's nice. I'll take it.

여 도와드릴까요?
남 네. 어머니께 드릴 선물을 찾고 있어요.
여 이 유리로 만든 파란색 찻잔은 어떠세요?
남 저는 마음에 들지만, 어머니께서 집에 같은 것을 갖고 계세요.
여 그럼 점토로 만들어진 이 예쁜 찻잔은 어떠세요?
남 꽃과 새들이 있는 찻잔이요?
여 네.
남 멋지네요. 그걸로 살게요.

03 ④

[해설] 촬영 시기(여름 방학), 촬영 장소
(Long Beach), 촬영한 사람(남자), 사진
속 인물(사촌 Emma)에 대해 언급했지만
인화한 장소에 대해서는 언급하지 않았다.

[어휘] cousin[kʌ́zən] 사촌
amazing[əméiziŋ] 놀라운

M Minji, do you want to see some photos from my summer vacation?
W Sure. Where did you go?
M My family visited my cousins in California. I took these photos in Long Beach.
W These photos are amazing. [Pause] Who is this girl?
M That's my cousin, Emma.
W Oh, I thought she was your sister.
M No. My sister is not in this photo.

남 민지야. 내 여름 방학 사진들 좀 볼래?
여 좋아. 너 어디 갔었니?
남 우리 가족은 캘리포니아에 있는 내 사촌들을 방문했어. 나는 Long Beach에서 이 사진들을 찍었어.
여 이 사진들 멋지다. [잠시 후] 이 여자애는 누구야?
남 내 사촌 Emma야.
여 아, 그녀가 네 여동생인줄 알았어.
남 아니. 내 여동생은 이 사진 안에 없어.

04 ③

[해설] 남자가 목도리를 주겠다고 했으므
로 여자는 장갑만 살 것이다.

M What are you going to do this winter vacation?
W I'm planning a trip to New York.

남 너 이번 겨울 방학에 뭐 할 거니?
여 나는 뉴욕으로 여행 갈 계획이야.

어휘 trip[trip] 여행
scarf[skɑːrf] 목도리
cf. scarves scarf(목도리)의 복수형
gloves[glʌv] 장갑
a few 몇 개의

M When are you <u>planning</u> to <u>go</u>?	남 언제 갈 계획이니?
W In January.	여 1월에.
M What is the weather like in New York in January?	남 1월에 뉴욕 날씨는 어떠니?
W It's <u>very</u> <u>cold</u> <u>and</u> <u>snowy</u>. Actually, I need to buy a scarf and gloves.	여 매우 춥고 눈이 와. 사실, 나는 목도리와 장갑을 사야 해.
M I have a few scarves. I'll give you one.	남 나 목도리가 몇 개 있어. 내가 하나 줄게.
W Thanks a lot. I just have to <u>buy gloves</u>, then.	여 정말 고마워. 그럼 나는 장갑만 사야겠다.

05 ②

해설 블라우스에 문제가 있어 환불받고 싶다는 여자의 말에 남자가 영수증이 있는지 물어보는 것으로 보아 두 사람이 대화하는 장소는 옷 가게임을 알 수 있다.

어휘 complain[kəmpléin] 불평하다
missing 빠진, 분실된
exchange[ikstʃéindʒ] 교환하다
get a refund 환불받다
receipt[risíːt] 영수증

M May I help you, ma'am?	남 도와드릴까요, 손님?
W I'd like to complain about this blouse.	여 이 블라우스에 대해 불평할 게 있는데요.
M What's wrong with it?	남 무슨 문제가 있나요?
W I wanted to <u>wear it for</u> my birthday party, but I couldn't wear it because 2 buttons were missing.	여 제 생일 파티에 그것을 입으려고 했는데, 단추 두 개가 없어서 입을 수가 없었어요.
M I'm so sorry. Would you like to <u>exchange it</u> or get a refund?	남 정말 죄송합니다. 상품을 교환해 드릴까요, 아니면 환불해 드릴까요?
W I'd like to <u>get a refund</u>, please.	여 환불받고 싶습니다.
M Do you <u>have your</u> receipt?	남 영수증 가지고 있으세요?
W Yes. Here it is.	여 네. 여기 있어요.

06 ④

해설 남자가 계속 지각을 하자 여자는 다시 늦으면 한 달 동안 교실을 청소해야 한다고 경고하고 있다.

어휘 promise[prámis] 약속하다
for a month 한 달 동안

W Matthew, do you know what time it is now?	여 Matthew, 너 지금 몇 시인지 알고 있니?
M Yes, ma'am. It's 9:30.	남 네, 선생님. 9시 30분이에요.
W By what time <u>should you come</u> to school?	여 몇 시까지 학교에 와야 하지?
M By 8:30. <u>I'm really sorry</u>.	남 8시 30분까지요. 정말 죄송해요.
W Do you know that this is your third time this week?	여 이번 주에 이번이 세 번째라는 걸 알고 있니?
M The third time? I promise I <u>won't be late again</u>.	남 세 번째라고요? 다시 늦지 않겠다고 약속할게요.
W If you're late again, <u>you will have to</u> clean your classroom for a month.	여 다시 늦으면, 너는 한 달 동안 교실 청소를 해야 할 거야.

07 ⑤

해설 여자가 남자에게 스웨터가 잘 어울릴 것 같다며 가격도 저렴하다고 하자 사겠다고 했다.

어휘 believe[bilíːv] 믿다
everything[évriθìŋ] 모든 것
used[júːzd] 중고의, 헌
look good on ~에게 잘 어울리다
cheap[tʃiːp] 가격이 싼

M There are so many things here at the market.	남 여기 시장에 물건들이 아주 많네.
W People came out to sell those because <u>they don't use them</u> any more.	여 사람들이 더 이상 사용하지 않은 물건들을 팔려고 나왔어.
M I can't believe everything here is used. Look at that bike. That looks new to me.	남 이곳에 있는 물건들이 전부 중고라는 걸 믿을 수 없어. 저 자전거를 봐. 내겐 새것처럼 보여.
W Yes. Are you going to <u>get something here</u>?	여 맞아. 너 여기서 뭐 살 거야?
M I am not sure.	남 잘 모르겠어.
W Look at this sweater. I think it'll <u>look good on you</u>. It's only $4.	여 이 스웨터를 봐. 너에게 잘 어울릴 것 같아. 겨우 4달러야.
M Really? That's so cheap. <u>I'll take it</u>.	남 정말? 엄청 저렴하네. 그거 살래.

08 ②

해설 남자가 숙제에 필요한 정보를 집에 가서 인터넷으로 찾으라고 했고 여자는 동의하며 책들을 대출하겠다고 했다.

어휘 topic[tápik] 주제
artist[άːrtist] 화가
century[séntʃəri] 세기
famous[féiməs] 유명한
at that time 그 당시
quarter[kwɔ́ːrtər] 15분
search[səːrtʃ] 검색하다

M What are you doing here, Vicky?
W I'm doing my art homework. I found some helpful books here.
M What is your topic?
W It's about artists of the 19th century. I am reading books about the paintings of famous artists at that time.
M It's 5:45. The library will close soon.
W Really? I didn't get enough information for the homework.
M Why don't you search more on the Internet at home?
W That's a good idea. I'll borrow these books first.

남 Vicky, 여기서 뭐하니?
여 미술 숙제를 하고 있어. 나는 여기서 도움이 되는 책들을 좀 찾았거든.
남 숙제 주제가 뭔데?
여 19세기 화가들에 관한 거야. 나는 그 당시 유명한 화가들의 그림에 관한 책을 읽고 있어.
남 지금 5시 45분이야. 도서관이 곧 문을 닫을 거야.
여 그래? 숙제에 필요한 정보를 충분히 얻지 못했는데.
남 집에서 인터넷으로 더 찾아보는 게 어때?
여 좋은 생각이야. 먼저 이 책들을 빌릴게.

09 ④

해설 나이(30세), 출신 학교(Yale 대학교), 전공(법학), 지원 분야(영화)에 대해 언급했지만, 연봉에 대해서는 언급하지 않았다.

어휘 graduate from ~을 졸업하다
law[lɔː] 법학
law firm 법률 회사
movie business 영화계

W Can you tell me about yourself?
M Yes, my name is Benjamin Smith. I'm 30 years old. I graduated from Yale University 3 years ago. I studied law in school and now I work at a law firm in Manhattan.
W How long have you been working there?
M For about 2 years.
W Why do you want to change your job?
M I've been interested in making movies since I was young. I'd really like to work in the movie business.

여 본인에 대해서 말씀해주시겠습니까?
남 네, 저는 Benjamin Smith입니다. 30살이고요. 3년 전에 Yale 대학교를 졸업했습니다. 학교에서 법학을 공부했고 지금은 맨해튼에 있는 한 법률 회사에서 일하고 있습니다.
여 거기서 일한 지 얼마나 되셨나요?
남 2년 정도 했습니다.
여 왜 직업을 바꾸고 싶으신가요?
남 저는 어렸을 때부터 영화를 만드는 데 관심이 있었습니다. 저는 영화계에서 정말 일하고 싶습니다.

10 ③

해설 달리기를 하는 중에 일어나는 부상을 막기 위해 스트레칭 하는 방법을 알려주고 있다.

어휘 stretching[strétʃiŋ] 스트레칭
follow[fάlou] 따라하다
floor[flɔːr] (방의) 바닥
spread[spred] 뻗다
put A together A를 모으다
bend[bend] 구부리다
forward[fɔ́ːrwərd] 앞쪽으로
ankle[ǽŋkl] 발목
deep breath 심호흡
get hurt 다치다
while[hwail] ~하는 동안

W Listen up! Stretching is good before running. Follow me. Sit down on the floor. Your legs have to be straight out in front of you. Put your feet together and bend your body forward. When you do that, hold your ankles and take a deep breath. If you do this exercise, you won't get hurt while running.

여 잘 들으세요! 스트레칭은 달리기 전에 하면 좋습니다. 저를 따라 하세요. 바닥에 앉으세요. 다리는 앞으로 뻗어야 합니다. 두 발을 모으고 몸을 앞으로 구부리세요. 그렇게 할 때, 발목을 잡고 숨을 깊게 쉬세요. 이 운동을 하면, 달리기하는 중에 다치지 않을 겁니다.

11 ④

해설 전주까지는 3시간이 걸려서 9시 30분에 도착한다고 했다.

어휘 leave[liːv] 떠나다
take[teik] (기차를) 타다, 시간이 걸리다
downstairs[dáunstɛ̀ərz] 아래층으로
arrive[əráiv] 도착하다
one way 편도
cost[kɔːst] 비용이 들다
round trip 왕복

M Excuse me, does the train to Jeonju leave at 7?
W No, it leaves at 6:30.
M Where do I take it?
W You have to go downstairs.
M How long does it take to Jeonju?
W It takes 3 hours, so you will arrive at 9:30.
M How much is the ticket?
W One way costs $25, and round trip costs $50.
M 2 round-trip tickets, please.

남 실례지만, 전주 행 기차가 7시에 떠나나요?
여 아뇨, 6시 30분에 떠납니다.
남 어디서 기차를 타야 하나요?
여 아래층으로 가셔야 해요.
남 전주까지 얼마나 걸리나요?
여 3시간이 걸려서 9시 30분에 도착할 겁니다.
남 표가 얼마인가요?
여 편도는 25달러이고 왕복은 50달러입니다.
남 왕복표로 두 장 주세요.

12 ④

해설 남자는 매일 한 시간씩 자신의 개를 산책시키기 위해 공원에 간다고 했다.

어휘 pretty[príti] 꽤
walk[wɔːk] 산책시키다
that's why ~. 그것이 ~한 이유이다.

M Hi, Susan. What are you doing here?
W I'm riding my bike with my friends. How about you?
M I'm going to the park. This is my dog, Max.
W He's pretty big. What kind of dog is he?
M He's a Jindo dog. He's 2 years old.
W I see. How often do you walk him?
M I walk him in the park for an hour every day.
W That's why you are going to the park.
M That's right.

남 안녕, Susan. 너 여기서 뭐하고 있니?
여 나는 친구들과 자전거를 타고 있어. 너는?
남 나는 공원에 가는 중이야. 얘는 우리 개 Max야.
여 좀 크다. 얘는 어떤 종이야?
남 얜 진돗개야. 2살이고.
여 그렇구나. 너는 얼마나 자주 개를 산책시키니?
남 나는 매일 한 시간 동안 공원에서 산책을 시켜.
여 그래서 네가 공원에 가고 있구나.
남 맞아.

13 ③

해설 두 사람은 경기 시작 20분 전인 2시 40분에 만나기로 했다.

어휘 gym[dʒim] 체육관
Me neither. 나도 그래.
cheer for 응원하다

M Do you have any plans for tomorrow afternoon?
W No, I don't have anything.
M Do you want to go to a basketball game at the school gym?
W Well, I don't know anything about basketball.
M Me neither. But it'll be fun to cheer for our school team.
W You're right. What time does the game start?
M It starts at 3:00. How about meeting 20 minutes before the game?
W Sure.

남 너 내일 오후에 계획이 있니?
여 아니, 아무 것도 없어.
남 학교 체육관에서 하는 농구 경기에 갈래?
여 음, 나는 농구에 대해 아무것도 모르거든.
남 나도 그래. 그런데 우리 학교 팀을 응원하는 건 재미있을 거야.
여 네 말이 맞아. 경기가 몇 시에 시작하니?
남 3시에 시작해. 경기 시작 20분 전에 만나는 게 어때?
여 좋아.

14 ③

해설 남자가 여자의 티켓을 확인한 후 공연 관람 시 주의사항을 안내하는 것으로 보아 두 사람의 관계는 극장 직원과 관람객임을 알 수 있다.

W Good evening. May I see your ticket, please?
M Yes, here it is.
W Thank you. Please do not take any photos or videos during the performance.

여 안녕하세요. 티켓을 볼 수 있을까요?
남 네, 여기 있습니다.
여 감사합니다. 공연 중에 사진이나 영상을 찍으시면 안 됩니다.

어휘 video[vídiòu] 영상
performance[pərfɔ́ːrməns] 공연
bottled water 병에 든 생수
restroom[réstrù(ː)m] 화장실

M All right. Can I bring this coffee inside?
W No. You can only bring bottled water into the room.
M Okay. Oh, can you tell me where the restroom is?
W It's around the corner over there.
M Thanks.

남 알겠습니다. 커피를 가지고 안으로 들어가도 되나요?
여 안됩니다. 극장 안으로 병에 든 생수만 가지고 가실 수 있습니다.
남 네. 아, 화장실이 어디에 있는지 알려주실래요?
여 저쪽에 모퉁이를 돌면 바로 있습니다.
남 고맙습니다.

15 ⑤

해설 남자는 동아리 모임 시간을 3시 30분에서 30분 뒤로 변경해달라고 부탁했다.

어휘 for a minute 잠깐
drummer[drʌ́mər] 드럼 연주자

W Hi, Anthony. Can I talk to you for a minute?
M Sure. What's up?
W We have a band club meeting at 3:30. Can you come?
M I'm sorry, I can't. I have a meeting with Mr. Evans at 3.
W You have to come because you're the drummer.
M Then, can we have it 30 minutes later?
W Okay. See you then.

여 안녕, Anthony. 잠깐 너와 이야기할 수 있니?
남 물론이지. 무슨 일이야?
여 우리 3시 30분에 밴드 동아리 모임이 있어. 너 올 수 있니?
남 미안하지만, 난 못 가. 나는 3시에 Evans 선생님과 면담이 있어.
여 네가 드럼 연주자라서 꼭 와야 해.
남 그럼 모임을 30분 후에 할 수 있을까?
여 좋아. 그때 보자.

16 ⑤

해설 남자는 학교 성적이 좋지 않아서 학업에 집중하기 위해 테니스 강습에 가지 않았다.

어휘 grade[greid] 성적
focus on ~에 집중하다
schoolwork[skúlwərk] 학업, 학교 공부
worry[wə́ːri] 걱정하다

W Mike, I didn't see you at the tennis lesson earlier.
M Right, I had to miss it today. Actually, I don't think I can play tennis for a while.
W What's wrong? Did you get hurt?
M No. I'm not getting good grades in school. So I have to focus on schoolwork.
W Oh, I'm sorry to hear that.
M Don't worry. I'll get better grades soon and start taking tennis lessons again.

여 Mike, 나 아까 테니스 강습에서 너를 보지 못했어.
남 맞아, 나는 오늘 강습을 빠져야 했어. 사실, 나는 한동안 테니스를 할 수 없을 거 같아.
여 무슨 일이야? 너 다쳤니?
남 아니. 나는 학교 성적이 좋지 않거든. 그래서 학업에 집중해야 해.
여 아, 그 말을 들으니 안됐구나.
남 걱정하지 마. 곧 더 좋은 성적을 받고 테니스 강습을 다시 시작할 거야.

17 ④

해설 도서관에서 이어폰으로 음악을 크게 듣고 있는 남자에게 여자가 소리를 줄여 달라고 하는 대화가 적절하다.

어휘 library card 도서 대출 카드
living[líviŋ] 생활 (방식)
section[sékʃən] 코너
turn down 소리를 줄이다
volume[váljuːm] 볼륨, 음량
loud[laud] 소리가 큰
I can't stand it. 견딜 수 없다. 참을 수 없다.

① W I'd like to borrow this book.
   M Can you show me your library card?
② W How long can I borrow these books?
   M For 10 days.
③ W I'm looking for books on cooking.
   M They're in the living section over there.
④ W Could you turn down the volume?
   M Sorry. I didn't know it was so loud.
⑤ W He is being noisy in the library.
   M I can't stand it any longer.

① 여 저는 이 책을 빌리고 싶어요.
   남 도서 대출 카드를 제게 보여주시겠어요?
② 여 책을 얼마나 오래 빌릴 수 있나요?
   남 열흘 동안이요.
③ 여 저는 요리 관련 책을 찾고 있는데요.
   남 그건 저쪽 생활 코너에 있어요.
④ 여 소리 좀 줄여 주시겠어요?
   남 죄송해요. 소리가 그렇게 큰 줄 몰랐어요.
⑤ 여 그가 도서관에서 시끄럽게 떠들고 있어요.
   남 더 이상 못 견디겠어요.

18 ③

[해설] 이름(Emily King), 가르치는 과목(과학), 담당 동아리(배드민턴), 성격(이해심 있고 배려하는)에 대해 언급하였지만, 사는 곳에 대해서는 언급하지 않았다.

[어휘] homeroom teacher 담임 선생님
married[mǽrid] 결혼을 한
understanding[ʌ̀ndərstǽndiŋ] 이해심 있는

M Let me introduce you to my homeroom teacher. Her name is Emily King and she is 35 years old. She teaches science. She is married and has a son. She is also a club teacher for badminton. She is the most popular teacher in school because she is very understanding and kind.

남 저의 담임 선생님을 소개하겠습니다. 선생님의 성함은 Emily King이고 35세입니다. 선생님은 과학을 가르칩니다. 결혼을 하셨고, 아들이 하나 있습니다. 선생님은 배드민턴 동아리 교사이기도 합니다. 매우 이해심 있고 친절하시기 때문에 학교에서 가장 인기 있는 선생님이십니다.

19 ③

[해설] 남자가 여자에게 문을 열고 잠깐 붙잡아 달라고 요청하는 말에 대한 응답이므로 수락하거나 거절하는 말이 와야 적절하다.

[어휘] present[prézənt] 선물
for a minute 잠깐 동안

M Clara, you look so busy. Is there something I can help with?
W Sure. Thanks. *[Pause]* Let's see...
M What are those boxes for?
W They're boxes of presents for club members. Oh, can you move those boxes for me?
M Okay. Where do you want me to move them?
W To Mr. Lee's office.
M All right. Can you open the door and hold it for a minute?
W Sure. I'll get the door for you.

남 Clara, 너 아주 바빠 보여. 내가 도울게 있을까?
여 그래. 고마워. *[잠시 후]* 어디 보자…
남 저 상자들은 뭐에 쓰는 거야?
여 동아리 회원에게 줄 선물 상자들이야. 아, 나 대신에 저 상자들을 옮겨줄 수 있니?
남 그래. 내가 그것들을 어디로 옮기면 될까?
여 이 선생님의 사무실로.
남 알겠어. 문을 열고 잠깐 붙잡아 줄래?
여 응. 내가 문을 열어줄게.

① 와 줘서 매우 기뻐.
② 응, 그 상자들은 나를 위한 거야.
④ 미안해. 너는 여기 있을 수 없어.
⑤ 아니, 괜찮아. 나는 도움이 필요하지 않아.

20 ③

[해설] 남자가 연체료가 얼마인지 물었으므로 이어질 응답으로 연체료가 얼마인지 답하는 것이 적절하다.

[어휘] check out (도서관 등에서) 대출받다
be allowed to-v ~하는 것이 허용되다
at a time 한 번에
fee[fi:] 수수료
[선택지]
return[ritə́:rn] 반납하다
per[pər:] ~당

M Excuse me. Can I check out these 5 books?
W No, I'm sorry. You are allowed to borrow only 3 books at a time.
M Oh, I see. I'll borrow these 3, then. And how long can I keep them for?
W For 3 weeks. If you bring them back late, you have to pay a fee.
M How much is the fee?
W It's 100 won a day per book.

남 실례합니다. 이 5권의 책을 대출할 수 있나요?
여 아니요, 죄송합니다. 한 번에 3권의 책만 대출이 허용됩니다.
남 아, 알겠어요. 그러면, 이 3권의 책만 대출할게요. 그리고 얼마 동안 가지고 있을 수 있나요?
여 3주 동안이요. 늦게 가져오면, 연체료를 내야 합니다.
남 연체료는 얼마인데요?
여 책 한 권당 하루에 100원입니다.

① 그 책은 10달러예요.
② 제시간에 책들을 반납하세요.
④ 그걸 지불할 필요가 없어요.
⑤ 집에 도서 대출 카드를 두고 왔어요.

01 ③	02 ①	03 ③	04 ③	05 ③	06 ④	07 ④
08 ④	09 ④	10 ③	11 ⑤	12 ③	13 ③	14 ②
15 ④	16 ⑤	17 ③	18 ⑤	19 ⑤	20 ③	

01 ③

해설 내일 아침에는 아름다운 햇살만 내리쬘 것이라고 했다.

어휘 changeable[tʃéindʒəbl] 변하기 쉬운
pour[pour] (비가) 마구 쏟아지다
not ~ anything but A A외에는 어떤 것도 ~아닌

M Good evening, everyone! The weather today was very changeable. It started with a light rain, but it was pouring in the afternoon. Luckily, we won't see anything but beautiful sunshine tomorrow morning, but it may become a little cloudy in the afternoon.

남 안녕하세요, 여러분! 오늘 날씨는 아주 변화가 많았습니다. 약한 비로 시작했지만 오후 들어 비가 마구 쏟아졌습니다. 다행히 내일 아침엔 아름다운 햇살만 가득하겠으나, 오후에는 조금 흐릴 수도 있겠습니다.

02 ①

해설 아날로그시계 중에서 둥글고 줄무늬 모양의 밴드가 있는 것으로 사기로 했다.

어휘 in particular 특별히, 특히
prefer[prifə́ːr] 더 좋아하다, 선호하다
popular[pɑ́pjulər] 인기 있는
then[ðen] 그러면
round[raund] 둥근

M What can I do for you, ma'am?
W I'm looking for a watch for my younger brother.
M Are you looking for anything in particular?
W I think my brother would prefer one with a simple design.
M Okay. These digital watches are really popular now.
W They look nice, but he already has one.
M I see. Then how about this round watch? The band has stripes on it.
W Great. I'll take it then.

남 무엇을 도와드릴까요, 손님?
여 남동생에게 줄 손목시계를 사려고요.
남 특별히 찾으시는 게 있나요?
여 동생은 디자인이 단순한 것을 더 좋아하는 것 같아요.
남 알겠습니다. 이 디지털시계들이 요즘 정말 인기가 좋습니다.
여 좋아 보이긴 하는데 동생은 이미 디지털시계가 있거든요.
남 그러시군요. 그럼 이 둥근 시계는 어떠세요? 밴드에 줄무늬가 있어요.
여 좋군요. 그럼 그것으로 주세요.

03 ③

해설 이름(Adam Brown), 예전 학교(Waterloo 중학교), 취미(체스 두기), 입고 있는 옷(검정색 셔츠)에 대해 언급하였지만 사는 곳에 대해서는 언급하지 않았다.

어휘 join[dʒɔin] 가입하다
chess[tʃes] 체스
hobby[hɑ́bi] 취미

M Mina, have you met Adam yet?
W Adam? Adam who?
M It's Adam Brown. Today is his first day. He's a new student from Waterloo Middle School.
W I didn't know there was a new student in our school.
M He is also going to join our chess club. Playing chess is his hobby.
W Great. [Pause] Oh, is that Adam over there?
M Yes, that's him. The one in the black shirt.

남 미나야, Adam하고 이미 만났니?
여 Adam이라고? Adam 누구?
남 Adam Brown이라고 해. 오늘이 그 애의 첫 등교일이야. Waterloo 중학교에서 새로 온 학생이지.
여 우리 학교에 새로운 학생이 있다는 거 몰랐는데.
남 걔는 우리 체스 동아리에도 들어올 예정이야. 체스 두는 게 그 애의 취미거든.
여 잘됐네. [잠시 후] 아, 저기에 있는 쟤가 Adam이니?
남 응, 걔야. 검정 셔츠 입은 사람.

04 ③

해설 남자는 넥타이를 아직 받지 못했고 신발은 반품을 신청했다.

어휘 fancy[fǽnsi] 고급의
clothing[klóuðiŋ] 옷, 의복
yet[jet] 아직
return[ritə́:rn] 반품하다
fill out (서식을) 작성하다
request form 신청서
delivery[dilívəri] 배달

[Telephone rings.]
W Thank you for calling Fancy Clothing.
M Hello, I ordered a necktie 3 days ago, but I haven't received it yet.
W Let me check your order. May I have your name, please?
M It's Chris Moon.
W The tie was sent today, so you should get it tomorrow.
M That's great. Oh, also I'd like to return a pair of shoes. How do I do that?
W First, you have to fill out a request form. Then we'll send the delivery man to pick up the shoes.
M All right. I'll do that. Thank you very much.

[전화벨이 울린다.]
여 Fancy Clothing에 전화 주셔서 감사합니다.
남 안녕하세요, 3일 전에 넥타이를 하나 주문했는데요, 아직 못 받았거든요.
여 고객님의 주문을 확인해 보겠습니다. 성함이 어떻게 되시죠?
남 Chris Moon이라고 합니다.
여 넥타이는 오늘 발송했으니까 내일 받으실 거예요.
남 알겠어요. 아, 그리고 신발을 반품하고 싶은데요. 어떻게 해야 하나요?
여 우선 신청서를 작성하셔야 해요. 그리고 나면 저희가 신발을 수거할 배달 직원을 보내 드립니다.
남 알겠어요. 그렇게 하죠. 정말 감사합니다.

05 ③

해설 여자가 양초와 커피용 머그잔을 구매하려는 것으로 보아 선물 가게에서 나누는 대화임을 알 수 있다.

어휘 candle[kǽndl] 양초
section[sékʃən] 코너, 구역
mug[mʌg] 머그잔
else[els] 그 밖의 다른

M Can I help you find anything?
W Yes, where can I find candles?
M The candles are behind this section.
W Okay. Do you also have coffee mugs?
M Yes. They are right next to the candles.
W Thanks. I want to get one for my mother.
M Is there anything else I can do for you?
W No, that's all. Thank you.

남 뭐 찾는 것 좀 도와드릴까요?
여 네, 양초는 어디에 있나요?
남 양초는 이 코너 뒤에 있어요.
여 알겠습니다. 커피 머그잔도 있나요?
남 네. 그것들은 양초 바로 옆에 있습니다.
여 감사합니다. 어머니에게 하나 사드리려고요.
남 그 밖에 제가 해 드릴 일이 더 있나요?
여 아니요, 그게 다예요. 감사합니다.

06 ④

해설 집에서 식사를 해야겠다고 제안하는 여자의 말에 남자가 동의하고 있다.

어휘 stay home 집에 머물다

M Are you ready to go, Mary?
W I'll be ready in about 5 minutes.
M Okay. [Pause] Oh no! It's pouring out there.
W Really? There was no rain in the forecast for tonight.
M I know. I can't believe it.
W Will it be safe to drive?
M I don't know if I'll be able to see anything.
W I think we should just stay home for dinner tonight.
M I think so, too. Driving in this rain is not a good idea.

남 갈 준비 되었나요, Mary?
여 5분 정도면 준비될 거예요.
남 알겠어요. [잠시 후] 이런! 밖에 비가 많이 퍼붓고 있네요.
여 정말요? 일기예보에는 오늘 밤에 비가 온다는 말이 없었어요.
남 맞아요. 믿기지가 않네요.
여 운전하기에 안전할까요?
남 제가 뭐라도 볼 수 있을지 모르겠어요.
여 오늘 저녁은 집에서 식사를 해야 할 것 같아요.
남 저도 그렇게 생각해요. 이렇게 비가 올 때 운전하는 것은 좋은 생각이 아니에요.

07 ④

해설 남자는 사자는 보았으나 호랑이는 없어서 못 봤다고 했다.

어휘 have fun 재미있게 놀다
see A close up A를 바로 옆에서 자세히 보다
for the first time 처음으로
trainer[tréinər] 조련사
explain[ikspléin] 설명하다
difference[dífərəns] 차이점
get to-v ~할 수 있게 되다
polar bear 북극곰

W Did you have fun at the zoo, Jason?
M Yes, Mom. I saw many animals close up for the first time.
W What animal did you like most?
M I liked the wolves and foxes most. The trainer there also explained the differences between them.
W That's nice. Did you get to see lions and tigers too?
M I did see lions, but there weren't any tigers.
W Oh, I thought they had white tigers there.
M The only white animal I saw was a polar bear.

여 동물원에서 재미있게 놀았니, Jason?
남 네, 엄마. 많은 동물을 가까이서 본 건 처음이었어요.
여 어떤 동물이 가장 좋았니?
남 늑대와 여우가 가장 좋았어요. 거기에 있는 조련사분이 둘 사이의 차이점도 설명해 주었어요.
여 좋았겠다. 사자와 호랑이도 볼 수 있었니?
남 사자는 분명히 보았는데 호랑이는 없었어요.
여 아, 그 동물원에 흰 호랑이가 있는 것 같던데.
남 제가 본 유일한 흰색 동물은 북극곰이었어요.

08 ④

해설 여자는 선생님에게 전화하기에는 이른 시각이라는 남자의 말에 동의하며 대신 문자 메시지를 보내겠다고 했다.

어휘 burn up (몸이) 펄펄 끓다. (열이) 몹시 나다
fever[fí:vər] 열
flu[flu:] 독감. 유행성 감기
make a call 전화하다
text message 문자 메시지
instead[instéd] 대신

M Mom, I haven't been feeling well since yesterday.
W Really? Then why didn't you tell me earlier?
M I thought I was just tired.
W Let me check. [Pause] Oh, you're burning up with a fever.
M I think I have the flu, Mom.
W I think you'll have to miss school today. I'll call your teacher now.
M But it's 6 in the morning. I think it's a little early to make a call now.
W Yes, you're right. I'll send her a text message instead.

남 엄마, 어제부터 몸이 안 좋았네요.
여 정말이니? 그런데 왜 진작 말하지 않았니?
남 그냥 피곤한 거라고 생각했어요.
여 어디 보자. [잠시 후] 아, 너 몸이 펄펄 끓는구나.
남 제가 독감에 걸렸나 봐요, 엄마.
여 너는 오늘 학교를 쉬어야 할 것 같구나. 네 선생님한테 지금 전화할게.
남 하지만 지금은 아침 6시예요. 지금 전화하기에는 조금 이른 것 같아요.
여 그래, 네 말이 맞아. 대신 문자 메시지를 보낼게.

09 ④

해설 디자인(단순한 디자인), 모양(사각형), 색상(검정), 주머니 개수(2개)에 대해 언급하지만, 재질에 대해 언급하지 않았다.

어휘 backpack[bǽkpæ̀k] 책가방
simple[símpl] 단순한
at least 적어도

W Isn't your backpack too small, Peter?
M Yes, Mom. I need a new backpack.
W What kind of backpack do you want?
M I want one that I can use in high school, too.
W Then, it should be a simple design.
M Right. I'd like a square one in black.
W Okay. Is there anything else?
M I also need at least 2 pockets.

여 네 가방이 너무 작지 않니, Peter?
남 맞아요, 엄마. 새 가방이 필요해요.
여 어떤 종류의 가방이 갖고 싶어?
남 고등학교에서도 쓸 수 있는 걸 원해요.
여 그럼 단순한 디자인이어야겠구나.
남 맞아요. 저 검정으로 된 사각형 가방이 좋겠어요.
여 알겠다. 또 다른 건 없니?
남 적어도 주머니가 2개도 필요해요.

10 ③

해설 지구 온난화의 위험성을 알리려는 행사로 마라톤 대회를 홍보하고 있다.

어휘 may[mei] ~일지도 모른다
sound[saund] ~하게 들리다
scary[skɛ́(:)əri] 무서운, 겁나는
global warming 지구 온난화

M Thank you for your time today. Before I let you go, I'd like to tell you about an event called the Green Day Marathon. I know the word "marathon" may sound scary to some of you, but you can bring your kids and just walk with them. We're trying to let people know about the dangers of global warming. This is a family event that all of you will enjoy!

남 오늘 시간을 내주셔서 감사드립니다. 여러분들을 보내 드리기 전에 녹색의 날 마라톤 대회로 불리는 행사에 대해 알려 드리고자 합니다. 마라톤이라는 말이 어떤 분들에게는 무섭게 들릴 수 있다는 것을 알고 있습니다만 아이들을 데리고 오셔서 같이 걷기만 하면 됩니다. 우리는 지구 온난화의 위험에 대해 사람들에게 알리고자 노력하고 있습니다. 여러분 모두가 즐기게 될 가족 행사입니다!

11 ⑤

해설 여행 기간은 10일이라고 했다.

어휘 whole[houl] 전체의
abroad[əbrɔ́ːd] 해외로, 해외에

W Have you been to Australia, Paul?
M Yes, I have. I went there 2 years ago.
W Really? Who did you go with?
M I went with my whole family.
W Was it a family vacation?
M Yes, it was. And it was our first trip abroad.
W Did you go to Sydney?
M Of course, we did. We took a picture in front of the Sydney Opera House.
W Wow, I'm sure you had a wonderful time.
M Yes, we did. It was a 10-day trip, but it felt so short.

여 호주에 가 본 적 있니, Paul?
남 응, 가 봤어. 2년 전에 거기에 갔었지.
여 정말? 누구랑 함께 갔는데?
남 가족 모두와 같이 갔어.
여 가족 휴가였니?
남 응. 우리의 첫 해외여행이었어.
여 시드니에 갔었니?
남 물론 갔지. 시드니 오페라 하우스 앞에서 사진도 찍었어.
여 와, 멋진 시간을 보냈겠구나.
남 응, 그랬어. 열흘 동안의 여행이었는데 너무 짧게 느껴졌어.

12 ③

해설 남자는 학교 도서관에서 하는 자원봉사를 신청하기 위해 전화했다.

어휘 leave a message 메시지를 남기다
volunteer[vὰləntíər] 자원봉사(자)
sometime[sʌ́mtàim] 어느 때
between A and B A와 B 사이

[Telephone rings.]
W Martha Middle School. How may I help you?
M Hi, my name is John Sales, and my daughter goes to your school.
W Do you want to leave a message for her?
M No, I want to know if you still need a volunteer.
W Oh, are you calling about volunteer work at the school library?
M Yes, I am.
W Wonderful! Can you come to the school sometime between 11 and 1 today?
M Sure. I will come by at 12:30.

[전화벨이 울린다.]
여 Martha 중학교입니다. 무엇을 도와드릴까요?
남 안녕하세요. John Sales라고 하는데요. 제 딸이 그 학교에 다녀요.
여 따님에게 메시지를 남기시겠어요?
남 아니요, 자원봉사자가 아직도 필요한지 알고 싶어서요.
여 아, 학교 도서관에서 하는 자원봉사일 때문에 전화하셨나요?
남 네. 그렇습니다.
여 잘됐네요! 오늘 11시에서 1시 사이에 학교로 오실 수 있으세요?
남 네. 12시 30분까지 갈게요.

13 ③

해설 방문 시간을 3시에서 4시로 바꿀 수 있는지 물어보는 여자의 말에 남자가 동의했다.

어휘 appointment[əpɔ́intmənt] 예약
repair[ripέər] 수리하다
instead[instéd] 대신에
pick up (차에) 태우러 가다
work for (시간 등이) ~에게 가능하다

[Telephone rings.]
W Hello.
M Hello. Can I speak to Mrs. Larson, please?
W This is she. May I ask who's calling?
M My name is James Carter, and I'm calling to check your appointment for repairing your TV.
W I think I made the appointment for 3 p.m. today. Is that correct?
M That is correct, ma'am.
W I'm sorry, but could you come at 4 instead? I need to pick up my son at 3.
M 4 o'clock works for me.
W Thank you so much.

[전화벨이 울린다.]
여 여보세요.
남 안녕하세요. Larson 씨 계신가요?
여 전데요, 누구신지 물어봐도 될까요?
남 James Carter라고 하는데요. 고객님의 TV를 수리하기 위해 방문 예약을 확인하려고 연락드렸습니다.
여 오늘 오후 3시로 예약한 것 같네요. 맞나요?
남 맞습니다, 고객님.
여 죄송한데 대신 4시에 오실 수 있나요? 3시에 아들을 태우러 가야 하거든요.
남 4시에 가능합니다.
여 정말 고맙습니다.

14 ②

해설 남자가 여자에게 정치에 참여하게 된 계기를 묻고 최초의 여성 시장이라고 했으므로 두 사람의 관계는 기자와 시장임을 알 수 있다.

어휘 pleasure[pléʒər] 기쁨, 즐거움
career[kəríər] 경력
be in school 재학 중이다
law school 법대
take part in ~에 참여하다
politics[pálətiks] 정치
mayor[méiər] 시장
female[fí:meil] 여성의
Time flies. 세월이 빠르다. 시간이 쏜살같다.

M Thank you for your time, Ms. Pederson.
W It's my pleasure, and I'm sorry I only have a few minutes.
M It's okay. I understand you are very busy. So, when did you start your career?
W When I was in law school.
M How did you take part in politics?
W I started working at the mayor's office.
M And now you're the first female mayor of this city.
W Yes. Time really flies.

남 시간을 내주셔서 감사드립니다, Pederson 씨.
여 제가 더 기쁘죠. 그런데 몇 분밖에 시간을 낼 수 없어 죄송하네요.
남 괜찮습니다. 사장님이 아주 바쁘신 것 이해합니다. 그럼, 경력을 쌓기 시작한 때가 언제였나요?
여 법대에 재학 중이었을 때였죠.
남 정치에 어떻게 참여하게 되었나요?
여 시장님의 사무실에서 일을 시작했습니다.
남 그리고 지금은 이 시의 최초의 여성 시장이시군요.
여 그렇습니다. 세월이 정말 빠르네요.

15 ④

해설 여자는 아빠의 생신 선물을 사기 위해 남자에게 같이 쇼핑몰에 가자고 부탁했다.

어휘 clothing[klóuðiŋ] 옷, 의복
delivery[dilívəri] 배달, 배달되는 물건
plan to ~할 계획이다
shopping mall(= mall) 쇼핑몰
anyway[éniwèi] 어쨌든, 아무튼

W I need to buy a sweater for my dad. His birthday is this Saturday.
M I know an online store for men's clothing.
W I don't think shopping online is a good idea.
M Why do you say that?
W There are only 3 days until Saturday. The delivery could take longer than that.
M You are right. Some deliveries can take 5 days.
W Yes, so I'm planning to go to the shopping mall later today. Can you come with me?
M Of course. I was going to go to the mall today anyway.

여 우리 아빠에게 드릴 선물을 사야 해. 아빠 생신이 이번 토요일이거든.
남 내가 남성 의류를 파는 온라인 가게를 알고 있어.
여 온라인으로 쇼핑하는 게 좋은 생각이 아닌 것 같아.
남 왜 그런 말을 하지?
여 토요일까지는 3일밖에 남지 않았어. 배달이 그보다 더 길어질 수도 있잖아.
남 네 말이 맞아. 어떤 배달 물품은 5일이 걸리기도 해.
여 응, 그래서 이따가 쇼핑몰에 갈 계획이야. 나와 같이 가줄래?
남 물론이지. 오늘 어쨌든 쇼핑몰에 가려고 했었어.

16 ⑤

해설 남자는 인터넷 연결에 문제가 생겨서 숙제를 하지 못했다고 했다.

어휘 miss[mis] ~을 하지 못하다
Internet connection 인터넷 연결

M When do we have history class today?
W I think it is after lunch. Why?
M I need to talk to the teacher before class today.
W Oh, are you leaving early before history class?
M No, I'm not. I didn't do my homework last night.
W You never miss homework. Did something happen?
M Well, there was something wrong with the Internet connection at home. So, I couldn't finish my homework.
W That's too bad.

남 우리 오늘 역사 수업이 언제지?
여 점심시간 이후인 것 같은데. 왜?
남 오늘 수업 시간 전에 선생님하고 이야기를 좀 해야 해.
여 아, 역사 수업 전에 먼저 가려고?
남 아니, 그렇지 않아. 지난밤에 숙제를 못 했거든.
여 너는 숙제를 안 하는 일이 없잖아. 무슨 일이 있었니?
남 음, 집에서 인터넷 연결에 문제가 있었어. 그래서 숙제를 끝내지 못했어.
여 안됐구나.

17 ③

해설 원숭이에게 바나나를 줘도 되는지 묻자 주면 안 된다고 하는 대화를 선택한다.

어휘 entrance[éntrəns] 입구
get[get] 사다
feed[fiːd] 먹이를 주다
allow[əláu] 허락하다
admission[ədmíʃən] 입장료

① M Excuse me. Where can I find bananas?
  W Fruits are right next to the entrance.
② M What do you think of this shirt, Mom?
  W You should get a larger one. It's too small for you.
③ M Excuse me. Can I give this to the monkey?
  W No, feeding the animals is not allowed in this zoo.
④ M Where do you want to go for lunch?
  W I know a really good Italian restaurant.
⑤ M Excuse me. How much is the admission?
  W It's $15.

① 남 실례합니다. 바나나가 어디에 있나요?
  여 과일은 바로 입구 옆에 있어요.
② 남 이 셔츠 어때요, 엄마?
  여 더 큰 것을 사야겠구나. 이건 너에게 너무 작아.
③ 남 실례합니다. 원숭이에게 이것을 줘도 될까요?
  여 안 됩니다. 이 동물원에서는 동물들에게 먹이를 주는 것이 금지되어 있습니다.
④ 남 점심 식사하러 어디로 가고 싶니?
  여 내가 정말 좋은 이탈리아 레스토랑을 알고 있어.
⑤ 남 실례합니다. 입장료가 얼마죠?
  여 15달러예요.

18 ⑤

해설 위치(Vermont 가와 3번가가 만나는 곳), 판매하는 카레 종류(20가지), 카레 가격(6달러 미만), 카레 요리의 장점(건강에 좋음)에 대해 언급하였으나 배달 주문 방법에 대해서는 언급하지 않았다.

어휘 real[ríːəl] 진정한
curry[kə́ːri] 카레, 카레 요리
be located ~ ~에 위치하다
avenue[ǽvənjùː] (도시의) ~가, 거리
under[ʌ́ndər] ~미만의
not only A but also B A뿐만 아니라 B인
pay A a visit A를 방문하다
disappointed[dìsəpɔ́intid] 실망한

W If you've never had real curry, you have to try the New Curry House. It is located on Vermont Avenue and 3rd Street. At the New Curry House, you can choose from 20 different kinds of curry from all over the world and they are all under $6! As you may know, curry is not only delicious but also good for your health. Pay us a visit, and you won't be disappointed!

여 만약 당신이 진정한 카레 요리를 못 드셔보셨다면 New Curry House에서 맛보셔야 합니다. 이곳은 Vermont 가와 3번가가 만나는 곳에 있습니다. New Curry House에서 전 세계의 20가지 카레 요리 중에서 선택할 수 있는데 모두 가격이 6달러 미만입니다! 여러분이 아시다시피 카레 요리는 맛이 좋을 뿐 아니라 건강에도 좋습니다. 저희에게 오시면 실망하지 않으실 겁니다!

19 ⑤

해설 9시에 올 수 있는지 묻고 있으므로 이 시간이 가능한지 여부나 시간을 조정하기를 원하는 응답이 적절하다.

어휘 make an appointment with ~와 만날 약속을 하다
counselor[káunsələr] 상담 교사, 카운슬러
class schedule 수업 시간표

[Telephone rings.]
M Hello.
W Hello, may I speak to Mr. Woo?
M This is he. May I ask who's calling?
W My name is Jennifer Baker from James Middle School.
M Yes, I left you a message about my daughter.
W You wanted to make an appointment with a counselor, right?
M Right. I need to talk about my daughter's class schedule.
W Okay. Can you come at 9 in the morning?
M Sorry, but can I come at 9:30 instead?

[전화벨이 울린다.]
남 여보세요.
여 여보세요, Woo 선생님과 통화할 수 있을까요?
남 전데요. 전화하시는 분은 누구세요?
여 저는 James 중학교의 Jennifer Baker라고 합니다.
남 네, 제 딸 때문에 선생님에게 메시지를 남겼었죠.
여 상담 선생님과 만날 약속을 잡기를 원하셨죠, 맞습니까?
남 네, 제 딸의 수업 시간표에 대해 이야기해야 합니다.
여 알겠습니다. 아침 9시에 올 수 있으세요?
남 죄송하지만, 대신 9시 30분에 가도 될까요?

① 아니요, 전화를 다시 드릴 수 없습니다.
② 네, 그녀는 15살이 됩니다.
③ 네, 만날 약속은 나중에 잡을게요.
④ 아니요, 메시지를 남기지 마세요.

20 ③

해설 사흘 전에 받은 성적표를 어떻게 했는지 묻고 있으므로 성적표가 어디에 있는지 대답하는 것이 적절하다.

어휘 report card 성적표
strange[streindʒ] 이상한
comment[kάment] 코멘트, 의견
grade[greid] 성적, 학점

W Have you received your report card, Jamie?
M No, I haven't, Mom.
W That's strange. I received an e-mail from your school saying that they sent the report cards.
M Oh, I received a report card 3 days ago, but something's wrong with it.
W What do you mean?
M Teacher comments were missing, so we're getting a new one tomorrow.
W But the grades were correct, right?
M Yes, they were.
W Then, what did you do with the one you received 3 days ago?
M I had to return it to the teacher.

여 성적표 받았니, Jamie?
남 아니요, 안 받았어요, 엄마.
여 그것참 이상하네. 성적표를 보냈다는 이메일을 네 학교로부터 받았는데.
남 아, 성적표를 사흘 전에 받았는데 문제가 좀 생겼어요.
여 그게 무슨 뜻이지?
남 선생님의 코멘트가 빠져 있어서 내일 새로 받아요.
여 하지만 성적은 틀림없잖아, 그렇지?
남 네, 맞아요.
여 그럼 사흘 전에 받은 그 성적표는 어떻게 했니?
남 선생님에게 다시 돌려 드렸어요.

① 저는 그것을 이틀 전에 엄마에게 주었어요.
② 그것은 다른 집으로 잘못 보내졌어요.
④ 저는 어제 과학 보고서를 완성했어요.
⑤ 선생님이 나한테 크리스마스카드를 보냈어요.

01 ④

해설 일요일은 바람이 강하게 불 것으로 예보하고 있다.

어휘 national holiday 국경일
trip[trip] 여행
during[djúəriŋ] ~동안
as usual 평소처럼
partly[páːrtli] 부분적으로
not ~ until .... …때가 되어서야 ~인
windy[wíndi] 바람이 부는

M This Friday is a national holiday, and many of you may be planning a trip during this long weekend. Friday will be sunny as usual, but it will be partly cloudy on Saturday. We won't have any rain until Monday, but it will become very windy on Sunday. I hope you enjoy the long weekend.

남 이번 금요일은 국경일입니다. 그리고 많은 분들이 긴 이번 주말 동안 여행을 계획하고 계실 것입니다. 금요일은 평소처럼 해가 나겠지만 토요일에는 곳에 따라 구름이 끼겠습니다. 비는 월요일이 되어서야 내리겠습니다만, 일요일에는 바람이 아주 강하게 불겠습니다. 긴 주말을 즐겁게 보내세요.

02 ⑤

해설 평평한 지붕에 굴뚝이 있고 옆에 차고가 있는 집이다.

어휘 fireplace[fáiərplèis] 벽난로
real[ríːəl] 진짜의
chimney[tʃímni] 굴뚝
unique[juːníːk] 독특한
triangular[traiǽŋgjulər] 삼각형의
shape[ʃeip] 모양
completely[kəmplíːtli] 완전히
flat[flæt] 평평한, 고른
separate[sépərèit] 독립된, 분리된
garage[gərάːdʒ] 차고

M Have you been to Claire's new house?
W Yes, I have. It's a beautiful house.
M It really is. There's a fireplace in the living room.
W I know. There's a real chimney on the roof.
M The roof of the house is unique, too.
W You're right. It doesn't have a triangular shape.
M It's completely flat. Claire has a separate garage for her car, too, doesn't she?
W Yes, she does. The garage is next to the house.
M I wish I could live in a house like hers.

남 Claire의 새집에 가 보았니?
여 응, 가 봤어. 아름다운 집이더라.
남 정말 그래. 거실에 벽난로가 있어.
여 맞아. 지붕에 실제로 굴뚝이 있어.
남 지붕도 독특하잖아.
여 네 말이 맞아. 삼각형 모양이 아니야.
남 완전히 평면이지. 걔는 차를 넣어둘 독립된 차고도 있지, 그렇지 않니?
여 응, 있어. 차고가 집 옆에 있어.
남 Claire의 집 같은 곳에서 살 수 있으면 좋겠어.

03 ⑤

해설 장소(Camping Land), 기간(3일), 참가 인원 수(100명 이상), 참가비(500달러)에 대해 언급했으나 활동 내용에 대해서는 언급하지 않았다.

어휘 be not all that 그다지 좋지 않다, 별로다
campground[kǽmpgraund] 야영지
participate[pɑːrtísəpèit] 참가하다
pretty[príti] 꽤, 상당히

W How was your summer camp, Jaden?
M It wasn't all that interesting.
W Really? Where was the camp?
M It was at a small campground, Camping Land.
W How long was the camp?
M It was for 3 days.
W How many people were there?
M A little over 100 people participated, and the camp price was $500.
W That was pretty expensive for a 3-day summer camp.

여 여름 캠프 어땠니, Jaden?
남 그다지 재미있지 않았어.
여 정말? 캠프 장소가 어디였는데?
남 Camping Land라는 작은 야영지였어.
여 캠프 기간은 얼마나 되었니?
남 3일이었지.
여 사람들은 몇 명이나 왔어?
남 100명 조금 넘게 참가했고 캠프 참가비는 500달러였어.
여 여름 캠프 3일 치고는 꽤 비쌌구나.

04 ③

해설 여자는 남자에게 피자를 가져올 것을 제안했지만 남자가 요리할 시간이 없어 애플파이를 가져가겠다고 했다.

어휘 potluck[pátlək] (여러 사람들이) 음식을 조금씩 가져와서 나눠 먹는 식사
throw a party 파티를 열다
share[ʃɛər] 나누다, 공유하다
host[houst] (손님을 초대한) 주인
dessert[dizə́ːrt] 디저트

W I'm going to have a potluck party at 6 on Friday. Do you want to come?
M What's a potluck party?
W I throw a party, but all the guests bring food to share.
M I see. Then, the host doesn't have to prepare all the food.
W Right. I heard that you could make good spaghetti.
M I like to cook Italian food. I usually make my own pizza, too.
W Really? Then why don't you bring pizza?
M I may not have time to cook on Friday. Can I just bring dessert?
W Of course. You can bring anything you want.
M Good. I'll bring apple pie.

여 내가 금요일 6시에 포트럭 파티를 열어. 파티에 올래?
남 포트럭 파티가 뭔데?
여 파티는 내가 여는데 손님들이 나눠 먹을 음식을 각자 가지고 오는 거야.
남 알겠어. 그럼 주인이 음식을 전부 다 준비할 필요는 없구나.
여 맞아. 네가 맛있는 스파게티를 만들 줄 안다고 들었는데.
남 나는 이탈리아 음식 만드는 것을 좋아해. 보통 내가 먹을 피자도 직접 만들지.
여 정말? 그럼 피자를 가지고 오는 게 어때?
남 내가 금요일에 요리할 시간이 없을지도 몰라. 그냥 디저트를 가져가도 되니?
여 물론이지. 네가 원하는 건 무엇이든 가지고 와도 돼.
남 좋아. 애플파이를 가지고 갈게.

05 ④

해설 여자가 금이 간 기타를 고쳐 달라고 하고 남자는 어떻게 수리할 것인지를 설명하는 것으로 보아 대화 장소는 악기 수리점임을 알 수 있다.

어휘 fix[fiks] 고치다, 수리하다
crack[kræk] (갈라져 생긴) 금
actually[ǽktʃuəli] 사실은
common[kámən] 흔한
replace[ripléis] 교체하다
whole[houl] 전체의
board[bɔːrd] 판
pay A for B B에 대해 A를 지불하다
cost[kɔːst] ~의 비용이 들다

M What can I do for you?
W Do you think this can be fixed?
M Oh, there's a small crack. This is actually a very common problem.
W Do you have to replace the whole board?
M No, I can just put a small piece of wood in the crack.
W I paid a lot of money for this guitar.
M I see. But this kind of crack happens only to this type of wood.
W I hope it won't cost too much to fix it.

남 무엇을 도와드릴까요?
여 이것이 수리가 될까요?
남 아, 살짝 금이 갔군요. 이건 사실 아주 흔한 문제이지요.
여 판 전체를 교체해야 하나요?
남 아니요, 금이 간 곳에 작은 나무 조각을 대기만 하면 됩니다.
여 저는 이 기타에 많은 돈을 지불했거든요.
남 그렇군요. 근데 이런 금은 이런 종류의 목재에만 생기죠.
여 수리하는 데 너무 많은 돈이 들지 않았으면 좋겠어요.

06 ③

해설 문을 열어 달라는 여자의 부탁을 남자가 들어주자 고맙다고 했다.

어휘 move in 이사 들어오다
floor[flɔːr] (건물의) 층
neighbor[néibər] 이웃, 이웃 사람
hold[hould] (사물을 특정한 위치에 오게) 하고 있다[유지하다]
appreciate[əpríːʃièit] 감사하다

M Are you moving in today?
W Yes, I'm moving in to the 8th floor.
M Really? I live on the same floor. We'll be neighbors.
W Oh, great! My name is Jennifer.
M I'm Jason. Do you need help with those boxes?
W No, thank you. But could you hold the door open?

남 오늘 이사 들어오시는 건가요?
여 네. 8층으로 들어옵니다.
남 정말요? 저와 같은 층이네요. 우리가 이웃이 되는 거군요.
여 아, 잘됐네요! 저는 Jennifer라고 해요.
남 저는 Jason입니다. 그 상자들을 옮기는 데 도와드릴까요?
여 괜찮아요. 근데 문 좀 잡아 주시겠어요?

	M Of course. *[Pause]* This is a very heavy door.	남 물론 그럴게요. *[잠시 후]* 이거 아주 무거운 문이네요.
	W I really appreciate your help.	여 도와주셔서 정말 감사합니다.

07 ④

해설 여자는 금성을 가장 좋아하지만, 남자는 태양계에서 가장 크다는 이유로 목성을 가장 좋아한다고 했다.

어휘 in particular 특별히, 특히
Mercury[mə́:rkjuri] 수성
without[wiðáut] ~없이
telescope[téləskòup] 망원경
Venus[víːnəs] 금성
Mars[mɑːrz] 화성
Jupiter[dʒúːpitər] 목성
Saturn[sǽtərn] 토성
planet[plǽnit] 행성
the solar system 태양계

W What are you doing, Timothy?
M I'm just looking at the night sky.
W Are you looking for anything in particular?
M I'm looking for Mercury.
W But can you find it without a telescope?
M Yes, you can also see Venus, Mars, Jupiter, and Saturn.
W Oh, I didn't know that. Do you have a favorite planet?
M Yes, my favorite is Jupiter. What's yours?
W My favorite is Venus. Why do you like Jupiter?
M Because it's the largest planet in the solar system.

여 뭐 하고 있니, Timothy?
남 밤하늘을 바라보고 있어.
여 특별히 찾는 게 있니?
남 나는 수성을 찾고 있어.
여 그건 망원경 없이도 찾을 수 있니?
남 응. 금성, 화성, 목성과 토성도 볼 수 있어.
여 아, 그건 몰랐네. 너는 가장 좋아하는 행성이 있니?
남 응, 내가 가장 좋아하는 건 목성이야. 네가 가장 좋아하는 건 뭐니?
여 나는 금성을 가장 좋아해. 너는 왜 목성을 가장 좋아하니?
남 그게 태양계에서 가장 큰 행성이기 때문이지.

① 수성 ② 금성 ③ 화성 ④ 목성 ⑤ 토성

08 ④

해설 발표 연습을 해야 하는 남자를 대신해 여자는 보고서 복사를 해주겠다고 했다.

어휘 presentation[prèzəntéiʃən] 발표
copy[kápi] 복사본
focus on ~에 집중하다

M Mary, are you busy right now?
W Not really. What's up?
M I have to practice for my presentation. It starts at 3 p.m.
W It's almost 1:30. You have enough time.
M Not really. I still have to make 30 copies of my report.
W Okay. I'll make the copies right now. Just focus on your presentation.
M Thank you so much, Mary.

남 Mary, 너 지금 바빠?
여 아니. 무슨 일이야?
남 나 발표를 연습해야 해서. 오후 3시에 시작하거든.
여 지금 거의 1:30이야. 시간이 충분하네.
남 그렇지 않아. 아직 내 보고서 복사본 30장을 만들어야 하거든.
여 알았어. 내가 바로 지금 복사할게. 넌 네 발표에 좀 더 집중해.
남 정말 고마워, Mary.

09 ④

해설 돌아온 요일(금요일), 여행 기간(7일), 방문한 국가 수(4개국), 총 여행 경비(3개월 치 월급)에 대해 언급하였으나 여행 동반자에 대해서는 언급하지 않았다.

어휘 must be ~임에 틀림없다
tight[tait] 빠듯한, 빡빡한
possible[pásəbl] 가능한
cost[kɔːst] 비용이 들다
salary[sǽləri] 월급, 급여
worth[wəːrθ] ~의 가치가 있는

W When did you come back from your trip?
M I came back on Friday. I'm really tired.
W You must be. How long was your trip?
M It was for 7 days. It was a very tight schedule.
W How many countries did you visit?
M I visited 4 countries.
W That's about 2 days for each country. How's that possible?
M That's possible in Europe.
W How much did the whole trip cost?
M It cost me 3 months' salary, but it was worth it.

여 너 여행에서 언제 돌아왔니?
남 금요일에 돌아왔어. 정말 피곤하다.
여 틀림없이 피곤하겠지. 얼마 동안의 여행이었니?
남 7일 동안이었어. 아주 빠듯한 스케줄이었지.
여 몇 개의 나라를 방문했니?
남 4개국을 방문했어.
여 대략 이틀에 한 나라씩 간 거구나. 어떻게 그게 가능했지?
남 유럽에서는 가능하지.
여 총 여행 경비가 얼마나 들었니?
남 3개월 치 월급이 들어갔어. 하지만 충분히 그만한 가치가 있었어.

10 ④

해설 체육관을 이용할 때 다른 사람에게 피해가 가지 않도록 복장, 신발과 이어폰 사용, 탈의실 문 닫기 등에 신경을 써 달라고 안내하고 있다.

어휘 attention [ətén∫ən] 주목
proper [prápər] 적절한, 적당한
noisy [nɔ́izi] 시끄러운
used [juːzd] 사용된
make sure 확실하게 하다
changing room 탈의실

M May I have your attention, please? The city gym is now open, from 6 a.m. to 10 p.m. Please wear proper gym clothes and shoes only. Also, use your earphones when you listen to music. Music can be noisy to others. You also have to put used towels in the basket, which is next to the door. Make sure you close the door when you enter and leave the changing room.

남 주목해 주십시요. 현재 시 체육관이 요즘 오전 6시에서 밤 10시까지 개방되어 있습니다. 적절한 체육관 복장과 신발만을 착용하시기 바랍니다. 그리고 음악을 들을 때는 이어폰을 사용하세요. 음악은 다른 사람들에게 시끄러울 수 있습니다. 또한 사용한 수건은 문 옆에 놓여있는 바구니에 넣어주셔야 합니다. 탈의실에 들어오거나 나갈 때는 문을 닫았는지 꼭 확인하시기 바랍니다.

11 ③

해설 Kent의 정체를 그의 여자 친구가 유일하게 알고 있다고 했다.

어휘 officer(= police officer)
[ɔ́(ː)fisər] 경찰관
secret [síːkrit] 비밀
episode [épisòud] (드라마 등의) 1회 방송분

W Have you seen the TV show *Officer Kent*?
M No, I haven't. What's it about?
W It's about a New York police officer named Kent who's also a superhero.
M That sounds interesting. Does anybody know that he's a superhero?
W His girlfriend is the only person who knows his secret.
M When is it on TV?
W It's on from 6 to 7 p.m. every Friday on channel 7.
M I'm busy this Friday. I'll watch it next week.
W This Friday will be the last episode.
M Oh, that's too bad.

여 TV 프로그램 〈Officer Kent〉를 본 적이 있니?
남 아니, 본 적 없어. 무엇에 대한 내용인데?
여 슈퍼 히어로이기도 한 Kent라는 이름의 뉴욕 경찰관 이야기야.
남 그거 재미있을 것 같다. 그가 슈퍼히어로라는 것을 아는 사람이 있니?
여 그의 여자 친구가 그의 비밀을 알고 있는 유일한 사람이야.
남 그게 TV에 언제 방영되니?
여 채널 7에서 매주 금요일 오후 6시에서 7시까지 해.
남 이번 주 금요일에는 바빠. 다음 주에 봐야겠다.
여 이번 주 금요일이 마지막 방송분이 될 거야.
남 아, 아쉽네.

12 ①

해설 남자는 잃어버린 모자를 찾기 위해 호텔에 전화했다.

어휘 check out (호텔에서) 체크아웃하다
earlier [ɔ́ːrliər] 앞서, 전에
hold [hould] (수화기를 들고) 기다리다
for a second 잠시 동안
give A a call back A에게 다시 전화를 하다

[Telephone rings.]
W Thank you for calling the Pine Tree Hotel. How may I help you?
M Hello. This is Mark Clayton. I checked out of your hotel earlier today.
W Yes, I remember, Mr. Clayton. What can I do for you?
M Can you check if there is a black hat at the counter?
W Can you please hold for a second? *[Pause]* I'm sorry, there aren't any hats here, sir.
M I'm pretty sure I lost it at the hotel.

[전화벨이 울린다.]
여 Pine Tree 호텔에 전화 주셔서 감사드립니다. 무엇을 도와드릴까요?
남 안녕하세요. 저는 Mark Clayton이라고 합니다. 오늘 아까 호텔에서 체크아웃을 했습니다.
여 네, 기억합니다. Clayton 씨. 무엇을 도와드릴까요?
남 카운터에 검정색 모자가 있는지 확인해 봐 줄 수 있나요?
여 잠깐만 끊지 말고 기다려 주시겠어요? *[잠시 후]* 죄송하지만, 여기에 모자는 없네요, 고객님.
남 그 호텔에서 잃어버린 게 확실해요.

W I'll give you a call back if we find a black hat.
M Thank you.

여 검정색 모자를 찾으면 다시 전화 드릴게요.
남 감사합니다.

13 ③

해설 남자는 점심시간이 끝나는 1시 30분까지 가겠다고 했다.

어휘 take an appointment 예약을 받다
see a doctor 의사의 진료를 받다
expect to-v ~할 것을 예상 [기대]하다
helpful[hélpfəl] 도움이 되는

[Telephone rings.]
W ABC Children's Hospital. How may I help you?
M Can I make an appointment for 2 p.m. today?
W I'm sorry, but we don't take appointments on Mondays.
M How long do we have to wait until we see a doctor?
W We're very busy on Mondays, so you should expect to wait about an hour.
M If we get to the hospital at 1 p.m., can we see a doctor at 2 p.m.?
W The hospital is closed for lunch until 1:30 p.m.
M I see. Then, we'll just have to get there at 1:30.
W I'm sorry I couldn't be more helpful, sir.

[전화벨이 울린다.]
여 ABC 어린이 병원입니다. 무엇을 도와드릴까요?
남 오늘 오후 2시로 예약할 수 있을까요?
여 죄송합니다만 월요일에는 예약을 받지 않습니다.
남 진료를 받으려면 얼마나 기다려야 할까요?
여 저희가 월요일에는 아주 바빠서요, 한 시간 정도는 기다리는 것을 예상하셔야 합니다.
남 오후 1시에 병원에 가면 오후 2시에는 진료를 받을 수 있을까요?
여 병원이 오후 1시 30분까지 점심 식사로 문을 닫습니다.
남 알겠습니다. 그러면 1시 30분에 거기에 도착해야 하겠군요.
여 더 도움이 못 돼서 죄송합니다.

14 ②

해설 수표를 현금으로 바꾸고자 하는 여자와 이것을 처리해 주는 남자의 대화로 보아 두 사람의 관계는 은행 직원과 고객이다.

어휘 in line 줄에 서 있는
cash a check 수표를 현금으로 바꾸다
bill[bil] 지폐
small bill 소액권, 잔돈
password[pǽswərd] 비밀번호
credit card 신용카드
specialist[spéʃəlist] 전문가

M Can I help the next person in line, please?
W Hi, I'd like to cash this check.
M Could you sign your name on the back?
W Yes, of course.
M Would you like 100-dollar bills?
W Yes. I need some smaller bills, too. Can I have three 100-dollar bills and five 20-dollar bills?
M Yes, of course. [Pause] Is there anything else?
W I also want to change the password for my credit card.
M I'm sorry, but you'll have to talk to a credit card specialist for that.
W I see. Thank you for your help.

남 줄에 서 계신 다음 분, 도와드릴까요?
여 안녕하세요, 이 수표를 현금으로 바꾸고 싶어요.
남 뒷면에 서명하시겠어요?
여 네, 그러죠.
남 100달러짜리 지폐를 원하세요?
여 네. 소액권 지폐들도 필요합니다. 100달러짜리 지폐 3장과 20달러짜리 지폐 다섯 장으로 받을 수 있을까요?
남 네, 물론이지요. [잠시 후] 또 다른 일이 있으실까요?
여 신용카드의 비밀번호도 바꾸고 싶습니다.
남 죄송하지만 그 문제는 신용카드 전문가에게 말씀해 주셔야 하는데요.
여 알겠어요. 도와주셔서 감사합니다.

15 ③

해설 집 근처에 좋은 중고 컴퓨터 가게가 있다는 남자의 말을 들은 여자가 주소를 보내 달라고 부탁했다.

W I need to get a new computer. My old one just stopped working.
M Let me see if I can fix it.

여 나는 컴퓨터를 새로 하나 사야 해. 내 오래된 컴퓨터가 방금 작동을 멈췄어.
남 수리할 수 있는지 내가 한번 볼게.

어휘 over[óuvər] ~이상
send A B = send B to A A에게 B를 보내 주다
address[ədrés] 주소
right away 당장

W No. It's <u>already</u> <u>stopped</u> <u>working</u> twice.
M You used that computer for over 10 years, right?
W Yes. It's time to get a new one.
M Why don't you get a used one? There's a really <u>good</u> <u>used</u> <u>computer</u> <u>store</u> near my house.
W That's not bad. Can you <u>send</u> <u>me</u> <u>the</u> <u>address</u>?
M Sure, I'll send it to you right away.

여 아니야. 벌써 두 번이나 고장 났는걸.
남 너는 그 컴퓨터를 10년 넘게 썼지, 그렇지?
여 응, 새것을 살 때가 되었어.
남 중고 컴퓨터를 사는 건 어떠니? 우리 집 근처에 정말 좋은 중고 컴퓨터 가게가 하나 있거든.
여 그거 나쁘지 않겠는데. 나에게 주소 좀 보내 줄래?
남 물론이지, 지금 당장 보내 줄게.

16 ①

해설 두 사람은 새해 첫날 일출을 보기 위해 일찍 일어나야 한다고 했다.

어휘 be up 자지 않고 깨어 있다
midnight[mídnàit] 자정
put on 착용하다
sunrise[sʌ́nràiz] 일출
clearly[klíərli] 선명하게
wake up 일어나다, 잠에서 깨다
New Year's Day 새해 첫날, 1월 1일

M Why are you still up? It's almost midnight.
W I'm putting on my contact lenses. These are the type of lenses I wear while I sleep.
M When did you get them?
W Last week. I want to <u>see the sunrise clearly</u>.
M Well, you need to sleep now. We have to <u>wake up early</u> to see the sunrise tomorrow.
W Okay. It's my <u>first time to see</u> a sunrise on New Year's Day.

남 왜 아직도 자지 않고 있니? 자정이 거의 되었는데.
여 콘택트렌즈를 끼고 있어요. 이것들은 제가 잘 때 끼는 콘택트렌즈예요.
남 그것들을 언제 샀니?
여 지난주에요. 일출을 선명하게 보고 싶거든요.
남 음, 지금은 자야 한단다. 내일 일출을 보려면 우리는 일찍 일어나야 하잖아.
여 알겠어요. 제가 처음으로 새해 첫날에 일출을 보는 거예요.

17 ②

해설 도서관에서 잡지를 빌리려는 여자와 대출이 불가능하다고 알려 주는 남자의 대화 내용을 고른다.

어휘 be allowed ~하는 것이 허락되다
delete[dilíːt] 지우다, 삭제하다
magazine[mæ̀gəzíːn] 잡지
copy machine 복사기
boring[bɔ́ːriŋ] 지루한, 따분한
stay awake 깨어 있다
bank account 은행 계좌

① M Taking pictures is not allowed here.
　 W I'm sorry. I'll <u>delete them</u> right now.
② M I'm sorry, but you can't borrow magazines.
　 W I didn't know that. Where is <u>the copy machine</u>?
③ M Are you ready to order, ma'am?
　 W Can you <u>give me another minute</u>?
④ M Did you like the movie?
　 W It was so boring. It was <u>difficult to stay awake</u>.
⑤ M I would like to open a bank account.
　 W I can help you with that. What is your name, sir?

① 남 여기서 사진을 촬영하시면 안 됩니다.
　 여 죄송합니다. 당장 지울게요.
② 남 죄송합니다만 잡지는 대출이 안 됩니다.
　 여 몰랐어요. 복사기가 어디에 있죠?
③ 남 주문하시겠습니까, 고객님?
　 여 시간을 좀 더 주시겠어요?
④ 남 그 영화 마음에 들었니?
　 여 영화가 너무 지루했어. 잠들지 않고 깨어 있는 것이 힘들었어.
⑤ 남 은행 계좌를 개설하고 싶습니다.
　 여 제가 도와 드리죠. 성함이 어떻게 되시죠, 고객님?

18 ④

해설 키(1미터 이상), 몸무게(최고 45킬로그램), 먹이(물고기), 서식지(남극)에 대해 언급하였으나 수명에 대해서는 언급하지 않았다.

어휘 world-famous 세계적으로 유명한

W Welcome to Penguin Land, everyone! The penguins in front of you are the world-famous emperor penguins. Adult emperor penguins <u>are over</u> 1 meter in height and can <u>weigh up to</u> 45 kilograms. They usually eat fish, and they <u>all live in</u> the South Pole. Now, let's go and meet the smallest penguins.

여 Penguin Land에 오신 것을 환영합니다, 여러분 앞에 있는 펭귄은 세계적으로 유명한 황제펭귄입니다. 다 자란 황제펭귄은 키가 1미터가 넘으며 몸무게는 45킬로그램까지 나갈 수 있습니다. 이들은 대개 물고기를 먹는데 모두 남극에 삽니다. 이제 가장 작은 펭귄들을 가서 만나 보세요.

emperor penguin 황제펭귄
adult[ədʌ́lt] 다 자란
height[hait] 키, 신장
weigh[wei] 무게가 ~ 나가다
up to (특정한 수) 까지
the South Pole 남극

19 ③

해설 남자가 여자의 생활 습관을 칭찬하자 그것을 실천해 보도록 충고했으므로 자신도 한번 해 보아야겠다고 말하는 것이 적절하다.

어휘 used to-v (예전에) ~하곤 했다
as soon as ~하자 마자
healthy[hélθi] 건강한, 건강에 좋은
instead of ~ 대신에
[선택지]
drink[driŋk] 술을 마시다
give it a try 시도하다, 한 번 해보다

W What do you drink in the morning, Paul?
M I drink coffee.
W I used to drink coffee, too, but now I just drink 2 glasses of water.
M It's not easy to drink 2 glasses of water in the morning.
W I drink one glass as soon as I get up. Then I drink another one after exercising.
M Wow, you have a very healthy lifestyle.
W You should also drink water instead of coffee in the morning.
M I guess I can give it a try.

여 아침에 무엇을 마시니, Paul?
남 나는 커피를 마셔.
여 나도 예전에는 커피를 마셨는데 지금은 물 두 잔을 마실 뿐이야.
남 아침에 물 두 잔을 마시는 것이 쉬운 일이 아닌데.
여 나는 일어나자마자 한 잔을 마셔. 나머지 한 잔은 운동한 뒤에 마시지.
남 와, 너는 건강에 아주 좋은 생활 습관을 갖고 있구나.
여 너도 아침에 커피 대신 물을 마셔야 해.
남 한번 시도해 봐야겠어.

① 알겠어, 차를 마시도록 노력해 볼게.
② 음주는 너에게 좋지 않아.
④ 아침에 전화할게.
⑤ 너는 커피를 너무 많이 마시는구나.

20 ⑤

해설 여자가 남자의 화난 친구에게 문자 메시지를 보내라며 제안하고 있으므로 보낸다고 하거나 이미 보냈다는 응답이 적절하다.

어휘 be mad at ~에 화가 나다
be supposed to ~하기로 되어 있다
lose track of time 시간 가는 줄 모르다
apologize to ~에게 사과하다
answer[ǽnsər] (전화를) 받다
text message 문자 메시지

M My friend John is really mad at me, Mom.
W What happened?
M I was supposed to meet him at the library, but I forgot.
W That's not good. Why did you forget?
M I was playing basketball with other friends, and I lost track of time.
W Have you apologized to him?
M I wanted to, but he's not answering my phone calls.
W Why don't you send him a text message?
M I already did that 30 minutes ago.

남 내 친구 John이 나한테 엄청 화가 났어요, 엄마.
여 무슨 일이 있었는데?
남 그를 도서관에서 만나기로 했는데 잊어버렸거든요.
여 그건 잘한 일은 아니지. 왜 잊어버렸니?
남 다른 친구들과 농구를 하고 있었는데 시간 가는 줄 몰랐어요.
여 그에게 사과를 했니?
남 그러고 싶었는데 그가 내 전화를 받지 않고 있어요.
여 문자 메시지를 보내는 것은 어때?
남 30분 전에 이미 그렇게 했어요.

① 내 전화기가 작동이 안 돼요.
② 걔의 이메일 주소를 잊어버렸어요.
③ 어제 그에게 사과했어요.
④ 걔가 자기 전화기를 도서관에 두고 갔어요.

01 ③

[해설] 목요일에 흐리고 쌀쌀해진 뒤 금요일에는 첫눈이 내릴 것이라고 예보하고 있다.

[어휘] fresh[freʃ] 새로운
lots of 많은 ~
than usual 평소[어느 때]보다

M Here's the weather forecast for the next 5 days. We will have lots of sunshine on Monday, Tuesday, and Wednesday. It will also be warmer than usual, but it will become cloudy and colder again on Thursday. And on Friday, we should have our first snow of the winter.

남 앞으로 5일 동안의 날씨 예보입니다. 월요일, 화요일, 그리고 수요일은 햇빛이 많이 나겠습니다. 또한 평소보다 더 따뜻하겠습니다. 하지만 목요일에는 다시 흐리고 더 쌀쌀해지겠습니다. 그리고 금요일에는 올겨울 들어 첫눈이 내리겠습니다.

02 ④

[해설] 여자는 바퀴가 작고 바구니가 달린 자전거를 사기로 했다.

[어휘] wheel[wiːl] 바퀴
even[íːvən] 심지어 ~조차[까지]
headlight[hédlait] 헤드라이트, 전조등
replace A with B A를 B로 대체하다

W Excuse me, I'm looking for a bicycle for myself.
M Okay, these are the bikes for women.
W Do you have bikes with smaller wheels?
M Yes, we do. They are over here.
W Oh, they have a headlight.
M Yes, but you can replace it with something else.
W Then, can you change the headlight to a basket?
M Of course.
W That's great. I'll take this one then.

여 실례합니다. 제가 탈 자전거를 찾고 있어요.
남 알겠어요. 이것들이 여성용입니다.
여 바퀴가 더 작은 자전거 있나요?
남 네, 있습니다. 그것들은 이쪽에 있어요.
여 아, 전조등이 있네요.
남 네, 근데 다른 걸로 바꾸셔도 됩니다.
여 그럼 전조등을 바구니로 바꿔 주실 수 있나요?
남 물론이죠.
여 좋아요. 그럼 이것으로 살게요.

03 ⑤

[해설] 색깔(갈색), 크기(8명이 앉을 수 있는 크기), 가격(500달러), 판매 장소(Tim's Furniture)에 대해 언급하였으나 재료에 대해서는 언급하지 않았다.

[어휘] dining table 식탁
seat[siːt] ~개의 좌석을 갖고 있다
furniture[fə́ːrnitʃər] 가구
inexpensive[ìnikspénsiv] 비싸지 않은

W We need to get a new dining table.
M What's wrong with the one we're using right now?
W I don't like its color. I want to have a brown one.
M How big a table do you want?
W I want one that seats 8 people.
M Really? That will be expensive.
W We can go and buy one at Tim's Furniture.
M Yes, that store has a lot of inexpensive furniture.
W We can get a good table for only $500 there.
M Okay, then let's do it.

여 우리 식탁 한 개 새로 사야 해요.
남 지금 쓰고 있는 것에 무슨 문제 있나요?
여 색깔이 마음에 안 들어요. 저는 갈색인 것이 좋거든요.
남 얼마나 큰 식탁을 원하는데요?
여 8명이 앉을 수 있는 것이 좋아요.
남 정말요? 그건 비쌀 텐데요.
여 Tim's Furniture에서 가서 사면 돼요.
남 맞아요. 그 가게에는 비싸지 않은 가구들이 많이 있잖아요.
여 거기에서 단돈 500달러로 좋은 식탁을 살 수 있을 거예요.
남 알겠어요. 그럼 그렇게 해요.

04 ④

해설 남자는 친구와 장난친 벌로 점심 식사 후에 구내식당을 청소했다.

어휘 as usual 평소와 같이
lie to ~에게 거짓말을 하다
cafeteria[kӕfətíəriə] 구내식당
spill[spil] 엎지르다

W How was your day at school, Jake?
M It was good as usual.
W What did you have for lunch?
M We had to choose between chicken and pizza, so I had pizza.
W What did you do after you had lunch?
M I played basketball with my friends.
W Don't lie to me, Jake. Your teacher called me.
M Oh, I'm sorry, Mom. I had to clean the cafeteria after lunch.
W What happened? I heard it wasn't the first time.
M I was just playing with my friends, and I spilled all my milk.

여 학교에서 오늘 어떻게 보냈니, Jake?
남 평소와 같이 좋았어요.
여 점심 식사로 무엇을 먹었니?
남 치킨과 피자 중에서 골라야 해서 저는 피자를 먹었어요.
여 점심 식사 후에는 무엇을 했니?
남 친구들과 농구 시합을 했어요.
여 거짓말 마라, Jake. 네 선생님이 나한테 전화하셨어.
남 아, 죄송해요, 엄마. 점심 식사 후에 구내식당을 청소해야 했어요.
여 무슨 일이 있었니? 처음이 아니라고 들었는데.
남 친구들과 놀다가 제가 제 우유를 모두 엎질렀거든요.

05 ②

해설 기차표에 대해 이야기 한 뒤 기차를 타기 위해 움직이고 있으므로 대화를 나누고 있는 장소는 기차역이다.

어휘 print out 출력하다
electronic[ilektránik] 전자의
convenient[kənví:njənt] 편리한

M Oh no! We're going to be late.
W We'll be fine. We still have 10 minutes.
M Do you have your ticket with you?
W Yes, I have it on my cell phone.
M On your cell phone? Did you print it out?
W Oh, it's an electronic ticket. You don't have to print it out. You can just show your cell phone.
M Really? That's very convenient.
W I know. Let's hurry. Our train's going to arrive.

남 이런! 우리 늦겠는데.
여 괜찮을 거야. 아직 10분이 남았어.
남 너는 표 가지고 있니?
여 응, 나는 내 휴대전화에 표가 있어.
남 네 휴대전화에? 그것을 출력했니?
여 아, 이건 전자 티켓이야. 출력할 필요가 없어. 휴대전화를 보여 주기만 하면 돼.
남 정말? 그거 참 편리하네.
여 맞아, 서두르자. 곧 우리가 탈 기차가 들어올 거야.

06 ②

해설 여자가 취소된 점심 약속을 취소되지 않은 것으로 착각한 것에 대해 사과하고 있다.

어휘 schedule[skédʒuːl] 일정, 스케줄
factory[fӕktəri] 공장
appointment[əpɔ́intmənt] 약속
cancel[kӕnsəl] 취소하다
confuse[kənfjúːz] 혼란시키다

M Good morning, Sara. How are you?
W I'm well, Mr. Willis. How was your weekend?
M It was great. So, what's my schedule for today?
W First, there is a meeting at 10. After a short break, you have to visit the factory. Then there is a lunch appointment with Mr. Peterson.
M Mr. Peterson? I thought we canceled the lunch with him.
W I didn't hear anything about it.
M Check it again. I'm sure I told you this before.
W [Pause] Oh, my mistake. I'm sorry that I confused you.

남 안녕하세요, Sara. 잘 지냈죠?
여 네, 잘 지냈습니다, Willis 씨. 주말을 어떻게 보내셨어요?
남 잘 보냈어요. 그래서 오늘 제 일정이 어떻게 되나요?
여 우선 10시에 미팅이 있습니다. 잠깐 휴식 후에 공장을 방문하셔야 합니다. 그런 다음, Peterson 씨와 점심 약속이 있네요.
남 Peterson 씨라고요? 그와의 점심 약속은 취소했던 것 같은데요.
여 그것에 대해서 아무것도 듣지 못했는데요.
남 다시 확인해 보세요. 전에 이걸 분명히 말했던 것 같아요.
여 [잠시 후] 아, 제 실수네요. 혼란을 드려 죄송해요.

07 ⑤

해설 남자는 음악을 전혀 좋아하지 않으며 노래 실력이 형편없다고 했다.

어휘 report card 성적표
surprising[sərpráiziŋ] 놀라운
not ~ at all 전혀 ~ 아닌
terrible[térəbl] 형편없는

W Did you get your report card today?
M I did. I think my grades are okay. How about you?
W Same here. But I got a C in art.
M Really? That's surprising. Isn't that your favorite subject?
W No, history is my favorite subject. What's yours?
M I don't have a favorite subject. I enjoy most of the subjects this semester.
W Is there a subject that you really don't like?
M Oh, I don't like music at all. I'm terrible at singing.

여 오늘 성적표 받았니?
남 응, 받았어. 내 성적은 괜찮은 것 같아. 너는?
여 나도 그래. 근데 미술에서 C를 받았어.
남 정말? 놀라운 일이네. 미술이 네가 가장 좋아하는 과목이 아니니?
여 아니, 역사가 내가 가장 좋아하는 과목이야. 너는 가장 좋아하는 과목이 뭐니?
남 나는 가장 좋아하는 과목이 없어. 난 이번 학기에 대부분의 과목들을 즐겁게 공부했어.
여 정말로 좋아하지 않는 과목이 있니?
남 아, 난 음악을 전혀 좋아하지 않아. 노래를 형편없이 못 부르거든.

08 ④

해설 여자는 궁궐에 대해 영어로 설명해 놓은 안내문을 사진으로 찍겠다고 했다.

어휘 palace[pǽlis] 궁궐, 궁
anyway[éniwei] 그건 그렇고
such[sʌtʃ] 대단히, 매우
whole[houl] 전체의

W How many times have you been to this palace, Junha?
M This is actually my first time.
W You live in Seoul, but you've never been here before?
M I've been so busy that I didn't have time to visit.
W Anyway, this is such a beautiful palace.
M I know. That's why I brought you here.
W Look! There's an information board in English of the whole palace.
M Wow, you can learn so much about Korean history by reading this.
W Let me take a picture of this, so I can read it at home.
M Good idea!

여 이 궁궐에 몇 번 와 봤니, 준하야?
남 사실은 이번이 처음이야.
여 너 서울에 살잖아, 그런데 여기에 전에 와 본 적이 없다고?
남 난 너무 바빠서 방문할 시간이 없었어.
여 그건 그렇고 여기는 정말 아름다운 궁궐이네.
남 맞아. 그래서 내가 너를 여기로 데려왔어.
여 봐! 궁궐 전체에 대해 영어로 된 안내문이 있어.
남 와, 너 이것을 읽으면 한국 역사에 대해 많이 배울 수 있겠다.
여 집에서 읽을 수 있도록 사진으로 찍을래.
남 좋은 생각이야!

09 ④

해설 이름(Mark Kidd), 직업(중학교 교사), 결혼 여부(미혼), 출생 지역(Boston)에 대해 언급하였으나 나이에 대해서는 언급하지 않았다.

어휘 neighbor[néibər] 이웃 (사람)
living[lívit] 생계 (수단)
geography[dʒiágrəfi] 지리
married[mǽrid] 결혼한
single[síŋgl] 미혼의, 독신의

W Have you met your new neighbor?
M Yes, I have. His name is Mark Kidd.
W What does he do for a living?
M He's a middle school teacher. He teaches geography.
W Is he married?
M I think he's still single. By the way, weren't you born in Boston?
W Yes, I was. Why do you ask?
M He said he was born in Boston, too.

여 너의 새 이웃과 만났니?
남 응, 만났어. 그의 이름은 Mark Kidd야.
여 그는 직업이 뭐니?
남 그는 중학교 교사야. 지리를 가르쳐.
여 그가 결혼을 했니?
남 아직 미혼인 것 같아. 그건 그렇고, 너 Boston에서 태어나지 않았니?
여 응, 거기서 태어났어. 왜 물어보니?
남 그가 자기도 Boston에서 태어났다고 말하더라.

by the way 그건 그렇고
be born 태어나다
have a lot in common 공통점이 많다

W Really? Can you introduce me to him?
M Of course. I'm sure you two will have a lot in common.

여 정말? 나를 그에게 좀 소개해 줄 수 있니?
남 물론이지. 너희 둘은 틀림없이 공통점이 많이 있을 거야.

10 ⑤

해설 플라스틱 제품을 보다 세심하게 재활용할 필요가 있다고 말한 뒤 라벨을 제거하고 유제품을 담았던 용기를 잘 씻는 등 올바른 재활용 방법을 제시하고 있다.

어휘 importance[impɔ́ːrtəns] 중요성
proper[prápər] 제대로 된
recycling[riːsáikliŋ] 재활용
separate A from B A를 B에서 분리하다
item[áitəm] 제품, 물품
remove[rimúːv] 제거하다, 없애다
label[léibəl] 라벨, 상표
bin[bin] 쓰레기통
wash out ~의 안을 씻어 내다
container[kəntéinər] 용기, 그릇
dairy product 유제품

M Today, I'd like to talk about the importance of proper recycling. Many of you are separating plastic items from glass bottles, cans, and paper boxes. However, plastic items need to be recycled more carefully. You should remove labels before you put plastic items in a recycling bin. And you should also wash out plastic containers for dairy products, such as milk and yogurt.

남 오늘 저는 제대로 된 재활용의 중요성에 대해 이야기하고자 합니다. 여러분 중 많은 분들이 유리병, 캔, 그리고 종이 상자들로부터 플라스틱 제품을 분리하고 계십니다. 하지만 플라스틱 제품은 더 세심하게 재활용이 되어야 합니다. 여러분은 플라스틱 제품을 재활용 쓰레기통에 넣기 전에 라벨을 제거해야 합니다. 그리고 여러분은 우유와 요구르트 같은 유제품을 담은 플라스틱 용기도 잘 씻어내야 합니다.

11 ④

해설 물병은 한 개에 5달러이다.

어휘 bottle[bátl] 병
carry[kǽri] 갖고 다니다
completely[kəmplíːtli] 완전히
just in case 만일을 대비해서

W Let's get this water bottle, Mike.
M You can't put hot water in here.
W That's fine. I don't need to carry it for hot water. I just need a small bottle.
M But isn't it too small? And it's completely black.
W I know it's small and black. That's why I like it. And it's only $5.
M Okay. How many bottles are you getting?
W I think I'll get 2, just in case.
M What is this on the bottle?
W Oh, I guess you can write your name on it.

여 이 물병을 사자, Mike.
남 이 안에 뜨거운 물을 넣을 수 없잖아.
여 괜찮아. 나는 뜨거운 물을 갖고 다닐 필요가 없어. 단지 작은 병이면 돼.
남 하지만 너무 작지 않니? 그리고 완전히 검정색이야.
여 나도 그게 작고 검정색이라는 거 알아. 그래서 내가 그것을 좋아하는 거야. 그리고 가격도 5달러밖에 안 하잖아.
남 좋아. 몇 개 살 건데?
여 두 개 사자, 만일을 위해서.
남 병 표면에 있는 이건 뭐지?
여 아, 그 위에 이름을 적을 수 있나봐.

12 ①

해설 남자는 책 사인회를 하는 작가를 만나기 위해 서점에 왔다.

어휘 wonder[wʌ́ndər] 궁금해 하다
miss[mis] 놓치다
look forward to v-ing ~하는 것을 기대하다
in person 직접, 몸소

W Can I help the next person in line, please?
M Hi, I was just wondering if there's a book signing here today.
W Oh, you just missed it.
M Wasn't the event from 3 p.m. to 5 p.m.?
W Yes, that's right.
M It's only 4:30. Did something happen?

여 줄에 서 계신 다음 분, 도와드릴까요?
남 안녕하세요. 오늘 이곳에서 책 사인회가 있는지 알고 싶어요.
여 아, 방금 놓치셨네요.
남 행사가 오후 3시에서 5시까지 아니었나요?
여 아니요, 맞아요.
남 4시 30분밖에 안 되었는데. 무슨 일이 있었나요?

W The author wasn't feeling well, so she left 10 minutes ago.

M I was really looking forward to meeting her in person.

W I'm sorry.

여 작가분이 몸이 안 좋으셔서 10분 전에 떠나셨어요.

남 제가 그분을 직접 만나기를 정말 기대했거든요.

여 죄송합니다.

13 ②

해설 두 사람은 입장료가 5달러인 11시 영화를 보기로 했다.

어휘 show[ʃou] 상영되다; 공연, 쇼
each[i:tʃ] 각각

W Would you like to see a movie tomorrow?

M Sounds good. What do you want to see?

W How about *Little Woman*?

M Oh, sure. What time is it showing?

W There are shows at 11, 3, and 7:30 tomorrow.

M How much are the tickets?

W Tickets for the 11 o'clock show are $5 and all other shows are $9 each.

M Then, I'd like to go at 11. Is that okay?

W Sure, that sounds fine to me.

여 내일 영화 보러 갈래?

남 좋지. 뭐가 보고 싶은데?

여 〈작은 아가씨〉는 어때?

남 아, 좋아. 상영 시간이 몇 시니?

여 내일은 11시, 3시, 7시 30분에 상영해.

남 티켓은 얼마야?

여 11시 티켓은 5달러이고, 나머지는 모두 9달러씩이야.

남 그럼 11시에 가고 싶어. 괜찮니?

여 그래, 나도 괜찮아.

14 ②

해설 남자가 딸에게 줄 책을 사고 있고 여자가 책을 추천한 뒤 가격을 말해 주고 있으므로 두 사람의 관계는 서점 직원과 고객임을 알 수 있다.

어휘 just[dʒʌst] 이제 막
turn[təːrn] (나이가) ~살이 되다
recommend[rèkəménd] 추천하다
come out to be (총계) ~이 되다

M Hi, I'm looking for a book for my daughter.

W Okay. How old is she?

M She just turned 6 last week.

W Is she just starting to read?

M Yes. She started learning to read a year ago, and she likes to read animal stories.

W Then, I would recommend *The Three Little Pigs*. The book is on sale right now.

M That'll be perfect! How much is it?

W With a 10% discount, it comes out to be $9.

남 안녕하세요. 딸에게 줄 책을 한 권 사려고요.

여 알겠습니다. 따님이 몇 살인가요?

남 지난주에 막 6살이 되었어요.

여 따님이 이제 막 읽기를 시작했나요?

남 네. 1년 전에 읽기를 배우기 시작했고요, 그리고 동물 이야기 읽는 것을 좋아해요.

여 그러면 〈아기 돼지 3형제〉를 추천해 드리고 싶네요. 이 책은 지금 세일 중이에요.

남 그거 좋겠네요! 얼마죠?

여 10% 할인해서 9달러 되겠습니다.

15 ⑤

해설 남자는 여자에게 교실 청소가 끝날 때까지 잠깐 기다려 달라고 부탁했다.

어휘 first[fəːrst] 먼저
third[θəːrd] 세 번째의
finish v-ing ~하는 것을 끝내다

W The study group meeting is in 10 minutes. Let's go.

M I can't leave now. I have to clean our classroom first.

W Why are you cleaning the classroom?

M I was late for school today for the third time this week, so I'm cleaning.

W Do you want me to help you clean the classroom?

M No, I have to do it myself. Can you wait for me until I finish cleaning the classroom?

W How long will it take?

M I think it's going to take only a minute or two.

여 스터디 그룹 모임이 10분 뒤에 있어. 어서 가자.

남 지금 갈 수 없어. 우리 교실 청소를 먼저 해야 해.

여 왜 교실을 네가 청소하는데?

남 나는 오늘 이번 주에 들어 세 번째로 지각을 했어. 그래서 청소를 하는 거야.

여 내가 교실 청소하는 것을 도와줄까?

남 아니, 내가 직접 해야지. 내가 교실 청소를 끝낼 때까지 기다려 줄 수 있겠니?

여 얼마나 걸리겠니?

남 1~2분 정도밖에 안 걸릴 거야.

16 ②

해설 남자는 어버이날에 어머니께 드리기 위해 카네이션을 샀다.

어휘 order[ɔ́:rdər] 주문하다
online[ɔ́nlain] 온라인으로
deliver[dilívər] 배달하다
celebrate[séləbrèit] 기념하다

W What beautiful flowers! Where did you get them?
M I ordered them online yesterday, and they were delivered about an hour ago.
W What are the flowers for?
M I bought these for my mother.
W Is it her birthday?
M In Korea, we give our parents carnations on Parents' Day.
W Oh, I didn't know that. I usually celebrate Mother's Day and Father's Day on 2 different days.
M Not in Korea. There is just one Parents' Day.
W I see.

여 정말 아름다운 꽃들이구나! 이것들을 어디에서 샀니?
남 어제 온라인으로 주문했어. 그리고 한 시간쯤 전에 배달되었지.
여 꽃들을 어디에 쓸 거야?
남 어머니께 드리려고 샀어.
여 어머님 생신이니?
남 한국에서는 어버이날에 부모님께 카네이션을 드리거든.
여 아, 나는 그건 몰랐어. 난 보통 어머니날과 아버지날을 각각 다른 날에 기념하거든.
남 한국에서는 그러지 않아. 어버이날 하루만 있어.
여 그렇구나.

17 ④

해설 여자가 공원에서 음식을 먹으려하고 남자가 이를 제지하는 대화가 적절하다.

어휘 lost and found 분실물 보관소
restroom[réstrù(:)m] 화장실
section[sékʃən] 구역, 부문
ride a skateboard 스케이트보드를타다

① M Excuse me. Do you have a lost and found here?
  W Yes, we do. What did you lose?
② M Here's the menu. I'll be back to take your orders.
  W Can I order now? I know what I want.
③ M Let's use the restroom before the movie starts.
  W That's a good idea.
④ M Excuse me. You can't eat in this section of the park.
  W Oh, I'm sorry. Where is the picnic area?
⑤ M I'm sorry, but you can't ride your skateboard here.
  W Where can I ride a skateboard in this park?

① 남 실례합니다. 분실물과 습득물을 취급하시나요?
  여 네, 그렇습니다. 무엇을 잃어버리셨나요?
② 남 여기 메뉴판입니다. 주문을 받으러 다시 올게요.
  여 지금 주문해도 될까요? 제가 주문해야 할 것을 알고 있어요.
③ 남 영화가 시작하기 전에 화장실에 다녀오자.
  여 좋은 생각이야.
④ 남 실례합니다. 공원의 이 구역에서는 음식을 드실 수 없습니다.
  여 아, 죄송합니다. 피크닉 구역이 어디죠?
⑤ 남 죄송하지만 여기서 스케이트보드를 타면 안 됩니다.
  여 이 공원에서 스케이트보드를 탈 수 있는 곳이 어디죠?

18 ③

해설 상품명(Sky Jump), 기능(더 빨리달리고 더 높게 점프할 수 있음), 가격(180달러), 할인율(10%)에 대해 언급하였으나 색깔에 대해서는 언급하지 않았다.

어휘 a pair of 한 켤레의
regret v-ing ~한 것을 후회하다
spend money on ~에 돈을 쓰다

M Do you want to become a better basketball player? Then, get a pair of these amazing basketball shoes. Why are they called Sky Jump? They will help you run faster and jump higher. $180 a pair may seem expensive, but you won't regret spending that money on a pair of Sky Jump. Order now, and you will receive a 10% discount.

남 농구를 더 잘하고 싶으신가요? 그렇다면 이 놀라운 농구화 한 켤레를 구매하세요. 이 농구화는 왜 Sky Jump라고 불릴까요? 이 농구화는 당신이 더 빨리 달리고 더 높게 점프를 하도록 도와줄 것이기 때문입니다. 한 켤레에 180달러라면 가격이 비싸게 보일 수도 있겠지만 여러분은 그 돈을 Sky Jump 한 켤레에 쓴 것을 후회하지 않으실 겁니다. 지금 주문하세요, 그러면 10% 할인을 받으실 수 있습니다.

19 ⑤

해설 여자가 빌린 책들을 반납했는지 묻고 있으므로 이어질 응답으로 책을 반납했는지 여부를 답하는 것이 적절하다.

어휘 as usual 평소처럼
give A a hug A를 껴안다, 포옹하다
receive[risíːv] 받다
return[ritə́ːrn] 돌려주다, 반납하다; 반납
borrow[bárou] 빌리다

W How was your last day at school?
M I guess it was the same as usual.
W Did you say goodbye to all of your friends?
M Yes. Some of them gave me a hug, and I also received a few cards from others.
W That's so sweet of them. Oh, did you return the books that you borrowed from the school library?
M Yes, I put them all in the return box.

① 물론이죠, 내일 그것들을 반납할게요.
② 아니요, 아직 카드를 읽지 않았어요.
③ 아니요, 오늘 학교가 문을 닫았어요.
④ 네, 책을 몇 권 더 빌렸어요.

여 학교에서 보낸 마지막 날은 어땠니?
남 평소와 똑같았던 것 같아요.
여 네 친구들 모두에게 작별 인사 했니?
남 네, 친구들 중 몇몇은 저를 껴안아 주기도 했고요, 다른 친구들에게서 카드도 몇 장 받았어요.
여 친구들이 정말 착하구나. 아, 학교 도서관에서 빌린 책들은 반납했니?
남 네, 반납 박스에 모두 넣었어요.

20 ④

해설 여자가 악기를 연주할 줄 아는지 묻고 있으므로 이어질 응답으로 연주하는 악기의 이름을 말하는 것이 적절하다.

어휘 free time 여가 시간
how to-v ~하는 방법
not ~ at all 전혀 ~아닌
instrument(= musical instrument)
[ínstrəmənt] 악기

M What do you usually do in your free time?
W I usually play the piano.
M Don't you play the guitar, too?
W Yes, I do, but I've only been playing for 2 months.
M I saw you playing the guitar last week at Jimmy's place, and you were really good.
W I can play a few songs, but I like to play the piano when I'm at home.
M Wow, I want to hear you play the piano. You must be great.
W Maybe later. What about you? Do you play any instruments?
M I play the drums and the bass guitar.

① 나는 집에 피아노가 없어.
② 나는 종종 체육관에서 농구를 해.
③ 기타는 내가 가장 좋아하는 악기야.
⑤ 나는 지난달에 피아노 연주하는 것을 배웠어.

남 여가 시간에 주로 무엇을 하니?
여 나는 주로 피아노를 쳐.
남 기타도 치지 않니?
여 아니, 기타도 쳐. 하지만 연주한 지 두 달밖에 안 됐어.
남 네가 지난주에 Jimmy의 집에서 기타를 치는 것을 보았는데 정말 잘 치더라.
여 기타로 노래 몇 곡은 연주할 수 있어, 하지만 집에 있을 때는 피아노 치는 것을 좋아해.
남 와, 네가 피아노 연주하는 걸 들어보고 싶다. 분명 잘 할 거 같아.
여 아마도 나중에. 너는? 악기를 연주할 줄 아니?
남 나는 드럼과 베이스 기타를 쳐.

01 ③	02 ③	03 ②	04 ④	05 ②	06 ③	07 ⑤
08 ⑤	09 ⑤	10 ③	11 ③	12 ②	13 ④	14 ③
15 ②	16 ④	17 ③	18 ④	19 ③	20 ③	

01 ③

해설 내일은 하루 종일 흐린 날씨가 될 것으로 예보하고 있다.

어휘 rainy season 장마철, 우기 · throughout the day 하루 종일 · raindrop[réindràp] 빗방울

M Good afternoon, everyone! I hope you're all having a wonderful weekend. We're finally getting lots of sunshine after the rainy season over the past few weeks. However, we won't have much sunshine tomorrow as it will be cloudy throughout the day. The good news is that we won't see another raindrop for the next 10 days.

남 안녕하세요, 여러분! 여러분 모두 멋진 주말을 보내고 계시기 바랍니다. 지난 몇 주 동안의 장마가 지나가고 드디어 햇빛이 많이 나고 있습니다. 하지만, 내일은 하루 종일 흐릴 예정이라서 햇빛을 많이 볼 수는 없겠습니다. 좋은 소식은 앞으로 10일 동안은 빗방울을 전혀 구경하지 않게 될 거라는 점입니다.

02 ③

해설 여자는 손잡이가 있고 장미가 그려진 컵을 사겠다고 했다.

어휘 follow[fálou] 따라가다 · in particular 특별히, 특히 · handle[hǽndl] 손잡이 · sunflower[sʌ́nflauər] 해바라기

W Excuse me. Where can I find cups?
M I'll show you where they are. Follow me, please.
W [Pause] Oh, there they are.
M Are you looking for anything in particular?
W I'm looking for something with a handle.
M There are the ones with handles.
W Do you have any with a picture of a flower?
M Yes. There's one with a picture of a rose and another with a picture of a sunflower.
W Perfect! Then, I'll take the one with a rose on it.

여 실례합니다. 컵은 어디에 있나요?
남 그것들이 어디에 있는지 보여 드리죠. 저를 따라오세요.
여 [잠시 후] 아, 저기에 있군요.
남 특별히 찾으시는 것이 있나요?
여 손잡이가 있는 것을 원해요.
남 손잡이가 있는 컵들은 있습니다.
여 꽃 그림이 있는 컵도 있나요?
남 네, 하나는 장미 한 송이 그림이 있는 것이고, 다른 하나는 해바라기 한 송이가 그려져 있는 것이에요.
여 좋아요! 그러면 장미 한 송이가 그려져 있는 것으로 살게요.

03 ②

해설 남자는 병원에 다녀온 여자에게 같이 있어 주기를 바라는지 물으며 걱정하고 있다.

어휘 just[dʒʌst] 방금, 막; 단지 · serious[síəriəs] 심각한 · run a test 테스트를 하다 · result[rizʌ́lt] 결과

[Cell phone rings.]
W Hello.
M Hi, honey. Have you seen the doctor yet?
W Yes, I have. I just came home.
M What did she say?
W She just told me to come back next week.
M That doesn't sound good. Is it something serious?
W The doctor ran some tests. The results will come out next week.
M Do you want me to come home and stay with you?
W No, it's okay. I'll be fine.
M All right. I hope it's nothing serious.

[휴대전화가 울린다.]
여 여보세요.
남 여보, 벌써 병원에 다녀왔어요?
여 네, 다녀왔어요. 이제 막 집에 왔어요.
남 의사 선생님이 뭐라고 하셨나요?
여 다음 주에 다시 오라고만 하셨어요.
남 좋은 이야기로 들리지 않는데요. 심각한 상황인가요?
여 의사 선생님이 몇 가지 테스트를 하셨어요. 결과는 다음 주에 나올 거예요.
남 제가 집에 가서 당신 옆에 있을까요?
여 아니, 됐어요. 저는 괜찮아요.
남 알겠어요. 심각한 일이 아니면 좋겠네요.

04 ④

해설 남자는 밸런타인데이에 친구들과 축구를 했다.

어휘 seafood[síːfud] 해산물
by[bai] ~ 옆에
amazing[əméiziŋ] 놀라운
eat out 외식하다
break up 헤어지다

W Hey, James. Did you have fun yesterday?
M Yes, I guess. How about you?
W It was the best Valentine's Day ever. My boyfriend and I went to this famous restaurant in the city.
M Do you mean the seafood restaurant by the river?
W Yes, the food was amazing, and the waiter was very friendly.
M I'm happy to hear that you had a wonderful time.
W What did you do? Did you eat out with your girlfriend?
M No, we broke up last week. I played soccer with my friends.

여 안녕, James. 어제 즐겁게 보냈니?
남 응, 그런 것 같아. 너는 어땠니?
여 지금껏 최고의 밸런타인데이였어. 남자 친구와 나는 시에서 가장 유명한 레스토랑에 갔어.
남 강변에 있는 해산물 레스토랑 말이니?
여 응, 음식이 대단했고 웨이터도 아주 친절했어.
남 네가 멋진 시간을 보냈다는 말을 들으니 좋네.
여 너는 뭘 했니? 여자 친구랑 같이 외식했니?
남 아니, 우린 지난주에 헤어졌어. 나는 친구들과 축구 시합을 했어.

05 ②

해설 남자는 아픈 곳을 보여주며 진통제를 받았고 여자가 병원에 가라고 했으므로 두 사람이 대화하는 장소는 약국임을 알 수 있다.

어휘 take a look at ~을 보다
swollen[swóulən] 부어오른
step on ~을 밟다
by accident 우연히, 모르고
make a fist 주먹을 쥐다
hurt[həːrt] 아프다
take[teik] (약을) 복용하다
pain[pein] 아픔, 통증
pain medicine 진통제

W What can I do for you?
M Could you take a look at my right hand?
W Oh, it's really swollen. What happened?
M Someone stepped on it by accident.
W Can you make a fist?
M I think I can. But it hurts more when I try to move my fingers.
W I think you should see a doctor.
M I will, but do you have anything I can take for the pain?
W Sure. [Pause] Here's some pain medicine.

여 무엇을 도와드릴까요?
남 제 오른손을 좀 봐주시겠어요?
여 아, 많이 부었네요. 어쩌다 그러셨어요?
남 어떤 사람이 실수로 밟았어요.
여 주먹을 쥘 수 있나요?
남 쥘 수 있는 것 같아요. 하지만 손가락을 움직이려 하면 더 아파요.
여 병원에 가 보셔야 할 것 같네요.
남 그럴게요. 그치만 통증이 가시도록 복용할 만한 것 없을까요?
여 있어요. [잠시 후] 여기 진통제를 좀 드릴게요.

06 ③

해설 남자가 함께 영화를 보러 가자고 제안하자 여자가 승낙하고 있다.

어휘 in particular 특별히
volleyball[válibɔ̀ːl] 배구
practice[prǽktis] 연습

M What are you doing tonight?
W Nothing in particular. I usually go to bed early on Fridays.
M Do you need to get up early on Saturdays?
W Yes, I have volleyball practice on Saturday mornings. But there's no practice tomorrow.
M Then, you don't have to go to sleep early tonight, right? Do you want to go to the movies with me?
W Sure, it's been a long time since I went to the movies.

남 오늘 밤 뭐 할 거니?
여 특별한 일은 없어. 나는 보통 금요일에는 일찍 잠자리에 들거든.
남 토요일에는 일찍 일어나야 하니?
여 응, 토요일 아침마다 배구 연습이 있지. 그런데 내일은 연습이 없어.
남 그럼, 오늘 밤에는 일찍 잠자리에 들 필요가 없구나, 그렇지? 나랑 같이 영화 보러 가지 않을래?
여 좋아, 영화 보러 간 지도 오래되었어.

07 ⑤

해설 여자는 짧은 휴가 기간에 맞게 한
국에서 가깝고 시차도 없는 도쿄에 가기
로 결정했다.

어휘 far from ~에서 먼
time difference 시차
either ~도 또한 아닌

M Have you decided where to go for your vacation?
W Not yet. It's not easy.
M Didn't you want to go to London?
W I went there last year.
M New York is a good place to visit in summer.
W But it's too far from Korea. My vacation is only 4 days.
M Then how about somewhere close, like Beijing or Tokyo?
W Actually, I've never been to Japan before.
M There is no time difference either. It'll be perfect for your short vacation.
W I'll go to Tokyo, then.

남 너 휴가 때 어디로 갈지 결정했니?
여 아직 못했어. 쉽지 않네.
남 런던에 가고 싶어 하지 않았니?
여 거기는 작년에 갔어.
남 뉴욕은 여름에 방문하기 좋은 곳인데.
여 하지만 한국에서 너무 멀잖아. 내 휴가는 4일밖에 안 되거든.
남 그럼 베이징이나 도쿄 같은 가까운 곳은 어때?
여 사실 나는 그 전에 일본에 가본 적이 없어.
남 시차도 없잖아. 너의 짧은 휴가에 딱 맞네.
여 그럼 도쿄에 가야겠다.

08 ⑤

해설 일기예보를 확인하라는 여자의 말
에 남자는 지금 바로 확인하겠다고 했다.

어휘 excited[iksáitid] 신나는
pack[pæk] (짐을) 챙기다
snack[snæk] 간식
extra[ékstrə] 여분의
make sure 확실히 하다, 확인하다

W Are you excited about this weekend?
M Of course, Mom. It's my first time to go camping with my friends.
W You should start packing today.
M I've already finished packing.
W Really? Do you need more snacks? I can bring you more.
M No, thanks. I think I have enough snacks.
W Did you pack an extra jacket and an umbrella?
M I packed extra clothes, but I don't think it's going to rain.
W You should check the weather forecast to make sure.
M Yes, you're right. I'll do that right now.

여 이번 주말을 생각하니 신나니?
남 물론이죠, 엄마. 친구들과 캠핑 가는 게 처음이에요.
여 오늘 짐을 챙기기 시작하렴.
남 짐은 이미 다 챙겼어요.
여 정말? 간식 좀 더 필요하니? 더 가져다줄 수 있는데.
남 아니요, 됐어요. 간식은 충분히 챙긴 것 같아요.
여 재킷과 우산도 하나 더 챙겼니?
남 옷을 하나 더 챙겼는데요. 비가 올 것 같지는 않아요.
여 확실히 하기 위해서 일기 예보를 확인하렴.
남 네, 맞아요. 지금 바로 할게요.

09 ⑤

해설 이름(Jacob's Bakery), 제빵사
이름(Jacob), 개점 날짜(2월 2일), 영업
시간(9시부터 7시까지)에 대해 언급하였
으나 위치에 대해서는 언급하지 않았다.

어휘 baker[béikər] 제빵사
business hour 영업 시간
on A's way home A가 집에 가는 길에

M Have you been to the new bakery in our building?
W Do you mean Jacob's Bakery?
M Yes. I wonder why it's called Jacob's Bakery.
W Jacob is the name of the baker.
M Oh, I didn't know that. When did it open?
W It opened on February 2nd. I heard the cookies are the most popular.
M Do you know the business hours?
W Yes. The bakery is open from 9 to 7.
M I'll get some cookies on my way home then.

남 우리 건물에 있는 새 빵집에 가 봤니?
여 Jacob's Bakery 말하는 거니?
남 응. 나는 왜 Jacob's Bakery라고 불리는지 궁금해.
여 제빵사의 이름이 Jacob이야.
남 아, 그건 몰랐네. 거긴 언제 개점했니?
여 2월 2일에 열었어. 쿠키가 가장 인기 있다고 들었어.
남 그 가게의 영업시간 알고 있어?
여 응. 9시부터 7시까지 열어.
남 그럼 집에 가는 길에 쿠키를 좀 사야겠다.

10 ③

해설 인명 구조원이 근무 중일 때만 수영장을 이용하고 뛰지 말아야 하며 물 외에는 먹거나 마시지 말라며 수영장 안전 수칙을 설명하고 있다.

어휘 pool[puːl] 수영장
safety[séifti] 안전
lifeguard[láifgàːrd] 인명 구조원
on duty 근무 중인
except[iksépt] 제외하고는, 외에는

W Before you start using the pool, it's very important that you know and understand our safety rules. First, use the pool only when there is a lifeguard on duty. Second, there is no running in the pool area. Lastly, eating or drinking is not allowed except water. I hope everyone will stay safe and have lots of fun!

여 수영장을 이용하시기 전에 안전 수칙을 알고 이해하는 것이 아주 중요합니다. 먼저, 인명 구조원이 근무 중일 때만 수영장을 이용하세요. 두 번째로는 수영장에서 뛰면 안 됩니다. 마지막으로 물 이외에는 먹거나 마시는 것은 금지됩니다. 여러분 모두 안전한 상태로 즐거운 시간을 보내셨으면 좋겠습니다!

11 ③

해설 다른 난방기가 더 저렴하다고 했다.

어휘 energy saving 에너지 절약형인
heater[híːtər] 난방기
reduce[ridʤúːs] 줄이다
heating bill 난방비
pay for itself 비용만큼 돈이 절약되다
warm up 데우다
instantly[ínstəntli] 즉시

M I'd like to tell you about our new heater today. This is an energy saving heater, so it will reduce your heating bills. Other heaters are cheaper, but our new heater will pay for itself in a year or two. It's very small and light, but it will warm up your room instantly.

남 오늘 저희의 새 난방기에 대해 말씀드리고자 합니다. 이것은 에너지 절약형 난방기여서, 난방비를 줄여 주게 됩니다. 다른 난방기들이 더 저렴하지만 1~2년 후에는 저희의 새 난방기가 비용만큼 돈을 절약해줄 것입니다. 저희 난방기는 아주 작고 가볍지만 여러분의 방을 즉시 따뜻하게 해 줄 것입니다.

12 ②

해설 남자는 식당 예약을 오후 6시에서 7시로 바꾸려고 전화했다.

어휘 reservation[rèzərvéiʃən] 예약

[Telephone rings.]
W Thank you for calling Martha's Kitchen. How may I help you?
M Can I talk to Elisabeth, please?
W She's not in today.
M She told me to call her if I needed to change my reservation.
W I can help you with that, sir.
M Oh, great! I have a reservation for tonight under my name.
W May I have your name?
M It is Henry Baker, and could you change my reservation from 6 p.m. to 7 p.m.?
W Of course. I'll make that change right now.

[전화벨이 울린다.]
여 Martha's Kitchen에 전화 주셔서 감사드립니다. 무엇을 도와드릴까요?
남 Elisabeth 좀 바꿔 주시겠어요?
여 그녀는 오늘은 일하지 않습니다.
남 제 예약을 변경하려면 그녀에게 전화해 달라고 했거든요.
여 제가 도와 드리겠습니다, 고객님.
남 아, 잘됐네요! 제 이름으로 오늘 밤 예약을 했는데요.
여 성함이 어떻게 되시죠?
남 Henry Baker이고요, 예약을 오후 6시에서 7시로 바꿀 수 있을까요?
여 물론입니다. 지금 당장 그렇게 변경해 드리겠습니다.

13 ④

해설 여자가 남자를 4시 30분에 만나서 차에 태워주기로 했다.

어휘 miss[mis] (탈 것 등을) 놓치다
get off work 퇴근하다

M Mom, I need a few things for math homework. Can you come and pick me up after school today?
W Sure, honey. Where are you going to get them?

남 엄마, 수학 숙제 때문에 필요한 게 좀 있어요. 오늘 방과 후에 오셔서 저 좀 태우고 갈 수 있나요?
여 물론이지, 아들아. 그것들을 어디에서 살 거니?

parking lot 주차장

M There is a store next to the school. But if I go there, I'll miss the school bus.
W Okay. I finish work at 3:30. How about 4 o'clock?
M Well, school finishes at 4, but I need time to go to the store and buy things.
W I see. How about 4:30? I'll wait in the parking lot.
M Okay. Thanks.

남 학교 옆에 가게가 하나 있어요. 하지만 거기에 가면 스쿨버스를 놓치게 돼요.
여 알겠어. 나는 3시 30분에 퇴근해. 4시는 어떠니?
남 글쎄요, 학교가 4시에 끝나는데, 가게에 가서 물건을 살 시간이 필요하거든요.
여 알겠어. 4시 30분은 어때? 주차장에서 기다릴게.
남 알겠어요. 고마워요.

14 ③

해설 엔진에 문제가 있는 것 같다는 여자의 말에 남자는 몇 가지 검사를 해야 한다고 했으므로 두 사람의 관계는 자동차 정비사와 고객임을 알 수 있다.

어휘 describe[diskráib] 말로 설명하다, 묘사하다
have a hard time v-ing ~하는 데 어려움을 겪다
start[staːrt] (차의) 시동을 걸다
hood[hud] (자동차의) 보닛

M How can I help you, ma'am?
W I think there is something wrong with the engine.
M Can you describe the problem?
W I had a hard time starting the car this morning.
M Can you open the hood? I'll take a look.
W Sure, I hope it's nothing serious.
M I don't think there's anything wrong with the engine.
W What is the problem then?
M I'll have to run some tests. Could you wait in the waiting room?
W Yes, of course.

남 도와드릴까요, 고객님?
여 엔진에 뭔가 이상이 있는 것 같아요.
남 문제를 설명해주시겠어요?
여 오늘 아침에 차 시동을 걸기가 힘들었어요.
남 보닛을 열어 주시겠어요? 한 번 볼게요.
여 그러죠. 심각한 일이 아니었으면 좋겠네요.
남 엔진에는 아무런 문제가 없는 것 같습니다.
여 그럼 뭐가 문제인가요?
남 몇 가지 검사를 좀 해야 할 것 같군요. 대기실에서 기다려 주시겠습니까?
여 네, 그러죠.

15 ②

해설 남자는 여자에게 좋은 영화를 추천해 달라고 부탁했다.

어휘 relax[rilǽks] 느긋하게 쉬다
no way 절대로 안 돼
not ~ at all 전혀 ~아니다
come out (신제품 등이) 나오다
recommend A for B B에게 A를 추천하다
text 문자를 보내다

W Do you have any plans for this holiday?
M I'm just going to relax at home.
W That sounds like a good plan. Why don't you read some books?
M No way. I'm not interested in reading at all.
W What are you going to do at home for 3 days then?
M I want to watch movies. I haven't seen any movies for 2 years.
W Really? A lot of good movies came out last year.
M Can you recommend some good movies for me?
W Sure, I'll text you the names of the movies.

여 이번 공휴일에 계획이 있니?
남 집에서 그냥 느긋하게 쉬려고 해.
여 그거 좋은 계획인 것 같다. 책을 좀 읽는 건 어때?
남 절대로 안 돼. 난 독서에 전혀 흥미가 없거든.
여 그럼 사흘 동안 집에서 뭐 할 건데?
남 영화를 보고 싶어. 2년 동안 영화를 한 편도 보지 못했거든.
여 정말? 작년에 좋은 영화가 많이 나왔는데.
남 나에게 좋은 영화들을 좀 추천해 줄래?
여 물론이지. 영화 제목을 문자로 보내 줄게.

16 ④

해설 여자는 전날 커피를 너무 많이 마셔서 잠을 자지 못했다고 했다.

M Megan, you look tired. Do you have a lot of work to do?

남 Megan, 피곤해 보이는구나. 할 일이 많니?

어휘 **for a while** 잠시, 한 동안
fall asleep 잠들다
happen to ~에게 (어떤 일이) 일어나다

W Well, I've been working on this art project for a while. But it will be done by this week.
M What time did you go to bed last night?
W I went to bed earlier than usual, but I couldn't fall asleep easily.
M Were you worried about your project?
W No, I wasn't. I just drank too much coffee in the afternoon.
M Oh, that happens to me, too.

여 음, 한동안 이 미술 프로젝트에 몰두했거든. 하지만 이건 이번 주에 끝나.
남 어젯밤에 몇 시에 잠자리에 들었니?
여 평소보다 일찍 잠자리에 들었지만 쉽게 잠들지 못했어.
남 네 프로젝트가 걱정이 되었니?
여 아니. 그렇지 않았어. 오후에 너무 커피를 많이 마셨을 뿐이야.
남 아, 그런 일은 나한테도 일어나.

17 ③

해설 식탁에서 소금을 건네 달라고 하는 상황이 적절하다.

어휘 **fork**[fɔːrk] 포크
napkin[nǽpkin] 냅킨
pass[pæs] 건네 주다
washing machine 세탁기
on sale 세일 중인

① M Do you know what time it is now?
　 W Yes, it's 5:30.
② M Can I get a fork and some napkins?
　 W Yes, I'll bring them right away.
③ M Could you pass the salt, please?
　 W Sure, here it is.
④ M Do you have these shoes in size 12?
　 W I'm sorry. 11 is the biggest size.
⑤ M Is this washing machine on sale?
　 W No, that's not on sale.

① 남 지금 몇 시 인줄 아시나요?
　 여 5시 30분이네요.
② 남 포크와 냅킨 좀 얻을 수 있나요?
　 여 네, 지금 바로 갖다 드릴게요.
③ 남 소금 좀 건네줄래요?
　 여 네, 여기 있어요.
④ 남 이 구두 12 사이즈로 있나요?
　 여 죄송합니다. 11이 가장 큰 사이즈에요.
⑤ 남 이 세탁기는 세일 중인가요?
　 여 아니요. 그건 세일을 하고 있지 않아요.

18 ④

해설 상품명(Balance Five), 무게(290, 310, 330그램), 색깔(검정색), 가격(90달러)에 대해 언급하였으나 길이에 대해서는 언급하지 않았다.

어휘 **among**[əmʌ́ŋ] ~ 중에서
weight[weit] 무게
less[les] 덜 ~한
pro[prou] 프로 (선수)

W Let me introduce our new tennis racket. Its name is Balance Five. You can choose from among 3 different weights: 290 grams, 310 grams, and 330 grams. It only comes in one color, black. However, it is less expensive than any other models. Get one today for only $90, and play like a pro!

여 저희 새 테니스 라켓을 소개해드리겠습니다. 이름은 Balance Five입니다. 여러분은 290그램, 310그램, 그리고 330그램의 세 가지 무게 중에서 선택할 수 있습니다. 오직 한 가지 색상인 검정색으로 출시됩니다. 하지만 어떤 다른 모델보다도 덜 비쌉니다. 오늘 단돈 90달러에 한 개를 구매하시고 프로 선수처럼 운동해 보세요!

19 ③

해설 집을 나서기 전에 TV를 끄는 것을 잊지 말라는 여자의 말에 남자가 미안하다는 말과 함께 잊지 않겠다고 말하는 것이 적절하다.

어휘 **noise**[nɔiz] 소리, 소음
downstairs[dáunstέərz] 아래층에서
forget to-v ~할 것을 잊다
turn off (TV 등을) 끄다

W Where is that sound coming from?
M What sound are you talking about?
W I hear someone talking.
M I think it's coming from the bedroom.
W But we just got home. Who could be in our bedroom?
M Let me check. The noise may be from our neighbors downstairs.
W [Pause] What was it?
M It was the TV. I forgot to turn it off when I left home.

여 저 소리가 어디서 나오고 있죠?
남 어떤 소리를 말하는 거예요?
여 누군가가 말하는 게 들려요.
남 침실에서 나오는 소리 같아요.
여 하지만 우리는 방금 집에 도착했잖아요. 누가 우리 침실에 있겠어요?
남 내가 확인해 볼게요. 아래층에 사는 이웃에게서 들리는 소리일지도 몰라요.
여 [잠시 후] 무슨 소리였어요?
남 TV 소리였어요. 제가 집에서 나갈 때 끄는 걸 잊었네요.

W Please don't forget to turn off the TV before you leave home.
M I'm sorry. I won't forget again.

여 집에서 나갈 때는 TV를 끄는 것을 잊지 마세요.
남 미안해요. 다시는 잊지 않을게요.

① 아니요, 그것은 좋은 생각이 아니군요.
② 우리 이웃 사람들은 아주 시끄러워요.
④ 제가 즉시 TV를 수리할게요.
⑤ 네, 당신은 그것을 기억해야 해요.

20 ③

해설 생일을 왜 슬픈 날로 생각하는지 묻는 여자에게 그 이유로 나이 먹는 것이 싫다고 말하는 것이 적절하다.

어휘 past[pæst] 지난
turn[təːrn] (나이가) ~살이 되다
celebrate[séləbrèit] 기념하다

W When is your birthday, Uncle Bill?
M It's November 9.
W It was just this past weekend.
M Yes, it was. I just turned 31.
W How did you celebrate your birthday?
M I stopped celebrating my birthday a long time ago.
W Why? It's your happiest day!
M Well, to me it's the saddest day.
W Why do you say that?
M Because I don't like getting older.

여 생일이 언제예요, Bill 삼촌?
남 11월 9일이야.
여 바로 지난 주말이었네요.
남 응, 그랬지. 나는 막 31세가 되었어.
여 생일을 어떻게 기념했어요?
남 나는 오래전에 내 생일을 기념하는 것을 그만뒀어.
여 왜요? 삼촌에게 가장 행복한 날이잖아요!
남 글쎄, 내게 가장 슬픈 날이야.
여 왜 그렇게 말하세요?
남 나이 먹는 것이 싫기 때문이야.

① 삶이 너무 소중하기 때문이야.
② 나는 내 생일을 기억 못 하거든.
④ 이번 주에 기념하려고 해.
⑤ 행복해지는 것이 중요하기 때문이지.

LISTENING Q 중학영어듣기 **모의고사 시리즈**

Listening Q 유형편

Listening Q 1

Listening Q 2

Listening Q 3

+

- 중학 영어듣기능력평가
  16개 대표 유형 분석
- 실전 모의고사 5회 수록

- 학년별 중학 영어듣기능력평가 대비
- 최신 기출을 완벽 분석한 유형별 공략 수록
- 실전 모의고사 20회 + 고난도 모의고사 4회 수록

영어듣기평가 완벽 대비를 위한

리스닝 큐 시리즈

01 <시·도 교육청 영어듣기능력평가> 최신 5개년 출제 경향 집중 반영

02 <유형편>으로 기본기를 다지고 <실전 모의고사>로 완벽 대비

03 매회 Dictation(받아쓰기) 구성으로 완벽 복습

04 개정 교과서 교육부 지정 의사소통 기능 및 발음 팁 수록

05 QR코드 하나로 3가지 배속 선택이 가능한 차별화된 음원 재생 서비스 제공

천일문 STARTER

중등 영어 구문·문법 학습의 시작

1 중등 눈높이에 맞춘 권당 약 500문장 + 내용 구성

2 개념부터 적용까지 체계적 학습

3 천일문 완벽 해설집 「천일비급」 부록

4 철저한 복습을 위한 워크북 포함

구문 대장 천일문, 중등도 천일문만 믿어!

3 in 1 구성

+ 본책   + 워크북

+ 천일비급

씨듀런 Mobile & PC
온라인 구문 문장 암기 학습권(유료)

중등부터 고등까지, 천일문과 함께!

예비중 ~ 중3	예비고1	고1	고2	고3
천일문 STARTER 구문 학습 첫걸음	**천일문 입문** 우선 순위 빈출 구문	**천일문 기본** 기본/빈출/중요 구문 총망라	**천일문 핵심** 혼동 구문 완벽 해결	**천일문 완성** 고난도 구문 뛰어넘기

쎄듀 초·중등 커리큘럼

	예비초	초1	초2	초3	초4	초5	초6
구문		신간 천일문 365 일력 | 초1-3 | 교육부 지정 초등 필수 영어 문장		초등코치 천일문 SENTENCE 1001개 통문장 암기로 완성하는 초등 영어의 기초			
문법				초등코치 천일문 GRAMMAR 1001개 예문으로 배우는 초등 영문법			
			왓츠 Grammar		Start (초등 기초 영문법) / Plus (초등 영문법 마무리)		
독해				왓츠 리딩 70 / 80 / 90 / 100 A / B 쉽고 재미있게 완성되는 영어 독해력			
어휘				초등코치 천일문 VOCA&STORY 1001개의 초등 필수 어휘와 짧은 스토리			
		패턴으로 말하는 초등 필수 영단어 1 / 2 문장 패턴으로 완성하는 초등 필수 영단어					
ELT	Oh! My PHONICS 1 / 2 / 3 / 4 유·초등학생을 위한 첫 영어 파닉스						
		Oh! My SPEAKING 1 / 2 / 3 / 4 / 5 / 6 핵심 문장 패턴으로 더욱 쉬운 영어 말하기					
		Oh! My GRAMMAR 1 / 2 / 3 쓰기로 완성하는 첫 초등 영문법					

	예비중	중1	중2	중3
구문	천일문 STARTER 1 / 2			중등 필수 구문 & 문법 총정리
문법	천일문 GRAMMAR LEVEL 1 / 2 / 3			예문 중심 문법 기본서
	GRAMMAR Q Starter 1, 2 / Intermediate 1, 2 / Advanced 1, 2			학기별 문법 기본서
	잘 풀리는 영문법 1 / 2 / 3			문제 중심 문법 적용서
	GRAMMAR PIC 1 / 2 / 3 / 4			이해가 쉬운 도식화된 문법서
		1센치 영문법		1권으로 핵심 문법 정리
문법+어법		첫단추 BASIC 문법·어법편 1 / 2		문법·어법의 기초
문법+쓰기	EGU 영단어&품사 / 문장 형식 / 동사 써먹기 / 문법 써먹기 / 구문 써먹기			서술형 기초 세우기와 문법 다지기
				올씀 1 기본 문장 PATTERN 내신 서술형 기본 문장 학습
쓰기	거침없이 Writing LEVEL 1 / 2 / 3			중등 교과서 내신 기출 서술형
		중학 영어 쓰작 1 / 2 / 3		중등 교과서 패턴 드릴 서술형
어휘	신간 천일문 VOCA 중등 스타트/필수/마스터			2800개 중등 3개년 필수 어휘
		어휘끝 중학 필수편 중학 필수어휘 1000개	어휘끝 중학 마스터편	고난도 중학어휘 +고등기초 어휘 1000개
독해		Reading Relay Starter 1, 2 / Challenger 1, 2 / Master 1, 2		타교과 연계 배경 지식 독해
		READING Q Starter 1, 2 / Intermediate 1, 2 / Advanced 1, 2		예측/추론/요약 사고력 독해
독해전략			리딩 플랫폼 1 / 2 / 3	논픽션 지문 독해
독해유형			Reading 16 LEVEL 1 / 2 / 3	수능 유형 맛보기 + 내신 대비
			첫단추 BASIC 독해편 1 / 2	수능 유형 독해 입문
듣기	Listening Q 유형편 / 1 / 2 / 3			유형별 듣기 전략 및 실전 대비
		쎄듀 빠르게 중학영어듣기 모의고사 1 / 2 / 3		교육청 듣기평가 대비